A DIARY OF BATTLE

The Personal Journals
of Colonel Charles S. Wainwright
1861 - 1865

EDITED BY ALLAN NEVINS

NEW FOREWORD BY STEPHEN W. SEARS

Maps by Rafael Palacios

DA CAPO PRESS

Library of Congress Cataloging-in-Publication Data

Wainwright, Charles S. (Charles Shiels)
    A diary of battle: the personal journals of colonel Charles S.
Wainwright, 1861–1865 / edited by Allan Nevins; new foreword by
Stephen W. Sears.—1st Da Capo Press ed.
        p.   cm.
    Originally published: New York: Harcourt, 1962.
    ISBN 0-306-80846-3 (alk. paper)
    1. Wainwright, Charles S. (Charles Shiels)—Diaries. 2. United
States. Army of the Potomac—Biography. 3. United States. Army
of the Potomac—Artillery. 4. Soldiers—United States—Diaries. 5.
United States—History—Civil War, 1861–1865—Artillery opera-
tions. 6. United States—History—Civil War, 1861–1865—Personal
narratives. I. Nevins, Allan, 1890–1971. II. Title.
E601.W15   1998
973.78′1—dc21   97-42224
                                                           CIP

First Da Capo Press edition 1998

This Da Capo Press paperback edition of *A Diary of Battle*
is an unabridged republication of the edition first published in
New York in 1962, here supplemented with a new foreword
by Stephen W. Sears.

Published by Da Capo Press, Inc.
A Member of the Perseus Books Group

FOREWORD
BY STEPHEN W. SEARS

The blunt, outspoken Confederate general Daniel Harvey Hill insisted, at the end of the Civil War, that if he were given Rebel infantry and Yankee artillery, he could take on and lick any army in the world. He had excelled in infantry-leading and knew the qualities of the men he had commanded. He knew also, from firsthand battlefield experience, the qualities of the Yankee artillery. Hill said, for example, that at Sharpsburg the Federal artillerymen had so completely commanded his position that they "concentrated their fire upon every gun that opened and soon disabled or silenced it."

There is no better way to understand the record and inner workings of the Yankee artillery that Hill so admired than to read Charles S. Wainwright's Civil War journal *A Diary of Battle*, as edited here by Allan Nevins. Indeed, so far as Union eyewitness accounts are concerned, there is nothing remotely like Wainwright's. It is the only work of its kind. Writing before Wainwright's diary was published in 1962, L. Van Loan Naisawald, historian of the artillery of the Army of the Potomac, remarked regretfully of his research, "Diaries and letters of artillery soldiers were extremely scarce." *A Diary of Battle* remains today as singular a work as when Nevins purchased it from Wainwright's heirs and arranged for its first publication.

When, on October 17, 1861, Charles Shiels Wainwright was commissioned major of the First New York Artillery and journeyed to the field with the Army of the Potomac, he was a volunteer in a volunteer battery, but he was hardly the typical volunteer. In contrast to the average neophyte in a branch of the service that required more training to become a competent officer than either the infantry or the cavalry, Wainwright started off with an understanding of the basic workings of his command from his days in charge of a battery in the prewar New York militia. To be sure, this had involved no experience under fire, yet simply by knowing a prolonge from a lunette, a handspike from a friction primer, he stood well ahead in the arduous labor of training farm boys to be gunners. The First New York Artillery got a prize when it got Charles Wainwright.

The army seems to have recognized this. On January 25, 1862, Wainwright was appointed chief of artillery for Joseph Hooker's division. On

April 30 he was promoted lieutenant colonel and just a month after that
he was a full colonel. By September 1862 he was in command of the artillery of Hooker's First Corps. Then, in May 1863, his command was organized into a semi-independent artillery brigade. Wainwright's brigade
remained in the First Corps under John Reynolds and John Newton until
the spring of 1864 when, in a major reorganization of the Army of the
Potomac, the First Corps was legislated out of existence. Wainwright's artillery brigade went then to Gouverneur Warren's Fifth Corps. Brevetted
brigadier general on December 6, 1864 (to rank from August 1), Wainwright continued to serve under Warren through Appomattox. At the con
clusion of the Grand Review in Washington in May 1865, Wainwright
wrote proudly on the closing page of his journal, "Several were kind
enough to say that my brigade was the best. I think so myself."

Beyond his obvious overriding interest in the artillery arm Wainwright
brought a highly bred intelligence to his war effort. Every page of his jour
nal reflects that intelligence. Like so many Civil War soldiers, he was from
the first intent on recording this momentous passage in his life. Unlike so
many of his fellows, he did not restrict himself to one of those ubiquitous
pocket diaries with a tiny space allotted for each day's entry. The reader
(and the historian) can be grateful that Wainwright elected instead to re
cord his impressions and thoughts in ledger-sized notebooks without re
gard to entry length. When he had a lot to say, as he often did, he had
room to say it. If a battle—Gettysburg, for example—raged on, he kept
quick notes as reminders in such free moments as he had until he could si
down afterward and record what he had experienced. He was conscien
tious in putting down everything that happened in the order it happened
"To the history of the day," he wrote at the start of a long, proud accoun
of his role in the fighting at Jericho Mills on the North Anna in 1864.

At year's end 1862, Colonel Wainwright (as he now was) looked back
on a full year of journal-keeping. "I think I have accomplished my objec
in the journal," he wrote, "which is to so fix the events of my soldiering in
time and place, that I may easily recall them in years to come, should my
life be spared." And he added, "I do not expect that anyone else will ever
see it." Due to that expectation he was always unsparing in his comments
on men and events. There is no evidence, for example, that he followed
the common practice of sending journal entries, with the proper patriotic
sentiments all in place, to be published in his hometown newspaper. He
was unmarried, with only a brother in the service and an elderly father for
family, and so he did not sugar-coat his commentaries for the sensibilities
of the folks at home. What Colonel Wainwright thought of his fellow soldiers, of his superiors, of his president were views he did not intend to
make public. It would have done his military career no good, for instance,
if it got out that in his considered opinion, "It would be pretty hard to find

three poorer division commanders than we have in this corps" (by which he meant Abner Doubleday, John Robinson, and James Wadsworth). On any given day in his journal we feel confident that this is just what happened to him, or what he was at pains to find out if he was not an eyewitness to some event. This is Civil War history right as it occurred, with no punches pulled.

Wainwright closely followed events in the newspapers, and he was high enough in the chain of command to be on familiar terms with ranking generals, and so the range of his commentary is both wide and well informed. He has his biases and prejudices (not uncommon ones in his day and in this army), but his judgments have the ring of fairness about them. To take just one example, allegations that General Hooker was drunk when in command at Chancellorsville angered Wainwright. Thrice in his journal he refutes the charge, and in no uncertain terms. He knew General Hooker well, and was with him frequently for long periods during the battle. He had not the slightest doubt that the commanding general was cold sober during the entire time. He had expressed his reservations about Hooker as a general, but he had no reservation on this particular question. Having read this far in the journal, we feel we know Wainwright well enough to respect that opinion fully, and to conclude once and for all (for the allegation still persists) that whatever were Joe Hooker's failings at Chancellorsville, he was not guilty of drunkenness.

Wainwright saw considerable fighting in his three and a half years of service, and had several close calls—a bullet slamming into a tree inches from his head, a Rebel shell striking only yards away and not exploding. He served first with Hooker in lower Maryland, and for about the first half of the Peninsula campaign of 1862 against Richmond. He then fell ill, probably with dysenteric diarrhea, the scourge of so many soldiers on both sides during this campaign. He was absent for two months, missing the Seven Days fighting. His command was entangled in the subsequent transportation bottleneck while evacuating the Peninsula and did not reach the front in time to be engaged at Second Bull Run. Afterward, in the hasty on-the-run reorganization of the Army of the Potomac during the Maryland campaign, Hooker sought Wainwright to command the guns of the newly designated First Corps, but the orders were delayed and he did not reach the Antietam battlefield until the fighting was over. From then on he served continuously until the end—at Fredericksburg, Chancellorsville, Gettysburg, the fall 1863 maneuvering, then in Grant's final campaign from the Wilderness and Spotsylvania through Petersburg to Appomattox.

Regarding himself a professional in the matter of arms, Wainwright had his moments of accomplishment on these battlefields. At Williamsburg on the Peninsula he was satisfied with his response when for the first time in his life he came under fire. Some of his men left their guns at the first shot, and he rushed after the fugitives and harangued them. "Never in my life was I so mortified, never so excited, never so mad," he wrote, and then concluded thoughtfully, "It had at any rate the good effect of making me forget my own danger." His description of Williamsburg, the first real clash between these two armies, is easily the best contemporaneous account on either side.

Chancellorsville in retrospect became the high point of his wartime service. Hooker had bungled the administration of his artillery in this campaign, and in the heat of the contest there was no guiding hand to direct the guns. Wainwright could see what was happening, and managed to push his way in to see his old commander to spell out the crisis for him. "You take hold and make it right," Hooker told the surprised artilleryman, and Wainwright abruptly found himself in temporary command of all the army's artillery he could reach. His is a unique record of a key moment in the battle, and he covers it fully and carefully in a long, five-page entry.

At Gettysburg Wainwright's guns were instrumental in holding Cemetery Hill on the Union right on the second day of the great battle. On the first day, after the incompetent Doubleday (as Wainwright judged him) succeeded the fallen Reynolds in command of the First Corps, Wainwright had gone ahead and posted the guns on his own, without waiting for orders he suspected would never come. In one of the journal's unique contributions to the history of Day One at Gettysburg, Wainwright reveals that the doomed last-ditch Union effort to hold Seminary Ridge, west of the town, was due to a literal misunderstanding. General Howard had sent a German staff member from the Eleventh Corps to the embattled front with orders to defend Cemetery Ridge, south of the town, at all hazards. In the man's broken English, however, it came out Seminary Ridge. In the inevitable collapse of the line Wainwright wrote, "There was not a doubt in my mind but that I should go to Richmond. Each minute I expected to hear the order to surrender."

During Grant's 1864 campaign Wainwright's artillery brigade had two outstanding days, on the North Anna in May, and in the fight for the Weldon Railroad during the siege of Petersburg in August. The latter fight offered Wainwright the professional an ideal opportunity to test a favored gunnery tactic: "My instructions were almost entirely to 'Fire low, low! low!!' The ground was good, and every shot must strike the ground before entering the wood; also 'Fire solid shot almost exclusively!' Never before had I had so good an opportunity to test this low flight of shot through woods, so I was determined to give it a full trial, in which it more than fulfilled my expectations." After the Confederates were repulsed, an aide went over the ground and said he had never seen anything to equal it, with hardly a tree "struck higher up than he could reach while on foot."

Wainwright was exceedingly conscientious in his duties and demanding of his subordinates in regard to training and proper military form. At the same time, he was careful to take advantage of all the prerogatives of his rank and position. He was determined that all possible creature comforts due an officer in the field should be his. His tent was always carefully located and in the winter it was snug and well heated, his mess featured a French chef when he could manage it, and he bathed at every opportunity. "Almost every day of this campaign," he noted in his journal in the spring of 1864, "I have been obliged to remark, even more than ever before, how superior is the position of a light battery officer to even a colonel of infantry, so far as comfort goes, in times of general discomfort." In an entry several weeks later, he intoned mournfully, "I have met with a great loss today." We soon discover that he has broken the stem of his favorite pipe. "Besides being the sweetest pipe I ever smoked, it was a real beauty and had coloured most wonderfully; everyone who saw it admired it, and at least half a hundred have petitioned for it should I get knocked over."

One of the special values of Wainwright's journal, as Allan Nevins points out in his introduction, is its vivid portraits of the high command of the Army of the Potomac. Perhaps the most valuable of these portraits is the one he paints of Joe Hooker. Wainwright served longer under Hooker than under any other general and indeed he flourished under his tutelage. He found him personally a pleasure to deal with, but was much discomforted by Hooker's public braggadocio. Yet on the whole his picture of this important general is far better balanced than the caricature often portrayed by historians.

Among other unusual portraits sketched in Wainwright's journal is his rendering of Gouverneur Warren of the Fifth Corps, under whom he served in the last year of the war. Warren is best remembered as one of the Union heroes of Gettysburg, and as the general terribly wronged by Phil Sheridan, who relieved him of his Fifth Corps command at Five Forks just days before the end of the war. In these pages Warren is hardly a hero, but instead a profane, mean-spirited, poorly skilled general whose tantrums Wainwright thought were "the result of a sort of insanity." After reading Wainwright's account, we see Warren's fate in a very different light.

Beyond all of these other merits, Wainwright's journal is unique in its remarkably detailed rendering of the slow and painful evolution of Union artillery tactics in this war. From the start, the Federal artillery had a marked advantage over the Confederates in the quality of its guns, its equipment, its trained manpower, and especially in its ammunition. It was because of these factors that Harvey Hill said he could lick any foreign army with the Union artillery at his command. In battlefield tactics, however, the North lagged well behind the South. After the failures of their guns in the Seven Days campaign, General Lee and his artillerists moved swiftly to reorganize the artillery arm of the Army of Northern Virginia. By regrouping the batteries in battalions and then evolving improved command and control over them, Confederate gunners proved to be far more effective than their better-equipped opponents in such battles as Second Bull Run and Chancellorsville. With his observant, innovative eye Wainwright made strenuous efforts to catch up to his adversaries.

Working with and through Henry Hunt, the army's chief of artillery, Wainwright was instrumental in evolving plans for artillery brigades within the corps structure. He campaigned against the exclusive control of batteries in battle by brigade and divisional infantry commanders. Their views were necessarily (and understandably) limited, he pointed out; what was needed was better centralized control of the guns by those expert in artillery management and tactics. It is these command evils that Wainwright describes so vividly in his account of Chancellorsville. Although by the closing campaigns great strides had been made in organizing the guns, their command in battle by those most expert in their use was only a partial reality. Sometimes, as, for example, Wainwright records on the first day at Gettysburg and later under Warren, the desired result was achieved by default; he went ahead and managed the guns of his brigade in battle himself without waiting for orders from his superiors.

On October 5, 1864, in a particularly introspective journal entry, Wainwright looked back on his "dreams and expectations" of three years earlier when he joined the First New York Artillery. "Fortunately I had not indulged in any very wild imaginations of personal glory; my highest ambition then was to earn a solid name in the army as a first-class officer in my own arm of the service. Indistinct visions of some occasion on which I might gallop half a dozen batteries into position at the decisive moment, as General Sénarmont did at the battle of Friedland, and so save the day, were soon dispersed by the densely wooded country in which all our fighting has been done. . . . The artillery is in fact an arm of defense rather than of offense; its glory is in coolness and obstinacy, qualities which do not excite general admiration like the dash of a charge." While that is a judgment on the field artillery of the Civil War that rings as true today as when it was written, it is also fair to say that this journal kept so faithfully by Charles Wainwright does most certainly excite our general admiration.

STEPHEN W. SEARS
Norwalk, Connecticut
September 1997

WAINWRIGHT AND THE ARTILLERY

When Lincoln, just after the attack on Sumter, called for 75,000 militia, and the War Department fixed New York's quota at seventeen regiments, the Empire State had several hundred thousand men on its militia rolls. Only a small fraction of them, however, had been well drilled and instructed. According to Silas W. Burt, one of the chief organizers of the state's military effort, the proficient men would not fill more than fifteen regiments. And when in midsummer Congress voted a volunteer army of 500,000, the problem of officering it seemed insoluble. The tiny regular army did not have enough officers to go around, and many of them were unfit, Southern in sympathies, or needed in staff rather than field commands. It was an hour in which capable men of some military experience were desperately wanted.

The nation's demands were well comprehended by two young men in the Hudson Valley, William P. and Charles Shiels Wainwright. They were prosperous, the family owning a small estate at Rhinebeck, just above Hyde Park; they had been well educated; and both had served as officers in the militia. Charles had traveled in Europe, paying special attention to his favorite military branch, the artillery. Two months after Sumter, William enlisted in the Twenty-ninth New York Infantry with the rank of major, and was soon in a Potomac camp. He did so well that within a year he was colonel of the Seventy-sixth New York.

Charles hesitated. For one reason, his father was now eighty-five and, though in fair health, wished to keep one son. For another, their farm, "The Meadows," needed careful management. That part of the Hudson Valley, developed under the leadership of the Livingston and Schuyler families, still supplied grain, fruit, and meat to New York City by steamboat and rail; farm production was part of the war effort. As still other reasons, Charles at thirty-four felt entitled to a responsible post and preferred the artillery, which the government at first neglected.

But he did not hesitate long. His father and two sisters could spare him; by August the grain and hay had been harvested. Soon after the call for a half-million men, Charles visited his old friend Marsena R. Patrick, military planner and inspector at Albany on the staff of Governor E. D. Morgan. Though a West Pointer and a veteran of the Mexican and Seminole Wars, Patrick had left the army some years since and taken up farming, finally accepting the presidency of the New York State Agricultural College at Ovid, an institution that opened in 1859. He and Charles had been active in the State Agricultural

Society. Now fifty, Patrick left the college to become brigadier general. He first encouraged Charles to try to recruit an artillery regiment. Though Wainwright had posters printed and set up a booth at the Dutchess County Fair, he met no response. Thereupon Patrick suggested that as Colonel Guilford D. Bailey, a graduate of West Point in 1856 and recently an officer of the Second United States Artillery, had just raised a light artillery regiment and needed a major, Wainwright should apply for the place.

Going to Elmira, one of the three principal posts of rendezvous in New York, Wainwright found Bailey receptive. "He is about my own height and build," wrote the applicant, who was tall and slender, "has black hair, a ruddy complexion, smooth skin, and as beautiful a pair of black eyes as I ever saw." Without delay Bailey sent Wainwright's name to Governor Morgan, who almost as promptly signed the commission in the First New York Artillery. "I am experiencing in my own person," wrote the elated new officer, "the good effects of some of the enthusiasm which pervades the whole country." Realizing that he would witness events of importance, he bought a large black book and on October 1, 1861, began his journal.

For when that month opened he was at Elmira again, ready for duty. He was equipped with overcoat, Mexican saddle, a pair of revolvers, telescope, blanket, uniform, saber, and flannel underwear; an outfit to which he soon added a folding cot and mattress. The regiment had practically filled its quota of eight hundred when he arrived, and he flung himself into drilling it with enthusiasm, for he had commanded a battery in the militia. Practice in the "manual of the piece" was at first limited by the fact that they had only four guns. But the men took turns at these guns in groups of thirty-six, while Wainwright made them master infantry tactics and hold regular parades. He was much pained by the awkwardness of most recruits and the ignorance of the officers whom Bailey and he directed. He tells in his early diary of the colonel of another regiment who, giving a wrong order, was corrected by a captain. They began to dispute the point, until at last the colonel, pulling a worn copy of Hardee's *Tactics* from his pocket, shouted to his troops: "Battalion, parade rest! Rest there, boys! Sit down on the curb until we look it up!"

On October 29 the artillery regiment set off for Washington. The eight hundred men filled seventeen cars, some of them dirty unventilated boxcars, and the journey consumed fifty hours. They arrived exhausted. It was his worst journey, Wainwright tells us, since "I made the trip from Hanover to Köln shut up in the middle seat of a diligence with five *bad*-tobacco-smoking Germans, who would keep the window shut!" The newspapers spoke much of "sumptuous collations" spread at different places on the road to Washington. "These places," he wrote, "must be on some other roads; we saw none of them, unless a distribution of cold coffee and sandwiches in the cars this morning was one." In Baltimore the regiment had to march from station to station, a good mile, between one and two A.M., and face the jeers of plug-uglies. Then in Washington their first camp experience was depressing. They had to quarter themselves in an open field about a mile northeast of the Capitol in pouring rain, with no breakfast, nobody to help get food prepared, and "everything wet and floating" as they huddled around smoky, sputtering fires. This was a foretaste of hardships to come.

Yet later that fall of 1861, as General George B. McClellan whipped his army into shape by incessant drilling, they found Washington an exciting place. New regiments kept pouring in. A decent array of guns, mainly Parrotts and old six-pounders, arrived and gave the First New York Artillery a sense of confidence. Some horses for battery mounts came from the North; others were selected by junior officers from a government corral containing a thousand beasts. Wainwright used $150 sent him by his father to buy himself a good steed. He began to live fairly well, with a tight tent, a little stove, his folding cot, and enough blankets; training his batteries by day and studying hard at night. He managed to find a servant, an Irishman, who for $20 a month blacked his boots, cared for the horse, and helped with meals. Up to New Year's the weather was almost uniformly fine, with skies so bright and roads so hard that impatient Northerners berated McClellan for failing to strike a blow. The general might at least clear the Potomac of rebel guns that blocked its navigation, they said. But Wainwright, who daily saw glaring evidence of lack of discipline, cohesion, and martial spirit in the loose volunteer array, sympathized with McClellan's insistence on full preparation.

The task of making true soldiers out of country recruits—for most of Wainwright's men came from the farms—was long and arduous. The major complained that his boys were "round-shouldered, stooping, and very slack in the joints; it would require a long 'setting-up' to give them the aplomb and sharp, almost jerky, movements of the real soldier." Constant admonitions were necessary, Colonel Bailey issuing rebuke after rebuke in general orders. The men had no soldierly pride, and no notions of respect. "The sentinels will lounge on their posts, and even sit down where they can whistle, sing, or talk with whoever comes along. Very few of the men think to take their hats off when they come into a tent, and hardly any of them salute." Wainright did not know whether the defect arose from the careless habits of a democratic education, or from a determination to permit as little difference as possible between the position of privates and that of officers. He inclined to think the whole national character responsible:

> It is astonishing how little snap men have generally. I suppose we have as good a lot of officers as any regiment among the volunteers; at Albany they say we are better officered than any other regiment from New York State, yet I have not come across more than half a dozen in the lot who can get fairly wakened up. Their orders come out slow and drawling, and then they wait patiently to see them half-obeyed in a laggard manner, instead of making the men jump to it sharp, as if each word of the order was a prod in their buttocks. This is doubtless in part owing to the miserable, sleepy, slipshod way everybody does business in our villages and small towns (Rhinebeck, for example); partly to the officers having raised their own men and known most of them in civil life. I am every day more and more thankful that I never laid eyes on a soul in the regiment until I joined it. . . . [Diary, December 12, 1861]

His regiment grew with the addition of more companies, until by the end of the year it had 1404 officers and men. McClellan's artillery chief, William F. Barry, gave Bailey and Wainwright just the direction and counsel they needed. "General Barry," writes the diarist, "is a tall, spare man about 45 years of age; very military in his bearing; apparently very reserved; a hard worker, systematic, and just the person needed to organise new artillery." In a long inspection of various artillery units on a cold December day, Barry sat his horse like a Spartan while Wainwright's teeth chattered; and he made it a very thorough inspection, too: "not a strap of the harnesses, a key of the carriages, or an implement in the boxes out of place appeared to escape his eye." When the Army of the Potomac held a grand review on November 20 for the President, it struck Wainwright as steady and adequate, though lacking in the glitter and precision of reviews of British and Continental troops that Wainwright had seen; for one reason, American uniforms were less showy. The insistence of McClellan and Barry on thoroughness, promptness, and neatness seemed to the major very important. Seeing some of his men, even officers, turning out with dirty shirts and unwashed faces, he wondered what "Old Wool," the disciplinarian John E. Wool, famous for inspecting the inside of soup kettles with white kid gloves, would say to them.

As 1861 ended, Wainwright was called upon to help in weeding incompetent officers out of the Army of the Potomac. Congress had authorized the War Department to appoint examining boards to pass on the skill, discipline, and efficiency of questionable men up to and including the grade of colonel. The mere announcement of these boards frightened numerous incompetents into resigning. McClellan sped the work of getting rid of "scrub" officers, and more than three hundred soon left or were dismissed. Wainwright gladly served as junior member of one board, acting also as recorder. It gave him some chagrin to see men whom he had regarded rather highly ousted, but much satisfaction to assist in dismissing ignorant, lazy, and stupid officers. It is plain that his own standards were high, and that he thought nobody should hold a commission who lacked ability, self-control, and some degree of breeding. Colonel Bailey had told him that he wished the First New York Artillery officered by "gentlemen," a prescription of which Wainright warmly approved. We find him expressing admiration for such men as his own Lieutenant John Fitzhugh, "an educated gentleman, just graduated from Yale College; ugly enough to look at, but like the countryman's horse, a good one to go."

Such labors varied the continuing drills and studies with which Wainwright occupied the early weeks of 1862. In these weeks the Army of the Potomac was immobilized by mud, bad weather, and the illness of its commander, for McClellan had been prostrated by typhoid. The impatience of the country and the Administration grew. Most Northerners thought that the army should move at once to clear the south bank of the Potomac of Confederate batteries down to the Chesapeake, capture Norfolk, and deliver a blow at the Southern forces in their winter quarters at Manassas. Lincoln believed that some early movement was imperative. Edwin M. Stanton, whom he appointed Secretary of War in January, shared that belief. News came of an important Western victory won by George H. Thomas at Mill Springs, Kentucky; Ulysses S. Grant was almost ready to move against Fort Donelson. When would McClellan's great force get under way? On January 27, spurred by the War and Navy Departments, the President directed a general advance against the enemy February 22; and a few days later he issued a special war order requiring McClellan to march against Manassas by that date. It was then certain that Wainwright would soon see action.

I

McClellan could not be accused of neglecting the artillery, for he had a clear comprehension of its importance, and with General Barry did his best to build its strength. By the beginning of 1862 the Army of the Potomac had seventy-three batteries, of 407 pieces. Of these twenty-nine light batteries, with 166 pieces, comprised the regular field force; eighteen batteries made a reserve corps; and one battery as well was attached to each division of the army. McClellan's 407 pieces included much siege artillery, for he intended to lay siege first to Yorktown and then Richmond. By the time of Chancellorsville the Army of the Potomac brought 412 guns to the field, with fewer siege pieces and more light ordnance. Of all the competent or semicompetent commanders of the army (John Pope and Ambrose E. Burnside were incompetent), Joseph Hooker alone showed an inadequate appreciation of the value of a prompt, powerful, well-directed artillery. But in proportion to its strength, the North accomplished much less with its guns than the Confederacy; and to the very end the War Department and high command failed in important respects, as Wainwright complains, to manage its artillery well.

The field artillery of both North and South was characteristically organized in four-gun and six-gun batteries, though a few two-gun or eight-gun batteries were found. The six-gun battery was regarded as best, with some variety in composition; say, four six-pounders and two twelve-pounders. First and last, both sides used a heterogeneity of cannon: brass guns, wrought-iron guns, and cast-iron guns; smoothbores and rifled pieces; muzzleloaders and breechloaders; and a variety of calibers. Secretary Cameron just after Bull Run had ordered three hundred iron guns for the army, two-thirds of them rifled, of three-inch caliber. No less an authority than Major Henry J. Hunt, who had collaborated with William H. French on the artillery manual used throughout the war, thought this order to private contractors a mistake, pronouncing the three-inch rifled piece "the feeblest in the world." But others, including Wainwright, deemed the three-inch gun excellent, and it was certainly important, as Cameron saw, to get a supply of artillery as quickly as possible. McClellan believed that the Napoleon, a copy of a field gun designed by Napoleon III, was the most efficient piece, easily handled and maintained.

"The basic field artillery weapons throughout the war," states L. Van Loan Naisawald in *Grape and Canister*, "were the 12-pounder light gun or Napoleon, the 10-pounder Parrott rifle, and the 3-inch ordnance rifle. All three were muzzle-loaders." The Napoleon was a smooth-bore muzzle-loading bronze gun, with a bore diameter of 4.62 inches. It could fire canister, shrapnel, solid shot, or shell, and could send its twelve-pound solid balls about 1,200 yards; but it was most effective with short-distance canister. The ten-pound and twenty-pound Parrott, a cast-iron rifled gun with a wrought-iron jacket, had a much longer range, but only the ten-pounders held their own long. As for the three-inch iron rifle, "long, sleek, slender-barreled," which was soon dubbed the "ordnance gun," it had the advantage over the Napoleon of lightness and range. It weighed only 820 pounds as against 1,227 for the Napoleon, and theoretically carried a ball some 4,000 yards. All three of the basic weapons carried into the field solid shot, shell, case shot or canister, and shrapnel.

McClellan in organizing the artillery for the whole Army of the Potomac authorized four field batteries to each division, with an artillery reserve for the whole army of a hundred guns, and a siege train of fifty heavy guns. He called for regular instruction in theory, practice, and tactics in all volunteer batteries, to be given by officers; and we shall find Wainwright laying much stress on such instruction, with the use of texts. But then Wainwright was an exceptionally conscientious officer.

Batteries had to possess much larger numbers both of men and horses than most people at the time realized. Roughly twenty men, expertly trained, were required for each gun. To mount a light battery of six guns properly, with a caisson to each gun, using six-horse teams, demanded eighty-four horses. A horse battery, in which the cannoneers were mounted, required 149 horses. Then additional horses were wanted for battery wagons and forage. We can understand why Wainwright constantly worried over the losses among his horses from bad treatment—overstrain, the wearing of harness day and night, insufficient shelter, and underfeeding. We can understand why Jennings C. Wise in his history of Confederate artillery, *The Long Arm of Lee,* writes: "Nothing became so tempting a prize to the Confederate artilleryman as the sleek teams of the enemy." On Wainwright's evidence, they were often far from sleek. After each action, the artillery commander first mournfully counted his dead and wounded, and then reckoned the number of his horses slain.

Some of the most important battles of the Civil War were decided, or largely decided, by the artillery. At Malvern Hill in 1862, Robert E. Lee's bloody defeat was attributed above all to the Northern guns. Colonel Henry Jackson Hunt used his fourteen light batteries and the numerous heavy pieces under Colonel Robert O. Tyler to disable the six or eight Confederate batteries that came upon the field; then, massing them effectively, he employed them to beat back the Southern infantry. The terrible punishment he administered the attackers taught Lee a memorable lesson. The Southern losses exceeded 5,000, and as D. H. Hill bitterly commented: "More than half the casualties were from field pieces —an unprecedented thing in warfare." At Second Manassas the artillery of Lee, splendidly handled at a decisive moment, played a great part in Pope's overthrow. Colonel Stephen D. Lee of the Confederate artillery called Antietam or Sharpsburg "Artillery Hell," and the fact that Lee fought McClellan to a standstill in that engagement was largely attributable to the two hundred guns that he brought to the struggle. Truly, writes Jennings C. Wise, "one might say that Sharpsburg was a day of glory for the Confederate artillery." At times the battle of Gettysburg became an artillery duel. In the last campaigns of the war the superiority of the Northern artillery was one of Grant's cardinal advantages.

As Wainwright writes, in the latter part of the struggle he witnessed the same scene again and again. The Confederate infantry would attack with brilliant impetuosity, advancing irresistibly through the woods and over the hills; then the Union artillery would come into position, get the range, and begin dropping its shells; exultant cheers would rise from the Union infantry, which would surge forward; and the Confederates would retreat. The three main principles of artillery action, surprise or concealment, economy of force, and concentration of strength, men like Hunt and Wainwright well understood. The fact that they could not be applied without a centralization of command in high-ranking officers, however, was not grasped by most army commanders. Such a centralization was opposed by most heads of corps.

General Hunt in his report on the role of the artillery in the battle of Chancellorsville, after acknowledging the invaluable services of Wainwright, condemned Hooker's mismanagement of the artillery arm in scathing terms. The general had scattered the batteries hither and yon, letting them fall into utter confusion until Hunt and Wainwright rescued them. "It will, perhaps, hardly be believed," writes Hunt, "that for the command and management in their operations of the artillery of the army, consisting of 412 guns, 880 artillery carriages, 9,543 men and officers, and 8,544 horses, besides their large ammunition trains, there were but five field officers in the army, and from the scarcity of officers of inferior grades these officers had miserably insufficient staffs. Add to this that there was no commander of all the artillery until a late period of the operations, and I doubt if the history of modern armies can exhibit a parallel instance of the crippling of a great arm of the service in the very presence of a powerful army, to overcome whom would require every energy of all arms under the most favorable circumstances." He adds that fourteen guns were lost before Colonel Wainwright or he took charge of the whole artillery; none afterward.

And later, in his official report on the artillery at Gettysburg, General Hunt pointed out that no line officer of that branch in the Army of the Potomac (he was staff) had a rank higher than colonel. In two corps a colonel did command the artillery; in one corps a major; in three a captain; and in one a lieutenant! Hunt went on:

> The most of these commands in any other army have been considered proper ones for a general officer. In no army would the command of the artillery of a corps be considered of less importance, to say the least, than that of a brigade of infantry. . . .
>
> Not only does the service suffer, necessarily, from the great deficiency of officers of rank, but a policy which closes the door for promotion to battery officers, and places them and the arm itself under a ban, and degrades them in comparison with other arms of the service, induces discontent, and has caused many of our best officers to seek positions, wherever they can find them, which will remove them from this branch of the service.

Wainwright became possessed by the conviction that for efficient management in camp, battles, and marches, the artillery of the army should be organized in an independent corps, under a general exercising full control subject to the army commander alone. This would put an end to the system under which any of a half-dozen corps commanders could order his share of the artillery about, and even division commanders could interfere. He himself rose to the brevet rank of brigadier general, but he never saw his dream fully realized. The Confederates did rather better. Their government in January 1862 authorized the appointment of brigadier generals and additional field officers in the Corps of Artillery. William N. Pendleton, Lee's Chief of Artillery, was not highly efficient; but at least the Confederates after Malvern Hill saw the necessity for high officers who could combine batteries and mass them for a concentration of fire on key points.

II

WAINWRIGHT'S rise was steady and points to brilliant qualities. The untimely death of Colonel Bailey early in the Peninsular campaign—possibly shot in the back by a resentful subordinate—gave him command of the regiment. He was soon Chief of Artillery in the First Corps, and later in the Fifth Corps, heading a brigade. In one action after another he distinguished himself. At Chancellorsville his force lost three officers, twenty-five men, and forty-three horses, and Hunt praises him warmly. At Antietam he was in the thick of battle, while his brother William had just been wounded at South Mountain. He was involved in John F. Reynolds' attack on Lee's right at Fredericksburg, in which Reynolds, crossing the Rappahannock well downstream, had to face Stonewall Jackson's forty-seven guns. The general had Wainwright bring every available gun to bear on the position, with the result that "a little after one o'clock the Confederate artillery there fell silent." General George G. Meade was able to move forward, but later had to retire. "About the only satisfaction Reynolds could find," writes E. J. Nichols in his life of Reynolds, "was in the handling of his guns."

At Gettysburg, Wainwright's artillery brigade did its heaviest fighting on July 1 and 2. On the first day his batteries lost eighty-three officers and men and about eighty horses. At dusk that evening he posted his guns on Cemetery Hill. He faced a still heavier encounter the next day, when the Confederates planted batteries in the wheat field 1300 yards away and opened the most accurate artillery fire Wainwright had yet seen from them. "We replied with our thirteen three-inch guns with good effect," he wrote in his official report. "It was an hour and a half, however, before we were able to compel them to withdraw, and then they hauled off their two right pieces by hand." That evening he had to withstand the heavy assault of Robert E. Rodes's troops, his men serving twenty-one guns as fast as they could load and fire. The cannoneers stood at their pieces even when Confederates drove into Michael Wiedrich's and James B. Ricketts's batteries, fighting the enemy off with fence rails and stones, and capturing a few prisoners. Thus they saved Cemetery Hill. As Hunt testified in his report: "The attack of Rodes was mainly repelled by the artillery alone."

Wainwright's losses were heavy in the campaigns of 1864 and 1865. In the three-day struggle for the Weldon Railroad alone, thirty-six artillerymen were killed or wounded. At North Anna it was the artillery that, firing canister, stopped the Confederate advance when a Union brigade turned and ran for cover; and the promptness and efficiency with which it came into action won general commendation.

All the while, overworked as he was, burdened with heavy responsibilities, and once very ill, Wainwright faithfully maintained his diary. The method he followed is indicated in an entry of December 31, 1862, in which he states of the record for the year just closed: "I might easily have found incidents enough to double it, but I am a slow writer and most of such incidents occurred when I had but little time to make the notes from which this is drawn off." That is, he made notes steadily when busy in the field, and then when he could find a few hours wrote his record in detail. In quieter seasons, he wrote every day; sometimes he mentions sitting up late to finish, and once he records that his new entry leaves him just ninety minutes for sleep before the army starts another movement. The freshness and authenticity of the journal are clear. At the same time, it is evident that Wainwright reflected upon his impressions before he set them down. Observant, methodical, and conscientious, he liked to ponder upon the scenes about him, and particularly the men.

Though he is conspicuously reticent about himself and his family, so that we get no real picture of his father, his soldier-brother, or his sister Mary, he does inevitably divulge a good deal about his personality and tastes. He is emphatically a gentleman, and very conscious of the fact. At one point he reflects upon how few officers in a gathering he has just left can be termed gentlemen. He is well read in English literature; at any rate, he mentions books that few but well-read men have seen. He is a powerful man physically; he once (June 13, 1864) threw a "coffee-boiler" from his campfire into the road, and his capacity to withstand fatigue on long marches, with little sleep, is remarkable. Punctual and exact in his own discharge of duty, he is a strict disciplinarian, maintains an austere front to his men, punishes derelictions sternly, and repeatedly registers his approval of the shooting of deserters. Yet he is conspicuously humane to beasts, expressing great solicitude for "my poor horses," and rejoicing when the batteries picked up enough corn on one march for an extra feed. When comfort is obtainable—good meat, good wine, warm shelter, a separate room, a servant—he makes the most of it; when he suffers hardship, which is half of the time, he says little about it.

The variety of the journal is appealing. Wainwright took a broad interest in most of the events of the war, military, political, and social, and had strong opinions upon most of them. Some of his convictions amounted to prejudices. He was so warm a Democrat that he cannot say a favorable word for Lincoln, his Cabinet, or the Congressional majority. One of his closest Rhinebeck friends was the Honorable William Kelley, the Democratic nominee for governor of New York in 1860 and owner of the splendid estate "Ellerslie" there; and Wainwright shared the Kelley-Tilden-Seymour political philosophy. Another strong conviction was that Eastern soldiers and generals were superior to Western, and that the fighting at Antietam and Gettysburg was much fiercer than that at Shiloh and Chickamauga. Yet only one general really extorted his admiration—McClellan. And he is emphatic in declaring as late as 1864 that it is impossible for any American general to find material for a really good staff, well trained in their duties. With what may be called the professional side of of the army he is always keenly concerned.

We find here his notes upon the aspect of nearly every town and village into which he marched; upon the topography of the battlefields and the state of the roads; and upon the weather, of which the diary probably gives a fuller account than any other book. He makes room in 1863 for a vivid description of gambling in the army just after payday, describing a gambling saloon in the woods at least two acres in extent, with more than a thousand men gathered around tables, some with large piles of banknotes by them. He takes note of the whores of Norfolk. He is careful to include comments on army diet, army medicine, and army straggling. Though Wainwright has little humor, he can draw a vivid sketch in a sentence or two, such as his characterization of Stanton ("a long-haired, fat, oily, politician-looking man") and his portrait of General Samuel P. Heintzelman: "a little man, almost black, with short coarse grey hair and beard, his face one mass of wrinkles," who "wears the most uncouth dress and gets into the most awkward positions possible." He could be very acid in his comments on the uneducated, the uncouth, and the dull-witted; and as a Hudson Valley aristocrat he had an unpleasant vein of supercilious superiority in his attitudes toward Negroes, Irishmen (especially after the Draft Riots), some "Dutchmen," and others whom he considered lesser breeds. On the other hand, he vastly admired a good fighter of any origin or national stock whatever. His frankness in commendation and criticism gives salt to his diary.

At two points, moreover, he gives us a record that goes beyond the mere jotting of diary notes. One is his careful portraiture of generals. Upon all the successive commanders of the Army of the Potomac he delivers a penetrating series of comments. He had especially good opportunities for observing McClellan, Hooker, Burnside, and Meade. "Little Mac" he thought not only a splendid military organizer, but a sound strategist. Hooker's character he found, on close acquaintance, to be bad. He was a braggart, a liar, a heavy drinker at times (at least by repute), and addicted to unjust attacks on fellow officers. Of Meade the diarist had a high opinion, noting only his two grave faults of slowness in movement and irascibility in speech: "Meade does not mean to be ugly, but he cannot control his infernal temper." Winfield Scott Hancock appears in these pages the brave and able commander he was; so does "Uncle John" Sedgwick, whom all loved. But we got such a convincingly unfavorable study of Gouverneur K. Warren—his profanity, his moodiness, his streak of meanness—that we cannot greatly regret the terrible calamity that overcame him in the last hours of the war. At the same time, Philip H. Sheridan emerges in a very harsh light.

Still more remarkable are Wainwright's studies of the great battles. He collected materials and critical points of view as if he intended to write a history of them. After Antietam, Chancellorsville, and Gettysburg he inquired for the impressions of other officers, so far as time permitted, and set them down beside his own. He was glad to escape Second Manassas because it was so full of blunders, and to share in Reynolds' frustrations at Fredericksburg rather than in the carnage before Marye's Heights. But all the other principal battles he saw. He had good opportunities to observe and judge Grant's strategy from the day he crossed the Rapidan in 1864 to the end, including the Wilderness, Cold Harbor, Spotsylvania, and the other bloody fields down to the cornering of Lee at Appomattox. What he saw did not give him a favorable opinion of Grant's s.rategic powers. The whole war, he thought, had proved the futility of frontal assaults on heavily fortified lines, and yet Grant continued to try them and to fail. The Illinois general ended the war, but he did it by sheer weight of numbers. In all future accounts of the Army of the Potomac, Wainwright's assessments of its defeats and victories will have to be carefully considered.

The keeping of such a record, amid the storm and stress of the conflict, was a remarkable achievement. Plainly, it is a remarkable man, a soldier of many gifts, who here at last lifts himself and his special view of the four years of war into the keeping of history.

❊ ❊ ❊

The facts in the military career of Charles Shiels Wainwright are recorded in abundant detail; those pertaining to his life before and after the war are not available in any printed work and have been difficult to ascertain in public archives. By his own statement when he applied for a pension November 28, 1902, he had been born in the City of New York on December 31, 1826. This confirms his assertion at the time of his enlistment, October 12, 1861, that he was then thirty-four years old. The census enumeration as twenty-five years of age, gives his occupation as farmer, and credits him with ownership of $50,000 in real estate and $13,800 in personal estate. Possibly the census taker guessed at his age. His pension application of 1902 shows that he was then living at 1715 G Street, N.W., Washington, that he had never married, and that since the war he had lived in Dutchess County, in Europe, and "for the past eighteen years" in Washington. He was wholly incapacitated by blindness and the effects of malaria.

He died at the George Washington University Hospital on September 13, 1907, and his body was taken to New York for interment. His death certificate gives his age as eighty-two and his occupation as retired army officer. It records one fact not elsewhere found, that his father and mother had both been born in Massachusetts. According to the brief obituary in the Washington *Post* of September 15, for some years after the close of the war "General Wainwright had a large farm and country place on the Hudson, near Albany"; he had been a member of the Metropolitan Club in Washington; and he was survived only by one brother and several nieces. The brother was of course William P. Wainwright; one of the nieces was Miss N. W. Bradley of New York. Charles Wainwright was a member of the Sons of the American Revolution by virtue of the fact that he was descended from Surgeon Thomas Tillotson of the Maryland Line. He was also related, on his mother's side, to the Robert R. Livingston family of New York.

This makes a pitifully meager record. Not many men, however, leave so imposing and valuable a monument for posterity to study as Charles S. Wainwright left in his diary. He came out of obscurity, for little is known of his career before 1861. After Appomattox, he disappears into obscurity again, for we know even less of his subsequent career. The important fact is that he treasured the diary on which he had expended so much effort, that it passed after his death into the hands of his brother, William, and that later descending to a nephew it finally became the possession of a great library on the Pacific Coast. Wainwright served his generation well in the war to preserve the Union. He has also served posterity in the magnificent record he made of the men, the events, and the emotions of that struggle.

The diary or journal that Charles Shiels Wainwright kept from October 1, 1861, through the Grand Review of May 23–24, 1865, is in five notebooks approximately eight by ten inches, each in hard mottled covers with black leatherette binding and corners. The whole record fills 1,700 pages and contains approximately 525,000 or 530,000 words. Although the ink is badly faded in places, the text is quite legible throughout. The volumes contain a few very rough diagrams of engagements, and statistical summaries of guns in the batteries, officers and men, and casualties.

The first volume, entitled "Journal No. I," covers the period down to December 31, 1862. The second notebook, "Journal During Rebellion," brings the narrative down to October 17, 1863. The third, also called "Journal During Rebellion," carries the story to June 30, 1864. These three are very much the same length, each containing from 120,000 to 125,000 words. The fourth volume comes down to December 31, 1864, and the fifth to the end of May 1865, these averaging about 75,000 words each.

At some unknown date the diary came into the possession of Colonel William P. Wainwright's son, Dr. Charles H. Wainwright, who was a surgeon in the New York Hospital. His widow, Margaret Gaire Wainwright, inherited it when the doctor died in 1948. From her it passed to a nephew, Mr. Harry Cronin, of the staff of the New York *Daily News*. Mr. Cronin offers a few reminiscences of his aunt, his uncle, and their home:

"I remember C. H. showing me the diaries off and on, years ago, but I never thought anything about them, and neither did he. A hardheaded former stockbroker, mentally very keen, he just did not get very excited about family background. . . . Originally 37 East Twenty-ninth was a five-story brownstone, complete with upstairs maids and downstairs maids. In the 1920's, when my aunt and uncle kept traveling around the world, they converted the lower two floors to commercial use and kept the upper three floors for themselves and their maid. The place was crammed with old family mementos, old swords, General Charles S. Wainwright's flagstaff, and so on. . . . My uncle-in-law was very orderly and kept track of an awful lot of material. I know that he would never have dreamed of selling the diaries. He merely kept them as family possessions which he undoubtedly deemed worthy of their rightful niche in the world."

The diaries were purchased in 1961 by the editor of this volume, who later presented them to the Huntington Library, with some related material. The New York Public Library has a small collection of the papers of Colonel William P. Wainwright.

The editor has selected from the diaries all the material that he deems of historical importance or general interest. Publication of the entire record would have required inclusion of so much arid and repetitive detail as to limit the appeal of this marvelous narrative, and would have served no good purpose. The integrity of the text has been scrupulously respected. General Wainwright abbreviated many words—battery, artillery, regiment, and so on—and these have been spelled out. He had a system of punctuation all his own, in which he regularly used colons for periods. Writing in haste, or when greatly fatigued, he occasionally misspelled a word or got a proper name wrong. The editor has corrected his errors, given some uniformity to capitalization and punctuation, and in general done just what any officer of a publishing house would do to prepare a present-day manuscript for the press. The quaint spelling of "havre-sack" has been retained. In no instance, however, has the author's meaning been distorted or modified in the slightest, and no liberties have been taken with his diction or style.

—A.N.

CONTENTS

—————⟨∞⟩————

LIST OF MAPS

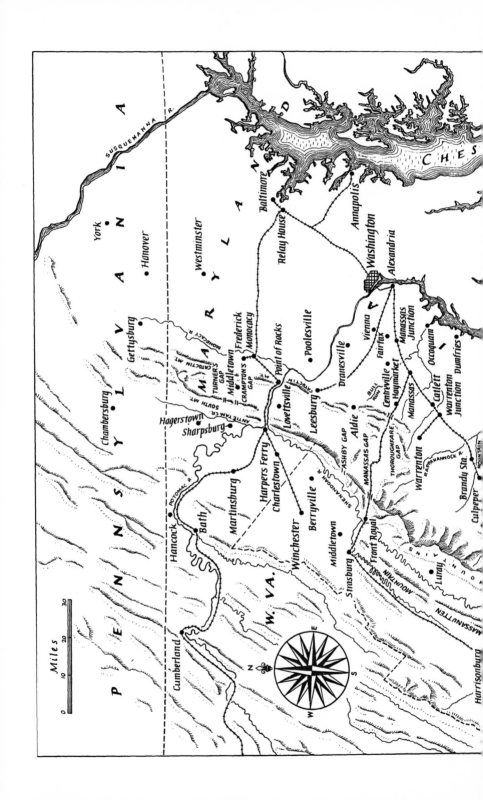

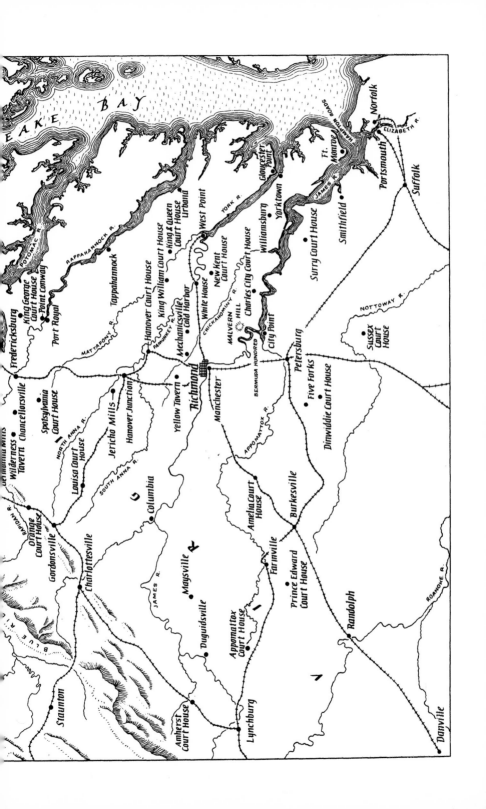

THE CLEARING OF THE POTOMAC

When Wainwright was commissioned a major in the First New York Artillery in mid-October 1861, McClellan had been in charge of the forces around Washington a little less than three months. In that period he had accomplished a remarkable work in organizing, disciplining, and inspiring an army. The fifty thousand troops of which he took command just after Bull Run had been little more than a mob, loosely grouped into brigades. McClellan stopped the desertions and straggling, got rid of incompetent officers, instituted systematic drill and instruction, and formed divisions of three or more brigades each. He also saw to the organization of adequate cavalry, engineering, and artillery establishments and to the planning of an elaborate system of defenses for Washington. By the time Wainwright entered the Army of the Potomac it comprised a hundred thousand men, well trained, properly equipped, and animated by a high spirit. "Had there been no McClellan," General Meade said, "there could have been no Grant; for the army made no essential improvement under any of his successors."

The organization of the artillery was entrusted to a New Yorker in his early forties, William Farquhar Barry, who had graduated from West Point in 1838 and fought in the Seminole and Mexican Wars. He had helped form the first battery of light artillery in the American army and, after serving at Bull Run, had been appointed brigadier general of volunteers. Under his direction field batteries normally of six guns were assigned not to brigades but to divisions; each division being entitled to four, one of which should be manned by officers and men of the regular army. Wainwright came under direct orders of the tirelessly efficient but genial Barry.

The army when Wainwright joined it had seven divisions on the Virginia shore of the Potomac opposite Washington, two up the river, and one in reserve. Late in October Brigadier General Joseph Hooker's newly formed division of about ten thousand New York and Indiana troops was sent to lower Maryland, on the north shore of the Potomac, opposite some of the

Confederate batteries that had closed the stream to Union navigation. Here, Wainwright by Barry's recommendation got his first important chance; he would be divisional chief of artillery. Throughout autumn and early winter the cautious McClellan kept his army inactive, though the weather was fine until January. Thus when Wainwright finally had an opportunity to see the river freed, it was not by Union action but by voluntary Confederate evacuation. But his first interesting duty, along with Colonel Robert Ogden Tyler, later a distinguished general at Chancellorsville, Gettysburg, and Spotsylvania, was on one of the boards weeding out incompetent officers.

❊ ❊ ❊

CHRISTMAS, DECEMBER 25, 1861, WEDNESDAY. Tomorrow I am to enter on a new style of work, being appointed one of an examining board under the Tenth Section of the Act of July 22, 1861. . . . Colonel Bailey will send a number of our officers before the board, and we shall doubtless have some others.

DECEMBER 29, SUNDAY. The examining board have met three times. . . . Colonel Bailey has sent up the names of Captains Tamblin, Cothran, and Slocum, and of Lieutenants Peabody and Eggleston of "M" Company, Seabury of "H," Cooper of "C," and Gansevoort of "E." We have made some way with the three captains. Cothran knew but very little of the tactics, but had so many excuses for not being better posted, and is so evidently a man of sufficient intellect and education to make a good officer that the board would not throw him, but recommended he should have another chance. Tamblin and Slocum have not been finished with yet. The latter made wretched work of it and will doubtless have to go. I am almost sorry, for the poor man has worked very hard to learn his drill, but cannot get over his lack of early education; he makes the most fearful blunders with the mounted drill and although I have some days spent two hours with him in my tent trying to explain the orders and movement so as to get it through his head, he makes the very same blunders the next day. There is no saying what his written statement will be, as he can hardly write at all, and cannot spell. We require each officer to make a written statement as to what opportunities he has had, a sort of short account of his official life up to the present time, so as to get some idea of his education.

As for old Tamblin, he has proved a much harder subject to deal with than I expected. He not only answered pretty much every question out of the tactics, but when corrected as to some reply about the use of artillery in action, shewed fight, and quoted from authors which none of the rest of us had ever heard of. We had finally to summon witnesses in his case. Colonel Bailey shewed that he was not able to impart his knowledge to others, however much he might know himself; and that he was greatly wanting in efficiency as an officer, not having the respect of any of his men. The law authorizes these boards to "examine into the capacity, qualifications, propriety of conduct and efficiency of such officers as may be brought before them." A pretty wide scope. Lieutenants Eggleston and Peabody were also before the board. The former was found totally lacking in every respect. The latter is evidently capable and intelligent, and was passed. Lieutenant Seabury who was to have come before the board has resigned instead. . . .

I saw General Patrick this morning. He tells me that I stand very high with General Barry, which is very pleasant, especially as I was a perfect stranger to him when I came down, and have never spoken ten words to him, except on business, nor used any outside influence whatever; so it can only result from what he has seen himself.

DECEMBER 31, TUESDAY. As I did not get home to camp until near 12 o'clock last night, this of course is not written the same day it is dated. My new duty as mustering officer kept me busy from 9 o'clock this morning until 11:30 at night, but I have got through it all except signing the muster rolls of the Rocket Battalion, and the Massachusetts Battery all of which were so full of mistakes that they will have to be made over again. Fortunately General Barry's order specified that there would be no review or inspection, which saved much time. . . .

After a late dinner I returned to the Germans in order to compare their muster rolls. I had been obliged to get one of their own officers to call the rolls for me, making bad work with their jaw-breaking names; neither did I do much better in going over the rolls though they brought in a couple of bottles of champagne to wash them down. They have a very nice camp here, being a part of the Artillery Reserve, which I find includes all the regular battalions camped in our neighbourhood; their horses are all well sheltered in good board sheds, and they have board shanties for their officers, mess rooms, and so on. All the officers of the battalion mess together; I was over-persuaded to go down to supper with them, on condition that we would return to work in ten minutes. But Colonel Brinckle* insisted on my taking the seat of honour, and gave my health in due form; as he held out his glass for the real German click, it brought back such recollections of the Rhine, Berlin, and all my journeyings there, that I could not help speaking of it. Immediately there was a shout, the major has been in "faderland"; every one of them wanted to know if I had visited his birthplace; and, as most of them were from the Rhine country, of course I had. Then came a lot more clicking of glasses on the part of all those from this or that town. The amount of it all was that instead of being ten minutes at supper, it was two hours or more before we got back to our work. . . .

* Colonel John Rumley Brinckle, Fifth U.S. Artillery.

Another month has been added to our camp life here; a month on which I look back with a great deal of satisfaction, as one well spent and resulting in actual, tangible progress in acquiring a good knowledge of our business, both on my own part and by those under my command. I am beginning to feel as if I really was a·soldier, and my straps to set easily on my shoulders. The weather has been wonderfully fine all the month, not more than two stormy days during the whole of it. All of our batteries have made good progress except "A" and "C." These two lag behind terribly. . . .

I have seen but little of the army beyond the artillery and cavalry which come to drill on the plain here. We have very, very few officers visiting us either, except some of the Colonel's old West Point classmates who drop in. Rumours of an advance on the other side of the river have been renewed every day, but have amounted to nothing at all so far.

Our monthly return today shows an aggregate strength of 1,385. This, of course, does not include Kennedy's and Robinson's batteries, which do not belong to the regiment. We have gained twenty recruits, had seven die and eight desert; the number of sick at this time is about the same that it was last month.

WASHINGTON, JANUARY 1, 1862, WEDNESDAY. While in the city this morning I met General Barry who said that General Hooker, commanding a division somewhere down the river, opposite the rebel batteries, which have closed navigation all winter, had written up asking that a good officer might be sent down to him as chief of artillery, and that if I thought I should like the place he would recommend me for it. The offer took me very much by surprise, as I had no idea of getting a command in the field before the Colonel did: so I asked for a day to think of it. Of course I have thought of nothing else through the remainder of the day; but after getting the advice of my most true friend, Patrick, and weighing the matter well, I have determined to accept. The pros and cons run something in this way. Cons: I shall be entirely cut off from the regiment, none of our batteries having been ordered to that division. The batteries there are said to be in very bad order, so that I should have to go through a long course of instructing again; Dan Sickles commands one of the brigades, and ranks next to General Hooker, consequently would take command should anything happen to the General: and, strongest of all reasons against going, Hooker's division does not lie with the rest of the army, and the chances seem to me to be against his moving with it. On the other hand, Patrick tells me that General Hooker is generally considered a pleasant man to serve with: that should the army move Aquia Creek way, this division may be the very first to push across the river; that Barry's offer of the position to me was a great compliment, there being but two volunteer officers holding similar commands; and, as a settler, that if I refuse this position I may not have another offered to me. How soon I may get the order to go I cannot say, but presume almost immediately, as General Hooker was very urgent in his request that he should have a chief of artillery sent at once.

WASHINGTON, JANUARY 5, SUNDAY. The examining board closed up its business yesterday. It was decided that Tamblin was too old a dog to learn new tricks. Slocum too must go, but the board softened his case down with a commendation of the poor fellow's efforts to learn, and informed him that he may do better in some less responsible post. Lieutenant Gansevoort resigned sooner than stand an examination, and Lieutenant Cooper on his plea of ill health was given another trial. This finished up those from our right. We had but one other case before us, that of Captain Bunting of the Sixth New York Infantry, a case in which I took a great deal of interest as his battery is one of my new command (if I get it) and he himself has been acting chief of artillery in Hooker's division for a couple of months past. Never did man's looks belie him more than did Captain Bunting's: a fine, military-looking man, evidently well educated and of good social standing. We were surprised to see him before the board. He has been in command of a battery over four months, and most of the time of several, but did not know the first thing; could not tell the proper intervals and distance in line; nor where the different cannoneers should sit on the boxes; indeed he at last admitted that he had never studied the tactics, so his was a very short and decided case. It was astonishing to me that such a man should have taken a position where he must become known, and then not even try to fill it respectably. . . .

Letters from home say it was very quiet in New York on New Year's Day; merchants being very blue over the bank suspension, and all feeling ugly as to affairs with England. Here there was not nearly so much calling as I expected to see, except on the public functionaries: great crowds were going in at the White House: some officers with epaulets and chapeau bras, things which I have not seen before since I have been down here. I did not pay my respects to the President or any of the other powers that be. General McClellan was sick, some reports said very dangerously so, but he is well enough to attend to business again now.

JANUARY 8, WEDNESDAY. To the press of work of last week has followed a spell of perfect idleness. On Sunday night we had an inch of snowfall, which has been followed by very cold weather for this latitude, almost freezing the Potomac over. The ground has been too slippery for mounted drills, and so all hands have been busy fixing screens of pine

and cedar brush around the picket ropes. As it is intended that all our
batteries shall be sent to divisions as fast as they are got ready, General
Barry will not give us boards to build stables with, such as the Artillery
Reserve have, and we are obliged to do the best we can by cutting
evergreens in the woods some two miles off and making a hedge around
our horses some twelve feet high. It will serve a good purpose to keep off
the wind, but is no protection against rain or snow. For our own
private horses we purchased enough boards to build a rough shed.
Boards are enormously high here owing to the blockade of the lower
Potomac, which shuts off pretty much all communication by water,
and forces everything over the single track railroad, which has as much
as it can do to bring down the troops themselves and provisions for this
vast army. Firewood too is very high. The government contractors
having made their bargain before the "rebs" shut up the river could not
possibly carry it on, did they not cheat us out of nearly half what we
are entitled to; but since officers and men have got stoves up, we manage
to get along very well, not requiring outdoor fires, except for the
guard. . . .

All the regiment have been vaccinated in accordance with orders;
small pox being a good deal about. Have gone through with the operation myself: the doctor pronounces mine a success.

JANUARY 12, SUNDAY.   Our cold spell broke up on Wednesday night with
a rain storm, followed by fog and muggy weather, which has taken
pretty much all the frost out of the ground again, so that our camp is
one sea of mud some six inches deep. It is next to impossible to move
about the camp behind our own immediate quarters, where we have
boards laid down, unless one goes on horseback. I went in to church
this morning and then stayed till near dark so as to get some exercise
on the dry sidewalks, as also a good dinner, our fare out here growing
worse instead of better. Met several New Yorkers in at Willard's, as I
almost always do whenever I go in there.

Today it has been very fine, almost like April, and a soft drying wind
blowing. Trust it will dry up the mud so that we can begin drills again,
for I am tired of doing nothing. Colonel Bailey too expects to be able to
take hold now, and means to have some battalion drills, which I am very
anxious for. Colonel Hunt, commanding the Artillery Reserve,[*] has had
several; and General Barry had Brinckle's battalion out once, when I
went with him. The regulars as well as the Dutchmen made pretty poor
work of it; but four well drilled six-gun batteries, whose captains
thoroughly understood the manoeuvres, would make a superb sight.

[*] Henry J. Hunt, West Point 1839, who had commanded the artillery defenses south
of the Potomac when McClellan took charge, was appointed head of an artillery reserve that McClellan expected to number 100 guns.

JANUARY 15, WEDNESDAY. We got a good drill on Monday in spite of a most cutting wind: but that night it snowed and then rained, so that we are all ice again. At present the roads are horrible, rendering any movement hereabouts impossible; and I am beginning to think that things in this department will remain as they are until spring; if, indeed, it is not intended to retain this army around Washington altogether for the protection of our blessed Congress. The radicals there seem determined to drive the President into the most extreme measures, and sometimes I fear he has not got backbone enough to hold out against them. If he will only stick to the programme he has laid down that this war is for the preservation of the Union, the putting down of armed rebellion, and for that purpose only, I feel sure that one good campaign will close up the whole business. But if he gives way to these "black Republicans," and makes it an abolition war, there will be an end to the Union party at the South, and I for one shall be sorry that I ever lent a hand to it. General Burnside is about starting from Annapolis; they say he has a splendid command. . . .

I hear nothing of my assignment to Hooker's division, and begin to doubt if I shall get it. The more I think of it, the more I am convinced that this division will see no service this winter, if it does at all; so I am not regretting the non-coming of the order so much, being quite willing to stay here yet if I can only get into the field with some of our own batteries by and bye. We hear that guns are now arriving in numbers, and are promised our full outfit so soon as the carriages get here. . . .

JANUARY 19, SUNDAY. The weather continues such as to prevent our drilling. On Friday I spent most of the day testing a new shell: the matter had been referred to Colonel Bailey, but as he cannot leave his bed he sent me out. . . .

We have sent off a recruiting party to try and fill up the regiment, Captain Crounse, and Lieutenant Barnes, with four enlisted men. It is to be hoped that they will succeed.

All is now anxiety as to the Burnside expedition which has at last got off from Annapolis: on its success I imagine depends whether a move will be made here or not, so soon as the roads will permit. On Friday night we heard the heaviest firing to the south and east that we have heard yet; heavier even than that from the rebel batteries down the river the night the new sloop of war *Pensacola* went down, some two weeks ago; it lasted for several hours, and appeared very distant. Many think that it must have been as far as Norfolk and that Burnside has gone there; but that is almost too great a distance for it fairly to shake the ground, which it did, waking me up; no easy job, by the way. . . .

Mr. Cameron, Secretary of War, resigned a week ago, and another Pennsylvanian, Edwin M. Stanton has been appointed in his place. Folks prophesy wonders from him. I hope they may prove correct, but I do not like his looks. I saw him in the box with President Lincoln the other night at the Opera: a long-haired, fat, oily, politician-looking man. It was the first chance I have had to get a real look at the President. It would be hard work to find the great man in his face or figure, and he is infinitely uglier than any of his pictures. When the audience rose and cheered on his entry, instead of coming forward and bowing like a gentleman, he sat down, stuck his head out over the edge of the box, and grinned like a great baboon. I was ashamed to think that such a gawk was President of the United States.

Met James Beekman, wife and daughter, at church this morning, also John Jay. Most of the visitors here though appear to be from northern New York and the lake borders: the flour merchants have made fortunes the past season and are spending them now. . . .

JANUARY 22, WEDNESDAY EVENING.   Whist has got to be an established institution with us now, the Colonel, Dr. Evarts, Major Van and myself, generally making up the set. Anything to kill time this bad weather. The sun has not shown itself for ten days: it rained on Sunday, Monday and Tuesday, finishing up with snow. It has not been cold, but all are suffering from ennui and want of exercise. The effect on the men and even the officers is very demoralizing; when it does dry up it will take a week to get them all up to the point they were at last month. . . .

We hear nothing of Burnside's expedition yet: but there is news of another success in Kentucky, at Mill Springs, something really decided as the rebel commander Zollicoffer was left dead on the field. It is to be hoped that Thomas will not now show that he deserves the soubriquet he had while at West Point, of "Slow Thomas," but will be able to turn the rebel flank at Bowling Green, while Buell attacks them in front.* One real big victory there now will not only open the whole Southwest, but make the rebs at Manassas shake in their shoes. . . .

* General George H. Thomas fought the battle of Mill Springs on January 19, 1862, as part of his campaign to recover eastern Kentucky from the Confederates. He had marched over wretched mountain roads to reach the place, which was about seventy miles northwest of Cumberland Gap, on the Cumberland River. The Southerners were commanded by George B. Crittenden, a Kentuckian who had graduated from West Point in 1832 but had become a lawyer, and by Felix K. Zollicoffer of Tennessee, a former newspaper editor and Congressman. Each side had about 4,000 troops, but despite this equality in numbers, Thomas' Minnesota and Ohio volunteers won a crushing victory, capturing twelve guns, 150 wagons, more than 1,000 horses and mules, and large stores. The success ended the Confederate threat to easten Kentucky, removed two Southern generals (for the drunken Crittenden saw his career ended), and greatly elated the North as the first substantial gain since Bull Run. But Thomas, a slow-paced veteran who had fought in the Mexican and Seminole Wars since leaving West Point in 1840, thought an invasion of east Tennessee—which was much desired by Lincoln—unwise if not impracticable, and turned back to Somerset, Kentucky.

JANUARY 26, SUNDAY. The long expected order for me to "report to Brigadier-General Joseph Hooker for duty as Chief of Artillery of his division" came yesterday, and I expect to go off Wednesday. I shall have to get some tents and other things to take down with me. . . . Were the roads any way decent I would ride down myself, but they are intolerable everywhere. General Barry informed me that there are three six-gun batteries with the division now, and that he would send me one of our own, whichever one I wanted, so soon as the roads were good enough to get it there.

BUDD'S FERRY, MARYLAND, JANUARY 31, FRIDAY. Here I am safely in my new quarters, or at least in my new command; for I am as yet sponging on some neighbours for a lodging; my own tents, bedding, and so forth, from some unaccountable reason, not having met me at the boat yesterday morning. The trip down here was anything but an agreeable one; the only boat running, one day down, the next up, is a Schuylkill stern paddle-wheel about as large as a big canal boat, and with a speed of some seven or eight miles an hour. It rained too until we got nearly down here, which did not add to the pleasantness of such close quarters. The boats land here at what is called Rum Point. . . . The Virginia shore here is steep, rugged and very broken by numerous small streams which empty into the Potomac. The rebel blockade batteries begin at Cockpit Point, a mile or so below Freestone, and are sprinkled pretty thick for some five or six miles down the river from there, mounting very heavy guns. The camps of Hooker's division are stretched along on this side for about the same distance, lying back a mile or more, however, from the river. They picket the river bank the whole distance from Mattawoman Creek to Port Tobacco, where we have a strong outpost. They say that the rebs fire largely at every vessel that attempts to pass up or down, and sometimes try to throw shell over into our camps, a distance of over two miles in a direct line. These shell our men pick up, if they do not burst, which they seldom do, and sell to curiosity hunters from New York and Boston; one man is said to have got $20 for an immense hundred-pounder or something of that sort. General Hooker told me that he estimated the number of shots they had fired, since the establishment of the blockade, at about 5,000, not one of which had injured a living creature.

I found an orderly with a horse awaiting me on the arrival of the boat, who shewed me the way to General's quarters, where we got about dark; worse than Camp Barry. I had never dreamed before how bad mud could be. You rise at once from the landing on to a sandy plain, which seems to extend all along this bank of the river. There must be a subsoil of blue clay or something of that sort, for the sand would not hold the water itself, and as I went in for a foot or two there can be no frost in the ground. The road for near the whole distance, some three miles they say, I thought it nine, runs through a forest of yellow pines: in places it is corduroyed, but everywhere horribly bad.

The General received me very pleasantly, and after a little chat turned me over to one of his aides, Lieutenant Lawrence, who gave me a spare bed there happened to be in his hut. General Hooker is decidedly a very handsome man, tall and portly, but very soldierly, with a florid complexion, bright blue eyes, and an expressive nervous mouth; I should think him about 47 years old; his hair is iron grey. He is a graduate of West Point, but resigned from the army after the Mexican War, and has been living in California of late years. The headquarters camp is located in a small grove, adjoining an equally small church. The officers have good sized log huts, say 14 by 20, with canvas roof and open wood fireplaces; they live two in a hut.

My horse arrived soon after I did, having left the day before; Edward says he was two or three times afraid he had lost him altogether, so deep down did he sink in the mud. This morning I rode on here about a mile where two of my batteries are camped, "H" First United States and the Fourth New York. After making myself known to the officers and receiving a very kind invitation from Lieutenant Eakin, commanding Battery "H," to occupy his tent until my own arrived, which I at once accepted, I went on another mile down the river to the camp of the Sixth New York. . . .*

FEBRUARY 5, WEDNESDAY. My traps only reached me today. The waggoner took them to the wrong boat, a quartermaster's boat that happened to be coming down the day I did; so they have been lying here, but at another wharf all the time. It will be some days yet before I get them up as I want to raise my two tents on logs so as to get a room big enough for recitations; meantime Lieutenant Eakin still allows me the use of his tent. And now let me try to describe the location here so that I shall be able to understand it years hence, should I read this then. "Budd's Ferry" used to be a simple row boat (perhaps they had a flat boat) ferry across the river, from in front of the Widow Budd's house to the mouth of Quantico Creek: up which creek some five miles or more lies the town of Dumfries. Colton's map of Maryland has a road marked on it from Port Tobacco through Milshead to this point. But I have very great doubts whether there were any public roads whatever in this whole district before the army came here, for a more uncivilized looking region I never saw. As it is, there is what we should call a farm road running from directly opposite my camp down to the widow's house, a

* Lieutenant Chandler P. Eakin was an officer in the First Regiment of Artillery in the regular army, and he and his Battery H did able service in a long series of engagements.

distance, including some small turns, of about one and one-fourth miles. Mrs. Budd has left her house on the river bank, the rebel guns pointing too directly at it; and it is now used by the officers and men of a section of artillery which is posted near to it to warm their fingers and their coffee in. It is by degrees coming to pieces, the men stealing the clapboard and flooring to make themselves bunks with. . . .

Directly opposite here at a distance of 2,400 yards is Shipping Point, a bluff some thirty feet high, and perhaps a mile long, stretching down from the mouth of Quantico; on it are the principal rebel batteries, mounting a dozen guns or more. As we see them from the Budd house they look very strong, there being an immense amount of new earth thrown up; we can also see the rebs at work on them, and marching about in their rear, the first sight of a "butternut" I have had. Whenever a vessel passes up or down the river, and I am surprised to hear that almost every night there are some go by, the rebs open on them, and though they have so far done no actual harm, sometimes force them to turn back. Two or three gunboats of ours lie in the river, above and below the batteries, to render relief should it become necessary. The section of little ten-pounders has also at times replied to the enemy's guns, and the officers and men say that have seen them carry off dead or wounded men afterward, but I have great doubt of our having done any more harm than their shot have. General Hooker has now forbid the firing of the section at all, unless the *Page* or some other boat comes out. Our men, for fortification, have dug a great pit in the sand for their guns, and cut embrasures to it so that they can hardly be damaged unless by a shell bursting directly over their heads. The camp where my own quarters are, "Camp Hooker" as it is named, lies on the north side of the main road, and about one hundred yards from it. . . . Both of the volunteer batteries complain that General Hooker would not allow them to draw boards for stables, while he approved the requisition of the regulars; which was making a most invidious distinction. The Sixth New York is camped about a mile to the east of this point, and near the "Excelsior" Brigade. Their camp is on a plain, but in the middle of a dense growth of small pines, which gives them most perfect shelter. . . .

The weather here has been much the same as it was all last month at Washington: rain rather better than half the time. Sunday night and Monday we had a fall of some four or five inches of snow, the heaviest this winter in this region of country. The roads are beyond any description I can give of them; on horseback you cannot go off a walk, and the poor teams have almost as much as they can do to draw an empty waggon. The forage for our artillery horses we pack up, two sacks of grain slung on a horse; of hay we get next to none. The General has issued an order forbidding the use of teams to haul supplies until the roads are better, fearing that they may all be used up. Very large details from the infantry are at work, making a new corduroy all the way from Rum Point, through the different camps to the extreme end of the Excelsior Brigade, some seven or eight miles in all.

FEBRUARY 9, SUNDAY. A bright sun and high wind all day give promise of something better in the way of getting about. I trust it will turn out so for they begin to talk of the army moving again. Foote's success at Fort Henry has woke everyone up once more and the cry is "on to Richmond." There is no use in talking though for the army could not possibly live ten miles from a railway and I doubt if they could get artillery along at all. General Hooker went up to Washington last week to Mrs. Lincoln's ball; all the division commanders were there, so rumour says the ball was a blind to a council of war.

✷ ✷ ✷

All the troops around Washington had by this time gone into winter quarters without waiting for orders and showed the ingenuity to be expected. A few conical tents with a hole at the top, like those that General R. B. Marcy had modeled on Western tepees, permitted the use of stoves. In others a clay hearth served as fireplace, with chimneys of stone or of barrels placed one atop another. Tents were at first raised on wooden floors and surrounded with boughs for warmth; then within a short time complete log cabins replaced many of them. As the Comte de Paris noted, most soldiers in the Army of the Potomac carried a few books, including a Bible, in their knapsacks; they wrote many letters—the Eleventh Massachusetts sent from its camp an average of 4,500 letters weekly, which the government transported free. The arrival and departure of the mail was a great event in camp life. "Together with the correspondence, the mail brought enormous packages of newspapers, which ragged boys, both on foot and on horseback, distributed in great haste, even to the remotest corners of the camp." Wainwright had brought to the front a servant, named Edward, whom he quotes as using a strong Irish brogue.

To his artillery McClellan attached special importance. By the beginning of 1862 his army was marshaling its seventy-three batteries of 407 pieces. Eighteen of the batteries formed an Artillery Reserve under Colonel Henry Jackson Hunt, who was later to command the guns that wrought havoc with the troops of Pickett's Charge at Gettysburg, and the others were attached to the divisions in the field. Each division was supposed, as we have noted, to have one regular battery of four guns and three volunteer batteries, making sixteen to twenty-two guns, well built, light, and easily handled. When the war began the government had not yet adopted effective rifled cannon, and although just after Bull Run the War Department ordered two hundred rifled pieces made of iron, many artillery officers to the end preferred smoothbores.

Hooker established his headquarters six miles northeast of Budd's Ferry on the lower Potomac, almost opposite the mouth of Quantico Creek, and distributed his command over the western half of Charles County, Maryland. He planted batteries on the river, built warehouses and wharves for supplies, established a telegraph line to McClellan's headquarters, and began to plan for action. He longed to distinguish himself, and before long was proposing a sly night expedition with his whole force against the Virginia shore, to take the Confederate batteries in the rear. This was forbidden. Meanwhile his division had its troubles. The men were accused of excessive addiction to whisky; he irritated many Northerners by refusing to hold runaway slaves; and he got on badly with the quarrelsome Daniel E. Sickles, second in command. His difficulties increased when Henry M. Naglee, a West Pointer in the class of 1835, a Mexican War veteran, and an inveterate troublemaker, one of McClellan's pets, arrived to command one of the brigades. Though wounded at Fair Oaks, Naglee was never to rise above the rank of brigadier general and was eventually mustered out of the service early in 1864.

❋ ❋ ❋

FEBRUARY 12, WEDNESDAY. No change in the weather; rain, rain, rain, and, of course, nothing for me to do. My house goes up very slowly in consequence of the bad weather; it is only about a dozen yards to the south of this tent, being about as central a position as I could get, and, having no staff, I am almost obliged to live with some one of the batteries. I shall continue to mess with Battery "H" so long as I remain here, but when we move expect to join headquarters. Our mess is very simple, more so even than at Camp Barry, but it is very cheap, only some $18 a month they say; and what there is is quite well cooked. I should like to improve it, but as I am a sort of invited guest do not feel at liberty to suggest an increase of the expense. All the servants, except my own, are taken from the enlisted men of the company. Edward did not like it at all when he first came down here, and gave notice that he should quit, but now he is quite contented and says "it is much better than it was at Camp Barry. There are no na-gers here." I have got him an "A" tent to himself and given him my stove, as I intend to have an open fireplace in my tent, so he ought to be quite comfortable. . . .

FEBRUARY 16, SUNDAY. News of victories continues to come in from south and west, making us doubly anxious for fine weather here that we may have our share in them. The capture of Fort Henry is officially announced, as also the taking of Roanoke Island by Burnside, after some pretty hard fighting. Today's papers say that Price's army is all captured in Missouri, and that Fort Donelson is taken. I hope that both are true though they have not been telegraphed down to General Hooker yet, as all important victories are. Rumours of all kinds as to our own movements are as plenty here as they were at Washington; but I do not believe that even General Hooker himself knows anything decided about the matter. He has a balloon here. The balloonist was on the boat the day I came down; we had quite a talk together; he claims to have already made most important discoveries as to the enemy's position, and promises much more. He was up today, seeing what he could see, the atmosphere being clear.

Have got into my new quarters and am very comfortable. The two wall tents, one being split down the back, are placed end to end on a log wall, raised between three and four feet from the ground: it gives me a room about 9 by 18 feet; rather out of proportion but quite comfortable and roomy. Have got a good door to it; floor and open fireplace; also a desk, pegs to hang clothes on and other like conveniences. Camped down right in the woods, we do not have to go far for fuel. My man cuts the trees down right at my door. Being a fresh importation, he is not very good at handling his axe, which gives him something to do. General Hooker is very particular about the men burning fence rails, but once in a while a few will disappear. . . .

FEBRUARY 19, WEDNESDAY. It has rained pretty steadily since Sunday; first a cold rain, and then a warm one. Of course we are again floating in a sea of mud, and there is an end to all hope of any mounted drills this month, for it will take a week of good weather to dry us up after it stops raining, that is supposing it ever does stop. The new road to the landing is completed, which is a great help to us in hauling forage and stores; but woe to the horseman who gets once off the corduroy! If he ever gets his horse on again he is a lucky man. We have another improvement too, in the substitution of a good side wheel steamer, the *Argo*, for the tub I came down in.

A new brigadier-general has also made his appearance here to take command of the First Brigade. Heretofore Sickles has been the only general officer, except General Hooker, in the division. General Naglee, I understand, graduated at West Point but resigned soon after, and has been living in California. I have not seen him yet, but his quarters are close by my own, and if he is a nice man he may prove an acquisition in the way of company; of which I am very much in want, not having as yet found any officers in the division I care to be at all intimate with.

The First Brigade was General Hooker's original command;* it consists of the First and Eleventh Massachusetts, Second New Hampshire and Twenty-Sixth Pennsylvania, all regiments which have been out since the commencement of the war. The Second New Hampshire is camped near general headquarters, and I think is rather a pet of the General's: the other three regiments are my near neighbours, the First Massachusetts being close to me. All these regiments are full, and in very good order except the Pennsylvania one.

Sickles's "Excelsior" is the Second Brigade; there are five regiments in it, of which I know almost nothing except that there seem to be an infinitude of courts martial among the field officers. I met Sickles one day in the General's tent, but fortunately he did not offer to shake hands. Have also seen one of their other officers up there, Lieutenant-Colonel Farnum, very drunk; "on dit" that Hooker, who has a weakness that way, is very sweet on Farnum's wife. This brigade is camped some three miles from here near Liverpool Point. The Third Brigade is composed of the Fifth, Sixth, Seventh, and Eighth New Jersey regiments, and is camped down towards Rum Point. Colonel Starr of the Fifth commands the brigade, a captain in the regular cavalry, promoted from the ranks.† Neither the Second nor Third Brigades are full, the regiments averaging from 700 to 900.

The good news from Fort Donelson proved to be true. Official information of its capture together with 15,000 prisoners, and Generals Johnston and Buckner, was telegraphed down here on Monday, and

---

* Most respectable citizens regarded Daniel E. Sickles, of an old New York family, former legation secretary in London, state senator, and Democratic Congressman, as highly disreputable. As his biographer W. A. Swanberg says, he was "always in some sort of crisis, be it financial, legislative, sexual, or homicidal." But this former friend of Buchanan had been roused like a lion by Southern secession and had thrown himself into the war with such zeal that Governor E. D. Morgan of New York had authorized him to raise a brigade of five regiments. When the national authorities disdained both Sickles and his regiments, the peppery leader appealed to Lincoln, and the President promised that a mustering officer would arrive to "take you all in out of the cold." Wainwright would naturally dislike Sickles, his politics, and the way he had thrust himself into the army.

Naglee had been a banker in San Francisco. Hooker, too, had been in California from 1849 to 1861 as soldier, impecunious rancher, and officer of the state militia. Like Sickles, he was fired to action by the outbreak of war and hastened to present himself to Lincoln, declaring with characteristic self-confidence that he would make "a damned sight better general" than the government had on the field of Bull Run. The Massachusetts members of Congress recommended him for a brigadier generalship, and this West Pointer of the class of 1837, with a good Mexican War record, forthwith took command of the four regiments which are here named by Wainwright.

† Colonel Samuel H. Starr commanded the "Jersey Blues," as the brigade was termed, but was shortly demoted for "conduct unbecoming an officer and gentleman." He called a private a "God damned sonofabitch" and struck him with his sword.

read that night at all the evening parades. All these victories have created quite an excitement in camp, the men are hurrahing and the bands playing half the time. Everyone is getting anxious for our turn to come; and something may possibly be done soon; but for our own division, we can only cross the river with boats and there is not the sign of one here yet. The radical papers, indeed nearly all the Republican ones, are beginning to find fault with McClellan; the *Post* is so outrageous in its abuse that I was glad to stop it. We get the *Herald* here regularly the day after it is published, and the Baltimore papers the same day. As I said once before, I know so little that I do not like to have any opinion as to whether we should have moved before this, should try it now, or wait; but until I can prove General McClellan to have been remiss, or mistaken, I am quite willing to believe he knows best, and has decided rightly. They say he is very active around Washington, and does an immense amount of work.

FEBRUARY 23, SUNDAY.   I have a large batch of letters today from New York and Boston; all full of the victories west and south. The cities seem to have been wild with joy, saluting, illuminating and all sorts of goings on; quite a panic in the cotton market, and some even thinking that the war is about over. I wish it was, though I must say that I should like to get a little taste of fighting myself first, just to see how it feels and to be able to say that I had been in an actual battle. . . .

Here we have nothing but continued rains, and so very heavy. Our last ones have been warmer than the previous, and as the frost is about all out of the ground they ought to settle it so that a few days would dry us up. The batteries have been able to get a few standing gun drills, none of them are as perfect at it as most of the batteries we had at Camp Barry; in many little things showing that they have not had anyone to explain matters to them. On Friday I commenced officers' recitations in my tent, and mean to have them three times a week. I have not required the attendance of the officers, only invited them; most of them were present, and took an interest in it.

Our new brigade commander is inclined to carry things with a high hand. The other night he visited all his pickets and arrested thirteen officers whom he found asleep. He also undertook to give some orders to the battery, but found he had got outside of his command. On Friday we received two Whitworth guns from Washington. They are not to belong to my command, but are sent down for General Hooker to practise with. The first fine day I hope to get a chance to astonish our opposite neighbours, as it is said that this gun will carry true six miles.* . . .

---

* The Whitworth rifled cannon, usually breechloading, had gained an international reputation. Various Confederate commands obtained them through the blockade, and Lee used four of the six-inch caliber in his Gettysburg campaign. Union forces im-

FEBRUARY 26, WEDNESDAY. Things begin to look decidedly like a move here; not that any actual orders preparatory have been issued, but there is a sort of undercurrent which tends that way. General Hooker has been up in the balloon two or three times, and today was out all day on the upper flotilla, sailing about and reconnoitering the opposite shore. All leaves are stopped, no matter on what ground they are applied for: he would not even permit me to go up to Washington where I was summoned today to appear as a witness in Captain Cothran's case. It may be some weeks yet before the movement takes place, but things certainly tend that way more decidedly than at any time heretofore. . . .

Yesterday afternoon we tried the Whitworths. I had a detachment of Bramhall's men down to work them. These guns are entirely different from anything we have. They are full six feet long, and not much over two inches bore; the rifling instead of being given by a number of grooves sunk in the sides of the bore, is obtained by making the bore itself hexagonal with a rapid twist, I do not know how much exactly. They are loaded at the breech, which swings open on a hinge and is fastened by a strong screw. Solid shot are the only ones used. These are some ten inches long, weigh about thirteen pounds, are rounded at the point, cut flat at the butt, and planed down to fit the bevels of the bore exactly. The powder is placed in a tin case which also fits the bore exactly, and is kept in by a wad of wax and grease, which cleans and lubricates the bore of the gun behind each shot; this tin has a flange at the bottom, by which it is withdrawn after firing. The guns were planted on the plain in front of the First Massachusetts camp, whence we had a good view of Cockpit Point, as also of Shipping Point or Possum's Nose as it is sometimes called. Altogether about forty shots were fired. General Naglee was there, made himself very officious, monopolised one gun entirely, and did two-thirds of the firing, very much to my disgust, and General Hooker's too I think. I only got six shots myself, all of them aimed at a house just in rear of the upper battery on Shipping Point, and so near it that the lower story was entirely hid by their earthwork. Of these, three we saw strike the top of the parapet; could see the dust rise; the others went over it, and may have struck the house for aught we know. The distance was a little over three miles; to Cockpit two and one-half miles. After some time the rebs tried to reply from their lower batteries, but their shot fell far short, much to the amusement of our

---

ported a battery of Whitworth fieldpieces, of smaller caliber, and carried them on the Peninsular campaign, but did not employ them. Later this battery was made part of the Washington defenses. The guns had remarkable accuracy and penetrating power and have been termed the finest artillery pieces on either side. But as the shape of the projectile was not adapted to a large charge of explosive, they used solid shot instead of shell as their principal ammunition.

men, who had gathered in crowds and cheered and jeered lustily. For accuracy and range these guns certainly surpass everything we have, but they are too long, too heavy, and too small calibre for general field uses; and as only solid shot can be fired from so small a calibre, except on dusty ground it is impossible to see where your shot strikes at these great distances.

FEBRUARY 28, FRIDAY.   Our expected move has all blown to the winds: it was to have been an actual move, a dash across the river to seize and destroy the batteries there and so raise the blockade. Sometime next week was the time the General intended trying it; but today all those who came down in the boat from Washington say it is talked of all over town, which of course renders a surprise impossible and quashes the whole thing. How it got out at Washington I do not know, but should not be surprised if it was let out on purpose as a gentle way of letting the General down, his plans not being approved of. I think its success very doubtful.

MARCH 9, SUNDAY.   I was writing a letter home about three o'clock this afternoon, racking my brain for something to say, and finding nothing, save that we were excessively stupid here, when I was aroused by a general shout of "good news," "good news," from the men outside. It was just about the time our newspapers should come along, and supposing they had something more from the West of victory I stepped up on the bank to secure one. The crowds of men in every tree top, and on the barrack roofs of the First Massachusetts, all gazing across the river, together with the dense volume of smoke which rose from all the rebel batteries, told the story at once. So soon as I could get saddle on my horse, I galloped down to our point, that being about the nearest point of observation.

On reaching the river bank I could see that most of the buildings at Shipping Point, the little steamer *George Page,* and two schooners lying in the creek near to her were all on fire; while columns of smoke were rising more or less from all the different batteries there and at Cockpit Point. They had evidently loaded the guns which they could not remove, and built fires over them in the intention to explode the guns and burn the carriages, for very soon the guns, as also evidently the magazines, commenced to explode. Some of the guns, however, could not have had their shot well wedged, for quite a number of shot fell in the river, well towards this side; showing that the guns had been discharged instead of bursting.

Lieutenant Henslow of "D" Company, who commanded the section on picket today, told me that he had noticed an unusual stir about the opposite batteries all day, and was very much tempted to open fire on the men who could be seen in numbers around the embrasure, had not

General Hooker's orders been so positive not to fire. I had heard firing in the direction of Cockpit Point for about ten minutes before the men started me out by their shouts, but supposed it was the old story of the rebs firing at some vessel which was running the blockade. Instead of which it was the gunboat *Yankee* shelling the point, previous to sending a boat ashore. The boat's crew were on the point when I got down to the river. Afterward the gunboat dropped down as low as Shipping Point and landed there. Company "A" First Massachusetts also took a large barge they have for "toting" their stores around from Rum Point to near their camp, and pulled across there.

Fearing that I might be wanted by the General, I rode up to headquarters, but found General Hooker was out on the lower flotilla. Finding I could learn nothing there except that the General had been receiving many communications from the gunboats all the previous night, and had started off very early, I came back to camp to await the return of the Massachusetts party. I went over to see Colonel Cowdin about nine o'clock. He told me that his men had asked permission to go over, but that he had refused it, so Company "A" had gone on their own account: I presume his refusal was only official. The party returned while I was there, each man bringing something in the way of a trophy; pots, pans, axes, shovels, and one even a wheelbarrow. Some too had a rough sort of bowie knife, evidently of home manufacture, but heavy enough no doubt in the eyes of its former owner, to kill a "damned Yank," if he could only get at one. The most interesting trophy to me was one of the Whitworth bolts I had myself fired over there. . . .

We have now had a week without rain; the nights have been frosty, but a strong wind almost every day has helped to dry up the ground a good deal, enough for all the battalions to get a mounted drill yesterday. Found them woefully rusty, but as all seemed pleased to get to work again, they will probably pick up again very fast, if the good weather will only hold on. Last night we had a white frost and today has been quite warm, but as the wind has got around to the east again, it is to be feared that we shall have another rain. . . .

This clearing out of the rebs puts an end to all our General's ideas of glory to be got by storming their works. He had determined on another attempt. Perhaps it was meant to co-operate with the move from up above; one thing is certain, that some thirty empty canal boats were sent down here from Washington, and the gunboats were increased in number. Six boat howitzers were also brought down on Thursday, with all their equipment for a landing party. Since then I have been busy instructing the officers and men detailed from the New Jersey Brigade, fifty to each gun, how to use them; manual of the piece, cutting of fuses, and so on. The intention was to cross these howitzers with the storming party, as it would not be possible to get the battery horses over then. I had got quite interested in my new scholars, but that is all over now.

We tried the Whitworth guns again, on Friday, at Cockpit Point. This time General Naglee was not there (he is off on leave) so the firing was much better: every one of the thirty shot fired struck in or very close to the battery. As they are so small and they do not burst, it is doubtful if we did any harm. . . .

MARCH 10, MONDAY. Under the new state of affairs here General Hooker sent up to Washington last night for orders but none have yet been received. One of the New Jersey regiments was sent across the river this morning to Cockpit Point, to dismantle the rebel batteries there of their remaining guns, and to destroy such other property left there as they were not able to bring off or was not worth it. They accomplished their work, throwing three guns, all that were left, over the parapet, down onto the beach where the gunboats can get at them, and bring them off. . . .

This afternoon we had news of the sad work made by the rebel iron-clad *Merrimack* among our fleet at Fortress Monroe. About eight o'clock this evening the General got word from the lower flotilla that there were reports of the *Merrimack* coming up the Potomac tonight. He determined to try our little Whitworths on her and sent up for me. It would not have been a very bad night to spend out on Stump Neck, being soft and springlike; still I am glad to go to bed instead. Stump Neck, where we were going to plant our guns, is a long low spit of sand formed by the debouch of the Chicamoxon about two miles above Budd's Ferry. We should have had everything most favourable for a chance to hit her below the water line, which I take to be her only vulnerable point, and as she would have been within range for at least half an hour, the Whitworth being so very accurate I think that there was some chance of our getting a hole through her. By ten o'clock, though, we got a telegram from Washington telling us how the *Merrimack* had been driven back into Norfolk by the little *Monitor;* a most glorious beginning for Ericsson's new style of gunboat.[*]

The rebels still have a force at Aquià Creek, and Colonel Hampton is said to be at Occoquam Village with a regiment or brigade. So Heintzelman, or whoever pushed down the river, did not follow to this side of

---

[*] It is interesting to note that Wainwright gives the correct official name of the *Merrimack,* which being named for the Massachusetts river and not the town had the final "k." With a draft of twenty-two feet, a speed of only four knots, and such poor maneuverability that it took her a half hour to turn around, the ship could never have been the menace to Washington that Stanton feared. But we can understand Wainwright's regret that he never had a chance to hole her with the Whitworths.

the creek. The blockade, however, is raised, and the river quite free for navigation now.

MARCH 11, TUESDAY. This afternoon I crossed over to Shipping Point, and had a good look at the abandoned works and camps there. The bluff is almost perpendicular, from twenty to thirty feet high, and flat cleared land on top. The batteries were sunk or half sunk in the bank, so that the lower part of the parapet was in the old bank, and from fifteen to fifty feet thick, making it impossible for the fire of our gunboats to injure them. Most of the batteries had but one gun, and all were semi-circular: the magazines had been cut into the solid bank. All the batteries had been well revetted with plank, and some of them nicely soldered on the parapet. They had loaded all the guns, wedging shot in them, and then built lumber and logs around and over them to which they had set fire. Two guns had been burst in this manner; in others the shot had not been well wedged, so that it was driven out by the explosion, and the gun thus saved, though the carriage was destroyed; in two or three cases the fire had gone out altogether, and no damage had been done. This was the case with the splendid English gun, a 120-pounder Blakely, which was in the battery farthest down the river. Our men had despaired of getting off this gun, it being near one hundred feet back from the edge of the bank, had wedged in more shot, and built a large pile of pine lumber around it, intending to fire it when they left this evening so as to destroy the gun. To thus lose such a piece would have been a great shame, so I hunted up the officer in charge, and shewed him how, by levelling the artificial part of the parapet and laying timber skids from the gun to the edge of the bank, it could without much trouble be run on log rollers from its carriage to the brink, there being a slight descent; which he promised to do tomorrow.

I went through a number of the camps, including those of the Twelfth and Twenty-Second North Georgia about a mile back from the river. There were but very few tents, most of the men having lived in hovels built in the ravines, which are numerous, with a roof of logs covered with dirt. They were wretched things and awfully dirty. I cannot think why they should have had such wretched huts, for there is a large steam sawmill on the point, and vast piles of lumber and scantling around it. Hundreds of entrenching tools and axes were lying in a pile about a mile back; and the men seem to have had a super-abundance of cooking utensils, especially bake ovens. I saw large quantities of corn, corn meal, rice and fresh meat lying around, but no flour. Judging from the number of half-worn shoes with which the camp was strewn, there can be little truth in the reports of their suffering in that line. There were also many blankets and articles of clothing left behind.

I cannot yet imagine why they should have left in such haste. It must have almost amounted to a stampede; in one or two huts it was evident the men had left their half-eaten meal behind. While I was over there our pickets brought in some twenty or thirty young cattle, and I had an opportunity of seeing the new mode of telegraphing by signal flags.* Ten minutes was sufficient time to report the capture of the cattle to General Hooker and get his orders to bring them across the river.

* The Confederates had left the Potomac in such haste because, anticipating Mc-Clellan's advance and having only 50,000 to 55,000 effective troops in northern Virginia, they thought it safer to gather their forces nearer Richmond. Joseph E. Johnston had in fact expected McClellan to march in concealment along the northern bank of the river, cross near Aquia Creek, and seize Fredericksburg, which would place him closer to the Confederate capital than Johnston's own forces. Hence the evacuation of Centreville and the James line.

Visual signaling by the army had been perfected by Albert James Myer, a graduate of Hobart College and a Buffalo medical school, who while serving in Texas was struck by the possibilities of such communication in the clear air of the plains. He successfully used his system in General E. R. S. Canby's campaign against the Navajos in New Mexico. Called to Washington to organize the Army Signal Corps, he established effective signal schools. Fort Myer bears his name.

OPENING THE PENINSULAR CAMPAIGN

The immediate passage of large steamers down the Potomac heralded, as Wainwright divined, a movement by McClellan's now powerful Army of the Potomac upon Richmond by way of the water route; that is, to Fort Monroe as a base, and thence up the Peninsula between the York and the James to a point near the Confederate capital. Lincoln and Stanton much preferred an advance by land directly across the Rappahannock to Richmond. Each path had advantages and disadvantages. The one chosen by McClellan shortened the supply lines, brought the Union army close to Richmond before meeting heavy resistance, and threw the Confederates completely on the defensive; but it necessitated the maintenance of a substantial body of troops before Washington to block any Confederate raids. Hooker had opposed the water route; but his troublesome subordinate General Naglee not only supported McClellan as a good friend, but maneuvered Hooker out of a conference of division commanders, which Lincoln convened on March 8 to debate the alternatives, and attended in Hooker's stead! The result was that the council voted eight to four for the Peninsular route. It was to prove far less easy than McClellan anticipated.

Lincoln's War Order Number Two, dividing McClellan's main army into four corps, placed at their head Generals Irvin McDowell, Edwin V. Sumner, Samuel P. Heintzelman, and Erasmus D. Keyes; men whom McClellan himself would not have selected. The first three had voted against the water route. Hooker's division was assigned to the Third Corps under Heintzelman, a Pennsylvanian of mediocre ability who had graduated from West Point in 1826 and served in the Mexican War. He was approaching sixty, and the impetuous General Philip Kearny was presently to refer to him as "an old fool."

❊ ❊ ❊

MARCH 12 [1862], WEDNESDAY. The excitement today has been the passing up the river of the steamboat *Bay State* and a dozen others, mostly large North River and Sound boats. The day was very fine, and the passing of the boats seemed to give us new life and bring us once more

into connection with the rest of the world. It is evidently the intention
to ship a part, if not the whole, of the Army of the Potomac to some
place where these river boats may go with safety. We have not yet received any orders as to what this division is to do. Report that our
troops have advanced to Manassas without any fighting. . . .

The weather being very fine now, we have settled down to our drills.
I wish I had a better lot of horses to enter on a campaign with, but
Captain Osborn* tells me that there are none to be had in Washington.
I require them to be exercised every day without fail, and hope with
extra care, the good weather and a larger supply of hay, which he ought
to get now, to bring up those that are really good for anything.

MARCH 14, FRIDAY. President Lincoln has issued three "War Orders"; a
high sounding title they have, at any rate. The first announces that he
himself is hereafter Commander in Chief, and so relieves McClellan of
all control of the Western and Southern armies. The second forms the
army into "Corps d'Armée." The third cuts down McClellan's command
still further, limiting it to the Army of the Potomac. We shall now see
how great Mr. Lincoln's military talents are. The whole thing is plainly
the result of the radical influence on the President; they have been very
bitter against McCellan lately, and he has yielded to them thus far. I
fear he has not overmuch backbone. The order organizing the Corps
d'Armée has not reached us yet, so I do not know what they have done
with this division.

General Hooker told me this morning that he was expecting orders
to cross the river at any moment, and on that ground refused to give
me forty-eight hours leave to run up to Washington. Some of our regiments cross the river every day to remove or destroy the stores there,
generally returning at night. On Wednesday night, however, two companies from a Jersey regiment went up to Dumfries, spent the night there
and brought back a few prisoners; but had no fight. The inhabitants all
fled at the approach of the dreaded "Yankees," but seeing that our men
did no harm soon returned. Some of them claim to have been good
Union men all the time. This morning two full regiments crossed over,
so I suppose a reconnoissance will be pushed out still farther towards
Fredericksburg. I had some hopes of attending church there next Sunday,
but have about given it up. The balloon was taken across the river today
and has been up to see what they could see.

* Thomas W. Osborn, of the First New York Regiment of Light Artillery, soon rose to
be a division artillery chief with the rank of major. He became in fact one of the most
noteworthy artillery officers of the war, and particularly distinguished himself at
Gettysburg as chief of artillery of the Eleventh Corps. See L. Van Loan Naisawald,
Grape and Canister (1960), 291, 298, 402, 424–25.

The weather still keeps mild and without rain, although yesterday and today have been cloudy. The river is alive all day long with steamers, large and small, passing up: the *Baltic* and several other large ocean steamers have gone by, as also quite a number of North River barges. On Wednesday Lieutenant Baum of the Twenty-Sixth Pennsylvania, an ordnance officer at division headquarters, went across the river and has not since been heard of; one of the signal corps who was with him is also missing. The supposition is that they have been captured by some lurking party of the rebel cavalry. These are the only men we have lost. Neither have we taken any number of prisoners, but lots of "contrabands," as the runaway niggers are now called, come back with our men almost every day. There is quite a camp of them at Rum Point, and another at Liverpool Point.

MARCH 16, SUNDAY. Rain again, and very heavy too nearly all day. The Chicamoxon, which runs through the ravine at the bottom of our camp, has spread out to the size of quite a respectable stream. I passed most of the day at headquarters, being caught up there when the heavy rain came on. Could learn nothing of importance except that no orders had yet been received directing any movements on our part. I also saw a copy of Army of Potomac order announcing . . . this division is in General Heintzelman's command instead of McDowell's as we at first heard. I am glad that we are not under the Bull Run hero, and if Heintzelman is moving down on the other side we shall no doubt cross over and join him. . . .

MARCH 19, WEDNESDAY. Have just returned from a short trip up to Washington. I got my leave for forty-eight hours on Monday, and left about daylight Tuesday morning. We have no regular boat running now, so had to go and return as I could get a chance, barely getting twenty-four hours in Washington, which was very little and drove me almost to death. A number of other officers went up in the same boat, the *Eagle,* a Philadelphia ferryboat, among them General Naglee and Colonel Marsden of the Second New Hampshire. The trips up and down were not unpleasant, though tedious. We met a large number of the steamboats coming down the river loaded with troops, and so crowded that they cannot possibly be going far, though their destination is not yet made public.

Washington was not so much deserted by uniforms as I expected to see it; still those there seemed to have more to do, and many of them had their horses in marching trim. At Camp Barry I found Colonel Bailey packing up to join Casey's division, not Sedgwick's as he had expected. He is much disappointed, as Casey's is said to be the poorest division as well as the smallest in the army, being composed entirely of regiments which have come down since January.* . . .

This morning General Hooker commenced to move across the river; at least the first brigade and two of my batteries had orders to pack up. Just as they got ready the order was countermanded, by telegraph from Washington. I should have been sorely put out if they had crossed while I was away. They have turned the First Massachusetts out of their barracks, which were much the best in the division, and made a general hospital of it where all the sick left behind will be placed. There is no doubt now that the whole Army of the Potomac is to be put in motion soon, and we among the rest, but whether this division is to be part of the water party or not I cannot yet say.

General McClellan has issued his address to his troops, in which he distinctly says that his object in keeping them so long inactive has been to make real soldiers of them; which he thinks they now are. Take it altogether, it is very good.

MARCH 23, SUNDAY.   We had a real equinoctial storm last week, and cold too at that. It prevented all outdoor movement except such as was absolutely necessary. We got orders of preparation for moving, but as yet do not know when we shall start: from what I can learn it will probably be about the middle of the week. Our transportation has been cut down to four waggons to a regiment, and one to a battery, for all camp and garrison equipage, officers baggage, papers, and so forth. I shall move up to General Hooker's headquarters tomorrow, as that will be my proper post on a move, and I have no transportation of my own. . . .

The river continues to be alive with troops and boats passing. We do not yet know where they have gone, but everything points to the neighbourhood of Fortress Monroe; certainly they have not gone far, as those boats which went down loaded on Tuesday passed up empty yesterday. The Third Division, Hamilton's, of our corps went by yesterday in some twenty-five boats. This would seem to indicate that we too are to be of the boat party; still the general opinion here is that we shall go to Fredericksburg. I think there is no doubt that General Hooker wishes to do so. Letters from home tell me that one hundred steamers were taken up in New York and sent off ten days ago; and that 100,000 men are to be carried to the mouth of the York River. That is a very large number, and will require several weeks to get down there with all their appurtenances unless a great many more boats are sent here.

---

* Silas Casey, who had graduated from West Point in 1826 and been wounded in the Mexican War, published in 1861 a useful two-volume work, *Infantry Tactics.* He was a Rhode Islander. The previous August he was appointed brigadier general of volunteers, and he was now to take part in the Peninsular campaign as a division commander in the Fourth Corps.

Meantime we learn that the advance from Washington had pushed out some twenty or thirty miles beyond Manassas without opposition, and had mostly returned. . . . There has been a terrible hard fight at Pea Ridge in Arkansas. And Burnside had succeeded in capturing New Bern, North Carolina, thus obtaining a safe base of operations there, much to the relief of many here who feared that he might be overwhelmed by troops sent down from the army which has left Manassas. Take it altogether Burnside has made quite a success of it; he gives all the credit of the plan to McClellan, and I feel pretty confident of the ability of our young commander if he is not interfered with by the powers at Washington. The War Orders of the President plainly show that they were not willing to let him have everything as he wanted it.

HEADQUARTERS HOOKER'S DIVISION, MARCH 26, WEDNESDAY. Am now living at division headquarters, where I am not nearly so comfortable as to quarters as in my double hut, but much better off in mess matters. Our fare in Company "H" was very poor, the company itself by no means pleasant, and such close companionship with officers under my command by no means tending to ensure the deference necessary. Here the General and all his staff mess together, and we fare very well, at least comparatively, with the addition of clean tablecloths and napkins. We had shad for breakfast this morning. The other day I dined with Adjutant Price of the Seventh New Jersey; a most capital dinner we had too, they having a good French cook, and the field officers being able and willing to pay for good living. The General's staff are all volunteer officers, knowing nothing of their business save what they have picked up in the service. Most of them are from the First Brigade, which was his original command; men of ordinary social standing, and very ordinary education, so I doubt if I shall find any of them much company for me. . . .

We have quite a number of orders coming in relation to organization and so forth in the field, as also with regard to our own preparation to move. One of the first prescribes the powers of corps commanders, and also designates flags for each headquarters. First Division's will carry a red flag 6 by 5; Second Division's blue; Third Division's red and blue vertical. Ours being the Second will have a blue flag. We are ordered to turn in all surplus stores at once to the depot quartermaster and come down to marching trim, so everyone has had enough to do this week packing up and making out invoices. The weather has been very fine again, and the General is looking hourly for transports and orders; but they do not come. We hear that they are very short of boats at Washington and that General McClellan is complaining of not being furnished with the amount of transportation promised him. We being down here will probably be the last to get off.

MARCH 30, SUNDAY. The superb weather of last week ended yesterday morning with a severe rain storm, alternating with snow. This change from the warmth of May to slush underfoot and icicles overhead is far from agreeable, and I wish myself back once more in my comfortable hut. The public mind here has settled down now that we are not to move at once, and all have been using the fine weather for drills. My batteries have been out every day: General Naglee and Sickles have been having brigade drills, and a grand review of the whole division is seriously talked of. Naglee managed his brigade pretty well, keeping it in two lines, but the field officers were all very ignorant of the manoeuvres. I was disappointed, too, in the appearance of the men. They were slouchy, especially the Second New Hampshire. I went down on Friday to see how Sickles managed; he had about 3,500 men out in one line, and what from want of room, and ignorance on his part as well as on that of others, he was able to do very little with them. Some of the regiments looked beautifully, but though raised as a brigade they were not all uniformed alike: the First, Third, and I think one other, had the New York State jacket and kepi, an infinitely trimmer and more soldierly dress than the United States frock and slouch hat. . . .

The papers state that the Senate have refused to confirm Sickles in his commission as brigadier-general, of which I am very glad, and so is General Hooker. No official notice of it, however, has been received here yet, so he continues in command. By the bye, from what I learned in our Jersey brigade the other day I am now convinced that the troops which we all admired so much at the grand review were Kearny's, the First New Jersey Brigade. When I was in Washington I learned that he had refused promotion to a division because they would not let him take his old brigade along. He has spent a vast amount of labour on it, and they say several thousand dollars. He has great reason to be proud of it, and I should not think would want to give it up.*

Two companies that went over the river brought back several very rampant "secesh" citizens with them; moving spirits in the bad work over there; they looked very down in the mouth on learning that they would be furnished free transportation to Washington. A party of signal officers joined the command yesterday, direct from Fortress Monroe: they report the peach trees there in full bloom; a change of climate from this which I wish they would hurry up and give us.

* Philip Kearny, a brilliant graduate of Columbia College who entered the army in 1837, had been an observer with the French forces in Algeria in 1840, had lost an arm in the Mexican War, and, after leaving the American service, had joined the French to win the Legion of Honor at Solferino. He was one of the best-trained officers on the Union side. Now a brigadier general of volunteers commanding a New Jersey brigade, he was soon to distinguish himself in the Peninsular fighting and to earn his promotion to the rank of major general.

Every day the river continues covered with boats. They say that forty went down on Thursday loaded to the guards. A number of them now have sloops and schooners in tow loaded with horses, batteries, and waggons.

BUDD'S FERRY, APRIL 2, WEDNESDAY. In order to pass the time I have entered on a new duty: sitting on a court martial. It is my first experience on a General Court, and from what little I know, hope it may be my last. General Naglee is president of the Court, with nine Colonels, two Lieutenant Colonels, and myself, so that I am junior member, and have to give my vote first when a vote is taken. We have now sat two days on the case of Colonel Small of the Twenty-Sixth Pennsylvania charged with any number of crimes or faults or whatever they may be called; enough at any rate to cover with the specifications half a dozen pages of foolscap. The evidence so far is not at all to the credit of the colonel. It is interesting and rather amusing to see the different traits of individual character come out in the members of the Court. Colonel Small is a lawyer himself, and lawyer fashion is constantly raising objections on all technical points. Whenever these would be of weight in a civil court they are strongly supported by the lawyer on the Court. Then when the question is one depending on discipline, he always finds supporters in one or two members from the Second Brigade, who are pretty hard characters themselves, and I suppose think they may be brought up on some similar question one of these days. My next neighbour on the Court is Lieutenant-Colonel Gershom Mott, of the Fifth New Jersey to whom I have taken quite a fancy: he is a fine soldierly-looking man; was, I believe, in the Mexican war; says little, but seems very sound in his military ideas.*

This Twenty-Sixth is the only Pennsylvania regiment in the division and most fully bears out the report I have all along heard, that the Pennsylvania regiments are the worst officered in the army. The colonel, lieutenant-colonel, and major are all now in close arrest, outside of their own regiment; of which Lieutenant-Colonel Fiske, of the Second New Hampshire, is in command.†

Last night General Hooker went on board one of the gunboats, expecting so to meet McClellan who was to pass down on the steamboat

---

* Gershom Mott of New Jersey was one of the many able officers who attained high rank without benefit of West Point. Now just forty, he had been active in banking and transportation. Commissioned a lieutenant colonel in August 1861, he fought efficiently throughout the war, becoming a brigadier general in 1862, a division commander in the spring of 1864, and a major general soon afterward. He was twice wounded, at Second Manassas and Chancellorsville.

† Francis Skinner Fiske of New Hampshire was brevetted a brigadier general for his services; he resigned in October 1862.

Commodore. The boat went down, but McClellan was not on board, only his staff. I presume General Hooker now knows exactly what is to become of us but we subordinates are still in ignorance. Things are in such a state of readiness with us that it will not take long for us to move when our transports do come.

APRIL 3, THURSDAY. This morning they telegraphed down from Washington that the boats for this division will be down tomorrow; so, unless there should be some unforeseen delay, we will get off by Saturday or Sunday at the latest. A circular has been sent out to know the number of men, horses, and so on for which transportation will be required in each regiment. My return calls for room for 463 men, 436 horses, and 59 carriages all told. Hall's and Smith's batteries are to be loaded at Rum Point, Bramhall's and Osborn's at Liverpool Point. I should have preferred to have had them all together, but the docks were too small; as it is, I think that those at Liverpool Point have sense enough to get along without me, so I shall look mainly to Hall and Smith. The First Brigade will load at Budd's Ferry, on five boats; there is no pier there at all. The Second at Liverpool Point on four boats; and the Third at Rum Point on five boats. . . . The cavalry regiment, Third Indiana, which has been with us all winter, will remain, and the Fifty-Sixth Pennsylvania is coming down to join them. General Hooker's orders are very strict against any slaves or contraband being taken along.

Bramhall got his new three-inch guns just in time. They are infinitely better than the James gun he has had. Battery "H" is also to have new guns, light twelve-pounders; I wish they were here, but we shall have to go without them now. I am short of both men and horses, and some of the horses we have are worth but very little. . . .

APRIL 6, SUNDAY. Still in the old quarters, but we break up tomorrow morning. General Hooker and staff go down in the *Argo.* I hope and expect to go with them; at any rate I shall send Edward, my horse and traps, on board tomorrow only holding on to my saddlebags and a single pair of blankets so as to be prepared for an emergency. It has been a most exquisite day; I have had thirteen hours' work, though some of it was rather play, and delicious enjoyment, having a boat to take me to and from between the two landings. All of Hall and Smith's batteries are loaded. . . .

LIVERPOOL POINT, APRIL 8, TUESDAY. Everything of mine is loaded at last, and an awful time of it we have had. It commenced snowing and raining at two o'clock yesterday afternoon and has kept it up pretty steady ever since. All day one has had to potter round in slush an inch thick, and any depth of mud underneath: cold too, and chilly, freezing the marrow in your bones. The dock here is very small and poor. Sickles's quartermaster claimed entire control of it as a brigade dock; had he not done so, and I had had a towboat to get my vessels alongside I could have been all loaded yesterday. But the quartermaster was very ugly, claimed to ship his waggons and the like first, and at the same time did not arrange his business so as to keep the dock occupied all the time. I managed to get a few boats loaded yesterday by the aid of a little gunboat that towed them in for me. But I was afraid to come to a downright quarrel with the quartermaster as he is a pet of Sickles's, and I should hate to have to have anything whatever to do with him. Today the order relieving Sickles came down, and Nelson Taylor is in command.* Hooker also stopped here on his way down, and so dressed down Captain Austin, the quartermaster, as to set me all right. It was eight o'clock this evening when we got through stowing our carriages on board the barge *Wallkill* of Newburgh, . . .

CAMP ON CHEESEMAN'S CREEK, APRIL 12, SATURDAY. In Virginia at last and part of the great army. We had an awful trip down: none of the other divisions could have fared so badly. Many of our men were on the boats six days and really suffered for want of food. My own little command all got down safely, and were landed yesterday and today. I believe we have lost three horses, and had one man injured, that is all.

For myself I missed the barge, and was obliged to beg quarters on the *State of Maine* with Colonel Dwight's command.† The Colonel received me kindly, and ordered his Adjutant to see that I had a berth, which I got, and managed very well, having my own blankets. The boat was very crowded; the men fairly lying on top of one another on the floor of the saloon. But it is the best ventilated steamer I ever was on board of, for even the lower cabin was by no means foul. The Colonel is a most strict disciplinarian, though very self-indulgent, rarely getting up before one P.M., and had all the men on deck for inspection each day, no matter how severe the storms, and the whole boat cleansed. The men also all had their hair cut close one day; the pile of dirt disclosed beneath the

---

* Daniel E. Sickles, already noted as a man of disreputable character, who had murdered Philip Barton Key and escaped penalty on a plea of temporary insanity, had been nominated a brigadier general in September 1861, but was rejected by the Senate in March 1862. Later on, a second nomination was confirmed and made retroactive to the first. Wainwright's contempt for him was widely shared. Nelson Taylor, of Connecticut origin, had served in the Mexican War and then settled in California. Just after Bull Run he was commissioned colonel of the Seventy-second New York. He was later to be elected to Congress from New York City, where he was practicing law.

† William Dwight, of Massachusetts birth, had left West Point before graduation to go into business. In 1861, at the age of thirty, he was made colonel of the Seventieth New York. He was destined to fight throughout the war, though at Williamsburg he was wounded three times, left for dead on the battlefield, and captured. He became a brigadier general and division commander, and during the Red River campaign was General N. P. Banks's chief of staff.

earlocks of some must have been accumulating all winter, and as the
pilot said, "would grow a hill of corn."

I made acquaintance with the captain and pilot on the ground of this
being a Newport boat, and spent most of my time in the wheel house
during the day, where I was out of the way of the men, and could see
what there was to be seen: my advances also procured me the best there
was to be had on board to eat, which was very little, this boat having
been seized by General Hooker on the way up the river, and not having
had any chance to lay in supplies. I don't know what we should have
done had it not been for a foraging party which went on shore at Port
Tobacco, the first night out, and robbed hen roosts and pig sties. I did
not approve the deed, but ate the pork none the less.

Our evenings were passed in the purser's room, playing whist. It was
a queer company, at least for me to find myself among. General Hall
of the Second Excelsior was on board with his wife, as also the wife of
the quartermaster. He and Lieutenant-Colonel Farnum were among
Walker's filibusters in Nicaragua, and had queer stories to tell of their
adventures there. Farnum too was supercargo on the *Wanderer*, during
her trip for slaves.* He is a singular character; has been engaged in pretty
much every big piece of rascality going in these days; takes a canteen,
three pints of whiskey every day, and as a consequence is drunk almost
every night. Still there is an openness and certain kind of truthfulness
about the man, which make it impossible not to like him to a certain
extent.

It blew so hard when we left on Wednesday that we only got twelve
miles down the river. And the storm continuing on Thursday we hauled
in at Point Lookout and remained there until it abated at sundown,
when we got off and anchored opposite the dock at Hampton by daylight
on Friday. . . .

As the fog up the James lifted, the cry was raised, "There comes the
Merrimack!!" and sure enough there she was just coming out of the
Elizabeth River, with two wooden steamers as tenders. Such a scatteration
of vessels as ensued was quite a sight: the roads were full of transports
of all sorts, steam and sail, and those which lay farthest up got underway
in a hurry. The men of war, too, of which I should think there were over

* Sickles' "Excelsior Brigade," the second brigade of the Second Corps in McClellan's
army, comprised six New York regiments and became famous for its heavy casualties,
losing nearly 900 men killed or mortally wounded during the war. John Egbert Farnum was a noted adventurer. Coming from New Jersey, he had been a private in the
Mexican War and later participated in the filibustering expeditions of both Lopez in
Cuba and Walker in Nicaragua. The slaveship *Wanderer* had landed about 420 Negroes
from Africa on the coast near Brunswick, Georgia, in December 1858, a bold crime that
produced great excitement in the South; two were exhibited at the South Carolina
State Fair in 1859. For his share in this affair Farnum had been indicted in Savannah.

twenty altogether, got under way and stood up the river, the *Monitor* leading. I had a very fair, though not near, view of both these now celebrated vessels. The *Merrimack* is large and unwieldly-looking, resembles an immense sperm whale half out of water, or a Noah's Ark; while no better description can be given of the *Monitor* than "a very large cheese box on a raft." The little *Naugatuck* too pushed up boldly, with almost nothing but her smoke pipe sticking out of water. The *Vanderbilt* started but did not go far: they say that she has been fitted with a tremendous iron stem, and her machinery protected with cotton bales. The Commodore is on board and has pledged himself to run the *Merrimack* completely under water, if he can once get a fair clip at her. There though is just the rub. The "reb" lay in the mouth of the Elizabeth, and invited our vessels to come up to her, which they would not do, so after an hour or more she paddled back. Meanwhile the two small gunboats ran in under the cliffs at Hampton, and they say captured a couple of boats with quartermaster horses on board. . . .

APRIL 14, MONDAY.   Our camp here is really a pretty one, the weather is delightful and everything calculated for real enjoyment for the few days in which we may be permitted to lie here to rest previous to moving up to our place in the lines around Yorktown. The division is camped along both sides of Cheeseman's Creek; their clean white little shelter tents sparkling amidst the young green of the woods, for the leaves are just beginning to come out. At night especially when the hundreds of camp fires are lighted the scene more resembles fairy land or a grand picnic than what one would expect of grim war. Cheeseman's Creek is celebrated for its oysters, the whole creek being one vast bed; the banks are studded with the little cottages of the oystermen, many of whom are natives of New Jersey. Our men have no respect for their reserved rights; in another day or two I fear there will be no oysters left. From daylight till dark hundreds of the men are in the water, and at low tide get even out to the middle of the creek. They dig the oysters with their hands and toes, and make bags of their shirts or breeches to carry them; such vast oyster roasts as have been going on here ever since our arrival were never known before. The Jersey men of the Third Brigade are particularly at home in the muddy water.

Our headquarters, by which I mean division headquarters as I shall be living there hereafter, are on the north side of the creek about three-quarters of a mile from its head. The tents are pitched in line, facing the creek, on a bit of smooth green sward and some twenty or thirty feet back from the edge of the bank, which is about ten feet high. I fear it will be a long time before we again light on so pleasant a spot. . . .

This morning I rode up to general headquarters, about three miles

from here. The whole country is flat, with an infinitude of small creeks
setting in in every direction, and a great deal of swampy land. At least
three-quarters of it is wooded; mostly large pines, and a terribly dense
underbrush. The roads are much like those we had on the Potomac,
and will have to be corduroyed, the whole of them, which nearly the
whole army are now at work at, giving the country the appearance of
one vast bee hive. McClellan's headquarters lie between the branches
of Wormley's Creek, on a large open field; they are beautifully laid out
and in superb order. The Reserve Infantry and Artillery, under General
Sykes, are camped directly in front of him; they are all regulars, except
the Fifth New York (Duryea's Zouaves), and Brinkle's German batteries.
They say that the Fifth New York is equal in all respects to the regulars
and better drilled; the men are a fine-looking set, and very showy in
their red trousers and white turbans. *

At headquarters I learned from General Barry something about the
position of the army and the way they got here. Most of them were
landed at Fortress Monroe, and moved up to their present position nine
or ten days since Porter's and Smith's divisions had the lead, but there
was no fighting to speak of, the enemy falling back over Warwick Creek,
which stretches nearly the whole distance across the Peninsula at this
point; flowing into the James. On the 5th Smith had a little more of a
fight at Lee's Mills, but without any decisive results. Battery "E" of our
regiment was in this fight, the first one to be really engaged. . . . Casey's
division is on the extreme left of our line, some six miles from where
we shall be, so I am not likely to see much of the Colonel. I was very
sorry to hear that Blenker's division had been taken away from Sumner
and sent to Frémont in the Valley of Virginia.†

Cheeseman's Creek will be the depot for most if not all the army. It
has suddenly become the most busy port in the whole country: thousands
of men are at work there night and day landing stores of all kinds. The

* Hiram Duryea of New York led a regiment from the metropolis that was famous for
its gay uniform modeled on that of the Algerian light infantry, for its precision in
drill, and in time for its fighting power. According to Mark M. Boatner, it excited the
admiration of regular troops when at Gaines's Mill, after sustaining sharp losses, it
deliberately paused under fire to count off and straighten its ranks. Duryea was brevetted a brigadier general after this action.

† Louis Blenker, a leader in the revolt of 1848 in the German states who had migrated
to America and become a New York businessman, was commissioned colonel of the
Eighth New York in April 1861 and fought bravely at Bull Run. He was soon afterward raised to the command of a division comprising three German brigades. John C.
Frémont was now commanding in West Virginia, and Blenker was ordered to leave
McClellan's force and join him. His march to the new area was attended with great
hardship, for the War Department neglected to furnish his troops the most elementary
necessities, and they arrived at their destination in deplorable condition.

ordnance department have a dock of their own, at which the siege train is now being disembarked. The First Connecticut Artillery, late Fourth Connecticut Volunteers, under Colonel Tyler, has charge of the trains; a better working set of men I never saw, judging by the way they were at it, when I was there yesterday. Colonel Tyler was the president of our examining board: one of Bramhall's men was commissioned in this regiment just before we left Maryland.

APRIL 16, WEDNESDAY. Went up to headquarters yesterday with General Hooker, to select a spot for the division to camp on. We took another road around by Back Creek, and across the head of the east branch of Wormley's. Passed a number of rebel camps and redoubts, which appear to have been abandoned almost as soon as completed. They had laid out an immense amount of work on them: the redoubts were very well built and beautifully finished: the huts were large, carefully put up, and roofed with split shingles. The fatigue parties are getting on grandly with the roads; almost finished now.

The spot allotted for our division is a part of the same open space occupied by general headquarters and the reserve. It is very contracted, and will not allow any opportunity for drilling. It lies directly north of the Hampton and Yorktown road, between a small branch of Wormley's Creek and a large house owned by one Clark. Only two brigades and my artillery can be got in here: the other brigade will have to go into the wood on the other side of the road, where our own headquarters will be. Heintzelman's corps occupies the right of the line: Porter's division lying nearest to the York River, ours next, and then Hamilton's. I could not wish to be better located to see all that will be going on, as it brings us directly in front of Yorktown, and the main works of the enemy: as also close enough to Army Headquarters to hear whatever may be allowed to leak out. General Heintzelman has his headquarters about half a mile up the road from us, close to a steam sawmill, one of two the rebs left uninjured and which are now hard at work sawing lumber and planks for us. It is said to be on the exact spot where Lafayette had his headquarters during the first siege of Yorktown. I hope we may be able to finish the matter up in as short time as Washington did, nineteen days, and with as good results.

This morning I rode over to Farenholt's house on the banks of the York River just below the mouth of Wormley's Creek; from which a capital view of Yorktown and its defences on the river front, as also of Gloucester Point, on the opposite side of the river, is obtained. A large battery is being erected here to mount several 100-pounder Parrotts and one 200-pounder. The reb flag, "stars and bars" as they call it, was floating over both Yorktown and Gloucester. Their batteries along the river on this side appear very extensive; I could make out one large water battery in a cove under the cliff, which I should judge to be forty feet high. A dock runs out a long distance into the river, at which there were some half dozen sloops and schooners lying: steamers run regularly from there up to West Point, so that the enemy can have no difficulty in getting supplies down from Richmond. It is hoped to interfere with this so soon as we get our big guns mounted. I think it could be stopped at once if we had half a dozen little Whitworths here, and told General Barry so: the distance cannot be over three miles. Two small gunboats steam up sometimes and shell the point a little, but without any effect. . . . ,

General Naglee moved his brigade up to the front this afternoon. An order is out forbidding all calls being sounded or beaten, or bands playing until further orders. I saw General Heintzelman when up there with Hooker yesterday: ugly as his pictures are, they flatter him; a little man, almost black, with short coarse grey hair and beard, his face one mass of wrinkles, he wears the most uncouth dress and gets into the most awkward positions possible. He talks way down in his throat too, having lost his palate, so that one can hardly understand him. I was much disappointed in him; could not see any signs of a great man.

❆ ❆ ❆

McClellan had moved very nearly 60,000 men and one hundred guns down the Potomac to the area of his new base at Fort Monroe, he himself arriving there April 3. Here he faced a force of at most 23,000 Confederates under Major General J. Bankhead Magruder, so disposed as to cover Yorktown and Williamsburg. McClellan later stated that he hoped "by rapid movements to drive before me or capture the enemy on the Peninsula, open the James River, and push on to Richmond before he should be materially reinforced." Unfortunately, he at once met three bitter disappointments. The navy, whose gunboats he expected to help batter down the enemy defenses at Yorktown, was so preoccupied with the *Merrimack* that it was almost useless to him. The terrain proved far more difficult than he had expected, with the Warwick River running athwart his path, not parallel to it; and Magruder had made good use of the streams, swamps, and woods in three lines of fortifications, some of them using the old British entrenchments of 1781. Finally, President Lincoln, concluding that the forces left to defend Washington were too small for safety, withheld McDowell's First Corps, some 40,000 men, which McClellan had expected to co-operate closely with him.

When McClellan arrived at Fort Monroe, he could readily have broken Magruder's Warwick River line and taken Yorktown. But, dismayed by the strong defenses and overestimating the strength of the enemy, he refused to make a frontal attack and settled down instead to a siege of the position. This he conducted with great skill, erecting redoubts, digging parallels, and using guns, mortars, and howitzers. In these operations Wainwright was of course involved. They were certain of final success—but meanwhile McClellan was losing a whole month of invaluable time.

✳ ✳ ✳

APRIL 18, FRIDAY. Our postal arrangements are now fully established, going out and coming in every day, so that we shall get letters and papers regularly. Received a large batch yesterday and today down as late as the 10th from New York. The excitement there does not seem to abate; the inefficiency of the blockade and escape of the *Nashville* troubles our merchants very much. There is said to be a good deal of secession feeling too in the city exhibited in various ways; while the abolitionists are doing their best through the *Tribune* and *Post* to turn this from a war for the Union into one for the propagation of their own notions. On the other hand, there are great rejoicings over the Western victories, the capture of Island No. 10, and Pope's countless prisoners—which those down here who know him I find have great doubts of. . . .

This morning General Hooker reviewed my batteries, and was pleased to express himself as very well satisfied with them. They looked tolerably well, having got a pretty good outfit of horses from the trains left behind in Maryland; but I fear there will be no chance now for us to have anything in the shape of a mounted drill. . . . Last night I had some trouble with General Naglee, he refusing to allow his commissary to issue to the batteries. The commissary was very impudent. On reporting the matter to General Hooker, he removed the commissary, and gave me all I wanted. Today Colonel Taylor, commanding the Second Brigade, had also to appeal against Naglee for refusing to allow him the camp ground assigned to him. Hooker had to go up there himself, and ended the matter by placing Naglee in arrest. Naglee feels his shoulder straps too much, and forgets that they do not give him command outside his own brigade. So all three of our brigades are under colonels again: Cowdin the First, Taylor the Second, and Starr the Third.

"CAMP SCOTT," BEFORE YORKTOWN, APRIL 20, SUNDAY. We, headquarters, moved up yesterday, and are tolerably located, having had a place cleared in the woods for our tents, a short distance off the road. It is not nearly so good ground as that we had on Cheeseman's Creek, being wet underfoot, and no sod. But we are here close to our work, where we have got to be, and must not spend too many thoughts on comfort now. . . .

On Friday night our first line was commenced in two places, or rather

an approach or zig-zag was so begun on our extreme right where there
are no woods to cover our operations. This goes from the west branch
of Wormley's Creek up to the Moore house; a small white building, in a
peach orchard, quite near the river bank, and which is noted as the
house in which Cornwallis signed his surrender. The land for half a
mile wide along the York lies level and almost entirely cleared. The
peach orchard around the Moore house has been the scene of all the
sharpest skirmishing so far, and has been really deadly to both sides. In
a few days now we expect to have entire control of it.

The corduroy roads back of us are pretty much finished; now the main
work is on the roads going from the camps to where our batteries are to
be. This west branch of Wormley's Creek, with its many little tributaries
is terribly in our way on the right, requiring three or four long bridges
over it; with scarped roads up and down its high banks on either side.
The worst part of it, as also the approach in zig-zag, is on the front of
Porter's division, but we have working parties on the roads there. There
is very little cannonading from either side as yet; most of the work so
far not being in sight of the rebel batteries. The pickets shoot at each
other whenever they get a chance, and very big stories are in circulation
as to the prowess of individual men: one of the Berdan Sharpshooters
is said to have hit thirteen of the enemy from his post, before he was
brought down himself by a ball right through his brain. On the other
side a nigger has had it all his own way for some days, keeping everything clear from his perch in a tree over near the peach orchard, until he
too met with more than his match, and dropped from his tree dead. . . .
APRIL 22, TUESDAY.   My batteries came up yesterday, as has been the
case in every previous move, they were met by a heavy storm, and they
as well as many another poor fellow had a wet berth of it last night:
nor has there been much chance for it to dry yet today. . . .

I rode out to the front today, and saw some of the batteries that are
being constructed there; two on the left of our road, Nos. 6 and 7 they
are marked. The first is almost finished; No. 7 just begun; No. 6 will
mount five four and one-half inch ordnance guns, which went up there
yesterday, and are now all ready to be mounted so soon as the platforms
are laid. I understand there are a number of other batteries building to
the right, all in the woods and out of sight of the enemy. I started to go
that way today but was ordered back by some general officer, on the
ground that my duty did not call me there; but as General Barry informs me that I have a perfect right to visit the whole of the lines in my
capacity as an artillery officer, I shall stand on the dignity of my red
shoulder straps another time.

From these batteries I struck into the woods and came around behind
our Third Brigade, which lies in rear of headquarters. I got into one

brigade of Germans, Hamilton's division, which was really set down in a swamp; at least last night's rain had made it so. The woods were full of men from the Engineer Brigade, making gabions and fascines, which now lie in great piles along the road sides ready for use. If as large details are made from all the other divisions as from ours, work ought to go on rapidly. . . .

APRIL 24, THURSDAY. Yesterday being fine, I made another visit towards our right, as far as Battery No. 3, one of the largest, and pierced for ten guns. This is as far to the right as the work of our division goes. . . .

Most of the weather the past week has been wet and cold; having no stoves to warm or dry our tents we are very far from comfortable. All the working parties on coming in receive a half gill of whiskey to each man. Many of the orders given show how purely volunteer we are; sometimes they are received by a captain who has been an old sergeant and at least knows the name of things. They tell a good story of a crotchety old fellow of this sort who commands a company in one of the Jersey regiments; an obeyer of orders literally and no more. He was sent out with a large party to work on a "redoubt" at such a spot. Finding no "redoubt," but a "redan" there, he sat his men down and rode about for two hours or more searching for a "redoubt"; not finding any which had not workmen enough, he returned to brigade headquarters to find that the adjutant-general had wished to show his knowledge of engineering when he wrote the order, but had never heard of such a thing as a "redan."

APRIL 26, SATURDAY. Another large batch of letters from home. They certainly have more to excite them there than we have; the papers telling all sorts of stories; a little truth buried in a mass of lies. There seems to be no doubt however now that McDowell's corps has been taken from McClellan's command and is not coming down here, as it has gone to Fredericksburg. They have, however, sent Franklin's division down to replace Blenker's in Sumner's corps; it arrived a day or two ago, but is still on shipboard. I hear that it was intended to land McDowell somewhere north of the York, and have him turn Gloucester Point: he had four divisions, near 40,000 men in his corps, and could easily have done it. The same thing may be tried with Franklin's division, as they are kept on board their boats; but I should doubt if his ten or twelve thousand are strong enough. . . .

This morning a part of our division had a little brush with the enemy. I have forgotten to mention before that General Naglee has been transferred to Casey's division; and that we have a General Grover in his place; a very different-looking man, and one that takes my fancy.* The

* General Cuvier Grover, a Maine graduate of West Point in the class of 1850, had already distinguished himself. Commanding at Fort Union in New Mexico in 1861 with the rank of captain, he had refused a Confederate demand for surrender, burned his

rebs had been busy at a new work to the left and front of our No. 6 in a place that was likely to make it troublesome. General Grover took five companies from the First and Eleventh Massachusetts and started to destroy it at daybreak. Keeping the rest of his little force in reserve, some one hundred men of "C" and "H" Companies First Massachusetts charged across the open, some four hundred yards, and carried the work. There were about seventy-five rebs in the work, but they fled as our men jumped into the ditch. Another one hundred with picks and shovels followed close, and soon levelled it, when Grover withdrew his force in good order, bringing fifteen prisoners with him. Our loss was three killed and twelve wounded. The men behaved well, and it is said that McClellan compliments the affair. . . .

I met General Kearny yesterday riding out to take a look at the lines: his brigade is in Franklin's division. Watts DePeyster was with him; is acting as volunteer aide on his staff. Colonel Bailey was here for a few moments this morning; as our Court was sitting. I could not see much of him. Casey's division has been some distance in the rear, but has now moved up to the left of the line, some four or five miles from here. . . .

APRIL 28, MONDAY. Yesterday and today the weather has been really fine. Here we are at the end of April and still deep in the mud; the season is now not very much more forward than on the Hudson. . . .

After our Court adjourned today, I rode with Colonel Farnum over to the extreme right of our lines. We have entire possession of the peach orchard there now, the parallel running along the front of it. The rebs make it a pretty hot place still, and one is obliged, by day, to keep down in the covered approaches. We got out to the Moore house where we are putting up two batteries quite close to the river; these are not over a mile from the enemy's main work. A large number of batteries for mortars as well as guns are going up over here. One very fine work on the creek for ten immense thirteen-inch mortars is just being finished. The First Connecticut were laying the platforms and landing the mortars today; they weigh near ten tons each: most unwieldy pieces of iron to handle. The battery is cut right into the bank some fifteen feet high in which is also the magazine. Mortar batteries are also going up on our front, and all are busy again; what with trench guards, pickets and fatigue parties, our division now sends out near half its numbers every day.

Today I received an order for one of my batteries to be on picket each night, near the "White House," going on after dark, and returning at daybreak, so as not to be seen by the enemy. I took all four of my

stores, and made a successful forced march to safety beyond the Missouri River. He was now, in April 1862, appointed a brigadier general in McClellan's Third Corps. Fighting to the end of the war, he was brevetted a major general in 1864.

captains out there this afternoon so as to explain fully to them where they were to go and what they were wanted to do. Seeing so many of us around the house, the rebs opened from one of their guns, the shot striking and burying itself about fifty yards to the left of the house. Captain Smith and I went to try to dig it up, when they fired a second. Remembering the sailor in Marryat's tale, I got right on top of the first shot, but the rascals made a very good line of it, and had they given a little more elevation it would have been unpleasantly close. . . . They fire quite lively in this direction at times now. One large shell came over as far as General Heintzelman's headquarters, buried itself within three feet of the telegraph tent, and bursting made a hole big and deep enough to bury a horse in.

APRIL 29, TUESDAY. We were all routed out in a hurry this morning about two-thirty o'clock with orders to get under arms as a heavy sortie was expected. A brigade and one battery also were to move out to the front. I lost no time, but footed it half dressed over to my command, ordered all to harness up, and Osborn to move out at once. Back to my tent, finished dressing, got my orders to report to General Martindale, siege officer of the day,* and mounted just as Osborn came by; twenty minutes by the watch from the moment I first left my tent. Pretty well for a seven months old battery with volunteer officers! Arrived on the plain beyond Heintzelman's headquarters. I hunted high and low for General Martindale, but it was dark as Erebus, and he was nowhere to be found. . . . As day fairly dawned, all idea of their making a sortie was given up, and our troops returned to camp. . . .

APRIL 30, WEDNESDAY. Muster day again, and the paymaster just down here to pay on the previous muster; two months behind. Fortunately for some of us he had an overplus of funds so that a number of officers, myself among others, got paid up to date. The four months' pay came very acceptable just at this time, as I not only wanted some to send home, but to pay for a second horse, an opportunity to procure one having just turned up. The Ninth New York Cavalry has proved good for nothing, is not to be mounted and all the officers are to be mustered out; consequently their camp, some mile or so from here, has been a complete horse fair the last few days. Many of our officers have purchased and I myself have got a big long-legged black; not much to look at nor

* John Henry Martindale, a New Yorker, had graduated from West Point in 1835 but resigned before seeing any active service in order to enter engineering and, later, law. He was given a brigadier general's commission after Bull Run, and after helping improve the defenses of Washington was assigned to Fitz-John Porter's division in the Army of the Potomac. After the war, in which he reached the brevet rank of major general, he became one of the prominent attorneys of upper New York and was elected attorney general of the state.

young, but with good underpinning, a fair mouth, and easy as a cradle on the trot; a change from my bay which is infernally hard..

My batteries appeared tolerably well on inspection: their camps in good order. Like most of the other troops they have got arbours up over their tents, also over the street between the tents and park, which they call "Wainwright Avenue." . . . Much is said in the papers about our immense force down here, and the radicals are very severe on our General for not having carried Yorktown by storm at once. *We* find no fault with him for wishing to take it with as small loss of life as possible, and doubt if it could have been carried by storm. . . .

The papers have a report, from reb sources they say, that New Orleans is ours.

CAMP "WINFIELD SCOTT," MAY 3, SATURDAY. Three days have gone by with absolutely nothing to note. The weather has continued much the same, but our work has gone on grandly, and may now be said to be finished. I went along all the right of the line this morning; found the guns mounted in nearly all the batteries, their magazines filled, and many of them in perfect readiness; on my return I stopped at general headquarters, and saw General Barry, who asked me to go over the whole lines with him tomorrow when he would explain everything to me, as the bombardment is to commence at daybreak on Monday. This is just what I wanted as it will give me a chance to learn a good deal, and as I shall have no part to take in the siege. At least no part to speak of, for I also learned that some Whitworth guns had come down, and that I was to have charge of them.

It will be a splendid sight when all our guns and mortars open, especially if the rebs reply lively; one worth half a lifetime to see, a sight I have dreamt of, but never expected to really witness.

MAY 4, SUNDAY. I did not ride around the lines with General Barry today, nor will we open the bombardment of Yorktown tomorrow. When I looked out of my tent this morning I was saluted with the cry, "The rebs have gone!" The news had just been received, for we are early risers here, our breakfast hour being five-thirty. All last night they kept up quite a lively cannonade, heavier than at any time before. So soon as it was light, our men not seeing the reb picket line, pushed out, and finding no resistance at all were soon in the works. Colonel Brewster of the Fourth Excelsior, Sixty-Third New York, claims that his men were the first in. It is also claimed by one of Parker's regiments; probably they went in at different points. The evacuation of their stronghold here will no doubt save many lives for the time, but I would much rather they had fought it out. McClellan's enemies, who are getting very bitter, will doubtless use it as an argument against him that he has allowed them to escape; though I cannot myself see any force in it.

Immediately after breakfast General Hooker rode over to head-quarters to ask that this division might be allowed to follow up after the enemy. Before nine he was back with his orders; all was at once astir. Unfortunately most of the command were out of rations, this being the regular day for issue, and their waggons had gone down to the landing for them; consequently the last of the division did not get off until noon. The brigades marched First, Second, Third, with three of my batteries following the First Brigade. Smith was to have followed the Second, but did not get ready in time and fell in rear of the column. The cavalry of horse batteries passed our quarters at nine-thirty o'clock, full trot: a most exhilarating sight. I remained with Smith's battery for some miles in hopes to get it up into its proper position, but without success.

We passed out by the Hampton road, skirted the works of Yorktown, and then on by the direct road to Williamsburg. For the first four or five miles the road was level, hard and dry. I did not have time to go inside the rebel works. Once when I rode over to watch them Heintzel-man, who was standing on the parapet, called to me to keep in the road, as the ground was full of torpedoes. Report said that these tor-pedoes were planted all over. I saw a dozen spots in the middle of the road marked by our men as torpedoes; all that was visible was a foot or two of telegraph wire sticking out of the ground, the idea seeming to be that men or horses would get entangled, and so pull the wire, which was to fire the torpedo.

About five miles or more from Yorktown we were stopped by a portion of Sumner's command coming in from the south; our infantry took to the fields, but the batteries were obliged to wait. Soon after I met two or three wounded cavalrymen coming back. They reported that they had got within sight of Williamsburg, when they were stopped, the rebs being strongly fortified there. A couple of miles farther on I found Colonel Bailey halted with his batteries for the night. From him I learned that they had known of the rebel retreat by three o'clock this morning; had started at sunrise, marched to the James River at Raspberry Point, and then here. I cannot see why General Sumner, who commanded all the left wing of the army, his own corps and Keyes's, should not have telegraphed his information at once to McClellan, when we too might have been moving by sunrise; much less why he should have abandoned the direct road to Williamsburg from Warwick Court House which he was on and have come way over here to the right with his whole force.

THREE

THE FIRST BATTLE: WILLIAMSBURG

While McClellan had been wasting almost a month on his siege of York-town, which he could have avoided by an early and determined assault, the Confederates had been concentrating their forces. As soon as Magruder's evacuation of the town was discovered, General George Stoneman's cavalry division set off in pursuit, with Hooker's division following. The troops were on their way by early afternoon of May 4, and before evening of that day had learned from Stoneman's men that the Confederates were blocking the Yorktown-Williamsburg road by heavy fire from a large redoubt that commanded it. Under a heavy rain the Union column halted some three miles from Williamsburg. Next morning Hooker flung his division against the formidable enemy line based on the huge earthen redoubt, called Fort Magruder. He did not know just how strong the resistance would be, but his fighting temper had been irritated by McClellan's caution, and he and his men were eager for aggressive action. As they moved into battle the steeples of Williamsburg could be plainly seen ahead. First the skirmishers engaged the Confederates, who held a number of small redoubts aligned on both sides of their major stronghold. Then, as Wainwright relates, the artillery came up. Captain C. H. Webber's First United States Battery be-haved badly under fire, and it was only after Wainwright had brought the officers and gunners of the First New York Battery to man the deserted pieces, and the Sixth New York Battery also pushed to the front, that the enemy's fire was silenced. Here the volunteers outshone the regulars!

Hooker's division fought stubbornly throughout the day and sustained almost three-fourths of the whole Union loss in the battle of Williamsburg. One Massachusetts regiment expended all its ammunition and fell back; other regiments became exhausted; and an enfilading fire forced a New Jersey and a New Hampshire regiment to retreat. The whole line that Hooker had first established became untenable. In the general retreat the batteries under Wainwright, after doing effective work, had to be abandoned, most of them being mired so deeply—for every discharge had forced them deeper into the mud—that they could not be carried off.

To forestall a rout, Hooker had to form a line of cavalrymen across the Hampton road with orders to cut down any able-bodied soldiers who ran away. He and General Grover succeeded in forming a new defensive line on which the Fourth New York Battery took position, firing canister at the charging Confederates with such effect that Grover later credited it with the chief role in saving the new position. Hooker rode along the line exhorting his men to stand firm, and Heintzelman at one point collected all the bandsmen he could find, ordering them: "Play! Play! It's all you're good for. Play, damn it! Play some marching tune! Play 'Yankee Doodle,' or any doodle you can think of, only play something!" Then in mid-afternoon Philip Kearny came into battle with his Michigan and New York troops, and delivered such spirited counterattacks that the Union forces recovered much of their lost ground.

General Winfield Scott Hancock meanwhile gathered the greenest laurels on the Northern side. Coming up to take position on the Confederate left, he first repulsed a fierce attack by Jubal A. Early's brigade, and then at just the right moment led so determined a countercharge that he achieved a brilliant victory. McClellan telegraphed his wife: "Hancock was superb." It was in consequence of this victory that the Confederates retreated. Next day, May 6, a beautiful spring morning, the Union columns marched through the streets of Williamsburg, pausing to gaze at the brick buildings of William and Mary College.

Wainwright begins his story at sunset on May 4, when, on the first day's march from Yorktown toward Williamsburg, he encountered Hooker at the head of his infantry column. The major reported that the advance across King's Creek was very slow, many infantrymen hesitating to wade it. Hooker ordered him to get his guns as far forward as possible toward Williamsburg: "If the enemy are there I shall attack early tomorrow morning." It was one A.M. before Wainwright could lie down for a little sleep.

❊ ❊ ❊

BATTLE OF WILLIAMSBURG, MAY 5, 1862, MONDAY. By three o'clock we were again stirring. Leaving orders for Bramhall and Smith to push on so soon as horses and men were fed, I rode on and routed up Osborn and Webber. The men were tired and wet, for it had begun to rain at two o'clock and was now pouring; cold too, the chill striking into one's very bones. The crossroad from the church was very muddy, and when we got into the Warwick Court House road it was so terribly cut up that it was with difficulty we could get along. Starting out the men, and moving the four or five miles, which seemed twenty, I made it after seven o'clock when I got up to where General Hooker had halted the infantry. He

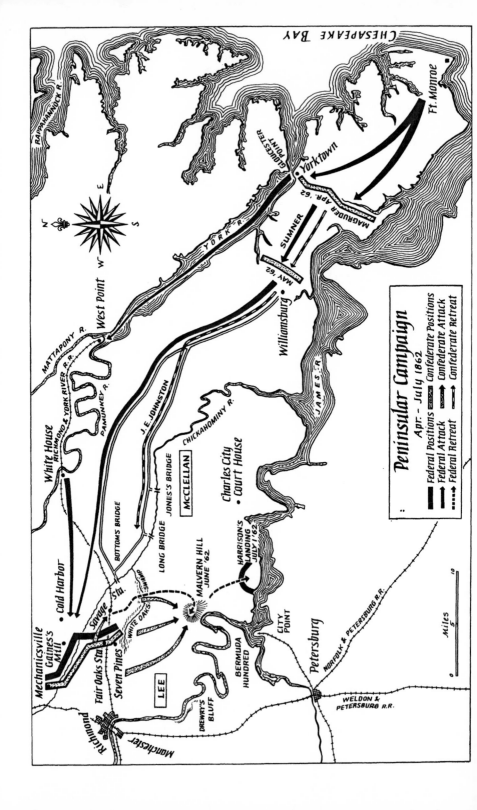

CHESAPEAKE BAY

Ft. Monroe

Gloucester Point

Yorktown

MAGRUDER APR. '62

YORK R.

SUMNER

MAY '62

Williamsburg

JAMES R.

West Point

MATTAPONY R.

RAPPAHANNOCK R.

PAMUNKEY R.

RICHMOND & YORK RIVER R.R.

White House

J. E. JOHNSTON

CHICKAHOMINY R.

McCLELLAN

Charles City
Court House

Cold Harbor

BOTTOMS BRIDGE

JONES'S BRIDGE

LONG BRIDGE

HARRISON'S
LANDING
JULY I '62

Mechanicsville

Gaines's
Mill

Savage
Sta.

WHITE OAK
SWAMP

MALVERN HILL
JUNE '62

CITY
POINT

Richmond

Fair Oaks Sta.

Seven Pines

LEE

BERMUDA
HUNDRED

Petersburg

Manchester

DREWRY'S
BLUFF

NORFOLK & PETERSBURG R.R.

WELDON &
PETERSBURG R.R.

Peninsular Campaign
Apr. - July 1862

Federal Positions
Confederate Positions
Federal Attack
Confederate Attack
Federal Retreat
Confederate Retreat

Miles
0   5   10

said that he was only waiting for me to come up in order to attack, and where would I put my batteries? As of course I had to look about me a little, the General rode up the road with me; but so soon as we emerged from the woods the rebs opened on us so sharp that we got off our horses, and proceeded out on foot and alone.

The rain was coming down in torrents, making all objects at any distance very indistinct. The road by which we had come up lay through a heavy wood for half a mile or more behind us; some hundred yards inside this wood it made a thorough cut of say thirty yards in length, the bank being six to eight feet high on either side. On both sides of the road the rebs had felled a large amount of the timber as it debouches into the plain in front of Williamsburg. Directly up the road, about eight hundred yards from where we stood at the outer edge of the felled timber, was a large redoubt from which they were firing quite lively. To the right and left of this one we could see a number of other earthworks in the distance; on our left there seemed to be a field battery behind the crest of a knoll (have since found that it was in a small redoubt built in a hollow so that the top of the parapet was about on a level with the top of the crest). On our side of the plain I could see nothing but woods on either hand with a heavy slashing of felled trees in front. The road was the only way to get on to the plain, and that would be ugly enough for some five hundred yards; the rebel redoubt, Fort Magruder, having a raging fire down it. Still I thought the open plain the proper place, and told the General so; but he said he could not support the batteries out there, his pickets only being at the outer edge of the slashing. On our left the slashing extended up the road about three hundred yards farther than it did on the right, a large triangular field having been lately cleared there, and planted in corn last year. Not being able to go out on to the plain, I told the General that the only place left one was this fallow lot; but I might get a couple of guns in the road. "Get them in then as quick as you can," were his orders.

Going back to the edge of the woods, where Captain Webber had halted his battery, I directed him to put his first piece out at the farthest corner of the slashing in the road; his second also in the road but some twenty yards to the rear, a slight bend in the road here placing them thus in echelon; and the other two sections in the newly cleared field to the right of the road: leaving his caissons in the wood. He at once moved out himself with the first section, while I directed the posting of the other two. Gaps in the fence were pulled down, and after a great deal of trouble from bad drivers and balky horses I got them all in. Almost before the first piece had turned into the field, Lieutenant Eakin fell at my feet terribly wounded in the shoulder. We were both of us on foot, he standing about four feet in front of me. A shell struck the road half a dozen yards from us and burst as it fell, a piece of it entering his left shoulder just below the collar bone; he fell against me, and at once called out that he was a dead man. I got a couple of men to carry him off, but had full occupation myself driving the horses of the guns up to the pulling point. At last, I had all four guns posted; when looking around what was my horror, on seeing that nearly all the limber had cleared off under shelter of the woods, and that there was not more than one or two men near each gun. This was an awful beginning for one's first battle, and knowing what a wretched battery this was, I reproached myself with having so far yielded to Webber's claims as senior officer as to have given him the advance instead of Bramhall.

Rushing back to the road, where the men had hid themselves behind the large felled trees, I met Webber, without his hat, covered with mud and almost wild. "Major," says he, "Lieutenant Pike and two men have been hit and I cannot get the others up to their guns." Though we slammed at them with our sabres, and poked them out with the point, it was no good; drive two or three to a gun, and by the time you got some more up the first had hid again. Never in my life was I so mortified, never so excited, never so mad. It had at any rate the good effect of making me forget my own danger, and the place was an awful hot one there in the road. There was a certain amount of excuse for the men. Their captain had just joined them; their other officers knew nothing; two of them were shot down at once, as also a couple of the men, and one horse of the leading gun killed; it was a very hot place for men to have their first experience in; and they were a wretched lot of men. Some of them did stick to their guns, but not enough to work them, and the drivers had carried the limbers way to the rear. The first piece had three men keep to it, who got off two or three shots; a wheel horse of their limber being killed, the drivers could not run away with it, so they ran off without it.

General Hooker meantime, it seems, was anxiously waiting for the battery to open. Seeing how things stood, for he was not far to the rear, he sent Captain Dickenson, his adjutant-general, to me to say that he would give me a company of infantry to work the guns. Looking at it coolly now, I have no doubt it was only meant, in good part, to get me out of my trouble; but then it appeared as a slur on the artillery, almost an insult, and made me very mad. "Thank the General," said I, "but I have artillery men that can and will man those guns." Running back to my horse, I rode to Osborn's battery, just in the rear of Webber's caissons; shouted to the men that General Hooker wanted to send infantry to fight our guns; called upon them for the honour of the First New York Artillery to save me, their own major, from such a disgrace; in short made them a speech, the first speech of my life; and closed by asking who would volunteer to serve the guns of an abandoned regular battery. The men were mounted on the chests, sergeants and officers at their posts. I have no doubt all heard me, for I was very much excited, and don't know now what I said; but almost before I had done, Sergeant Horn of the first or second piece, whom I had often had occasion to praise on drill, standing up in his stirrups, replied, "Every one of us, Sir." The men jumped from the boxes, officers dismounted, detachments were regularly formed, and marched to the abandoned pieces as if on drill. A more beautiful thing it was impossible to see, not a man flinching; the infantry on the roadside gave them three cheers, and wasn't I a proud man?—proud of the First New York Artillery.

Fire once opened, the enemy's shots were not nearly so sure and it became comparatively safe to be about there. It was just about eight o'clock when we opened fire; half an hour later Bramhall came up, and I at once moved his battery into the fallow lot, to the right of Webber's. One of his pieces had been left behind stuck in the mud, and though it came up later in the day, was not put in position. Webber's men kept coming back as they got over their fright, but there were not over five of them to a gun at any time during the day. The rain made all objects at any distance very indistinct. At no time could we see any large body of the enemy; our work was simply to silence and keep silent their artillery. They seemed to have three guns in Fort Magruder and three or more in the sunken redoubt. Occasionally a shot would come from a third work still farther to their right, but their works to our right did not trouble us at all during the day. In an hour we had silenced them totally, at least for a time, and held up our own fire. . . .

Half an hour, perhaps, after we had ceased firing, long rolls of musketry were heard at this point to the left. Every moment I expected to see our men rush into the open, but after a time we found the firing to recede into the woods, as if our men were being beaten instead of gaining ground; so I turned my four left pieces to the left, and opened on the corner of the woods. Infantry officers tell me that shell fell directly in the rebel column, and burst with great effect. It was now my turn to get it hot and heavy from all three of the rebel batteries; the redoubt away to our left opening very strong, which forced me to throw Bramhall's right far forward in echelon. How long this fight lasted I do not know, but it seemed to me all day. At last, however, we got their fire under, and shortly afterward, all being quiet, I spoke to General Hooker about dispositions for the night, thinking it must be near sundown. He thought too it was late, and we were both astonished when Captain Dickenson told us it was twenty minutes passed eleven!—the day not half through. It seemed a good week since I got up.

This time they left us quiet for an hour or more, so that one had a little time to look around. I proposed to General Hooker to get my two

twelve-pounder howitzers around to where the infantry were, so as to
fire down the ravine by which the enemy's columns came up, if possible,
but he said there was no road by which he could get them there that he
knew of. Since then I have been sorry that I did not go to look for myself, as there was a small wood road, I find, which led in that direction.
General Hooker stayed all the time just where the road came out of the
wood, and did not go over to the place where our infantry were engaged at all. On passing around among my guns, I found that two of
Bramhall's pieces were disabled by shot wedging in the bore. One of
them we replaced with his sixth piece which had been stuck on the road
coming up; the other shot, I believe, they got home after a time. One of
Webber's howitzers had cracked so badly as to render it unsafe, and was
hauled off. This left us ten guns in position, but my men had got the
range, and worked admirably. . . .

During this lull General Hooker sent word to Sumner on our right
that he was holding the enemy here, and begging him to attack. Captain
Benson commanding "M" of the Second Artillery took the message,
passing out on the open ground in front of the wood. He got back safely,
and brought his saddle in, but left his horse dead on the plain. Many of
our officers said they could hear firing to our right, quite early in the
day; though I did not hear any myself. It seems it was Hancock's attack.
Had old Sumner followed him up with the whole of Smith's division as
he asked, and as Smith himself wanted to do, there is not a doubt in my
mind that Williamsburg could have been carried, the heavy losses in
our division saved, and probably very many prisoners, and a good part
of their train captured. I hear that Wheeler with "E" Company of our
regiment was in with Hancock, and that the latter did grandly.

About twelve-thirty o'clock the enemy made a second charge on our
infantry, driving them back some distance into the wood at one time;
their artillery fired but little, and I could render but little aid for
fear of firing into our own men. General Hooker was a good deal
worried at one time, and much excited. Taylor's brigade was sent over
to reinforce the others, and drove the rebs back again. Whenever there
would be a regular succession of volleys the General would rub his
hands, and exclaim "That's Dwight, that's Dwight." This fight was
doubtless a hard one, but when it was over everything settled down and
remained so quiet that I began to hope it was over for the day.

My own men were very tired, some of them completely broken down;
they were all unaccustomed to fighting and doubtless worked harder
than was necessary. Finally we were getting short of men at some of the
guns, so many being required on account of their sinking and the
badness of the ground; and as everything was so quiet I asked the
General's permission to ride back and look up Smith who had not yet

made his appearance, though he had no farther to come than Bramhall and should have started at the same time. Some three hundred to four hundred yards back in the woods I passed our field hospitals where the wounded were receiving their first dressing, and then sent back in ambulances about a mile or so to where the main hospital was established in and around a fine large house occupied by the overseer of "Buck" Allen, who has large plantations around here. Our little Doctor Goddard remained all day at the front, and gave his first care to our wounded almost among the guns where they fell. The road was now awful; my horse sank to his knees at almost every step. Ammunition and hospital waggons were stuck all along. . . . When we got to within a mile of the front, I heard heavy firing for the first time since I had gone back. Pushing on as fast as I could alone, just as I reached the hospital I met the first of a string of ambulances, waggons, and other vehicles, just breaking into a run; the men too were starting, hospital attendants and such like. In fact, [this was] the commencement of a stampede. The road was so narrow at this point that but one waggon could pass at a time. One of my limbers was first; all were yelling and hollering to their horses and to those in front to get on. Drawing my sabre, I rode right at the lead driver of the limber, and brought that up short, so stopping the whole concern. The firing at the front was diminishing, and the stampede died out in a few minutes. Just then Chauncey McKeever came galloping back, waving his sword and swearing like a demon, "Shoot the cowards!" In a few minutes a couple of squadrons of cavalry, who had been sent around by a road to our left came back. McKeever insisted they should fire on the waggoners, though I told him that the fright was all over. The man seemed crazy, so fearing the officer in command of the cavalry might be as great a fool as himself and fire, I pushed on to the front out of the way.

There I found a sad change for the worse had taken place during my absence. The enemy, reinforced it is said by Longstreet's whole division, which had come back from six miles beyond Williamsburg, had attacked at the old point, and driven our men entirely back to the road. Colonel Starr had withdrawn his regiment from the slashing on the left of my guns, and gone to help our infantry. The enemy pushed on over the felled timber to our left, and through the woods behind it, until they had possession of the road in rear of the batteries. All was up then at once with the guns, there being no exit, at least that we knew of, for horses; and had there been they could not possibly have hauled the pieces out of the soft ground of the field. Bramhall turned his guns at once towards them and fired canister until they were directly on him, when he withdrew his men over the slashing in his rear into the wood, and so across to the other road where General Sumner was, and reported to him, getting most undeservedly cursed for his pains. Our infantry had fought nobly, Dwight's regiment especially. It lay in the slashing, and held their ground until all their ammunition was gone, Dwight and Farnum both wounded, and the rebs all but surrounding them.

By the time I got up the fighting was over. We had lost possession of all the slashing on the left of the road, but held the woods for some distance in that direction. General Heintzelman was there in consultation with Hooker. Osborn had got a dozen or so of his men together, and manned one piece which he had planted in the road just in front of the little thorough cut. So soon as Smith came up, to hurry whom I sent Lieutenant Ames back, I put two of his Parrotts and his section of six-pounders in position on . . . a little knoll, and comparatively open; they had perfect command of the road but nothing more. We did not have to wait many minutes. It was perhaps half an hour after the other guns were captured when the rebs charged in column down the road; my five pieces were all loaded with canister, but I held fire until the head of the column was well down to within about 150 yards of us, and two whole regiments were plainly in view. Three rounds to a gun then blew the whole thing away, except small parties which got into the slashing on the left of the road, and picked off my cannoneers so badly that after trying two or three rounds of canister on them I was obliged to let the men cover themselves behind the trees. Finding no infantry at all near my guns to reply to these fellows, I went back to General Hooker, and asked him to send some, which he promised to do. After waiting ten minutes or so, and finding that the rascals were working up nearer and nearer to me all the time, I again went back and found General Grover, to whom I made the same request, and from whom I received the same promise. Still no supports came. Four of Smith's men had been hit, and I began to be anxious lest another attack should be made, as I could find no infantry within 100 yards to my rear. Going a third time, I found the head of Kearny's column just come up. To Kearny I put my request. This time, instantly he turned to the First Company of a Michigan regiment: "Captain, you will take your company, and put them wherever Major Wainwright here says"—which was done as promptly as it was ordered, and I saw no more of my friends in the slashing. . . .

Shortly before sunset the whole of our division was withdrawn, Kearny's taking our place, and Thompson's battery of the Second Artillery relieving Smith's on the knoll, which with Osborn's I moved back to an open field about three-fourths of a mile to the rear where we bivouacked for the night.

Thus ended my first fight. In looking back to it, I cannot but first of all be grateful to Providence that I escaped unhurt. For a good part of ten hours I was exposed to more or less artillery and musketry fire; when we ran the gauntlet with Kearny, and when the canister was fired over our heads, it was almost a miracle that I was not hit. Besides this, I was kicked over by one of "H" Company's horses while trying to force them into the field, his hoof striking me just below the stomach, and throwing me halfway across the road; an inch higher or lower would have ruined me for life if it did not prove fatal. Quite early in the day a minie ball carried off my left stirrup, slitting the wooden side of its whole breadth, but not even cutting the shoe. My good bay was equally fortunate, escaping unhurt, a mere shaving of one hoof only being cut off.

Of my officers, Bramhall and his lieutenants were all that I could have asked of them, cool, quiet, attending closely to their business and taking good care of their men. When they were not actually firing, the large stumps left in the field afforded excellent cover; and to the fact that their officers required them to use this cover, it must be attributed, together with the softness of the ground, which swallowed up the enemy's shot as it were, and the fact that the large part of their fuses were not cut at all, that there was not a single man hit in this battery. Osborn was slow (as I expected), but did capital service. He astonished me, when in the evening I told him to move to the rear, by replying in his drawling way, "Major, I shan't go until I get that gun out." The gun he spoke of was one that lay buried in the mud on the side of the road, just in front of the knoll in a small hollow where at the time the rebel shot and shell were falling so fast, that I told him he might leave it till morning, as there was no fear of Kearny being driven back. He did get the gun, though with the loss of a man; and I learned that there was a good deal more grit in him than I thought. . . .

I saw but two or three cases among the men of the volunteer batteries of any inclination to shirk, while the very admirable behaviour of Sergeant Horn, and of Sergeant Doran with his Irishmen, almost wiped out the disgrace the men of "H" Company brought on themselves at the beginning of the fight. One of these men I found afterward with a musket he had picked up hunting around for cartridges and fighting it out on his own account.

The total loss in our division was 1,576 out of not more than 8,000 actually engaged. I have heard of but one field officer killed, Major L. M. Morris, of the Eighth New Jersey. Seven out of nine captains in this regiment, I hear, were killed or wounded. My own loss was four killed, and twenty wounded, one mortally. It is wonderful that it should have been so small. One man also is missing, but may turn up. At night I was much worried as I did not know what had become of Bramhall's men or Webber's either.

Wet to the skin and very tired, I lay down at night with the officers of Osborn's battery under a paulin, but could not sleep much for the cold, and for thinking. I had often asked myself how I should feel in my first fight, and expected to be a good deal frightened, though I knew pride would keep one up to the mark. The sight of blood often making me feel faint, I was more afraid of the effect the sight of dead and wounded would have on me than of anything else. Whatever may have been the cause, whether it was having so much to do, or whether it was excitement, or both together. I know not, but I cannot recall having felt the least personal fear while under fire. After I got back to the rear after Smith, there was some reluctance to go to the front again, a sort of nervous lassitude, but the instant I heard the heavy firing this was over. The excitement too was different from what I expected; I certainly never was more conscious nor did my mind ever see things more coolly or reason clearer. As to seeing men shot, dead or dying, I had no feeling but one of perfect indifference. When Lieutenant Eakin fell against me, and cried out that he was "a dead man," I had no more feeling for him, than if he had tripped over a stump and fallen; nor do I think it would have been different had he been my brother.

As to my official acts, I see but two that I wish had been different. First, that I did not go over myself on to the ground where our infantry were, and see whether it were not possible to get my howitzers around there; and second, that I should have gone to the rear for Smith's battery. To be sure, it is very doubtful whether he would have got up at all had I not gone; neither can I see that anything more could have been done or saved had I remained; but the guns were lost during my absence, and I confess it, I am a little ashamed to have been to the rear at that time.

General Hooker was in the road just to the rear of my batteries, and under fire all day, as brave as brave could be beyond a doubt. But he seemed to know little of the ground where his infantry were fighting; and I must say did not impress me at all favourably as to his powers as a general. His great idea was to go ahead quick until you ran against the enemy, and then fight him; the spirit of Heintzelman's order of the night before, "not to let Sumner get into Williamsburg first," seemed to be his main rule of action. Kearny on the other hand was calm and deliberate, and would not put a man into position until he had examined his ground, and knew what he had to do. Old Heintzelman did not get there until about one P.M. or later; he may have done a great deal without my knowing it. . . .

Soon after the enemy's second attack, which took all our troops to drive back, say by 12:30 o'clock, General Hooker sent to Heintzelman and Sumner for reinforcements. None came until Kearny arrived, he says at two o'clock; I feel very sure it was nearly if not quite four o'clock. He came up all the way from Yorktown. General Sumner had the whole of

Keyes's corps, three divisions, only a mile or two to our right. . . . As early as ten o'clock in the morning Hancock with his brigade attacked the extreme left of the enemy, drove them back, and shortly afterward got possession of one of their works, when he sent back word to General Smith, his division commander, that if he would give him another brigade he could push around to the rear of Williamsburg. Smith at once ordered up the whole division, but was stopped by Sumner who would not let Hancock go any farther; and lay there all day with his 30,000 doing nothing. It is very hard to understand such things. I know there is an awful amount of jealousy among our leading generals, but hardly think it can go so far; at the same time, it is equally hard to suppose they are actual fools.*

CAMP NEAR WILLIAMSBURG, MAY 6, TUESDAY.   It did not rain much last night, and today it has cleared off. Kearny and some other troops pushed on this morning several miles beyond Williamsburg; had a small fight with Johnston's rear guard, and brought in some prisoners, and a few abandoned guns, mostly old iron ones. Our own division is camped tonight around the sunken redoubt, and has had large fatigue parties out all day bringing in the wounded, and burying the dead, both our own and the enemy's. Williamsburg is full of rebel wounded, with a goodly number of our own. We also have several hundred prisoners there. Hooker claims to have captured representatives of forty-three regiments, which would go to show that our division fought at different times during the day, two, if not three times our own numbers.†

* Edwin V. Sumner, who had been born in Massachusetts in 1797 and was failing in vigor, held second rank in the Army of the Potomac. McClellan, who had not expected a serious battle on the first day of pursuit and therefore remained at Williamsburg, sent him to the front to hold command until superseded. Later some critics held Mc-Clellan responsible for the close issue and heavy losses of the battle on the ground that he should have been on the field. Others, with more reason, held Sumner responsible because he failed to furnish systematic direction. It was certainly fought on the Union side without plan, without efficient marshaling of superior numbers, and without such management of the various divisions as to minimize losses. Sumner was to continue to show lack of method and foresight, though he distinguished himself at Fair Oaks, and his voluntary retirement from the Army of the Potomac early in 1863 was a relief to others.

It is dismaying to find suspicion already arising that certain jealous Union commanders might be more eager to defeat each other than the enemy. But General Alexander S. Webb, who became Chief of Staff of the Army of the Potomac, writes in his history of the Peninsular campaign of this very battle: "The tone of certain passages in Heintzelman's report, and the sensitive reply of Sumner, indicate, as between these two officers, an undercurrent of jealousy or unfriendliness existed, which, on a subsequent occasion, came near working mischief."

† Hooker later declared that he had fought the whole Confederate army on the Peninsula; but actually, as his biographer Walter H. Hebert states, he had opposed only six brigades under James Longstreet. His casualties, however, were very serious; the 1,575

I was awfully tired and stiff this morning. The rain had got down inside my rubber cape, and had wet me from head to foot; it was impossible to get dry clothing, so a good part of the night was spent standing over the fire. Soon after I started out this morning, I met Bramhall and his First Lieutenant Martin; I had heard nothing of them, since the capture of their battery, and was more affected at finding them alive and safe than by all the casualties of the day before. On riding up to my position of yesterday, in the fallow field, I found Bramhall's five guns, and one of Webber's Parrotts still stuck in the mud; they had sunk down so deep that the rebs were not able to carry them off. Here too I saw a most wonderful exemplification of the nature of the ground in this field. Shortly before the guns were captured one of the wheel horses of a limber was shot dead. The men did not have time to get the harness off him, and the rebs only carried away the lead and swing teams so that the other wheel horse was left standing in the traces all night. The weight of his dead mate bearing on the pole had caused the live horse to sink in the ground feet-first until it reached halfway up his chest, and suffocated him. When I got there he was quite dead; the surface of the ground coming up to the cantle of the saddle, his tail and rump sunk quite out of sight. The whole of the land hereabouts is underlain by a bed of shell marl which again lies on a subsoil of heavy clay; the soil above the marl is a very light sand, and in places not over a foot or two thick. The immense rains we have had all this spring, sinking directly through the sand and finding no outlet from the marl, have converted it into the consistency of soft mortar; so that when a heavy substance once breaks through the top soil, there is nothing to stop its sinking until it reaches the hard clay.

As I looked over the ground, and saw how thick the cannon balls lay, I was more and more filled with wonder at our small loss in the batteries. I counted thirteen projectiles lying on a piece of ground which could almost be covered by a wall tent. Most of them were six-pounder shell and case with Beauman fuses, not one in ten of which had been cut. The paper fuses did not work well with them or us either, it being almost impossible to drive them without wetting the powder. My own notion, as formed from yesterday's experience, is that the smooth-bore guns are the most accurate within a range suited to them. The firing of my two twelve-pounder howitzers was perfect, and uniform; this may be partly owing to the ammunition for them having been made before the war

---

men reported killed, wounded, and missing were one-fifth of the division. With pardonable anger, he declared in his report that he had suffered these murderous losses unaided while 20,000 troops stood idly by. It was true that 30,000 might have been marched to help him but were not, but the fact was attributed mainly to Sumner's failure to comprehend the situation, not to any malice.

broke out, when it was manufactured with much more care than now. I have got my batteries together now, and find them in a pretty bad condition. "H" Company has lost so much in material that it will be impossible to make it good in time to move forward with the rest. So Webber is to move back to Yorktown, and there await an entire new outfit; he will get the twelve-pounder Napoleon guns, which were promised me before we left Budd's Ferry. . . . The enemy carried off three Parrott guns, one howitzer, and one caisson body of Webber's; and one limber of Bramhall's.

MAY 7, WEDNESDAY. Fighting a battle, I find, is the smallest part of a campaign. The repairing of damages, writing reports, and getting ready to go at it again is infinitely more fatiguing. Another day's work and I am only just beginning to see daylight. Rode into the town this morning, and saw General Barry; he was rather gruff at first over the loss of the guns, but Webb took my part, and Barry concluded to wait until he had seen the ground himself. McClellan's headquarters are in Williamsburg; Franklin's and Porter's divisions are to come by water. The cavalry are out beyond the town reconnoitering, but the army cannot advance until we get rationed up. It is too far to haul all the way from Shipping Point, or even from Yorktown, with the roads in their present condition: a temporary depot is being established at the mouth of Queen's Creek.

I took a look at several of the redoubts this afternoon. Fort Magruder is the largest and quite a formidable affair. They are all very well built, and placed so as to cover one another: the line stretching entirely across the Peninsula, which is quite narrow at this point. The line in itself I think as strong as the one they held at Yorktown save that the flanks can be turned by water. The rebs evidently meant at one time to hold this line, or they would not have expended so much labour on it. But it is now pretty certain that they would have passed right on had we not pressed them so close. I found Bailey camped with his command about half a mile north of Fort Magruder. They all appeared really sorry that they did not get into the fight. Our men are still at work burying the dead. Our own are pretty much all interred. They say that they lay very thick in the slashing, and that a number had evidently been bayonetted by the rebels, after they were shot down. I cannot think that there were many such cases. The rebel wounded in our hands, and our prisoners generally, express much surprise at receiving such kind treatment: they had been told by their leaders that they would all be murdered. I saw several hundred rebel prisoners in Williamsburg. They were a seedy-looking lot, most of them in grey or butternut clothes, and all sorts of slouch hats; you could hardly call it a uniform at all.

MAY 9, FRIDAY. Our first mail received since we left Yorktown. It brings me no letters of later date than May 1st, and of course nothing with regard to what is said or thought of matters here. Yesterday's New York papers have nothing more in them either, and the division is feeling somewhat sore at all the glory going to Hancock, who did but very little fighting. It is said that General McClellan has sent a second telegram to Washington correcting his first, and complimenting Hooker and his men. General Hooker is busy getting up his report, and says that he means to see that his men have all the credit they deserve.

The firing yesterday was as I supposed. Franklin, after quite a sharp little fight, landed his division at West Point. Today all the army, except our division, start "on to Richmond" way. West Point will give us a good base for supplies as it is a railroad terminus. Our division is under orders to move at eight o'clock tomorrow. The First Brigade, however, remains behind to garrison Williamsburg until some other troops come up, when it will join us. Bramhall too has to wait for horses, so I shall only have two batteries to start with; but as we are to be in the rear, there is not much likelihood of my needing any.

This afternoon I took a ride all through the town of Williamsburg; visiting the college, where Grover has his headquarters. It is a queer old place; apparently has not grown any since the last century. Many of the buildings are very old—that is, for America—and everything indicates a perfect stagnation for years past. Most of the wealthier inhabitants have cleared out for Richmond, leaving all their furniture and servants behind. In the house that Grover has, the old servants wait on him just as they did on their old master. Many of our officers have picked up servants here.

CAMP TEN MILES FROM WILLIAMSBURG ON POST ROAD, MAY 10, SATURDAY. Our march out this far today was quite pleasant, the weather being fine and the road good. Our headquarters tents are pitched in the door yard of a small abandoned house. Most of the furniture was gone out of the house, the negroes on the place having appropriated much of it to their own use, and were indulging in all the luxury of cushioned rocking chairs. One room in the house was strewn with paper, letters, bills, and the like, many of them dating away back to Revolutionary days, and bearing the signature of men who figured largely then. I picked out several for my autograph collection, but my conscience would not let me carry them off.

TURNER'S FARM, MAY 11, SUNDAY. We came six miles to this place this morning; have our tents pitched in a nice grass field in front of Mr. Turner's house, who claims to be a Union man. He has a fine farm here in good order save where damaged by the passing of armies. They gave a number of us quite a nice dinner today, and supplied headquarters with ice and fresh milk in abundance. McClellan's orders for the protection of private property are very strict, even to forbidding the burning of fence rails; but it is very hard to enforce them. Several of Mr. Turner's pigs and calves have fallen under the shots of our men today, but when it could be got at the carcass was returned to him. My battery horses are enjoying a good bite of clover, this sort of poaching being quite legitimate.

We have reports today, nearly official, that the rebs have cleared out from Norfolk; leaving without a fight so soon as our forces landed. The iron-clad *Merrimack*, it is said, they have blown up, while their smaller gunboats have gone up the river to Richmond.* The James as well as the York is now open to us, so that we have both flanks covered by our navy, and can make our supply depots on either river.

MAY 12, MONDAY. We are lying quietly in camp today; a rest which I for one am very glad to have, for somehow I do not get over the fatigue of the battle and afterwork, and have felt very miserable until today, when after a long night's rest I am much better. . . . The ill feeling in the division on account of the newspaper reports of the Williamsburg battle continues very strong. The more I think of it, the more credit our men seem to me to deserve; but the less generalship I see in Hooker, and more to blame in old Sumner and perhaps in Heintzelman too.

BARHAMSVILLE, MAY 13, TUESDAY. We made a little march, only a couple of miles, to this place this afternoon. I do not know what advantage was gained by moving us so short a distance, and do not like the change in our camp at all. At Turner's we had a beautiful quiet site, in an open green field; here we are stuck down by the roadside in a wood of scrub oak and pine.

The country here is much better farmed than it is lower down the Peninsula. No tobacco is grown, and many of the farmers seem to understand the use of the shell marl, which lies under all their land. . . . Not more than a quarter of the land is cleared, though it has all evidently been under the plough at one time or another; as the corn rows and dead furrows can be seen plainly in the woods, even where the trees have the largest growth. Nearly half the inhabitants have abandoned their houses and moved on Richmond way. In all these cases their dwellings have been pretty thoroughly pillaged, first by their own negroes and then by our men. Where the people have remained, nothing in

---

* McClellan's movement up the Peninsula made Norfolk untenable. Lincoln himself, with Secretaries Stanton and Salmon P. Chase, went down the Potomac to help direct the operations for recapturing the place. On May 10, after General John E. Wool landed troops to take the Confederate fortifications in reverse, the Confederates evacuated the town, setting fire as they left to buildings and material of war. Commodore Josiah Tattnall, being unable to take the *Merrimack* up the James River, thereupon destroyed her; an unavoidable if somewhat too precipitate step that caused great elation in the North and consternation in the South.

their houses has been touched. Most of these are lukewarm Union men, but none are young and able-bodied. All such have already gone into their army, either willingly or forcibly.

MAY 14, WEDNESDAY. There was a military execution near here yesterday afternoon, a negro hung for rape committed on a white woman. I did not go to see the execution, having no taste for such sights. McClellan is doing his best to make our men behave themselves; his orders are very strict against everything like pillage, or any offence to the inhabitants. But he is not well supported in it by all his subordinate commanders, many of them allowing their feelings of hatred to the rebels to interfere with their obedience of orders, and some even condemning him for too great leniency towards them. For my own part, I think the General right on every ground: militarily, because pillage always produces demoralization, and lax discipline; judicially, or as just, because whatever may be the crime of the inhabitants, it is not right for individuals, whether officers or privates, to judge and punish them; and politically, because this is our own country, and the inhabitants our fellow citizens though they are rebels. Our object is to put down the rebellion, not to open wider the breach of estrangement, or to impoverish our own country. It appears very strange to me that so many men, sensible ones too in most matters, should be so shortsighted, and allow their feelings so entirely to get the better of their judgment.

An order came down from Army Headquarters the other day for the provost-marshals to seize and turn over to the provost-marshal general "all animals or other property in the hands of officers, men, and followers of the Army, acquired on the march, the possession of which cannot be properly accounted for." Under it, Captain Young, our division provost, has been gathering them up for some days, and this afternoon started for headquarters with a most heterogeneous cavalcade; rawboned Rosenantes, scrub ponies, donkeys and donkey carts. His guard are mostly New York City b'hoys, and turned the whole thing into a tatterdemalion parade, drawing shouts of laughter from the crowd of spectators along the road.

NEAR SLATERSVILLE, MAY 15, THURSDAY. We moved to this place this morning, starting at six o'clock. The order of march directed that the Third Corps would "be concentrated at Cumberland Landing"; but that our division would keep the rear; the consequence of which was that we could not get any farther than this point. Somehow or other our marches seem to be very badly managed, the different divisions continually running into each other. Whether the fault lies at headquarters in the arrangement or in the division commanders, in the carrying out, I cannot say, as I only see the orders for our own division. I feel sure though that it could be obviated, as the weather has been fine, and the roads good so far. It commenced raining about an hour before we got into camp, and is horribly wet and cold this afternoon.

I know almost nothing of what has been going on in the other parts of the army, since we left Williamsburg. Our place away to the rear keeps us as ignorant of what is doing at the front as if we were in New York. Rumours of all sorts daily float through the camp, to be either contradicted the next day, or allowed to die a natural death. There has been no battle since West Point; though the cavalry have had a number of little skirmishes and one of some magnitude near this point, in which I hear that Bailey's classmate, Sanders, quite distinguished himself. Porter's division is said to have landed at Cumberland, on the Pamunkey, where our present supply depot is.

We have New York papers of Tuesday, giving an account of the capture of Norfolk, and so on. President Lincoln's landing first was quite an extensive piece of buncombe in a new line for this country. It seems to me the rebs might have made an obstinate defence there, as well as at Williamsburg to good advantage, at least in the gaining of time. . . .

MAY 16, FRIDAY. It cleared off warm this morning, and has been a fine May day. The spring has been wonderfully cold for this latitude, not warmer on an average than we generally have it up the Hudson. Letters from home say it is uncommonly cold and wet there too. We remained quietly in camp all day; and I hope the roads will dry up before we move again. Grover's brigade, the First, which we left in Williamsburg, and Bramhall's battery came up today. This gives me three batteries, of sixteen guns; all I am likely to have for some time, as Webber seems to have made no progress in getting his new outfit yet. Brigadier-General Abercrombie took command of the Third Brigade today, so that all our brigades are now under general officers.* . . .

Slatersville consists of less than half a dozen houses, or is about the size of all the other "villes" we have come across. It lies on the Post road two miles east of New Kent Court House, which place is marked on the maps in large letters but really consists of a Court House and jail (both are now burnt), a vile-looking tavern, and three or four dwellings. It is about halfway between Williamsburg and Richmond. We are picketing several roads which lead down to the Chickahominy on our left, crossing it at Jones Bridge, and may be left here for some days to cover the rear from any attack from that quarter.

* John J. Abercrombie, a Tennessean who had graduated from West Point in 1822 and been wounded in the Mexican War, was now a brigade commander in the Army of the Potomac and fought well at Fair Oaks (where he was wounded again) and Malvern Hill. But he was almost sixty-five, and after the summer of 1862 was kept on duty in the defenses of Washington and in administering army depots.

FOUR

THE ADVANCE ON RICHMOND

In moving up the Peninsula from Williamsburg toward Richmond, McClellan's army could use either the York or the James River as a supply line. He chose the York, apparently under the advice of Stanton, who wished him to keep his right wing north of Richmond so that he might readily unite it with McDowell's corps, which was to march through Fredericksburg upon the Confederate capital. The distance between Williamsburg and the new base immediately in front of Richmond was only about forty miles. In arguing with Lincoln and Stanton in favor of the Peninsular movement, McClellan had minimized the difficulties of the route.

The army began its advance on May 8, with Keyes's corps and Stoneman's cavalry leading the way. Hooker's division, which had needed a special period of recuperation, set out a little later. The roads were few and wretched; day after day heavy rains fell; the weather was unseasonably cold. But the troops pushed stubbornly through New Kent Court House, until on May 15 McClellan was able to establish headquarters and a permanent depot at the White House, an old Virginia mansion on the Pamunkey River. That date, as we have seen, found Hooker and Wainwright halfway to the new base. In this vicinity the army was concentrated by May 21, confronting Richmond at a distance of only seven to twelve miles. As more rain fell, the troops began to suffer from exposure. Heintzelman's corps, of which Hooker's division was part, was at first kept in a reserve position on fairly high ground called Poplar Hill and met less hardship than other units.

Ever since Williamsburg, which might fairly be called a check if not a defeat, McClellan had been complaining that his army was too small. Because of casualties and sickness, he reported on May 14 that he could not bring more than 80,000 men at most into battle; and he was sure that Johnston, the Confederate commander, had a far stronger force. Actually, at the time of the siege of Yorktown McClellan had possessed 112,000 troops against Johnston's 60,000, and he was still far the stronger. But he reported to the President that the Peninsula had been stripped of fighting men, who were all in the Southern ranks. "I ask for every man that the War Department can send me," he wrote. He would fight no matter what the odds; but "the greater our force, the more perfect will be our combinations, and the less our loss." The real question was whether he could so dispose of his superior force as to make the most of his greater numbers and better equipment.

About May 15, as Wainwright notes, McClellan formed two new provisional corps under firm friends, not to say favorites. One was William B. Franklin, West Point, 1843; the other was Fitz-John Porter, West Point, 1845. Both later became centers of controversy. Franklin had a sharp quarrel with Burnside after Fredericksburg, while Porter figured in the most famous court-martial in American army history.

* * *

MAY 17 [1862], SATURDAY.   Another day in camp: so I got permission to go out on a ride, hoping to pick up some news, or at least to get some idea of matters in the army as I am tired of lying here in total ignorance of what is going on. I went as far as "White House" where general headquarters now are, and Franklin's corps is encamped. Franklin and Porter both have corps now; "provisionary corps," McClellan's order calls them, the arrangement being subject to the approval of the President, and numbered Fifth and Sixth. Porter's, the Fifth, consists of his old division, which was very large, and the reserve of regulars; Franklin's, the Sixth, of his own and Smith's divisions. This does not, of course, increase the size to the capacity of their commanders, and raises two generals to that command who have not shown themselves hostile to McClellan. I hear that McClellan was not in favour of making Corps d'Armée so soon, knowing how bad a frequent change of high officers is, and wishing to test his generals before any were selected for such responsible posts. But Mr. Lincoln overruled him in this, and made corps commanders out of untried men; of whom the three in this army are veritable "old fogies," if not something worse.

The "White House," a small low building, standing near the bank of the Pamunkey, on a flat of two or three hundred acres of cleared ground, originally belonged to the Custis family, and is now the property of Robert E. Lee, a general of note in the rebel army.* It was here that Washington courted his wife, the widow Custis. The house and garden are under strict guard, and in no way injured; the clean rows of young

* Actually the Custis family had bequeathed the White House to Robert E. Lee's son, Fitzhugh or "Rooney," it being an estate of about 4,000 acres. Lee's principal position at the time Wainwright wrote this passage was military adviser to President Jefferson Davis.

vegetables in the garden looked very inviting. About a quarter of a mile above the house the Richmond and York River Railroad crossed the Pamunkey, but the rebs burned the bridge before they left. Fortunately for us the river is navigable for steamboats to this point, so the destruction of the bridge does no harm. Our men are busy building piers here and this will doubtless be our base of supplies hereafter as we can use the railroad to get them to the front; unless we should shift over to the James. The railroad is held by the Second Corps for some six or eight miles beyond "White House," or nearly to the Chickahominy. The Fourth Corps is on the Post road, and reached the Chickahominy at Bottom's Bridge today. The reb pickets are on the other side of the stream, and will have to be driven back before the bridges can be rebuilt, as doubtless both Bottom's and the railroad bridges are destroyed.

I was rather surprised to find the roads generally very bad; that from Cumberland Landing to the "White House," along which Porter's command were trying to march, was almost impassable, quite so for artillery, I judge, as I met the reserve just turning back. The country does not seem to dry up at all, owing I suppose to the subsoil of marl being full of water; and the immense amount of wood. I said that not over a quarter of the land is cleared. I doubt now if there is much more than one acre in ten. Still there are some really good farms: I went through one on my way home that was in capital order; a good house, on a fine airy knoll, with large and thrifty orchards of both peaches and apples; the grain looking well, and the best field of clover I have seen in Virginia, in full bloom. Such a place they tell me was worth about $25 an acre before the war. . . .

General Hooker has finished his report of the battle and sent it up. He read it to me piecemeal as it was written. It hits somebody very hard; is correct in the main, I should say—speaks very flatteringly of his chief of artillery and shoulders all the responsibility of Starr's withdrawal of his regiment and the loss of the guns. With regard to Colonel Starr, he told me that the old man had acted according to the best of his judgment, trying to do his duty conscientiously, and that whenever any of his officers did so he could ask no more of them. It is very pleasant to feel one has that kind of a commander; one who will not make a scapegoat of you should you commit an error of judgment, but says, do the best you can, I will support you. Indeed, all my intercourse with General Hooker has been of the pleasantest kind, and I have found him a delightful man to serve with. I do not, however, like the way he has of always decrying the other generals of his own rank, whose every act he seems to find fault with.

PREVOST'S FARM, MAY 18, SUNDAY. Being Sunday and a fine day of course we had to march. Since we left Budd's Ferry, I believe we have had but two Sundays in camp, and on both of those it rained. The order again designated Cumberland as our point of destination, but again we were halted some two miles short of it, the Second Corps being in the way. Though we were five hours on the road, we did not make over half a dozen miles, owing partly to the state of the roads, but mainly to other divisions being in the way. Our present headquarters has a splendid outlook, being on the top of quite a high cleared knoll. All round at our feet lie the troops of the division; and in the distance we can see the Pamunkey winding about among the trees, and studded with the white sails of vessels. In many places, too, where the river itself is not visible, the sails are seen moving to all appearances through the middle of a thick wood. The Second Corps, at least a part of it, lies on another knoll about a mile off, their tents and fires making quite a picture at sunset. . . .

BALTIMORE CROSSROADS, MAY 19, MONDAY. Another little move today of six miles, right up the Post road, which brings us within half a dozen miles of Bottom's Bridge, and some twenty of Richmond itself; just a nice afternoon's drive with a pair of good trotters before a light wagon, were the roads good and no obstructions in the way. . . .

MAY 30, TUESDAY. No move today, nor is one likely to be made for several days. The gunboats failed in their attack on Fort Darling,* and have fallen back down the river. As yet we have no particulars, and know nothing as to the strength of the rebel position; still one cannot help thinking that if another Farragut had been in command things might have been different, and the enemy's works passed if they could not be destroyed. It is said that another trial will be made, but it must be some time first. Meanwhile I suspect we shall make our movements quite independent of it and this will necessitate the thorough bridging of the Chickahominy, and opening of the railroad; a work of several days at least. . . .

The doctor on whose farm we are camped is one of the rich and thriving men of the neighbourhood, owning near 100 negroes and farming some 700 acres. He was an original secessionist and member of the convention that passed the ordinance of secession. Our provost-marshal grumbles a great deal at having to furnish a guard to his house, and says the men ought to hang him. I agree with him as to the hanging, if done after proper trial, but not that our men should be allowed to turn into common thieves and murderers. I have not been up to his house myself,

---

* This was the battle of Drewry's Bluff on the James. Union gunboats, attacking the shore batteries here fifteen miles downstream from Richmond, were repulsed; but not before they caused a great deal of confusion and fright in Richmond. General Joseph E. Johnston now decided to withdraw his army south of the Chickahominy and resist McClellan near the city rather than north of the stream.

but Lieutenant Martin tells me the old man lives very well, and is quite communicative. Joe Johnston spent the night at his house before our men came up and was almost captured by our cavalry, a body of them getting within a few hundred yards of the house before he knew it. . . . MAY 21, WEDNESDAY. A really warm day, more like such weather as one expects down here at the end of May than any we have had before. Remained quietly in camp, for somehow or other I do not seem to get rested; not that I feel at all ill, only worthless. General Kearny rode up in the afternoon, and spent a couple of hours or more with Hooker: I was present all the time. The battle of Williamsburg was the topic of conversation, and the reports of it telegraphed and written. Kearny asked to see the General's report, and mine; the former he praised very highly. He also related a conversation he had had with General Sumner, in which that general gave his version of the battle; one entirely new to me, and which while it explains a great deal before unaccountable, by no means increases my respect for Sumner as a general though it partly relieves him from blame for not reinforcing Hooker.

Sumner told Kearny that McClellan was mistaken in supposing it a mere affair of the heads of his columns, and Hooker in supposing that the attack on him was meant for the main one. That he, Sumner, penetrated the enemy's design, which was to decoy our men out into the plain by a partial attack on our left, and then to break through our centre. That seeing where they intended to make their attack he had prepared for it, drawing his men up in five lines, so that finding they could not carry out their plan the enemy withdrew. The old man claims that it was a great battle, a great victory and that he was in command. Perhaps General Sumner is right, and he is a great general, but I do not want to serve under him in another fight if this is a specimen. How in creation did Johnston know anything about his "five lines" which lay half a mile back in the woods, and never drew trigger? The enemy were retreating, and our position did not interfere with their retreat; why then should they attack? and who ever heard of "five lines" of battle drawn up in a dense wood before? . . .

Why McClellan should have remained at Yorktown until so late, when he must have heard the firing and known that a battle was going on, puzzled me at first. But I have since learned from an officer who was with him that Sumner's reports were frequent, and all described matters as progressing most favourably (his "five lines" back in the woods still held their ground!). It was not until three o'clock or near it, that he got any intimation of the real state of affairs; and then through a citizen, an old gentleman who had come down from the front, and told him that he thought he could not know the real state of affairs and was able to explain enough to set McClellan off for the front like a rocket. . . .

MAY 22, THURSDAY. This morning I took another ride around to see what I could learn. Striking right across to the railroad, I followed up the track for perhaps five miles to the bridge. The road is evidently new, and in perfect order; not a rail had been removed or a culvert broken so far as I went. Of the railroad bridge over the Chickahominy, not more than twenty or thirty yards has been destroyed, though it must be fifty feet high and is quite long; all trestle work too. A couple of miles before reaching the bridge I passed a steam sawmill, apparently in perfect order, and surrounded with the largest piles of fine white oak timber and planks I ever saw: just what we need to repair the bridge and all ready for use. It is very singular that they should have left this and the railroad uninjured. I found some of the Second Corps along the railroad, and Couch's division at the bridge. They threw strong parties across the river yesterday: as did Casey's division at Bottom's Bridge. From there I came around to Bottom's Bridge, where the Post road crosses, and found this bridge almost rebuilt. The Chickahominy is here only some fifteen feet wide, running between mud banks some six feet high! But they say it rises wonderfully after even a few hours' rain; and after a heavy storm spreads over its banks so as to become a torrent of half a mile in breadth. Keyes's corps, the Fourth, has the advance here, and will all cross, it is said, so soon as the two bridges are passable for infantry. Sumner lies on Keyes's right, and Franklin still farther up the stream, which as the stream makes quite a bend here must bring him within some eight miles of Richmond. . . .

NEAR BOTTOM'S BRIDGE, MAY 23, FRIDAY. A damp, cold day, with drizzling rain in the afternoon. We moved up here, some four miles, getting our tents pitched shortly before dark, close to a great tumbledown old house, about half a mile from the bridge, and which looks as if it might have been a tavern at one time. The house is now used as a hospital by some of Casey's division. Every abandoned house we have come across during the last ten days we have found occupied in this way by Keyes's corps. There is a great deal of sickness in the army, but the Fourth Corps seems to be pre-eminent in this way. This sickness is owing to the wetness of the ground, cold rains, and the fact that none of the men are seasoned, or know how to take care of themselves. In fact, the surgeons themselves know little more; many (most of them) being poor hands at their trade, and pretty much all treading on new ground. One whole campaign will doubtless rectify much of this, and season the men, but I fear the loss from disease must be heavy meantime. The attacks are mainly diarrhea and southern fever, a species of typhoid.

Keyes's corps crossed the Chickahominy this morning and pushed on a couple of miles or so. This makes rather a bad dividing of the army until we can get a number of bridges thrown across, which will take some days. . . .

MAY 24, SATURDAY. A steady hard rain all day, turning the whole country into a sea of mud and rendering the roads almost impassable. About noon, just in the midst of the heaviest pour, orders came for us to send one brigade and a battery over the river to support Keyes, who was having a fight. Grover was sent with his brigade and Bramhall's battery, and I got permission to ride out with them. After going about two miles beyond the bridge, the troops were halted, formed in line of battle, and ordered to entrench themselves. . . .

The rain has stopped this evening. Grover and his troops have returned to camp. The first locomotive on the railroad is now, 7:00 P.M., whistling at Dispatch Station about a mile from here, so we shall now be saved the fifteen miles hauling of supplies. This being the case, and as tomorrow will be Sunday, we shall doubtless have to march again. I have forgotten to mention that Sickles has been confirmed as a brigadier-general and returned to take his old command this week, the Second Brigade, relieving General Abercrombie.

WHITE OAK SWAMP, MAY 25, SUNDAY. As I expected, we have marched again today. As we ceased thereby to be the rear guard and moved up on to the left of the line, we marched with a battery in rear of each brigade, and all the train in rear of the division. After crossing Bottom's Bridge we turned short to the left by the first road, and went due south some three or four miles, nearly to White Oak Swamp bridge, which we are to watch. The swamp lies higher up; at this point the stream, which still bears the name of swamp, is a small affair, running through a wide grass bottom, with quite a high sloping bluff on this side, about half a mile from the bridge. On this high ground the First and Second Brigades are camped: the First in line of battle, with the Second in column in its rear. Smith's battery is in position on either side of a house here, in which one Brackett is living. The position is a lovely one if attacked in front, which it is not likely to be; of its flanks I know nothing save that there appear to be vast woods both ways. The Third Brigade, Osborn and Bramhall, and our own headquarters lie near a mile to the rear, directly opposite to where the road Savage Station comes in. The country on this side of the Chickahominy is not so much cleared as on the left bank. Still it is not as I expected to find it, a swamp, but quite broken, and with a good deal of tolerable grass in the hollows, which to be sure are soft and wet. . . .

MAY 26, MONDAY. Our headquarters tents are pitched in the dooryard of an abandoned house; the house is not a large one, about the usual size around here, with lots of out-buildings, but no cellar. We use it as a kitchen and dining room. Most all the furniture was gone when we arrived, but it was disgusting to see officers at work carrying off what little remained; even to a lieutenant-colonel running away with a great hair sofa, and a flat iron. The men would very soon have pulled all the out-buildings to pieces for the boards had they not been stopped.

I rode out with General Grover to examine the country on the right of our position, but could discover nothing save an endless wood, intersected by innumerable small roads. It will require constant sharp watching in that direction. In front it is quite open too and on the opposite side of the stream. I do not know whether our picket posts communicate with those of Kearny, who lies somewhere on our right but suppose they do. General Orders 118 received today indicate an early battle is expected by McClellan, as it not only requires that all waggons shall be left on the other side of the Chickahominy, except ambulances, and that the men shall leave their knapsacks with the waggons, but also speaks distinctly of "the approaching battle," and finishes with an exhortation to officers and men.

This evening we are having another heavy rain; and a very cold one too, for the season. The water comes down most tropically, in sheets instead of in detached drops as it does farther north.

MAY 27, TUESDAY. There has been a great deal of firing pretty much all day, away off on the far right. We know nothing as to whether they have had a fight there, or if it has been a mere cannonading. Everything hereabouts has been perfectly quiet, making it hard work to kill time. . . .

MAY 28, WEDNESDAY. General Hooker was over at Army Headquarters, and gave me quite a budget of news on his return, some good, some not. The worst is the awful amount of sickness in the army, amounting to a full quarter of our total force. Indeed, he says that we have but 68,000 effective men now, Keyes's whole corps not reaching 12,000. It is not nearly so bad in my own batteries, not more than one in ten being reported sick. As yet only one of my officers, Parker, junior lieutenant of Smith's battery, has been attacked; but he, poor fellow, is very sick. The good is that McDowell is at last really on his way to join us. McClellan's object in coming by the York instead of advancing along the James was to effect his junction; but for a week past the camp has been full of rumours that McDowell did not want to come, and was raising all sorts of difficulties. Now we know officially that he has his orders from Mr. Lincoln to start this morning, so he ought to join us by Saturday at the farthest. The firing yesterday was from quite a little battle at Hanover Junction, whither a portion of Porter's corps was sent to destroy the railroad bridges over the North Anna so as to prevent the enemy concentrating on McDowell before he gets within supporting distance of us. It was quite a brilliant affair they say, and entirely successful. The news that McDowell is coming with his 40,000 men is already spread throughout the camps, and is causing great rejoicing. I think it will be impossible for the enemy to hold Richmond long after he joins us; though there is not much chance now of our getting in by the 1st of June, the day I had fixed upon.

Monday's *Herald* tells us of great excitement in New York caused by Banks's retreat to Harper's Ferry. We had heard that he had fallen back there in consequence of all his troops save 5,000 being transferred to McDowell, but according to the newspaper accounts, he was tumbled back pretty roughly by the reb General Jackson, and they seem to think it doubtful if he can hold his own there. If McDowell will only hurry up, and enable us to get Richmond it will matter but little what happens in the rest of Virginia.

* * *

It was not true that Washington's orders for the disposition of troops had constrained McClellan to advance by the York instead of the James; he had long since chosen the York and Pamunkey Rivers of his own free will. He maintained that choice of his own volition. As late as May 19 McClellan held a conference with the commander of the Atlantic blockading squadron, Louis M. Goldsborough, on a possible transfer to the James, but decided against it. Stanton advised the York River base, but merely advised.

McClellan labored under the illusion, created partly by his bad intelligence service, that the Confederates had overwhelming strength. He reported in mid-May that he himself had 102,236 troops. But, he declared, he would have to fight "perhaps double my numbers" in order to take Richmond, and wanted heavy reinforcements. The Administration was then anxious to send McDowell with his 38,000 men to reinforce McClellan. On May 17 Stanton issued an order to McDowell at Fredericksburg: "Upon being joined by General Shields' division you will move upon Richmond by the general route of the Richmond and Fredericksburg Railroad, cooperating with the forces under General McClellan, now threatening Richmond from the line of the Pamunkey and York Rivers. While seeking to establish as soon as possible a communication between your left wing and the right wing of General McClellan, you will hold yourself always in such a position as to cover the capital of the nation against a sudden dash of any large body of the rebels." Lincoln was quite right in holding that one primary duty of the Union forces was to protect Washington; its capture would have come near paralyzing the government.

At this point, unfortunately for McClellan, Stonewall Jackson executed the brilliant strategic diversion in the Shenandoah Valley that did so much to wreck the advance on Richmond. On May 8, pushing forward from

Staunton, he defeated a Union force at the village of McDowell; on the 13th he fell upon and destroyed another force at Front Royal, and he then pressed on against Banks, defeated him at Winchester, and threw his army in headlong retreat to the Potomac. Reports of this flight and of Jackson's own arrival on the Potomac not far northwest of Washington caused a panic in the capital. Though McDowell had already begun his march to join McClellan, he was ordered on May 24 to turn back, and much the greater part of his force was dispatched to the Shenandoah to join Frémont in an effort to capture Jackson's army. McClellan, already in trouble because he had not foreseen the difficulties which a rain-swelled Chickahominy might present, was left to fight without the expected aid. He actually had great superiority in numbers; but did he have the requisite generalship?

Governor John A. Andrew of Massachusetts had meanwhile, on May 19, responded to Stanton's request for more regiments by a letter of very radical tone. After accusing the Southern troops of fighting "by all the means known to savages," he had declared that the Union should not only liberate the slaves in invaded areas, but enlist them—"let them fight, with God and human nature on their side." If it did this, asserted the impetuous governor, "the roads will swarm if need be with multitudes whom New England would pour out to obey your call." This letter aroused the resentment of conservative officers in McClellan's army; of McClellan himself—and Wainwright.

* * *

MAY 29, THURSDAY. I tried to find Colonel Bailey today, the weather being fine, but did not succeed. I got over as far as Savage Station. Most of the country is covered with woods. On my way I passed Kearny's camp, and made him a little visit. In course of conversation he let out some traits of his character which were very amazing. He asked me if I had seen Hooker's report, and then spoke of it as a wretched affair, entirely unintelligible, a complete muddle of words. He evidently forgot that I was present when he read it, and heard his exclamations of "capital; I say Hooker, this is clear as crystal," and other like praises. Had he remembered it he would hardly have expected me to swallow his after blarney about my own report, which he told me was "the only plain, military report of the fight" he had seen.

There is a great deal of talk in camp about the reply which Governor Andrew of Massachusetts telegraphed the President in answer to the new call for troops. Even the abolitionists say it is ill-advised at this time, while all others are indignant beyond measure, Colonel Mott of the Sixth New Jersey even going so far as to say that "he would like to march up into Massachusetts and teach them that though they have done well, they are not yet quite the hub of Creation." For one, I shall wish myself at home if the war is to be turned from its original purpose into an abolition crusade, and I believe most of the army have the same feeling.

We are almost beginning to feel settled here, as if we were not to move for some time, and all are getting their wardrobes washed up. The railroad bridge is finished, so that we now draw our supplies from Meadow Station. . . .

MAY 30, FRIDAY.   Rode over to Army Headquarters today along with Lieutenant Price; we crossed the railroad at Meadow Station, and the Chickahominy by a new bridge Sumner's men have just laid about two miles above the railroad bridge. The bridge proper is not more than thirty or forty feet long, but is approached by over half a mile of corduroy across the flat on this side, which has been a big job to make as the ground will not support a horse, much less a waggon. I am told that there are three or four more such bridges higher up; enough to secure an easy and speedy junction of the army on either side the stream. At present the Third and Fourth Corps are the only ones that have crossed; both are under the orders of General Heintzelman, as the left wing of the army. The other three corps are stretched along the north bank, reaching as far up as Mechanicsville, which is only five miles from Richmond. Porter holds the extreme right.

McClellan's headquarters are at the Gaines house, about a mile from "New Bridge," and a good twelve miles from our camp by the road we have to come. The country round there is very different from what it is in this part: the land lays high, is much of it cleared, and well farmed, the houses are large and numerous. We hold down to the river at New Bridge, but not the other side at all, I believe; neither do I know exactly how far we do come up on both banks. The heavier guns of the reserve are posted on the high ground commanding all the old crossings, so that Brinckle's Dutchmen get plenty of firing. . . .

We had quite a spread for dinner; lamb, green peas, asparagus, and lots of good things. . . .

BATTLE OF SEVEN PINES, MAY 31, SATURDAY.   This has been a sad, sad day for the First New York Artillery. Our glorious and much loved Colonel is dead: shot down at his post, close to his guns. It is as glorious a death as a man can die, but hard for one so young, with such abilities, and in his first fight. Hard too for us who are left behind, and who in eight short months of intercourse had come to esteem him so highly; to love him so much. It will be almost impossible to make good his place in the regiment; while his loss is one that really affects the whole army. There were few men of more promise among us; more likely to shed lustre on our arm of the service, and on the army. General Casey leaned on him much, consulting him on nearly all occasions, and often entrusting him with important matters outside his own command. For myself, I feel as if I had lost one of my nearest and dearest friends, so strong a hold had he taken on my heart. . . .

Last night we had another of those rains in which the very sluice gates of heaven seem to be opened, and the water drops in masses for hours. This morning it was clear again. I felt better than I did last night, but determined to try a day in bed; hoping thereby to shake off entirely this miserable feeling. At 3:00 P.M. Major Moses, of Heintzelman's staff, rode up with orders for a part of our division to move at once, saying that the whole of Keyes's corps was routed; completely destroyed, for all the good they could do. The first brigade was left to hold White Oak Bridge, with two sections of Smith's battery; the other section together with the Seventh and Eighth New Jersey were moved back about half way to Bottom's Bridge, where a small work has been thrown up commanding some roads that come in on our rear at that point. Sickles's brigade, the Fifth and Sixth New Jersey, and Bramhall's and Osborn's batteries were ordered to move instanter, leaving tents and knapsacks behind. The infantry were so long getting under arms that I got permission to go on with the two batteries; which I did at a good rate, as the road had not been travelled at all by wheels until we had passed where Kearny had been encamped. About halfway up we began to meet hosts of stragglers and runaways, many of them frightened half out of their wits, together with some slightly wounded men. One of these last, with the chevrons of an artillery sergeant, was the first to tell me that Bailey was killed. . . .

About five hundred yards in front of the station, that is towards Richmond, Kearny's batteries were halted behind a belt of wood. So I halted mine there too, and passed out through the wood some two hundred yards, on to a large open plain; large at least for this part of the country, being I should think half a mile wide, east and west, and near a mile the other way. The Williamsburg Postroad runs through the middle of it, and the railroad along the north side. . . .

It was about five o'clock when I got up. Half an hour or so later our infantry arrived, and Sickles was at once pushed up to the far side of the plain to relieve one of Kearny's brigades. He did not go through the woods beyond, nor were his men engaged, except as skirmishers. My batteries remained where I first halted them; and myself, at the outer edge of the wood along the east side of the plain, where the remains of Keyes's corps were drawn up, behind some partly finished breastworks, with their batteries in position. About six o'clock very heavy musketry firing commenced on the right of the railroad and continued until it got too dark to see. This was Sumner's corps attacking. He had brought them over the bridge I crossed yesterday, and went in with a will. The old man seemed to be making up for Williamsburg. The fighting there at times was evidently very desperate, but it was equally clear that the enemy were being driven slowly. Here Lieutenant Mink of "H" Company found me. From him I learned that Casey's division was in the advance, that they were taken completely by surprise, and whipped almost before they knew it. Colonel Bailey was killed by a small piece of shell, or a bullet passing through both temples. He was commanding "A" Company at the time, which fought well, but lost all their guns; he breathed for half an hour after he was hit, but was not sensible at all. . . .

Nothing more was done by us, but it was nine o'clock before I was permitted to unharness where we stood, and lie down myself in the mud close along the roadside. Even then sleep was almost impossible owing to the eternal braying of mules in a train which hauled up close along side of us.

BATTLE OF FAIR OAKS, JUNE 1, 1862, SUNDAY. We were harnessed up at daylight, and I at once reported to General Hooker, for orders, leaving the two batteries where they were. Very soon after the firing on our right, in front of the Second Corps, began. The battle raged there furiously till three or four P.M. I heard nothing of what was going on, and knew from the direction of the smoke and noise that Sumner was gaining ground slowly. . . . After Sickles had advanced his right the rebs fell back from the open ground directly in front to a bit of wood and slashing beyond, some 500 or 600 yards. . . . Soon after this half a dozen of the Fire Zouaves captured a four-horse omnibus which the rebs were using as an ambulance. It was marked "Exchange Hotel," and was one evidence of the advantages they now have over us in being so close to their base, their wounded only having to be carried seven or eight miles into Richmond, and all the vehicles of the city being at hand for transportation. The New York b'hoys drove their prize in style, one standing up behind, and shouting in real old fashioned style, "Broadway, ride up here!"

General McClellan came over along our lines, after the fight of the Second Corps had subsided; having been with Sumner all day. He did not pass near enough to where I was to enable me to get a good view of him. At sunset I got the batteries into something more like a park than we could last night, picket ropes stretched, and paulins spread for shelter. I turned in with Bramhall, but had just lain down when an order came for me to send one battery out to Sickles. On going to the General, however, I easily got the order rescinded. All was then quiet until about midnight when they got a scare in Casey's division in the left of the line of works, and made a fearful stampede of it. Some loose cattle, or stray orderlies got in among them and overturned a few tents; the disturbed men thought it was reb cavalry, and raised the cry which started two or three whole regiments. They went through the batteries like a flash, many of them without coat, hat, or shoes, and could not be stopped; even those who shot over the picket rope got up only to run the harder. So soon as the fun was over we turned in again, for it was raining, and I for one was very wretched.

* * *

The two-day battle of Fair Oaks or Seven Pines cost the Confederates 6,135 and the Union forces 5,030 casualties without any substantial advantage on either side; for though the Confederates gained a little ground, they promptly gave it up. It had been brought on by a Confederate effort to crush the two corps of McClellan's army which had been placed in an exposed straddle on the south bank of the Chickahominy.

In E. D. Keyes's corps, Silas Casey's division had taken a position just in front of Seven Pines, with Darius N. Couch's division supporting him; in Heintzelman's corps Philip Kearny's division placed itself at Savage Station, while Hooker's division, as noted in the diary, was close by at Poplar Hill. The storm of May 30 described by Wainwright had almost completely separated the two-fifths of McClellan's army on the south side of the Chickahominy from the three-fifths on the north side. If Joseph E. Johnston could smash Keyes and Heintzelman, he would reduce the Union forces to a helpless condition. He made a promising start when he overran Casey's division, which broke under the first sudden shock of the advance. Wainwright's account of this particular "skedaddle" goes far toward supporting the newspaper accounts of the panic. Only the determined movement of General Sumner, who brought his corps over the flooded Chickahominy in the nick of time to check the Confederates, averted a disastrous defeat.

Next morning, June 2, Hooker took his infantry forward past Casey's former lines to show what a determined attack could accomplish. The artillery found the ground too soft to advance. But when he reached White Oak Swamp, and one of Casey's brigade commanders told him that a crossing was impossible, Hooker blazed: "Get out of the way! I have two regiments here that can go anywhere!" This was the spirit that made Wainwright and others admire "Fighting Joe." Both Hooker and Kearny deplored the failure of McClellan to order an energetic thrust after Fair Oaks directly against Richmond, and became increasingly disgusted with the caution of the general.

The most important event of Fair Oaks was the wounding of Joseph E. Johnston, which brought Robert E. Lee into command of the Army of Northern Virginia.

❊ ❊ ❊

NEAR SAVAGE STATION, JUNE 2, MONDAY. Why this place is called Seven Pines I could not see, unless it is seven miles from Richmond—that being just about the distance by the road. Fair Oaks Station is almost on a line with it—not a mile off, and is five and one-half miles by rail from Richmond. It was a very queer place to post a division according to my ideas. The open ground cannot be much over one hundred acres with woods on every side, and roads coming in on each flank. A thousand men or so to watch the roads would have been all well enough, but with no supports on either flank there was very small show for a successful fight. To make the matter worse, Casey had just been moved out here from a similar opening in the rear, of about the same size, into which Couch's division was then moved: and while he was in the first opening he had cut down most of the wood between the two, so that it now made an impassable slashing, through which his men could not fall back in any order. A very small redoubt, with rifle pits running from it on both sides, had been commenced near the middle of the field, but they were only a foot or so high as the ditches filled with water so soon as the diggers got down a few inches.

The following is what I can make out of the accounts I get of the fight: mostly relating to the part taken by the two batteries of my own regiment. On Saturday morning General Casey pushed out a small reconnoissance, but discovered nothing new: the party captured an aide-de-camp of General Johnston's. A little after noon, while the men were getting their dinner, his pickets were rapidly driven in. Naglee's brigade was at once drawn up on the right of the post road, about 100 yards in front to the right of the redoubt, the open ground on that side the road running farther up. Spratt's battery was with them. They held the enemy in the wood, the battery doing good work, until their right flank was turned completely, and they were exposed to a heavy cross-fire, when the men retired in a good deal of disorder. Captain Spratt and Lieutenant Howell were wounded, and Lieutenant Mink was obliged to leave one gun behind, about all its horses being killed. Battery "A" was in position behind the works; four guns in the redoubt, and two on the left of it. So soon as Naglee's brigade gave way, the rebs charged the redoubt, and another party coming in on the left flank at the same time, the whole division cleared out. Couch's division made considerable of a stand in their own camp, but they too were turned on both flanks, and forced back, though in rather better order than Casey's men. Kearny came up before they got out onto the big plain, and stopped them here after a good deal of trouble, while their further attempts to turn to our right were defeated by Sumner.

A number of officers are down on General Keyes. One of Casey's aides told me that when they sent back to him for reinforcements, he was much more engaged in looking after his personal effects (he was camped with Couch) than his command, and cleared out without doing anything. Old Casey himself was brave as a lion, and remained while his men would stand; he lost everything but the clothes he stood in. . . .

The day has been intensely hot, and the stench from the dead bodies of men and horses beyond conception. I counted forty-one dead horses around "A's" positions, one of them the big bay Rumsey brought from Elmira with him.

JUNE 3, TUESDAY.   I was about used up when we got back to camp last night, and today am what I suppose is called absolutely sick. General Hooker has gone out to Seven Pines again today, and will reoccupy the place I believe. I am not able to go with him, and have turned over my command to Captain de Russy, of the Fourth Artillery. When I heard last night that Captain de Russy had reported with his battery, I did not like it, as he is an officer of twenty years' experience, and ought not to serve under a tyro like myself. Now I can leave my batteries under his command, knowing that they will be as well, if not better managed than I could do it myself.

As our headquarters camp was broken up this morning, I went back to the station to spend the day with Dr. Evarts, who has his tent pitched there. Found the doctor as miserable as myself, but as he had nothing to do we managed to work through the day. He has been hard at it night and day ever since Saturday noon. Near 1,100 wounded men passed through his tent in twenty-four hours; some four or five civilian surgeons aided him. The medical director of Casey's division seems to be quite worthless, so that Evarts had to go on his own hook entirely. . . .

On returning I found our headquarters tents had been pitched on the big plain, about 250 yards in front of the works, and the same distance to the right of the road. It was in an oat field where the ground was so soft that my camp stool sank a couple of inches or more in it by my weight, and so wet that the holes so made filled at once with water on removing the stool. I went to bed so soon as my tent was ready. At dusk some scare occurred in the works to the right and rear of where I was, and a general fusilade followed. I was frightened enough, real downright fear this, for I thought I had got between the two fires. Still I was too wretched to move, and the whole thing passed over in a few minutes.

PRIVATE HOSPITAL, JUNE 8, SUNDAY.   I call this "private hospital" because

Dr. Evarts and myself are the only inmates. It is a small abandoned house back somewhere about halfway between Savage Station and White Oak bridge, and nearly opposite a Dr. Carter's house. We have cleaned out the room, hung blankets over the windows where we could not mend them, and have our cots standing about six feet apart with the medicine chest between them. Here we lie nearly all day, Evarts doctoring himself as well as me. On Wednesday Dr. Simm, our medical director, advised me to apply for a sick leave, and gave me a certificate; but I thought then I should get better after a little. In that I have been mistaken, as I have grown very weak, and worse each day. Today I have sent up my application and hope to get a leave by tomorrow. . . .

BALTIMORE, JUNE 12, THURSDAY. My leave came on Monday afternoon, and as Dickenson sent over an ambulance with it we left at once for Savage Station. After remaining there at Heintzelman's headquarters for several hours, we got down to "White House" by a return train, and there went on board one of the hospital boats for the night. Lieutenant Brown, of Bramhall's battery went down with us and did all he could. It commenced to rain before we got down to White House, and rained all night and the next day: indeed, it has done little else than rain ever since this month commenced. As the boat for Fortress Monroe was very crowded on Tuesday, and it was so wet, Dr. Evarts thought we had best wait over a day. The doctor was able to move about, but I have been getting weaker every day, and lay quietly in my berth pretty much all the time. The boat had not many on board. There were a lot of volunteer women nurses on board, ladies I suppose I ought to call them, who no doubt wanted to be very kind, but I would rather they had left me alone. In the afternoon, however, Mrs. Joe Howland came over from another boat to see me, and did me a world of good. I wonder whether most of the sick men appreciate the difference between a real lady and one so called. Mrs. Howland's sweet face and pretty manners must enable them to appreciate her at any rate. . . .

NEW YORK, JUNE 30, MONDAY. At last I am getting on my legs again; have been pretty sick they say: still I managed to get down stairs every day. The first time I was able to walk so far, I went in to the grocer's and got weighed; just turned 106 lbs!* Now I am so much better that I expect to go up home tomorrow or next day. . . . I hear, though not officially, that I have been promoted to fill Bailey's place; the official

---

* While Wainwright does not state explicitly what his prostrating ailment was, various of his remarks suggest that it was dysentery, or to use a term commonly employed by army surgeons, dysenteric diarrhea. The Civil War authorities reported more than 1,700,000 cases. It resulted in great emaciation in the worst seizures, many men becoming mere shadows. At the same time Wainwright seems to have had a seizure of malarial fever, also common in the army.

notice, I suppose, is down at Hooker's headquarters, from what Osborn writes me. Watts DePeyster has been appointed major in my place. His father wanted me to recommend him, but I could not do it, knowing he is totally unfit for the place. . . .

THE MEADOWS, JULY 31, THURSDAY. Another whole month at home; and yet hardly fit to go back to camp. I started a fortnight ago, but got a relapse from over-exertion in New York, and had to ask for a further extension of twenty days. I should not have got the certificate from the surgeon in New York if Dr. Satterlee had not been in the office, as they have become very strict in that line now. I hope to start on Monday. Have been up to Albany to see about my commissions, and if any men can be got for the regiment. Could do nothing in the matter of men, but got a certificate of my promotion to lieutenant-colonel April 30th, and colonel June 1st. . . .

I felt very sore at being away during all the hard fights of a month ago. From what I can learn of them they were terrible. Osborn kept me well posted as to the part taken by my own command in them; it was only engaged at Savage Station, and Malvern Hill, and did not lose a single man either killed or wounded. "B" and "E" Companies of the regiment seem to have both distinguished themselves. There has apparently been some change in the arrangements of the artillery in the army, one battery having been taken from each division to form a Corps Reserve. Not having been there, I know almost nothing as to the pros and cons for McClellan's abandonment of his position near Richmond; but supposing him to have started on right grounds, the change of base appears to have been most admirably executed, and gives me a much higher idea of McClellan's abilities as a general than I had before. His enemies, however, see nothing in it but what they find fault with and are very much down on him. . . .

WASHINGTON, D.C., AUGUST 7, THURSDAY. Came yesterday, and shall remain until tomorrow. This morning I was remustered as lieutenant-colonel and as colonel to date back according to my commissions. This remustering on promotion is something new; a great farce I think. When once accepted into the U.S. service as an officer for three years, I cannot see why they should require you to go through the same formality on each promotion. However, I had to submit, and then draw my pay for three months, which came to quite a little sum. The weather here is very hot. Everything is quiet and not many uniforms about the street. . . .

❋ ❋ ❋

Taken North on sick leave after Fair Oaks, Wainwright had missed the Seven Days' battles, the very crisis of the Peninsular campaign. McClellan wrote after Fair Oaks, on June 7: "I shall be in perfect readiness to move forward and take Richmond the moment McCall reaches here and the ground will admit the passage of artillery." George A. McCall with a fine division called the Pennsylvania Reserves began landing his 9,000 troops at the White House base on June 11. But McClellan still delayed his final movement against the enemy, and informed his wife that he expected to make his next battle "mainly an artillery combat."

While he waited, "Jeb" Stuart made a spectacular cavalry raid clear around the Union army. Lee strengthened the fortifications of the Confederate capital, and obtained about 25,000 fresh troops from North and South Carolina and Georgia; so that he soon had the largest army he was ever to command. Then, when the moment was right, he seized the initiative; he brought Stonewall Jackson's 25,000 men in a rapid march down from the Shenandoah Valley, intending that they should fall upon the flank and rear of the Union array while he struck in front. McClellan, learning of Jackson's movement from a Southern deserter, himself ordered an advance on June 25. Thus, after some sporadic fighting, the two armies clashed in full force on June 26 at Mechanicsville.

In the ensuing encounters, the most bitterly fought battle was Gaines's Mill, where the North and South lost a total of more than 15,500 men killed and wounded. Immediately afterward McClellan informed his corps commanders that he had decided to transfer his base to the James, and proceeded to move his 85,000 troops, with some 25,000 tons of supplies, across country to Harrison's Bar on the wider stream, where his new camp would be protected by Union gunboats. Lee, unaware of the true character of McClellan's movement until too late, failed to block the operation. By July 1 all the Union forces were united at Malvern Hill above the river; and a terrific Confederate assault there was repulsed with 6,000 or 7,000 casualties.

Northern confidence in McClellan had now sunk to a low ebb. He had been in a position, with an army of more than 100,000 men, to capture Richmond and perhaps end the war. His delays, his overestimation of enemy forces, his failure to understand the perils of the treacherous Chickahominy until too late, and his clumsy handling of his corps, had not only cost him victory, but had several times placed him in danger of overwhelming defeat. Lincoln and Stanton, advised by General Henry Wager Halleck, decided to recall McClellan's army from the James. They placed Pope in command of the newly formed Army of Virginia in front of Washington, and by an order of August 3, which was temporarily kept secret, directed McClellan to withdraw his forces to Aquia Creek.

❋ ❋ ❋

HARRISON'S LANDING, AUGUST 10, SUNDAY. Back in camp once more, having been absent just two months. Found all my traps safe on board the boat, except one box of claret; had a fine sail down the bay and a good night's rest, the first since leaving New York—Willard's being very hot and mosquitoeish. Made our connections all right at Fortress Monroe, and had a good day to come up the James. We had a gunboat as convoy after getting about halfway up, as the rebs have several times planted batteries on the shore, and fired at passing steamers. We met five or six steamers coming down loaded with field artillery, and schooners with horses. What does it mean? Is it simply because they have too much up here, or does it portend the moving of the whole army? Osborn and Pettit met me at the landing. I reported at once to General Hooker, and received a very warm welcome, but as they were so short of tents at headquarters, I could not get one there, and had to return, and put up my cot with Osborn last night.

My command now consists of Webber, Smith, and Osborn. They are camped in rear of the division along a small stream, and in a narrow belt of woods. Some of their guns are in position along the front. The batteries appear to be in pretty good order, but are short of men, and their horses are almost eaten up by the flies, which surpass anything I ever saw before. At night they settle on the inside of the tents so thick that it would really be hard work to find a spot without them as big as a half dollar. They make sores on the horses, and then fairly eat into them; the poor brutes have stamped all their flesh off. . . .

This evening we received orders to be ready to move tomorrow at 2:00 P.M. in the lightest marching order; all knapsacks to be shipped on board vessels here, as well as every article of quartermaster stores which can possibly be rendered surplus. I am stopping with Lieutenant-Colonel Samson, Sixteenth Massachusetts, tonight, they having a spare tent. I find his camp the coolest about, being right out on the open ground where there is plenty of air; it is a great mistake to get into the woods in hot weather.

AUGUST 12, TUESDAY. Still here, though the order to be ready to move has not been rescinded. I can find out nothing as to which way we are to go, but the continued shipment of stores points Washington way. Yesterday I rode to Army Headquarters to see General Barry. He was more than usually affable, but I could get nothing out of him as to the move. . . .

I have not been about much, not thinking it well to expose myself more than is necessary. From what I do hear the army is quite as devoted to McClellan as ever, and look upon the change of base as a wonderful affair. All the corps and division commanders have been made major-generals. Hooker does not look on it as much of an honour, being so wholesale to good and bad. General Sumner is said to be very feeble, and failing fast; he has never got over the severe fall from his horse he had last winter. Should he go on the retired list, Hooker may get his corps. General Casey has been ordered on more fitting duty for so old a man, and General Peck has his division.

About one-half the land, so far as I can see, within our lines is cleared, the whole being high above the river and rolling. Everything in the shape of grass has been trodden out long since, so the ground is all white dust. The whole line of our front is only some three miles I understand, so that it is not far to any part of the army. . . .

AUGUST 14, THURSDAY.   Still here but have orders to start at 6:30 tomorrow morning: there is not much doubt now as to our destination being Washington. Have remained quietly in camp pretty much all the last two days trying to straighten out regimental business, which I find Colonel Bailey seems to have given little attention to since he left Camp Barry. No monthly or other return has been made out for the regiment since March, nor have many been received from the companies; so that I am quite in ignorance as to the condition of the regiment, and its strength in either officers or men, but hope to get the matter straightened out soon. . . .

This afternoon I rode over to Kearny's quarters, spent an hour with him, and started to ride with him to Charles City Court House, but my stirrup breaking down, returned to camp. He is full of the possibility of our capturing Richmond at this time; says he could do it with his division, and that two or three divisions could do it easily. He talked very wild, as usual. Still, there may be something in what he says.

FIVE

FROM POPE'S DISASTER
TO McCLELLAN'S RESTORATION

As the military historian John C. Ropes states, the Lincoln Administration had three powerful reasons, after the Seven Days, for its distrust of McClellan. The first was his insubordinate temper. He seemed to believe that he was entitled to deal with the President and War Department as an equal contracting party, laying down his own terms. "Instead of doing his work as well as he could with the means he had or could procure, he was constantly attempting to drive the Administration into a corner; to fasten upon it the responsibility for the ill-success of his military movements; to threaten it, even, with the consequences of this or that failure to do what he desired." Thus when the War Department declared that McDowell must keep independent command of his corps, McClellan asserted that if he could not fully control all his troops, "I want none of them, but would prefer to fight the battle with what I have, and let others be responsible for the results." He would dictate the terms of his services, no matter what happened to the country. The second reason was that McClellan had a strong political bias. He was a Democrat. He went out of his way to write Lincoln a long lecture on his proper political policy. He even dared to tell the President that "a declaration of radical views, especially upon slavery, would rapidly disintegrate our present armies"—a veiled threat. And in the third place, he had made it plain that he could never be counted upon to fight. No matter how large his army was, he would always fancy the enemy stronger; no matter how favorable the situation became, he would always want to wait until a better moment arrived.

It was because of this well-earned distrust that his army was ordered back from Harrison's Landing on the James, while another army was formed under General John Pope in front of Washington. It was clearly the hope of Lincoln and Stanton that Pope would prove himself such a valiant and skillful general that public sentiment would acquiesce in the transfer to him of the main command in Virginia. And now McClellan furnished still a fourth reason for mistrust. When Lee learned of the impending evacuation of the army from the James, he left a small force in Richmond and hastened to move against Pope's smaller and still imperfectly assembled command. In vain did Lincoln, Stanton, and Halleck beseech McClellan to move fast and transfer his forces back to the vicinity of Washington in all haste; his best units would be needed to reinforce Pope. McClellan dragged his feet, or rather his decisions, until the orders became too imperative to be ignored any longer. Even then, he took his time. When Lee and Jackson flung their troops upon Pope, that unlucky general received only 23,000 men—some of them also tardy—as reinforcements from the Army of the Potomac.

Wainwright had counted it a piece of hard fortune that his illness cost him any chance of participation in the Seven Days and Malvern Hill. He might well count it good fortune that he was kept waiting far from the field as Lee concentrated his forces against Pope's weaker and badly exposed army on the Rappahannock, for he thus escaped sharing in one of the saddest defeats of the war. McClellan began his slow return on August 14; Wainwright fell into the movement the next day.

❊ ❊ ❊

CAMP NEAR JONES BRIDGE, AUGUST 16 [1862], SATURDAY. Yesterday morning we started at 6:30 A.M. Marched through Charles City Court House, and halted that night about a mile from where the road to this place turns off. The road was good but we had many detentions at the start from the troops ahead of us. To the Court House the road runs about a mile back from the river; most of the country was cleared, and we passed some really fine houses. The white oaks surpassed any I have ever seen before in size and number. Indeed, trees of all kinds, which we would consider giants at home, are common here in Virginia. The division marched with a battery in rear of each brigade; also its ambulances, and the few waggons allowed.

The Third Corps is marching on the left of the rest of the army which goes directly down the river road to Fortress Monroe, so that should there be any fighting at all we are sure to get it. General Hooker says there is not the least danger of any, but I wish he would make his march less carelessly even if it was only for the looks of the thing and as instruction to his men. The division has been awfully strung out today, a good mile at times between the brigades, and no pickets have been stationed on the roads coming in from the left. Kearny is ahead of us, and left strong posts on all the incoming roads until we came up. . . .

CAMP NEAR WILLIAMSBURG, AUGUST 18, MONDAY. We have got back here after a little over three months. The men generally grumble a good deal at thus taking the back track. I overheard a sergeant in one of the regiments today consoling them by the information that "we had only been on a big reconnoissance towards Richmond." Yesterday we reached the Post road again, and camped for the night near Slatersville. Now we are lying on the west side of and quite near the town. Porter's corps, which led the other column, passed here on Saturday. We have had an easy and rather pleasant march of it, there being no obstructions, and the weather continuing cool; at least it would have been quite pleasant had it not been for the dust. Colonel Averell with a brigade of cavalry covered our rear after we reached the Post road, as he had our left flank up to that time. From him, through my Adjutant Rumsey, I first heard that it had been intended to try Richmond when the order was given to be ready to march last Monday.

General Hooker afterwards told me all about it. The returned prisoners reported that there could not be more than 20,000 troops in Richmond; so McClellan determined to try it. Hooker and Kearny were very urgent for it. But Monday morning orders came from Washington reiterating those of a fortnight previous, to move the army there at once. McClellan went down to the telegraph station on the eastern shore and begged for permission to delay until he had made this trial, but Halleck forbade it, so the attack was given up. General Hooker said he still urged McClellan to try it, in spite of his orders, telling him that they meant to deprive him of his command under any circumstances, and that he might as well die for an old sheep as a lamb. If the attack failed they could no more than behead him, while if he succeeded in capturing Richmond, they would not darè to do it. However, McClellan would not directly disobey orders.

The country has suffered as much or more from our march back as it did from our march up. The corn being just in silk, the men have cleaned the fields pretty well of roasting ears. . . .

NEAR YORKTOWN, AUGUST 20, WEDNESDAY. My own little command, and indeed all the artillery of the corps, is camped here on the east side of the town, quite near to the edge of the bluff on York River and just outside of our old lines of last April. The infantry of Kearny's division sailed today, and our own go tomorrow as early as possible, but no waggons or ambulances were taken, and but very few horses; a whole brigade went up in the steamship *Baltic,* and General Hooker along with them. We have no papers, but as the infantry were sent off in such a hurry, and from what I could gather in a few minutes at headquarters, I fear that General Pope is getting worsted. . . .

AUGUST 22, FRIDAY. I am left here now I may say on my own hook, not having received orders to report to anyone. The batteries are getting men, horses and carriages washed; and the horses, freed from the flies and with plenty to eat, are already beginning to look better. We are all of us enjoying the salt-water bathing, though there is no surf, and the beach for some little way out is very bad, being covered with broken shells and sharp stones; some, too, complain of the crabs biting their toes. . . .

The "Enfants" and the Eighth New York Militia are camped between us and the town. Fred DePeyster* is with the latter as assistant surgeon. He gives a terrible account of the "Enfants," and says that two hundred of them have deserted; some twenty tried to desert to the enemy right after the first pay day but were captured. Most of them are foreigners, the roughscuff of New York City. Yorktown itself is very small, containing only some thirty or forty half-ruined houses all of which I should think were built before the Revolution. There are no shops or any signs whatever of any business transacted here before the war. Yet the York River is a superb stream, with any required depth of water, and the country on this side alone ought, if well developed, to support a town quite as large as Poughkeepsie. Enterprise certainly has not troubled this part of our country heretofore, and I doubt if the inhabitants of the Peninsula number many more than they did a hundred years ago. It is really sad to see two such superb rivers as this and the James with next to no commerce, though there is a back country which, if well developed, would produce enough to employ a quarter of all our shipping to carry it to market. . . .

AUGUST 26, TUESDAY.   Four days of perfect quiet since my last entry, with little or nothing to do. We have now been here a full week, and all are beginning to want to get away again, especially as what little news we get through the papers indicates a probability of active work in central Virginia. . . .

ON BOARD STEAMER *George Peabody,* AUGUST 29, FRIDAY.   I got my batteries shipped on Wednesday, as I expected, but did not start until yesterday morning. . . .

ALEXANDRIA, AUGUST 30, SATURDAY.   Got all the batteries landed today, but have not over 200 horses for the five. The schooners with the others on board were cast loose by the steamers having them in tow, during the gale on Thursday night, so that I do not know when they will be here. The carriages and waggons I have had hauled, by the horses we have, a short distance out of the town and have gone into camp there. Had a

---

* The DePeysters were a prominent family of New York, concerning whom much information may be gleaned from the diary of George Templeton Strong. Wainwright approved of J. Watts DePeyster as a civilian aide to General Philip Kearny, but was dubious of his capacity in higher posts. He and the Fred here mentioned were sons of the "fluent and venerable" Frederic DePeyster active in various metropolitan organizations. The "Enfants Perdues" were an independent New York City regiment recruited in 1861 by Felix Confort.

great deal of difficulty in getting my vessels up to the wharf, there being scores of schooners and what-not in the river with waggons and other material belonging to the rest of the army, and all anxious to get unloaded. Everything is in confusion. . . .

They say there has been much heavy fighting out at the front today. McClellan does not seem to have any actual command at present, but only charge of forwarding the troops out to Pope, as fast as they arrive. The town is full of stragglers. I met Colonel Brewster in the street trying to get those of our Second Brigade together so as to take them out to the front. Near half his own regiment is here, and a thousand or more from the division; most of them went off and got drunk so soon as they landed. We had one of these fellows up by our tents this evening, an Irishman, dead drunk; bewailing in the most bitter terms his comrades all being out fighting and getting "kilt intirely," while he was not with them, and cursing himself most loudly as a coward. We could not get him to clear out, and finally had to tie him hands and feet and pack him down to the city guard. He insisted on taking off all his clothes, and it was only by knocking him down first that Bramhall's men could get them on again.

AUGUST 31, SUNDAY.   No more horses yet. I was obliged to report to General Williams that I could not get off with Sumner last night, and he directed me to go with Couch's division this afternoon if I got my horses; which I did not. There has been heavy firing again pretty much all today. In the evening I went into town to see Captain Bramhall's mother at the hotel. While there some seven or eight very rough-looking men came in, who said they were officers (though they had privates' blouses on) of Ricketts's division. They reported that division as all cut to pieces, and scattered to the winds, and the whole army as in full retreat hitherward. Of course, they had themselves performed prodigies of valour, but from what I could make out of their account, all their division behaved badly. . . .

ALEXANDRIA, SEPTEMBER 1, MONDAY.   All of my horses have arrived now, except Smith's; somehow he is always behind hand, even when, as in this case, it is, at least partially, a matter of luck. The five batteries are under my command, by McClellan's order. All today has been spent in trying to gather up some news of the fights from the stragglers and trains which have arrived. . . . There are any quantity of rumours as to the death of generals; the papers mention, among others, Kearny and Patrick as being killed. . . .

On all sides I hear of how well that part of the Army of the Potomac which was engaged fought, especially Hooker's division; a cavalry orderly of McDowell's told me he had never seen anything like it. McDowell's corps seems to have fought badly or to have been badly handled. It is very hard to have been so near the battle as to hear the cannon, and yet not be able to take part in it. But light batteries are altogether dependent on having horses, and I could do nothing myself without my guns. Tomorrow I have a fair prospect of getting off, if the whole army is not going to fall back within the works. Would they only put McClellan in command I believe we could yet gain a great if not decisive victory.

SEPTEMBER 2, TUESDAY. It seems as if the whole of Pope's army were poured in upon us today as stragglers. Such a sight I never saw before and never want to see again. I rode two or three miles out the Fairfax pike, a fine wide road, to see what I could see. It was full of waggons and wheel vehicles of all sorts coming in, mostly empty, or with men in them. Many of the drivers seemed not to have got over their fright yet, and were driving as if all Stuart's cavalry were after them. There were runaways from every corps and division in the army, if not from every regiment. All these are stopped at the line of forts, organized into provisionary companies, and set to man the works. Rumsey went up to see General Slough this afternoon, at Fort Lyon. He is in command at this point, and told Rumsey that 13,000 stragglers had already been picked up, and placed in the works. The skedaddle and fright must be quite equal to what it was after the first Bull Run.

Captain McKeever stopped at my quarters at dusk; says the whole army is falling back to the line of works. That there was a great deal of fighting by divisions of corps at a time, and that everything was abominably managed. Pope had his army scattered miles and miles apart, out of supporting distance and so far off that he did not know where they were. At one time a good part of Lee's army was between him and Washington. On Saturday or Sunday night a number of the generals were at Heintzelman's quarters when Hooker openly said that "if they had left McClellan in command this never would have happened." This was a great deal for Hooker to say, as he has no love for McClellan. Here all are loudly calling for his restoration, and from what I hear and see by the papers I judge that the people are doing the same. McKeever says that Kearny is dead. He rode off alone to examine some ground, or to find his connection with the troops on his right, and went right into the enemy's lines. He was shot dead while trying to escape; the ball entered near the foot of the spine, and as he was lying down on his horse, it traversed nearly his whole body. His body was sent in today. General Stevens was also killed; I think he belongs in Bank's corps.

NEAR ARLINGTON HOUSE, SEPTEMBER 3, WEDNESDAY. Moved four of my batteries here this morning, by McClellan's orders. Smith is still waiting for his horses. The army has been coming in all day, and camping around the forts. I understood that the Third Corps was to come in near Alexandria; so I do not know whether I am to consider myself as still attached to it or not, having been ordered off here. There are large numbers of new regiments constantly arriving, very large, but very green. Several are camped quite close to me here, among them a Philadelphia regiment, under Colonel Prevost, who was Patterson's adjutant-general on the Peninsula. A fine-looking body of men, and with uncommonly good field music, French drums and trumpets: their tattoo tonight was the best I have ever heard.

Of course the one topic of conversation is still the late battles: little pieces of news concerning them can be picked up, but I have not yet got any connected account. From what I can learn there was a total want of generalship on the part of Pope and McDowell, who seem to have held separate commands. Neither do our men appear to have fought as well as they did on the Peninsula, from want of confidence in their leaders, I suppose; while the rebels did even better than usual. Ricketts's division which held the extreme left on Saturday did very badly according to all accounts. On the other hand, all are loud in praise of our division, and the star of "fighting Joe Hooker" is quite in the ascendent. Sykes, with the regulars, had a very hard fight at Bull Run: young Chamberlain I hear was killed there. Well as the regulars are said to have fought, some of their officers tell me that the Fifth New York surpassed them.

There is an immense amount of ill feeling all through the army, especially against Pope; and the cry for "little Mac" grows louder every day, not only from his own old army, but from all the other troops. I hear that he has been put in command of the defences of Washington, and all the troops within them, which must now include all Pope's and Mc-Dowell's commands as well as the Army of the Potomac, except the garrisons up the river. . . .

* * *

After Pope's debacle at Second Manassas, it was imperative to give the Army of the Potomac a new commander. Without loss of time, Lee swung his victorious troops to the invasion of Maryland, and an efficient general had to be found to stop him. It was clear to the Administration that McClellan bore a large share of responsibility for the Union defeat. To the last he had delayed the dispatch of reinforcements to the hard-pressed forces under Pope. "Not a moment must be lost in pushing as large a force as possible toward Manassas," Halleck had telegraphed at 3:30 P.M. on August 28; and McClellan had replied at 4:45 P.M., "Neither Franklin's nor Sumner's corps is now in a condition to move out and fight a battle." The evidence is clear that he and his closest lieutenant, Fitz-John Porter, both wished to see Pope fail. Lincoln, it is recorded, was never so angry as when he heard reports dealing with their conduct. He did not go so far as

Secretary Salmon P. Chase, who burst out, "McClellan ought to be shot!";
but he told the Cabinet that McClellan's conduct had been "shocking" and
"atrocious."

Nevertheless, Lee's imminent invasion of the North precipitated a crisis
that could be met in but one way. The only general who could rally the
forces about Washington and inspire them with a new fighting spirit was
McClellan. Four Cabinet officers—Stanton, Chase, Caleb B. Smith, and
Edward Bates—had united in a statement that "it is not safe to entrust to
Major-General McClellan the command of any army of the United States."
Lincoln himself felt the deepest repugnance to him. Nevertheless, in this
hour of dire national peril circumstances offered no alternative. On September 2, the President sadly told the Cabinet that he had just notified McClellan to take command of all the forces about Washington. Pope, as his army
was consolidated with that of McClellan, was exiled to an unimportant
command in the Northwest. There was no time to waste; on the night of
September 3–4 Lee's regiments began splashing across the Potomac fords
between Harpers Ferry and Washington. "McClellan has acted badly in this
matter," Lincoln told John Hay, "but we must use what tools we have."

Since Irvin McDowell, head of the Third Corps, had fought stupidly and
ineffectively in the recent battle, Hooker was now raised to its command.
He had three division commanders, all brigadiers: Rufus King of New
York, a former Milwaukee editor who had organized the Wisconsin "Iron
Brigade"; James Bremerton Ricketts, another New Yorker whose experi-
ence had been with the artillery; and ablest of all, John F. Reynolds of
Pennsylvania, a West Point graduate in the class of 1841 who had been
captured in the Seven Days' battles, and had just returned from Libby
Prison.

❊ ❊ ❊

SEPTEMBER 4, THURSDAY. We have a nice spot for our camp here, on the
flat, directly in front of and under Arlington house. It is clean and quiet,
and yet not much over a mile from the end of the Long Bridge, so that
we can get to Washington very easily, where we have to send a number
of times every day for stores of all kinds, as also marketing. Have got a
cook at last, such as he is, and started a mess for the adjutant and myself.
We at least fare better than before, and get plenty of fruit and vegetables
from Washington though not very good.

SEPTEMBER 5, FRIDAY. Got quite a budget of letters today, from home
and elsewhere, which have been accumulating ever since we left Harrison's Landing, three·weeks ago. All the letters are full of enlisting and

who is coming to the war. "H" says that in Boston the shops are all closed at 2:00 P.M., the bells rung, and the people gather on the Common. Massachusetts has about filled her quota. In New York City too they seem to be making great efforts, and expect to be able to avoid the draft. On some accounts I am sorry for it, as we shall not now get the old regiments filled up, and besides, I think drafting the fairest and most equitable mode of raising men. "H" says that the losses in the Second Massachusetts at Cedar Mountain fell very heavily upon their best people there, but that a number of the young men are going out with the new regiments who have not been before. The season has been almost as wet on the Hudson as in Virginia. Haying was only finished ten days ago. . . .

SEPTEMBER 6, SATURDAY. The report now is that Lee has gone up the Potomac and is trying to cross into Maryland. The greater part of the army has therefore gone over to the Washington side and now lies around Tenallytown and in that direction. I rode down to Alexandria this afternoon to see General Hooker and find out if possible just where I belong; I had not seen him or any of his officers since they sailed from Yorktown. I found the General's headquarters just broken up and Hooker himself on the point of stepping into a four-horse ambulance, which had been sent over for him in great haste, to carry him to the First Corps which he is to command, vice McDowell, either relieved, or unwilling to serve under McClellan. I was able to get only five minutes' conversation with the General, who was in capital spirits; just long enough to say that if he was satisfied with me so far I should like to go with him to his new command. He replied that he intended to apply for me at once. So I have good prospect for a change; which I am desirous of as it is not pleasant to be thrown under a new commander, and I like Hooker to serve with, though I do not think him a great general. Still more am I anxious to avoid the chance of being under Sickles, who may very likely get the old division, although he has always managed to be absent when it was hotly engaged. "On dit" that he is very spooney on Mrs. Lincoln, and that his strength lies there.

Hooker told me that Grover made an actual bayonet charge at Bristoe, the most brilliant thing of the whole war; and that had Ricketts's division behaved well, he would have captured "Stonewall" Jackson. As the General said that the whole army was to move at once up into Maryland I hurried back to camp without going over to the division. The four batteries with me are now pretty well refitted. . . .

NEAR FORT LYON, SEPTEMBER 7, SUNDAY. Did not get over to Washington after all today, for I received orders to rejoin my division with the batteries. So we broke up our pleasant camp near Arlington house and moved over here. The road was very dusty, and the march, though short, anything but agreeable. My own three batteries are now camped quite near to Fort Lyon, a large work some half mile east of the Fairfax turnpike. The division lies near by, and with it are a couple of New York batteries which were with it under Pope, Bruen's* and a Dutch battery. Both look like wretchedly poor affairs, and they tell me they are; I hope that they will not remain with us.

General Grover is now in command of the division, as senior officer present: were I sure he was to continue in command I should not object to remain here, as I have a very high opinion of him as a general. Hooker took all his own staff with him, and Grover has brought his up from the First Brigade. He expects to get the division and certainly deserves it. The division is very much reduced in numbers, and there seems but little prospect of the New York regiments being filled up. The First Massachusetts has been filled to the maximum since they got here: the Second New Hampshire received 600 recruits when they passed through here on the way out to Pope; and the Eleventh Massachusetts has also received several hundred. . . .

Captain Bates writes that he has got seventy recruits for his battery, and expects to have one hundred within the week, which, with his old men, will fill "A" Company to the maximum again. Had he shown the same energy in managing his battery as he does in recruiting it, he need never have had it broken up, in the way it has been. "F" and "H" Companies are at Yorktown and Gloucester Point; Dr. Pardee, our Second Assistant Surgeon, has been assigned to take charge of them. Should I be made chief of artillery of a corps I shall endeavour to get as many of the batteries of my own regiment with me as I can.

SEPTEMBER 8, MONDAY. Received two orders today which will give me something to do for a few days to come. The first, from Heintzelman, appoints me Acting Chief of Artillery of the Third Corps in the absence of de Russy. The second, from McClellan's headquarters, calls for an immediate and full report as to the condition of all the batteries belonging to the corps; which will require a pretty close inspection. The two batteries I found here yesterday have gone off to the Twelfth Corps, I believe. General Barry has been relieved from the position of Chief of Artillery, Army of Potomac, and is announced as Inspector General of Artillery at Washington. I do not know whether it is to be regarded as purely a piece of promotion or whether he and McClellan did not get along together. Colonel H. J. Hunt succeeds General Barry; he has been in command of the Artillery Reserve, and stands very high, as one of the best artillery officers in the Army, especially as to the handling of light

* Lieutenant John T. Bruen served in the Tenth Independent Battery of New York Artillery.

batteries in action. Barry's reputation, on the other hand, was more as an organizer, and in office work.*

Hooker has applied to have his old division transferred to his present command. Such transfers are very much objected to at the department, but Hooker's star is so completely in the ascendant now that there is no saying what they may do for him. Colonel Nelson Taylor of the Seventy-Second New York and J. H. H. Ward of Thirty-Eighth New York were made brigadier-generals today. They have both been commanding brigades pretty much all summer. Taylor's is a most excellent appointment I know, and Kearny always spoke in the highest terms of Ward.†

SEPTEMBER 9, TUESDAY. We are lying here perfectly quiet, with almost nothing to do, and hearing nothing of what is going on up in Maryland, save what little is published in the papers, and the War Department now keeps them from announcing any of the movements of our forces, as is very proper, for there is no doubt that heretofore the rebs have obtained a great deal of valuable information through this source. I hoped to have heard something from General Hooker before this in regard to my being ordered to the First Corps, for I should like amazingly to be with them now. It is rather hard to miss all the fighting, having seen so little of it owing to my two months' sickness and then to the want of transportation from the Peninsula. Not that I greatly regret being absent from the Pope campaign, but I should have liked to have been through the fights in front of Richmond and especially at Malvern Hill, where the artillery had such a grand chance to show off. . . .

I was very much disgusted with Smith's officers today.** A couple of German peddlers complained to me that they had been robbed, and one of them knocked down, while offering their wares in that battery. I at once went over there and directed Lieutenant Mairro, the Captain being absent, to have all the men in line, and the roll called. The Germans designated three of the men as the aggressors, and we then searched the

---

* Barry was to remain as Chief of Artillery in the defenses of Washington until March 1864. Then he became Sherman's Chief of Artillery in the Georgia campaign, the capture of Atlanta, and the march to the sea and northward through the Carolinas. Hunt, who was promoted to be brigadier general this month, was to fight ably at Antietam and Fredericksburg. We shall see later that Hooker dealt unwisely with him, and paid a penalty for this at Chancellorsville.

† Taylor we have already noted as the New Yorker who settled in California after the Mexican War, returned East to lead the Seventy-second New York, fought through the Peninsular campaign, and later became a Democratic Congressman. John Henry Hobart Ward, also of New York, was destined to make a remarkable record as brigade and division commander, fighting well in nearly all the great eastern battles, and receiving four wounds before he was mustered out after Spotsylvania.

** Captain James E. Smith commanded the Fourth Independent Battery of New York Artillery.

camp, and found about half of the stolen articles in one of the tents. The peddlers afterward seemed uncertain as to which were the guilty men, but I ordered them in arrest, and directed charges to be preferred against them. The disgusting part of it was that the officers of the battery were very loath to make the search, and arrest the thieves. Smith himself, on his return, came over to my quarters and talked very properly: whether or no he will act as well remains to be seen.

NEAR ALEXANDRIA SEMINARY, SEPTEMBER 14, SUNDAY. Have again moved camp a short distance and am now located a few hundred yards in rear of the seminary. The land here lies high and healthy, with fine views, but my camp ground is not itself quite so good as that we left near Fort Lyon. . . . Heintzelman's headquarters are at Arlington house. The cause of our move was the stretching of the troops along the line of works, General Halleck being apprehensive of an attack here. He thinks that when Lee has tolled McClellan off to a distance, he may recross the Potomac and make a dash at us here. I rode along a good part of the lines held by this corps yesterday in order to make myself acquainted with them against any attack that should be made. Some forts are quite large and most of them well located; the country around them is well cleared, and our men are now at work joining the detached forts by a line of rifle pits. There is no chance of this division being sent to Hooker, so long as there is the slightest danger of an attack here; even if they grant his request at all, of which we hear nothing. Neither do I get any intimation that Hooker has asked to have me sent up to him; which I certainly expected before this.

We are still without news as to what McClellan is doing or where he is. From what yesterday's papers say, it looks as if Lee really meant to push up into Pennsylvania. It would be a very daring move on his part should he attempt it, and I should be sorely disappointed if McClellan did not make it cost him dear. . . .

————••◁∞▷••————

ANTIETAM AND AFTER

Great events had taken place while Wainwright was kept waiting near Washington. Lee, fired with the hope of seizing much-needed shoes and clothing in Maryland and of gaining a new victory that might increase Northern war weariness to the point where Southern independence would be conceded, or that might alternatively bring about Anglo-French intervention, reached Frederick, Maryland, on September 7. He had with him about 60,000 effective troops, whose discipline and restraint won general admiration. To maintain his communications, he was compelled to seize Harpers Ferry and thus keep open his Shenandoah Valley line. He accomplished this feat by one of the most daring strokes of the war. Dividing his army, he sent three divisions under Stonewall Jackson and three others under other generals to surround Harpers Ferry and take the heights commanding it. They carried out this mission so successfully that at dawn on September 13 Colonel D. S. Miles, the Union leader, surrendered 11,500 men, seventy-three cannon, and a great quantity of small arms and camp equipment to them. Wainwright's scornful censure of this officer, who could either have held Maryland Heights above the town or have gotten away with his large force, was entirely deserved.

Lee had dared to divide his army in the face of the enemy because he was certain that McClellan would be dilatory, and so he was. Complaining that he was outnumbered and asking for 25,000 reinforcements, he moved forward in Maryland with great deliberation. He thus gave Lee ample time to place his main army in a good defensive position along South Mountain, the prolongation of the Blue Ridge into Virginia. Here, on September 14, the day before Wainwright received his orders to join Hooker, a hot battle raged. The Union forces pressed up South Mountain along a wide front. Franklin's Sixth Corps carried Crampton's Gap, a pass across the ridge, and Jesse Lee Reno's Ninth Corps and Hooker's First Corps took the high ground commanding Turner's Gap. The result was that the Confederates, who lost heavily, had to fall back. But Lee gained what he most needed, time; time for Stonewall Jackson to complete his movement against Harpers Ferry and march to reunite the Southern army.

Retreating in exemplary order, Lee's troops formed their new lines near Sharpsburg, close to the Potomac, on September 15, the day Wainwright left Washington. Here, early on the 16th, Jackson rejoined him. By a rapid forward thrust, McClellan might have caught Lee while he was still off-balance. But he did not get his troops up into position before Sharpsburg until the evening of the 15th, and spent the whole ensuing day in fixing his positions and reconnoitering. The battle of Antietam therefore did not begin until daybreak on the 17th. Hooker's corps was in the thick of the fight from the beginning.

❋ ❋ ❋

WILLARD'S HOTEL, SEPTEMBER 15 [1862], MONDAY. About noon received a telegram from Heintzelman's headquarters, directing me by "order of General McClellan, to proceed at once to his Headquarters, Frederick, Maryland, and report to Major-General Hooker for duty as Chief of Artillery to his Corps." I had almost given up all hopes of receiving the order, for which I was getting anxious as rumour says that Sickles is to have the old division. General Grover, too, means to leave if Sickles comes, and has thrown himself out from his old brigade by assigning Cowdin to it, who has just been made a brigadier-general. My waggon had gone into town when I got the order, so we were detained some hours before we could get it off. By four o'clock we had started the waggon, our horses and servants in charge of Whitney, sergeant-major, to go by the road to Frederick as quickly as possible, where we shall meet them; the adjutant and I going up by rail tomorrow.

On getting over here, we found all excitement with the news of a battle and victory yesterday, at South Mountain. McClellan's telegrams were posted in the hotel which was crowded with officers and civilians. Hooker's name was on every lip, for the telegrams gave him great praise. The main part of the fighting seems to have been done by the First Corps and Burnside's old corps under General Reno, who is reported killed; Burnside was in command of both corps. Quite a batch of prisoners were taken, while our loss does not appear to have been very heavy. It was no half victory this time, the enemy being driven completely over the mountains. I do not know now where I shall find the army, but doubtless beyond Frederick City. . . .

FREDERICK, MARYLAND, SEPTEMBER 16, TUESDAY. We reached here at 2:00 P.M.; had to foot it from the Monocacy Bridge, which was burnt by the rebs when here. It was difficult to find any place to get into in the town, all the hotels being full of quartermasters and what-not. At last we got a room between us in a private house; quite clean and comfortable. On our way up we met two of General Wool's staff going up to learn about

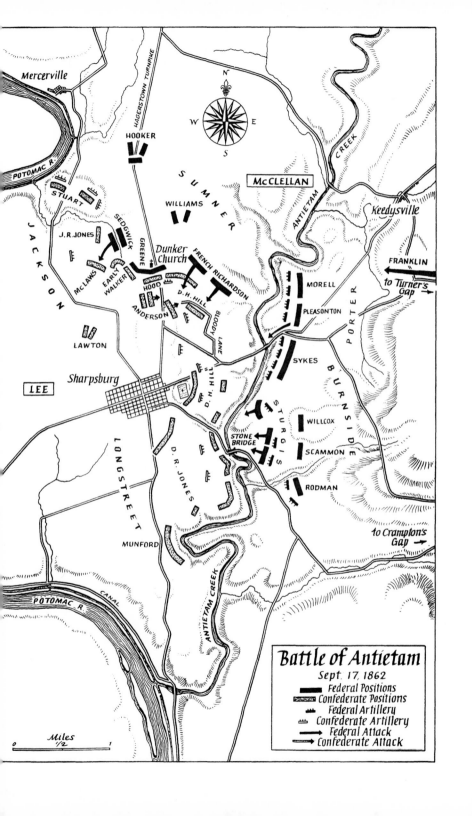

Mercerville

POTOMAC R.

HOOKER

STUART

JACKSON

J.R.JONES

SEDGWICK

McLAWS EARLY WALKER

HOOD

LAWTON

LEE

Sharpsburg

HAGERSTOWN TURNPIKE

S U M N E R

WILLIAMS

GREENE

Dunker Church

FRENCH RICHARDSON

D.H.HILL

ANDERSON

BLOODY LANE

D.H.HILL

N
W   E
S

McCLELLAN

ANTIETAM CREEK

Keedysville

MORELL

PLEASONTON

FRANKLIN

to Turner's Gap

SYKES

P
O
R
T
E
R

B
U
R
N
S
I
D
E

STONE BRIDGE

S
T
U
R
G
I
S

WILLCOX

SCAMMON

RODMAN

LONGSTREET

D.R.JONES

MUNFORD

CANAL

POTOMAC R.

ANTIETAM CREEK

to Crampton's Gap

Battle of Antietam
Sept. 17, 1862

▬ Federal Positions
▬ Confederate Positions
Federal Artillery
Confederate Artillery
→ Federal Attack
→ Confederate Attack

Miles
0   1/2   1

the Harper's Ferry affair. From them I first heard of the disgraceful surrender there, and what particulars are yet known. Everything indicates
that Colonel Miles either was at his old practises and drunk, or else that
he was a fool if not a coward. Ten thousand men in such a position certainly should have been able to hold out for forty-eight hours, in half of
which time they would have been relieved; or his whole command might
have cut their way out as Colonel Davis did with the cavalry. It is a
terrible piece of bad news, coming, too, right on top of such a victory as
South Mountain. General Franklin, with his corps, it seems, crossed the
mountains some distance south of the rest of the army and not many
miles from Harper's Ferry, at Crampton's Gap, and quite near enough
for the sound of the battle to be heard by Miles before he surrendered.

The army is said to be twenty or thirty miles on towards Hagerstown,
at which place the last reports place Hooker with the right wing. Lee's
main force is supposed to be at Williamsport and in considerable fear of
an attack before they get across the river; which they will doubtless have
if Hooker is after them. I fear it may be some little time ere I catch
them as my horses have not yet arrived. Can learn nothing of our losses
at South Mountain; nor can I hear anything of William.

MIDDLETOWN, SEPTEMBER 17, WEDNESDAY.   Frederick is quite a thriving
place of some 15,000 inhabitants. I had a good chance to walk around
it this morning and talked with a number of the inhabitants. They all
say that the portion of Lee's army which was in the city behaved well,
and did but very little harm, paying for what they took, but in Confederate notes; shoes and leather were the most coveted objects, as also
drugs. Our landlady, who is a strong Union woman, says she was obliged
to let them have a number of pounds of honey, and to take their worthless money for it. But she put on a price according, and then sold half
the bills to a secessionist neighbour who is foolish enough to believe that
Lee will be back again within a week, and in that way got the full value
of her honey. The town is full of soldiers. Most of the paroled officers
from Harper's Ferry are here, who are all very indignant at Miles, and
say they could have held out as well as not—that they only had some 200
killed and wounded. Quite a number of regiments have passed up today,
and one whole brigade or division, while stragglers have been passing up
in a perfect stream all day. As also waggons and ambulances without
number. Saw quite a number of rebel prisoners at the Court House, a
very thin, shabby and dirty set, but much more hardy and lively looking
than our men.

Those coming from west of the hills reported quite early that a fight
seemed to be going on towards Williamsport; we could not, however,
hear the firing here in town. This put me in a fever to get off, my horses
not appearing. I tried to hire or borrow, and offered to pay well to be

taken up in a waggon, but found that nothing in the way of horseflesh was to be had in the town. . . .

HEADQUARTERS HOOKER'S CORPS, SEPTEMBER 18, THURSDAY. I forgot to mention that so soon as we got outside the town yesterday afternoon, we could hear the firing very distinctly. Just before reaching Middletown we met the adjutant of the Third Pennsylvania Cavalry, who Rumsey knew, bringing in the body of his colonel. From him we heard that the battle was the most severe of the whole campaign; that General Hooker was wounded, but not badly, and that our forces were victorious.

This morning we started early, through Middletown and across the mountains. I tried to find some signs of Sunday's fight here but could not. The road we were on is the great National road, wide and good; at Boonesboro we turned short to the left, down to Keedysville, and then by a byroad away round to the right again. The whole of the way up we travelled in the middle of an army; so many men straggling forward were there that it seemed as if one-half the army must have been left behind. A number were without shoes, and a good many appeared to be really trying to get up; but I fear the greater portion were in no hurry to rejoin their regiments until the fight was over. Soon after crossing the mountains we began to meet trains of ambulances and waggons with the wounded, and many also on foot. Most of the people here are good Unionists and the women were out everywhere giving bread and butter and the like to the men. Near Keedysville we overtook a large body of troops moving up, and among them Barnes's battery.

We struck our rear line of battle in Sumner's corps, and followed it along to the extreme right of the army. It was very evident that we had not lost ground at the close of yesterday's battle, for I passed large numbers of rebel dead in places lying in rear of our present lines. On the right of Sumner I found Franklin, and from him learned that General Meade was in command of Hooker's corps, as also where I would find him. When I reported to General Meade he, with a number of other generals, was trying to learn from some citizens exactly where the river was. It seemed to me they could easily have found out by sending an officer over to see, but they seemed still ignorant of the exact position of the rebs. General Meade received me very pleasantly, pointed out the line held by the corps, and said there were no orders for a move of any kind at present.

After getting a lunch of bread and cheese with Captain Reynolds, whose battery was in position right where we were, I went with Rumsey along the whole of our line, to ascertain the condition of my new command. We found nearly all of them in position; seven full batteries and two odd sections. Most of them seem to have been roughly handled in the Pope campaign, and not to have got refitted before coming up here;

and one, at least, "B" Fourth Artillery, was very roughly handled here yesterday, losing about thirty killed and wounded. All complain of being very short of men and horses. I could do nothing except make myself acquainted with their positions, and direct them to take steps to fill up their chests, which I found some of them had not attempted to do since yesterday's fight. . . .

There has been no fighting today other than little spurts on the part of our skirmish line to make sure that the rebs were still there; and now and then a cannon shot. We did not put our tents up tonight, but slept under some large elms in a valley. I saw Patrick for a few moments; quite well. General Hooker was shot in the hollow of the foot; not at all dangerous, they say, but very painful.

❊ ❊ ❊

The battle of Antietam ended without decisive result. It was one of the bloodiest combats of the war; of the 130,000 men engaged in the two armies, at least 21,000 or 16 per cent were killed or wounded. "The corn and the trees, so fresh and green in the morning," writes a Massachusetts colonel, "were reddened with blood and torn by bullet and shell, and the very earth was furrowed by the incessant impact of lead and iron." In the cornfield on the Union right, where Hooker's division advanced, and where the Confederate troops had taken partial shelter, every stalk had been cut as if by a scythe. The dead, said Hooker, lay in rows precisely as they had stood in line a few minutes before the action commenced. Sumner marched a Union division into a Confederate ambush where the fire from front, flank, and rear stretched nearly two thousand men prostrate in a moment. At the end of the day, when Hood reported that he had no men left, Lee asked him what had become of his splendid division. "They are lying on the field where you sent them," replied Hood. "My division has been almost wiped out."

If McClellan had moved promptly and fought with instant decision, he might have destroyed the greater part of Lee's army. If he had used his troops, particularly on the right, as a unit, instead of letting them deliver piecemeal attacks, he could have demolished Lee's left wing. As it was, when the battle closed, the Confederates had been forced back on their left by more than a mile, and on their right by about a half mile; but they still held a strong defensive line passing through Sharpsburg. On September 18, the day after the battle, many on both sides expected McClellan to renew the attack. He had an overwhelming superiority in troops and equipment. But he lay still—and that night the Southern forces withdrew across the

Potomac, quite unmolested. He was content with checking Lee; he had no desire to overwhelm him.

The check of course accomplished great objects. It gave the North, after a long series of defeats, new encouragement. It gave Lincoln his opportunity to issue the Emancipation Proclamation; and it and the Proclamation together made foreign intervention impossible. The North had lost at South Mountain a brave corps commander, Jesse Lee Reno, a veteran of the Mexican War who had fought at Second Manassas. It had a new war hero in Hooker, whose impetuous attack at the opening of the combat had fairly confirmed his sobriquet of "Fighting Joe." But doubts as to McClellan's capacity and energy persisted. While Lee fell back to the Winchester area in the Shenandoah Valley, McClellan did not begin putting his army of more than 110,000 men across the Potomac until October 26.

❊ ❊ ❊

NEAR SHARPSBURG, SEPTEMBER 19, FRIDAY. On turning out of my blankets this morning, I learned that Lee had escaped across the river during the night. Orders soon came for us to move down to near Sharpsburg, which we did by the small byroad near the river which I was on yesterday, and pitched our camp about three-fourths of a mile from the town. We passed across the extreme left of where their line of battle had been, and in their rear of where the heavy fighting was. I did not go off to see the carnage in the worst places, but saw enough of it to satisfy me. In one place, even on the back road by which we marched, the corps had to halt until it was cleared of dead. The rebs had buried none, and only carried off those of rank enough to warrant their bodies being sent home. We found sixteen of their wounded left in a house by the river, with a surgeon and two attendants in charge, but the other doctors had carried off all the medicines and surgical instruments. The men said they had been told that the "Yanks" would bayonet them, and they expected to be killed. . . .

In the afternoon I rode with General Meade as far as McClellan's headquarters at Sharpsburg, and then went on to Keedysville, to see Hooker, who is lying there. Found him in bed, but in very good spirits; expects to leave for Washington tomorrow. He told me that he was hit while posting the First New Hampshire Battery and that if I had been there to attend to it he should have escaped; when he is confident that he could have driven the enemy into the river. He talked a great deal about McClellan not renewing the attack yesterday; said that Pleasonton reported Lee as crossing at four in the afternoon, but that Porter contradicted it. I wish I could tell when Hooker is really speaking the simple truth; but he so universally finds fault with everybody, not under himself, that one can attach but little consequence to what he says. From what I can learn, nearly if not quite all our other generals expected Lee would make an attack on us yesterday. They say too that our men were used up, and that they could not have been got to attack with any hope of success; our loss too was very heavy especially in this corps and the Second. Our field return today does not show 7,000 men present: 6,729 the number.

General Richardson lies in the same house with Hooker; he was shot through the bowels and cannot possibly live. He seemed in great pain as I could hear his groans the whole time I was in the house.*

SEPTEMBER 20, SATURDAY.   General Porter with a good part of his corps crossed the river this morning without opposition, and advanced a mile back, when he was attacked, and driven in with some loss. Last evening a detachment from his corps crossed and charged some batteries the rebs had planted on the bank to cover their retreat, capturing several guns. I rode down to the crossing this afternoon. The whole road from Sharpsburg to the river was lined with abandoned guns, caissons and waggons; while every house, barn and shed was filled with rebel wounded, and many more lay under trees, or wretched apologies for tents. Sharpsburg itself is a small place, with very comfortless looking houses, though most of them are stone or brick; a few have holes through them, made by stray cannon balls, and all are crowded with rebel wounded.

I stopped at McClellan's headquarters on my way back to report to Colonel Hunt, our new chief of artillery. I have only seen him a few times before, while we lay at Camp Barry. He received me very pleasantly, but it was hard work to get him to come down to business; friends were coming in all the time to see him. In this respect he certainly is not equal to General Barry, who was one of the most thorough business men I ever met with. One of my principal objects was to find out what my duties and powers are in my new position. Colonel Hunt takes very different grounds on this point from what they did at Heintzelman's headquarters, where the corps chief was only considered as a sort of inspector of artillery. He tells me I am responsible for the efficiency of the batteries of the corps in every respect. This will give me plenty to do, but I do not see exactly how I am to carry it out with the batteries attached to the several divisions, and subject to the orders of the division commanders. The Colonel wants an immediate, and most minute inspection made, and the exact condition of each battery reported to him. This will take me a couple of days to do.

* Israel Bush Richardson, a graduate of West Point in the class of 1841 who had shown exceptional gallantry at Cerro Gordo, had fought through the Peninsular Campaign, gaining promotion to the rank of major general. Wounded at Antietam, he died on November 3.

SEPTEMBER 21, SUNDAY. I was announced in orders today as chief of artillery of the corps, so can go to work now. It is also announced that this will be hereafter designated as the "Twelfth Corps," wherein I think that General Meade has misinterpreted the War Department order; which, however, is like all the others coming from there as indistinct as it can possibly be. I believe the corps should be called the First as it was when under McDowell. General Meade is now the ranking officer of the corps, but neither Hooker nor McClellan considered Ricketts, who is competent. Meade only commanded a brigade in the Third Division when it was down on the Peninsula. He is a West Pointer and Major of Engineers; a fine, soldierly, somewhat stiff-looking man, and the most thoroughbred gentleman in his manners I have yet met within the army. I do not know whether he will retain command of the corps, but doubt it as there are so many senior to him.

The corps consists of three divisions. The First Division is properly King's, but he being away wounded, General Doubleday now is in command. It contains four brigades; the first, under General Gibbon, is composed entirely of Western troops; the Second is Doubleday's own, and all the colonels being away sick or wounded, is now commanded by a lieutenant-colonel; the Third, General Hatch also absent wounded, is commanded by a colonel; the Fourth is Patrick's, all New York two-year regiments.*. . . General Hooker brought most of his own staff with him and took it away again. Those at present here are partly General Meade's and partly the proper corps staff. I have watched them with a good deal of anxiety as my social relations with them must be pretty close for some time to come. As yet I can form no judgment concerning them. . . .

SEPTEMBER 22, MONDAY. I finished the inspection of the batteries serving with the First Division today. I find that in this division, one battery is attached to each brigade, and subject to the orders of the brigade commander, although such an arrangement is in direct violation of orders. . . .

SEPTEMBER 24, WEDNESDAY. I find that of my twelve batteries, five are

---

* John Gibbon, who had graduated from West Point in 1847 and served in the Seminole War and on the border, was a North Carolinian who had thrown in his lot with the North although three brothers fought for the Confederacy. Now a brigadier general, he had shared in the Seven Days, Second Manassas, and Antietam. Abner Doubleday, also a West Point graduate (1842), had an equally redoubtable record; the Mexican and Seminole Wars, Fort Sumter, Second Manassas, and Antietam. His worst ordeal awaited him at Gettysburg. John Porter Hatch, West Point, 1845, had been at Winchester and Second Bull Run before he was severely wounded at South Mountain. Marsena Rudolph Patrick (West Point 1835), as previously noted, had been an Erie Canal driver, Mexican War soldier, railroad official, and college president before he re-entered the service and went on McClellan's staff. A man of stern Presbyterian convictions and powerful personality, he was an old friend of Wainwright's.

from Pennsylvania, four from New England, one from New York and two regulars. The nine here have forty guns, but are short of men as a whole, though nearly all have more or less infantry attached. They are also sadly in want of horses, a large number being unserviceable, and of stores of all kinds; one-half the horses are without shoes. In a week we ought to be able to get all these things from Washington, so that they can be ready for service again. The nine batteries have 930 aggregate present, 520 of which are with the four batteries of the First Division, and 370 total absent, or one-quarter of their whole number. The batteries of the First Division have not seen as much service as those of the Third, nor been so roughly handled as those of the Second. At present they are in the best order individually.

* * *

Wainwright's strictness in discipline is illustrated by his accounts, too long and detailed to be presented in full, of the dozen batteries of Hooker's corps which he was now supervising. He found the First Rhode Island Artillery, Battery "D," very creditable in outside appearance; "but there appears to be a good deal lacking inside, and I fear that when I come to know it better I shall have a good deal of fault to find." The captain was "uppish and overbearing, and I think very conceited in all things." The First New York Artillery, Battery "L," was "no credit to the regiment, everything slipshod and slovenly; the men made no appearance at all on parade; still they seemed to understand their duty so far as essentials are concerned." When Wainwright went to see the captain in charge he was shocked to find a number of privates in his tent, "as also a free and familiar way with his men, for which I had to haul him up." The First New Hampshire Artillery were "a very clean, bright-looking set, but not well instructed," a large number of them being new recruits. One of the Pennsylvania batteries had for captain "an old Scotch sergeant from the English army, excellent in action they say," but with a slovenly, ill-disciplined body of men. Of another unit, the First Pennsylvania Artillery, with no captain and only two junior officers for 110 men, Wainwright writes: "Things generally in a very loose order; camp dirty and discipline apparently very lax. I was by no means favourably impressed here."

Clearly, Wainwright intended to substitute firm order and stiff attention to cleanliness, promptness, and precision for an all too general laxity. But he was worried by the vagueness of his authority over the battle-weakened artillery scattered through the three divisions. Could not the division commanders always overrule him?

* * *

SEPTEMBER 25, THURSDAY. Took my reports up to Colonel or General Hunt, for there seems to be some uncertainty what his title is, though he still signs himself colonel. I had a long talk with him, not only about my batteries, but about the powers of a corps chief of artillery, and especially where he comes in conflict with the division commander—as I have already with General Doubleday—in regard to his batteries being attached to brigades. While with a division, the batteries were my own command, and I could give orders with a certainty of their being obeyed. But now if a battery commander or division chief does not like my orders, he may get his division general to give him contrary ones, and I cannot interfere. For instance, I want now to bring all the batteries of the First Division together, and to consolidate their ammunition train. To effect this, I had a long talk with General Doubleday, but he refuses to give his consent, and I am powerless. I told Colonel Hunt that the only way I could see to carry out his ideas would be to unite all the batteries of a corps into a brigade, at least while not in the actual face of an enemy. He does not approve of that idea, but says that if General Doubleday will not make the proper changes, I must get an order from the corps commander.

It is said that the enemy left more of their dead unburied on the ground here than our total loss in killed. Some ten or twelve captured guns and a number of caissons are parked in the field adjoining general headquarters.

SEPTEMBER 26, FRIDAY. The weather continues dry and fine; but the nights are right cold, with heavy dews or fogs; last night we must have come very near a frost. There is said to be a good deal of suffering among our men for want of clothing, especially blankets and shoes. The losses in the Pope affair have not been made good yet. Many of the men are quite barefooted, and others are without a blanket. The necessary requisitions for them have been made, but none have yet been received. As for horseshoes, I doubt if one is to be had in the army. General Meade sent an orderly off to get half a dozen for his own horses; the man got them way beyond Boonesboro, and paid twenty-five cents apiece for them.

The rebels still lie directly opposite to us, and have now a strong picket line along the river, for the whole width of the valley, while ours extends equally far on this side. Franklin's corps is up at Williamsport, Sumner's down at Harper's Ferry, which we reoccupied without opposition; the rest of the army lies between these two points. Lee's force and our own are said to be about equal. What the next move will be I do not know, but suppose that something will be done, so soon as we get our necessary supplies.

This corps has been filling up by the incoming of stragglers, and arrival of some recruits, so that we now have twice as many men present as we had a week ago. Still not half of those borne on the company rolls are present. The last return shows 46 regiments of infantry in the corps, with about 28,000 men on their rolls, or only some 600 men to a regiment; yet of these 16,000 are absent, and 12,000 only present. Our regiments average 260 officers and men in the field. This is a horrible state of affairs and something ought to be done, not only to stop the straggling but the paying of so many useless men. . . .

SEPTEMBER 30, TUESDAY. The last three days have been days of quiet, warm and fine. I did not expect we should have remained here so long as this, doing nothing. But they say that our supplies do not come; my batteries, I know, have not received the first thing either from the Ordnance or the quartermaster's department. I went up to headquarters again to see if something could not be done to give me horses and horseshoes, for without these I am almost helpless, but I could get no further satisfaction than that they were promised from Washington. This corps has now been two months since receiving any supplies to speak of, and I suppose it is the same throughout the army. Had they simply been marching, it would have nearly used up the old stores; but when to the long and hard marches you add the losses of half a dozen battles, our men are in a bad state indeed. Our medical director tells me that nearly the whole of his hospital tents are gone in one way and another, and that should we move and then have a battle, he would be unable to cover his wounded.

There have been some changes within the last few days. General Meade has gone back to the Third Division and Brigadier-General John F. Reynolds commands the corps. I have not yet seen enough of him to say how I like the change. He is an old light-battery captain, and ought to know how to take care of his artillery. General Patrick has gone up to Army Headquarters as provost-marshal, an office which I think he will fill to perfection. We have moved our headquarters camp, as also that of some of the divisions, to a greater distance from the dead of the battlefield. We now are on a fine little knoll where we get a good view across the river, though not of the Potomac itself. The tents are all in one row, facing west; mine are on the left flank. General Méade has his division headquarters on the same knoll facing the other way. His own tent is only some fifty yards from mine. We have two new Pennsylvania regiments added to the Third Division.

Among the War Department orders we have received of late are two containing proclamations by the President. One of these, after opening with a very short reassertion that the object of the war is the restoration of the Union, goes on to change it into an abolition one virtually, by the threat that if the rebellion is not over by the 1st of January, all slaves in the then rebellious states shall be free. I do not hear much said here in the army on the subject, but all think it unadvised at this time; even those most anti-slavery. It has been very evident that this was what the radicals have been driving at for some time past, but I had hoped that Mr. Lincoln would have had force enough to resist. The other proclamation suspends the writ of habeas corpus in respect to all military offenses. It is to be hoped that this will enable them to return some of the many men absent at home without leave, and who are really deserters. . . .

OCTOBER 1, WEDNESDAY. Rode up to Hagerstown today along with the corps commander, quartermaster and medical director. The distance from here is a good thirteen miles, so we had quite a ride there and back; the road was good, being all macadamized, but very dusty. The country through which we passed is a rich limestone, with hardly any streams, and, of course, very little grass land. The houses, barns, and whole country reminded me strongly of Pennsylvania. . . .

OCTOBER 2, THURSDAY. President Lincoln was to review the corps today. The line was formed right after dinner almost on the battlefield itself, that is but a few hundred yards to the rear of where the rebel line of battle was. Two o'clock was the hour appointed. After waiting an hour, General Reynolds rode with most of his staff to meet the President. He was to come from McClellan's headquarters, which have been moved some two or three miles below Sharpsburg. We had got halfway there when we met the "great mogul" riding in an ambulance with some half dozen Western-looking politicians. Republican simplicity is well enough, but I should have preferred to see the President of the United States travelling with a little more regard to appearances than can be afforded by a common ambulance, with his long legs doubled up so that his knees almost struck his chin, and grinning out of the windows like a baboon. Mr. Lincoln not only is the ugliest man I ever saw, but the most uncouth and gawky in his manners and appearance.

After the General had been presented and said a few words to the President, we rode on still farther to meet McClellan, who came up with a large part of his staff, when we wheeled in with them and soon again were up with the Presidential chariot. It was the first time I had seen McClellan near enough to know what he looks like, though I have been under his command now for near a year. He has a good face, open and manly, set on a very thick, short neck, and is what may be called thick-set altogether. I should not, from his looks, set him down as a great man by any means. The General rode a splendid bay horse, a trotter, and rode him well; he shows to advantage on horseback. At one time in the afternoon, he went down a steep hill at such a pace that only three or four of us kept up with him.

The first place we halted at was on a high knoll where McClellan took his post during the battle. Here we all dismounted, and the President got out. McClellan commenced to explain to him his arrangements and what took place during the battle. I stood near enough to him to hear all that he said, but was astonished to notice how little interest Mr. Lincoln took in the recital. Indeed he did not allow McClellan to more than open the fight when he turned off to his ambulance, and said, "Let us go and see where Hooker went in." McClellan seemed annoyed, and I was very much disappointed. We then rode across the fields to near the spot where I first reported to General Meade, while the ambulance went around by the road. Here we waited and waited without the President coming. McClellan sent one after another of his staff to look for him, but without avail and it was not until dark that we found out Mr. Lincoln had suddenly changed his mind, and driven back to camp.

It was near eight o'clock when the troops were dismissed, having stood half a day under a hot sun, in momentary expectation of the President's arrival. A specimen of Western bad manners, rather than of the much talked of Republican simplicity.

OCTOBER 3, FRIDAY.   Our review came off today. It was ordered for eleven o'clock, but we again had to wait until three. Mr. Lincoln was on horseback. He rode along the lines at a quick trot, taking little notice of the troops, and half the time not even looking at them. Not a word of approval, not even a smile of approbation; for that matter the army has not received the smallest official acknowledgment from Washington of their late victories. The men looked well, considering we have yet been unable to get any new clothing, but many of the regiments were terribly small. It took the President about thirty minutes to ride around the lines, when he at once cleared out, not waiting for the corps to march in review.

I got back to camp very hot, very tired, and utterly disgusted, a feeling which I think was pretty general throughout the command. There was not the slightest enthusiasm on the part of the men; and how could there be for a President who did not show the smallest interest in them?

❋ ❋ ❋

"The time passed away," writes Regis de Trobriand in *Four Years with the Army of the Potomac* of the period just after Antietam. "The fine days of October, the finest weather of the pleasantest season in the United States, slipped away without any indication on the part of General McClellan of any intentions to profit by them. More than a month had passed since the battle of Antietam, and the army was immovable. It was impatient at the long inaction. The country was astonished by it. Everywhere, it was asked, 'What is McClellan doing?' " It was to find out what he was doing, or rather why he was not doing anything, that Lincoln visited the army. And as de Trobriand adds, he returned to Washington convinced that he must issue positive orders to overcome the persistent inertia of the general. On October 6 Lincoln sent McClellan formal directions "to cross the Potomac and give battle to the enemy, or drive him South." Halleck, who transmitted the order, telegraphed: "Your army must move now while the roads are good." But alleging a shortage of supplies, McClellan sat still. The army did not move until October ended and November began.

Wainwright, one of the many conservative Democrats who thoroughly condemned Lincoln's extension of the objects of the war to cover emancipation, gives a prejudiced account of the President's visit. Other accounts mention his awkwardness, but speak of his patient anxiety to learn the facts. McClellan in his *Own Story* describes the meeting in pleasant terms, testifies to Lincoln's courtesy, and writes: "During this visit we had many and long conversations alone." But Lincoln's intimates knew that he was sick at heart as he saw the great host of soldiers lying idle before him. The Army of the Potomac, by its official report of September 30, 1862, had 303,959 men. Of these 101,756 were absent and 73,601 were with Banks's force; but McClellan still had 100,144 men present for duty, or far more than Lee. One morning during the visit Lincoln pointed out to his friends the white tents glistening for miles in the sunrise. "Do you know what this is?" he demanded, and supplied his own answer: "It is only McClellan's bodyguard."

❊ ❊ ❊

OCTOBER 5, SUNDAY. I have heretofore said nothing about the battle of Antietam, as I was trying to get some idea of it myself. I cannot get an exact account of the whole affair of course, but I have learned a number of things which I have not seen in print, and which seem to me to have a very important bearing on the result. My inquiries of course have been confined mostly to the part taken by this corps, but as the Second attacked at nearly the same point, and this was the main part of the fight, its attack was to a certain extent included.

On Tuesday, the second day after the battle of South Mountain, the rebs were found holding the line of Antietam Creek. After a heavy cannonading they were driven back so soon as our men got into position; and then we advanced to near their main line, which ran from the banks of the creek down toward its mouth up through Sharpsburg and then a short distance in front of the Sharpsburg and Hagerstown pike for near two miles, when it bent off towards the Potomac. McClellan's main attack was to be on their left flank, and Hooker was sent that same evening to feel them and see where the flank rested. Sumner was to join him by daylight the next morning, and the two corps stretched out so as to turn them if possible, get their own flank on the river, and attack together. Meantime Burnside with the Ninth and one other corps was to attack their right by the bridge some one and one-half miles below Sharpsburg.

Hooker pushed around, drove in their skirmishers, and found their left where they turned to the river. But not content with fulfilling his orders he drove so hard that his men got hotly engaged, and could not be separated at night. A newspaper reporter told me that he slept in a barn that night with General Hooker: that our men and the enemy were so mixed up that they lay down together, and so soon as they could see, commenced the fight again themselves. He said that he himself woke General Hooker up, and that the fight had become quite brisk by that time. In this way Hooker did not have all his corps in hand, and was forced into fighting at once though Sumner had not come up. Not that I suppose he was at all sorry to thus avoid being subject to General Sumner's orders. It was the same as at Williamsburg: an attempt to get all the glory himself. As it was, the rebels were driven some distance; their right completely across the pike and into the yards beyond. This wood comes up to the road at a small church, runs along the road to our right for four or five hundred yards, then falls straight back about one hundred yards, and then to the right again for a couple of hundred yards more. The limestone rock comes up all along this wood, cropping out three or four feet, the ridges running parallel to the road and dipping towards it; thus affording the rebs a most admirable natural breastwork. This corps made one or two attempts to carry the position, and Gibbon ran his own battery down the road to within 150 yards of the corner of the woods, where it remained about ten minutes. It was an awful place to put a battery; in front of two haystacks, and with its flank within easy musket range of the enemy. I cannot see how Gibbon could have placed it there, especially when there was quite as commanding a position and a safe one only some 300 yards farther back.

Sumner, who was ordered to start at three o'clock, did not move until after daylight, and then so slowly that notwithstanding McClellan sent constantly to hurry him up, he did not reach the point until this corps was about used up, and he had to go in alone. His men did not all behave well at first, but they had a hard fight of it and lost tremendously, over 5,000. They drove still more of the enemy's line across the road, and at one time penetrated nearly through the wood, but were unable to hold it. There seems to be no doubt that if McClellan's orders had been carried out, had Sumner been on time, and Hooker not too anxious to do it all himself, the attack would have been so complete a success that but little of the rebel army would have escaped. Sumner could have attacked at the point on the road, while Hooker could have stretched as much farther to the right which would have brought him down to the river. I noticed one open knoll here, within two fields of where our troops were, and which I find commands the whole rear of the rebel line. They had only two guns on it at any time, but it was too far to the right to reach our line.

Burnside, who was to have attacked at the same hour, did not attempt anything until afternoon, so that Lee was always able to concentrate on the point where the attack was made. Had we carried the line along the pike, it is said that Lee would have fallen back to the ridge on which our tents are now, where he could have got a strong position, with both flanks on the Potomac, and a short line. He could not have done it, however, without a very heavy loss in prisoners and guns if we had got the high knoll I speak of. Some say he should have adopted the shorter line at first.

Antietam was a victory, and a glorious one when you consider that but seventeen days before this army was running most disgracefully from the same troops over which they were now victorious. Why it was not a more complete victory seems to me to be owing to the three cases of disobedience of orders on the part of corps commanders, especially to Sumner. This is the second time "Old Bull" has allowed the rebs to escape by his stupidity or pigheadedness, and it is queer to me that he is kept in command. Still one cannot forget how splendidly he behaved at Fair Oaks.

At last I have got all my back mail, down even to the 2nd of this month. The President's abolition proclamation seems to cause a good deal of excitement in New York, as do all the radical movements. It seems sometimes as if these fellows, having now got the power in their own hands, meant to force all their vile notions upon the country as war measures. Lincoln, if one could judge from his early speeches and sayings, does not approve them. Still, he appears to be gradually yielding to their constant pressure. The weather continues fine and clear, but very dry. Up to last night it was really hot at times; the wind changed about ten in the evening, and today it is quite cool.

OCTOBER 10, FRIDAY. The whole of the week so far has been spent in making another and more close inspection of my batteries, in accordance with an order from headquarters requiring such inspection to be made of all the troops in the army. It extended even to their books and the management of all their affairs, while every officer and man borne on the rolls had to be fully accounted for. Two batteries a day was about as many as I could possibly get through with. I was surprised to find how loosely and inaccurately almost all the books were kept. Indeed, there was not a single battery where they were all properly written up, and their returns all made; while I found the best set of books in a battery

which passed a very bad inspection in every other respect. Not one of the
batteries was what it ought to be and most of them very far off from it.
It looks like a hopeless job to improve them under our present system
of affairs. If I had a good field officer for chief of artillery in each division, one who camped with the batteries and really looked after them, I
might hope to do something. But as it is, with the division chiefs also
in command of their own battery, having this extra labour to perform
without its bringing promotion or other reward, and changing frequently
as a senior captain joins or leaves the command, it is impossible to get
them to do anything more than forward a few reports. The corps chief,
living at headquarters, is separated even miles from some of the batteries
and can have no direct oversight of them. Another trouble lies in the
uncertain manner in which they are obliged to draw their supplies, generally through some brigade quartermaster and commissary, who not
liking the extra labour thus put upon him is very apt to do as little as
he can. All these things have made me think more of the idea which occurred to me in talking with General Hunt, when I first came here, viz:
to form all the batteries of a corps into a regular brigade, with its own
staff, and have them all camped together while lying as we do now, so as
to give the chief of artillery a chance to refit and instruct them. During
an engagement or when necessary on the march they could be sent to the
divisions, either all of them or a part. I have talked as well as thought
the matter over a good deal. In General Seymour I have found a strong
advocate for my plan (for it has almost got to be a plan). . . .*

The papers, I see, are getting very impatient, and the old cry as to Mc-
Clellan's slowness is again being raised. I was much surprised at first myself that we did not cross the river at once, but the more I know of the
condition of the army, and other matters, the less certain does it appear
that we could have done so to advantage. This corps as yet has received
next to no supplies, and is just as badly off as directly after the battle.
None of my batteries have yet had their ordnance requisitions filled, nor
have we drawn any horses, and though there are standing requisitions at
both Hagerstown and Harper's Ferry for horseshoes, we have not got a

* This proposal of Wainwright's was so important that it was unfortunate he gained
no influential support for it until late in the war. The chief of artillery in each corps
had limited powers. He was expected to inspect, equip, and supply his batteries, but to
exercise no command without orders from the general in charge. Division artillery
chiefs were similarly restricted. The batteries were so scattered about that even in rest
periods the artillery chief had imperfect oversight and control. Barry, early in the war,
had pleaded for the appointment of two brigadiers of artillery, but the adjutant
general had declared this illegal. Wainwright was trying to break out of a shortsighted, hidebound administrative system that fettered him to the injury of the service.
See Naisawald, *Grape and Canister*, 30, 31.

single shoe. Where the fault is I do not know; either at Washington or on the road, I presume.

The newspapers, in their wisdom, are congratulating us on the river being so low, while our generals are wishing it were extra high, so as to do away with the many fords which now require guarding. Were the river high we could concentrate and cross at Harper's Ferry without fear of Lee recrossing into Maryland at Williamsport and above there. As it is, the Potomac is no barrier at all.

The army has been increasing somewhat in strength by the arrival of recruits and new regiments and by the sending back of deserters and men kept too long in the hospitals. This system of always raising new regiments is a very bad one. No one not actually in service can understand how bad it is. It is almost as bad as commencing all over again, where we were a year ago. There is some doubt of General Hooker again coming to this corps; we hear that he is made very much of at Washington, Mr. Lincoln and Secretary Chase being particularly sweet on him. He may very likely get a separate command. . . .

OCTOBER 14, TUESDAY. The difficulty of guarding all the fords, and the way in which we should leave this whole country open should we move from here before the river rises is shown by the raid which Stuart has just made completely around us. It is a burning disgrace that with 2,000 cavalry he should have been permitted to ride rough-shod through so well settled a country, and not a shot fired at him, as it is that our cavalry should have allowed it. It is said that what little cavalry we have is so badly off for horses that they can do nothing. But with the exception of the few regulars and two or three other regiments, I fear our cavalry is an awful botch. . . .

OCTOBER 19, SUNDAY. We are still here with orders to be ready to move at any hour, but still we are not ready. This corps got a certain amount of clothing last week, the first we have received worth speaking of; still the men are very badly off for shoes and blankets. It seems almost as if they purposely kept them back at Washington, or else they have not got them. I have been unable to procure any horses yet, and have received but one keg of shoes. Not a single battery has yet got their ordnance requisition filled. . . .

The papers are full of reports of McClellan's removal, and I fear they will prove only too true. His enemies are very bitter, and will see no good in him, though there is not a doubt that no other man in the country could have saved Washington last month. They have been using a letter of Kearny's as very strong against McClellan, but foolishly have allowed the whole letter to be published. It is as mad a letter as any sane man could write; pitches not only into McClellan, but into every other general of any prominence in the army. It has afforded a vast deal of amusement to the old army men here, for there was a certain amount of truth in all he said, and none of our generals here were high enough at that time to stand in Kearny's way. I was very sorry to see the letters myself, for they have damaged the writer terribly. I am not so strong an admirer of McClellan myself but that I can see he falls short of being a really great general, such a one as we ought to have in command of this army, but I do think he is head and shoulders above any other man we have. Indeed, if you put the question, "Who is better?" to any of those who are most bitter, it silences them at once. Burnside and Hooker are the only two I have heard spoken of as his successor; the first has been offered the position and declined it, stating fairly that McClellan was better fitted for it than he was. Hooker I do not think is at all capable of filling the position. . . .

I was witness the other day to a queer and rather amusing scene, in which General Meade was the actor. I had heard that he had a hot temper, which he certainly displayed in this instance. Very strong orders have been issued against pillaging, we being among friends now, and Meade has shown himself particularly zealous in carrying them out. This day he was sitting by the fire in front of his tent, as I was in front of mine, when a private belonging to his division came along with a great bundle of corn leaves on his back. Up jumps the General, and himself demands, "What are you doing with that corn?" Finding the man had stolen it, instead of having him arrested, Meade commenced to talk to him, then to swear at him, and finally, as the steam got up, struck him aside of the head, and almost knocked him over. The man, who was a big fellow, picked himself up, and turning to the General said, "If it warn't for them shoulder straps of your'n, I'd give you the darn'dst thrashing you ever had in your life." On which Meade, very much ashamed of himself, cleared out.

OCTOBER 23, THURSDAY. Four days of entire quiet, with absolutely nothing to do. The weather today is really cold, and very uncomfortable. The high winds make our outdoor fires almost of no good, blowing the smoke in your face on whichever side you get. Fortunately we have been able to change our linen tents for cotton ones, almost new; had we not, it would be hard work to keep warm at night. My man is quite sick, with a sort of scurvy, and has been obliged to go to the hospital today; which is another great nuisance just as we are about to move, when I shall need him most. . . .

BURKITTSVILLE, OCTOBER 26, SUNDAY. Off at last, though still with many of our men barefooted and more than half my horses shoeless. Captain Lowry got me a few horses around our old camp, and has now gone up into Pennsylvania to see what he can do there as a last resort. We broke camp this morning soon after sunrise in a heavy southwest storm, terribly cold. I had nothing to do with the marching of the batteries, and so lay around until the General was ready to ride. . . .'. The march to this place was a very hard one on the men; the road rough, this limestone soil very slippery, and all drenched to the skin. The rain did not hold up at all until we got here, just at sundown; and the men had to spread their blankets in the wet ploughed fields. Some of us rode on ahead and secured a house for the General and another for ourselves. We were made very comfortable by a Pennsylvania Dutchman, a tanner, whose house stands just at the entrance to the village from Crampton's Pass. We dried ourselves by his stove, and the "frau" gave us a most capital supper, and very clean beds. The night was right cold and windy.

The country all along today, so far as one could see through the rain mist, was very rough and stony, but mostly cleared. Crampton's Gap is where Franklin had his fight the same day that the rest of the army fought at South Mountain. Burkittsville is a little village on the west or rebel side of the pass, lying very prettily in a valley a couple of miles wide. Our host's house shows many marks of bullets, and here and there of a cannon ball.

BERLIN, OCTOBER 27, MONDAY. We came this far today, not a long march, but a hilly one; the day was cold and lowering but no rain. We have our tents pitched within a couple of hundred yards of the river on the flat, with the railroad between it and us. The troops of our own corps and several others are camped on the hills around us. The view of the river from here is very beautiful. It may be a quarter or perhaps a third of a mile wide at this point. . . .

OCTOBER 29, WEDNESDAY. We have lain here now two days, getting a certain amount of supplies. Among others, Captain Lowry brought me in some forty horses, a mere drop in the bucket of my wants, but better than nothing: neither are the horses by any means such as we ought to have, though he says they are the best he could get. The whole army is still short of almost everything, and should we have a big fight would be at once reduced again to a state of inaction, and unable to follow it up. With the lack of discipline which pervades all our troops, it is impossible to make the men keep up to the mark unless they are fully supplied. Every man thinks that he is conferring a favour on the government by being here at all, and commences to pout and hang back so soon as government fails to furnish him with everything he is entitled to. I do not know that this can be remedied in so free a country. Discipline of any kind, save that of public opinion, is unknown in the country, and contrary to the whole education and general habit of our people. The officers too are little better than the men. If they have political influence, they need not fear what their superiors may do: vide the case of Captain Cothran, and hosts of others, who, dismissed by sentence of court martial,

are immediately reinstated by the President. The commanders of corps
are appointed by the President, really by Stanton, and cannot be removed by McClellan; while any other general officer, if relieved of his
command, has only to go to Washington and cry loudly against McClellan to be either reinstated or given a better position. As to shooting
deserters and cowards, whether men or officers, by court martial, that is out
of the question, as all such cases have to go to Washington and Mr. Lincoln always pardons them. An army to do really great things must be a
despotism, and entirely under the control of its commander, even to the
life of every man in it. If he abuses his power, let him answer for it with
his head. . . .

The Ninth Corps crossed the river yesterday, and the Reserve Artillery
today. The Sixth Corps is here with us; the Second and Fifth are to cross
at Harper's Ferry and go up the other side of the mountains. I have heard
nothing of Lee's whereabouts. This afternoon two citizens came up to
General Reynolds as we were standing in front of the tents, and introduced each other as reporters for *Times* and *Tribune,* and then asked
many questions as to our future movements; saying all the time that
they understood perfectly that it would not do to publish such information now; they only wanted it for their own guidance. I was delighted
to see the General receive them coldly, and after telling them that they
must apply to General Williams for such information, for he had none
of any kind to give them, turn his back and walk off.

❋ ❋ ❋

Wainwright's readiness to have cowards and deserters shot, and his hostility to press correspondents, shows that he had an imperfect grasp of the
conditions under which the American democracy had to wage war. In Prussia it would have been all very well to execute straggling soldiers, sleeping
sentries, and skulkers in battle in a rather sweeping fashion. But Lincoln
knew that if he allowed military commanders to begin shooting the boys of
the great volunteer army in this way, he would quickly hear from the parents of these troops; the Northern people would lose heart in the war. Discipline might have been better if more deserters had been shot; but some
highly unjust executions, as Walt Whitman reminds us, did take place.

Similarly, the American people had to be kept informed of the progress
of the war and the achievements and failures of the military leaders; and
the press was the logical instrument for this purpose. It showed immense
energy and devotion, its hundreds of reporters giving a far better contemporaneous account of the war than any previous conflict in history had
received. They ran the same perils in battle as the troops; some were killed,

some wounded, and some captured. General John F. Reynolds probably snubbed the correspondents of the New York *Times* and *Tribune* because he knew that both journals were sharply critical of McClellan and his sluggish movements. General Seth Williams, of course, was the adjutant general of the Army of the Potomac. The country was demanding progress in the war, and the army was not furnishing it. As Wainwright notes, the North had been greatly humiliated when J. E. B. Stuart with 1,800 hard-riding Southern cavalrymen made a daring raid October 10 into Pennsylvania, occupying Chambersburg for a night, and then sweeping back again into Virginia with prisoners, 1,200 fresh horses, and valuable information.

McClellan's army, crossing the Potomac at Harpers Ferry and Berlin, marched south to the Warrenton area in Virginia. He moved at so leisurely a pace that Lee was able to leave the Shenandoah, cross the Blue Ridge, and establish himself at Culpeper between McClellan and Richmond. It had never been certain that McClellan wished to force a battle; at the beginning of November wintry weather set in; and Lincoln gladly acted to remove the general.

* * *

FOUR MILES BEYOND LOVETTSVILLE, OCTOBER 30, THURSDAY. We broke camp and started across the pontoon bridge at an early hour this morning. The day was superb, the first of Indian summer; the air soft and balmy, the smoky mist hanging on the mountains, and the country rolling beautifully into rich knolls, all contributed to make the day's march more like a pleasure excursion than a part in the great tragedy of war. The view from the height above the bridge was a perfect picture. The still running water, with the long line of troops crossing it and then winding away into the country, was beautiful beyond my powers of description. We have left the limestone country, and are now in a high rolling grassy region, largely cleared and well watered. I have passed through no such farming region before, in either Virginia or Maryland, as we have here in Loudoun County. Although Lee's army marched through here there are many haystacks left, so that the horses are well supplied tonight. Everything is bought, the inhabitants being mostly loyal. We passed by the camps of the Ninth Corps around Lovettsville. General Burnside's headquarters were in the village, where I saw Colonel Richmond for a few minutes.

This part of Loudoun County is settled mostly by Quakers from Pennsylvania, nearly all of whom are good Union men. A Mr. Schooley, who has a fine farm adjoining the one on which we have our headquarters, is strongly loyal; at least his children are, which is a surer sign than a great display on his own part. His three daughters, fine buxom women, one of them really handsome, were on the stoop waving their handkerchiefs all day. Old Sanderson* could not resist such attractions; he had to dismount and make a call, which resulted in the General and most of us dining there. We had quite a good dinner and the warmest kind of a welcome, the girls seeming to enjoy it as much as any of us. After dinner the General had a game of grace sticks with the pretty one, but though he did manage to get the hoop over his head, his courage failed him. I do not believe she would have been very angry, had he persevered in getting his kiss.

OCTOBER 31, FRIDAY. Another fine day, during which we have lain in camp waiting for the other corps to move into their proper places. We called on our hosts of yesterday, and invited them to come over to headquarters in the evening for a tea drink; they having expressed a great longing for some good tea, which they say they have been without for a year. We got about half a dozen ladies altogether; Sanderson, as master of ceremonies, was untiring; had the office tent ornamented with flags, and from all our mess stores managed to make quite a decent spread of it. After tea we got a band up, and had some dancing and all the national airs we could think of. The girls enjoyed it amazingly, and were very patriotic. It will be quite an event in their lives.

It is just one year today since I arrived in Washington with my regiment, and really commenced my military life. When I look back upon it it is hard to realize all that has happened during that time. I little thought then that inside of the twelve months I should be colonel of the regiment, and holding so high a post as that I now occupy. I certainly have had no cause to complain of bad treatment; for I have found friends in those over me all the time, and without doing aught to gain their favour either, but simply working hard to perform my duty. All my intercourse with Barry and Hooker was of the pleasantest kind, and it promises to rest on the same footing with Hunt and Reynolds; but I cannot expect them to place the same confidence in me until after I have been tried in a fight.

NEAR PURCELLVILLE, NOVEMBER 1, SATURDAY. Another pleasant march to this place today, some fifteen miles, with fine roads and a beautiful country. We passed the Ninth Corps about halfway up, and stopped half an hour at Burnside's headquarters. General Willcox is commanding that corps, Burnside having charge of the two.† Our men march remarkably

---

* This was Major J. M. Sanderson, who had been one of the managers of the New York Hotel. He had been appointed a commissary of subsistence, a post he was well equipped to fill; O. R., Series I, Vol. II, 42, 45.

† Orlando Bolivar Willcox, a graduate of West Point (1847) and veteran of the Mexican War, had become an attorney in Michigan. As colonel of the First Michigan he was

well; much less straggling than there was on the Peninsula, owing to several reasons: mainly I suppose to the good roads, fine weather and open country; partially to the many and stringent orders McClellan has issued against it, and also in some measure to our having a younger and more active set of generals. Reynolds certainly is indefatigable, he looks after the whole corps on the march more closely than Hooker did after his division; he certainly will never be caught napping. So far, I am exceedingly pleased with him.

I find one advantage in being at corps instead of division headquarters; I know very much more of what is going on all over the army. I should judge that McClellan has now quite as large a force as he had at any time in front of Yorktown. . . .

NOVEMBER 2, SUNDAY.   For a wonder we are having a quiet Sunday, at a time when there is marching going on. It has been a most lovely day, clear and warm, with a soft gentle wind blowing and a sense of rest pervading all nature. We have a nice, clean camp on a good timothy sod, a few yards from the road, along which the Ninth Corps marched past us from about nine this morning until two in the afternoon. Tomorrow I suppose it will be our turn to move, while the Ninth rests. This is by far the best plan of marching when circumstances permit, as the men get a great deal more rest, and the roads do not block so badly. . . .

Everything so far has gone well, so far as our movements are concerned, but I find a terrible disease breaking out among the battery horses, which seems to be spreading very fast. The captains tell me that they first noticed it five days ago at Berlin, and already a large number in all the batteries are dead lame. The hoof cracks right around the crown, in some cases so badly that you can put your finger in between it and the crown. Should it spread much more we shall be helpless. General Ricketts has left the corps; politely relieved, by being placed in command at Berlin.* General Gibbon has his division. . . .

NEAR UNION, NOVEMBER 3, MONDAY.   The weather changed last night, and today has been right cold, cloudy and with a high wind. We did not start very early, and met many detentions on the way, owing to uncertainty about the roads. . . .

RECTOR TOWN, NOVEMBER 5, WEDNESDAY.   About fifteen miles march to

---

wounded and captured at Bull Run but soon exchanged. Promoted to be brigadier general, he commanded a division at South Mountain and Antietam and was to do valuable service with the Army of the Potomac until the end of the war.

* Brigadier General James Bremerton Ricketts, who had received his second wound at Antietam, was kept serving on commissions and courts-martial until the spring of 1864, when he took active command first of a division and then a corps in the Army of the Potomac.

this place today. The roads are still good, though more narrow, hilly and rough than farther down the valley. The country is fine, rich and quite well farmed. . . .

WARRENTON, NOVEMBER 6, THURSDAY. From Rector Town to Salem we had a rough march this morning through the hills, but from there on a good smooth road all the way. . . . Our corps is posted on the southwest side of the town on either side of the road to Warrenton Sulphur Springs, and about a mile from the centre of the town. The ground is high, falling off to the southwest gradually. The country beyond is quite open, and the road visible for a mile or two; a beautiful position. . . .

NOVEMBER 7, FRIDAY. A week ago summer appeared to be coming back to us: today one might easily fancy it midwinter. This morning I found the water in my tent coated with ice. At nine o'clock it commenced to snow, and continued to fall thick and fast until well on into the afternoon. Fortunately we are not moving today, and one can manage to keep tolerably warm in one's tent, by the aid of pans of hot charcoal, frequently renewed from the large campfires outside. This snowstorm may close our spell of cold weather, for it is too early yet for it to last so far south as this: but if we move tomorrow we shall have bad roads, I fear. We may remain here or hereabouts for several days, as the railroad is not open beyond Manassas much, and we must get our supplies that way now. We shall hardly get between Lee's main force and Richmond this time, though I doubt if he will be able to offer us much resistance this side of the Rapidan. Advancing from your base and opening your line of communication is a much slower process than falling back along that line and towards your base. . . .

We have no later papers than those of Tuesday, the day of the New York election, so do not know the result; rumour says that Seymour was chosen Governor.* A few days will now show whether they have been waiting until this election is over in order to remove McClellan.

---

* Horatio Seymour was elected Governor of New York by a majority of about 11,000 over General James S. Wadsworth, a Republican of radical leanings; and the New York Democrats won seventeen seats in the House of Representatives against fourteen taken by the Administration. Many elements had played a part in the election—high prices, high taxes, the draft, apprehension of Negro invasion of the labor market, and arbitrary arrests; but the principal cause of the Administration reverses in New York, New Jersey, Pennsylvania, and Ohio was the discouraging lack of success in the war effort.

SEVEN

BURNSIDE REPLACES McCLELLAN: FREDERICKSBURG

Lincoln's removal of McClellan was regrettable, and perhaps a mistake; but if so, it was a mistake which the general's faults and errors had made practically unavoidable. He had fought Antietam September 17, and many officers thought, like Wainwright, that he should have attacked the next morning and hotly pursued Lee's withdrawing army. But he did not move. Halleck demanded, Lincoln ordered, and the press beseeched him to advance and attack, but he lay immobile for six and a half weeks, or forty precious days. When he did move, it was with some idea that he might take his army to the Peninsula again if he found it impossible to get supplies forward beyond Culpeper by rail. Now, bidding his troops farewell, he returned to New Jersey to take no more part in military operations, but to play an ill-starred role in political affairs.

His successor, Ambrose E. Burnside, was popular and had a favorable record. He had won an important victory at Roanoke Island and New Bern. He had invented a breechloading carbine of superior quality and had manufactured it at Bristol, Rhode Island. If his management of McClellan's left wing at Antietam had been mediocre, he was credited with an earnest desire to renew the battle on the following day. A modest man, he had twice refused a proffer of the leadership of the Army of the Potomac. After all, Lincoln's range of choice among tested generals was small.

The new commander at once adopted a battle plan of his own. He decided to march his army east, seize Fredericksburg by throwing his troops across the Rappahannock by pontoon bridges at that town, and make it his base in an advance upon Richmond. This plan aroused uneasiness in the minds of Lincoln and Halleck. Could Burnside proceed with sufficient celerity to make sure of the possession of Fredericksburg before Lee's forces established strong positions there? Halleck finally sent Lincoln's authorization for the move, telegraphing, "he thinks that it will succeed if you move rapidly; otherwise not."

❀ ❀ ❀

NOVEMBER 8 [1862], SATURDAY.   The reports that Lincoln was only waiting for the New York election to be over before he again relieved General McClellan have proved to be only too true. Last night he received
the order again depriving him of his command, and directing him to
turn it over to General Burnside. I am inclined to think, however, that
Burnside is not just the man they want, and that they only use his popularity in the country to counter-balance McClellan's. I know that Burnside does not want the command, and think that before long it will be
turned over to Hooker or Meigs, as more pliable tools. The greatest indignation is expressed by everyone here, even those who have blamed
McClellan. Most say the change is a bad one, and the time chosen worse.
Yet they none of them can say who they would like to have in command
of this army, while any change just at this time will have the effect of
dampening the ardour of the men, and causing much delay, just as everything was going on so well. William reached here at two o'clock this
afternoon. He spent last night at McClellan's headquarters; says they
are all terribly blue there this morning. . . .

NOVEMBER 9, SUNDAY.   The disease among my battery horses, which first
broke out at Berlin, has got to be quite a serious affair. With some of
the horses the hoof is almost off; a few are attacked in more than one
foot, and can barely stand, much less can they march. The same disease
or some other attacks the horse in the mouth, which becomes quite
black and covered with pustules, while the tongue swells so that they
can hardly shut their mouths. I made an inspection through all the
batteries this morning, and found 315 horses attacked more or less, about
half of which are absolutely unserviceable. It seems to be spreading, and
is very rapid in its attacks. I cannot tell what we shall do if it continues
to spread.

Warrenton in the spring and summer (before the war) must have been
a really very pretty place. The country round is beautiful, the village
well built with a number of very nice villas around it; rather out of
order, though, just now as most of their negroes have run off. Among
these is the residence of "Extra Billy" Smith.* The inhabitants are intensely secessionist; several of the most prominent generals are from here,
and pretty much every able-bodied man in the place has gone into their

* William Smith, who had been a member of Congress 1841–43 and 1853–61, and a governor of Virginia 1846–49, rose to be brigadier general and major general on the Confederate side. He was again governor in 1864–65 and supervised the removal of the
administration to Lynchburg and Danville. He gained his nickname from the fact that
he established a line of mail and passenger coaches through Virginia, the Carolinas,
and Georgia early in the 1830's, and with each extension got an extra payment from
the government.

army. There are some 150 of their wounded still here from Bull Run fight. We have to issue them rations to keep them alive. I could not find that there was service in any of the churches today. The place must have had perhaps 1,500 inhabitants before the war.

NOVEMBER 10, MONDAY. McClellan took leave of this corps today; he had previously bid adieu to the others. About noon the whole corps except the pickets and guards was drawn up in rear of the camps of the Second and Third Divisions. Accompanied by General Reynolds and both their staffs, he rode slowly along the lines, the men all saluting as he passed. Such a sight I shall never see again. Not a word was spoken, no noisy demonstration of regret at losing him, but there was hardly a dry eye in the ranks. Very many of the men wept like children, while others could be seen gazing after him in mute grief, one may almost say despair, as a mourner looks down into the grave of a dearly loved friend. The General himself was quite overwhelmed, as well he might be, to see such affection and devotion testified towards him. Napoleon's farewell at Fontainbleau may have been more impressive—doubtless it was, for the French are great at scenic effect. But I could not have supposed there would be such a display of feeling from Americans. I do not know how the feeling was shown in the Second, Fifth, and Sixth Corps, but it must have been quite as strong as in this, which, except the Third Division, has only been under his command for two months.

After the review, the General passed an hour or two at our headquarters, and bade a personal farewell to all the officers who gathered there, of whom there must have been sixty or more. I remained near him the whole time, determined to see for myself just how he acted, and to hear just what he said. All on being introduced expressed their great regret at parting with him, some using expressions with regard to his removal which they had no right to use, and a few even going so far as to beg him to resist the order, and saying that the army would support him. These last he reproved gently but strongly. To everyone personally he expressed his high opinion of General Burnside, and begged them to transfer to him all the devotion and zeal they had ever shown for himself. Whatever might be their opinion of McClellan as a general, no one who saw and heard him today as I did could help pronouncing him a good and great man: great in soul if not in mind.

There were several European officers present, to whom the whole [affair] was utterly unintelligible. They repeatedly said: "I cannot understand you Americans; here we see a large army with officers and men devotedly attached to their commander, and yet they allow him to be taken from them without a remonstrance. Why don't the army march to Washington, and make the President reinstate him?" Doubtless that would have been the way were we French or Germans, but our people are naturally too law abiding. McClellan went directly from our camp to the cars. . . .

FAYETTEVILLE, NOVEMBER 12, WEDNESDAY. Today we moved to this place. . . . Almost immediately on leaving Warrenton we got into the pine country again, sandy and barren. This is about as desolate a looking region as one can well imagine. Burnside's headquarters were being moved up to near Warrenton, as we came through there. I saw General Hunt, who said that horses were expected up soon. General Hooker too was there, just come up from Washington. He looks well, and has been assigned to the Fifth Corps, instead of this one, General Porter being relieved on account of his friendship for McClellan, I suppose. On the whole I cannot say that I am sorry, for I think I shall like Reynolds quite as much, and have a good deal more respect for him. . . .

NOVEMBER 13, THURSDAY. Quite a mail came for me today, and papers down to Tuesday from New York. Why letters from New York should be nearly a week in reaching here I cannot see, the railroad being open to Warrenton Junction. Letters say that our snowstorm of last Friday extended to New York. All are full of Seymour's election. It seems to have been brought about by the solid, conservative men, and been meant more as a reproof to the radical tendencies of Mr. Lincoln, than as any sympathy for the Democratic party itself. They report everything as rising very rapidly in price, especially cotton goods of all kinds, including paper. . . .

NOVEMBER 14, FRIDAY. Have had a day of hard work and worry, on top of the worst return of my old fever since I left New York. On riding this morning over to the First Division I found the picket ropes of the batteries stripped of half their horses. Asking Captain Gerrish what he meant by it, he told me that General Doubleday had directed him to send down all his condemned horses by the men going for others this morning, and turn them in; he had accordingly sent off 140 of them. Here was a pretty kettle of fish: twenty-four guns at the front, with not four horses to a carriage to draw them in case of necessity. I at once saw General Doubleday, who corroborated Captain Gerrish's statement. As this brought me into direct conflict with a division commander, I could do nothing except report the case to General Reynolds. The General was mad enough, and sent me right off to Warrenton to get the old horses back if the new ones had not arrived. I went on the gallop, but got there too late. Lieutenant Hobbs, having them in charge, had already turned the horses in, and they had been shipped for Washington; neither had the others yet arrived. . . .

NOVEMBER 15, SATURDAY. Up to Warrenton again today to look after horses; managed to get some sixty or eighty altogether, but hardly a real good one among them. All were horses that had been condemned, and only about half cured. . . .

Burnside has made a new organization of the army into three "Grand Divisions" and a reserve, the commanders of which are to have all the powers as to interior matters which formerly rested in Army Headquarters. In other words, the Grand Division is the real corps, according to the European idea. This corps and the Sixth will form the left Grand Division, under General Franklin; the Second and Ninth Corps the right Grand Division under Sumner; and the Third and Fifth the Centre Grand Division under Hooker. . . .

Halleck is out with a letter, backed by another from Quartermaster General Meigs, with regard to the reports of delays in supplying this army after Antietam; the greater part of which letters are prevarications, if not downright lies. I *know* that this corps received no clothing whatever to speak of until within a week of our starting, and that all its requisitions have not yet been filled; that my batteries did not get a single horse from the quartermaster department nor receive one of their ordnance requisitions up to this time. Even now many of the horses want shoes. Halleck was here on Wednesday concocting the plan of the new campaign with Burnside.

NEAR MORRISVILLE, NOVEMBER 17, MONDAY.   Yesterday we lay quietly in camp, with a fine, moderately warm day. Today we commenced our change of base to Fredericksburg and Aquia Creek. This was not McClellan's plan, which, from what General Reynolds tells me, was to have pushed on at once as far as Culpeper and Madison Court House in hopes to cut Lee's army in two, before he could get it all concentrated behind Rapidan. General Reynolds has no doubt now that he would have succeeded in the plan, in which case the results might have been something very decisive. Now so much delay has been caused by the change of a commander that it is too late to do that, and we are going to try the Fredericksburg route, I suppose as a sort of compromise between McClellan's Peninsular route and Mr. Lincoln's overland. Well, if we succeed here and then push on we shall get right down to Cold Harbour again, on to the old ground of last June, and have the White House as our nearest base of supplies. The James still seems to me to be the proper line for an attack upon Richmond, but until they can give up their great fear for the safety of Washington, there is no hope of any commander being allowed to try that route.

Our march today has been a pleasant one; but through a most wretched country. Most of it deserves the name of pine barrens, very little is cleared, and that little is poor and sandy. The few houses are miserably poor, and the inhabitants literally "poor white trash." They have evidently suffered by the war, but it is equally evident that they have always been uneducated and slovenly. . . .

ACCOKEEK CREEK, NOVEMBER 18, TUESDAY. We left the direct road from Bealton to Falmouth, and bore off more to the northward, through rough byroads to this place, three miles from Stafford Court House. The weather and the country continues much the same as we had it yesterday, though we passed some two or three quite decent-looking houses. . . .

NOVEMBER 20, THURSDAY. We have not moved the last two days, but shall probably go as far as Brook's Station tomorrow. The delay is caused by the railroad not being open. I am told that so long ago as the 6th of October, McClellan wrote to Halleck requesting that the pier at Aquia Creek might be rebuilt; this railroad opened as far as possible, and supplies of all kinds, together with a pontoon and siege train be ready to send down here at once; in any case he should find it advisable to change from the Orange Railroad to this one: but not a thing was done. Perhaps it was because they meant to remove him, perhaps it was only another instance of the incompetence of the heads of all the departments at Washington. One thing is certain, that no steps whatever were taken towards it until after Halleck and Burnside had their interview at Warrenton a week ago. There is one other thing I cannot understand: why the bridges on this road, and the erections at Aquia Creek, should have been destroyed at all by our troops when they abandoned it last August. They could in no way be of the slightest benefit to the enemy, who, to be sure, would probably have destroyed them themselves; but they might not have done it, and any rate that was no reason why we should. As it is, this delay is likely to be fatal to our success here. . . .

BROOK'S STATION, NOVEMBER 22, SATURDAY. We moved to this place yesterday, where we have a very nice spot for our headquarters camp, and good open fields for the divisions to camp on. . . . The Sixth Corps lies at Stafford Court House, where are also Franklin's headquarters. . . . The rest of the army lies between here and Falmouth. We have wood and water in abundance here, and are close to a railroad station, beside being not very far from Aquia Creek landing itself; all of which are great advantages considering that we are likely to remain here a week or ten days if not longer. The weather is fine, and we are losing it all for lack of proper energy or will at Washington; had this road been restored and everything ready when we first arrived, we might now be south of the Rappahannock (which we cannot cross for want of pontoons) and ready to start for Richmond. . . .

NOVEMBER 24, MONDAY. Still at Brook's Station. I rode up to Burnside's headquarters today; about six miles from here on the road to Falmouth. . . . The country between here and headquarters is mostly wooded;

but there is some good land along the creek bottoms. The road is hilly and clayey, and so soon as it gets to be used much will be very bad. This soil washes as I never saw any other. The gullies worn on the roadsides in some steep descents are six or eight feet deep.

NOVEMBER 26, WEDNESDAY. Having got General Hunt's and General Reynold's verbal approval to the plan, I today wrote out a formal application to the former for permission to try the brigade organization in this corps: which I shall have copied and sent up tomorrow. In it I speak of the difficulties I have met with from counter-orders being given by the division generals; the impossibility of seeing that the regulations with regard to straggling and the packing of the carriages are carried out when the batteries are so scattered on the march; the great fatigue to the horses caused by the continual momentary halts of the infantry; my inability to look after the drill, discipline and internal management of them while in camp, owing to their being so widely scattered; the impossibility of my knowing where the reserve ammunition may be so long as it is carried with the division train over which I have no control; and the many difficulties attending the present system of supplying the batteries. I propose to consolidate all the batteries of a corps into one command, with its own quartermaster and commissary, under the corps chief of artillery. . . .

What the success of my application will be is very doubtful; I have not much confidence in it, but this will start the ball rolling, and others may take hold and urge it on afterward. The batteries are getting into fair condition now. We have most of our needed stores of all kinds, and the hoof disease among the horses has to a great extent disappeared.

NOVEMBER 27, THURSDAY. This is Thanksgiving Day in all the loyal states; here in camp it cannot be much observed, especially as we are having a heavy rain. We determined though a week ago to have a good dinner, if such could be got; and gave Major Sanderson carte blanche for our headquarters. The Major came fully up to his reputation as a caterer, and set out a really excellent dinner when one considers our situation, and destitution of proper cooking arrangements. His cook did himself great credit. We had the table spread in the office tent; the furniture of all the messes and the servants of all the officers put in requisition. . . .

Sanderson got his "Bill of Fare" up in style, not so long or varied as what he used to furnish at the New York Hotel; nor was the "Wine List" as extensive, being limited to champagne, which however was both good and abundant. The canvasback ducks were the "pièce de résistance," and they were equal to what could be got anywhere, cooked to a turn and served up hot. The soup, too, was quite a success; and boiled mutton is always our cook's strong point. I was fortunate enough to have in my private stores a bottle of sherry for the soup, and currant jelly for the ducks. But here is a copy:

BILL OF FARE

Fresh oysters, not on the shell.

Green turtle soup, a la tin can.

Leg of mutton, cut in capres.

Roast turkey, a la "Hard Tack," and cranberry sauce.

Sweet potatoes, aux cendres.

Haricots, farcis aux vents.

Riz, a la Dixie.

Pommes de terre, a la Smash.

Canvasback ducks, au feu d'enfer, and currant jelly.

Lobster salad, rather doubtful.

Mince pies, a l'essence de pommes.

Pumpkin pies, au New England rum.

Almonds—no raisins—apples.

Ginger, "hot in the mouth."

Fruit cake.

Coffee and whiskey

NOVEMBER 30, SUNDAY. Still at Brook's Station; it is now twelve days since the army arrived in these parts, and there are no indications of an advance. As McClellan is not in command, it is doubtless all right, and the delay is either a wise thing or else unavoidable. The papers tell us that the President "is determined to prosecute the war with renewed vigour." I only wish he would begin not by "renewing" but by instituting a little vigour, or system or knowledge of some kind, into the departments at Washington. McClellan's reorganization of the army a year ago did not begin high enough up; though I do not suppose he had power to change the heads of departments. In the adjutant-general's, the quartermaster's, and the ordnance departments there is a total inability manifested to take in the great increase in the army. . . . The commissary and medical departments are a great deal better managed; the latter especially has been wonderfully improved within the last few months.

The weather has grown somewhat cooler, but by no means actually cold yet. There has, too, been a good deal of rain the last week which makes us very thankful that we do not have to haul our stores any great distance. Our own camp is very comfortable; sheltered from the north winds; with a good sod under foot. Most of us too have got up small stoves in our tents. Many of the men have "logged up," so as to raise their shelter tents, and make a close hut. . . .

BROOK'S STATION, DECEMBER 3, WEDNESDAY. There is little to mark the days one from another as we lie here in a state of waiting: one is exactly like another, except perhaps in the state of the weather, or if I ride off somewhere. . . .

Yesterday I rode up to headquarters, and from there over to Falmouth and a little beyond. Burnside has moved his headquarters about half a mile nearer the river than they were before. General Hunt showed me Hooker's application for me, and his own endorsement, disapproving the transfer as I had requested him to. He had laid my brigade application before General Burnside, but without success. Burnside said that he was unwilling to make any changes in McClellan's organization; neither would he hold us out any hopes, although Hunt assured him that McClellan was intending to issue an order doing something of the kind, at the time he was dismissed. I did not care about my own plan being adopted; any other, which would have given me control of the artillery of the corps, would have suited me as well, or nearly so.

The village of Falmouth is a wretched straggling old place, very dirty and now deserted almost entirely. There have been mills of considerable size here; indeed, the buildings are still standing though they look as if they had not done much work for years. There is a broad dam across the river at this point, which (the river) I should think is 200 yards wide. I went a mile or two farther up to see Pettit's battery, which is in position on the heights. He was busy building works for his guns, and was making a beautiful job of it; they were laid out in a really scientific manner, and shew that he understood his business. His guns were in superb order, and he had made pendulum hausses long enough to get fifteen degrees of elevation. But his horses were wretched, uncleaned and uncared for; his camp dirty, and the men's tents stuck down just wherever it suited the occupants to put them. Pettit pointed out to me the position of the enemy's batteries on the other side, every one of which he had made himself as thoroughly acquainted with as he could by aid of a large and powerful glass. He says that his was the first battery to arrive here and that he had quite a little duel with those on the opposite side, driving them back from the river bank.

From what I can learn we are again indebted to the incapacity of General Sumner for not being in possession of Fredericksburg and the heights above it. The head of his column reached here the day after we left Fayetteville. At that time the enemy had not over 2,000 or 3,000 men on the opposite side, nor did they get any force there to speak of for at least three days after. He had no pontoons, it is true, and gives that as his reason for not crossing: but with such an army of mechanics as ours it is impossible that he could not find men among his 30,000 who were able to contrive and build a temporary bridge. Indeed, I am told that one of his officers offered to do it in a night. At any rate, the river can be forded near the dam, and with 30,000 men stone enough could be carried by hand to have raised a causeway to within a couple of feet of the surface. On the dam the water is only some six inches deep; and it is wide enough to push a narrow column across. Sumner is very much blamed for his not acting at once as the possession of the heights opposite would have saved us a fight at this point.

Now Lee is well entrenched along the hills above the town. Fredericksburg lies on a flat or bench of land some 40 feet above the level of the river, and perhaps a mile wide. The hills on which the enemy are entrenched rise 300 or 400 feet higher and make a quarter circle back of and above the town, reaching to the river about three miles up. Just below the town a small stream comes in through a deep gully; and below that again I could see a vast flat of apparently fine land with the range of hills running along its south side, but more broken, and lower than they are back of the town itself. The lay of the ground on this side of the river is identical in its general features with that on the other side, though more irregular, and both the first and second bench are proportionally lower. The land on this side is poor; a heavy clay, and washed into deep ravines. There is a large house standing on the river bank, known as the "Lacy house," which was and they say is still a very fine place. It is celebrated as having been at one time Washington's residence, I believe. Back of it on the high bank stands a new brick house, just built by a Mr. Phillips. It is in the cottage gothic style, and supplied with furnace, bathroom, and other luxuries unknown in Virginia generally. General Sumner has his headquarters there now. . . .

DECEMBER 7, SUNDAY.   Still at Brook's Station, ready to move for the last four days but waiting the final order to start. It was found that there was but this one road to the front from Stafford Court House without going a long way round, and as General Smith* is ranking corps commander, the Sixth had the right of way. They started at daylight on Thursday morning, and their rear guard passed here at noon today. What the trouble has been I do not know, but if it is going to take four whole days for one corps to march ten miles, I fear it will be a long time before we reach Richmond. Thursday the weather was fine, and unless stopped by other troops blocking the road, I can imagine no

* William F. Smith, who had been called "Baldy" since his West Point days although he had a fair supply of hair, had fought from First Manassas through the Seven Days and Antietam; he now commanded the Sixth Corps. Few officers were as able, but he was handicapped by a contentious personality.

reason why they should not have reached the river that day. It is well perhaps that they did not, as we should then have had to start on Friday, when the long delayed storm came on us with a vengeance. It commenced with a heavy rain, turning into snow towards night, and then clearing off cold, so that the snow still lies near an inch deep on the ground. I have no thermometer so cannot say exactly how cold it is or has been, but the snow has not melted at all today; and last night it creaked under the feet of the sentry in front of our tents in a way to show that the thermometer would have been somewhere down among the teens.

It is all very well for newspaper editors and correspondents to sit at home, and write about winter campaigns; neither do I doubt that such have taken place, but doubt if any ever were successful in such a country as this, and with so large an army. In Europe an army, whether moving through a friendly or hostile country, is almost always billeted in villages at night. To bivouac is a hardship not expected of them for more than two or three nights in succession. Our men may be said always to bivouac, their only tent covering being a small piece of thin canvas which can keep out no cold, and not more than half the rain; the same provision too is made for all the company officers, their only advantage being that each one has a whole shelter tent instead of half a one. In Europe magazines are formed as the army advances, the supplies being almost always found in the country. I certainly know of no instance where an army of much size had to get all the horse fodder even from a base scores of miles distant. With us not a thing is to be had in the country; on the contrary, hosts of the half-starved inhabitants look to our commissary for food and to keep them alive.

I asked our quartermaster how many waggons there are in this corps; he says 600. I think that there must be more, but even that number would make from 4,000 to 4,500 in the army, to give us the full supply of rations for the men, and the third allowance which our horses get. Add to these 1,000 ambulances and medical waggons, and quite as many artillery carriages; then move the whole over two or at most, occasionally three roads—which roads will for half the time be barely wide enough for two waggons to pass; never sufficiently broad for two to march abreast. The streams are very numerous, not large to be sure, but the banks on either side are low and marshy for a width of from 200 yards to half a mile. Any one of them it would require a whole day to make a new road over. There is another trouble with the roads here which I have not seen mentioned. The hills are very precipitous, so that the road is always carried up them by a thorough cut sometimes as much as twenty feet deep, and seldom wide enough for two waggons to pass. A stoppage in one of these cuts necessarily stops all behind. Now if all our officers and men knew as much as they ought to know, and worked as hard as they ought to work, no doubt all these difficulties could be overcome; but they are only human beings, not educated or disciplined to this business. . . .

DECEMBER 8, MONDAY. Still another day here. There seems to be a hitch somewhere, what it is I do not know. It is somewhat milder today. . . .

We get the papers very regularly and quickly here, and letters arrive in a shorter time than when we were up in Maryland. From New York they write me that there is a great deal of despondency felt among the merchants since McClellan's removal. The ravages of some of the rebel privateers, too, excite an immense amount of indignation against "Grandmother" Welles of the Navy Department. One of Burnside's aides, home for Thanksgiving, tells them that he expects to be within five miles of Richmond in twenty days. The newspapers are full of the President's message and the meeting of Congress. The first is very non-committal and wordy. In Congress the radicals are already beginning to raise the cry of traitor against every man who does not think as they do. The trial of General Fitz-John Porter for disobedience of orders and misbehaviour before the enemy is also exciting a great deal of talk. I have not read any of it, for it is as plain as the nose on a man's face that he will be found guilty whatever the evidence before the court may be. Had they dared to pursue the same course with McClellan, Porter would have escaped, but as they did not, they visit their anger on his friend. Some scapegoat, too, must be found for Pope's blunders. The Prince de Joinville is out with a pamphlet on this army, which tells a great many things, before unknown to the world generally, thus throwing a new light upon the Peninsular campaign.* He says a great many true things about the characteristics of this army, and is remarkably fair in his judgment of it generally. I have been as much surprised as he was to find a lack of energy almost universal among us, the last fault one would have expected among Americans.

Lieutenant-Colonel Warner of this regiment and Major Doull, Second New York Artillery, are announced in orders as inspectors of artillery for this army. General Hunt is out with a very strong order regarding the wasteful expenditure of ammunition, and directing that in future no officer will be excused in withdrawing his battery on the plea that he is out of ammunition. . . .

NEAR WHITE OAK CHURCH, DECEMBER 9, TUESDAY. We moved at last this

---

* The Prince de Joinville, son of Louis Philippe, had joined McClellan's army in September 1861, at the same time as two of his nephews—one of them being the Comte de Paris, later the ablest early historian of the war. McClellan appointed the nephews, the Comte and his younger brother, the Duc de Chartres, members of his staff. The pamphlet by the Prince de Joinville was now translated from the French by William Henry Hurlbert to make a 118-page volume, *The Army of the Potomac: Its Organization, Its Commander, and Its Campaign.*

morning, and a right cold day we have had of it for our march, which was a long one. The snow still lies on the ground. One quite large bay we could see was covered with ice, and I found the small streams frozen hard enough in places to bear my horse. But the sun was bright and the air bracing.

Our present camp, a mere temporary one, is about a half mile west from White Oak Church, on the Falmouth and Prince George Court House road. I do not know how far we are from the river, which is not in sight, and our orders are very strict to keep all hands on this side of the high land between us and it. This evening I received orders for five of my rifled batteries to report to Captain de Russy tomorrow evening at sunset; they are to move so as not to come within sight of the river until after dark, and report to de Russy at Pollock's Mills. As these batteries are to cover our crossing, it is plain that the crossing will not be made until day after tomorrow, and that it is likely to be somewhere near Pollock's Mills. Tomorrow I shall try to ride around there and examine the lay of the land. The batteries to report to de Russy are Reynolds, Hall, Thompson, Amsden, and Ricketts, twenty-two rifled three-inch guns in all.

Our corps will take over about 15,000 men; say 6,000 in First Division under Doubleday, 4,500 men in the Third Division under Meade, and 3,500 in the Second Division under Gibbon. . . .

DECEMBER 10, WEDNESDAY. We have a fine day for our preparations, not so cold, as it has been. We move tomorrow before daylight; the Sixth Corps is to have the advance at our crossing which is to be at Pollock's Mills, below Fredericksburg; while the rest of the army crosses at the town itself; so I hope this time we are to be the ones that will come in fresh and turn the tide of battle.

This morning I rode around by the river, where we are to cross, with Dr. Heard, who I find to be a most pleasant, gentlemanly companion. At "White Oak Church" we took a road which leads directly down to the river. The church is a very small building not bigger or more pretentious than one of our country school houses. There is considerable open ground between it and the heights this side the river, which is about two and one-half miles from the church by the road. The high ground on this side the river is broken by knolls, which at Pollock's Mills come quite close down to the bank. A good wide road runs along at the foot of these knolls. Just above the mill the first bank or bench spreads out to be from 200 to 300 yards wide; and is quite level. The heights behind it are mostly cleared, but without houses. On the other side of the river the first bench, a little higher than ours, spreads out into a fine plain a mile or more wide. The heights on that side seem to end about three miles down. We rode along up the river road for a couple of miles or so, and then turned up again by a road, a very bad one, which brought us out at general headquarters. . . .

* * *

Burnside had to get his pontoon bridges for crossing the Rappahannock sent down the Potomac from near Harpers Ferry and then taken by wagon to Falmouth, on the river bank opposite Fredericksburg. It was essential to make haste. If his army and the bridges arrived on the north bank of the Rappahannock together, quickly and stealthily, he could easily seize the town. If either were delayed so that Lee arrived first to fortify the south bank, he might be repulsed with heavy losses. And as Wainwright's diary has indicated, almost inexplicable delays did occur. Burnside had planned to occupy Fredericksburg, fill his large wagon trains with at least twelve days' provisions, and advance directly upon Richmond. But he completely failed in his first objective.

He had set the three Grand Divisions of his army on the march November 15 and 16, a magnificent array of some 127,000 men, with an ample supply of artillery attached to each division. General E. V. Sumner, leading the way, reached Falmouth on the 17th. General W. B. Franklin brought the Left Grand Division up to Stafford Court House, ten miles northeast of Fredericksburg, on the 18th. On the 19th Hooker's Center Grand Division arrived at Hartwood, not more than ten miles northwest of Fredericksburg. Sumner proposed to cross the river by fording it without waiting for pontoons, but Burnside forbade him to try—this decision being his first great mistake.

For the pontoons were preposterously delayed. Their movement was delayed by Halleck's confused orders, by carelessness about details, and by general confusion—the red-tape blundering of which Wainwright so repeatedly complained—so that they did not get to Aquia Creek until the 18th, and were not delivered on the Falmouth shore until the 25th. They were too late! By the 25th a large part of Lee's army under Longstreet had arrived at Fredericksburg, and the next day found the rest of it rapidly coming up. The weather turned bad, with the rain, cold, and snow described in the diary. Conditions by December 10 were highly unfavorable for an attack.

But Burnside knew that the country and the Administration expected him, with his 120,000 effectives and 312 guns facing Lee's force of 72,500 men, to make an effort. He did not pause to devise any real plan of battle. On the night of December 9–10 he laid about two-thirds of two pontoon bridges across the river in front of Fredericksburg and prepared to make a frontal assault. General Hunt had meanwhile placed forty rifled guns in a line along the river below Falmouth. Wainwright, who as a member of Franklin's Grand Division was expected to cross about a mile downstream from Fredericksburg, relates the sequel.

❊ ❊ ❊

BATTLE OF FREDERICKSBURG, DECEMBER 11, THURSDAY. Not very much progress made today; our bridge is down, and a division (I should think) of the Sixth Corps is on the other side, but Sumner has not been able so far to get his built. At the place where ours crosses I should think that there has been a flatboat ferry, as a kind of road leads down to the river bank on both sides. On the opposite side there is a flat of perhaps fifty acres below the bank and almost level with the river. Here the head of our bridge rests. A couple of hundred yards higher up the river there is a wooded ravine coming down to it, and on the bank directly over this ravine are two or three small houses with trees around them. . . . Ransom's and Simpson's batteries were posted just above the foot of the bridge to cover it from attack, and a very strong skirmish line with supports was stretched all along our bank. The rest of the troops were kept back on the high ground out of range of the rebel guns. The enemy did not bring any batteries down on to the plain, or indeed make any serious opposition to our crossing. The plain on their side was too open to give them protection, and had they brought any body of troops down upon it, they would have suffered terribly from our artillery. Their batteries back on the hill could not see our bridge, and only fired at a venture once in a while. . . .

Our headquarters tonight are on the high knolls above the bridge. I hear they have not been able to do anything above.

DECEMBER 12, FRIDAY. Everything here remained quiet until about noon. I rode up to the upper crossing to see how they were getting on. I found the bridge *not* built when I was there. Two light twelve-pounder six-gun batteries were firing on the houses low down near where the bridge head was to rest; one of them was firing solid shot at wooden houses! I suppose the captain had read in books that solid shot were used to destroy buildings, and had not common sense enough to distinguish the difference between those of wood, and those of brick or stone. On the high knolls a short distance above our crossing I found my old friends the Germans, with whom I had such a jolly New Year's Eve a year ago: they have seven large four and one-half inch guns in position, and some twenty-pounder Parrotts. The upper bridge was thrown soon after I was there. I hear that Major Doull, getting tired of reasoning, at last as a staff officer, in General Burnside's name, ordered a party across in boats. In twenty minutes we held the house which had detained the whole army a day and a half, and the bridge was quickly built with small loss.

So soon as both bridges were finished we all commenced crossing, the Sixth Corps going first. As the troops reached the plain the line was at once deployed, and advanced. This corps followed directly behind the Sixth forming on its left. Gibbon had the right of our line, and Doubleday the left. Each division was formed in three lines with its batteries in rear; those which had been sent to de Russy did not cross. The deployment was the most beautiful sight I have seen yet, something really like the movement of troops on the open battlefields of Europe. By sundown all were across, and our lines formed for the night. The Sixth Corps had advanced nearly or quite to the Bowling Green road, which runs parallel to the river, with their right resting on Deep Run. Our Second Division was in prolongation of the line of the Sixth Corps, but had not advanced to the road, a small ravine about one hundred yards this side of the road lying in their front. Meade and Doubleday lay at right angles to the road some two hundred yards below the Bernard house; Doubleday massed on the river bank.* I cannot understand why the rebs spent so few shot on us. The deployment on the open plain of 35,000 men certainly afforded a good mark; and, it seems to me, might have been made an ugly job.

We spent the night in Mr. Bernard's or Barnard's house. It is a splendid establishment, far superior to anything I have seen elsewhere in Virginia. The central building is some fifty feet square or more, with semi-circular wings running out on each side; the whole is of stone, and not only pretentious but realizing what it pretends to. The interior is handsomely finished, and has been well furnished, but most of the furniture has been removed. All of our headquarters staff, as also General Howe of the Sixth Corps and his staff,† occupied the drawing room. We had a good coal fire, and lots of light from candles in the handsome gilt candelabras. It seemed a sin to take possession of so handsome a drawing room; but we did not injure anything, and as I stretched my blankets on the fine Bruxelles carpet, and looked around at the handsome pictures and bright fire, I for once thanked my stars that I was a staff officer. Bernard himself is in the house. He is a bachelor

---

* All this was well downstream from Fredericksburg, on the left of the Union army, facing the Old Richmond Stage Road. Some maps identify the house mentioned by Wainwright as Burnett's not Bernard's.

† Albion Parris Howe, of Maine, West Point, 1841, now brigadier general and division commander, took part in many battles and became major general, but is best remembered as one of the guard of honor over Lincoln's body on the long funeral journey to Springfield.

between fifty and sixty, and lives here with his mistress in very considerable style: the mistress, though, has been sent away for safe keeping. So soon as our troops had possession of the house he was put in arrest, but representing himself to General Franklin as a good Union man, he released him. When Reynolds came over, however, who knew him of old, he clapped him under arrest again. Franklin and the corps commanders are occupying another part of the house. . . .

DECEMBER 13, SATURDAY. The fight commenced very early up on the right, and was heavy all the morning. About nine o'clock we commenced to move, swinging our line around, so that gradually the line of the Sixth Corps along the Bowling Green road was prolonged by nearly the whole of ours, while our extreme left always rested on the river. As I mentioned last night, our corps then lay on the hither side of a small ravine. This ravine begins almost directly in front of Bernard's house. . . . We found a pretty good road across it directly east of the Bernard house. Below the ravine is another large farm belonging to a Mr. Pratt, called "Smithfield," who has a good brick house on it, near the river. As Gibbon's division swung around on to the road, his left just came to a stone wall which I take to be the east boundary of Bernard's farm. Meade swung round on Gibbon's left, his line stretching to a farm road which runs from the front of Pratt's house straight to the Bowling Green road, and across it at right angles. As there is quite a little rise some one hundred yards in front of the road along here, both divisions advanced at once across the road, and up behind this crest. Some five hundred yards in front of this little crest runs the railroad to Richmond, parallel to the Bowling Green road. Just at this point, the ground slopes from us a little down to the railroad and then rises on the other side gradually to near the top of the crest, which is well wooded. The rebel line of troops, and batteries, was just in the edge of this wood, about 1,000 yards directly in front of where Meade was. In Gibbon's front the woods came nearer, say to within six hundred yards. . . . The enemy had no batteries immediately in front of either Meade or Gibbon, but quite a number to the right of Gibbon, and about a dozen guns to the left of Meade, so that they got a severe cross-fire on us here.

The first battery which I got into position was Hall's, Second Maine, six three-inch guns; I got it across the road and posted it on Gibbon's left. He had just come from across the river, and was moved over the ploughed ground so fast that his cannoneers could not keep up with the pieces. At one moment I had some fear of a repetition of "H" Company's performance at Williamsburg, especially as he had two horses killed while getting into·position. But men and officers all behaved splendidly, though with more of excitement than is well, and soon opened a severe fire in reply to the rebel battery about 1,600 yards off

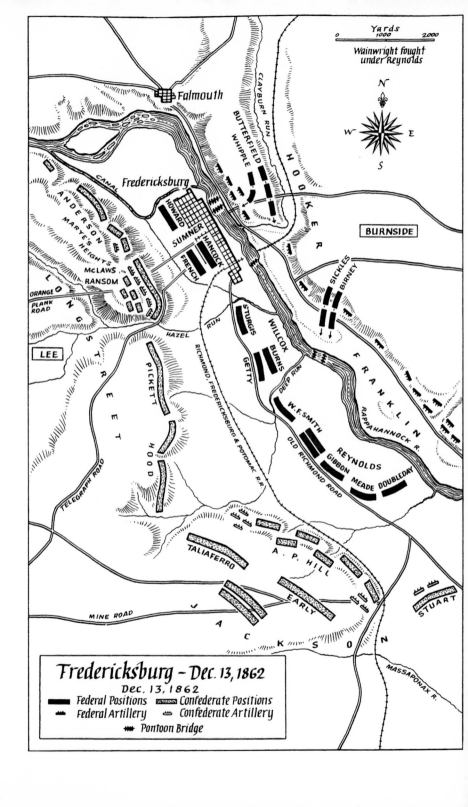

Fredericksburg – Dec. 13, 1862
Dec. 13, 1862
Federal Positions ▰▰ Confederate Positions
Federal Artillery ⚓ Confederate Artillery
〰〰 Pontoon Bridge

on his right front. The Sixth Corps batteries also opened on the enemy's
to our right. So soon as I had got Hall well going, I passed on to the
next field where Meade's batteries were just going in on his left.
Ransom I put on the right of the farm road leading from Pratt's
house and Cooper about one hundred yards to his left; they opened on
the enemy's guns to our left front. . . .

About noon General Reynolds told me that Meade was going to attack,
and directed me to shell the wood along our whole front. I at once
portioned the woods off between Hall, Ransom, Amsden and Cooper,
in all eighteen guns. The rebs soon replied, and their guns to our left
front taking Simpson in flank forced him to change front again; when
he was pushed up on a line with the other batteries. The firing was now
very sharp, the distance not being on an average over 1,000 yards. The
enemy soon again tried to enfilade us by getting six or eight guns in
the road (or behind), leading to Hamilton's directly on our left flank.
This sent me off to try and quiet them with some of Doubleday's
guns. . . .

* * *

Franklin's Grand Division on the Union left faced a powerful force of
Confederates under Stonewall Jackson and John Bell Hood, holding a
strong position on the ridge described by Wainwright, with the Richmond,
Fredericksburg, and Potomac Railroad in front of them, and woods in
front of the railway. The Southerners had an effective artillery force, part of
it under the command of the dashing Major John Pelham. Early on the
morning of December 13 Burnside sent Franklin a confused and con-
tradictory order, the most important parts of which were injunctions to
"keep your whole command in readiness to move at once," and to "send
out a division, at least," to seize if possible the heights occupied by the
enemy, "taking care to keep it well supported and its line of retreat open."
Franklin ordered Meade's division to make the attack on the ridge. His
troops formed on the Richmond Stage Road (called by Wainwright the
Bowling Green road), removing fences and bridging drains to let the
artillery cross. As it did so, it came under heavy fire from Confederate guns,
which Wainwright had to silence before Meade could advance.

Meade's attack was pressed with great gallantry. His first brigade drove
through the woods and across the railway, finally reaching and passing the
crest beyond. His second brigade met so sharp a fire from the flanks as it
climbed the ridge that only a small part of it established a position beyond
the crest. The third brigade accomplished little. The charge has been compared with that which Pickett later made at Gettysburg, and was quite as

spirited. Like Pickett's troops, those of Meade penetrated the enemy line
only to find themselves surrounded on three sides by fire, and were compelled to withdraw. Pickett's division lost three-quarters of its men, and
Meade's lost two-fifths. The troops of both Meade and Gibbon, in fact,
were so severely mauled that they retreated in disorder, heedless of officers
who tried to rally them. For this failure Franklin was harshly blamed,
though the real fault lay with Burnside. That Wainwright handled the
artillery with great effectiveness there can be no doubt.

The worst disaster on this tragic day meanwhile fell on the Union center,
where Sumner's Grand Division was thrown against the heights above
Fredericksburg. Six times did the troops charge, and six times they melted
away and receded under a murderous artillery and infantry fire. Of Hancock's 5,000 troops, who did the hardest fighting there, he lost 2,000.

✳ ✳ ✳

The rebel guns in the Hamilton Crossing road fell back some three
hundred yards to the southeast and again took position behind a fence
there. I now moved Gerrish's First New Hampshire Battery over the
ditch on to a small crest about halfway between the road and ravine, and
directed him against the same; as also Reynolds, who came up soon
after, giving me fourteen guns with a good oblique fire on them which
they could not stand long. Finding Captain Walcott looking for a position for his battery, I put him in on the right of the First Division
behind the Bowling Green road. This road along our front is very
nearly straight and about fifteen yards wide. The fence on either side is
made, like those in Devonshire, by throwing up an earthen bank about
two feet high, the dirt being here taken from the roadside. All along on
this bank are growing numerous cedars, and that on the north side is
farther raised by a wattle fence of a couple of feet; affording a most
complete screen though no other protection. I directed Captain Walcott
to cut embrasures in the wattle fence, and run his guns close up to the
bank, which he did. Just as his first gun was fired a Parrott shot came
through the fence, struck No. 1 at the second piece, cutting him right
through both thigh joints, and striking the axle of the piece, broke it and
exploded, killing one more man, and wounding three others.

All this took much less time to do than it has me to write it. For
some half an hour now the cannonading on both sides was very heavy.
I had now thirty-five guns in position and hotly engaged at short range,
and though there was no infantry fire the loss was quite severe. So soon
as the rebel guns were in a measure silenced, General Meade's division
charged the woods. I was still at the left of our line at that time, there

being most for me to attend to there, but from conversations since then with General Meade and others, am able to give some account of the charge. It was about ten or eleven o'clock when Burnside sent an order to Franklin pretty much in these words: "You will attack the enemy near Hamilton's house with one division, supported by one or more." Franklin shewed the order to Meade and directed him to make the attack, and Gibbon to advance in support. These were the two smallest divisions in Franklin's whole command. General Meade expostulated, saying that the mistake of Antietam was in one corps attacking at a time and here they were committing the same fault; that he had little over 4,000 men in his division, and that though he believed he could carry the heights he could not hold them. Franklin's only reply was, that is General Burnside's order. Meade accordingly went in with his division, directly in front of where it stood. His two leading brigades were in line, the third one in column, right in front, under General Jackson. This brigade, so soon as it had entered the wood, was to face to the left and sweep the crest to Hamilton's Crossing; which it did not do, General Jackson being killed on the railroad. . . . The other two brigades carried the crest, and passed through the woods into the opening beyond; when the men finding there were no other troops coming and that they were near a mile beyond our lines, turned around and came back. As they came out of the woods, the rebs again manned their guns and opened on them. General Meade says his loss is over one-quarter of his force.

General Gibbon, as I said, was to advance in support of Meade. It will be remembered that a stone wall perpendicular to their line divided the two divisions and that the woods extended down this wall much nearer to Gibbon that to Meade. Gibbon had his men in three lines, General Taylor's brigade composing the first. They were advanced slowly towards the wood at the time Meade attacked. Taylor (from whom I have this account) went to Gibbon and asked permission to fix bayonets and charge; but Gibbon would not let him, saying his orders were to advance in support of, not to charge with Meade. The rebels were hid by the wood and covered by a slight breastwork; thus protected, their fire was very severe while our men could do them but little harm. Taylor's brigade wilted under the fire until his men were all gone. Again he made the same request for the second line to charge; but Gibbon would not consent, and it was not until this brigade had pretty much disappeared also that he allowed Taylor to take the only one remaining and charge as he had requested. It was at once done, and the rebel work carried with some two hundred prisoners. Half the division had scattered or been shot, and Gibbon did not advance any distance into the wood. He withdrew his men as Meade fell back and, getting an ugly shot in the hand just at that time, turned over his command to Taylor and left the field. Apprised by the reopening of the rebel batteries and by their cheers that our men had been repulsed, I hastened once more to our extreme right. As I crossed the road, leading into the cornfield where Hall's battery was, I met General Gibbon coming out. As Gibbon's division advanced, he pushed Hall's battery forward to within three hundred yards of the woods, where I found him still holding his position, under a heavy fire from the rebel infantry, who had advanced from the wood, though his supports had fallen back. I at once ordered him back to his first position. . . .

About half an hour before sunset the enemy opened from all their batteries with vigour; which was replied to by ours with equal good will: darkness alone put an end to the conflict. After dark I withdrew all our batteries, by General Reynolds's order, to the north of the road. Shortly before this Sickles's division came up, and took position in the cornfield where Gibbon had been.

Thus ended our fight for the day. We had gained no ground, and had done but little to attempt it; the Sixth Corps had done nothing whatever, save a little skirmishing and keeping up a distant artillery fire. Meade had suffered very badly. Gibbon's division as well as his was much broken and scattered, so that stragglers covered the whole river bank under the ridge. The First Division had only been exposed to artillery fire, but had suffered unusually from it. Birney boasts that there was not a straggler with the Kearny badge. But General Reynolds collected several hundred of them, thinking by the red patch in their caps they were his stretcher bearers; and I myself routed near a dozen out from a ditch where they had hid under a small bridge. The batteries of the corps had suffered very severely in both men and horses. Hall had lost thirty horses, and was so reduced in both men and horses that he could make but three guns efficient. . . .

The day had been mild and misty, a heavy fog veiling everything until ten o'clock in the morning. We hear that they have met with even worse success on the right than ourselves, and with a fearful loss. Tonight we bivouac under the big chestnut trees in front of Bernard's house, as also do Generals Smith and Franklin. All my batteries are nearly out of ammunition. . . .

DECEMBER 14, SUNDAY.   Nothing was done today by this wing of the army; no advance made, save pushing our skirmish line out a little; the batteries have been but little engaged, only replying to the rebs when they opened, which they did with most vigour about half an hour before sundown again.

Meade's division and Gibbon's lay in reserve all day, reorganizing; that is, the infantry, for I find that General Reynolds pays but little respect to the division general's control of his artillery when it comes to the fight, and certainly has given me full swing. . . .

So soon as the fog lifted a little General Franklin rode around our lines for the first time. About eleven o'clock Burnside came over and examined them also, but nothing was done. To me the plan of attack here seems simple, but it would not be proper for me to make suggestions unasked. They may very possibly know more of the ground than I do; beside which, if my idea is at all feasible, it has doubtless suggested itself to some who are entitled to advise. This is what I should have done. The Massaponax Creek comes into the Rappahannock some six hundred yards below the extreme left of our skirmish line: from the river up to the crossing of the Bowling Green road it is not fordable, as we can see from the other side. There it bends around to the right somewhat as the railroad does, which crosses it a few miles beyond Hamilton's. All the land between the railroad and the creek appears to be cleared and level. I would have pushed out a good skirmish line with strong supports yesterday afternoon well down to the creek (the enemy only had a few sharpshooters on this ground), and then have examined my ground and marked just where my lines were to rest. Soon after dark the bridges should have been floated down to near where our left now rests; and by daylight I would have had the whole Grand Division ready to attack obliquely to the rebel right at Hamilton's house. With the two divisions of the Third Corps we have 40,000 men here, and over one hundred guns. Thirty guns would soon have silenced those of the enemy on the crest, and afterward have covered our right flank. As many more I would have had advance with the line in rear of its left flank, the ground here being all open; while the rest, with the aid of de Russy's, would have prevented their making any attack from the other bank of the Massaponax. I can see no reason why such an attack should not have succeeded in sweeping all the heights below the town if well seconded on the right where we have at least 40,000 more men. At any rate, I should like to have seen it tried, as it would have given a most glorious chance for our artillery to show what they could do.

The enemy kept up an intermittent fire of artillery all day. Every time it would break out on the left Reynolds would ride off with all of us (his staff), and remain on the lines until it was over. I suppose we made near a dozen of these trips around our lines during the day. On our return we always found Bayard and Smith sitting under the trees talking to Franklin.* . . .

About noon the enemy opened from a Whitworth gun away off below the Massaponax. Its bolts flew far into our lines, some of them travelling

* George Dashiell Bayard of New York, West Point, 1856, a cavalry officer, had been a brigadier general since April 1862.

at least three miles before they struck. Coming so far and directly down the length of the line, they caused quite a fright among some of the men at first, but I cannot learn that they did any harm. I saw three of them in succession strike within a few feet of the Fourteenth Brooklyn, who were lying down; one of which went directly through a knapsack, which its owner had only partially thrown off: the soldier was terribly frightened, but not hurt. This gun they had so well screened from the other side of the river that it could not be seen at all. Hall fired a number of shot at it, but without effect, which brought a curse from General Reynolds on the three-inch guns, and a wish for Parrotts. My prejudices being all the other way, I dismounted to try my own luck, and to see if I could still keep up my reputation as a cannon marksman, won in old militia times. The distance I estimated at about 2,700 yards; so great (and their gun being in a little clump of cedars) that I had to aim with my telescope. The very first shell flew and burst beautifully; the second went equally well and true, when they limbered up and cleared out. I was a little proud of my shooting, but much more of my favorite three-inch guns. . . .

DECEMBER 15, MONDAY.   Just such another day as yesterday. Nothing doing except to keep a sharp lookout on the enemy, and an occasional cannonade. Sickles's men fraternized with rebel pickets, and at one time I saw a large number from both sides sitting and talking at the neutral ground. Franklin put a stop to it, so soon as he found it out. . . .

As sundown General Reynolds informed me that we were to withdraw so soon as it was dark enough. About eight o'clock we commenced by sending off the troops and batteries lying in reserve. The night was cloudy and very dark, with a strong south wind blowing. . . .

NEAR WHITE OAK CHURCH, DECEMBER 16, TUESDAY.   We have moved our camp back nearly to where it was before we crossed; our tents are pitched in the middle of a dense grove of young pines which afford us capital shelter from the wind. The troops still lay on the hills towards the river, it not being yet fixed exactly where they are to go.

So soon as it was daylight this morning I rode down to the bridge; one had been removed, and they were just commencing to take up the other. As it grew lighter the rebs discovered that we had gone and pushed their skirmishers over the plain. It was an hour' after they had commenced to remove the last bridge before all our stragglers were got over in the boats. The last of them were jollily frightened, and no doubt some skulkers, who thought they had got into comfortable and safe quarters for the night, did not awake until it was too late to get away. The enemy did not offer us any hindrance in removing our boats, and before noon the whole river bank was again abandoned to the pickets.

While they were moving camp I rode around by Army Headquarters and found all my friends there safe and well. In a day or two when I get a chance for a quiet talk with Hunt and Patrick I shall be able to learn something about how things were managed on our right. Our total loss is now estimated at 15,000; a large number, considering that none were taken prisoners. The rest of the day was spent in writing letters, and resting; no one can tell how welcome a good dinner was, as also a bath and clean clothes. None of General Reynolds's staff were injured, though even the surgeon and commissary were always with him, and he exposed himself in the most reckless manner.

DECEMBER 18, THURSDAY. We have got a very nice headquarters camp here, except that the ground is somewhat wet; it is, too, a long way off from the troops of the corps, which have been ordered down towards Belle Plaine somewhere, though I doubt if their location is fixed for the winter, even if we do not make another attempt to progress towards Richmond. I do not like being so far off my batteries, for it is a day's journey for me to visit them all, and they cannot get to me without a good deal of trouble. The last two days I have been pushing forward their refitting, and trying to get from them the fullest kind of reports. I am anxious to send General Hunt a model in the last respect.

In thinking over our part of the fight, I feel exceedingly well satisfied with my batteries. I had them all except Leppien, Thompson, and Ricketts in what may be called hot places; and all, officers and men, behaved well. The only approach to shirking I saw was in the last New Hampshire and "G" Pennsylvania, but even there it was so slight as to be uncertain. Both these batteries left their posts without permission under the excuse of being out of ammunition; but the first had lost severely in men. . . .

The more I think of it, the more inclined I am to blame Franklin. It is a sore disappointment to me, for though I could not claim him as a personal friend, I have known him for years through William, and had been led by the opinions of officers who knew him in Mexico to look upon him as one of the most able men we have. He has been spoken of both in the army and in the papers as likely at some time to have command of this army; and I cannot understand why he should have allowed such a grand opportunity to place himself in a position to get it to escape him. It can only be accounted for on the supposition that his natural laziness has become too strong for him to conquer. I hear that he justifies himself on the explicitness of Burnside's order, "you will attack with *one* division." But, in the first place he knew that Burnside had not personally examined the point of attack, and could not judge accurately how strong a force it would require to carry it; second, a division is theoretically 12,000 men, but in an army like ours where regiments are not filled up, it may be of any number less than that. Meade had but 4,500. And third, Franklin commanded a wing of the army, and was entitled to use his own judgment in a case like this, which would have been sufficient reason had he failed; while success would probably have put him in Burnside's place almost at once. Generals Reynolds and Meade seem to me to have done everything within their power. The latter says that he got within sight of Lee's reserve ammunition train, and that had he had a real division, ten or twelve thousand men, he could have captured it all, and held the ground. This alone would have given us the victory in the end. But why not have put in the whole Grand Division at once? A small force of infantry, with our superabundance of artillery, could have covered their rear and secured the bridges; and what was the use of the 20,000 men of the Sixth Corps standing in line for near four days, a mile off from the enemy? Perhaps Burnside did not intend originally that we should attack at all. If so, it is singular that he should use one-half of his army to make a mere demonstration. But the more I think of it, the more provoked I get, so let us have done.

DECEMBER 21, SUNDAY. Have just finished my detailed report to General Hunt, a copy of which I will send to General Reynolds, for I mean so far as possible to do all that lies in my power to look upon Hunt as my actual commander, and the artillery as simply attached for service to the corps. The report gave me an excellent opportunity to show some of the bad workings of the present artillery system, especially in that the corps chief of artillery has no control over the extra ammunition. I might have gone farther and shown what blunders General Doubleday made, and some on Gibbon's part too. Meade, when Ransom went to him for orders, told him to go to me, that he had nothing to do with the artillery. If our division chiefs of artillery had more rank, and it was distinctly understood that they held their positions because they were supposed to be particularly well acquainted with their own arm of the service, so that the division commander would rely on their judgment and take their advice, it would be different. But as it is they do little more than look after their own battery, and do not dare to state their objections to anything their division commander may order. I might too have enlarged on the fact that batteries of all the divisions were posted with the First on Sunday and Monday, and that on Saturday the firing of the First Division batteries had but little to do with the movements of that division. . . .

We read all the accounts in the papers of the fight; none of them seems to lay the blame at Burnside's door. The radical papers are very quiet, labouring hard to make it out a victory. The others are very severe on the Administration; even the *Times* pitches into Halleck strongly. My letters are very despondent—the great loss of life appalls the people at home. In the army the effect has been, so far as I can see, to take all life out of it: it is not really demoralized, but every bit of the enthusiasm which was so marked as we came down through Loudoun County is gone. Very little is said about Burnside, but neither officers nor men have the slightest confidence in him. It is singular how plainly this is apparent, and yet I cannot point out how it is shown, unless it is by a universal distaste to talk about the future. General Reynolds is very different from Hooker, in that he never expresses an opinion about other officers. I can get nothing out of him, but now that my reports are all in shall ride around, and find out what I can. . . .

DECEMBER 25, THURSDAY. I want to apply for a leave of absence, so as to be at home for New Year's Day; indeed, I had some hopes of getting off yesterday, but had to wait until all my reports were in of ammunition expended, matériel lost, and so on, and now General Reynolds has been summoned up to Washington and I do not like to make my application until he gets back. Brigadier-General Wadsworth is in command of the corps during his absence. Wadsworth having been defeated in his efforts to be governor of New York gets the First Division as a balm. He commanded a brigade in it while McDowell had the division last winter, but has been in charge of Washington ever since, and has not seen any active service. I know nothing of his natural ability, but it ought to be very great, as he knew nothing of military matters before the war, is not a young man, and has had no experience in battle to entitle him to so high a position.* Doubleday has gone to the Third Division in place of General Meade, who has been assigned to command of the Fifth Corps, he and Reynolds having both been made major-generals. I am very sorry to lose General Meade from this corps, for I look upon him as one of our very best generals; but he certainly deserves the promotion, and will fill his new position well.

Mr. Lincoln is more flattering to this army when defeated than when victorious. He had not a word to say to it after South Mountain and Antietam, but now he hastens to tell us that "though not successful, the attempt was not an error, nor the failure other than an accident." Some say that Burnside did not want to attack at the time and place exactly, but that the orders from Washington were peremptory; which may account for Mr. Lincoln being so particular to tell us that the attempt was not an error. He also "congratulates us that the number of killed and wounded is comparatively so small." Compared with what, I

* James S. Wadsworth, who had commanded brigades early in the war, was indeed a man of great natural abilities, as his leadership in the Republican party indicated. Returning to the army as a division commander, he did excellent service before he was mortally wounded in the Wilderness fighting of 1864. His gallantry at Gettysburg attracted national attention.

wonder; with the loss of the enemy? Or with the advantages gained? Or with our losses in previous battles? The rebel loss cannot be much over a quarter what ours was; our advantages gained are an entire loss of confidence in our command! This army has never lost so heavily in killed and wounded before in any one battle, or series of engagements. Burnside himself is said to be very much cast down. As a man he has behaved beautifully, clearly and unreservedly at once taking himself all the responsibility of the battle. I wish that I could feel that he did as well as a general before and during the fight, but so far as I can learn he seems to want decision, and knowing his own wants, to take refuge in obstinacy, like all weak-minded people when they become conscious of their failure.

I learn that he kept his plan of attack so secret that even Hunt did not know exactly what it was to be until within twenty-four hours of the time the move commenced; that he did not consult at all with his corps commanders, if he did with those of his Grand Divisions. One consequence of this was that he knew nothing of the country opposite save what could be seen from this side. Reynolds, Patrick, and a number of intelligent field officers in this corps were in and around Fredericksburg for four months last summer, and knew every foot of the ground, and yet he did not even consult Patrick, who is on his own staff; the consequence of which was that his whole plan of attack had to be altered after his troops were across the river. It was intended to push up the river bank after getting across, and then to turn the heights at the point where they come quite close to the river, but on getting there they found their way barred by a canal.

Patrick tells me that had Burnside consulted him or allowed him to know anything as to what his plans were, he could have explained to him the exact lay of all that land. Finding the heights could not be turned, they were stormed directly up the face. Our men are said to have charged most gallantly a number of times, but did not reach the first main line of rebel works. Humphreys's division of entirely new troops quite rivalled the old Second Corps.* Our losses in these charges were fearful, for they all happened in a very short space of time. From what I can learn at Hunt's headquarters I had about all the artillery

---

* All military historians agree that no better fighting was done at Fredericksburg than that of the Third Division of the Fifth Corps under the veteran engineer officer Andrew Atkinson Humphreys, West Point, 1831, who later became Meade's Chief of Staff. He led a charge against Marye's Heights above the town that swept close to the stone wall sheltering the Confederate line before heavy losses brought it to a stand. Humphreys had one horse disabled and another killed under him. He survived until 1883 as one of the most distinguished engineers in America or, indeed, in the world.

fighting of the army, and the batteries on this corps front lost more men
and horses than all the others put together. . . .

* * *

Wainwright's animadversions upon Burnside were just, and his criticisms
are fairly stated. The general could have obtained excellent advice on both
topography and strategy from the subordinates whom Wainwright names,
and others as well. In fact, General Franklin, commanding the powerful
left wing, with more than half the strength of Burnside's splendid army,
strongly advised his leader on the night of December 12 to get two divisions
over the Rappahannock on his front during the night, and attack with
30,000 men at dawn the next morning. Such an attack would have had
great chance of success, for the Confederate right was not yet at full strength.
Burnside, states Franklin, promised the necessary orders but did not write
them. Instead, on the 13th he sent Franklin the confusing and limiting
instructions that brought about the belated attack by three brigades only,
while he launched Sumner's command in the frontal assault on enemy lines
above Fredericksburg, which broke down after so appalling a butchery.

It is a fact that the general had no plan. General Francis W. Palfrey
writes in his history of the battle: "It is a pitiful picture, but is probably a
true one, that Burnside passed the evening of the 12th riding about, not
quite at his wits' end, but very near it. As far as can be made out, he finally
came to the conclusion that he would attempt to do something, he did not
quite know what, with his left; and if he succeeded, to do something with
his right. . . . But bad and vague as the plan was, the orders issued were
worse and vaguer." Wainwright has criticized Franklin rather too harshly.
But he did deserve some criticism. Palfrey adds: "But while it is easy to
defend Franklin and impossible not to sympathize with him, it is not easy
to feel entirely satisfied with him. . . . Franklin might have done something more than he did, with the large force under his command, if he had
been impelled by the energy of the strongest natures."

Lincoln's statement on losses was certainly indefensible. On the Union
side 12,700 men were slain or wounded in a force of about 106,000; on
the Confederate side 5,300 out of 72,500. But Lincoln just after the battle
faced one of the most dangerous political crises of his Presidency. As a
storm of grief and anger swept the North, the radicals of the Senate made a
determined drive to force the moderate William Henry Seward out of the
Cabinet—in fact, to force a complete reorganization; and it required all
Lincoln's skill and determination to maintain control of the situation. He
was anxious to place a moderating hand on public discontent. After warn-

ing Burnside that he would fail unless he moved promptly, he had resolutely abstained from sending him any messages, much less orders. The responsibility for the defeat was Burnside's alone, and Wainwright errs in guessing at unwise Presidential directives. But Lincoln was ready to stand by Burnside until he could get another commander.

* * *

DECEMBER 28, SUNDAY.   I have got all my reports made at last, even to accounting for each round of ammunition expended, and every strap and priming that were lost. I think that General Hunt will be satisfied with the fullness and completeness of these detailed reports, as he says he is very much pleased with my general report which I accompanied with a rough map of all the ground occupied by our corps. My batteries, including Ricketts on this side of the river, and not counting Walcott, fired 5,782 rounds of ammunition: 3,986 rounds of three-inch, and 1,796 of twelve-pounder. Hall fired 1,100 rounds, the most of any battery; Stewart 192 rounds, much the least considering where he was placed. I estimate that one-quarter of the amount fired was thrown away by the excitement of officers and men. The loss of matériel is very small considering that Hall had two limber chests destroyed and a great deal of harness cut up, but nothing serviceable was left behind by any of the batteries. I feel very much pleased and well satisfied with the behaviour of the batteries and the part taken by the artillery of this corps all through the late fight.

General Reynolds has not yet returned from Washington and as he is now expected to be absent for several days yet, I must give up all idea of getting off home for New Year's Day. I have letters from home as late as Christmas evening. The hard times do not seem to have quite dried up the purses. There is a box on its way down here, which it is to be hoped will have better luck than some of my previous ones. . . . Our good cook though has gone, and we are temporarily getting on the best way we can with Sanderson's nigger "Ben." Sanderson means to try to get us a French cook from New York. I could not get one last summer, but he is so well known among them he may very likely have better luck. We have fixed up our camp here quite prettily, and as the weather is again moderate are very comfortable. . . .

DECEMBER 31, WEDNESDAY.   Today closes the year, and with it the first volume of my journal. Some 380 pages for fifteen months of life in active soldiering is not very much. I might easily have found incidents enough to double it, but I am a slow writer and most of such incidents occurred when I had but little time to make the notes from which this is drawn off. I think I have accomplished my object in the journal, which is to so fix the events of my soldiering in time and place, that I may easily recall them in years to come, should my life be spared. I do not expect that anyone else will ever see it.

On Monday I went over to see General Hooker; found him near Stoneman's Switch, on the Aquia Creek Railroad. He received me very pleasantly, and talked as wildly as ever in condemnation of everybody. I confess that I was able to sympathize with him more than ever before in a great deal of what he said. I did not, however, join in his vituperations, but only listened. He had nothing to say against McClellan this time, unless his saying that "McClellan was too good a man to command an army in this country" is considered to be against him. Once before he told Colonel Lamson that "McClellan had not enough of the devil in him." I am afraid there is a great deal of truth in this opinion, but it is one which rather tells against others than McClellan, and even if it does in any way militate against his qualities as a general, it exalts him as a man. So far as possible, Hooker is bound in honour not to speak against McClellan for he owes his promotion in the volunteer service, and his commission as brigadier-general in the regular army, to McClellan. I am sorry though that such considerations have but little influence with him. . . .

The monthly inspection reports from the division chiefs of artillery are rather more satisfactory than they were in November. Ransom's is the best, and gives a pretty fair statement as to the four batteries in that division: not putting them all as excellent, except his own as he did last month; but distinguishing somewhat. Cooper's battery he reports "excellent"; his own and Simpson's "good"; Amsden's "indifferent"; and Clark's ammunition train "bad." I am much inclined to think that this is about the order in which they ought to stand, but doubt Cooper being entitled to the term "excellent." Leppien's report is a mere statement as to the condition of the batteries in the way of supplies. Reynolds who now is chief of the First Division makes a pretty good report; he seems to be more willing to perform all the duties of division chief of artillery than any other I have yet had. All report the horses in very low condition; we have had no hay to speak of since we left Loudoun County, and the five days and nights spent in harness on the other side of the river was very hard on the poor beasts. The guns and carriages on the other hand are all reported in perfect order, and the supplies of ordnance stores complete or required for. In the rapidity with which the batteries have renewed their supply of ammunition, and made good all their losses, I can see that there is a great improvement over what it was after Antietam, and that I have not worked at them altogether to no purpose. This is part of my report to General Hunt.

----·-<∞>-·----

EIGHT

HOOKER REORGANIZES THE ARMY:
CAMP GAIETIES

As the year 1863 opened, the Army of the Potomac sorely needed two progressive steps: the appointment of a vigorous new commander, and comprehensive reorganization. Burnside showed a manful spirit when he wrote Halleck a letter assuming full blame for the Fredericksburg debacle: "The fact that I decided to move from Warrenton on this line, rather against the opinion of the President, Secretary of War, and yourself, and that you left the movement in my hands, without giving me orders, makes me responsible." Yet he then took a series of rash steps, which Wainwright in part chronicles, showing anew that he was unfit for high command. He decided on a movement up the Rappahannock to the fords above Fredericksburg, where he would cross the river and engage Lee again. When his principal subordinates protested to Lincoln that this advance might be ruinous, the President telegraphed Burnside: "I have good reason for saying that you must not make a general movement without letting me know of it." But Burnside still wished to march, and after receiving grudging approval from Halleck and Lincoln—the President writing, "be cautious"—he started the army forward on January 20. That night a tremendous storm set in which made the road impassable for artillery and pontoons, stalled the supply wagons, mired the ammunition trains, killed horses and mules, and halted the marching infantry in knee-deep mud. The army had to drag its way back to camp. Angered by the hostility of some of his principal subordinates, Burnside then on January 23 prepared orders dismissing Hooker and three other generals, and relieving Franklin and four others. At this point Lincoln decisively interfered. Calling Stanton and Halleck to the White House on January 25, he told them that he would immediately transfer the army from Burnside to Hooker.

Stanton and Halleck concurred with the removal of Burnside, but the selection of Hooker was the President's act alone. He might have been chosen at the time of McClellan's ouster but for his imperfect recovery from his wound, his violent utterances against "Little Mac," his position

below three senior corps commanders—Burnside, Sumner, and Franklin—
and the fact that both Stanton and Halleck opposed him. Now the army
and the public received the appointment well. But a number of generals,
like Wainwright, thought Hooker unfit for the place. Darius N. Couch,
Oliver Otis Howard, "Baldy" Smith, and Meade were all privately critical.

The way was now open for the much-needed reorganization. In fact, the
need was urgent and appalling. A consolidated report for the army on
January 31, 1863, showed 145,800 infantry, 14,000 cavalry, and 17,900
artillery present for duty, including 21,200 men in the Washington defenses. But Hooker told the War Department that when he took charge,
85,123 officers and men were absent without leave. With many units ill
clothed, ill fed, and ill sheltered, troop morale was at a low ebb.

* * *

WHITE OAK CHURCH, JANUARY 4, 1863, SUNDAY. The new year opens with
fine weather, all the threats of a storm having passed off without being
realized. Everything remains quiet as yet, though rumours of another attempt to drive Lee from Fredericksburg are so rife that there must be
something in them. What shape the new move will take I know nothing
of, for I make a point never to seek such information from those above
me, lest I receive a rebuff; nor do I think that they ought to make the
plans known to a single individual beyond those to whom the knowledge
is necessary for the perfect execution of the plan. As for the reported
plan of movements which generally circulates among those who ought
not to know, I never give it a second thought.

General Reynolds did not return until last evening. He has been before
the Committee on the Conduct of the War, and in consultation with the
authorities there. The General is not at all communicative, but it is
easy to see from what little he lets fall that he has a very low opinion
of the said committee, and of the manner in which they conduct their
examinations. . . .*

On the 1st I rode around to the old division and called on a few of
my old acquaintances there, also to see Patrick, from whom I learned
many things to confirm me in my opinion with regard to the late battle
across the river. On Friday I visited the camps of all the batteries. Most
of them were in quite good order; those of the First Division decidedly
the best. Stewart's example is a great thing for the other batteries there,
though they are still very far behind him in all their internal manage-

* Reynolds had already publicly stated that Franklin had read his orders too narrowly,
and that in his place he would have thrown Smith's corps in along with Reynolds's
own corps; an implied censure. See Edward J. Nichols, *Toward Gettysburg: A Biography
of General John F. Reynolds* (1958), 155, 156.

ment. He has got up most excellent huts for his men, some of them quite large, covered with old paulins and tent flies; now his men are at work putting up a stable for his horses. Most all of the batteries have got some sort of huts up for their men, as have also the infantry; still no orders have been issued putting the army into winter quarters yet. . . .

I was over at headquarters today for some time. I never before heard the authorities at Washington spoken of so severely; a number of officers have been up before the Committee on the War, and they all bring down the hardest stories as to the feeling towards this army on the part of both Stanton and Halleck. Having got rid of McClellan does not seem to satisfy them; they would have every man killed off that ever served under him. The speech of Halleck that "the army must go to Richmond, if every man had to go on crutches" is about the mildest of all those reported of him.

General Orders No. One, War Department, for this year, contains the President's abolition proclamation, declaring all the slaves free in those parts of the country held by the rebel armies. To my mind he is thus only doing all in his power to estrange the whole population of the Southern states, to turn into rebels those who have heretofore been Union men, and to still further embitter the feelings of all; while it will tend to divide the people of the Northern states and may make rebels of Maryland and Kentucky. Mr. Lincoln is said to have declared that the proclamation is no more than the Pope's Bull against the moon, and that practically it can work nothing; which is virtually admitting that it is issued to please the radicals.* What is to become of us with such a weak man at the head of our government, be he never so honest? —one who tries to be all things to all men, and turns off things of the most vital interest with a joke. . . .

JANUARY 8, THURSDAY.   Four days, I might say, of intense quiet. The rumours of a move here seem to have died out in a great measure, although the weather still continues fine and the roads most excellent for this country. It has been somewhat colder than it was last week, and at one time today it threatened snow, but did not amount to anything, only a few flakes falling. Meantime the news from the West is quite stirring. Rosecrans was more successful the second day at Stones River than the first, and although he pretty much used up his own army in doing it, he

---

* What Lincoln had said was that he did not wish to issue a proclamation if it were to be as impotent as the Pope's bull against the comet. But the Emancipation Proclamation outlawed slavery in all of eight states and the greater part of Virginia and Louisiana, so that as far as Union armies progressed in these areas slavery died. It also encouraged slaves to escape to the Union lines. And it irrevocably committed the United States to the early extirpation of slavery everywhere. Wainwright expressed the view of many conservative Democrats, but a host of Northerners rejoiced in the great liberating document.

has fairly driven Bragg out of Murfreesboro, and so freed east Tennessee to a great extent.* . . .

JANUARY 14, WEDNESDAY. Today I am resting, and shall attack (inspect) the Third Division tomorrow. The weather continues wonderfully fine, and today is so mild that we can keep our tents open and our fires down until dark. The natives say it is unusual to have such weather at this time; last year we were up to our eyes in mud at this time. The south wind now blowing may bring us up rain, which will quickly change the aspect of the country if it comes, and probably knock in the head the movement which is now evidently in contemplation, for we have just received orders to be ready to start tomorrow morning. There is a certain something though which makes me doubt if we get off quite so soon.

JANUARY 18, SUNDAY. I was right in thinking that we should not get off on Thursday. Before morning the order was countermanded, and the move put off until tomorrow morning; now it is again postponed, and it looks a little doubtful if we get started at all. The intention is to cross the river at Banks's Ford and so turn Lee's right; but he must know by this time that something is in prospect, and so be on his guard everywhere along the line. Even the New York papers plainly intimate that Burnside is about to make another attempt, though they do not announce it in so many words. Today we have a change in the weather. It is quite cool, but as the little rain we had is not enough to make the roads bad, the change is, if anything, an improvement for active operations, over the damp, warm, muggy atmosphere we have been having. Meantime the delay has enabled me to complete my inspections, and today I have written out all the reports in full, so that I am quite ready for whatever may turn up. . . .

JANUARY 19, MONDAY. We are now under orders to start tomorrow morning: part of the army moved today. Banks's Ford is our destination, so far as I can learn. I know that a number of batteries have started for that place, where they are to go into position to cover the crossing. I went over to Franklin's headquarters today. Both his staff and Smith's are talking outrageously, only repeating though, no doubt, the words of their generals. Burnside may be unfit to command this army; his present plan may be absurd, and failure certain; but his lieutenants have no right to say so to their subordinates. As it is, Franklin has talked so much and so loudly to this effect ever since the present move was decided on, that he has completely demoralized his whole command, and so rendered failure doubly sure. His conduct has been such that he cer-

* Wainwright spells the names of the general and the battle "Rosecrantz" and "Stone River." His Christmas boxes arrived on this date, "great bulky things enough to frighten one, especially when the limited transportation allowed in the army is remembered."

tainly deserves to be broken. Smith and they say Hooker are almost as bad. We shall soon see what we shall see. The weather continues very fine. . . .

ON THE MARCH, JANUARY 20, TUESDAY. We started off at sunrise this morning; meeting the divisions near the Pollock's Mill house, about one-half mile back of general headquarters. We crossed the railroad at Stoneman's Switch, and then struck off for Banks's Ford. The roads were not bad at any point, but we were much detained by other corps on the road; so that the head of our column did not reach this point (wherever it may be), until after dark. We of the staff got here just at dusk, and as it began to rain at that time we all busied ourselves to fix some sort of a cover of boughs, fearing that our waggons would not be up. They did reach us, however, about nine o'clock when we got some tents up, and a sort of supper.

The day has been a good one for marching, but our First Division had quite a distance to come, and the stoppages on the road have been very fatiguing to the men. We are here in the woods, which is about all I know of our whereabouts: they say that it is not more than three miles to the ford, and that the main road from Falmouth to Culpeper is only a little way from us; but it looked, in the dusk, as if we were lost in an endless wilderness. This rain is likely to close up the whole affair and send us wading homewards through the mud tomorrow, for it is falling very steady; a regular northeaster. On the march today the disaffection produced by Franklin's and others' talk was very evident. The whole army seems to know what they have said, and their speeches condemning the move were in the mouths of everyone.

❈ ❈ ❈

The army had now been started on the movement that was to become famous as Burnside's "mud march." The rain that Wainwright describes lasted thirty hours without cessation. "To understand the effect," writes Regis de Trobriand, "one must have lived in Virginia through a winter. The roads are nothing but dirt roads. The mud is not simply on the surface, but penetrates the ground to a great depth. It appears as though the water, after passing through a first bed of clay, soaked into some kind of earth without any consistency. As soon as the hardened crust on the surface is softened, everything is buried in a sticky paste mixed with liquid mud in which, with my own eyes, I have seen teams of mules buried. That was our condition on the 21st of January, 1863."

Wainwright had been busy for practically a week beginning January 11 in making a careful inspection of all the batteries of his corps; that is, Reynolds' First Corp⌐. He did this with characteristically strict attention to discipline. Nearly all officers, but especially those of rural and small-town background, he found, had two great faults—"a want of the habit of command and of thorough system." Wainwright scrutinized everything closely: the cleanliness of the camps, the character of the shelter given the horses, the grooming, the polish of the men's shoes, the condition of the company books and papers, the clothing even to the men's underwear. Nothing was ever perfectly right. He found one Maine battery in exquisite order, the artillerymen showing marvelous quickness and accuracy when he questioned them on tactics. "Still, there is always a screw loose somewhere; here I found the camp not regularly laid out, the men's quarters partly sunk in the bank, and consequently a large amount of sickness."

Out of his eleven batteries, Wainwright rated two as excellent, three as good, three as fair, two as indifferent, and one as bad. They encountered a rough test in the "mud march."

* * *

JANUARY 21, WEDNESDAY. This has been about as stormy a day as it is possible to get up: cold, with a high wind and heavy rain. Our men, who had arrived last night after dark and when the rain had already begun, had straggled very badly, and sought shelter under the thick pines. This morning they could neither be got into their ranks or even found. General [Nelson] Taylor told me that he could get but 1,800 men in line in the whole Second Division. Still Burnside would not give up the attempt until near night. About eight o'clock I rode down to where the crossing was to be. The batteries to cover it were most of them in position under charge of General R. O. Tyler, who commands the Artillery Reserve. A few pontoon boats were in the water, but many more were still struggling to get through the sea of mud down to the place of crossing. The teams, even when more than doubled, could do nothing, as the animals could get no foothold in the slough. Hundreds of men were then put on to drag ropes, but with very little better success; for their will was not in the work, and our discipline is not strict enough to make man do such work on such a day without the will. I went from there to Franklin's headquarters where I found him, Smith, and their staffs, in quite a comfortable camp; doing nothing to help things on, but grumbling and talking in a manner to do all the harm possible. They may be correct in their ideas as to the absurdity of Burnside's attempt, and in thinking that it can only lead to another slaughter pen; but however well convinced of it they may be, they have no right to express such opinions even to a single member of their own staffs. Franklin's position is high enough to justify him in protesting formally against the move to Burnside himself. If his protest was not heeded and he was still sure it could only lead to disaster, he should ask to be relieved. So long as he, or anyone else, holds a command, it is his duty to exert himself to the *utmost* to carry out the orders of his commander. His staff talks very freely about Franklin's having command of the army in Burnside's place. This failure will no doubt depose Burnside, but I cannot think so badly of Franklin as to suppose that he has been working for that object. Neither do I think he has any chance of succeeding to the command. He lost that at Fredericksburg; had he done as he might have there, there is not a doubt but what he would have got the place.

All the afternoon we lay in our tent, as uncomfortable as it was possible to be. The rain fell in torrents; everything was wet and nasty. We got a stove up which helped to dry us somewhat, and an old pack of cards killed off some of the time. But the ground was too muddy to unpack our waggons, and the rain would not allow any outdoor cooking so that coffee, hard tack, and sardines were pretty much all we could get to eat. Last night we slept four in the tent, and tonight we have to take five.

JANUARY 22, THURSDAY.   We have our headquarters tents pitched in the old place again tonight. Some cavalry have had their horses here during our absence, and have made the spot pretty dirty, but we shall probably move over nearer to our troops before long. It has not rained much today, but the roads have been incalculably bad. Still the fact that men, artillery, and pontoons could get miles, at least, on their way *from* the river shows that had they willed it the pontoons could have been got the short distance *to* the river yesterday. Some of them, though, are sunk so deep in the mud that they can only be got out by digging. A vast deal of the delay is caused by the ignorance of drivers and officers, a case of which I found in the Fifth Maine Battery this morning when I rode around to see that all had started. The battery waggon had sunk deep where it stood in park, and Lieutenant Whittier had a dozen horses on it trying to get it out for half an hour, but could not budge it. Seeing at once that the horses had no foothold in front of the carriage, I had it unlimbered and turned around by hand, so that when again limbered up the horses had fresh hard ground to pull from, when the regular team carried it off at once. . . .

JANUARY 25, SUNDAY.   The whole army has, I believe, got back to its old quarters at last. All Friday and yesterday men and teams were straggling in. . . .

The opinions among the men and regimental officers with regard to the late attempt are almost entirely against it. They do not want to make a winter campaign, and the slaughter of Fredericksburg has deprived them of all confidence in General Burnside, so that their minds were just in a state to be influenced by such talk as Franklin's. General

Hunt thinks that our chances of success were good had there been no disaffection in our own ranks, and I believe Reynolds thinks the same. For myself, I do not know enough of the matter to form an opinion of my own. Burnside is furious. He drew up an order dismissing Hooker from the service entirely, and relieving Franklin, Smith, and most of the Sixth Corps generals from their commands. Although the order was not issued, it is known all over the army, and causes great talk. I believe most of them deserved it. The newspapers are very severe on Franklin. His chances of promotion are now all gone; this affair, his behaviour at Fredericksburg, and his replies before the investigating committee have killed him entirely. . . .

The court martial order in the case of Fitz-John Porter is just out. He is found guilty of violation of the Ninth and Fifty-Second Articles of War, and cashiered in the most severe manner. The papers have been full of the trial, but I have not read the proceedings. From the manner of getting up the charges and of the formation of the court, I made up my mind at once that the case was to go against him. It was necessary for the Administration that it should: some scapegoat had to be found for the shortcomings of their pet, Pope, and in Porter they could hit a friend of McClellan at the same time. He may have been guilty of everything charged against him, or he may have been perfectly innocent, of this I know nothing; his condemnation was a foregone conclusion.*

Today I got a short leave of absence from General Franklin, or rather I got *ordered* up to Washington and New York on regimental business; no leaves being granted. . . .

NEW YORK, JANUARY 31, SATURDAY. I left camp on Monday morning; stopped in Washington long enough to draw my pay, and see C——, and reached here early on Tuesday morning. At the station near Falmouth I got into the car with General Hancock and introduced myself. The first thing I heard was that Burnside was relieved, and Hooker appointed to the command of the army in his place. Sumner and Franklin were also relieved. The appointment of "fighting Joe Hooker" to the command of the Army of the Potomac has given great satisfaction and raised great expectations in the civilian world; the papers are loud in his praise. I cannot say that my own expectations are so high. Hooker may have learned a great deal since I left him, but judging from what I saw, I do not think him much of a general in the higher branches of that position. His bravery is unquestioned, but he has not so far shown himself anything of a tactician,

* Wainwright's statement is highly unjust to the judges who tried Fitz-John Porter, who included General E. A. Hitchcock, Rufus King, James A. Garfield, James B. Ricketts, and Silas Casey—men who would never yield to political motives. General David Hunter presided over the court-martial. Long years afterward, a board of review was, however, to report in Porter's favor (1879).

and at Williamsburg he certainly did not appear to be master of the situation. One great quality I think he has, a good judgment of men to serve under him. I am asked on all sides here if he drinks. Though thrown in very close contact with him through six months, I never saw him when I thought him the worse for liquor. Indeed, I should say that his failing was more in the way of women than whiskey.

I found all my friends here at home well; and the warmest kind of a welcome for myself which has given me a most delightful week of it. But I have not succeeded so well in the regimental business which served as an excuse for my order. This was to induce Watts DePeyster to resign. He is in no way fitted for the position which has been forced upon him, and his ill health now would be a sufficient excuse for him to resign with honour. I urged it on him as strongly as I could, for I fear if he comes back into the field he will be dismissed by an examining board, if nothing worse happens; but it was of no avail. . . .

CAMP NEAR WHITE OAK CHURCH, FEBRUARY 6, FRIDAY.   Returned safely to camp today; found headquarters still in the old place (but about to move tomorrow), and so far from any fault being found that I had over-stayed my leave four days, surprise was expressed at my getting back so soon. . . .

There have been no changes in the camps of any of the troops during my absence. Just before I left Brigadier-General Robinson reported to the corps and was assigned to the Second Division.* Taylor was much provoked at it as he expected to retain that place, if Gibbon did not come back; he sent in his resignation at once, and went home in the same train that I went up by. It was pretty hard on Taylor to have a man thus put over him, for he is a first-rate officer, and though his commission as brigadier-general only dates from August, he has commanded a brigade since April last. I doubt very much if the change has been any improvement.

Among my orders I find Burnside's farewell and Hooker's inaugural. The former evidently found it hard work to know what to say; Hooker speaks with great confidence, and well, much less conceitedly than I feared he might. In forming his staff, Butterfield has been made chief. It is said that Hooker wanted General Stone, who has at last been found not to blame for the Balls Bluff disaster, and who is considered the best organizer in the army; but Secretary Stanton would not consent, and

* This was John Cleveland Robinson, who had studied at West Point, fought in the Mexican and Seminole Wars, and served in the expedition against the Mormons; a New Yorker. He was destined to command a division so effectively at Gettysburg that he has a statue there, to leave a leg at Spotsylvania, and to retire from the army with the rank of major general and with the Medal of Honor.

Major J. Watts DePeyster, mentioned above, had become commander of the artillery of the Second Division of the Sixth Corps, with two batteries under him.

Butterfield was taken as the second best man. I should think he would fill the post very well, provided he confined himself to the mere internal administration of the army and does not attempt to meddle in matters of strategy or grand tactics. There is one other danger too: coming out as colonel for a three-months' militia regiment, which by his indomitable energy and good common sense he made remarkable for its drill, discipline, and soldierly behaviour on the streets of Washington, Butterfield has been pushed forward faster than almost any other civilian who has not been an avowed political appointment; and there is great danger that his head has been turned, and he may believe himself a military genius, and so attempt to originate, instead of simply applying his good sense and energy to the carrying out of other people's ideas. The rest of Hooker's staff, except his personal aides, are the same that McClellan left. General Williams has been reinstated as adjutant-general.*. . .

Orders No. Three regulates leaves of absence: allowing two line officers from a regiment, one from a battery, and two enlisted men from every hundred present to be absent at a time. A most excellent order, though hardly liberal enough; even this small number of leaves will tend greatly to make all contented and amiable, especially if used with judgment in the selection of those allowed to go. Orders No. Six does away with the Grand Divisions (a blesssing), and announces the corps commanders as follows: First Reynolds; Second Couch; Third Sickles, temporarily; Fifth Meade; Sixth Sedgwick; Eleventh Sigel; and Twelfth Slocum. The Ninth Corps has been taken from this army and ordered out West; they are just leaving now. . . .

NEW CAMP, FEBRUARY 8, SUNDAY.   Yesterday we moved our headquarters camp to this place. It is on the left of the road between White Oak Church and Belle Plaine, about three miles from the former, and four or more from the latter place. The Third Division lies quite near to us; the First and Second are still from two to three miles off, but very much nearer than to our old camp. Sanderson picked out this spot for our camp, and has made a good selection: off from the road far enough not to be disturbed by passers, the tents are pitched under the brow of a hill, which, being crowned with small pines shuts off all the north wind. The office of the adjutant-general, a hospital tent, is pitched at the head of the street, and the other tents in two rows facing inward. On the left of the office tent as you come out of it are the adjutant-general's, General

---

* Daniel Butterfield of New York, a graduate of Union College, had led a militia regiment to Washington in the month of Bull Run, and gone rapidly up the ladder. He made a notable war record in first the Eastern and then the Western theater, was wounded at Gaines's Mill and Gettysburg, and became major general. But he is best remembered as composer of "Taps" and originator of the badges for identifying corps. Seth Williams remained Adjutant General of the Army of the Potomac under Hooker and Meade.

Reynolds's, the inspector's and aides's tents, five in all. On the other hand mine is the first, then Heard's, Bache's, Sanderson's, and Painter's; just our own mess, with our cook and dining tent behind Sanderson's, so that he can look after it, and our horses beyond that again. General Reynolds is not at all of the fancy order, so we shall probably have nothing better than our tents to live in all winter; still, we can be quite comfortable if the weather does not prove more than ordinarily cold. I have my tent pitched very carefully, so that it shuts snug, and at the same time is stretched perfectly true, which gives it the maximum of size. On the ground, after having it levelled, I have some two inches of small cedar boughs laid carefully, and over this a good piece of Brussels carpet. My table and desk set against the tent-pole at the head; my bedstead occupies one side; trunk and washstand the other; while a strong cord stretched from pole to pole answers to hang coats and towels on. But I pride myself most of all on my patent bath-tub. Just on the left of the tent-pole I sunk the ground for about three feet in width and running back say four feet; the front of this place is say three inches deep at the edge of the tent, where it empties into the outside gutter, running back to nothing. Over this I throw my India rubber blanket doubled, and with a sponge half the size of a bucket I can enjoy as good a bath as at home. The excavation is so very slight as hardly to be noticeable; it is just enough to raise the edges of the rubber, keep the water from running all over the tent, and to carry it outside. As I look around my little nest tonight I feel very snug and really comfortable. I know of no tent anywhere that looks so nice and inviting.

While the camp was being moved yesterday, I rode up to Army Headquarters, to report to General Hunt, and pay my respects to Hooker. Received a warm welcome from both. Hooker was in capital spirits, and, so far as I could judge, has agreeably disappointed the old officers at headquarters. I trust that he will do better than even his best friends expect, and as the President is said to have taken a great fancy to him, he may be better supported at Washington than any of his predecessors have been. Still, he has a big job on hand, and it requires a good deal of a man to fight and manoeuvre 100,000 men. General Hunt has become a complete convert to my plan of a brigade organization of the batteries in each corps, and has already urged it on Hooker, but without success. I tried my hand with the General, and brought up his promise to me when he applied for me as chief of artillery of his Grand Division; but with no better success. . . .

FEBRUARY 12, THURSDAY. The weather this week has been very mild, taking all the frost out of the ground. Tuesday was a complete April day, so soft and springlike in feeling, and with the bluebirds chirping up in the pines around our camp. They have made their appearance a good month earlier than they did last year over on the other side of the Potomac. Yesterday we had rain, and more is promised by tomorrow. But compared with a year ago, this winter has been dry and mild, comparatively free of mud.

My inspections are completed, and Whitney is copying out the reports to go up tomorrow. I have but ten batteries now: eighteen guns in First Division; twenty-two in the Second; and twelve in the Third. Our First Division is much the strongest now, though Patrick's old brigade has been taken away: for the Second Division has always been small, and the whole of the Pennsylvania Reserves are ordered up to Washington. All the batteries show more or less improvement over the last inspection, "F" Pennsylvania and "L" New York most decided; while none were in really bad order. The condition of the horses, though, was poor throughout, owing to short supplies of hay. I found them all looking much worse than they did a month ago, although they have had nothing to do. Captain Thompson returns but an average of twenty-seven and one-third ounces of hay per horse for each day's feed in January. Many of the oats, too, are musty, and the horses are falling off at such a rate that from fifty to one hundred (replacements) a month will be required to keep the batteries efficient, unless our quartermaster's department turns over a new leaf. I have forwarded full statements and complaints to both Generals Reynolds and Hunt, and hope to produce some good effect. . . .

FEBRUARY 16, MONDAY. More rain has made the roads very muddy. Still, they are not nearly so bad as they were at this time last year, and as there are no fences left in this part of the country while the woods are rapidly disappearing, one can pretty much always pick out a tolerably good track across country. . . .

Hooker seems to be gaining the confidence of his generals by degrees. Many of his orders are good, but he is rather imposing upon us by the number of reports he calls for. My communications with regard to hay have at least raised a breeze in the quartermaster's department: the twenty-seven ounces per horse impressed Hooker, and he stirred Ingalls up with a long pole.* Complaints must be put in a shape to strike; the statement that so many tons of hay were issued to each battery in the month of December had no effect, but talking of ounces opens their eyes. We are promised an improvement, which cannot come too soon. . . .

Foster's move on the coast has been a failure; some say old Hunter was

* Rufus Ingalls of Maine, West Point, 1843, was Chief Quartermaster of the Army of the Potomac from July 1862 to June 1864, and as such always a figure of controversy. Of his efficiency, however, there was no question. McClellan in his *Own Story* pays tribute to his "remarkable skill and energy," and Colonel Theodore Lyman in *Meade's Headquarters* says that he handled his huge army trains as if they were perambulators on a smooth sidewalk.

the cause. Burnside, with the Ninth Corps, is consequently detained from going out west. Meanwhile the Administration, with its good, honest, *weak* President and rascally Cabinet, is every day sinking deeper into the clutches of the radicals.

General Wadsworth returned today from a little expedition down the neck as far as Westmoreland Court House. They did not find any body of rebels there, but picked up some eight or ten stragglers, a small lot of contraband goods, and a mail from Richmond. They also brought in about a hundred horses and mules, of very little value, and were followed by a goodly number of contrabands. Wadsworth is one of the nervous sort, who must be doing something all the time which will show. Quiet, unostentatious preparation he does not appreciate.*

I have been hard at work on my regimental monthly returns, and expect now to get some of them off soon. The number of returns called for from headquarters together with my regimental business make it rather heavy work without an adjutant, so I have made another effort to get Rumsey out of the regiment. Captain Spratt has been made lieutenant-colonel of the Tenth New York Heavy Artillery: have recommended Mink to fill his place. I have also sent up the name of Sergeant D. L. Smith of "E" Company for a second lieutenancy. Smith was most highly spoken of by Barry, and Ayres at Lee's Mills, for his bravery in quenching the fire in an ammunition chest, blown open by one of the enemy's shells. Captain Cowan, in whose battery he is now serving,† speaks of him as a most industrious, conscientious, and religious man. I had him over here, and was rather disappointed in not finding him bright, but it may be diffidence, as he says himself that he doubts his capacity to be an officer. So soon as I get some of these monthly returns off, I shall try what can be done towards straightening out "E" Company: and getting some at least of the men back.

FEBRUARY 19, THURSDAY.   On Tuesday we got the heaviest snowstorm of the season. Yesterday morning it lay nearly six inches deep over the

* Brigadier General John B. Foster, a Maine man who had graduated at West Point in 1846 and had at once distinguished himself in Mexico, had helped capture Roanoke Island and New Bern early in 1862. He was now commanding the Department of North Carolina, and undertook several local operations of some note. James S. Wadsworth, who had succeeded Abner Doubleday, went out on repeated expeditions to repair the lack of forage noted by Wainwright. As a strong antislavery man, he rejoiced to bring back Negroes, whose liberation Wainwright did not like.

† These men were Captain Joseph Spratt, originally of the First New York Light Artillery; Brigadier General Romeyn B. Ayres, who commended Smith; and Major Andrew Cowan, originally of the First New York Independent Battery. Lieutenant Charles E. Mink was getting the recognition he so well earned. Major Alexander Doull, mentioned below, was Hunt's capable inspector of artillery.

whole country, but it finished off with rain, which carried off most of the snow, and turned the rest into mud. . . .

Tomorrow I have to go over to Stoneman's Switch, some ten miles, being ordered on a board "to examine and report upon a plan for the organization of Reserve Ammunition trains for Artillery and Infantry which has been presented by Major Doull, Second New York Artillery." By a report I made yesterday, I find that there are but 817 men present with my ten batteries, belonging to them, and 362 attached infantry. The batteries need 480 recruits to fill them up on the present basis for six guns each, even if none of the 173 men reported absent are dropped. The chances of getting any recruits are very small. Several of the batteries have had men off all winter without securing a single one.

One of Mary's long letters came tonight full of all the goings-on in New York. She is more than good to me; I know not what I should do without her letters, shut off as we are from all intercourse with society. New York seems to be more wild with gaiety than ever; money is worth nothing a bushel, and "shoddy" reigns supreme. These letters are even more than usually welcome just now as we are temporarily cut off from the newspapers, owing to the permits of our newsboys being stopped, they having been found smuggling whiskey into the corps. . . .

FEBRUARY 22, SUNDAY. On Friday I went over to Stoneman's Switch. The board consisted of General Griffin, Major G. L. Andrews of the Seventeenth Infantry, and myself. Doull's plan for carrying the reserve ammunition is essentially the French system, namely in caissons. Griffin was as overbearing and supercilious as usual;* he had examined the plan, and did not approve it (having one of his own in fact); consequently there was no more to say on the matter. Major Andrews and myself did manage, however, to give Doull a hearing. I was very much disgusted with Griffin, but as we all agreed in our conclusion, did not think it worth while to make a fuss. My objections to the change are that it would require more men and more horses than our present plan, the two things which we are most short of already.

Sanderson got back from his leave yesterday, and brought a French cook with him. My man John, too, has come back with a lot of convalescents. He managed, I suspect, to pass himself off as a soldier, and so avoid all expense, even drawing a complete suit of new clothing. I asked no questions and consequently was told no lies; which would most probably have been all I should have got, had I attempted to investigate

---

* Charles Griffin of Ohio, a West Pointer of the class of 1847, was noted for his gruff and choleric temper, and readiness to take offense. He commanded at this time the First Division of the Fifth Corps. Later he fought in all the important battles of the Army of the Potomac, becoming a major general and helping supervise the terms of surrender at Appomattox.

matters. John Brown, Sanderson's contraband, is to be waiter for the mess now, so that we can have things decent and live something like gentlemen if our cook turns out good for anything. . . .

FEBRUARY 28, SATURDAY. The month has closed with what may pass for a stormy week. At least we had a heavy snowstorm at the commencement and several rains since, all of which have contributed to make the roads pretty bad. The winter is now nominally over, and the much talked of winter campaign not yet begun. Compared with last year, the weather has been fine' and the roads passable; this army is about as strong in numbers, while officers and men are infinitely better acquainted with their duties. McClellan, that "slow coach," that "over-cautious general," that "lukewarm patriot," has been removed over four months; and what have we gained under the new regime? How much progress have we made since his removal? And how much more brilliant has the campaign of this winter been, than was that of a year ago? Twenty thousand more men lost is about all the difference; nor is there now much more prospect of an early move this spring. . . . Vicksburg is not taken, nor anywhere near it; nor Charleston either for that matter, although Hunter has proved himself radical enough to suit the most extreme, and great talk is made about his negro regiments. Congress is speechifying and introducing resolutions of the most violent order. I trust we shall not get quite to rival the French Assemblée under Robespierre. The country I judge is very desponding, though many try to talk loud in order to keep their own courage up. In our army everything is very quiet. Since ten days ago Stuart tried to make a raid around our rear, and did stir up our cavalry pretty well up by Hartwood Church; but we hardly heard of it at all down here, and it did not amount to anything nearly so much as what the newspapers try to make it out.

I received a sort of left-handed compliment the other day from General Hunt, in a note concerning the inspections made some ten days since. He says, "None of the batteries under your command are reported in *bad* order; the only corps in the army so reported. Fifth Maine, 'L' New York, and 'F' Pennsylvania are the best." I was rather nonplused by the last part of it, but find that the General was particularly pleased at there being regular recitations held in these three batteries. He tells me that but one other battery in the army has had them. I was enough pleased with the compliment, such as it was, to send copies of the General's note to all the batteries, which I backed with an order, or as much of one as I have power to give, stirring them all up to new exertions. . . .

Efforts are to be made to recruit up the old regiments to their maximum, and I have been requested to recommend officers and sergeants from the various batteries of mine to go on recruiting service. I doubt if it will amount to anything. Still it may, as Congress is likely to pass the law for a draft now before it. Could a regular system of drafting once be organized and fully enforced, it would be infinitely better than this depending on volunteers. Our numbers would then be certain, good men would be secured, and they would, or at least could, be assigned where they would be most useful. Congress has already made one mistake, in calling it a "conscription" law. The word is anti-Republican, and will make the act very unpopular.

Our mess is now running very nicely. Our French cook gives us an excellent soup every day; his Juliennes, made with desiccated vegetables, are almost equal to Delmonicos. Sanderson is making arrangements to send his clerk up to Washington about once a fortnight, when he will bring down with him poultry, game, and so on, and we expect to live like fighting cocks so long as we remain in our present quarters. Through all the storms of the last week I have been very comfortable in my tent: it is perfectly dry, and so well pitched that all draughts are shut out. The other officers think me very particular and pokey, but they none of them manage to be so comfortable. We have made arrangements with the mail agent to supply us with newspapers so that the *Herald* is in my tent every day when I return from dinner. Take it altogether the *Herald* is about the best paper now, and the least *un*reliable in its war news, though half of what it publishes is not true.

MARCH 4, WEDNESDAY. The first day of spring was worthy of the name, clear and warm, with a strong, drying wind from the southwest. The snow has all gone, and the roads are really drying up; the high wind to-day must have helped greatly, though it has made it very disagreeable getting about. The whole winter has passed with hardly one day in which it has been uncomfortable under canvas and only three or four when a topcoat was needed. . . .

I think that some improvement in the army is beginning to result from Hooker's orders; not much as yet perhaps, but still a little. We have received an order today, No. Eighteen, which will create quite a stir; it is founded on the inspection reports of last month. It specifies certain regiments and batteries as having "earned high commendations from the inspecting officers," and certain others as decidedly in bad order. The first have the number of leaves of absence allowed them increased to three in the hundred, while the others are cut off entirely. . . .

My returns of horses show the complement for the ten batteries to be 1,088; on hand 863 serviceable, and 84 unserviceable, total 947; 225 horses needed. All the horses are looking far from as well they ought to, those we have drawn this winter being wretchedly poor. A very ugly disease has also broken out among them, a violent distemper or lung fever, quite contagious and almost as bad as glanders. . . .

✳ ✳ ✳

Hooker had done a remarkable work in reorganizing the Army of the Potomac, improving its discipline, and raising its morale. When he took command, its health, its spirits, its confidence in its chiefs, and its devotion to the national cause were all at a low ebb. Carl Schurz reported to Lincoln that he had heard officers and privates declaring that they expected to be defeated anyhow, that all their sufferings and losses went for nothing, and that they might as well go home. The sickness rate was horrifying, and men were actually dying of scurvy. With the roll of absentees at the 85,000 mark, desertions continued at an estimated rate of two hundred a day.

Abandoning Burnside's four grand divisions, Hooker regrouped the troops into the corps enumerated by Wainwright above; and five of the corps commanders, John F. Reynolds, Darius N. Couch, George Gordon Meade, John Sedgwick, and Henry W. Slocum, were capable officers. Not so much could be said for Daniel Sickles or Franz Sigel, but Sigel was soon relieved in favor of O. O. Howard, a West Pointer of thirty-two who won the sobriquet of "the Christian General" because he never drank, smoked, or swore. Hooker kept the troops busy with drills, reviews, and inspections, which bettered their tactics and their dispositions alike. He concentrated George Stoneman's cavalry into a single corps of about 10,000 men, a marked improvement over the old distribution among divisions. He also let it be known that the artillery was to be considered a separate corps though, as Wainwright states, he neglected to regroup and re-officer it. Perhaps his greatest error was to reduce the authority of his chief of artillery, Henry J. Hunt, who became simply an advisory officer.

Meanwhile the general increased the quantity of food and improved its quality, seeing that the men got fresh bread twice a week, good beef, and ample supplies of fresh vegetables. He built new hospitals and raised the efficiency of the old ones. By frequent furloughs to those who had earned them, and by allowing small festivities, he produced a far more cheerful temper among the men. Army equipment was bettered. New recruits came in, many of them full of zeal. As General T. W. Hyde of Maine says in *Following the Greek Cross*, a history of the Sixth Corps, by the time that spring brought drying roads, "the discipline and morale of the army were about perfect, confidence in Hooker was unbounded, and when we moved out of our dismantled winter homes, we felt that the war was going to be ended this time."

* * *

MARCH 8, SUNDAY. It is just one year today, counting by Sundays, since the "rebs" cleared out from Shipping Point opposite our then camp at

Budd's Ferry. On that day a hundred men of the First Massachusetts crossed the river and visited the abandoned camps. Today the First Massachusetts is encamped within twenty-five miles of that spot; having advanced just that distance on the road to Richmond in one year! . . .

In yesterday's paper is a list of nominations to major and brigadier-generalcies, sent in to the President for confirmation by the Senate. Reynolds and Meade are both among the first, but Sickles and others of that ilk are also in the list. Of those recommended as brigadier-generals some are excellent, and others miserable. What has become of the act of Congress requiring aspiring generals to have distinguished themselves in the field? Mr. Lincoln would have hard work to designate the place and time in which some of his candidates won their laurels. General Reynolds returned today. The enemy have fairly got at least one privateer afloat. The capture of the ship *Jacob Bell* by the *Florida* has made a great stir in New York, sending marine insurance away up, and scaring our shipowners half out of their boots. A swift steamer can no doubt do a vast amount of harm, and must be very hard to catch, especially as all the European nations are more than half on the rebel side. Home letters complain of the scarcity of change; silver has disappeared entirely, and even copper is at twenty percent premium in New York. Postage stamps compose the only small money of any real value now in circulation. Everything has risen to double or treble the old prices, but this does not appear to have stopped extravagance. . . .

MARCH 12, THURSDAY. The weather continues as changeable as is possible even in March. Monday and Wednesday were soft, lovely spring days, while Tuesday and today have been stormy and disagreeable enough. The event of the week so far has been the great anniversary dinner on Tuesday, it being one year since the organization of the corps. . . . The dinner was given by the staff, the invited guests being McDowell as first commander of the corps, Hooker as second, Meade as third and Reynolds; also the present division commanders, Wadsworth, Robinson, and Doubleday, and Butterfield as Hooker's chief of staff. Those now with the corps were the only ones who came, Meade being kept away by the storm, and Hooker having been summoned up to Washington.

The dinner went off well notwithstanding the storm. By the aid of our French cook the spread was superior to our Thanksgiving dinner, and the whole thing was got up in much more style. But the company was not so pleasant, and rather too much was attempted, making it less sociable, and consequently hardly so great a success. Sanderson had worked very hard at it ever since he came back from his leave. A large log hut was put up at the end of the camp opposite to the adjutant-general's office, the floor of which was covered with pine boughs and the sides hung with flags; but the day was cold and stormy, our roof leaked, our chimney smoked, and it was impossible to keep quite warm. My man John acted as chief butler, and won Sanderson's warmest commendations. Some eight or ten of the most intelligent of the contrabands, got up in white chokers and thread gloves, were under John's orders and were quite effective. The cravats and gloves were some that Sanderson had left over from the supply he got for the Prince of Wales's service while he acted as his purveyor in Canada. Sanderson had drawn out a list of toasts with quotations from Shakespeare to each; but our party were neither wits, nor much accustomed to public dinners, so that this part of the affair fell very flat. . . .

The last four days have brought up absolutely nothing worthy of noting here. . . . It would be pretty hard to find three poorer division commanders than we have in this corps; that is, in my opinion. Doubleday knows enough, but he is entirely impractical, and so slow at getting an idea through his head. Wadsworth is active, always busy at something, and with a good allowance of common sense, but knows nothing of military matters. Robinson appears to be one of those old regular officers who have made no progress since they left West Point, and whose main exertions are expended in grumbling at and trying to get around whatever order they may receive from their superior. . . .

MARCH 15, SUNDAY. Reynolds dined with our mess today. We certainly are living very well now. Our cook is a good plain cook without being anything very extra: his soups are excellent, and in addition to the simple joint he can fix us up a number of nice little dishes of meat, as also desserts. We have four courses every day, and on Sunday always an extra spread. When Sanderson's clerk comes down from Washington we have oysters, fish, poultry, and game as long as it will last, and champagne almost every Sunday, eking it out by a mixture of claret. . . . Our dinner hour is five. We have a stove in the tent, and a chandelier composed of two crossed sticks with a candle in each of the four ends, and suspended by a bit of red tape. With a clean tablecloth and a good dinner we look and are real comfortable. It is generally near eight o'clock when we get up from table, having nothing to do now. Bache is a tremendous talker. Sanderson has no end of stories to tell, and not infrequently opens my eyes widely with regard to persons whom I have known or heard of. His hotel experience is almost equal to a doctor's in this respect without the pledge of secrecy. After dinner we always adjourn on weekdays to one of the tents and play whist till ten o'clock; when we close with a little cake, candy, or fruit, and occasionally a toddy. We are rather a remarkable mess in that except Sanderson, none of us are drinkers, or card players for money, and all like to go to bed early.

The first note of preparation for the coming campaign has been sounded, in the shape of an order cutting down transportation, and requiring the turning in of extra baggage. . . .

MARCH 19, THURSDAY. Went up to Washington on Monday, and returned yesterday. . . . I had but little to do beyond drawing my pay and getting a few small items of saddlery and the like. . . . Did not hear anything new of importance, but the feeling amongst officials is evidently a buoyant one, and they look forward with great confidence to the operations of the coming summer. Mr. Lincoln declares that the new draft law shall be fully carried out, and the war prosecuted with renewed vigour. He has made this declaration so often before, without any results following, that there is not much confidence to be placed in these promises.

A raid from our side has been completed during my absence, Averell with a body of cavalry completely encircling Lee's army and getting pretty close up to Richmond. No great amount of damage was inflicted, and the loss was about equal on the two sides, but I understand Hooker claims the raid to have been a success; that it accomplished all he expected, and brought him all the information he wanted.* . . .

MARCH 22, SUNDAY. This is the first spring day we have had for over a week now. The sun has been bright and warm, since the mist cleared off this morning. . . . Preparations are beginning to be made for a move; nothing, however, which indicates a very early day for it. Last year the Army of the Potomac was in full motion at this time, and we had excitement enough watching the transports crowded with troops as they passed down the river. So far the question of transportation worries them the most, if one may judge from the great number of orders issued on the subject, many of which are extremely absurd. For instance, they require me as a staff officer to share my tent with another; while each six-gun battery is allowed three tents, so that Stewart and Davidson, both second lieutenants, have three tents for the two. . . .

General Reynolds has gone up to Washington again, having been summoned before the investigating committee on Franklin's conduct during the "mud march." The investigation will probably amount to nothing as the old army officers stick to each other like brothers. In fact, these committees of investigation seldom are really just. They are appointed and start with a foregone conclusion on the subject in hand, one way or the other; call their witnesses and put their questions accordingly.

---

* General William Woods Averell of New York, West Point, 1855, commanded the Second Cavalry Division in Hooker's army. He used his force in repeated small raids in Virginia, and on March 17, 1863, fought a spirited action at Kelly's Ford in which he showed brilliant leadership and proved that thereafter Jeb Stuart's cavalry would encounter stubborn resistance. It was in this engagement that John Pelham was mortally wounded.

This is especially the case with the Congressional Committee on the Conduct of the War. They will not allow those brought before them to volunteer information: a plain answer, yes or no if possible, without any explanation, is all they permit their witnesses to give.

Hunt has just made an improvement in reducing the number of heavy spare parts, felloes, spokes, and so forth, carried in the battery waggons. Only one spare wheel to a section is to be carried hereafter, which will also save some horseflesh. The horse batteries, too, are to have but one chest on their caisson bodies hereafter: an excellent change for the three-inch guns, the ammunition chests of which, when loaded, are very heavy. . . .

MARCH 25, WEDNESDAY. The quartermaster's department still occupies their attention at headquarters, and Hooker, or rather Butterfield, I imagine, has got quite a new kink in his head. All the waggons are to be drawn by mules instead of horses, and pack mules are to be substituted for waggons so far as possible. These last are to be used for pretty much all communication between the waggon train and the troops while in action, or in the immediate presence of the enemy, as well as carrying up ammunition as other articles. I have my doubts of the success of this experiment (not but what it is excellent in theory), on the simple ground that our mules are totally unbroken to the carrying of packs, and our people totally unaccustomed to the use of them in this way. When the English introduced pack mules during the Crimean campaign, they got well-broken animals from Spain and hired Spanish muleteers to manage them. Some half dozen were sent over here from headquarters one day, with a man to show how to pack on three boxes of ammunition, and now there is great amusement in the trains, trying to get the mules accustomed to their new burdens, and the men used to their animals. . . .

Old General Sumner died on the 21st at Syracuse, New York. He was on his way to St. Louis to take command of that department, when he was taken sick quite suddenly and died in a few days. "Old Bull" Sumner, as he was called in the regular army, is a most appropriate nick-name. Owing to his incompetence to fill so large a post as a corps commander, we lost the chance to destroy Johnston's army at Williamsburg last May; Antietam was but half a victory; and the heights of Fredericksburg were not secured in December when we first came here. But the old soldier was as honest as the day, and simple as a child. The fault was not so much his, as of those who put him and kept him in such a place, while the glorious way in which he pushed across the half-gone bridges to the relief of Keyes at Fair Oaks suffices to cover all his faults. He was one of those whom every one must hate to find fault with; yet whose removal from the command of a corps was generally looked on as a relief. . . .

MARCH 28, SATURDAY. On Thursday I went over to the races got up in the Third Corps; they were as rivals to those held by the Irish brigade on St. Patrick's Day. Birney's staff, I believe, were the main movers in the matter, together with Ward, Graham, and others. The racecourse was located about a mile in rear of Army Headquarters; the ground was fair for this country, and considering the small amount of preparation it could receive. General Ward presided, and there were many of the general officers present all day; and most of them, including Hooker, for a time. How they managed to scare up such a number of females I cannot imagine: there must be a large number of officers' wives down with the army now. Mrs. Salm-Salm and Mrs. Farnum, of course, were on hand.* Both have been handsome women in their day, and are still good-looking enough to stand very well in the eyes of General Joe. The camps are full of stories about them both.

The sports opened with flat and hurdle-races, for officers riding their own horses. Some of the riding was quite good on the flat, but the horses shew that they were none of them much accustomed to jumping. Prince Salm-Salm was badly thrown, and so much injured that the first report was it would kill him. After the horse racing was over there was foot and sack racing for the men, a greased pole to climb, and "fighting cocks." The last furnished the most amusement, and was decidedly good. Two men are bucked, and then set on their feet when they try to butt each other over; their seconds setting them on their feet again whenever either one is upset. As a whole, the affair went off exceedingly well for this country, where we are not much accustomed to these sports. . . .

MARCH 31, TUESDAY. Here we are at the end of March, with the season apparently no farther advanced than it was at the commencement. Yesterday and Sunday were cold and windy enough for winter days down here, and today we have had a heavy storm of rain, snow, and sleet. . . .

General Hunt is doing his best to have the artillery at least in good order when the campaign opens. Most of his instructions are excellent, and if we can only carry them out, the artillery will do more service than ever before. But I have so little control over the batteries in this corps, nor do I suppose others are better off, that it is impossible to see that these instructions are fully carried out. Had I a good, reliable field officer in each division it could be done, but I have not one of any sort now. . . . Hardly a week passes without my visiting all the batteries informally, and by keeping my eyes open I learn much more about their actual condition than I can from a regular inspection. Taken altogether I believe they are in quite good order; those of the First Division are really highly creditable. Reynolds has not only worked hard on his

* Prince Felix Salm-Salm, of Prussia, had offered his services to the Union in 1861 and was assigned to General Louis Blenker's Division of troops, mainly Germans.

own battery, but makes the best division chief of artillery I have had with me yet. . . .

All the batteries are well supplied with stores. They have had their harness repaired and well oiled, carriages mended and painted, and so far as material is concerned are in excellent order. The ground has allowed but very little chance for battery drills. Section drills and harness drills have been pretty well kept up, and my orders to exercise the horses daily have been generally observed, especially in the First Division. All the batteries report having had recitations three times a week.

The newspapers are full of all sorts of rumours, reports, and sensations: the last one is a repetition of the old story, that Richmond is being abandoned. I believe there is no doubt but that its inhabitants are suffering considerably, but do not believe that Jeff Davis has any idea of giving up Virginia yet awhile. Farragut has run his fleet up past Port Hudson so as to co-operate with General Grant, who has succeeded Sherman in command of the army operating against Vicksburg. Burnside goes out to Ohio or Kentucky. I hear but very little as to which way we are to move when we do go, but they say we are to go with a rush whichever way it may be. One report in circulation is that this corps will be left here to guard the depots; but I doubt it, for though the corps itself may not be one of the best, its commander certainly is. General Reynolds has been confirmed as major-general. . . .

CAMP THREE MILES FROM BELLE PLAINE, APRIL 5, SUNDAY. We are still undisturbed in our winter quarters and several reasons are plain for our remaining so for at least a week to come. First the weather which is very uncertain and stormy; all day yesterday and extending through last night, we had one of the most severe storms of the season, wind, rain and snow. It was much like the one we had last year during the time I was loading my batteries at Liverpool Point, except that one was longer and more severe. Then General Hooker has just commenced to review the different corps of the army, and cannot well get through under a week: while the War Department has ordered a general muster of all the troops on the 10th, for the use of the provost-marshal in making drafts to fill up the regiments, and so forth. . . .

This corps was reviewed by General Hooker on Thursday. The troops are so scattered, and the ground hereabouts so broken that we could not get the whole corps out together, so it was reviewed by divisions. The Third Division was formed about half a mile from our headquarters here. Doubleday made bad work of it, for the ground was very much cramped even for his little command of only some 3,000 men. . . . The next day, Friday, I went over to see the Sixth Corps reviewed. The whole of it was out together, though the ground it formed on was very rough. It is a larger corps than ours, and certainly made a much better appearance, but I hear that General Hunt says my batteries looked decidedly the best. There is no doubt that the Fifth and Sixth Corps under Porter and Franklin were much better instructed and disciplined than any of the others. Another cause for its superiority over this corps lies in the great proportion of Pennsylvania regiments that we have; which as a rule are, without doubt, worse officered than any others in this army. Major DePeyster is now on duty with Howe's division of the Sixth Corps; and made himself very ridiculous at the review by his strutting manner, which called attention to him, while he not only did not mount his cannoneers, but also commanded "present sabres" when he passed in review. Every officer of my acquaintance whom I met after the review congratulated me on my major. The Twentieth New York met General Hooker about half a mile from the review grounds and marched up with us as a sort of escort; for the purpose of shewing the excellence of their drill. It is said (and I believe truly) to be the best drilled regiment in the army; their marching, and changes from company front to the flank, and their wheeling into line on Friday were certainly wonderful. It is a German regiment, raised in New York City, and commanded by Colonel Von Vegesack (I don't know how to spell the name) an officer of standing in the Swedish service, and a very nice fellow in every way.*

I hear that the President is expected down today. In case he comes, we may very likely have all our reviewing to go over again on a grander scale. Hooker has considerable liking for that sort of thing when he can make it pay; and is said to have boasted a good deal while at Washington; declaring that he "had the finest army on this planet" and that "he could march it straight to New Orleans." Whether or no he will prove capable of taking it as far as Richmond remains to be seen, to say nothing of going to New Orleans. By the bye, Farragut's success on the Mississippi does not turn out to be quite so great as at first reported. The news looks anything but very brilliant from both west and south. Consequently, the expected capture of Charleston, Port Hudson, and Vicksburg is again postponed; and gold is once more on the rise.

APRIL 8, WEDNESDAY. President Lincoln came down on Saturday afternoon instead of on Sunday, and arrived at headquarters quite unexpectedly. It is said that their arrival created quite a commotion on Hooker's back stairs, hustling off some of his female acquaintances in a most undignified way. Mrs. Lincoln and one of his sons came down with the President. The object of his visit seems to be to review the army, which according to present appearances will keep him here all this week. The Cavalry Corps under General Stoneman was reviewed first, on Monday.

* Baron Ernest Mattais Peter Von Vegesack, a captain in the Swedish army and a veteran of the Danish-Prussian War over Schleswig-Holstein, joined McClellan's staff and became a brigade commander. He returned to Sweden late this summer.

It was probably the largest body of cavalry ever seen together on this continent, there being 11,000 out, it is said. Some of the regiments looked quite well, but many were little better than ridiculous. The country here is not calculated to make fine cavalry. Our men are far too slouchy, the "setting up" and bearing of the real soldier showing much more on horseback than on foot; and the plain, simple uniform now worn in our army prevents any attempt at style, especially on such wretched horses as we have here. The horse batteries were much more creditable, and looked really finely. They are all regular batteries, except one, and in most cases are commanded by old light artillery officers. The one volunteer battery is the Sixth New York which was with me on the Peninsula. Bramhall has resigned, and Martin is now the captain. Even in the midst of the old regular batteries they keep up their reputation, in camp as well as in the field. I have been to see them several times on my way to Army Headquarters, the shortest road leading almost through their camp, and always meet with the warmest welcome.

Today the Second, Third, Fifth, and Sixth Corps were reviewed together, and made really a splendid show. There must have been 50,000 men out; the ground was fair, and the arrangements capital. It would be hard to say which of the four corps made the best appearance: the Third has, if any, turned out in a little the best style, and Sickles deserves credit for getting so good a line formed; and for the manner in which the whole corps saluted at one time by bugle command. I rode around with General Hooker and the reviewing party, as did several ladies, of whom there were a large number present. . . .

APRIL 12, SUNDAY.   The reviewing is over, the President gone back to Washington, and all once more quietly waiting for orders to move which will probably be the next excitement. On Thursday the whole of this corps was marched down to the plain on which the First Division was drawn up last week, and was there reviewed by the President. The day was fine, the view of the Potomac beautiful, the ground most capital. Reynolds and everybody worked hard, so the troops looked and marched well; and our efforts were repaid by the generally expressed opinion that it went off altogether better than any of the other reviews. There was one new feature in it, at any rate. The whole of the artillery was massed, and passed in review as one body, so that I appeared in my proper place, as an actual commander. It was General Reynolds's own proposition, without any request on my part; whether it arose from his really approving the brigade organization, or was only done for convenience and effect, I do not know. The ten batteries made quite a display, marching battery front, and looked well, although some being six and others four-gun batteries rather broke the column. Hunt was much pleased with it. After the review, the President, most of the general officers present, and their ladies had a lunch at our headquarters, which Sanderson got up, and capped the satisfaction already felt with our review. . . .

We do not yet get any direct accounts of the attempt on Charleston: the reports through rebel sources are that Dupont's fleet was repulsed and the monitor *Keokuk* sunk. I fear it may be true, as Charleston is almost as precious to them as Richmond, and every effort will be made to save it; while on our side we have anything but a desirable commander of the land forces in old Hunter.

Everybody is reading the first report of the Congressional Committee on the Conduct of the War. It is quite voluminous, and comes down to the close of last year. I am trying to get through it, but its unfairness, partiality, and in very many cases absolute falseness make me so nervous that I can make but little progress. The radical party, who have complete control over the Cabinet and do pretty much what they please with our weak President, seem to be determined to stick at nothing in order to punish every official who does not go all lengths with them. A small instance of this has just come out in a War Department order dismissing a volunteer lieutenant for what they call treasonable sentiments expressed in a private letter to his uncle in China!

NINE

CHANCELLORSVILLE AND AFTER

The Northern press was radiant in April 1863 with news of the bold movements of Grant and Admiral David Dixon Porter against Vicksburg. Grant had marched his army along the west bank of the Mississippi to a point below the fortifications of the town, and Porter had run the batteries with gunboats and empty transports to be placed at Grant's service. On the last day of April Grant landed 30,000 troops on the east bank at Bruinsburg, ready to strike into the interior of Mississippi, living off the country, and besieging Vicksburg from the rear. N. P. Banks meanwhile executed some successful marches in Louisiana. Lincoln, Halleck, and the Northern public were anxious to see equal progress made on the Eastern front by Hooker.

The government knew that the Army of the Potomac was more powerful and efficient than ever. Hooker had not far from 125,000 troops present for duty, or about twice as many as Lee had collected in his lines behind the Rappahannock. The troops were ready to fight again, and Hooker himself kept all the self-confidence that had marked his bearing and speech in the recent grand reviews. The army's intelligence service had been markedly improved, so that the commander was thoroughly informed of the movements of the Confederates. He meant to make the most of his overwhelming numerical advantage.

His initial plan was to send Stoneman's 10,000 cavalry up the Rappahannock and across it to cut in behind Lee's rear; thus severing his supply lines and forcing him, since he was believed to have only three days' rations, to retreat. "Let your watchword be Fight! and let all your orders be Fight!," Hooker instructed Stoneman. He would attack the retreating Lee when his forces were in confusion. However, when rains swelled the Rappahannock and delayed the cavalry blow, he decided upon a larger strategy. He would march three corps far upstream to cross with the cavalry beyond the Confederate lines, and use them to turn Lee's flank by a rapid and well-masked advance. Meanwhile, one corps was to hold the river at Falmouth opposite Lee's center, and three corps were to push across the stream there and attack. Thus Lee would be caught between two massive forces of infantry, each as large as his whole army.

The weather continued for a time to delay Hooker. It was cold, wet, and gloomy, as Wainwright writes. It turned the roads for a time into such bogs that wags declared that the only feasible direction was downward. Hooker had to order postponement after postponement. But finally the muddy red hills and valleys began to dry out, and the troops could begin to move.

* * *

APRIL 15 [1863], WEDNESDAY. A rainy day enables me to write up, and the prospect of a move now at any moment admonishes me to do so. On Monday we received orders which really looked like a start. The men are to carry five days' rations of hard bread, coffee, sugar, and salt in their knapsacks; and three days' in their havresacks; making eight days on the persons of the men. Each man is also to carry sixty rounds of ammunition; ninety more to go on mules and in the waggons. Of course, with such a load of rations and ammunition the men will be able to take but little else, and the amount of extra clothing is accordingly reduced to one extra shirt, a pair of socks and drawers. Today all the extra tents above the number allowed by existing orders were turned in, and I believe we are ready to start now on twelve hours' notice. How the orders cutting down transportation and so forth have been carried out in other corps I do not know, but General Reynolds obeys orders literally himself, and expects all under him to do the same.

Stoneman started with nearly the whole Cavalry Corps on Monday morning. He was to cross at Rappahannock Station, and go as far as Culpeper. This much I know, but whether his movement is meant simply as a blind, while the rest of the army is to cross here or below, or whether we are all to cross above, I know not, but am inclined to think that this corps at least will probably be thrown over somewhere hereabouts, as I have been out several times with General Reynolds and made a thorough examination of the banks for some five miles below where we crossed in December. His attention seemed to be most closely given to a spot which would land us on the other side about two miles below the mouth of the Massaponax. . . .

The newspapers pretend to have a great deal in them just now; but when one knows that the greater part of it is false there is but little satisfaction in reading them. According to their accounts of the numbers of the rebel armies in different parts of the country, Jefferson Davis must have at least one million of men under arms. Have finished the "Committee on the Conduct of the War" report this evening, and cannot remember a more bare-faced distortion of facts, and concealment of truth, than it is composed of; so far at least as my own personal observation and knowledge made me acquainted with matters and things. The War Department seems to feel it necessary to justify itself regarding the Fitz-John Porter court martial, as almost every colonel in the army is being supplied with several copies of Judge Holt's review of the proceedings. On the other hand, a large number of the *National Intelligencer*, with Reverdy Johnson's summing up, sent down to Porter's personal friends, were taken out of the mail! Another little evidence of the strength of our freedom when those in power choose to trench upon it.

APRIL 19, SUNDAY.   We are still in peace and quietness. The very heavy rain of Wednesday I take it to be the cause of it. It raised the river seven feet at Rappahannock Station, where Stoneman is still waiting to get across, and is now reported to be out of forage. His part of the move is by this time fully known to Lee as a matter of course. Even the privates seem well informed about it, so that we get as late news through rebel deserters as we do direct; while their pickets call across the river to ours, asking what is the matter with our cavalry that it does not get across. . . .

I was at Army Headquarters yesterday and had a long talk with General Hooker. He is very confident of success, though the blocking of Stoneman at Rappahannock Station has somewhat interfered with his plans. He did not tell me how it was to be accomplished, but said he was sure he could carry the position opposite with but little loss. He told me too that when the President was down here he told him that he (Lincoln) has commenced this campaign tail end foremost: that he should have allowed him (Hooker) to attack Lee first, and as he was sure to whip him badly, Charleston and Vicksburg could then have been approached to good advantage. It is well for a commanding general to have confidence in himself and in his plans, but I fear that Hooker has too much of it. He certainly talks too much about what he can do; it sounds very much like braggadocio, and should he fail, great will be his fall.

General Hunt told me of a conversation between a Swiss general who was down here, General Butterfield, and himself on artillery organization. Butterfield, it seems, was the main cause of Hooker's not approving the brigade plans, and Butterfield's opposition was founded on what they do in Europe; where they do have batteries attached to divisions. He had read that much, and thought he knew all about it; nor would he believe Hunt until the Swiss assured him that, excepting as to their position in camp, on the march, and in battle, the division commanders had nothing whatever to do with the artillery, the batteries being in all other respects controlled entirely by artillery officers. Now Butterfield wants Hunt to urge the matter on Hooker again, but is not willing to come out and admit plainly that he was wrong in his opposition.

This army is now in good order to commence operations. There has been a large amount of drilling going on for the last month, and though neither officers nor men are quite so anxious for a fight as they were last spring, both are much better seasoned to the hardships and know much more about their business. In numbers we are about thirty percent stronger than McClellan was in front of Yorktown; that is, the Army of the Potomac now numbers 110,000 men, in round figures. Not one of the old corps commanders remains; and but two of those now commanding corps had more than a brigade a year ago. Although I cannot say that they have very great confidence in him, there is none of the jealousy towards Hooker, on the part of his lieutenants, that was manifested towards McClellan. The different corps commanders have just been permanently fixed by direction of the President. Reynolds the First, Couch the Second, Sickles the Third, Meade the Fifth, Sedgwick the Sixth, Howard the Eleventh, Slocum the Twelfth, and Stoneman the Cavalry. All but Sickles and perhaps Stoneman I should think were first-rate men; and Sickles may do better than I expect. Howard, who succeeds Sigel in the Eleventh, is brave enough, and a most perfect gentleman. He is a Christian and an enthusiast, as well as a man of ability, but there is some doubt as to his having snap enough to manage the Germans, who require to be ruled with a rod of iron.

This morning I had all the batteries out for inspection in full marching order. Each battery is to take two waggons with it exclusively for forage; 120 pounds of grain is to go on each spare horse, and two days' rations for the team on each off horse. I cannot say that I like the packing part of it, but am anxious to keep my carriages as free of encumbrance, and as light as possible. . . .

APRIL 23, THURSDAY. It is still rain, rain, rain, with a regular pour today, which will make the roads and river impassable again for days to come. This corps was not on the Peninsula last year, and many of its officers are very bitter against McClellan, even hinting that he did not want to move faster; while these same men consider the present difficulties of weather quite insurmountable. Yet even these rains are not equal to what we then had. Stoneman was still on the north side of the Rappahannock yesterday morning, and will hardly get over the river for some days to come, as the rain of today has doubtless raised the river quite as much as it did last week. Had our cavalry got over when they first reached the station they would have run a good chance of catching Fitzhugh Lee, who was on his way up into Loudoun County with 2,500 men and 175 waggons on a foraging expedition.* . . .

* Robert E. Lee's second son, William Henry Fitzhugh ("Rooney") Lee, who graduated from Harvard in the same class with Henry Adams, had served with Jeb Stuart on various expeditions, including the raid on Chambersburg, Pennsylvania. Two months after

The two-year regiments, of which there are near forty from New York, will soon be going home, as will the nine-months' men raised last summer. It will reduce this corps nearly one-quarter in number, most of the loss falling on the First Division. The calling out of the nine-months' men at the end of last summer was one of the most absurd things the wiseheads at Washington have done. Any fool could have told them that the regiments would not be fit for service until last year's campaign was over, and that their time would be out just as this year's commenced. . . .

APRIL 26, SUNDAY. Yesterday and today have been clear and windy, drying up the country very much, so we shall doubtless soon get off now. The rain of Thursday made a great freshet in all the streams, and carried away the bridge over Bull Run, so cutting off Stoneman's supply of forage. We may have to wait until this and other damage is repaired. Meantime we are all packed up and waiting patiently for orders. All but the very minimum of baggage is to be left behind until the result of the first battle is made certain, so we are cut down very close in our culinary department. Still our French cook gave us as good a soup and fillet of beef today as I want to see, even though we did have to eat it off of tin plates. . . .

I cannot make out exactly what the Administration is driving at. Many of their steps would indicate that they were heart and soul with the rankest radicals, while others look as if they were by no means sure of their position. Of these last are the sending of Holt's review of the Porter court martial to the army, and the issue General Order No. 100, just received, which under guise of "Instructions for the Government of Armies in the Field" is a defense of its radical abolition principles. The "Instructions" are drawn up by Professor Francis Lieber, a very learned student and bookworm no doubt, and revised by Major General Hitchcock, an old theoretical fool.* I would not give a fig for the opinion of either of these gentlemen on practical politics, though they are both very well posted as to all German theories. So far as I can see, the President's abolition proclamation has only served to unite the people of the rebel states, and so give strength to the rebellion. . . .

BIVOUAC, APRIL 28, TUESDAY. We are off at last. It was two weeks yesterday since the cavalry started, so we cannot expect to make much of a

Wainwright's entry he was captured while recovering from a wound and kept prisoner until early in 1864.

*Ethan Allen Hitchcock, grandson of the Green Mountain hero, had been commandant of West Point, from which he graduated in 1817. He had published since his resignation from the army in 1855 a number of books on Swedenborg, Shakespeare, Dante, and Spenser, of no real value. But he did good war service, chiefly in connection with the care of prisoners. Francis Lieber (1800–72) held a chair in Columbia College, was a pioneer in the American study of both political science and military law, and was a close friend and adviser of General Halleck.

surprise of it. Though I doubt if Lee knows now just how Hooker means to move upon him. I am sure I do not; except that the Third, Sixth, and our own corps are to make a crossing hereabouts tomorrow morning, and that the rest of the army has gone up the river to Banks's Ford or higher.

We moved from camp at noon today; all the divisions being ordered to rendezvous at White Oak Church. Just as we rode out of camp the General ordered me to direct all the batteries to report to me at the church. I told him I had no power to issue such an order; when he directed Colonel Kingsbury to send it to the division commander. Consequently, on reaching White Oak Church I found all the batteries massed there, and under my orders. Whether General Reynolds means that I shall have control of them through all the coming operations, or only to cover the crossing of the river, I do not know; but take whatever I can get in this way, and shall try to prove that it is the best way.

From the church we moved down the direct road towards the river and are now bivouacked about halfway down immediately in rear of the belt of wood on the high ground. Every precaution possible has been taken to prevent an alarm being given to the other side; but as there must undoubtedly have been more than usual passing on the river road, they are probably on the lookout across the stream. . . .

Our pontoons lie in the road as far to the front as they could be taken before dark, without coming into sight. The idea is to carry the boats down to the river by hand during the night, so as to make no noise whatever. Wadsworth, with all his division, is detailed for this purpose. . . . He called upon me as I was trying to get into a snooze, for it is now late and we must all be stirring before daylight tomorrow. The men can't get the pontoons down by hand; they are too heavy and unwieldy. . . .

BATTLE OF CHANCELLORSVILLE. Shall write by days as heretofore, though of course not actually at the date indicated.

NEAR FITZHUGH HOUSE, APRIL 29, WEDNESDAY. Was stirring before daylight: the fog hung so thick that it was hard work to find one's way about. To the west of the road leading down from White Oak Church is a piece of wood; beyond this again is a high open bank, on which de Russy had his batteries in December. Here I posted Cooper, Amsden, Hall, and Reynolds, with twenty rifled three-inch guns, all under charge of Major Matthews. The position is fine, just above where Pollock's Mills used to be, and commands all the opposite plain as far up as "Smithfield." To the east of the road the second bank is not quite so high, but is still very good, and rises abruptly up from the river road. Here, directly in front of the Fitzhugh house I put in Edgell Thompson and Ricketts with fourteen rifled three-inch. Lieutenant-Colonel Warner reported at daylight with Taft's twenty-pounder Parrotts* and another battery from the reserve; these he took down the river about a mile to "Traveller's Rest," where he could command the lower bank of the Massaponax. . . .

Meanwhile the Sixth Corps threw its bridges at Franklin's old crossing, as did Gibbon his at Fredericksburg, without any opposition, and all was ready to cross above us. Old General Benham, who had charge of laying the bridges, came up now and was very loud in his talk. He had been up all night and taken so much whiskey to keep himself awake that he was tight as a brick; had fallen off his horse once and scratched his face badly. Ransom and Stewart were now moved down onto the lower bank right where the bridge was to start from, and I then rode to the upper batteries and had them open slowly on the rifle pit. General Reynolds was getting nervous at being behind time. . . .

Finding the engineers could not or would not work, two regiments from the First Brigade, First Division, the Sixth Wisconsin and Twenty-Fourth Michigan went over in boats, General Wadsworth going with them himself. They landed without very much difficulty and rushed up the bank about the time that we got a good range on the main rifle pit. Nothing but legs could now save the rebs on the bank, and they made the best of it. I never saw men run faster. It was amusing to see our men too rush on. Two of them pushed up the bank alone and took the men out of the smaller pits; they would only take their muskets away from them, tell them to run to the rear, and then, throwing down the captured muskets, rush on to the next pit. In this way they went up as far as "Smithfield." Such is the excitement of success, and so much does a man's bravery depend on the fact that his enemy are running away from him. The remainder of the brigade was quickly pushed over in the boats and the bridge laid, when the whole of the First Division crossed, and formed a sort of bridge head on the other side. . . .

General Reynolds has his headquarters tonight on a small knoll just at the junction of the road from White Oak Church with the river road. From this spot we have a most excellent view of the whole plain opposite and the hills beyond. We have no tents up, but as it has begun to rain I have got a paulin from Leppien whose battery lies in rear of us, and (with) our own mess are quite comfortable. The General has been quite nervous during the day, and has sworn pretty hard when things did not go to suit him. . . . General Gibbon occupies the town of Fredericksburg with his division of the Second Corps. One division of the Sixth Corps lies around the Bernard house; and the Third Corps has moved down to the rear of the Seven Sisters. General John Sedgwick has command of all the troops here, some 45,000, I should think. What we are to do

* Captain Elijah Taft of New York commanded a reserve battery of four twenty-pounders.

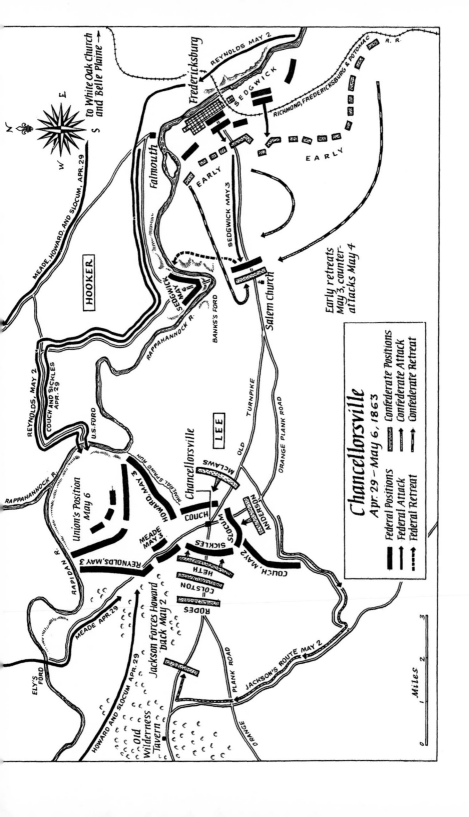

Chancellorsville
Apr 29 – May 6, 1863

Federal Positions
Federal Attack
Federal Retreat

Confederate Positions
Confederate Attack
Confederate Retreat

Fredericksburg

REYNOLDS MAY 2

SEDGWICK

RICHMOND, FREDERICKSBURG & POTOMAC R.R.

R.R.

EARLY

Falmouth

EARLY

SEDGWICK MAY 3

Early retreats
May 3, counter-
attacks May 4

Salem Church

SEDGWICK MAY 4

BANK'S FORD

to White Oak Church
and Belle Plaine →

MEADE, HOWARD AND SLOCUM, APR. 29

HOOKER

RAPPAHANNOCK R.

REYNOLDS, MAY 2

COUCH AND SICKLES
APR. 29

U.S. FORD

RAPPAHANNOCK R.

RAPIDAN R.

Union's Position
May 6

REYNOLDS, MAY 3

MEADE
MAY 2

HOWARD, MAY 2

Chancellorsville

MINERAL SPRING RUN

McLAWS

LEE

OLD TURNPIKE

ORANGE PLANK ROAD

ANDERSON

COUCH

SICKLES

SLOCUM, MAY 2

HETH

COLSTON

RODES

COUCH, MAY 2

ELY'S FORD

MEADE APR. 29

HOWARD AND SLOCUM APR. 29

Jackson forces Howard
back May 2

Old
Wilderness
Tavern

JACKSON'S ROUTE MAY 2

PLANK ROAD

ORANGE

0   1   2   3
Miles

exactly, now we have our crossing I do not yet know, or whether we are to do anything here.

APRIL 30, THURSDAY.   It rained a good part of last night, and is a heavy, muggy morning; the roads are very bad, and the fields so soft as to make the moving of batteries difficult. It was noon before we could get a sight of the rebel position beyond the Bowling Green road. . . . So soon as it cleared up I crossed the river with General Reynolds, to lay out our line there and put in Stewart's and Ransom's batteries. . . .

About five P.M., the rebs opened on our bridge, and on the Second and Third Divisions, which lay massed on the low flat between the road and the river. Reynolds and all of us were in Robinson's quarters down there at the time. They dropped their shot very true, and did a good deal of damage, killing and wounding a number of the men. One shell burst in a large puddle of water quite near us as we mounted our horses. Another shot struck one poor fellow, a sergeant, as he sat on the ground clasping his knees, taking off both legs and both arms. The two divisions were then withdrawn under cover of the hills, when the rebs turned their attention to our batteries in front of the Fitzhugh house, and to the lines across the river. They fired from four Parrott twenty-pounders and some smaller guns. . . . So soon as all was again quiet we went up to the knoll on which our headquarters were. Two shot had ricochetted over the spot early in the affair and had sent all the servants off on the double quick. Even his soup, just on the fire, could not keep our cook; and one of the niggers seized an officer's horse that happened to be fastened nearby, and rode for dear life nearly up to the church. They all came back after a time, and we finally got our supper. . . .

Near midnight I was awakened by an officer reporting to me with Battery "C" of the Third Artillery, a horse battery with six three-inch guns. Reynolds had sent for some heavier guns, and Butterfield sent these. I do not want them, but ordered him up where Taft's section was, and directed him, as I had all the others, to have his men at their posts at the first break of day. The only casualty in my command today has been one man in Stewart's battery severely wounded.

* * *

Hooker had finally gotten his advance in motion late on the afternoon of April 27, 1863, when three of his corps, numbering 42,000 men, set out toward the upper Rappahannock. They were to cross the river at Kelly's Ford thirty miles above Fredericksburg, at the same time that Stoneman's cavalry crossed still farther upstream; and the combined infantry and cavalry were to fall upon Lee's left flank. Of course Lee quickly learned all about the movement, for Jeb Stuart on the 28th notified him that a large force was on its way up. The plan was that these Union troops under Slocum, Howard, and Meade, once across the Rappahannock, should execute their flanking move along and across its tributary, the Rapidan. While this operation against the Confederate flank was being carried out, the Second Corps under Darius N. Couch was to hold the center at Falmouth; and the First, Third, and Sixth Corps under Reynolds, Sickles, and Sedgwick respectively were to cross in the Fredericksburg area to strike Lee's main force on his right. As these three corps totaled 59,000 men, or almost as many as Lee had altogether, Hooker hoped they would crumple him up, and throw him back against the force coming in from the Rapidan on his left. It was a good plan—if it worked! The main difficulty was that its success depended on Lee's waiting until the Union attack began. And Lee, realizing that some such pincers strategy was contemplated by his opponents, had decided to attack early and attack hard.

The reader should remember that Wainwright was in Reynolds' corps (and very happy to be with that efficient general); the division commanders being Wadsworth, a radical whom Wainwright distrusted as a friend of Stanton and the "abolitionists," John C. Robinson, and the undependable Abner Doubleday. Sedgwick was placed in top command of the three corps that were to cross in the Fredericksburg area. He laid his bridges in a heavy fog, after a four-hour delay attributable to the intoxication of Hooker's West Point classmate of the Engineers' Brigade, General Henry Benham— whose drunkenness is mentioned by Wainwright in indulgent terms. The troops began crossing. "Hooker was satisfied," writes his biographer Walter H. Hebert, "that Sedgwick had carried out his part of the plan well, and he sent a dispatch to Slocum telling him that the enemy anticipated the main attack at Fredericksburg; therefore, Slocum was to advance as far as Chancellorsville, where he would be joined not only by the Fifth Corps (Meade's) but probably by the Second (Couch's) and Third (Sickles's) as well."

As Hooker's strongest forces were thus concentrating by various lines at Chancellorsville crossroads, Lee realized that they meant to crush his left. Four Union corps would presently be there. Just where, in response, should Lee attack? He decided to assult Hooker's right at the point of concentration. The brick mansion called Chancellorsville stood in a fifty-acre clearing almost directly south of the intersection of the Rappahannock and Rapidan, at a distance of something over five miles. West of this the Confederate attack, with Stonewall Jackson leading, would fall.

❀ ❀ ❀

MAY 1, FRIDAY. The day has been a fine one, and perfectly quiet along here; not a shot fired on either side, unless it may have been a few exchanged between the pickets. I sent the horse battery back to the reserve. . . .

Yesterday should have been muster for pay; so having nothing else to do, the men were mustered today, and the monthly returns made so far as possible. All three of the corps lie in full view of the enemy, but as we have now been here three days doing nothing and they must know ere this of the movement of the rest of the army, they doubtless guess our object is only to keep them here, and will not stay. In fact, we have seen a large body moving up the river along the road on top of the ridge. The General thinks it Jackson's corps which was sent down to Port Royal after our threatening that point. Our signal men counted nine batteries of forty guns in the column. At General Reynolds's request I passed sometime on top of Pratt's house watching the column. It came into full view, and the division between brigades and other units could be easily seen with a good glass.

From General Hooker we have an order saying that the "operations of the Fifth, Eleventh, and Twelfth Corps have been a series of splendid achievements," and that he has got Lee just where he wants him. I trust that Hooker is not hallooing before he is out of the woods. He is now at "Chancellorsville," wherever that may be: about fifteen miles, I believe, above Fredericksburg on the road to Gordonsville. Some of the corps crossed as high up as Kelly's Ford, I hear. The Third Corps went up to join them last night. I cannot learn that they have had any fighting to speak of yet.

MAY 2, SATURDAY. About seven o'clock this morning an aide of General Sedgwick's came to us, with his horse all in a foam, with orders for the corps to proceed at once to United States Ford, and join General Hooker. The order from Hooker required us to be there by daylight this morning, but it was over twenty-four hours in getting to Sedgwick by some mismanagement somewhere. We at once commenced to withdraw; a division of the Sixth Corps moving down as if to re-enforce us for an advance at this point. So soon as the enemy saw that something was up (8:00 A.M.) they opened a heavy fire on our bridges, and a very accurate one, too. . . .

It took some time to get the troops in motion, lying as the whole corps did exposed to the fire of the enemy's guns, without drawing down an attack upon us. Had it been night, or even foggy, as all the other mornings have been, we could have cleared out at once; but a good amount of marching and counter-marching was required to keep them in ignorance as to just what we were doing. . . . It was about noon when I got off, and passing by Army Headquarters struck off by an inner road. I was determined to take this opportunity to see how orders were carried out as to the packing of carriages, straggling, and so on. I found I had a job on hand, but there was a certain amount of fun, and a great deal of satisfaction in it. The first haul-up I gave them was at a momentary halt some two miles beyond headquarters, just to make certain which of two roads I was to take. Here one half the men started off from their batteries under excuse of getting water: and were wonderfully astonished when I forced them to go back, and wait for permission. Many of the carriages were much overloaded, and the day being warm, the men hung on to their overcoats, havresacks, and even canteens. I halted two or three at a time from the head of the column to water their horses; and then had the captains overhaul their carriages, with the full understanding that any article found on them afterwards not allowed by orders would be thrown away. The field where the three Pennsylvania batteries were halted was literally covered with overcoats which the men would not carry. . . .

It was long after dark when I reached United States Ford. General Reynolds, I found, had gone out to Chancellorsville, some five miles, and left no orders for me. So finding that there was small chance of my getting my command to the front on account of the road being blocked by infantry, I halted in a large open space soon after midnight, near to a brick house used as a hospital about half a mile from the bridges. I was heartily tired as I wrapped myself up in my blankets under a large tree, but got very little sleep, being constantly disturbed by officers looking for General Reynolds. Even his staff did not know where he was and some of them remained with me through the night.

We had heard more or less firing ever since we came near the bridges; at times very heavy, and lasting all through the night. Lee had turned Hooker's right in the afternoon; the Eleventh Corps, which held that position, is said to have run away bodily, and the Twelfth too have been very badly cut up. From what I hear it is to be feared that Hooker is not doing so well as he expected and that his congratulatory order was issued rather too soon.

* * *

As late as the evening of May 1 Hooker had seemed to possess an easy advantage. He had nearly 50,000 men under Sedgwick holding the Rappahannock in front of Lee, well entrenched and well protected by natural cover. He had thrown more than 50,000 more around and behind Lee's left flank, and had others coming to join them. He himself had taken up headquarters at Chancellorsville House. He thought he had good reason for issuing his boastful General Orders Number 47, declaring that the operations of the past three days "have determined that our enemy must either ingloriously fly, or come out from behind his defenses and give us battle on our own ground, where certain destruction awaits him."

But as Lee and Jackson conferred in great anxiety that night, Stuart brought them word that the Union right, where Slocum and O. O. Howard commanded the Eleventh and Twelfth Corps, was badly exposed. It had come up hastily from its crossing at Kelly's Ford; it had no hill or stream to protect it; and it had dug no entrenchments. If Lee threw part of his army by rapid and well-concealed marches around it, he could surprise it from the rear. Soon after dawn Jackson's column of perhaps 20,000 effective men was on its way. Early in the afternoon he and Fitzhugh Lee, reconnoitering Howard's lines, found him totally unprepared. The men had built imperfect defenses facing south, with no protection on the west; they were playing cards, eating, or sleeping. This particular corps contained a large number of German-born troops, who had till lately been commanded by Franz Sigel, and who resented the fact that Howard had taken Sigel's place.

Attacking with a rush, Jackson's forces completely defeated the 10,000 men of Howard's corps, and sent them flying through the woods west of Chancellorsville. The German troops fled in utter rout. Only as night came on did the Union lines stiffen and halt the Confederate advance. It was plain that a decisive change in the situation had occurred. The Union army that had tried to flank the Southerners was itself outflanked; the offensive had passed from Hooker's troops to those of Lee and Jackson. For this fact Howard was highly censurable.

But it quickly became clear that Hooker had himself committed an almost inexplicable error. He had gotten his army across the Rappahannock with admirable skill, and so maneuvered it that swift action might well have enabled him to crush Lee. But at the critical moment he lost his nerve and pulled his advancing troops back from the open country beyond Chancellorsville into the tangled wilderness that partly surrounded the house. He thus lost his power to continue handling his forces freely and handed the initiative over to the Confederates. As he put it, Joseph Hooker had suddenly "lost confidence in Hooker." As he did so, he lost the battle.

* * *

MAY 3, SUNDAY. A cup of coffee from one of the batteries and then I started in search of General Reynolds. Batteries had been coming in from the front all night, and quite a number were now parked in the open as well as my own. I therefore only ordered them to be ready to move the instant they received orders. Several artillery officers from the other batteries came up to me, asking where they could procure ammunition; no one appeared to know anything, and there was a good deal of confusion. . . .

I found the First Corps just taking position along the road leading to Ely's Ford, on the extreme right of the army. Reynolds with one of the divisions had been out to Chancellorsville, but was ordered back to cover the right flank, Hooker being afraid that Lee was trying to push around that way, and get between us and our bridges. All our line was through a heavy wood, with hardly a place for artillery. Near its centre was one little opening of a couple of acres, and where our line turned to the right, leaving the road about five hundred yards before it crosses Hunting Run, was another. The General desired me to bring up the twelve-pounder batteries for these positions. I therefore again went to the rear, and ordered up Stewart, Ransom, and Leppien. The road was very much blocked, and progress slow. On my return I found that Leppien, who had started first, was not there. He had either missed the road or been sent elsewhere; very heavy fighting was going on at the front.

Reynolds was in bad humour. Two Dutch batteries he had seized on had cleared out after being posted. I told him that it seemed to me all the artillery of the army was running around loose. I had met half a dozen batteries going to the front, and as many more going to the rear, blocking the road to no purpose; while Best still stuck in his old place. On my way out I met Ames, with "G" Company, who told me he had been three times ordered to the front by his division commander, and on reaching the Ely's Ford road sent back again by order of General Hooker. General Reynolds desired me, after posting Ransom and Stewart, to go to General Hooker and tell him the condition I found matters in, especially the behaviour of the Dutch batteries. I found General Hooker in a tent near a small white house at the junction of the road from Chancellorsville with the Ely's Ford road. He had been stunned by a pillar falling on him at the Chancellorsville house, and was lying down. The sentry refused me admittance, but reported a messenger from General Reynolds. Soon after General Meade came out and said I could not see the General, but he would take my message in. I gave it to him as regarded the Dutch batteries, but at the same time placed myself before the tent opening so as to catch Hooker's eyes if possible. In this I succeeded, and so soon as he saw me he called me in, when the following conversation took place, as near as I can remember it.

GENERAL HOOKER. "Well, Wainwright, how is the artillery getting on?"

SELF. "As badly as it well can. Batteries are being ordered in every direction, blocking up the roads; and no one seems to know where to go. Where is General Hunt?"

GENERAL HOOKER. "What is the matter?"

SELF. "As near as I can understand, every division commander wants his own batteries, and battery commanders will obey no one else's orders. It is just the condition I told you of and wanted to provide against, by giving artillery officers of rank actual command, so that they could order any battery. The ammunition trains, too."

GENERAL HOOKER. "Well, we have no time to talk now. You take hold and make it right."

SELF. "Where is General Hunt?"

GENERAL HOOKER. "At Banks's Ford. You take his place."

SELF. "I would rather you should give it to Griffin or Ayres. They are old artillery officers; have rank, and are better known than I am."

GENERAL HOOKER. "I know nothing of them as artillery officers; I do you, and wish you to take it. General Van Allen will write the order. What do you want?"

SELF. "I will do the best I can, General. I must have power to put batteries with other divisions than their own, and to fill them from any ammunition train."

GENERAL HOOKER. "Van Allen, write the order. Colonel Wainwright, First New York Artillery, will take command of all the artillery and ammunition of this army. No officer whatsoever will give any order which may conflict with his arrangements. Will that do, Wainwright?"

SELF. "Perfectly, Sir."

I left the tent rejoicing, yet with a weight of responsibility on me such as I had never had before. Rejoicing at such an admission of the principles of artillery organization which I had been contending for; and feeling the responsibility of so much authority, and also the need that I should use it in a way still further to advance the principle that the artillery should be subject to the orders of artillery officers. I determined not to interfere with the dispositions of corps or division commanders, except so far as might be absolutely necessary. My first business was to report the order to General Reynolds, that I might be relieved from duty with my own corps. . . .

The fight of the morning had been a very severe one. Our troops were driven away from the Chancellorsville house, and by the time I again reached it, the whole army had fallen back to the Ely's Ford road, the new line being formed along the south side of that road. The First Corps still held the right of the line; next came the Fifth Corps, its left reaching to the opening at the White House, some seventy acres or thereabouts. This was the exposed point, the road from Chancellorsville coming in here, our line making an obtuse salient angle. Here I found that Captain Weed, artillery chief of the Fifth Corps, had got a number of batteries in position, without reference to where they belonged. I shewed him my order, at which he was at first rather huffy, but I explained to him that I did not mean to interfere with his dispositions, and on the contrary would give him full command at this point, and a right to retain whatever batteries he needed in spite of orders from their division commanders. I then saw each battery commander there, and directed them to obey Captain Weed's orders. I found they were from every corps in the army, and, the emergency being over, some of them were anxious to rejoin their own divisions.

I also enquired particularly into their condition. I found several had not obeyed orders as to filling up with ammunition, and one Ohio battery was reduced down to its gun limbers half-full. The lieutenant in command was a good deal frightened when I reminded him of General Hunt's orders, and informed him that he would have to remain, should there be another attack, even if he had not a round of fire.

The corps commanders all received my order and explanations kindly, especially when I told them I did not intend to interfere. Sickles I had no occasion to see. His corps, having suffered badly in the morning, was in reserve. Howard said he was rejoiced at such an order, and at once called up his principal staff officer, and directed him to accompany me along his lines, shew me the dispositions which had been made, and aid me in carrying out whatever alterations I might think best. There were only two or three batteries in position on Howard's line, but one of which I changed slightly: asking, however, that the timber in their front might be cut in certain places, so as to give them a better range. I could readily believe that the Eleventh Corps had run away *bodily* the night before, for it seemed to be all here in line now; their organization in no way disturbed. While I was with Howard I noticed one thing I have not seen in any other command in our army: a division staff officer rode up and reported that a certain order had been carried out. In these really essential military points our army is very remiss. Staff officers generally do not even consider it necessary to report that they have delivered an order with which they have been sent; much less do the subordinate commanders report when the order has been executed; so that the General cannot know with certainty how things stand.

The left of the army rests upon a high open knoll, a few hundred yards from the river, and commanding the road, a small one, leading to Banks's Ford and Fredericksburg for a couple of miles. Here I found Captain Randall of the First Artillery, with two batteries. Like Weed, he had taken them without reference to the infantry posted here. Indeed, I do not know that I found a single battery with its own corps. The position was a beautiful one to look from as well as to fire from. The officers had a couple of tents pitched in rear of their guns, the men were lying under the trees, and things looked like anything but a fight. I dismounted and rested here for half an hour, being very tired. Randall was kind enough to give me some coffee and fried ham. Who would not be a light battery commander? No General, not even Hooker, is half as well off, as Randall here lying on the soft grass under his tent, with nothing to worry him, and no responsibility unless the enemy came into actual sight of his position. . . .

Returning again to the front, I passed along the whole line of our own corps to the extreme right, and then down along the river to the bridges, so as to make myself acquainted with all the roads so far as possible. All over this country to the rear I met stragglers from all the corps, but by far the most from the Twelfth Corps. The fights of yesterday afternoon and this morning seem to have scattered this corps to the winds. Wherever I have been today I have come across officers and men belonging to it, by scores, and but very little of it was in line of battle. The Third Corps must have been very badly handled too. On one of my rides to the front I met General Revere, about a mile in rear of the line of battle, with what was left, as he said, of my old division; taking it back to reorganize. General Berry, its commander, he told me was killed, and Mott wounded.[*]

When I got again to the front I found the enemy making another attempt to break through at the point held by Captain Weed. The woods opposite were only about 300 yards distant; so that the batteries were under easy musketry fire. Weed had unhitched all his horses, and was moving about among his guns with actual delight beaming on every feature of his face. The rebs came out from the woods but being within easy canister range of the batteries were quickly sent back. Weed had about thirty guns at this point. I found "F" and "G" Pennsylvania of my own batteries here; also "K" of my regiment, under Captain Fitzhugh, whom I was delighted to see alive and well. He told me they had had an awful fight at Chancellorsville in the morning, that "B" and "D" of the regiment had been in the thick of it, and that General Hooker had openly declared there that he owed the salvation of his army to the good behaviour of his artillery. . . .

* Joseph Warren Revere, a grandson of Paul Revere, had been a midshipman, but left the navy to become a rancher in California. In 1861 he was appointed colonel of the Seventh New Jersey. For his conduct at Chancellorsville, where he moved a division to the rear for rest in the midst of battle, he was court-martialed and dismissed; but Lincoln mitigated the sentence by allowing his departure to be recorded as a resignation. Hiram G. Berry of Maine, who has appeared before and was now a major general, was slain leading a bayonet attack on May 3. Gershom Mott received his second wound at Chancellorsville, but survived for much hard fighting in Virginia under Grant.

When I was out at the left with Randall, heavy firing could be distinctly heard down the river, which has continued all the afternoon. Sedgwick, I learn, carried the heights of Fredericksburg early this morning and is pushing up towards us. Tomorrow morning we shall no doubt have a heavy fight, as Lee will be sure to attack Sedgwick before he joins us, and that will be the time for Hooker to pitch in. General Hunt has some batteries and a brigade at Banks's Ford, so as to open communications with Sedgwick so soon as he gets that far up.

No one can imagine how tired I and my poor horse were when soon after dark I brought up at General Hooker's headquarters for the night. For the last two hours my best efforts had been unavailing to get more than the slowest trot out of "Billy," and every step had been accompanied by a dig of the spurs. I had lost my glass somewhere, very likely torn from my back in the woods without my knowing it, so stiff was I, and aching in every limb. Hooker made his headquarters about 100 yards to the left of where the United States Ford road comes into the Ely's Ford road, and in rear of the left of the Fifth Corps. His spring waggon had just come up as I got there, and he had a half bottle of champagne opened. How good it was! None of his staff were with him but Lawrence, and the General was as communicative with me as in the old Peninsular days. He told me that he should give Lee tomorrow to attack him, and "then if he does not," said Hooker, "let him look out." . . .

I had almost forgotten to mention the most horrible thing of the day. The woods were on fire around Chancellorsville, where hundreds of our wounded must have lain, and been absolutely burned to death. We can only hope that many of them crawled, or were got off before the fire reached them, and that it made quick work with the others. The dry leaves in the woods catch like tinder at this season. . . .

* * *

As late as the morning of May 3 the struggle still remained undecided. Stonewall Jackson had been mortally wounded the night before; part of the Confederate forces were in confusion, and all were tired; while large sections of the Union army had not been used at all. Two divisions of Sickles' corps stood on high ground at a point called Hazel Grove between Lee's main army and the force he had detached under Jackson. Had they been reinforced and sustained they could have kept the enemy divided, and Lee might still have been defeated. But Hooker fatuously ordered the troops to fall back from Hazel Grove. Ambrose Powell Hill at once seized the hill, and Jeb Stuart placed artillery on it that swept the Chancellorsville lines below. The house was set afire, and the Union forces were pushed back into the Wilderness.

The desperation of the fighting on this second day of Chancellorsville was horrifying to onlookers. Men struggled like demons, and left windrows of slain and wounded behind them. Hooker, who had been stretched senseless across the sill of Chancellorsville House when a cannonball struck the pillar against which he was leaning, was for a time completely incapacitated. While half of his army battled fiercely, the whole corps moved only to fall back. De Trobriand in his memoirs completely supports the position that Wainwright takes in his diary. "Thus we find the army paralyzed," he writes, "at the very time when the capture of Fredericksburg Heights by Sedgwick, and his approach to the rear of Lee, should have been a signal to us for the redoubling of efforts, the decisive moment to throw the First Corps on the flank of Stuart, while the Fifth and Eleventh Corps strike the center of Lee. . . . Everything could yet have been saved; yet all was lost. Hooker was no longer Hooker."

The story of May 4 was equally sad. Lee, seeing that Hooker was inert, reinforced his lines in front of Sedgwick and attacked with all his energies. The Union commander found himself with about 20,000 men on a line six miles long sustaining an assault by about 25,000. No aid came from Hooker and the main army. It was with great difficulty that Sedgwick held on until night and a heavy fog enabled him to fall back across the Rappahannock.

On the evening of the 4th a council of war was held to discuss the question of retreat by the entire Union army. Meade wished to remain; so did the badly humiliated Howard. But Sickles and Couch voted for retreat, and Hooker decided to recross the Rappahannock. He was back where he had started, with losses of 12,000 men killed and wounded, fourteen guns, 20,000 small arms—and his reputation as a warrior.

❊ ❊ ❊

MAY 4, MONDAY. The first thing after daylight was to report to General Hunt what I had done the day before and turn matters over into his hands. We got a little breakfast, and then I went over the whole line with General Hunt. He approved of all the dispositions I had made, and finding that there was still trouble about getting ammunition, desired me to go down to the bridges and straighten that matter out; which I did as well as I could, though I was completely fagged out, and would much rather have gone quietly back to my own corps. When I got across the river I found the trains all in confusion, the rebs having brought a battery down to the river bank, and shelled them with a good deal of accuracy, so that they had to move their park.

As General Hunt had just come up from Banks's Ford and had the last news from Sedgwick, all those who knew him along the line were anxious to hear what he had to tell. We talked thus with pretty much every general officer of mark in the army. On hearing that the Sixth Corps had reached Banks's Ford, only ten miles off, they without exception made the same remark: "Lee will draw off heavily to attack Sedgwick and of course we shall pitch in this afternoon." That we should do it I had not a doubt; the merest tyro in military knowledge knows that having our army divided, it was Lee's business to attack the weaker division, and also that it was the business of the other division to move to the relief of the one attacked. Still we did nothing all day, though the noise of the attack on Sedgwick was plainly heard along our whole line for several hours before dark. Why we did not move I cannot say. I can only hope that Hooker has something very wise and deep on hand for tomorrow, to fulfill his speech to me last night. Our corps has pushed out two reconnoissances today; one for a couple of miles through the woods to our front, and the other to Ely's Ford, without either of them finding a sign of the enemy, save a few stragglers whom they brought in. . . .

My business with General Hunt occupied me till noon today, and since then I have been around among my own batteries, and examining the line held by our corps. The Fifth Maine is so badly used up that I have sent it back to Falmouth; they lost six men killed outright, and twenty-two wounded. At sunset I went back into the woods with my man, took a good sponge bath in a little streamlet, and got on clean underclothes, which refreshed me exceedingly. As I was coming back to headquarters, a heavy musketade broke out on the right of our line, where the nine months' Jerseymen were. It lasted about five minutes and then ceased entirely. Our lines along there are zig-zag, and one of the privates in his modesty had gone well out to the front; as he rose from his haunches, some of his comrades thought it was the enemy and fired. The line on the opposite face of the angle, in the dusk thought the fire was from the rebs, so they were soon in full blaze at each other. Two or three men were killed, and several wounded, but the man whose modesty caused it all escaped.

MAY 5, TUESDAY. Slept pretty well last night, and got up this morning, feeling a little rested. Like everyone else who knew the state of affairs, I expected this would be a busy day with a good deal of hard fighting. Sedgwick had been so hard pushed by Lee yesterday afternoon that he was obliged to withdraw across the river at Banks's Ford at dark. Hooker had assured me that he would make Lee smart today. I therefore felt sure that something would be done. Opinions were divided as to what was best. Some were in favour of bringing the Sixth Corps up here, and attacking with all our force, while others thought we should withdraw from here, and crossing again at Fredericksburg, where Gibbon's division still held the heights, push on between Lee and Richmond. But all have been disappointed. Today, like yesterday, has passed without moving a foot. Meade and Reynolds have been up at headquarters a great part of the time. Reynolds does not say what went on there, but lets fall enough to show that he wants to fight. General Hunt speaks much more openly in favour of it.

I got some dinner with William about two o'clock and remained there some time under a shelter tent as a heavy shower came up. An hour or so later, after I got back, we had another still heavier and lasting an hour. Never did I see it rain so hard before except during the night before Fair Oaks. The water actually ran down the hillside on which we were in one sheet an inch deep. Some twenty of us got under a single tent fly, spread like the roof of a lean-to. It was but very little protection, but being in the middle row I got off pretty well; those over and under me were wet through. The rain continued at intervals all night.

At seven P.M. we got orders to withdraw and cross the river. Wiedrich and Reynolds I sent off by a byroad which started directly in their rear, and joined the main road about halfway to the bridges, near an old mill. . . . On reaching the mill I found the head of the column of batteries halted and was told that it was done by General Hunt's order; he was near a fire in the woods close by. I rode over there and found Hunt with Meade and Reynolds. He told me that the river had risen so much the ends of our bridges were under water, and it was doubtful if we could get across. General Hooker had gone over and could not get back, nor was there any communication except by signal.

We stood around the fire there for nearly an hour. Being alone, the three generals expressed themselves pretty plainly against the withdrawal. By that time word came that the bridges had broken loose, and we were to go back to our old position. Meade's exclamation was: "What an act of Providence! Perhaps the salvation of the country will be brought about by this." I at once turned the batteries around, and took them back to their old positions. It was one o'clock when I reached headquarters. Everyone was asleep, the tent fly was full. I had no blankets; was very wet, and utterly miserable. Finding nothing else for it, I build up the fire, almost out, piled what little brush I could lay my hands on into a sort of seat to keep me off the wet ground, and sat down on it, expecting to keep guard all night.

In half an hour an orderly came with a note to General Hunt, which I took to him, feeling sure, as proved to be the case, that it contained orders to withdraw. We got off a second time now, and went clear across the river. It was raining and cold; my legs were wet as they could well be, and I was fearfully tired. The batteries lumbered on slowly through the mud, and the infantry with them; men and horses were all more than half asleep. When I would get a short distance ahead of the batteries I would dismount by some fire and try to warm a little life into my feet and legs. Perhaps I stopped in this way four or five times. The fires were surrounded by men who had straggled off to warm themselves. I was very much struck by hearing almost identical remarks from the men wherever I stopped. All appeared to feel that our retreat was a disgrace, and none could understand it, but each conversation concluded the same: "If Little Mac had been here we never should have gone off this way." The confidence of the men in their old commander certainly is not yet shaken.

MAY 6, WEDNESDAY. The day was just beginning to break as we got down onto the flat around the bridges. Here I found Captain Fitzhugh with several batteries, who informed me that he was ordered to say that no more artillery would cross the river until further orders; at the time there were more batteries there than could be used. I halted mine there, and then crossed the river myself to look for Reynolds or Hunt. Finding neither, I pushed on up the hill to Hooker's headquarters, where, everybody being asleep, it was after a good deal of trouble that I got hold of Colonel Sharp, Patrick's assistant. Never in my life before was I so tired and sleepy. It was with the greatest difficulty I could even think. Everyone else, too, seemed to be in about the same condition. I managed to tell Sharp the state of things, and at the same time told him it was utterly impossible for me to go across the river again, so he kindly offered to see to matters. I got off my horse at a hospital tent near by where I found some doctors that I knew, and fairly dropped down asleep on some blankets. For the first time, I was totally used up. It was just one week since we broke camp. During that time I have never had more than 6 hours sleep out of the 24, and last night none; I was tired half to death, wet to the skin, and nearly frozen.

I got about three-quarters of an hour sleep, when General Reynolds sent for me, and ordered me to see that all the batteries not needed by General Hunt were sent home to their respective divisions. I was lucky enough to find General Hunt easily, who only wanted two rifled batteries. Cooper and Thompson were left, they not having been in position since we came up the river. After starting the others off, each on his own hook, I set off to find my way home alone, even without an orderly. The rain had stopped, but it was not yet clear; the mud was almost knee deep, and "Billy," as tired, sleepy, and hungry as his master, could with difficulty be urged to move at all. At the church I met Dr. Bache. He had spent the night at a house a mile or so farther, had a good sleep, and breakfast for himself and horse. Having no business to take him to the ford, he went back to this house with me, where I managed to dry myself be-

fore a large wood fire, got something to eat, and then a two hours'
sleep in an old rocking chair by the fire. At the same time Bache's orderly
fed and groomed my horse, so that a little before noon we started again
for camp.

Going by an inner road we escaped meeting any large body of troops,
and reached Army Headquarters by three or four in the afternoon. None
of their tents had been struck, so Warner gave me a good dinner,
and afterwards I got another sleep of an hour or so. General Hunt came
in about dark, from whom I learned that our bridges were all safely
up, without any trouble from the enemy, save that they posted a few
batteries about 8 A.M., and tried to annoy us on this side in the removal
of the last from the river bank. Our batteries replied and finally drove
them off. Officers were continually arriving at the General's quarters,
whose hospitality embraced them all. The opinion was universal that
we might have done better, and that the failure would doubtless cost
Hooker his place. Some half dozen of us, in talking over his successor,
all agreed on Meade as the fittest man in this army, with Warren as chief
of staff. From what I had seen of Meade during the three days I was
at Chancellorsville, and from my previous knowledge of him, I had given
him the preference, and was glad to find that there were others, good
judges, who agreed with me. Of Warren I know but very little.*

"WALLACE HOUSE," MAY 7, THURSDAY.   After every action one feels kindly
to every one you know, and it is hard work to pass them without stopping
to speak. After such a battle as we have just come from, amounting almost to a campaign, there will be a vast amount to say. Every tongue
in the army seems today to be wagging its fastest. The greater part
of what is said they would do much better to leave unsaid. Nearly all
are very bitter on Hooker, and many accuse him openly of being drunk.
When I saw him he shewed no signs of having drunk at all that I
could see, and I saw a good deal of him on Sunday; the idea certainly
never entered my head that day. The General has just issued a rather
extraordinary Order No. 49, in which he "congratulates" the army "on
its achievements of the last seven days," and says "that the reasons" of
its failure "are well known to the Army." It is these very reasons that
everyone I have met is looking for; what they are no one seems able to
conceive. This is bad enough, but he goes on to boast of our achievements, captures, and so on, while the balance is altogether on the other

---

* Gouverneur Kemble Warren, of New York, a graduate of West Point in 1850, had
been only a regimental commander until Yorktown, after which he led a brigade. He
had fought in the Seven Days, at Second Manassas, Antietam, and Fredericksburg; and
early in 1863 he was appointed chief topographical engineer of the Army of the Potomac. He was to perform memorable service to the Union at Gettysburg, where his
monument stands on Little Round Top.

side, and the army more nearly disgraced than it has ever been before. Such braggadocio is worse than ridiculous.

It is reported that Stonewall Jackson, "Lee's right arm," was mortally wounded in the fight of Saturday night.

NEAR WHITE OAK CHURCH, MAY 10, SUNDAY. Am once more beginning to feel somewhat settled, and to see my way clear towards completing the reports, etc., of our late doings. We moved here on Friday; have a fine open airy location, far enough from the road to escape the dust and annoyances of passing teams but no more. The weather is now so mild that we shall only occasionally need a little fire to stand around of an evening. Our tents are arranged much as they were before; and are to have an arbour of evergreens built over them. . . .

Have letters from home written since they received news of our failure. They seem to have as hard work making head or tail of it as we do. The newspapers, they say, each tells a different story, and probably none of them the true one. The *Tribune*, Mary writes me, is very severe on its pet, Hooker. Here we are not allowed to see any paper except the Washington *Chronicle*, which tries to make out a glorious victory. This attempt to keep newspapers from our men is a very absurd step on the part of the Administration; they are not, like Europeans, content to remain in ignorance, and the very stopping of the papers excites their curiosity to see what is in them, which, if not satisfied, will make them believe it worse than it really is. The privates discuss the cause of our failure quite as much as the officers, their little knowledge of course leading them to seize on the most tangible reason, without any very close examination into the cause. So one hears them asking on all sides, why the troops around Washington were not sent down to help us: "If Davis could spare every man from Richmond, why could not Lincoln run the same risk in Washington?" Had our defeat been owing to the want of men, their reasoning would be perfectly good, but it was not. On the contrary, Hooker had more than he could manage, and the First, Second, and Fifth Corps took almost no part in the fight. Save the Sixth Corps, which was perfectly successful, and Hooker's own old division, no part of the old Army of the Potomac was heavily engaged. The Eleventh Corps skedaddled, and the Twelfth—well, I believe the Twelfth did better than the Eleventh, but they are undoubtedly the two poorest corps in the army. Then he put in his old division, which fought well, but was eaten up; and there the fight ended so far as Hooker was concerned.

I do not yet know what our loss is, but think it will mount up to about 15,000; of whom some 5,000 were captured. They have requested us to send over for many of our wounded as they have not medical force enough to attend to them; a string of ambulances went up and brought them off. General Gordon, who was in command there, was very un-communicative, and would not allow anyone to go back into the country far enough to judge at all of their loss.*

MAY 12, TUESDAY.   Yesterday I completed my detailed report of what my batteries did in the late operations. It was a short report, for while under my own command they were not engaged of consequence. I also yesterday sent the batteries to report again to their several divisions. On going up to General Hunt's after this, I learned that Hooker had at last determined to adopt the brigade organization for the artillery. It came quite unexpected . . . but none the less welcome, though it will be difficult now to get the thing properly organized before we have to start again, and the whole winter has been to a certain extent lost. I feel that if I had had my batteries close under my eye for the four months we lay at Belle Plaine, I could have done a great deal towards instructing and disciplining them, which now I shall not have time for.

* Military authorities are in wide disagreement on numbers and losses in the Chancellorsville fighting. Major John Bigelow in his masterly book on the battle puts the Union army at 133,868 aggregate, and its killed, wounded, and missing at 17,278, the strength of the Army of Northern Virginia at 60,892 aggregate, and its killed, wounded, and missing at 12,821.

TEN

LEE INVADES PENNSYLVANIA

As grief and depression overspread the North after Chancellorsville, Lincoln sent Hooker a patient letter. The general's movement had now failed, he wrote. "What next? If possible, I would be very glad of another movement early enough to give us some benefit from the fact of the enemy's communication being broken; but neither for this reason nor any other do I wish anything done in desperation or rashness. . . . Have you already in your mind a plan wholly or partially formed? If you have, prosecute it without intereference from me." Hooker made it plain that he could not move at once. His army was reduced by the withdrawal of nearly 23,000 men who had enlisted for two years or nine months, and he thought the enemy forces larger than his. Lincoln agreed that it might be best to recuperate the army, and merely "keep the enemy at bay and out of other mischief, by menaces and occasional cavalry raids, if practicable. . . ."

But Lee was not willing to be kept at bay. He meant to strike a blow. It was impossible to attack Hooker in his strong positions opposite Fredericksburg with much hope of success. He should therefore march into the Shenandoah Valley to rescue its people and resources and, if circumstances favored, press on to transfer the scene of hostilities north of the Potomac. Thus drawing the Army of the Potomac northward, he might find an opportunity to assail it on the march. And if he won another great victory north of the Potomac, he might capture some large Northern city; or bring the French and British governments up to the point of intervention; or so discourage the Northern people that they would lose heart in the war.

Lee's decision was not ratified by Jefferson Davis' Administration without strong opposition in his Cabinet. Grant was pressing Pemberton's army hard before Vicksburg. James A. Seddon, Secretary of War, had proposed that two or three of Lee's brigades be sent as a reinforcement to the Army of the West. In a crucial Cabinet meeting on May 26 John H. Reagan of Texas pleaded for rescuing Vicksburg rather than invading Maryland and Pennsylvania; but Davis and the majority decided in favor of Lee's plan. Hooker wrote the President on May 28 that the enemy was about to make a movement of some sort. Meanwhile, the North got a little comfort out of some cavalry operations first under Stoneman, and then under his successor Major General Alfred Pleasonton.

* * *

MAY 14 [1863], THURSDAY.   The weather continues fine and warm; really hot in the middle of the day. The evenings are perfectly charming, and after a hard day's work followed by a good dinner, the sitting out in the starlight and soft balmy air has been a pure enjoyment. We had a heavy shower today followed by a change of wind to the north.

Yesterday the new organization of the artillery in this corps was announced in orders, putting me formally in command. A quartermaster was also assigned to me, who is to act as commissary as well, in the person of Captain Cruttenden. He was depot quartermaster at Belle Plaine all winter, and is said to be a first-rate man. . . . I issued my first order today as a brigade commander, directing the batteries to move their camps to a spot about two hundred yards from these headquarters. The place is a pretty good one, though the camps cannot be arranged with any general symmetry. General Hunt's order carrying out the new organization directs that the batteries retained in the corps be raised to "110 enlisted men for four guns, and 150 enlisted men for six guns" from the attached infantrymen belonging to the corps.

MAY 17, SUNDAY.   Have got my new concern pretty well started. . . . When I was at General Hunt's today he asked me if I could turn my brigade out for review tomorrow for an English officer visiting here, Lord Abinger. I told him that my horses were wretched, but that I was not ashamed of the command in any other respect. I fear, though, that we shall not make much of a show.

There are no indications of an early move on our part yet, and so far as I know all is quiet on the other side of the river. Stonewall Jackson is certainly dead; he was severely wounded late in the attack on Saturday afternoon and died three or four days afterward. Regrets for the man himself are as freely expressed by all who knew him personally in our army as they can be on the other side. Every one of his old acquaintances whom I have heard speak of him say that he was one of the purest, most honourable and conscientious men that ever lived. He was sincerely religious, verging a little perhaps on the fanatic. Like Lee and many other of the best officers they have on the other side, Jackson was decidedly opposed to secession, but Virginia having seceded he believed that it was his duty to fight for what he considered his country, sacrificing his feelings to what he conscientiously believed to be his duty. It is impossible to look upon this class of men in our Southern states as actual traitors. They are so most certainly in deed, but not in heart; on the contrary, it is their very patriotism which makes them traitors. For my own part I believe that the same idea of allegiance to their state is in fact almost as prevalent at the North as it is at the South, and were the shoe on the other foot, would not trust Massachusetts any sooner than I would South Carolina, or Pennsylvania sooner than Mississippi. To the rebels the loss of Stonewall Jackson is almost equal to a defeat. Full of energy, prompt, obedient and lightning quick in his obedience, worshipped by his men, and fully appreciated by his commander, he well deserved the name of "Lee's right arm"; a "right arm" which had never failed him whether the blow was to be struck near by, or hundreds of miles away.

At last the New York papers are allowed to come down to the army after being kept out for nearly three weeks. I cannot yet understand why the newsboys were not allowed to bring them for those sent by mail were not stopped, and hundreds were brought down every day by officers and men coming from Washington. The news contained in them is little if any more reliable than that in the Washington *Chronicle*, the latter being made up entirely from the former, but then we get both sides, and do not have to take only just such lies or rumours as Stanton and Forney choose to give us.* If I may judge of the correctness of their information by the letters from their correspondents in this army, at least three-quarters of it must be incorrect; so the befogged state of the good people at home is not to be wondered at. . . .

A very good sanitary order has been drawn up by Dr. Letterman, medical director of this army.† I particularly like what he says against

* John W. Forney (1817–81), a Pennsylvania journalist and politician, had established the Philadelphia *Press* in 1857, at first as a supporter of President Buchanan. When the Lecompton issue became acute he joined Stephen A. Douglas in assailing the President, and by 1860 had become a Republican. In 1861, when secretary of the Senate, he founded the Washington *Sunday Morning Chronicle*, which the next year he converted into the *Daily Morning Chronicle*. It actively supported Lincoln, Stanton, and the general policies of the Administration. Despite Wainwright's disparaging remarks, the *Chronicle* was widely regarded as the best newspaper in the capital. For several days after Hooker's defeat the War Department imposed a censorship on all news from the army. To elude the censors the correspondents of New York dailies had to find their way out of the lines and go direct to their newspaper offices with their reports. On Tuesday, May 5, Henry J. Raymond's *Times* had a full account of the fighting on Saturday and Sunday; and on Tuesday the 6th Horace Greeley of the *Tribune* knew all about the disaster. With white face and trembling lips, he exclaimed to his associates: "My God, it is horrible, horrible! and to think of it, 130,000 magnificent soldiers so cut to pieces by 60,000 half-starved ragamuffins!" The censorship was not lifted until May 7. Some of the reporting of the battle was confused; but then, as Wainwright states, most of the officers on the field were badly confused.

† Jonathan Letterman (1824–72), a Pennsylvania physician of long army experience, had been appointed medical director of the Army of the Potomac by McClellan in

camping in the woods, and believe that it is cooler as well as more healthy on the open hilltops. Every item in the order is sound sense, except that requiring all sinks to be dug eight feet deep! The doctor probably does not know how much eight feet is, and has no idea of the labour of digging a hole to that depth.

In General Order No. 53, Hooker prescribes division and brigade headquarters flags, carrying out the idea of the distinguishing badges ordered some time since, which I do not remember mentioning here. It is said to be an idea of Butterfield's, and is a good one, but not original with him; only a carrying out of Kearny's red patch. By these orders the corps of this army will be distinguished from one another hereafter by symbols to be worn by all the officers and men on the cap, painted on the covers of all waggons, and displayed on all general headquarters flags. These symbols are: for the First Corps a disk (what Butterfield calls "a flat sphere"); the Second a trefoil; the Third a lozenge; the Fifth a Maltese cross; the Sixth a Greek cross; the Eleventh a crescent; the Twelfth a star. The different divisions in each corps are distinguished by the colour of the symbol, red for the first, white for the second, and blue for the third. For corps headquarters we have adopted a gold enamelled disk, with the red, white and blue dividing it Ⓐ. This was General Reynolds's own idea and has been followed by most of the other corps headquarters. A rectangular flag designates a division, triangular a brigade; a white ground with red symbol the first division and its brigades; a blue ground and white symbol the second; and a white ground and blue symbol the third. Different brigades in the division are designated by a blue or red border to their flag. No special badge has been ordered for the artillery; but most of them have adopted the corps headquarters badge. I have not ordered it, but allow my men to wear it when they choose. I mean them all to wear their crossed cannon and letters on their caps which will mark them all sufficiently.

MAY 21, THURSDAY. The weather continues perfect, warm and most charming. All remains quiet so far as I hear. . . .

On Monday I had my little command out for parade and review for the first time; it looked quite creditable save in respect to horseflesh. General Hunt came up, and I supposed was to review, but he made Lord Abinger receive the salute, with which "me Lud" was much flattered. After the review they all came and dined with us. I was much pleased with Lord Abinger, who shewed himself a sensible fellow, well

---

June 1862, and had accomplished a memorable feat of reorganization. He had established mobile hospitals and created an effective system of ambulances for battlefield service. Now he was taking in hand the sanitary regulations of the army. His scientific proficiency, insight into army problems, and administrative skill had a world-wide effect on military practice.

informed on military matters for an English officer. He was through the Crimean war on the staff of his uncle, General Scarlett,* who was one of their best division commanders there. I believe his present rank is lieutenant-colonel of the Fusilier Guards, but am not certain. Fortunately our Frenchman had not left us, but it was one of his last days. We had fresh lamb and some other matters down from Washington, so he sent us up a really good dinner and our guests were pleased to pronounce him a veritable artiste for an army cook. Altogether I had a very pleasant day, and really enjoyed having visitors.

Our French cook has left us; offered a place at the West Point Hotel, he says, for the summer. But I suspect he does not like active campaigning, where he not only has a hard life, but nothing to cook, and nothing to cook it in. Sanderson has written for another. In the meantime his contraband "Ben" is acting cook. It is hard work to come down to nigger grease, after living so well as we have for months, but the chances are we shall have to endure it now for the whole summer.

Have been working up regimental business as well as my brigade affairs since my return, and have at last got squared up. On Monday received notice of the promotions and appointments I had recommended, and was really rejoiced when it was settled that Reynolds and Osborn were to be the majors, as I heard that there were several trying for these positions. . . . We completed the arbour over and in front of our tents today, so that our camp now looks very inviting. This artificial shade is much preferable to going into the woods, as it does not cut off any of the wind.

MAY 24, SUNDAY. The great topic of conversation of the newspapers for a week past has been Grant's victories in Mississippi. Today we have official information on the subject in a dispatch from Grant sent down to us from general headquarters. From the time he ran the blockade with his vessels and landed at Port Gibson he seems to have marched from one victory to another. . . . I judge that the rebels have shown but little fight in the battles of Grant's, from the low figures at which he places their loss in men while he reports large captures of artillery. The dispatch mentions five distinct battles in seventeen days, in which Grant estimates the rebel loss in killed, wounded, and prisoners at 9,100; while he captured 68 pieces of field artillery. In his fight with Joe Johnston on the 14th he captured 17 pieces, and yet put Johnston's loss at only 400,

---

* The Scarlett family was distinguished in England. James Scarlett, first Baron Abinger, had been one of the most successful advocates of his time, and became lord chief baron of the exchequer in 1834. Sir James Yorke Scarlett, his son, led the desperate charge of the heavy brigade at Balaclava in the Crimean War, and with 700 men defeated 2,000 Russian cavalrymen. Every American officer who read Kinglake's history of the war, as many did, knew of his exploit. Another son achieved some repute as a diplomat.

barely enough men to man the guns captured. Both Lee's army and this one would think itself disgraced to lose a larger proportion of artillery than 1 piece to 1,000 men killed and wounded.

I do not want to detract from General Grant's success, but it does "rile" one a good deal to have the stay-at-homes contrasting his rapid victories with our little or no progress. They either do not or will not comprehend that the whole strength of the rebellion is concentrated in our front, and that their Western armies are made up in men and matériel of what is left over after furnishing Lee. Lieutenant-Colonel Bankhead was with Buell until Christmas, and Captain Comstock of the engineers has been sent out to Grant lately. Warner has just received a letter from the latter, who is with Grant, and he confirms all that Bankhead, and every other officer I have seen, says as to the vast inferiority of the Western armies on both sides compared with those here. . . .

The papers and the army continue to discuss the battle of Chancellorsville. Some of the papers are very severe on Hooker, and insist upon it that he was drunk, which I do not believe. Others go quite as far the other way, and try to screen him from all blame, seeking to throw it on one or the other of his subordinates. The attacks on General Howard are outrageous. He had been in command of the Eleventh Corps but a month before the fight, and was previously unknown to its officers and men. On the Peninsula he won the name of an excellent officer and brave man. He is the only religious man of high rank I know of in this army, and, in the little intercourse I have had with him, shewed himself the most polished gentlemen I have met. I know that he was very anxious to attack Lee on Monday, and together with Couch, Reynolds, and Meade was decidedly opposed to our withdrawal on Wednesday night. Sickles was the *only* corps commander who I have heard it said favoured the withdrawal. Of Slocum's opinion I am ignorant.*

We remain here in a perfect state of quiet. About all of the two-years' men, and a good part of the nine-months' men have gone home: a whole division of the latter, Humphreys's, from the Fifth Corps. Some of the troops around Washington have been sent down to replace them, among others the division of Pennsylvania reserves which used to be in this corps. Reynolds and Meade both applied for them; the latter was successful. The accession, however, by no means keep up our strength to its numbers a month ago, and the newspapers overestimate it at least 30 per cent. Leaving out the cavalry, I doubt it we have over 70,000 men at this time. Our best men are still left, though few in numbers, the old "Army

---

* Slocum did not reach the council of war until after it ended, and Sedgwick was busy fighting. Reynolds and Howard were certainly in favor of fighting on; so was Meade. But Couch wanted an advance only under certain conditions, and stated later that he voted against it.

of the Potomac." Properly handled by a general in whom officers and men had confidence, I believe we could now whip Lee. But there is only one man in whom this army would have entire confidence, and no chance of his ever again having command, unless Lee is once more knocking at the gates of Washington.

My batteries are getting along nicely, except that we want some better horses. We get a fair allowance of hay now. The loss in ordnance stores has been made good, and the Fifth Maine is filled up with men. The division commanders, of course, do not like the batteries being taken from them, so Robinson being called upon for the detail of 35 men, sent over the offscourings of some of his regiments. I had them examined by my little doctor, who reported 30 of them physically unfit for artillery service, which report was sent up to corps headquarters with the men, and at last Stevens obtained a passable set.

MAY 28, THURSDAY. Have had a change in the weather. All the first of the week was cloudy, damp, and cold, though without rain, so that fires were in demand, around which we shivered all the evening. Today it cleared off and is mild again. Everything continues quiet here, though there are rumours that Lee is stirring, and many of us believe that our next move will be in the direction of Washington. . . .

This war, it seems, does not confine the ravages of death to those actually engaged. I heard the other day that it had carried off my old friend James Bolton, away out in England. James, though born in England, and not in this country for near twenty years, was intensely American in all his feelings. Since the commencement of this rebellion he has spent all the leisure moments he could get from the duties of his parish in trying to enlighten the English as to the true state of matters here. Night and day, his wife says, he was able to think of little else, and his physicians attribute his death to his anxiety and nervousness on this subject, preventing his rallying from a comparatively slight attack of illness. He was true, whole-souled, earnest, brave with the highest courage. A more manly man, a purer, more cheerful, more real Christian, or a more loving, faithful, jolly friend I shall never meet with in life. The world will not acknowledge it, but his death was as real, as noble a sacrifice to the cause of our Union, as if he had fallen on the field of Chancellorsville.

Yesterday we were quite stirred up by orders to get ready to start instanter. This was however soon followed by orders to draw rations, have quartermaster waggons packed, and be in a constant state of readiness. I have not been able to learn exactly what was the cause of these orders, but suppose they were brought out by reported moves of Lee. I believe that my command is as near ready to move as I can make it, except in the matter of horses, which we are promised from the quartermaster trains so soon as mules arrive from Washington to replace them.

MAY 31, SUNDAY.   General Hooker has just left us: he came over to see Reynolds, who however went up to Washington this morning, summoned up by the President or somebody. Old Sanderson saw the General ride up and invited him to dismount, which he did, and sat an hour with us. I confess to being old fashioned, undemocratic, or whatever it may be in my notions enough not to approve of the commander-in-chief of an army making visits to the staff of his subordinates. An occasional friendly call on his corps commander, or even on individuals of lower grades if they are old friends or have distinguished themselves, is right and proper; but to sit an hour drinking and talking with a whole staff is too much of a coming down to please me. All in camp of course gathered around the General, who did the talking. . . .

The General sat with us for an hour, and spent that time in an attempt to justify himself as to the result of Chancellorsville. I cannot begin to write down half what he said, for he always talks in a very rambling, unconnected way. He based his defence for not attacking Lee on Monday, first that he expected Lee would attack his own right. That Stonewall Jackson in striking the Eleventh Corps on Saturday evening only did so in passing around to turn our right and get between us and our bridges; and he cited a letter from Jackson to his wife, which has been published in the papers, as evidence that he was correct in his surmise, and that Jackson's fall alone prevented that plan being carried out. He, Hooker, did not know that Jackson had been wounded; consequently, expecting the attack on his right, placed and kept the First and Fifth Corps there in readiness to meet it.

This sounded well and farseeing. But Jackson would in that case have attacked our right by Sunday morning, or at the very latest sometimes that day. Whereas Averell's cavalry came in from that direction on Sunday evening, and the First Corps pushed out strong reconnoissances on Monday without seeing a sign of the enemy. So that this was no reason for not attacking on Monday afternoon, when Lee had gone to pitch into Sedgwick; which is the time, it has always seemed to me, Hooker was most to blame for not taking advantage of. This reason of his for keeping so many men out of the fight makes me think of Sumner's holding his 30,000 in reserve at Williamsburg. Had Reynolds been allowed to put his fresh corps in at Chancellorsville house, as he wanted to, on Sunday morning, and been supported by Meade, who knows what the result might have been? I know that this is what Reynolds thinks ought to have been done, and what Hooker himself would have advocated had he been a subordinate. . . .

The second excuse which Hooker brought up was worse than the first, being an attempt to throw the whole blame on General Sedgwick. He was very bitter against "Uncle John," accusing him of being slow and afraid to fight; also of disobeying orders directly. Now for a general to make such charges against an absent subordinate, in defending himself before a lot of young staff officers, while he takes no official notice of it, is—well, I hope Hooker was drunk while here, for his own sake. I said nothing in reply to his statements; but my feelings were divided between shame for my commanding general, and indignation at the attack on so true, brave, and modest a man as Sedgwick.

A day or two ago I saw McMahon, adjutant-general of the Sixth Corps, who told me the other side of the story; and as we were down here part of the time, I know much of what McMahon said is correct. For the rest he says the orders and dispatches are on file in his office. That Sedgwick did not do what Hooker wanted him to there is no doubt, I believe; but this was more from Hooker's fault than his, owing as it was to the indistinct, even nonsensical wording of the orders received, and the fact that they were delivered from twelve to twenty-four hours later than they should have been. This last is attributed to some new plan of Butterfield's, I don't know what, but certainly a poor substitute for the telegraph.

The first order about which there was trouble was the one for our corps to be at United States Ford by daylight on Saturday; which, as I have mentioned, was not received until twenty hours after it ought to have reached us. On Saturday morning Sedgwick received two dispatches in both of which General Hooker informed him that the enemy were in full retreat down the Bowling Green road, and directing him to cut them off. Now, the Sixth Corps had had its pickets on this road for three days, and the only enemy they had seen were those in the trenches opposed to them, and Jackson's corps marching *up* on Friday. The Bowling Green road, too, commences at Fredericksburg, twelve miles or more from where Hooker was; so these dispatches were nonsense, to say nothing of the fact that Lee had at no time shown any sign of a retreat by any road whatever. Sedgwick could not make out what they meant, but as Hooker seemed to want him to do something, he crossed another division over the river, drove in the rebel pickets and placed his line of battle on the Bowling Green road before dark; and then went to see Butterfield, who remained in the old headquarters camp until Monday.

Soon after midnight on Saturday, and while Sedgwick was still absent, an order came directing him to cross the river at Fredericksburg, attack the heights, which were nearly abandoned, and be at Banks's Ford by morning. This is the main point on which Hooker rests his blame of Sedgwick; that he only reached Banks's Ford at nightfall instead of in the morning of Monday. But even had there been no force to oppose him except the few cavalry which Hooker supposed to be in the trenches, Sedgwick could hardly have moved twelve miles through that country, where he would have at least been in danger of an attack, to Banks's Ford so as to have got there in less than twelve hours from the time of receiving his order. As it was there were enough rebels on the heights back of Fredericksburg to make a good fight by the aid of their strong position, so that it required daylight to dislodge them. And then they held a second line on Marye's Heights which they stuck to pretty obstinately, the two fights costing Sedgwick several thousand men. As he was obliged to wait until daylight before he could attack, it seems to me that he did pretty well to carry two such strong positions and drive the opposing force twelve miles in fourteen hours, even though he had three men to their one.

This order, too, was very queer in that it directed Sedgwick to cross at Fredericksburg, while he was already over the river two miles below, and to have come back and then crossed again would have taken him at the very least four hours, probably six. Immediately on receiving the order the troops were got under arms, so that an hour later when Sedgwick got back the advance was made from their then position at once. From all that I can learn, so far from any blame resting on Sedgwick, he deserves the highest commendation; and all the glory of the late engagements belongs to him and his corps, save what the artillery corps won by such hard work at Chancellorsville.

On Monday afternoon, too, he held his own against Lee himself, until Hooker ordered him to withdraw at Banks's Ford. Hooker says that this order was countermanded and that there was no occasion for Sedgwick to withdraw. But at the time the countermanding order was received, most of the corps had already crossed to this side: and Sedgwick and his division generals say that it would have been certain destruction to have remained there.

It seemed to me worth while to write this out this afternoon; for I got my information on both sides as direct as possible, and as yet have not seen any of it in print. It does not throw any light on the question why Hooker did not make an advance on Monday, nor explain his conduct in any way. The queer orders sent to Sedgwick give more colour to the report of his being drunk than anything else I have heard. Still I cannot believe it, and do not hesitate to say that he was perfectly sober every time I saw him on Sunday.

CAMP NEAR WHITE OAK CHURCH, JUNE 4, 1863, THURSDAY. Last night we were stirred up about midnight with orders to be ready to move half an hour after daylight this morning. It did not result in anything more than keeping us up the greater part of the night, so that everyone is very sleepy and cross this morning. By 9 or 10 o'clock all were settled down again in quietness. I have not learned the cause of the stir yet, but presume that it was owing to some reported movements on Lee's part. I hardly know what to think about the probabilities of Lee's taking the offensive before the fate of Vicksburg is decided. Should Johnston succeed in forcing Grant to raise the siege we shall no doubt have him down upon us at once. But so long as the prospects continue favourable for us there, I hardly think that they will risk a double defeat, which would shake their cause to the very centre. The Richmond papers of Tuesday, which reached us the same evening, had not a word of news from Vicksburg, except such as they copied from New York papers.

Yesterday afternoon I went over to Williams's camp, about half a mile off from here. . . . On my way over there, I saw how the poor privates of the army dispose of their money, the paymaster having been down here lately. Under the shade of a fine wood, I came across a gambling saloon of at least a couple of acres in extent, literally covered with men gathered around checkered cloths and ring-boards. There must have been over a thousand of them, and some had large piles of bank notes alongside of them. This vice has been growing very rapidly in the army both among officers and men; even the contrabands are at it half the day instead of attending to their masters' work. No women being allowed in the army, and there being next to none in the country around, the men are shut off from all excitement in that line; whiskey too is pretty difficult for the privates to get: and the absence of these two sources of entertainment may drive them more strongly into gambling. Some of the head gamblers make a great deal of money out of it. I have heard of men sending home $1,000 at a time. Many of the losers too seem to have funds at home, on which they draw when their pay is exhausted. . . .

Butterfield moved Army Headquarters this week. They needed it badly, for the old ground had got to be very filthy. Their present camp . . . has been laid out and cleared up quite tastily, but is located in the middle of a dense wood of young pines, where they cannot get a breath of wind, so that these hot days it is almost intolerable. Had he moved there last February, it would have made lovely winter quarters for them. But going into such a position now is simply absurd, to say nothing of its being in direct contravention of their own order as to camping in the wood. Butterfield has not made so good a chief of staff as I expected. Much to my surprise he does not seem to have practical common sense in all points, the very trait of character in which it was supposed he would excel. He is most thoroughly hated by all the officers at headquarters as a meddling, over-conceited fellow. They say that Hooker would be a delightful man to serve with if he would only get rid of "the little Napoleon."

* * *

Lee's invasion was now fully under way. He had been reinforced by James Longstreet's two divisions and a large number of conscripts, for the South was rigidly enforcing the draft; so that by May 31 his reports showed that he had 88,754 men, of whom 68,352 were ready for battle After Stonewall Jackson's death he reorganized this large force in three corps under Longstreet, Richard S. Ewell, and Ambrose P. Hill. Temporarily leaving Hill with 20,000 men to guard the Rappahannock line, he concentrated his forces at Culpeper, skillfully swung them into the Shenandoah Valley, and moved north behind the rampart of the Blue Ridge.

Meanwhile Hooker, who still had about 100,000 men, was alert to the situation and kept fairly well informed by his superior intelligence service. He had Sedgwick throw troops across the Rappahannock to ascertain if Lee's main body had really departed, but A. P. Hill responded so briskly that Sedgwick mistakenly concluded they had not. Then Hooker ordered Pleasonton to use all the Union cavalry in a reconnaissance toward Culpeper, to find out how large a Confederate body was being gathered there. The sequel was a collision between Pleasonton and Jeb Stuart in the heaviest cavalry battle of the war, Brandy Station. Though Stuart drove Pleasonton back and captured three guns, the Union leader accomplished his main object—he learned for a certainty that Lee was on his way toward Maryland and some unknown Northern objective.

With another great battle impending, the question whether Hooker should be kept in his command was still unsettled. The Cabinet divided on this issue. Salmon P. Chase supported the general; perhaps Stanton for a time did so. William H. Seward, Montgomery Blair, and Gideon Welles believed that he should be displaced in favor of another general. The Congressional radicals, including a majority of the Committee on the Conduct of the War, remained favorable to Hooker. "I believe he can and will whip the Rebels in the next fight," Senator Zachariah Chandler wrote his wife. If a new leader was to be appointed, the choice lay between Meade and Wainwright's immediate commander, Reynolds. Till the very end of June the question remained undecided.

Hooker's first plan was to attack Lee's rear and move upon Richmond, but the Administration forbade this, ordering him to keep his army north of the Rappahannock. He therefore moved his main forces north and west, paralleling Lee's march. Reynolds' corps, including Wainwright, marched back across old battlefields—Manassas, Chantilly—near Washington to a point on the Loudoun & Hampshire Railroad due west of the capital and close to the Potomac.

* * *

JUNE 7, SUNDAY. Something is certainly in the wind from the other side, for we of this corps are kept in a chronic state of readiness to start off on a gallop,'while some parts of the army are actually stirring. Yesterday and this morning we were under orders to be ready to move at daylight; men's tents were struck and all horses and teams harnessed and kept so until 9 or 10 o'clock. On Friday the Sixth Corps moved down to the river, and threw one division over at what is known as "Franklin's Crossing." The cavalry, I hear, are to make a grand reconnoissance or demonstration towards Culpeper today, and two brigades of picked infantry have been sent up to aid them, while the Third Corps is said to have moved up as far as Kelly's Ford in support. . . .

What all this movement means I do not know. The report in New York yesterday, it is said, was that Lee had evacuated and Hooker was in full pursuit. If Lee is leaving the other side he is not going towards Richmond, that is certain; but is rather trying to get around our right somewhere and either make an effort for Washington, or another dash into Maryland the same as he did last year. All Hooker's movements, especially the stretch of the army up the river, the threatening with a division of Sedgwick's over the river, and the cavalry move on Culpeper indicate that this is his notion. The cavalry will probably find out something on which we can act with certainty. I hear that Mr. Lincoln has been down here, and that finding the "Seven Sisters" could not reach a fifty-pounder the enemy have on the heights opposite, he declared he would send down a hundred-pounder on his own responsibility. I should think that, if we have to move in a hurry, Hooker might find it very much like a present of an elephant.

JUNE 11, THURSDAY. We are again under orders to move tomorrow morning, and this time I think we shall really get off. The first order came this morning, and directed that especial care should be taken to have the column as disembarrassed with waggons as possible, and all in a condition to move with great rapidity. This evening we have a corps order, saying that we will go in the direction of Bereah Church, the first division leading off at three o'clock, the second following at four, and the third at five o'clock; the artillery in rear of the first division. This gives us an early start, and should enable us to make quite a stretch if the roads are not blocked by other troops. What is in the wind I cannot say, nor which way we shall go from Bereah Church; but I do not believe we are bound for the south side of the Rappahannock again. The chances are that ours is a counter-move to one of Lee's.

I heard this morning that Pleasonton had a big fight on Tuesday at Brandy Station; decidedly the largest cavalry fight this war has yet produced. Hooker calls it a victory, though on what grounds exactly I cannot see. The numbers seem to have been about equal on the two sides, and the fighting has been back and forth. First we drove the rebel horse back on to their infantry supports, and then they drove ours back in the same way. The first is proved by our capture of Stuart's camp and baggage; the latter by our loss of two guns, and leaving most of our wounded on the field. . . .

Sedgwick's division still remains quietly on the other side of the river; they have thrown up a slight earthwork, pitched their tents, and made themselves quite at home. The pickets are on the most amiable terms, and save a few shots now and then from the long-range guns on either side, there is no disturbance. Mr. Lincoln's hundred-pounder has come down, and was hauled into position today, I hear.

The three deserters which were to have been shot in the Fifth Corps a week ago are still alive, having received a fortnight's grace from the President. Whether this will be followed up by entire pardon or not remains to be seen. We have had a general court martial sitting in the brigade; it took all the officers we could scare up in the command to compose the court. The prisoners were men of Stewart's battery charged with robbing a sutler, burning down his tent, and firing at him. Some half a dozen are implicated in the matter; whiskey the moving cause.

DEEP RUN, JUNE 12, FRIDAY.   We were all packed and ready to start, on time this morning, but did not get off until near 8 o'clock, the road being blocked by other troops. It was very tedious waiting so long with nothing to do to amuse one, especially when it happens so early in the morning. If one has to get his breakfast at break of day, it should be followed up by excitement or occupation enough to keep him awake. We got our quoits out at last, and killed some time that way. While we were waiting Reynolds shewed me a trait in his character which is to a certain extent commendable, but not always agreeable to others. He sent for me and desired me to send an order around to the battery commanders to feed up any hay they might have over, while they were waiting, instead of leaving it behind. A very right and wise thing for them to do; but this giving of orders about little things on the part of a corps commander is a sort of reflection on the ability of the subordinate, to whom he gives them, to understand and attend to his own business. I should have thought it an insult to my battery commanders to send such an order around to them; an officer who had not brains enough to think of such a thing as that, is not fit to have charge of a battery. I rode around, however, as I had to do something, and found, as I expected, that the matter was already attended to. It is a great mistake not to place confidence in those under you. Well enough to keep an eye on them until you know they are competent; but if you are interfering in every little matter they will never have confidence in themselves. . . .

We reached "Hartwood Church" about noon, and halted there for a couple of hours. General Meade's headquarters were close by, the Fifth Corps having been guarding United States and Banks's Fords since the cavalry were sent up the river. They do not move until tomorrow or next day. Webb gave me some dinner, and we had quite a talk. He told me that Hooker came over to see Meade soon after Chancellorsville, and tried to throw the blame of the failure on him. Meade talked very plainly, and getting mad, damned Hooker very freely; so much so that he, Webb, cleared out and called off the rest of the staff, fearing that a court martial might ensue. He says that Meade's temper is intolerable. Webb has just received a commission as brigadier-general, and is to have a brigade in the Second Corps.*

BEALTON STATION, JUNE 13, SATURDAY. Another fine day and a clear road. We made but twelve miles, and as we started early were in here soon after noon, and this time pitched all our tents as we may remain for some little time. Our camp is in a small wood about half a mile from the railroad. Some of the army are getting on to familiar ground again, as it was not far from here that Pope commenced his famous "victorious retreat" last year. . . . We are still in ignorance as to exactly what Lee is after. At least I am, and our uncertain movements indicate that General Hooker knows very little more. . . .

CENTREVILLE, JUNE 15, MONDAY. It would be hard to divide our march to this place from Bealton into days, as yesterday's march did not end until three o'clock this morning. We started quite late yesterday morning, but about noon received orders to push on as rapidly as possible, which caused our traveling so late, and made a long march of it up to Manassas Junction. The Third Corps moved at the same time, and as the country along the railroad is quite open we moved in a number of columns, which made a very pretty sight of it, and inspired a rivalry in the different commands as to their order in marching. I saw our first division at one time when I could take in the whole length of it, and have never seen so many men march so well before.

I have to keep at my battery officers all the time about their men straggling. They do not seem to know what it means. Cooper said to me at one time near Warrenton Junction that battery men never straggled. I pointed out a couple of his own two fields off, and asked what he called that. He said they would not straggle!—that he had never known any of his men to be absent when the battery got into camp at night. What a

---

* Alexander Stewart Webb, a New Yorker (West Point, 1855), had been in much of the fighting in the East, and had been chief of staff of the Fifth Corps at Antietam. A man of fine leadership, he rose to be major general, gained the Medal of Honor at Gettysburg, and has a well-earned statue in the Bloody Angle of Spotsylvania. After the war he was president of City College in New York for more than thirty years.

totally unmilitary, unexact people we are! Here was a good officer of near two years' service, who really thought that straggling only meant lagging behind, and that if his men were present at evening roll call it mattered not where they went meantime. I ordered him to call these men in, and informed him that he must keep each detachment on a line with their own pieces, and near to them, so that the sergeants can have their eye on them all the time. I do not want to put the screws on my officers too strong at the start, but shall first try to get right notions into their heads, and pique their pride. It is going to be a hard job to bring them up to the mark I aim at. . . .

JUNE 16, TUESDAY. We are lying quietly in camp today, waiting orders and what shall be decided on. A good part of the army is said to be about in this neighbourhood, as also general headquarters not very far off. The Eleventh and Twelfth Corps came direct across from Stafford Court House by way of "Wolfe Run Shoals," and the Fifth is also in. The Sixth Corps, too, is on its way, our demonstration across the river below Fredericksburg not having served to keep Lee there. Nor did Mr. Lincoln's hundred-pounder frighten him much: I hear that it was fired once and then started on its journey back to Washington. There is no doubt now that Lee's whole army has moved up into the Loudoun and Susquehanna Valleys. Whether he will take it all across the Potomac above Harper's Ferry, or only enough to attempt to draw us up there, and then strike for Washington by this line, is I presume what we are now waiting to ascertain. If the former proved to be the case we shall probably have some pretty tall marching.

I have ridden around today, and examined the ground hereabouts. Why Pope did not make this his standpoint instead of the south side of the run, I cannot imagine. That the army could not be rallied here after first Bull Run is comprehensible, on the ground that they were too badly whipped. But Pope was on the defensive and might have chosen this position just as easily as the one he did. In my journeyings to and fro so far, I have not seen anything equal to it for defence except the heights of Fredericksburg, and I doubt if they give as good a sweep for artillery fire. To fight a large army here would no doubt require some clearing of the woods, but that is easily done. . . .

The draft has not yet been enforced anywhere that I can hear of. It is very much talked against and great efforts are being made, by offering large local bounties, to fill up the quota without having recourse to it. I think that this is all wrong, as it tends to excite rather than allay the feeling against drafting; which we shall have to come to eventually if the war lasts for some years longer. Drafting, too, is the fairest and cheapest way of raising the men. As yet we are getting no recruits in this army, and I fear much that they will take to raising new regiments again, instead of filling up the old.

HERNDON STATION, JUNE 17, WEDNESDAY. Moved again today, not very far, to this place on the Loudoun and Hampshire Railroad. Our march was only fourteen miles, but was a most fatiguing one upon the men. I have never before seen so many actually used up. We were all ready to start at three o'clock, but did not get off until five. The day was intensely hot and the road very dusty, so that the loss of those two hours in the early morning told very heavily on the men. Our first orders were to go to Goose Creek, some four miles this side of Leesburg, but we were turned off to the right when about halfway, and took a byroad to this place. On our way we passed over the Chantilly battlefield, but I could not find anyone who was present in that fight to explain it to me. A large part of the road was through the woods, and when we struck off to come across here we had two miles, at midday, through a very dense growth of young pines, the branches almost meeting over our heads. The air was very hot and close out on the open; for those two miles it was intolerable—absolutely difficult to breathe. Finding the road pretty clear, I pushed through on a gallop, riding after breath, for I felt as if I should suffocate while there. The sides of the road were lined with men, who had dropped from exhaustion. There must have been near a thousand of them, many of whom had fainted entirely away. The surgeons had their hands full, and will, I fear, report a vast many candidates for the ambulances tomorrow morning, if we are called upon to move. . . .

GUILDFORD STATION, JUNE 19, FRIDAY. We moved the half dozen miles to this place this afternoon. The camping ground is better here, especially for my batteries, as we have tolerable pasture, and an abundance of water in "Broad Run." I have pitched my tent close to the batteries this time, as they are half a mile from corps headquarters, and we may possibly remain for a day or two. Shall go over for my meals, but think that I shall hereafter camp separately, as I do not like to have my officers too much around corps headquarters. We have a nice shady spot for our tents under three or four large trees. There is something which is certainly pleasing to one's vanity in being head of a command however small.

The fight on Wednesday was, as I supposed, at Aldie, and between the cavalry of both sides; not a large affair, nor did our men go clear through the gap. Pleasonton claims to have obtained a decided advantage over Stuart, and to have brought off some eighty prisoners. The affair at Brandy Station certainly did a great deal to improve the morale of our cavalry, so that they are not now afraid to meet the "rebs" on equal terms.*

* The engagement at Aldie on the 17th had importance in that Pleasonton, by driving Fitzhugh Lee back and occupying the pass or gap in the Bull Run range there, gained

Yesterday we had the first rain since Chancellorsville near six weeks ago. It commenced with very heavy thunder, and fell in detached showers all the afternoon and through the night. Today it is muggy, close, and unsettled, so that we shall probably have more rain before it clears off. The country is very dry; the crops, were there any, would be suffering from the drought on this sandy soil. As it is, the armies are about the only ones concerned. To them the rain is most welcome, if we do not get too much of it, as it will lay the dust, and make better marching. They say that it is equally dry up on the Hudson. . . .

JUNE 21, SUNDAY. The weather has been unsettled ever since the shower of Thursday, and a good deal of water had fallen at intervals. We now have as much rain as we want for the present, the dust being well laid and the streams as high as will be convenient for us to cross. Yesterday it was really cold, so that fires did not feel at all uncomfortable.

We lay very quietly yesterday, making out our trimonthlies, and so on. Today we have been in a sort of semi-quiescent state; that is, half packed up and ready to move on ten-minutes' notice. This, I suppose, is owing to the fight which was evidently going on a good part of the day over in the direction of Aldie. . . .

Last night we received our mail and papers, so had plenty to read and talk about today, though we did not get the back numbers. The papers say that Lee's plans are quite clear. I confess they are not so to me; but then I cannot pretend to know as much as a newspaper writer. That a part of his army has gone up into Pennsylvania there is no doubt, but I hardly think he can mean anything more than a raid. Once east of the Susquehanna River he would stand but small chance of getting back again, and there is no point of importance west of that, unless he intends to make a bold push for Pittsburgh. To strike across there and then to Cincinnati, if possible, has always seemed to me to hold out great attraction to him. There are no forces to speak of on the road; he could have at least three days start of us, and could destroy the Pennsylvania Railroad, while his left flank would be quite free for him to fall back into the mountains of Virginia. At Pittsburgh he could strike a severe blow. The destruction of the United States foundries there would be a great inconvenience, at least; and should he burn all the iron-works it would make the war felt more at the North than it has been heretofore.

A mere move up to Chambersburg and towards Harrisburg would only serve to get supplies, and frighten the people in Washington. This last seems to have been pretty effectually accomplished already: people there say the city never was in so much danger; which we in the army do not believe. Pennsylvania and New York are in a great stew, mobilizing

---

possession of Loudoun County northwest of Washington, just under Frederick, Maryland, and so pushed the Confederate advance farther to the west than its best route.

the militia, and raising men. I am delighted at Seymour's promptness in forwarding troops. From the reports in the papers of the arrival of militia at Harrisburg, and so forth, New York seems to have forwarded as many regiments as Pennsylvania has companies. Considering that Governor Curtin is the idol of the radicals, while Seymour is called a "copperhead" this is doing pretty well.

The Washington *Chronicle* had a report that Governor Seymour has ordered all the militia regiments to be filled up by a draft. If he will do this thoroughly, or what would be much better, make a state draft of men at once to fill up the New York regiments in the field, he would take the wind completely out of the sails of the radicals, give the lie direct to the talk of copperheadism, secure prestige enough to demand what he chose at Washington, and make a big step towards the next Presidency. He might do it too on strict party grounds, as disapproving of and in order to prevent the enforcement of a United States draft in the state.

Many of the papers and some public bodies also are now calling loudly for the reinstatement of McClellan. Some say, why does not the army demand him? An American army cannot do that: there is a feeling against an army dictating to the government in this country which our people do not get over even when they put on uniform and become a part of that army themselves. Such an idea could not be carried out, if attempted, and no one would frown upon it more than McClellan himself. It is true though that nine-tenths of us would look upon McClellan's being placed in command as better than a reinforcement of 25,000 men. . . .

JUNE 24, WEDNESDAY. There is almost nothing with which to make an entry here tonight though it is three days since the last. We have lain here in perfect quietness, and a good deal of comfort. My batteries have all got washed up, and their horses are quite refreshed. Have had them all out for battery drill each day, there being a tolerable field close by. It is the first good chance I have had to see them at it. As I expected, they are all very rusty at it. . . .

The cavalry fight on Sunday was quite a success. Monday morning Butterfield telegraphed an account of it to all the corps, closing his dispatch thus: "A disastrous day to the Rebel cavalry. Many charges made and the sabre used freely to great advantage to us"—which sounds very buncombe-ish. . . .

Army Headquarters are at Gum Spring about six or eight miles from here. Could I get over there I might learn something more as to what is going on, but it would not do for me to leave camp for so long a time as the ride would require. All the army is lying somewhere about here; the Eleventh Corps between us and Goose Creek, the Fifth at Leesburg.

To counter-balance our success at Upperville, we have news of worse losses on our part at Winchester, where things seem to have been managed worse than they were under Banks last year. I cannot make much out of what the papers tell us, except that Milroy blundered fearfully and lost everything; those of his men who did not run away were captured. The news from Vicksburg is rather encouraging.* . . .

BARNESVILLE, MARYLAND, JUNE 25, THURSDAY. At last some conclusion seems to have been come to, and the whole army was started across the Potomac this morning. There is therefore no doubt but that Lee's whole force is on this side. So far as I can learn the fear now seems to be that he is pushing for Washington by way of Frederick. We crossed at Edward's Ferry, without much delay, and came on to this place, an easy day's march, especially as it did not prove so warm as it promised at the start. There has been a drizzling rain all the afternoon: not enough to wet the men, however, and it is quite warm. The road was good, and the country quite open compared to that we left in Virginia. Hooker seemed to have some fear that he was behind time, and to apprehend an attack before he got footing fairly on the other side. . . .

General Reynolds is again in command of a wing; this time he has the Eleventh Corps along with his own instead of the Third.† I should have preferred the former arrangement, for I have not much faith in the "Deutschman," however much I may like Howard.

JEFFERSON, JUNE 26, FRIDAY. A disagreeable and hard march today though it was not a long one, only sixteen miles. The drizzling rain which commenced yesterday afternoon continued through last night and up to the present time. The road led over the Catoctin Mountains, and was narrow, rough, stony, steep, and muddy pretty much the whole way. The pulling was very hard on the horses, for they had no foothold in the slippery clay. I have seldom seen man and beast more tired: never after so short a march. The infantry fell out very badly all along the road. . . .

The change into this country from that in which we passed the winter is very great. Here there are no signs of war, not even any of Lee's

---

*After the fight at Aldie, Union troops drove Stuart's cavalry back toward the main Confederate army in the Shenandoah Valley, and on the way struck him first at Middleburg and then at Upperville. Generals John Buford and John I. Gregg fought effectively on the Northern side; Wade Hampton ably supported Stuart on the Southern. Though the Union cavalry lost 613 men at Aldie, Middleburg, and Upperville against Confederate losses of 510, it accomplished its main object of throwing Stuart back into the Valley.

† Reynolds' corps, it will be remembered, was the First, Daniel E. Sickles' was the Third, and O. O. Howard's was the Eleventh. Since the rout at Chancellorsville the German-American troops under Howard had been severely criticized, and one division commander, Julius Stahel, was replaced by General N. C. McLean, a former Ohio attorney.

raiding parties having been over it. The valley into which we entered on this side of the Catoctins appears very rich; the fields of grain are superb, especially the wheat which is ripening fast. The greater civilization has, however, brought with it its attendant evils. Even yesterday it was evident that we had got into a country in which the men could procure whiskey. Today there were a good number of them royally drunk, the hill over which we passed being noted for its distilleries.

The Eleventh Corps came over the same road, and we now made the left wing of the army of which our general is in command. Lee we hear has withdrawn all his forces to the other side of the South Mountains; so he does not mean to try for Washington and Baltimore.

MIDDLETOWN, JUNE 27, SATURDAY. We had a nice march today, one really to be enjoyed. The weather had cleared off fine, but not hot; the road was capital, wide and smooth; and the country exquisite. Well does this valley deserve the name of "Pleasant," by which it is known. As a farming country, if one may judge from the crops now on the land, and as real rural scenery, I have never come across its equal in this country. We passed a number of fields of wheat which will yield over thirty bushels to the acre, and some of them will go forty. Clover, oats and corn look equally well. The whole of the land is cleared, the farm houses are good, large, and fresh painted, and everything denotes thrift and prosperity. Perhaps all this strikes us the more coming out of such a dilapidated region as we have been in; but apart from that, the valley is lovely, lying so quietly between the two ranges of hills, which are a great beauty in themselves. As for fruits, the country is full of the most thrifty trees of all sorts. Cherry trees as big as oaks line the road for a good ways, so that half the corps have been eating cherries all day, and stand a very good show for an attack of stomach ache tonight.

We got into camp by two o'clock this afternoon. My brigade is literally "rolling in clover," for I parked them on two sides of a fine field of it and turned the horses loose for a couple of hours. . . .

ELEVEN

GETTYSBURG

On June 25 the troops of A. P. Hill and Longstreet united at Hagerstown, Maryland, and two days later they reached Chambersburg, Pennsylvania, while Richard S. Ewell's forces occupied Carlisle. Other Confederate units tore up sections of the Pennsylvania Central Railroad, entered York, and penetrated to within about a dozen miles of Harrisburg. Stuart's cavalry captured a trainload of supplies on its way to Frederick, Maryland. The war was at its crisis. Some Northern leaders feared that Lee would cross the Susquehanna, seize Harrisburg, and place Philadelphia in peril. And at this moment the Administration chose a new commander for the Army of the Potomac.

Hooker had heightened the latent distrust in which he was held by asking repeatedly for reinforcements, offering exaggerated estimates of the Confederate strength, and giving an impression of uncertainty in his movements. He crystallized this distrust into Administration hostility when he asked that the garrison of about 10,000 men at Harpers Ferry be withdrawn and added to Slocum's corps to operate in Lee's rear against his communications. It was a sensible request; but Halleck, the President's principal military adviser, who had an old dislike of Hooker dating back to their California days, had decreed that the troops were needed at Harpers Ferry, and sternly refused the general's request. Thereupon Hooker offered his resignation.

Gideon Welles, in his diary, presents an account of the scene when Lincoln on June 28 laid this resignation before the Cabinet. "The President said he had, for several days, as the conflict became imminent, observed in Hooker the same failings that were witnessed in McClellan after the Battle of Antietam—a want of alacrity to obey, and a greedy call for more troops which could not, and ought not to be taken from other points. He would, said the President, strip Washington bare, had demanded the force at Harpers Ferry, which Halleck said could not be complied with. . . ." The Cabinet went through the form of discussing Hooker's successor. But it was plain from the outset that Lincoln, Stanton, and Halleck had already decided for Meade as they had decided against Hooker.

* * *

FREDERICK CITY, JUNE 28 [1863], SUNDAY. This morning it was stated pretty positively that we should not move. I therefore rode up to Army Headquarters, which are just outside of this place, to see General Hunt, and learn what I could, this being the first chance I have had to get away from camp since we left White Oak Church. While I was there I learned that the corps was ordered up here, and at once returned, reaching Middletown just in time to meet the head of my brigade filing into the road. We are camped about a mile to the north of the city, and as my batteries are camped close by, my tent is again pitched with headquarters.

But the event of the day, which I learned so soon as I reached headquarters, is the removal of General Hooker, and the placing of Meade in command. It took me entirely by surprise, as it is going on to two months since Hooker made his fiasco at Chancellorsville, and I have not heard of his doing anything else since then which could cause the Washington authorities to change their minds. It is said that the reason assigned is a demand on Hooker's part for the withdrawal of the garrison at Harper's Ferry, and that it, with all the other troops in Maryland should be subject to his orders. Whatever reason may be assigned, from all I can learn, the removal was done in the same dirty manner in which Stanton does everything of the sort. He seems to take special delight in being as offensive as possible. Hooker feels his removal very much; all the more, no doubt, just at this time when we are on the point of another big battle, in which he might wipe off the opprobrium attached to him for his last. His farewell order is excellent, the most modest of all his productions.

General George G. Meade was my candidate for Hooker's successor immediately after Chancellorsville, I believing him to have the longest and clearest head of any general officer in this army. But I had very little expectation then that he would get the command, and feared that they would bring on some of their Western generals, who, having no idea of how Lee's men can fight, might prove a second Pope. The change of commanders just at this time I do not like: it is a very dangerous experiment on the eve of battle. Meade's order assuming command reads a little involved but contains one good sentence: "As a soldier in obeying this order, I have no promises or pledges to make." Such an expression is good policy, but I know Meade well enough to be sure that such was not his idea in writing it. He meant that he had received the order, and should obey it in the best way he could, without trying to curry any favour by promises, or seek popularity by loud talking. At our own headquarters where Meade is known, the appointment is very favourably received.

Butterfield remains with him at present, but Warren I understand will be the new chief of staff. Sykes succeeds to the command of the Fifth

Corps. Hancock is in command of the Second. I met Weed and Webb at headquarters each shining in the glory of their just acquired "stars." Two most excellent promotions. General Birney afforded a good deal of amusement today by the manner in which he passed through the city at the head of the Third Corps. First was a line of orderlies with drawn sabres to clear the way; then a band of music, and in due time Major General Birney with all his staff riding in order behind him. He certainly means to have all the "pomp and circumstance of war" he can get. Such feats are not common in this army, and do not take. Sickles came up today, so Birney will go back to his division.*

EMMITSBURG, JUNE 29, MONDAY.   Our new commander is determined not to let the grass grow under his feet, and his dispositions would indicate that he has some pretty certain ideas as to where Lee is, and what he ought to do himself. There is no doubt now that Lee has passed Chambersburg with the whole of his army, and that a good portion of it is east of the hills threatening York and Harrisburg. All the papers report this in a way to indicate that they are right for once. It seems to me a very bold proceeding on his part; but as our movements are kept very quiet, he may believe that the government will not allow us to go far from Washington. If so, he will find himself mistaken this time, for the whole army has been streaming north today, on as many different roads as there are corps; and Meade, having received the powers which they denied to Hooker, has ordered everything he can lay his hands on in the same direction.† . . .

We came along swimmingly all day, the road being good, about one half of it a turnpike, and reached here a couple of hours before dark. The men are in fine spirits, marched lively, and behave themselves quite well, considering how lax the regulations have become in regard to injuring private property since the radical program of destruction has been adopted. The people along the road sell everything, and at very high prices; fifty cents for a large loaf of bread, worth, say, twenty; fifteen to twenty-five cents for a canteen, three pints, of skimmed milk; how much for pies I do not know, but they were in great demand. I saw one man empty his whole three days' rations from his havresack in order to fill it with these leathern luxuries. Many of the inhabitants, though, will

* Gouverneur Kemble Warren has already appeared. George Sykes, West Point, 1842, bore the nickname of "Tardy George," and was assigned to the unimportant Department of Kansas early in 1864. Stephen H. Weed of New York, West Point, 1854, had taken part in the battles of Antietam and Chancellorsville, and was to find his grave at Gettysburg. David B. Birney, a lawyer, son of the eminent Abolitionist leader, had also fought in a number of battles. He was to take over the Third Corps at Gettysburg after Sickles was wounded, making a very creditable record.

† When Meade asked for the 10,000 men at Harpers Ferry, Halleck gave them to him without demur.

not sell, but give all they can; and we are cheered through all the villages by good wishes and pleasant smiles. Whiskey too is rather abundant; I caught several of my own men drunk, and had them tied by the hand to the rear of a gun so as to insure their keeping up. So soon as I found it out I rode ahead as we approached each village, and emptied all the liquor in the taverns and shops I could put my hand on. This was the provost-marshal's duty, but he contented himself with giving a warning not to sell, instead of removing the evil in toto. . . .

General Reynolds told me today that the command of this army was offered to him when he was summoned up to Washington a month ago; but he refused it, because, to use his own expression, "he was unwilling to take Burnside and Hooker's leavings." I learn too that it was mainly on Reynolds's recommendation that General Meade received his appointment. For my part, I think we have got the best man of the two, much as I think of Reynolds. He will do better at carrying out plans than at devising them, I think. As for the men, they are not at all satisfied; indeed the greater part of them will not believe that Meade's taking command is anything more than temporary until McClellan can be sent for. Much as I believed the heart of the army to be still with its first commander, I did not expect to hear the strongest political Republicans express their wish for his return so decidedly as they did today. . . .

IN PENNSYLVANIA, JUNE 30, TUESDAY. We are across the line now, north of Mason and Dixon's; the first time that this army, or any other of our large ones, has had to go into what is called a Northern state. We only came some six miles this morning, starting at eight o'clock, and are now resting peaceably, and getting up our monthly returns. The Second and Third Divisions are camped nearby where I am; the First is some three miles farther on where the road crosses Marsh Creek. The Eleventh has joined it. Buford with his Cavalry Division are in Gettysburg, out of which they drove some of the rebels this morning early. I hear that the Sixth Corps has moved to Manchester, and that Army Headquarters are at Taneytown. General Reynolds has his about a mile up the road. Though Doubleday is supposed to be in command of the corps, all our orders come from Reynolds direct, and he looks as closely as ever after everything himself. . . .

The Pennsylvanians do not give us an over-warm welcome; they are much more greedy than the Marylanders. Butter has gone up to fifty cents a pound, and skimmed milk to twenty-five cents a canteen. Yet they are running with complaints if a single fence rail is burned. I had a long talk with the man in whose field I am camped; he wanted half as much as his land is worth for the poor crop of clover destroyed. I proved to him, by his own admissions, that it would not have cleared him more than $15. He then fell back on the statement that his wife had been up

all night baking bread for the men, and had "guv" them all the milk
and butter she had. Which "guv"ing I found to mean selling at from
three to ten times their market value. I then dismissed him with a piece
of my mind as to himself and Pennsylvanians in general. They fully
maintain their reputation for meanness. . . .

* * *

By nightfall of June 30 Meade knew from his scouts and other sources that
Lee's army was concentrating at Gettysburg. The Confederates, after moving into Pennsylvania behind the northward extension of the Blue Ridge,
had poured east through the passes. Meade's troops, following Lee on an
inside line to protect Baltimore and Washington, had come up to the
Gettysburg area. Reynolds and the First Corps, including Wainwright's
artillery brigade, were at Marsh Creek, well in the van. And Reynolds was
determined to fight as soon as possible. He was a Pennsylvanian, he was
anxious to prevent devastation of his state, and he had the spirit of a born
fighter. He determined, on the evening of the 30th, to march into and hold
Gettysburg. To that end, as he commanded the whole left wing of the army,
he ordered the Eleventh Corps to join the First, and recommended that the
Third Corps come up as support. The capable Union cavalry commander,
John Buford, was then holding the ridges west of Gettysburg.

Thus it was that at dawn on July 1 the battle began. A trooper of
Buford's division was astonished to see Confederate soldiers—an advance
guard of General Johnston Pettigrew's brigade—moving down the Chambersburg Pike toward the town. The Southerners were equally astonished.
It was at 5:20 A.M., a mile and a half west of Gettysburg, that the first shots
were fired. The battle rapidly grew in volume. General Henry Heth's division of Confederates, numbering four brigades, deployed against Buford's
two cavalry brigades. The Southerners had the advantage of numbers; the
Union forces had the advantage of position on the ridge, where Buford
used the Lutheran Seminary as an observation post. As losses grew heavy,
Buford sent for help from Reynolds and the First Corps, advancing from
Marsh Creek.

Arriving on the scene, Reynolds climbed to the belfry of the Theological
Seminary and at once grasped the seriousness of the situation. Wadsworth's
division had accompanied him. Buford's line was being forced back, and
Reynolds disposed Wadsworth's regiments to support it, posting one element
in Wainwright's outfit—Hall's Second Maine battery—on the road facing
the Confederates. Before long part of Wadsworth's command was outflanked, and he directed two regiments to retire to some woods nearer

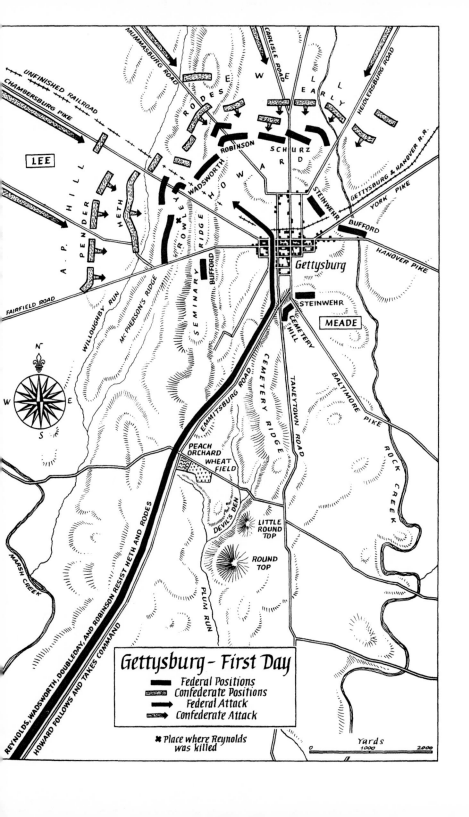

MUMMASBURG ROAD

CARLISLE ROAD

HEIDLERSBURG ROAD

UNFINISHED RAILROAD

CHAMBERSBURG PIKE

RODES

E W E L L

EARLY

ROBINSON

SCHURZ

H O W A R D

LEE

WADSWORTH

ROWLEY

STEINWEHR

GETTYSBURG & HANOVER R.R.

YORK PIKE

BUFORD

A. P. HILL

PENDER

HETH

SEMINARY RIDGE

BUFORD

Gettysburg

HANOVER PIKE

FAIRFIELD ROAD

WILLOUGHBY RUN

MC PHERSON'S RIDGE

STEINWEHR

MEADE

EMMITTSBURG ROAD

CEMETERY HILL

CEMETERY RIDGE

TANEYTOWN ROAD

BALTIMORE PIKE

ROCK CREEK

N
W E
S

PEACH ORCHARD

WHEAT FIELD

DEVIL'S DEN

LITTLE ROUND TOP

ROUND TOP

PLUM RUN

MARSH CREEK

REYNOLDS, WADSWORTH, DOUBLEDAY AND ROBINSON RESIST HETH AND RODES

HOWARD FOLLOWS AND TAKES COMMAND

Gettysburg — First Day

Federal Positions
Confederate Positions
Federal Attack
Confederate Attack

✶ Place where Reynolds was killed

Yards
0   1000   2000

town. Doubleday, division commander in the First Corps under Reynolds, tells the sequel in a way that illuminates Wainwright's story:

"As Wadsworth withdrew them [the two regiments] without notifying Hall's battery on the road, or the two regiments posted by Reynolds on the left, both became exposed to a disastrous flank attack on the right. Hall, finding a cloud of skirmishers launched against his battery which was now without support, was compelled to retreat. The horses of the last gun were all shot or bayonetted. The non-military reader will see that while a battery can keep back masses of men, it cannot contend with a line of skirmishers. To resist them would be very much like fighting mosquitoes with musket-balls."

In the midst of the battle Reynolds fell from his horse dead, with a sharpshooter's bullet through his brain.

* * *

BATTLE OF GETTYSBURG, JULY 1, 1863, WEDNESDAY. We breakfasted soon after sunrise, but it rather promised then to be a quiet day for us. I was just finishing up my monthly return when the order came to move at once. The order was from Doubleday, and placed the Third Division on the lead, and the First at the rear. So soon as my command had hauled out, as they had to wait for the Third Division in rear of which they were to march, I rode on ahead to learn what I could as to the prospects of a fight. I saw General Reynolds, who said that he did not expect any: that we were only moving up so as to be within supporting distance to Buford, who was to push out farther. At the corners where Reynolds had his headquarters the Third Division was turned off by him on a road to the left. General Reynolds then rode on, and took the First Division ahead with Hall's battery, which being camped near three miles in advance had an hour's start of us. We moved along very quietly without dreaming of a fight, and fully expecting to be comfortably in camp by noon. So confident of this was I that, for the first time, I threw my saddle bags into the waggon, and was thus left without my supply of chocolate and tobacco, without brush, comb, or clean handkerchief. My horse "Billy" cast two shoes on the road. I had no hesitation in stopping at a farm house with one of my forges until they could be replaced and even sat there ten or fifteen minutes longer until a heavy shower was over. I then rode up to the head of my brigade, where I found General Doubleday.

This was about two miles before coming to Gettysburg, and between ten-thirty and eleven o'clock. We were speaking of General Meade's promotion, and Doubleday was just saying that Sykes was his junior, and that they ought to give him a corps, when my attention was called to the smoke of shells bursting in the air. On listening we would hear the sound of cannon apparently some three or four miles off, which we supposed to be from Buford's cavalry. In a few minutes, however, an officer, I have forgotten whom, came up with orders for us to push on as fast as possible, as Reynolds was engaged over beyond the seminary.

I at once started my three batteries, Reynolds leading, and after going along the road about half a mile turned in to the fields on the left, where I saw that other troops had gone, and which took me directly towards the seminary. Halfway there I met Craig Wadsworth, who merely said, "The General is killed; Reynolds is dead." Shortly after I met his body being brought off. I halted and uncovered as he passed; it was all there was time for then. I had no confidence in Doubleday, and felt that he would be a weak reed to lean upon; that it would not do for me to wait for orders from him, but that I must judge and act for myself. Even at this time Doubleday was riding at the head of the Second Division, waiting orders I suppose.

On reaching the seminary I found that General Wadsworth had again occupied the ridge beyond, from which we had fallen back. Buford had cavalry on the flanks, and a strong reserve. What dispositions were to be made I knew not. No two divisions of the corps had yet got together, the Third being on a road which would pass to our front. Should the enemy be in force enough to drive right ahead, they would eat us up piecemeal; if they were not strong, the Third Division might come in on their flank. All I could do then was to put my batteries in a position where they could be got at easily, have them send their battery waggons and forges to the rear, and wait in condition to start at a trot the instant orders came. I then rode along the ridge on which the seminary stands, and afterwards out to the one beyond.

The seminary building stands upon a narrow ridge or rise of ground, formed by the outcropping of the rocks which run very near north and south. It is rather over half a mile to the west of the town; the ridge stretching away a long distance to the left of the seminary, while it ends in a broken, rocky knoll some 300 yards to the right. This knoll is covered with wood. A fine grove stands in front of the college building, and a belt of trees crowns the ridge for all its length to the left so far as I could see. The ground falls rapidly behind the ridge on the side towards the town; in front it slopes more gradually. The position, though wanting depth, was not a bad one on which to resist a front attack, if we should not be outflanked. The bottom of the little valley which lies between this ridge and the one beyond is somewhat moist and soft. About seventy-five yards north of the seminary and close to one of the houses the turnpike leading to Cashtown and Chambersburg crosses the ridge, and thirty or forty yards farther is a thorough cut through it for a railroad. The ridge beyond is wider and much more rolling; the greater part of it is cleared. Just where the Cashtown pike crosses it there stands a large farmhouse and barns, with an orchard to the left of it, and then some six or eight acres of wood.

It was here that General Reynolds was killed by a minie ball through the head of the spine. He fell from his horse, and expired instantly. So far as I can learn Wadsworth's leading brigade was pushed on much beyond this in support of our cavalry, when they were driven rapidly back; the enemy also opening with a six-gun battery. At this point, General Reynolds made a stand, getting Hall's battery into position on his right. This stand was quite successful, until they turned his right and the General himself fell, when our men gave way. The flank attack was made directly upon Hall's battery, and though he was successful in checking it, until he could withdraw after the infantry, he was obliged to leave one piece on the field, all six of the horses being shot down as they stood. Four of the horses to another piece were also killed, but this he got off part of the way by hand.

I did not like this advanced position at all, its right flank being exposed to a high ridge to the north, and approached by a number of ravines which afforded excellent cover to an attacking party. General Wadsworth had ordered Hall back again, but I took the responsibility of forbidding him to put his battery there until I knew there were troops to cover his right flank; at the same time directing him to get off his abandoned piece, which the enemy had not disturbed. While I was on the ridge, our Third Division came in on our left front, having been turned off the road by an order of General Reynolds. I placed Cooper's battery in position on the open ridge about where I thought the left of the division would rest, and ordered him to wait events.

Passing then to the right of the railroad cut, on to the wooded knoll, I found that it had just been occupied by Robinson's division, and Cutler's brigade. The lay of the ground was very intricate, so that it took me some time to make out the disposition of our troops; which proved to be all sorts of ways. As I was coming out I saw a line of rebels advancing towards Cutler's flank, and rode back to tell him, as I had no one with me, having sent Matthewson to put Stewart and Reynolds into position south of the seminary. As I came out again I saw a portion of the Eleventh Corps moving forward in line facing north, so that the two corps formed a right angle at the knoll where Robinson was. They had two batteries with them which were just opening fire.* . . .

* Wainwright here allots three paragraphs to the movements of his batteries, relating that one of his captains had an eye taken out by a case shot, and that he himself came within inches of losing a leg by another that grazed his ankle. He complains that

Somewhere about three o'clock, I should think, a long column of rebels came out of the wood a mile or so in our front, and filed off to our left. This was soon joined by another column, which when they faced into line formed a second line for them. They marched along quietly and with confidence, but swiftly. I watched them from the battery, and am confident that when they advanced they outflanked us at least half a mile on our left. So soon as they were within range I opened on them with the four guns, but a brigade of the Third Division sent to support the battery persisted in getting in front—that being its commander's idea of supporting. The rebel lines advanced rapidly. There was not the shadow of a chance of our holding this ridge even had our Third Division commanders had any idea what to do with their men, which they had not. I therefore soon ordered Lieutenant Bower to take his four guns back to the Seminary Ridge, to the position he had previously occupied about a hundred yards south of the college.

While I was with General Doubleday, one of Howard's German aides rode up, and told him that General Hancock, who succeeded Reynolds in command of the two corps, wished that the Cemetery Hill should be held at all hazards. What with the aide's broken English and our being on this hill and not knowing that there was a *cemetery*, I thought it was the *Seminary* Hill we were to hold. I had therefore strung my batteries out on it as well as I could, only having four now; and when I sent "L" Company to its old position, went myself to where Cooper had been ordered. Wadsworth's division was falling back as I got there, the rebs pushing rapidly on and cheering. They were also attacking the Eleventh Corps at the same time. The Cashtown road being our most important point, each one had aimed to take care of it. Robinson had ordered Stewart to take post on each side of the railroad. Doubleday had ordered Stevens from where I had placed him at the left to the road itself. Cooper had his four guns immediately in front of the main building, and Wilbur's section came down the road with Wadsworth's divsion. Thus there were eighteen pieces on a frontage of not over two hundred yards.

But there was no time now to make changes, for the rebs were coming steadily on down the ridge in front only some five hundred yards off, and all the guns were blazing away at them as lively as possible. In a little time I went to the right and front of Wilbur's section, one piece of which was on the Cashtown road. I there found that Lieutenant Davison had thrown his half of Battery "B" around so as to get an oblique, almost enfilading fire on the rebel lines. His round shot, together with the canister poured in from all the other guns, was cutting great gaps in the front line of the enemy. But still they came on, the gaps being closed by

General James Wadsworth, anxious to have his front protected, kept interfering with the proper placing of the guns.

regiments from the second line, and this again filled up by a third column which was coming over the hill. Never have I seen such a charge. Not a man seemed to falter. Lee may well be proud of his infantry; I wish ours was equal to it. When I returned I found the Fifth Maine limbering up. I stopped them, when Lieutenant Whittaker told me that General Wadsworth had said they had better withdraw. Remembering what I had supposed to be Howard's order to hold the Seminary Hill to the last, I had no notion of going off, and rode around to see that none of the guns moved. An officer now informed me that a rebel line was advancing on our right. Looking at it, I was sure that it was the Eleventh Corps, and could not be convinced to the contrary until they opened fire on a portion of that corps—which I could now see making for the town. At the same time I discovered that our own First and Second Divisions were filing through the railroad cutting, and making in the same direction. Indeed, most of them had gone when I found it out.

I then at once ordered all to limber up and move at a walk towards the town. I would not allow them to trot for fear of creating a panic among the infantry with which the road was now crowded. But I had very little hope of getting them all off, for the rebs were close upon us; so near that a big fellow had planted the colours of his regiment on a pile of rails within fifty yards of the muzzles of Cooper's guns at the moment he received his order to limber up. As I sat on the hill watching my pieces file past, and cautioning each one not to trot, there was not a doubt in my mind but that I should go to Richmond. Each minute I expected to hear the order to surrender for our infantry had all gone from around me, and there was nothing to stop the advancing line.

Just as the last of Stewart's caissons was coming into the road (fortunately the other batteries did not have their caissons with them), a number of the enemy's skirmishers, sweeping around the south side of the college buildings, opened fire across the road at about fifty yards distance. Our infantry did not return the fire, so there seemed no chance but what they would kill all my horses. Perhaps, though, it was as well for me that our infantry instead of making fight took at once and in a body to the left, over the railroad which here makes an embankment. This cleared the road, and I shouted "Trot! Gallop!" as loud as I could. It did not take long for the whole eighteen pieces and six caissons to be in full gallop down the road, which being wide allowed them to go three-abreast. As I saw the head carriages already at the turn of the road just before entering the town, I felt that now all were safe. And my next duty being to look out a new position for them I galloped to the front. In order to get by the batteries I was obliged to climb over the railroad and enter the town by another street.

I had hurrahed a little before I was out of the woods. The rebs pulled off the skirt of my coat; that is, after I left the road they got some pieces on the crest we had just left, and fired into the tail of our column, smashing up three of Stewart's caissons. The rascals south of the road, too, killed the off-wheeler of Lieutenant Wilbur's last piece; and when he had just got him cut out, and was starting again, they shot down three more horses, his own horse, and one of the drivers. So the gun was abandoned. I was terribly grieved when I heard of it, for I had begun to look upon our getting off from that place as quite a feat, and wished that it could have been without loss of a gun. The more I think of it, the more I wonder that we got off at all. Our front fire must have shaken the rebel lines badly or they would have been upon us. The gun lost was No. 1, the first three-inch gun accepted by the ordnance department.

The streets of the town were full of the troops of the two corps. There was very little order amongst them, save that the Eleventh took one side of the street and we the other; brigades and divisions were pretty well mixed up. Still the men were not panic stricken; most of them were talking and joking. As I pushed through the crowd as rapidly as possible, I came across General Rowley, who was in command of the Third Division. He was very talkative, claiming that he was in command of the corps. I tried to reason with him, showing that Wadsworth and several others ranked him; but soon finding that he was drunk, I rode on to the top of the Cemetery Hill, the existence of which I now learned for the first time. Whether Rowley would have handled his division any better had he been sober I have my doubts. . . .

I reached the top of the hill almost as soon as my first battery. Here I found General Howard, who expressed pleasure at seeing me, and desired me to take charge of all the artillery, and make the best disposition I could of it: saying that he would instruct Major Osborn to take his orders from me. The General pointed out to me how he should form the two corps; stating that this spot must be held until the rest of the army came up. I have since heard it said that General Hancock claims to have been in command at this time. I neither saw nor heard anything of him, and the troops certainly were posted as General Howard told me he meant to put them.*

Cemetery Ridge is directly over the town to the east, straggling houses running part way up its western slope. The ridge proper may be said to begin at this point, and to extend off to the south for a mile or two, sinking gradually as you get farther in that direction. The Baltimore pike comes directly up the hill from the town, passes over it, and runs off nearly due east. This was the ground which I occupied during the rest of the battle. Standing in the road now just at the commencement of its

---

* After Reynolds's death, questions of command seemed perplexing. But "Hancock the Superb," as McClellan had called him at Williamsburg, took charge with full power to hold the field or fall back—and decided to hold it; Doubleday very briefly directed the First Corps; and Howard continued to head the Eleventh.

descent, you look down on to the town, but cannot see into any of the streets; the road turning short to the right immediately on getting down the hill. On your left hand is the gateway to the cemetery, two brick towers with a connecting arch. The cemetery occupies some ten or fifteen acres of the highest point on the ridge, running along its summit. On your right hand the ridge ends about fifty yards from the road, sloping off quite sharply to the north. Some three hundred yards to the right and the same distance to the rear is Culp's Hill; a large, thickly wooded rise, encircled on the east, north, and west by a wet valley in which are two small runs. From its south side it is connected with the road by a sort of neck, partially wooded.

On the ridge General Howard had placed Von Steinwehr's division, and three of his batteries, so soon as he came up. These had not been at all engaged. I now had Major Osborn move four of his batteries into the cemetery itself, so as to command the direct approach from the Seminary Hill on the south side of the town. Four of Stewart's guns I planted to fire directly down the road. At the angle or corner of the hill I found Wiedrich with his four guns, and left him there, only throwing his guns well in echelon so that he could fire either to the west or north. Around the corner of the hill and facing north was Cooper, a stone wall between him and Wiedrich; on his right Stewart's other section, and then Reynolds's five guns, Breck commanding. They were twenty yards farther back than Cooper's, owing to the nature of the ground. On the neck of Culp's Hill I posted Stevens, who thus had a fire along my north front. The First Corps, what remained of it, was posted on this neck and Culp's Hill. The Eleventh held the cemetery, and furnished a support for the batteries outside the gate. All my caissons were parked in the rear of the cemetery.

When I had got this all arranged, and had given instructions to my officers, especially that they should not waste ammunition, and should not take orders from any man with a star on his shoulders who might choose to give them, I felt quite comfortable. We still had near an hour of daylight, and the moon was near its full, so that there was a good chance for the enemy to attack if they felt like it. I could give them a hot reception at the angle, and I thought could hold it if they did not come up through the town; in which case they would be almost upon me before I could know it. This I trusted they would not attempt, for beside the women and children there, the town was full of our wounded. It worried me very much to decide how to act should they attack from the town direct.

After dark I got a cup of coffee and a hard tack from some of the men, for none of our waggons were up, and consequently generals and staff officers were in a bad way. My man had kept with the battery waggons and forges, so I had my blankets, for which I was thankful. About eleven o'clock I turned in in one of the rooms of the gate house, along with General Ames, who was in command of the division of the Eleventh Corps holding this point,* and got some sleep.

The enemy had made no attempt to attack us after we got on to the Cemetery Hill. They were probably waiting for the rest of their army to come up. By morning I trust the whole of ours too will be up. The Third Corps commenced to arrive about dark, and took position in prolongation of the Eleventh on the ridge. The Twelfth also came up and was posted on Culp's Hill. All were protected, as also the batteries, by slight breastworks.

The day had been a most unfortunate one for us, our greatest misfortune being the loss of General Reynolds. To his death much of our loss afterwards was doubtless owing. Not that I think we should not have had to fall back here had he not been killed, for the enemy outnumbered us three to one; but it would have been done in better order, with half the loss to ourselves and much more to the enemy. Of the force opposed to the Eleventh Corps I know nothing, nor how well the Deutschmen fought; when they gave way, of course there would have been no chance for our holding on under any circumstances, as it would let the enemy opposed to them in behind our rear. But setting their doings aside we could have made much better fight if only a brigade of observation had been sent to the outer ridge, and the rest of the corps properly posted on the Seminary Ridge, with our flank extended by the cavalry, and all covered by such breastworks as could have been thrown up. We could have made a good fight of it, and if we succeeded in breaking their left, directly in our front, might by a sharp counter-charge have made it hard work for their right wing to get off. Under any circumstances had we withdrawn by order, it would have been in an orderly manner, and we should have lost but few sound prisoners.

The loss of the corps today is put at 7,000, some 3,000 of them being sound prisoners, captured at the last charge, and stragglers picked up in the town. All our wounded, and nearly all our surgeons, were prisoners in the town, including Heard and Bache, and my own little doctor. My own loss is four officers wounded, and about eighty men killed, wounded and prisoners—eleven of them prisoners. . . . The enemy's loss must have been quite considerable, for our fire on the Seminary Ridge was very severe. We also captured a thousand prisoners or more, for they evidently were not expecting a fight at this point any more than we were. The First Division took three regiments and General Archer, before Reynolds fell;

---

* Adelbert Ames, West Point, 1861, a hero of Bull Run and a brigadier-general at twenty-three, commanded a division under Howard with an efficiency which Wainwright well describes.

and Robinson captured about all of the brigade which I had seen coming
upon him.

* * *

The first day's battle at Gettysburg had on the whole seemed favorable
to the Confederates. Until one o'clock most of the fighting on the Union
side was done, as Wainwright indicates, by Reynolds's First Corps, which
won some initial successes. Then Howard's Eleventh Corps came up, and
he posted Carl Schurz's and Francis C. Barlow's divisions on the right of
the First Corps, covering Gettysburg on the north and northwest. Unhappily, he extended his lines so far that they were thinly held in places
and weak. When the Confederates made a general advance about three
o'clock, they broke through the Union center, throwing the left of the
Eleventh Corps and the adjoining right of the First Corps back in confusion. These troops retreated in disorder into Gettysburg. Thereupon General Jubal A. Early, following hard behind them, captured about five
thousand prisoners.

Fortunately for the Union cause, General Winfield S. Hancock arrived
at this critical moment, not with his Second Corps, but alone, with full
power to assume command until Meade came. He soon restored order, and
oversaw the placing of the Union forces, which were growing every hour,
on the most advantageous position possible. This was the famous fishhook
line of the Cemetery Ridge, a string of eminences extending south from its
head at the town. The hook or crotchet was formed by Cemetery Hill and
Culp's Hill, the latter a rocky forested knob with Rock Creek at its base.
The stem was the well-defined ridge running southward from Cemetery
Hill for about three miles, ending with the high rocky peak of Round Top,
near which rose the rough bald spur called Little Round Top. This was to
be made the Union line on the second day's battle.

The two generals, Lee and Meade, both arrived on the scene late on the
night of July 1; Meade even after midnight. The Union forces had been
slower than the Confederates in concentrating, and were shaken by their
ill fortune on the first day. But for the second day they would hold the
tremendous advantage of fighting on the defensive. When Lee had marched
into Pennsylvania he had told intimates that he intended to compel the
Northern army to attack him on ground that he would choose. Now he was
compelled to attack on ground fixed by accident and not design.

* * *

JULY 2, THURSDAY. General Meade came along our line between one
and two o'clock this morning. General Hunt was with him, and I ex-

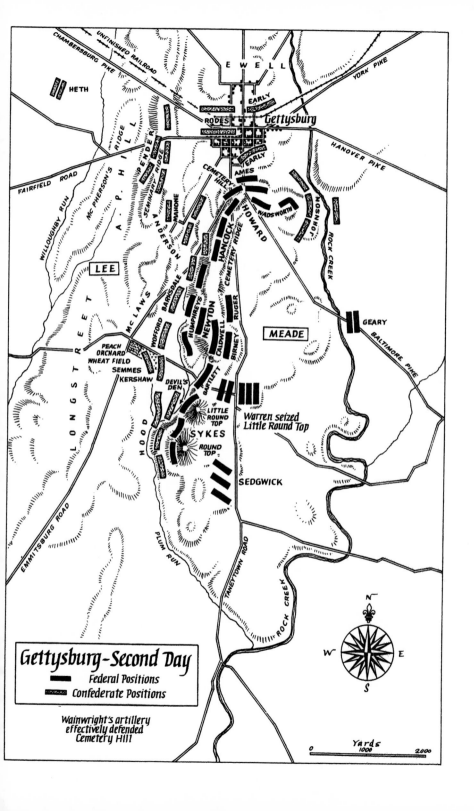

UNFINISHED RAILROAD

CHAMBERSBURG PIKE

YORK PIKE

EWELL

HETH

EARLY

RODES

Gettysburg

FAIRFIELD ROAD

HANOVER PIKE

MC PHERSON'S RIDGE

A. P. HILL

SEMINARY RIDGE

PENDER

ANDERSON

MAHONE

CEMETERY HILL

AMES

YEARLY

HOWARD

WADSWORTH

JOHNSON

ROCK CREEK

WILLOUGHBY RUN

LEE

MC LAWS

HANCOCK

CEMETERY RIDGE

HUMPHREYS

BARKSDALE

WOFFORD

NEWTON

CALDWELL

BIRNEY

RUGER

MEADE

GEARY

BALTIMORE PIKE

PEACH ORCHARD

WHEAT FIELD

SEMMES

KERSHAW

DEVIL'S DEN

BARTLETT

LONGSTREET

HOOD

LITTLE ROUND TOP

SYKES

Warren seized Little Round Top

ROUND TOP

SEDGWICK

EMMITSBURG ROAD

PLUM RUN

TANEYTOWN ROAD

ROCK CREEK

N
W   E
S

Gettysburg–Second Day

███ Federal Positions

░░░ Confederate Positions

Wainwright's artillery effectively defended Cemetery Hill

Yards
0   1000   2000

plained to him, as well as I could, the dispositions I had made here. It was not light enough to see much and they did not stop long. As they rode along the line towards the left, the rumour spread among the men that McClellan had arrived; whole lines sprang up and cheered. Even late in the morning some of the men believed it, so fixed was it in their minds that Meade's appointment was only temporary. The Second Corps arrived about seven o'clock, and went into position where the Third had been; Sickles moving along at the left. Our Second and Third Divisions had been placed on the left of the cemetery, next to the Eleventh Corps, Wadsworth remaining with his on the neck of Culp's Hill. The Fifth Corps arrived at noon, and the Sixth soon after. The last corps claims to have come thirty-four miles in twenty hours.

The morning was almost perfectly quiet, each side apparently marshalling their forces. The whole Army of the Potomac was now up, and all of Lee's too. Everything showed that we were to have a big fight; but this time Lee was to attack, and the country was open. My batteries opened at times on small bodies of infantry passing our north front towards Culp's Hill, but were not seriously engaged until four P.M. During the morning we strengthened the epaulements in front of our guns, and got everything straight so far as possible. I could not replace the ammunition spent, our waggons having all gone back to Emmitsburg. Nor could we get any more forage: but all had enough for today, except Stewart, who had thrown his off, as well as the men's havresacks when they first went into position today. His men and horses were without anything to eat today save what they could beg or borrow. Ames's division (Barlow's) was massed more today outside the gates; lying in two lines behind stone walls on both my fronts. On the north front they were in advance of the guns, at the bottom of the hill. Of Ames himself I saw a good deal; in fact, we were alongside of each other pretty much all day. I found him the best kind of a man to be associated with, cool and clear in his own judgment, gentlemanly, and without the smallest desire to interfere. We consulted together, but during the whole time we were here he never once attempted to presume on his superior rank. Ames is a gentleman; and a strange thing in the army, I did not hear him utter an oath of any kind during the three days!

About four o'clock the enemy planted four twenty-pounder and six ten-pounder Parrotts on a high knoll opposite our north front, and opened with a well-directed fire. To this I was able to reply with thirteen three-inch guns, so that the weight of metal was about equal, when you add an occasional shot which Stevens was able to get in from his left section. In every other respect the rebel guns had the advantage of us. They were on higher ground, and having plenty of room were able to place their guns some thirty yards apart, while ours were not over twelve; and the two faces of our line meeting here, the limbers stood absolutely crowded together. Still we were able to shut them up, and actually drive them from the field in about two hours. Their two right guns we could see them haul off by hand; they left twenty-eight dead horses on the ground, while we did not lose over a dozen. How it was they did not kill more horses I cannot understand, huddled together as we were, for their fire was the most accurate I have ever seen on the part of their artillery, and the distance was just right, say 1,400 yards. Some of their guns afterwards took position more to our left, at about 2,000 yards, but were soon silenced, I being reinforced by a section of twenty-pounder Parrotts which took position in the cemetery.

I saw during this artillery duel two instances of the destruction which can be caused by a single twenty-pounder shot: both of which happened within ten yards of me as I sat on the stone wall between Cooper's and Wiedrich's batteries, along with General Ames. One of these shot struck in the centre of a line of infantry who were lying down behind the wall. Taking the line lengthways, it literally ploughed up two or three yards of men, killing and wounding a dozen or more. Fortunately it did not burst, for it struck so near where we were sitting that it covered us with dust. The other was a shell which burst directly under Cooper's left gun, killed one man outright, blew another all to pieces, so that he died in half an hour, and wounded the other three. Here I had a specimen of the stuff this battery is composed of, and forgave Cooper and his men their utter unmilitariness and loose ideas of discipline in camp. So soon as the shell burst I jumped from the wall, and told Cooper to put on another detachment, that General Ames would let some of his men carry off the wounded; not a murmur was uttered, but five other men at once took place over their dead and wounded comrades, and fired before they could be removed. I was very proud of it. The man who was so badly blown to pieces lost his right hand, his left arm at the shoulder, and his ribs so broken open that you could see right into him; he was removed to the well, just inside the cemetery gates, and died there. Cooper came to me and asked permission for his brother, who was their bugler, to go and remain with him while he lived. The bugler, who had nothing to do, would not go sixty or seventy yards from his battery to see his brother in his last moments without permission, nor would his captain give the permission without asking mine. Yet were they in camp, hardly a man in the battery but would go off for all day without permission to see a well brother, and Cooper would think it all right.

I had two pretty narrow escapes myself, one the closest I have ever had. And in both cases I realized afterwards how indifferent one becomes to the danger when you are accustomed to the flying around of cannon balls, even to feeling that they are harmless, for in both cases the danger was the result of carelessness. In one case I was standing to the left of Wiedrich's battery, when a rifled shell struck about six yards from me and directly in line, burying itself deep in the ground almost under my feet. I waited quietly to see if it would drive out by the hole it entered when it burst, or would break out straight up. It never occurred to me that should it come right up it would certainly hit me, until it had safely blown out by its entrance. In the other case I was passing from the right of Reynolds's battery, but forgot that the left piece stood to the rear of the others, and passed to the front of it just at that instant it was fired. One step more on my part, and they would have blown their colonel as far as ever the British blew mutinous Sepoys. The flash fairly burnt my face; a sudden stop, an exclamation of "close shave," and I went on. In neither of these cases was it bravery on my part, or actual indifference to danger, but an unconsciousness of it at the moment. In neither case did I realize that my escape was any more than from perhaps a knockdown or a little bruise.

Cooper's and Reynolds's batteries fired beautifully. Ames, who himself belongs to the Fifth Artillery, several times spoke in admiration of the former. Wiedrich on the contrary made wretched work of it: his Germans were all excitement, and stood well but were utterly ignorant as to ranges, and the old man knew little more himself. I had to go to each piece myself, set their pendulum haussée, and show them just what length of fuse to use. I found one piece firing fifteen-second fuses at five degrees of elevation, while another was using eighteen-second fuses for four degrees of elevation.

Our artillery duel here was a mere divertissement, the rebels making their charge on our left, where Sickles had thrown his corps in advance of the rest of the line. I saw nothing of the affair, so shall say nothing, save that from what I can learn, the position chosen by Sickles was a bad one. He lost a leg. Our men were at length driven back to where they should have been at first, and held their own there, a good part of the Fifth and Twelfth Corps being sent over there. So soon as the latter was mostly withdrawn from Culp's Hill the rebs made a push for our works there. They tried the west front first, but failed; then the north and east, where they did succeed in getting something of a foothold. While they were trying the west front General Wadsworth sent over to know if I could not fire into the woods so as to strike the enemy. I sent back word that I could not without endangering our own men. Wadsworth then came over himself, and pointed out the spot where he said the rebs were and where he wanted to fire. I still insisted that it was within our lines, but he said that he had just come from there, and knew exactly where our lines were. I had been over there in the morning, and thought differently. But not wishing to be ugly, I had one of "L" Company's guns pointed there, and then insisted on Wadsworth's aiming himself at the point he wanted to hit. So soon as he had seen one shot fired, he galloped off, quite happy. I had that gun fire slowly, watching it myself, for I could not believe I had made so great a mistake in spotting our position on the hill. We had not fired half a dozen shots when a major of the Twelfth Corps came over and said that we were dropping every shot directly into their line, and had already disabled half a dozen men. It was just as I supposed, the rebs were around the corner, where I could not get at them.

About sundown Captain Ricketts reported with his battery. General Hunt, who had visited me during the fight and seen that we were having a hot time of it, had sent him up to relieve any of my batteries I chose. . . . He had everything in very beautiful order, and came up the road as if moving onto a parade ground. General Ames was much struck with it and asked what regular battery that was, which tickled Ricketts greatly.

About an hour after sundown, the moon shining brightly, the enemy made a push for our position. Dr. Mosser, who was in the town, tells me that the attack was made by the "Louisiana Tigers" and another brigade, the lines being formed in the streets running north and south, and marching out by the left flank. So soon as I caught sight of the head of their column coming out, I sent Lieutenant Matthewson over to Stevens's battery to direct him to open on them, and had the other batteries do so as the advancing columns came into view. They marched straight out of the town, and then facing to their right rushed for the hill. So soon as the rebels began to fire, the two lines of Deutschmen in front of the batteries began to run, and nearly the whole of them cleared out. As the enemy advanced we commenced firing canister, depressing the guns more and more, until it was one continual shower straight down the hill. The night was heavy, and the smoke lay so thick that you could not see ten yards ahead; seventeen guns vomiting it as fast as they can will make a good deal of smoke. Feeling sure that no enemy could get up that front, I now passed down the road beyond Stewart's four pieces, so as to get a view townward, for I could not get over my fear of an attack from that quarter. All was quiet, and Stewart keeping a sharp lookout. . . .

I pitied General Ames most heartily. His men would not stand at all, save one. I believe not a single regiment of the Eleventh Corps exposed to the attack stood fire, but ran away almost to a man. Stewart stretched his men along the road, with fence rails! to try to stop the runaways but could do nothing. Officers and men were both alike. Stewart's men however got a supper (they had been without food all day) for when they knocked a Deutschman down, they took his havresack from him. But on the other hand, the men of "I" Battery, also Germans, fought splendidly, sticking to their guns, and finally driving the rebs out with their handspikes and fence rails. Dr. Mosser tells me that a rebel soldier whose wounds he dressed in town that night said that he was on the hill, and that he saw one of the battery men snatch a musket out of the hands of one of their men and drive the bayonet right through his (the rebel's) captain. This would show that the Germans have got fight in them; the fault must be in the officers, most of whom are adventurers, political refugees, and the like.

As the attack was now evidently over, I ordered firing to cease so that the smoke might clear off. While I was passing this order along the line, and cautioning them at the same time to be prepared for a second attempt, a lieutenant-colonel rode up and desired me to cease fire as Carroll's brigade of the Second Corps was going to charge down the valley along my front on the rebel flank. I told him it should be done, the order to cease firing having been already given, but that I did not think he would find many live rebs there. Which proved to be the case, though Carroll did strike the rear of their retreating column, and brought off perhaps a hundred prisoners. . . .

Tonight our lines remain to all intents the same as they were established when the troops first came up, save that our left has been driven back from the Emmitsburg road to the top of the ridge, which at this point is quite low, and that the enemy have got some foothold on our extreme right, around the east side of Wolf Hill. Lee's attack today was a determined one, but not in sufficient force; he could hardly have supposed that he had the whole Army of the Potomac opposed to him. General Meade does not altogether like our position here. He thinks that a better one would have been on the ridge some half a mile farther back, where the line would have been nearer straight. General Hunt came over this morning and explained it to me, adding that it had been determined to hold our present position, but if driven from it we should then take up the other. He desired me to ascertain well the ways of getting there, as, if we were forced back, everything would depend on the artillery holding the new line until the infantry could be formed. This proposed line would have its right on Wolf Hill, instead of Culp's, and could be covered along nearly its whole front by Rock Creek, a small stream.

I turned in about midnight with Lieutenant Breck under one of his tarpaulins. I had had almost nothing to eat since yesterday morning; two cups of coffee and a couple of hard tack begged from the men was all. I did not like to sponge upon my officers, as they are likely to run short. But whether from the excitement or what not, I did not feel hungry. My greatest want has been tobacco, and officers and men are beginning to get short of it. I have managed to get a little here and there today; tomorrow Ricketts promises to fill my pouch, as he has a good supply in his battery cart. My man John has done beautifully, and has not been out of call all day; even in the heaviest fire he only took the horses a little distance under cover of the hill. He has been a real comfort to me, and worth a month's wages.

One of the corps staff informs me that General Newton has been put in command of the corps. I know nothing as to what sort of a general he is; nor have I seen him, he having nothing to do on this part of the line.* In fact, I have received no orders today except from General Hunt. Howard has been along several times, but I have been allowed to run my own machine. Speaking of Howard reminds me that after the charge of Carroll's brigade he himself tried to get two strong regiments to push down the hill near to the town so as to cut off some three hundred rebs who had sought shelter from our fire behind a little knoll. Some had escaped from them there, and knew just where they were. Not an officer of rank in either regiment could be found when the order was given to advance. I said to General Howard, why don't you have them shot? The General answered, "I should have to shoot all the way down; they are all alike." I begin now to believe the hard stories told of the Eleventh Corps' behaviour at Chancellorsville.

* * *

The Confederates had missed their greatest opportunity on the second day of Gettysburg when they failed to take and hold Little Round Top, which has well been termed the key to the battlefield. When the impetuous Sickles placed his corps in an eccentrically exposed position, John B. Hood, who commanded one of Longstreet's divisions, sharply attacked it, and thrust his troops between the left extremity of Sickles' line and Round Top. This movement placed the whole Union army in the greatest danger. If Hood had at that moment taken possession of the outlying spur, Little Round Top, which was quite unoccupied, he might have decided the issue of the battle. Fortunately for Meade's army, Gouverneur K. Warren, its chief engineer, climbed to the top in the nick of time. Some signal officers there were folding their flags to flee before the Confederates. Warren stopped them, and brought up reinforcements that reached the crest just as Hood's Texans arrived there. In the desperate struggle that followed, the volunteer regiments from Michigan, New York, Pennsylvania, and Maine stubbornly maintained their stand.

When the third day of the battle opened, the Union line was still intact

---

* John Newton, West Point, 1842, a veteran of many of the previous battles, was to continue leading the First Corps until the spring of 1864, and was then to serve ably in the Atlanta campaign. Doubleday felt humiliated to be displaced July 2.

in its fishhook position running from Culp's Hill and Cemetery Hill south to Little Round Top and Round Top. The First Corps was almost in the center of this line. As Wainwright indicates, he had played an important part on the second day in helping repel the attack launched by Early on Cemetery Hill. In fact, his batteries had been indispensable, and their gallant behavior is praised by most historians of the conflict. Now the First Corps was directly opposite Lee's main force of guns, and he had to play another important role.

Lee had failed in his attacks the second day on the two flanks of the Union line; that is, on Cemetery Hill and Round Top. He had a choice between withdrawing south, or assailing the Union center. For various reasons a retreat seemed inexpedient. The Confederate leaders therefore spent most of the morning assembling their artillery along Seminary Ridge for a heavy bombardment, and their columns of infantry for a massive attack to follow it.

❋ ❋ ❋

JULY 3, FRIDAY.   We were started up at daylight this morning by artillery fire on our right. During the night the batteries of the Twelfth Corps and some from the reserve were posted so as to rake the valley between Wolf and Culp's Hill, and the eastern face of the latter along which the rebs had made their lodgment. This was soon followed by musketry, and for four hours there was a steady roll of small arms. Such a feu d'enfer I never heard; there was not a time during the whole four hours when there was a let-up long enough for one to draw a breath. I hear that some of Geary's division fired forty rounds per man. At least two-thirds of this ammunition must have been needlessly wasted. Such a vast expenditure speaks badly for the pluck of the men, and cannot ever be necessary with good troops; most certainly not on the part of an attacking force. The ground was, however, eventually regained, and our lines established as before about eight o'clock.

By ten in the morning it began to be evident that Lee was preparing for an attack on some point of our main front. We could see them getting batteries into position all along the Seminary Ridge, and still farther to the north bodies of troops, too, could be seen sweeping around from those who had opposed the Twelfth Corps. On these latter I opened a slow fire whenever we could get a good chance. But they were too far off to do them much harm, and ammunition was valuable.

General Hunt passed along the whole line, seeing that the batteries were properly posted, and directing all the battery commanders to spend very little ammunition on the rebel batteries, but hold their fire for the infantry; not merely in order to keep their men fresh for the close quarters, but also because our ammunition was running short.

At one o'clock the rebel artillery opened with a fearful roar, along their whole line. It is said that they had 140 guns in position. We had 110 and soon replied slowly from most of them. For two hours the roar was continuous and loud as that from the falls of Niagara. The enemy fired full three shots to our one. I have never known them to be so lavish of ammunition. Lee must have given special orders, and have placed much reliance on this fire. But it was by no means as effective as it should have been, nine-tenths of their shot passing over our men. Officers tell me that the case and pieces of shell came down like hail, so high over their head did they burst. My own command took but little part in this grand artillery duel. Wiedrich's four guns were all I could get to bear upon the Seminary Ridge, with a couple of Ricketts's; so after half an hour's engagement with our friends of yesterday, who took position at longer range this time, the other batteries had nothing to do.

I should have liked to have had a better view of the grand conflict, but it would not do for me to leave my post, besides which it is foolish to go into unnecessary danger. From where I was we could only see the ridge on which the rebel guns were, not the valley between.

After about two hours of this work General Hunt sent words around for our guns to cease firing. The rebs kept it up a short time longer and then charged. Of all the hard fight which ensued along our centre of charges and counter-charges we saw nothing. Ames and I waited in intense anxiety, listening to the volley of musketry and the now sharp, quick reports of our guns (the ring of the brass twelve-pounders was easily distinguishable) and the alternate cheers and yells of the contestants. Before five o'clock it was all over, and we soon knew that Lee had met with a fearful repulse, leaving thousands of prisoners in our hands, including several generals. At one time it was positively asserted that Longstreet was among them, but this proved not to be true. I wanted now more than ever to go over, and learn who of my acquaintance had suffered, and how the batteries of my regiment had fought, but did not think it quite safe to leave. Several of my officers rode over to the spot where the main attack was made. They tell me that the ground was covered with dead in front of the Second Corps. Company "B" of my regiment is said to have been all cut to pieces.

At dark, when all was once more quiet, a great relief seemed to rest on the minds of everyone; a sense, as it were, that the worst was over. Not a certainty that the fight was done, or even that Lee might not try it again tonight or tomorrow, but a feeling that he had done his worst and failed. How great our victory had been, or what loss we had inflicted on the enemy we had little idea of, at least along the part of our line where I was. Rumours of the most exaggerated kind were floating around everywhere. General Meade, with a large staff, rode along the lines at dusk and was well received by the men. So far as I can learn as yet Meade handled his army well, so far as there was anything to do. Each point was strengthened as it needed it, without at any time weakening the rest of his line, if we except the withdrawal of two divisions of the Twelfth Corps last evening.

I have not heard of any generals of distinction on our side being killed today. Hancock was wounded, and several other general officers. Poor Weed was killed yesterday; he wore his star but a very short time. Several other artillery officers are said to have gone. It is a wonder that General Hunt has escaped, for he has been on the line all of both days, and it is said charged with our troops at the close of the fight, and was the only officer who did so on horseback. His horse was killed under him.

Just before dark Captain Hall rode up on his seventeen-hand horse, with half a loaf of bread and a great slice of raw ham, half an inch thick, in his hand. Hearing that I was short of something to eat, he brought this over to me. The excitement which had made me forgetful of hunger was over now, and I felt ravenous as a bear in the springtime. John borrowed a frying pan, cleaned it with a bit of newspaper, and cooked the ham to a turn; with the help of some leaves of lettuce dipped into the ham gravy, and a tin cup of coffee, I made a meal fit for a king. At least I thought so then. Had anyone asked me if I was excited before, I should have said no; but now the reaction showed to what a tension every nerve had been drawn for three days. While the revulsion brought a most pleasant feeling, it was one almost of lassitude, like the removal of a fever from the system. A feeling of intense enjoyment, but not of activity.

JULY 4, SATURDAY. As usual, we were up by daylight this morning, but it was not ushered in by a volley of cannon and musketry as it was yesterday. On the contrary, our pickets in the outskirts of the town soon reported that there was no enemy in their front. Very soon after I saw Heard and Bache trudging up the hill on foot, and joyfully went down to meet them. They said that the rebels had withdrawn from the town during the night, their pickets just gone at daylight. How far they had gone, they did not know. All our severely wounded' of the first day and those of the enemy were left in the town, as also all the surgeons of the First and Eleventh Corps who were caught there on our falling back. They only stopped with me a minute or two, and then went on to report to General Newton and General Meade. Others soon succeeded them, as also a few officers and men who had managed to hide during the rebel occupation. Among these was one man of "L" Company who, speaking a little American Deutsch, got an old fellow to pass him off for his son.

The old man had a son about the same size, who was absent from home, in the army perhaps, so was able to fit our boy out in citizen's clothes.

After making sure that we should not get orders to move for some time, I took Stewart and an orderly and rode down through the town to look for his three abandoned caissons.

On the way we stopped at a house in which Captain Reynolds and Lieutenant Davison lay. Both of them were doing well. The former's right eye is completely gone, and the right ankle of the latter is so shattered that it must always be stiff, if he does not have to lose his leg. Every house and church was full of wounded. The Eleventh Corps had pushed some pickets down into the town, but we had no difficulty in passing these and riding out the Cashtown pike to where the caissons were. These we found in exactly the state in which they were left. While we were examining the one farthest out, more than halfway to the seminary, I saw a man in rebel uniform standing on the top of the hill. At first I could not make out what he meant, for I supposed they had cleared out altogether. But as we started to ride up the hill a woman in one of the houses told us not to go any farther or we would get shot, for the rebels were still on the hill. Why they did not shoot at us I cannot say, for we were all of five minutes within easy musket range. I directed Stewart to leave his orderly there and send down teams to get up all the sound part of his caissons. This he did, but before the teams got there the rebs commenced firing at the houses, seeing our pickets pushing out, and drove the orderly in, so that nothing could be done that day.

On returning to the hill I got off a couple of notes home to say that I was alive and well, and then went all around the base of Culp's Hill to see the effect of so much firing yesterday morning. All the trees on the northeast side of the hill were full of bullets way up to their tops, big branches actually cut off by them; it was very apparent how wild the firing had been. It had not all been thrown away, however, for I passed several hundred of the rebel dead lying around among the rocks and boulders. In one place they lay really thick around. The ground was very broken, covered with great detached rocks lying on the surface—a hard place for a line of battle, but capital for a cool marksman. . . .

I have no fondness for looking at dead men, and less for seeing those who are suffering from wounds; consequently, I do not relish going over battle grounds. This, though, is the great battle of the war so far, nor is there likely to be one in which I shall get so good a chance again to see what slaughter is. I therefore rode to our left to take a view of the line where the main attack was made yesterday. In the cemetery itself, the only signs of the enemy's fire was in the tumbled down monuments and broken railings. Beyond that the dead rebels began to show in small numbers over the fields in our front. A short distance before reaching

the right of the Second Corps, I found Captain Fitzhugh with his battery. Here the dead of both sides began to lay quite thick, for the burial
parties were only just beginning work. Indeed, so numerous had they
been, the stretcher bearers were still bringing in the wounded. Just in
front of this was where "B" Battery of my regiment had been badly
posted by Captain Hazard of the Rhode Island Artillery. He had got
provoked at them for leaving a position the day before without orders,
and had purposely put them in a most exposed place, when there was
just as good a one under cover. Their withdrawal the day before was
the fault of Captain Regan, who had been placed in command of the
battery a day or two before, simply because Colonel Tyler did not know
what else to do with him. Captain Regan had no business with the battery, and even if it had been improperly withdrawn by its own commanding officer, he should have been placed in arrest, instead of a petty spite
being visited on the whole battery. They had four guns, and consequently
about sixty men in action; were in this position some fifteen minutes,
and then got out. Regan was killed outright, Lieutenant Sheldon shot
through both legs, nine men killed and fifteen wounded; nearly half of
all present. The proportion of killed was enormous.

A little beyond this I found Webb, already in command of a division,
though but a few weeks a general. It was in his front that the hardest
fighting was. Here the rebels had penetrated our first line, and some
thirty or more lay dead inside of it. Webb told me that when the enemy
reached the wall all his lines began to shake, and for a moment he
thought they were gone; but most of the rebs stopped at the wall. Seeing
this, he ordered his men to charge, which they did. That halt at the wall
was the ruin of the enemy, as such halts almost always are; yet so natural
is it for men to seek cover that it is almost impossible to get them to pass
it under such circumstances. Outside the wall the enemy really lay in
heaps; far more so at least than dead often do on the battlefield, for historians draw largely on the imagination when they talk of heaps of slain,
and rivers of blood. There was about an acre or so of ground here where
you could not walk without stepping over the bodies, and I saw perhaps
a dozen cases where they were *heaped* one on top of the other. A captain
lay thus across the body of a lieutenant-colonel. Both, especially the latter, were very handsome men. A wounded reb told me the colonel's name,
but I have forgotten it; he was from Norfolk.

While I was here General Hunt came up. He said that he wanted to
go out and see the effect of our artillery fire at a certain point, but we
were unable to reach it as it was under fire of the rebel pickets. Our
skirmish line now lay along the Emmitsburg road. General Hunt told
me that one of the corps or division commanders, Hancock I think,
nearly ruined himself by insisting that the batteries along his line should

keep up a heavy fire, after he, Hunt, had ordered them to cease. The consequence was they expended all their ammunition, and had none when the tug came. Fortunately Colonel McGilvery, an old Maine sea captain, had command of four or five batteries from the reserve on his right, and refused point blank to obey. I say fortunately, for when the enemy got close up, McGilvery, having all fresh and ready, poured in the ugliest kind of oblique fire on him.

The greater part of the wounded of both sides had been brought in, but there were a number of poor rebels still out on the ground. One poor fellow, an officer, had been shot in the mouth; his lips were fairly glued together with the gore; another one begged me for some whiskey, but I had none; most of them asked if I could not have them moved. For this I was powerless, save to blow up some of the regimental surgeons who, when I spoke to them on the subject, objected that they did not belong to their regiment. I fear that I should be very hard on such fellows if I had the power. As a rule the wounded of both sides are treated alike by our surgeons.

Our troops lay in the lines all day, as Lee was evidently still in front of us. Rations were issued, as also ammunition, and everything possible done to restore damages. It was hard work keeping the battery men in their places; all wanted to go around and see the sights. At night I again slept in the gate house.

JULY 5, SUNDAY. Lee has cleared out; gone off to the westward during the night with all his army. He evidently waited yesterday to give Meade a chance to attack him; perhaps, too, in order to get his trains well started on the way. Meade was too wise to try the attack and so Lee cleared off. A number of our generals I know think that we ought to have attacked. I for one am glad that he did not. Lee had doubtless lost very heavily, but we had suffered almost as much, and our men were quite as much exhausted as his. In every respect the two armies are so well balanced that the assaulting party is sure to fail if the other has time to post itself and do anything at entrenching. This has been shown in every battle so far, unless the generalship was very bad. Here Lee had a position quite as strong or stronger than ours; was entrenched and had his 140 pieces of artillery in position. He was probably somewhat short of artillery ammunition, but not of small arm or canister. Americans of both sides are not elated by success or depressed by defeat as most people are. The Saxon bulldog blood in them would have made the rebels fight harder than ever to pay off the scores of Friday; while I could plainly see that our men thought they had had fight enough for once. On strictly scientific grounds perhaps we ought to have attacked, but taking the composition of the two armies into consideration, I feel sure that Meade was right in not doing it.

Early this morning the runaway inhabitants of Gettysburg began to
return. Nine-tenths of the men had cleared out, leaving the women behind them, and gone off to look after their own safety. Now the danger
was over, they came back; great strong able looking fellows most of them,
but not one had courage enough to take a musket in hand for defence
of his own home. Hundreds from the country around, too, came down
in their waggons to see the sights, to stroll over the ground, and gaze and
gape at the dead and wounded. But not one lifted a finger to help the
tired soldiers remove the one or bury the other. Nor were any seen
travelling over the ground with aught to relieve the poor fellows who
had (some of them) been lying where they fell for three days and nights.
One man was found selling pies at twenty-five cents to the poor fellows
by Dr. Bache. Gettysburg may hereafter be classic ground, but its inhabitants have damned themselves with a disgrace that can never be
washed out. Had it not been for the wounded and women and children
left in it, I should rejoice had it been levelled with the ground. I think
that Meade might and should have seized every able-bodied citizen he
could get his hands on, and forced them to do all the burying. I would
have armed cavalry with cowhides and driven them like slaves to the
work.

Instead of helping us, they were coming in shoals with their petty complaints of damages. One man wanted a dead horse removed out of his
stable! Another demanded twenty dollars for bringing half a dozen
wounded cavalrymen some seven miles. Fortunately the quartermaster
to whom he applied was not weak, and instead of paying him the money
took his horses for government use, and left him to walk home. But we
are said to be among friends now, and our generals are afraid of complaints to be made at Washington. Mild, quiet Howard is the only one
I have heard of who has dared to do anything. He gave Major Osborn
permission to take any good artillery horses he might find; giving a receipt for them.

During the morning I rode out over the ground of the first day's fight.
Very few of our dead were buried and some of their own even had been
left lying where they fell. The bodies presented a ghastly sight, being
swollen almost to the bursting of their clothes, and the faces perfectly
black. Burying parties were out gathering all the dead, but the work of
burying them was very ineffectually done, for twenty or more were put
in a trench side by side, and covered with only a foot or two of earth.
The details from the different corps for this work were very large. I hear
that they report this evening near 5,000 rebel dead buried, including
1,200 around Culp's Hill. This last I do not believe, from what I saw
there myself yesterday morning. . . .

As yet I have heard no estimate of our own loss. It must be very heavy, though hardly equal to that of the rebels. They took very few prisoners after the first day, when they got between five and six thousand from the two corps. The loss in my own brigade sums up nine men killed, four officers and eighty-three men wounded, and eleven men missing: total 103. To these should be added a dozen or fifteen in Wiedrich's and Ricketts's batteries. . . .

* * *

All day July 4 the Confederates remained in their positions anticipating a Union attack that never came. Lee, indeed, had thought it might immediately follow the repulse of Pickett's charge. So did Longstreet, who wrote later: "When this charge failed, I expected that, of course, the enemy would throw himself against our shattered ranks and try to crush us." General E. P. Alexander of the Confederate artillery declared long afterward: "I have always believed that the enemy here lost the greatest opportunity they ever had of routing Lee's army by a prompt offensive."

Yet Meade never for a moment contemplated any such movement; he was too fearful of disaster. General James Wadsworth, as Pickett attacked, sent an aide to ask that he be allowed to throw in his division; and his disappointment when he met a refusal was doubled as he saw that Meade was preparing no counterblow. "To his mind," says his biographer, "the repulse of Lee should at all hazards be taken advantage of on the instant." Abner Doubleday felt outraged; Meade, he comments, could at least have ordered Sedgwick's corps into battle, for even if it were checked it could deal the enemy crippling blows. Warren took the same view. The disappointment of Lincoln over Meade's dilatory behavior was intense. He believed that Meade had thrown away an opportunity to close at one blow a bloody war that, as time proved, was to endure nearly two years longer.

When Lee on the night of the 4th, in a fearful storm, moved back toward the passes behind him so that he might retreat to the pontoon bridge he had left on the Potomac at Williamsport, Meade had two possible lines by which to pursue him. He, too, might go across the Blue Ridge extension (South Mountain) and follow directly down the Cumberland Valley. Or he might strike along the east side, a longer but safer route. He chose the latter line. On July 6th a great part of the army marched from Gettysburg toward Emmitsburg, and the remainder followed next day. It is true that Sedgwick's Sixth Corps did try to press the Confederates as they moved off through the South Mountain range, but he was soon recalled.

Meade's tardy march did not bring him within striking distance of the Confederates until July 12, and then he delayed an attack. Before he was ready to move on the 14th, the Confederate army had made good its escape across the Potomac.

❊ ❊ ❊

NEAR EMMITSBURG, JULY 6, MONDAY. The army started to head Lee off this morning. The Sixth Corps, which has had less of the fight this time than any of the others, along with the cavalry, went in *direct* pursuit yesterday. Our corps was one of the last to get off, and are to take the same road we came up by. We started about noon, and halted here for the night, some two miles north of the town. The men have even a more dirty appearance than usual. As for myself, I never was so dirty before in all my life. From what reason I do not know, our corps headquarters waggons have not come up since the fight, and now I hear they have been sent around to Frederick by another road. General Newton has his own waggon, but the old staff are entirely without. Six days without even a clean pocket handkerchief is awful. I had to stop by a brook to-day, and wash mine, hanging it over my head to dry as we rode along. I also sank my rank for once, and washed my feet by the roadside, like a private. But in spite of my best endeavours, I feel horribly nasty.

The men of course were still talking about the fight, and were loud in their curses of Pennsylvanians. If their curses could do this people any harm, the lot of Gettysburg would be as bad as that of the cities of the plain. All are rejoicing that we are once more out of the state. On the road we met several large waggons filled with Sisters of Charity from the convent here, and with the good things they were taking up to the wounded. Even the white coverings of the baskets did one good in the midst of so much dirt. We had to leave a strong force of surgeons behind, though large numbers are said to have come down from the cities. . . .

General Newton is another undersize, smooth face, and light hair; he seems a gentlemanly man, and quite affable. He brought his adjutant-general, Russell, and two aides, Bliss and Jackson, with him from his old division. The first of these, Russell, is already making himself very disagreeable, by finding fault with everything and everybody in the corps, and talking very largely as to what he will do to bring them up to the mark. What sort of men he had to deal with in his old place I do not know; but there are a number here who will not put up with his airs. . . .

HAMBURG, MARYLAND, JULY 7, TUESDAY. We started early this morning, passing the Eleventh Corps at Emmitsburg. I sent Lieutenant Matthewson on ahead to buy me a pair of socks and a couple of handkerchiefs in the town. He got them, the socks very large, and the handkerchiefs very small; the latter as well as the former of cotton. When we got into Emmitsburg I found our new Major Russell giving orders to some of my batteries, and swearing a good deal. I quietly asked him if he was transmitting orders from General Newton, and informed him that if he was I was the proper person to receive them; if not, that this was my command, and I allowed no interference. Almost directly afterward I heard General Robinson pitching into him in less civil terms. The Major will soon find that he is too big for his boots, and have to shrink into his proper proportion. . . .

We followed the road we marched up on, between the turnpike and the mountains. . . . About two-thirds of the way down the infantry were turned off to the right up the hill by a bridle path, which it was said would cut off some eight miles. The batteries had to go around, nearly down to Frederick, and then climb the hill from that direction. . . . The climb up the Catoctins was very steep, but the road was good, and no one else on it; so by taking it quietly and doubling teams where necessary, we reached the top soon after dark, and with only some half dozen horses of the Fifth Maine giving out. The carriages came in rather straggling, but were all parked for the night by ten o'clock, and only just in time, for as the last one got into the field it began to rain, and poured pretty much all night.

Lieutenant Jackson told me that General Newton was greatly tickled at our arrival. It seems that the Sixth Corps had been recalled from the direct pursuit of Lee and was following close behind us, Colonel Tompkins having turned off his batteries to follow mine. General Sedgwick was talking to Newton on top of the hill, his infantry just beginning to arrive, when Tompkins rode up and reported that it was impossible to get the artillery up that night. His batteries, he said, were close behind mine, and I had got off the road and was stuck for the night. He got his permission to halt and Jackson was sent down the road to meet me. He had to go but a very little distance, and in twenty minutes after Tompkins reported me stuck I passed the generals with the leading batteries. Newton crowed, and Uncle John was mad. . . . They say that my march today was thirty-two miles.

SOUTH MOUNTAIN, JULY 8, WEDNESDAY. We made two marches today. The first was in the morning down the mountain to Middletown, where we expected to halt for the night; and, our waggons 'having made their appearance, we got our tents up and opened out for a wash. Who can tell the luxury of that wash, and the clean clothes that followed it! A whole week of sleeping on the ground, riding in the dust; dirt, powder smoke, and sweat. I thought my wash in the wilderness of Chancellorsville could not be equalled, but this has surpassed it, for though not so tired, I was infinitely more dirty. I had sent orders around to the batteries to wash carriages and harness, and had camped them on the bank of the stream on purpose. Some of them had just begun work when we got orders to start again, and came to this place on the top of the pass where the great National Road goes through the mountain. . . .

JULY 9, THURSDAY. We have lain quiet in the pass all today. A large number of the cavalry passed during the morning, and in the afternoon drove the rebel cavalry back beyond Boonesboro. I rode out a few miles to see what I could, having never before had a chance to look at a cavalry fight. From where I was I could see many miles over the country, which is quite open. There was no large engagement, but several quite pretty little charges, and a good deal of cannonading. Our men brought in a few score of prisoners. General Buford was in command; many say that he is the best cavalry general we have. He resembles Reynolds very much in his manners, reserved and somewhat rough.

Lee must be somewhere over in the direction of Hagerstown. A great many of the prisoners that were captured from us are escaping; I hear of several officers arriving every day. Even old Colonel Whedock got off, though he is as big and old as Jack Falstaff; the old fellow shewed good pluck in running. We have got some reinforcements from the troops which garrisoned Harper's Ferry, and others. . . . We are beginning to get a few orders, and letters and papers from home. Among the former is one from General Meade thanking the army for its behaviour in the late battle, but as yet not a word from Mr. Lincoln. It would be too much of a knocking under for them to utter a word at Washington in praise of the Army of the Potomac. . . . The papers tell us that ours was not the only victory which crowned the national anniversary; Vicksburg too has fallen, and Grant's army is set free to aid at Port Hudson, where Banks is said to be making most wretched work of it.

FOUR MILES BEYOND BOONESBORO, JULY 10, FRIDAY. We moved this far today, and have gone into position on the hills at this place along the line of a small creek; Beaver Creek I believe it is called. The right of our corps, and I know of none beyond it in that direction, is about a quarter of a mile from a small village, and mill. We have a good position here, if our flanks are only taken care of, but I do not suppose that there is a possibility of Lee's attacking us. The men, I suppose by the advice of their officers or at any rate with their aid and consent, commenced piling up rails and digging earth the instant they were formed in line; even before orders came down from General Newton to do so. I was sorry to see so much anxiety to make themselves secure; it does not speak well for the morale of the men. I fear they are more willing to be attacked than they are to attack, which is not a good sign just now, for if there is any more fighting at all we must be the attacking party. Perhaps this feeling is not so much to be wondered at, when one takes into consideration the three last battles, and the tendency of Americans to reason on everything. They see that victory has been with the defensive, and wish to be always in that position.

There is a difference between the people of Maryland and those of Pennsylvania. A man of some fifty or more stood looking at our men pull down the fences to start their breastworks, and carrying off the sheaves of wheat just cut here for their beds. Having a fellow-feeling for the owner as a brother farmer, I spoke to the man and said it was hard on the owner of the land to destroy his crops and fences so. "Oh," says he, "you may destroy my whole farm if you will only whip the rebels." If the eastern Marylanders are the most bitter of the rebels, those west of Frederick are the truest Union people I have met with anywhere. This same willingness to sacrifice and give was apparent through this country in the Antietam campaign as well as in this one; their kindness was shown to the men as well before as after our victories.

The weather has been muggy, with more or less fine rain ever since the battle. It is not enough wet to interfere with us, save that the fields are very muddy, but it prevents the farmers from getting in their grain, and you can hardly stop the men from taking the sheaves to sleep on when the ground is so nasty. . . .

JULY 11, SATURDAY. We have not moved at all today: waiting, it is said, for the left of the army to move up to its position at or near Bakersville. . . . They say that some of the militia are coming down to join us, and that the Seventh New York is in the South Mountain pass. Also that Couch is coming down on to Lee's rear with a large body of them. I hear, too, that some of our advance claim to have destroyed Lee's pontoon train, so that he cannot get across the Potomac, which is very much swollen. How much of all these reports to believe I cannot say, but two things are certain: first, that Lee has not crossed into Virginia yet; and second, that if he does not clear out soon we shall have another fight. It would nearly end the rebellion if we could actually bag this army, but on the other hand, a severe repulse of us would give them all the prestige at home and abroad which they lost at Gettysburg, and injure our morale greatly. I trust therefore that General Meade will not attempt it, unless under circumstances which will make our chances of success at least four out of five. . . .

FUNKSTOWN, JULY 12, SUNDAY. Last night I expected that we should have got orders to move at daylight this morning, but they did not come until nine o'clock, and then, just as we were all ready, we were directed still to wait. It was after noon when we got off; so I got a last meal at our friends in the little hamlet where I also breakfasted this morning. The Eleventh Corps was in front of us, and they forced the bridge over the Antietam this morning with very little trouble. We crossed the stream by this bridge at Funkstown and formed our line just beyond. . . .

JULY 13, MONDAY. I fully expected that we should have a fight this morning, but the whole day has passed without one. There was a council of war at Army Headquarters, when all but Warren and Wadsworth were opposed to fighting. General Newton was sick and sent Wadsworth up in his place. Warren was present as chief of staff. Meade was in favour of waiting until tomorrow, as Couch would then be in Lee's rear with his militia, and considerable reinforcements are expected up for ourselves tonight. My informant as to what took place in the council was General Wadsworth, who talks very freely on the subject, and loudly against the decision. Could the General infuse his own courage and spirit of fight into each of the men, it would be well enough to drive ahead without taking anything into consideration. But there are very, very few, among either officers or men, who have it. There is something to be admired in the old man's earnestness, and did it concern no life but his own, it would be grand. His only idea seems to be that war means fight. Yonder are the enemy; pitch in. I know nothing about the left of our line, but Lee's position in front of us is very strong, and so far as we can see well mounted with artillery. My opinion is most decided that we could not carry it.

About three o'clock in the afternoon we had a tremendous rain, which made the fallow fields in such a state that it was difficult even to walk about them. To have kept the batteries supplied with ammunition or to have charged in line over them would have been impossible. After the rain was over the enemy fired several shot from a couple of twenty-four-pounder howitzers, as if just to show that they were still there. This was about an hour before dark. . . .

* * *

Wainwright's statement as to Meade's council of war requires amplification. Held on the evening of July 12, it was attended by Meade; his chief of staff, A. A. Humphreys; the seven corps commanders of the Army of the Potomac; the chief engineer of the army, Warren; and the head of the cavalry, Pleasonton. Wadsworth represented the First Corps, for Newton was not available. Meade was for attacking Lee the next morning. Wadsworth, Howard, Pleasonton, and Warren were also in favor of an attack, Warren making an able argument for it. But Sedgwick, the ranking officer after Meade, with Slocum, Sykes, William H. French, and General William Hays, the temporary commander of the Second Corps, were emphatically against attacking. The whole roster was thus five to five (Humphreys not taking a stand), but the corps commanders voted seven to two against a battle, and Meade said he would not take the responsibility of provoking it against the advice of so many of his commanders.

Lincoln felt the bitterest disappointment over Meade's continued inaction. He had instructed the general to press Lee tenaciously. Sending Meade news on July 7 of the surrender of Vicksburg, he had declared that if he would "complete his work so gloriously prosecuted so far, by the literal or substantial destruction of Lee's army," the war would end. Subsequently he had Halleck telegraph Meade: "You are strong enough to attack and defeat the enemy before he can effect a crossing. . . . Call no council of war. It is proverbial that councils of war never fight. . . . Do not let the enemy escape." Lincoln's biographers Nicolay and Hay write that the council should never have been called. They also state that if three corps commanders of tested fighting spirit—Reynolds, Hancock, and Sickles—had been present, they would have stood for energetic action; but Reynolds was dead, Hancock and Sickles wounded. It might be added that Abner Doubleday, also wounded, would have voted emphatically for a battle. Doubleday in his book on Gettysburg quotes the old military maxim that a fleeing enemy must be given a wall of steel or a bridge of gold: "In the present instance it was unmistakably the bridge of gold that was presented."

❊ ❊ ❊

WILLIAMSPORT, JULY 14, TUESDAY. This morning when we turned out Lee was gone clean over the Potomac into Virginia again. People at home of course will now pitch into Meade, as they did McClellan after Antietam, for letting him escape. My own opinion is that under the circumstances and with the knowledge General Meade then had he was justified in putting off his attack until today. Everything went to prove that the enemy could not cross the river until it fell, as General French reported having captured the whole of their pontoons. It seems, however, that he did not get them all, for Lee had enough left to make one bridge with the help of some canal boats. I hear that a citizen came into our lines in the afternoon and reported Lee withdrawing then. I know that none of his guns in front of us were removed until after the rain, for I examined all the tracks this morning. Had we attacked anytime before dark we should have encountered the whole of their artillery. As the guns on his left had the farthest to go to reach the crossing, they certainly were not the last removed.

We pushed on to this place at a pretty good rate, passing directly through their line of works. These were by far the strongest I have seen yet; evidently laid out by engineers and built as if they meant to stand a month's siege. The parapet was a good six feet wide on top, and the guns, which were very thick, were all placed so as to get a perfect cross fire and to sweep their whole front. When shall we learn to put up such field works? It is just as easy to put them up right as wrong, but ours are never laid out with an eye to their whole length, or even to the length of a corps. Brigade commanders are directed about where to place their men, and even the best of them only look after their own front; there is no reliance on mutual support and protection. The only way a proper line could be taken up would be to have an engineer officer at corps headquarters, and have it thoroughly understood that he was responsible for the position of all field works, and no division commander could say him nay, or interfere with him. There is a curious jealousy in our army, a grasping after power which does not rightly belong to them, which must be owing to our new-fledged generals not knowing the exact duties and powers of their position, and consequently being afraid that they will not get all they are entitled to. . . .

* * *

Competent accounts of the battle of Gettysburg give great credit to Wainwright for his intrepid management of his artillery on the first day, and effective fire from Cemetery Hill the second. A metal marker near where Reynolds fell singles him and Thomas Osborn out as mainly responsible for the silencing of the Confederate guns the second day.

A TIME FOR MEDITATION

Heavy Eastern fighting ended for 1863 with Gettysburg. Lee retired to the Rapidan, where he felt so safe that he detached two divisions of Longstreet's corps to fight at Chickamauga in Tennessee. Meade followed at his leisure, taking up a line along the Rappahannock. Lincoln had lost hope for the Army of the Potomac under its existing leadership. "I have no faith that Meade will attack Lee," he remarked late in July. "Nothing looks like it to me." And on September 21 he spoke still more despondently to Gideon Welles: "It is the same old story of the Army of the Potomac. Imbecility, inefficiency—don't want to *do*. . . . Oh, it is terrible, terrible, this weakness, this indifference of our Potomac generals, with such armies of good and brave men." General Wadsworth was so disgusted that he asked to be relieved and was sent on an inspection tour in the Mississippi Valley by Stanton. He paused long enough in Washington to remark to David Hunter: "General, there are a good many officers of the regular army who have not yet entirely lost the West Point ideas of Southern superiority. That sometimes accounts for an otherwise unaccountable slowness of attack."

Public attention now turned to the West, and to the fierce battles of Chickamauga, Chattanooga, and Lookout Mountain, which gave an emphatic answer to men who, like Wainwright, fancied that the Western troops were inferior to those of the East. They at least fought tenaciously, and they had a habit of winning. In Virginia the initiative was actually first taken by Lee, who in October began an offensive centering around Bristoe Station, where a sharp battle was fought. The campaign amounted to little; but in its course Meade, though outnumbering the Southerners eight to five, was compelled to retreat forty miles. Nor in the abortive Mine Run campaign in the Rapidan area that followed in November did Meade cover himself with renown. He marched, he saw the Confederates, and he retreated.

During this relatively quiet autumn Wainwright found opportunity for more general reflection than in the heat of the previous fighting, and set down some interesting and acute conclusions on the character of the war.

* * *

TWO MILES FROM BERLIN, MARYLAND, JULY 16 [1863], THURSDAY. We are lying here on the wheat stubble tonight, and are to have at least one day, I believe, to get our supplies renewed. These rains have made this country very nasty for camping on, as there is no sod, and the grain stubble gets very quickly trodden into mire. The rest of the army is coming in or already here; the Second Corps under General Gibbon, quite near to us. From the orders issued, I should imagine that supplies not only of commissary stores, but of shoes and clothing have been already sent up to Berlin and Sandy Hook. Very different from what it was last year, when after waiting six weeks we had to march without them.

The New York papers we get here tell us that they have had, perhaps are still having, actual serious rioting there on the draft question. At least the enforcement of the draft is made the excuse, by those who in a large city always profit by such disturbances. I am very sorry to see it, not merely on account of the damage done and the disgrace to the city, but also because it is just what those in power in Washington wanted. No part of the country has so strongly protested against the radical tendencies of the government, and now they will raise the cry that the protestors are disloyal, and unwilling to have the army filled up. If Governor Seymour does not toe the mark, I should not be surprised to see any measures taken against the city. Chase and Stanton would be only too glad to have the appointing of a military government in the city; and I, for one, do not believe them any too good to incite the riot for the sake of putting it down, in the same way that such things are constantly done in Europe. The rioters' main object of hatred seems to have been the negroes, of whom they are said to have killed a number, and have burned down the negro orphan asylum. This shows that the draft was only an excuse, not the foundation of the trouble.

JULY 17, FRIDAY. We lay quiet today filling up our supplies. I have done a good day's work myself, in that I have got off all my reports of the Gettysburg fight. It is difficult for me to get off a report of any action which pleases me; to have it give a clear and exact statement of the affair without being too long, and to claim such credit as my command actually deserves without appearing to derogate the claims of others or to indulge in buncombe terms. A report full of "Captain so-and-so most gallantly . . . ," "the men bravely stood," and so forth, is simply disgusting. . . .

My report of expenditures and losses is very complete. The five batteries expended 4,460 rounds of ammunition, or 160 rounds for each of the 28 guns. The amount of canister fired was tremendous. Stewart fired 116 rounds and Stevens 103, or more than the usual supply carried with each battery. The three-inch batteries fired, Cooper 80 rounds, his full supply, Hall 40, and Breck 53. The loss in harness was very heavy, and in all matériel. Stewart did not have the means to secure his damaged caissons, and consequently had to report them as lost, though they will be gathered up by someone on the part of the government. Six of the three-inch axles broke by the recoil of the guns; they are made altogether too light. Hall had two of his guns so much damaged that he was obliged to turn them in, and I consequently have but thirteen rifled guns now.

A good deal of talk is made about a fight on Tuesday last at Falling Waters, in which General Kilpatrick claims to have charged a large body of rebel infantry in breastwork and to have captured two cannon, three battle flags, and some 1,500 prisoners. It sounds like a big thing for the cavalry, but the fact that Kilpatrick makes the report leads to some doubt of its accuracy; that general's reports being great in "the most glorious charges ever made," "sabring right and left," and such stuff. They tell me at headquarters that General Meade required a reiteration of the report, before he was willing to send it up.* Our cavalry has done some very good service on this campaign, much more than ever before, and a man would hardly be a cavalry officer if he did not talk big. That seems to have been one of their characteristics in all ages and all armies. Some of our cavalry under Gregg had another fight on the Virginia side the day before yesterday; it was a much harder fight, but not so successful as Kilpatrick's.

Another order is out respecting transportation which is certainly the bugbear of our army. This order, like all the others, allows one wall tent for personal use and office of commanding officers of corps, divisions, and brigades, a perfect absurdity, for it will not begin to hold the clerks needed at either corps or division headquarters, to say nothing of the commanding general's tent being made an office at any time. Corps and division headquarters are allowed a spring waggon, and several saddle horses for contingent purposes, but not brigade headquarters. They would be a great convenience, especially the waggon. They also mean to do all they can towards supplying the army from the country; we may get a little in this way as we go through Loudoun County, but not beyond that. General Wadsworth has left the corps. . . .

* Hugh J. Kilpatrick of New Jersey had graduated at West Point only in 1861, and had gone at once into the war, being wounded at Big Bethel in June. He soon gained a reputation for "notorious immoralities" (Jacob D. Cox) and reckless fighting. Sherman was later reported to have said that he knew Kilpatrick to be "a hell of a damned fool," but he wanted just that type of man to command his cavalry; and the general served ably in the Atlanta campaign and march to the sea. At Falling Waters the Confederate commander Henry Heth, whose division had suffered terribly at Gettysburg, was helping cover Lee's withdrawal over the Potomac. He fought off Kilpatrick's troopers, losing, according to Douglas Freeman, only five hundred stragglers.

WATERFORD, VIRGINIA, JULY 18, SATURDAY. Once more we are on the "sacred" soil, as they call it. We started at four this morning, crossed at Berlin just as we did last year, and brought up at this place in good time. . . . The country here is as beautiful as ever. We manage to get a little hay at night, which is very much needed by our horses, they having grown very poor. The fields are full of blackberries, almost equal in size to the New Rochelle; the men will wander off to pick them, let me do my best. When we halt for ten minutes or more I have no objection to their picking blackberries if they are close by. Indeed, I gave them special permission to do so one time today when we halted alongside of a field, over the whole of which they were growing as thick as if it was the cultivated crop proper there. I got a good pull at them myself, too, and hardly had to move in order to find as many as I wanted.

As I change the leading battery in column each day, I ride near enough to its commanding officer to see how he marches his men. The great tendency of battery men is to straggle ahead, which they often do without knowing it, owing to the frequent momentary checks in the march caused by the infantry ahead. I do not find one of my officers who, riding at the head of his battery, is not constantly allowing them thus to pass ahead right under his nose without his seeing it. . . . I am rapidly coming to the belief that there are very few men who have their senses about them all the time: they seem to be dreaming or thinking of something else. As for the men, I am bound to stop straggling, and at one time today had ten men tied behind the guns of "L" Company. A whole day's march at the tail of a gun, where he has no chance to pick his steps, or even to jump a puddle of water, is not as light a punishment as it seems. . . .

HAMILTON, JULY 19, SUNDAY. We got in here today in time for me to do some writing. I also received some letters and papers. They had begun to get the fuller account of our battle and to realize what it was. The feeling seems to be growing there as well as here in the army that McClellan must be put in Halleck's place. Even those who do not think him fit to command an army in the field, admit his ability as a strategist, and in all the theory of war. . . .

The riots in New York were really of a most serious nature, much worse than any we have ever had there before. A large number of men were killed, and quite a determined resistance made to the troops when they got there. All the best militia regiments were away at the time, so that the mob had comparatively full sway. It was composed entirely of the lowest class of foreigners, not one in ten of whom were subject to draft, and was really, as most riots are, an anti-property riot. All they wanted was a clever leader to have done an immense amount of harm. Governor Seymour shewed to very bad advantage in the repressing of the riot: issuing proclamations, and asking the Archbishop to plead with them. He is said to have asked McClellan, whom he summoned to his aid, to address the mob, but he would not, and finding that the Governor would not act, left. It was a grand opportunity to have killed off a large number of the worst rowdies and scoundrels in the city, and should have been taken advantage of. . . .

MIDDLEBURGH, JULY 20, MONDAY. Our march today has been to the east of the district of country we came down last autumn; indeed, our corps is hugging pretty closely to the Bull Run Mountains, and has about all the army to the right of us. But, although we are thus supposed to be separated from the enemy, we found today that Mosby's men could strike any who were too venturesome over here. The bridge over Goose Creek being gone, and the ford at that point being too deep, Major Russell was sent upstream to try another; old Sanderson went with him; an orderly came back to say that the ford was good; but nothing has been heard of the others, who are now doubtless heading straight for Richmond. . . . Everyone is sorry for Sanderson; still, the idea of his going to the Libby, with his love of good eating and for little comforts, is so ridiculous that everyone laughs when they first hear of it.* . . .

JULY 21, TUESDAY. No move for our corps today. General Newton ordered the commissaries to take advantage of the halt to gather enough fresh vegetables in the neighbourhood to issue one ration to the troops, but I have not heard of enough being gathered even to supply the headquarter's mess; we certainly have seen nothing of them in our mess. Dr. Bache has consented to run the mess for a time, but there is precious little that can be done towards a decent table now, with nothing to cook, and a bad cook to do it. Some of the commissaries managed to get a few barrels of flour in the village, and forced the people to bake it; they grumbled terribly, and some were quite obstreperous, but so much has been said about this army now living on the country that Newton was determined to try what could be done in that way. . . .

There is a good deal of talk being made about War Department Order No. 207, regulating the giving of parole by prisoners. It does not admit of any parole being binding which is not given at the regularly appointed places of exchange. The thing had been much abused, no doubt, by paroling men on the battlefield, as also by officers who gave their parole in order to escape going to Libby. But the present order should have

---

* Major John S. Mosby had organized a corps of Partisan Rangers that carried on a ruthless guerrilla warfare in the Loudoun County area of northwestern Virginia. The record published as his *Memoirs* contains a report to Jeb Stuart dated simply July 1863, in which he notes that he is sending in 141 prisoners "that we captured from the enemy during their march through this county." Wainwright's friend Sanderson, formerly manager of the New York Hotel, was probably one of them.

its exceptions as in the case of a badly wounded man, whose chance of recovery would be very small if he should be moved.

WHITE PLAINS, JULY 22, WEDNESDAY. We reached this little, intensely "secesh" village a few hours before dark, and are very comfortably camped near the centre of the place. We got a most excellent supper at the house of the principal inhabitant. The good lady's husband is in the rebel army, but she was none the less willing to do the best she could for the general commanding, and gave us the best meal I have had for a long time. The corn bread surpassed any I have ever seen, being as light and delicate as any sponge cake. General Newton differs very much from Reynolds in his love for the comforts of life, and for good eating. Baked beans and cayenne pepper will never satisfy him for a meal. . . .

The Manassas Gap Railroad runs through this place. The road is open—at least a train has come through from Washington with supplies —but we have had no mail either go out or come in. The rest of the army is stretched along the railroad to the right of us, and Meade's headquarters are about six or eight miles off. I hear nothing of what Lee is about, but presume he is pushing for Culpeper faster than we are. . . .

WARRENTON JUNCTION, JULY 26, SUNDAY. We moved to this place yesterday afternoon.* I was sorry to come, as it is a wretched hole; low and flat, not nearly so pleasant as Warrenton itself. I have my batteries in a bit of wood about a quarter of a mile from the junction and directly north of the Warrenton branch. We are close to the depot of supplies at any rate, which is some advantage, as we stand a better chance of getting hay for our horses, which have become very low in condition. Corps headquarters are across a field directly in front of me. My own tents are pitched with the batteries, but I go over to corps headquarters for my meals.

This morning General Newton sent for me and asked me to ride around the country and report to him how he had best post his divisions. This I again respectfully declined to do, stating plainly that my business was to advise with regard to the posting of the artillery: that I should, of course, examine the position the first thing and would report to him my observations, but that I was unwilling to take the responsibility of posting his corps for him. Finally he concluded to go himself, and we rode together all around. I was much pleased with the General's observations regarding the lay of the land and so on. He knows enough theoretically at any rate, but is intensely lazy. It is very easy to see now how Major Russell managed to get such control, General Newton being only too glad to leave matters in the hands of anyone who would take

* Entries for July 23 and 24 had recorded the march through Monte to Warrenton, where one of the bands gave an evening concert "which brought out all the niggers and a number of white girls too."

all the trouble off of his shoulders. When we came in from our ride, we found the Eleventh Corps just arrived and going into camp on the left of the railroad. . . .

By home letters and the papers we learn that the riots in New York have at last been entirely put down. Nearly all the regulars in this army were sent on there, and are now camped in the city. It must be queer in the eyes of the New Yorkers to see their streets full of soldiers, and sentries pacing at every corner. The loss of life on both sides has been quite considerable, and the loss of property much heavier. The Common Council have voted two and a half million to pay substitute money for poor men who may be drafted. Philadelphia and other places have done the same. In Providence, where the draft has been enforced, it is said that but *one* man has been mustered in; all the rest have paid. We shall get a large army at this rate.

JULY 29, WEDNESDAY. The immediate pursuit of Lee has most certainly been given up, as the whole army is still lying here quite quietly. The Eleventh and ourselves are at the junction; the Twelfth about a mile to to rear of us; and the other four corps stretched out to the right as far as Waterloo. We have got or are getting our stores quite rapidly. . . .

A lot of ninety horses have just come in for me: this quite sets me on my feet as full two-thirds of them are really good; twenty of the other third are entirely worthless, but that is a much smaller number than what we generally have. As a rule, one-half the horses received from the corrals are totally unfit for artillery use; this is the best lot I have drawn this year. . . .

JULY 31, FRIDAY. We have now been in this spot nearly a week, so I suspect no one will be sorry to move out of it tomorrow, which we have orders to do in the direction of Rappahannock Station. The weather is really warm, hot one may call it, and this low spot very close, with the woods all around us. The whole army I believe is to move up to the line of the river. . . .

The War Department has a heavy business on hand now, and it is not at all to be wondered at that they should make bad work of some of it, but I am surprised that they so seldom do anything right or wisely. The whole manner of conducting the draft and raising recruits seems to be about as bad as it can well be, the main object all through being to please everybody, and curry favour all around. The act of Congress itself is no doubt faulty, but I think that it might be carried out better. Perhaps when they get the Invalid Corps fully organized they may do better; it will certainly put the means of doing so in their hands by stationing the companies of the First Battalion where needed, and putting the officers in as provost-marshals. By this means, and filling all the other offices with ex-officers who have shown some real pride in the army, no man being assigned to duty in the district in which he lives, politics could be kept out, and really good men sent to the army.*

The organization of a Cavalry Bureau to have entire charge of the organization and equipment of all the cavalry, and provide its mounts and remounts, is a step in the right direction. I say a step, for much depends upon how it shall be carried out, and how far it will be interfered with by the older established departments. Something of the same sort we want for the artillery; a general consolidation of it into one corps under one head, who should have entire control of it. . . .

AUGUST 2, SUNDAY.   An intensely hot day, and a great deal to do. Why is it that in every hot spell Sunday is always the hottest day in it, if there is any Sunday included? I was out nearly the whole day with General Newton examining the lay of the land across the river, selecting sites for batteries, and explaining to the officers to be posted over there what they were to do. The sun came down pelting all the time, and not a breath of air; but there was no occasion to ride fast, and being dressed as light as an officer can be on duty, I did not suffer much. My blouse I find most comfortable; it is not regulation, but is much more decidedly dress than those ordinarily worn, which are just like the ones issued to privates. Mine is a real German blouse of blue flannel; the many plaits keep it loose even when buttoned up close into the neck, so that it always looks neat and trim, and with only a thin knit silk shirt under it, it is very cool. . . .

I am pretty well tired tonight with the day's labour, but feel vastly satisfied now I know our position so well, and have got everything arranged, and their special duties explained to each commander of my little brigade. One can hardly imagine the immense advantage it is to be well acquainted with your ground before a fight. For myself, I have entire confidence tonight in our ability to hold all Lee's army at bay here until the rest of ours could get up.

The first batch of conscripts for this corps reached here today, 108 men for the Ninetieth Pennsylvania. I have not seen them, but judge that they did not come willingly, as one jumped from the cars on the way

* The War Department had issued an order on April 28, 1863, establishing an Invalid Corps, the name later being changed to Veteran Reserve Corps. Officers and men who had left the army for disability were invited to enlist. Those who were fit for light-armed duty were placed in a First Battalion and those less vigorous in a Second Battalion. In October 1863, the War Department authorized the organization of sixteen regiments, and at the end of that month nearly 500 officers and 18,000 men had enrolled. The corps, growing to a strength of more than 30,000 before the war ended, proved very useful. It provided guards at important depots of supplies, prisoners' camps, and other points, and garrisons in areas where resistance to the draft was feared, and at installations behind the front lines in the field.

down to get off, and several others have tried to desert; the jumper was shot dead by the guard.

AUGUST 3, MONDAY. Another piping hot day; rather more breeze, however, than there was yesterday, and a few clouds passing to obscure the sun at times. . . .

The house around which we are camped belongs to Mr. Bowen, a rebel, but is now inhabited by a man by the name of Smith, from Culpeper, a good Union man, and Stoneman's guide on his last raid towards Richmond. It is a large house of considerable pretensions outside, with a dooryard of fine sod on which our tents are pitched. The general has a room in the house; his staff tents are along one side and my two just to the right of the front door. We have an excellent well of water in the yard, which is a great thing in this part of the country. Today we managed to get a little ice, but our claret is all out, and though we have six or eight boxes in Washington, we cannot get it down yet.

AUGUST 6, THURSDAY. Three days of intense quiet, I might almost call it. The weather continues hot, but not quite equal to what it was the first three days we were here. This lying in an advanced position where one may be attacked at any moment, while at the same time the chances are twenty to one that you will not be attacked at all, is about the most tiresome position one can be in. Having to be always ready, neither men nor officers can go any distance away from their camps. And drills, at least for my batteries, which are all in position, are impossible. . . .

The army . . . encloses completely a vast rectangle, stretching from the Rappahannock to Centreville, with the railroad running through the middle of it. This will completely secure our railroad communications, and keep guerrillas out of our lines. It is just a year since Major-General Pope commenced that "victorious (!) retreat" of his from a point a few miles beyond where we now lie. There is no danger of a repetition of the affair, for Meade does not boast of having no line of retreat, nor is he likely to scatter his army all over the country as Pope did. Our cavalry too is vastly improved, and will at least be able to bring us in some information as to the rebel movements, if they do move.

Army Headquarters are at Germantown, so-called; there is no town, but there may have been a post office somewhere around before the war. It is some seven miles from here, quite a long ride. General Hunt complains that Meade is treading in the old footsteps and fights shy of giving him control of the artillery. When Hunt was here the other day he wanted a copy of the order Hooker gave me on the field at Chancellorsville, as a proof that in time of a general engagement it was necessary to have a chief of artillery with actual powers. I regret exceedingly that I have lost the original order, for it was a paper to be proud of. It was written in pencil on a scrap of paper, and must have got pulled out of my pocket by accident somehow. I was only able to give him as accurate a transcript of it as I could remember. . . .

AUGUST 9, SUNDAY. We may be said to have gone into summer quarters at this place; every thing indicating that no move will be made on our part for some weeks to come. The posting of the army, as indicated in my last entry, points very plainly in that way, as do the orders we receive, and the fact that the surgeons are having the camps moved out of the woods onto the open ground, where it is more healthy. Many of the commands are sinking wells, so as to get good water for the men. . . .

The troops continue very healthy so far; very much more so than they were last year at this time in any part of Virginia. This is owing to many reasons. The season is very different, this year being dry, while last was a constant pour. Again, the greater part of our men have become acclimated, the weak and sickly ones in a great measure weeded out. But the main reasons for the better health of the army lie in the facts that the men themselves as well as their officers have learned how to take proper care of themselves, and that our medical staff is infinitely superior to what it then was. The entire ignorance of the army last year with regard to making themselves comfortable and guarding against the fevers of this country was a necessary consequence of the whole army being recruits from another district of country, and entering upon a life new to every one of them. Had the officers known their business, it could doubtless in a measure have been prevented. Still, men will learn ten times as rapidly from the example of their comrades, as they will from any orders of their superiors. The medical staff has changed vastly from what it was a year ago; fully one-half of the old regimental surgeons have been sent home, and better ones come out in their place. Those that had brains enough to hold their commissions have learned their duties, the business part of which was totally new to every one of them, as well as the different mode of treatment required for troops in this climate from that needed by people living in houses farther north.

Still, the number of men borne on the rolls as absent sick is very heavy. In my own brigade it amounts to one-fifth of the whole; the infantry regiment will shew from a quarter to a third. But among these are included the wounded of Gettysburg and Chancellorsville not yet returned; and a larger number who have died in or deserted from the hospitals, but were not so reported to their companies. The men have a good time of it bathing in the river this warm weather. Bache and Heard propose that we should go down and have a swim some time if it is possible to find a spot out of sight of the men, which is not likely. . . .

AUGUST 11, TUESDAY. Yesterday we got an order from Army Headquarters calling attention to the number of officers and men absent sick and otherwise, and also to the great number reported on special extra and daily duty. The exact duty on which men so reported are engaged, as well as those on detached service, is required to be given. . . . The aggregate of the corps present and absent is about 17,500, and less than 7,000 of these are returned as present for duty. Hard upon one-third of the whole corps, 5,783, are absent sick, and less than half of the aggregate are available for the line of battle. If they get a detailed report of those on detached service and on extra and daily duty, I have no doubt it will show some very queer details.

It is often hard work to know exactly how men should be carried on the reports. The aggregate present and absent is worth nothing as showing the strength of the army, even when the report comes from a brigade headquarters much less that of the whole army. I have no doubt that the aggregate of this corps is 1,000 greater than the actual number borne on the rolls. I know of many cases in which the officers and men must be reported twice under our present system. For instance, all the infantry serving with my batteries, amounting to half the numbers carried in my report, are also carried in the reports from their own regiments as "on detached service within this army." Officers detailed at headquarters are reported twice in the same way.

So few of our officers have had a real business education that you cannot make them understand the necessity for exactness in their reports, or get through their heads the why and wherefore of the matter to such a degree as would enable them to make their reports out properly and uniformly. Still I feel sure that it would be easy to devise some other form which would give all the information the present one does, and yet be a much truer report. Our army though is but a temporary one, almost every officer and man feeling it to be so. It is hardly fair, therefore, to expect them to give the same attention to their business as if they were in it for life; it would be asking too much of human nature. . . .

AUGUST 16, SUNDAY.   The weather has been warm again since Thursday; hot, in fact, though not equal to what it was a week or ten days ago before the rain. Most people call it very hot now, but having little to call me out in the sun, it is about such weather as I like. The nights are getting cooler, so that there is no difficulty in sleeping while it is dark; but as soon as daylight comes the flies begin to bite, so that one is forced to get up in self-defense. These pests have multiplied with wondrous rapidity since the rain. It cannot be otherwise in a hot climate where there is so much decomposing animal matter as there must be around the camp of an army that remains in the same place for a few weeks. The only way to keep clear of them in the summertime is to be constantly moving onto fresh ground. . . .

I have another reason now for wanting to get home. My man John is going to leave me, and I must try to get me another white man, as I

cannot possibly stand these wretched "niggers." Nearly all the officers
here have contrabands for servants. Hardly any of whom were house
servants before they ran away, and consequently are as ignorant of their
business as farm hands might be expected to be. To this ignorance must
be added the natural laziness, lying, and dirt of the negro, which surpasses anything an ordinary white man is capable of. They never do a
thing until told to, so that when their master orders his horse, he has to
wait until his boots, spurs and equipments are cleaned, or else go with
them dirty. The only way he can have matters otherwise is by constantly
running after his servant, and making himself the greater slave of the
two. You may show them over and over again how you wish a thing done,
but they will not learn, simply because they do not care. Their whole
time is spent around the kitchen fire, talking, laughing, and playing
cards. There are some fifteen or twenty of them properly belonging to
our corps headquarters, which number is quite doubled by stragglers,
hangers-on, and the servants' servants.

These last are quite an institution. Seeing a strange nigger hanging
around our kitchen fire for several days, we called him and asked where
he belonged. "To headquarters," says he, with a grin and a nod of his
head over towards the horses of the corps staff. "Whose boy are you?" was
the next question. "I'se Jim's boy, sir." "Who's Jim?" "Colonel Bankhead's boy, sir." Bankhead pays his boy, Jim, fifteen dollars a month;
Jim attends to his master's tent, saddles and leads up his horse, and hires
the other nigger for five dollars a month to do the rest of his work!—
the Colonel feeding them both of course. How well he is served can
easily be imagined. A negro in their present state has no ambition to get
money, and no foresight in providing for the future. Enough to eat and
drink, with a few dollars to gamble, is all he wants; idleness is his
heaven, which no mere bribe can tempt him out of. Education will
doubtless do much to counteract this evil, but not everything. It is so
ingrained in their nature that several generations will be required to
breed it out. The present generation cannot get rid of it, and left to
themselves will die like sheep with the rot, simply because they are too
lazy to live.

My man John has a most thorough hatred of the nigger, and looks
down upon them with all the disdain of a thoroughbred English servant. He has not a lazy bone in his body. With the first break of day
he is up and about his work, talking to himself and rousing all the
niggers about him. He has a voice like young thunder which constantly
wakes up half the officers as soon as it does their men. But as he is
most amusing in his observations no one objects. I often lie awake for
half an hour, laughing until my bed shakes at his droll remarks. To me
he is invaluable, keeping everything about me exactly as I like it, so that

I hardly have occasion to speak to him unless it is to order my horse. In camp he never goes out of sight of my tent, but watches over my things like a house dog, so that the only articles I have lost were during the battle at Gettysburg, when his saddle and my blankets were stolen. All these he got back, except one woolen and the India rubber blanket. At night he sleeps between the two horses, just behind my tent, and is on foot in an instant if anyone comes near them. . . .

Drafted men, or rather substitutes, are coming in slowly. This corps has only received about five hundred so far, nearly one hundred of whom will never do a week's duty; the rest may be broken in in time. The surgeons and provost-marshals pass anything in the way of a substitute. Being appointed in the district in which they live, and most of them being political aspirants, their object is to fill their quota, not to get good men for the army. Anything that can stand in the shape of a man passes muster with them; but our surgeons are sending back a lot of them, which will give the Washington folks a chance to show whether they care most for popularity in the rural districts or to put down the rebellion. Some of the other corps are said to have received more men than we have, but I do not hear that they are of any better quality.

We got a letter yesterday from Colonel Sanderson dated "Libby Prison, Richmond." He says but little more than that he is well and is making the best of it. The inmates have chosen him chief cook, but there is no great choice of viands to cook. . . .

AUGUST 20, THURSDAY. Four days have elapsed since my last entry here; a longer time than has occurred since we left White Oak Church, which seems an age ago. Yet I am almost without anything to say tonight, as we have been perfectly quiet; even the rumours of our advance to Culpeper having blown over. . . .

We have had several orders this week from Army Headquarters regarding sutlers, purveyors, newsboys, and what not, which it is to be hoped will give us a better supply than we have had heretofore. The corps headquarter purveyor goes up every week, but I find I cannot agree to his terms for bringing things down. I know now how he manages to feed the staff at so low a figure, and yet so luxuriously as he does; a plan pursued by all the purveyors of the army I understand. Officers' stores coming down by government transportation while sutlers have to bring their own goods, and the former being often admitted when the others are not, the purveyor makes out a list of such stores as he wishes to sell to the men; these he divides into as many small lists as there are officers at his headquarters, who after adding what they may want for their own use, "certify on honour" that the whole list is thus for their individual use. I could not agree to any such imposition; neither could Heard or Bache, so our mess is not at all in favour with the corps purveyor. It is astonishing how few officers there are who consider it wrong to defraud the government in little matters, or dishonourable to get around an order, where they can add to their own ease and comfort by so doing.

AUGUST 23, SUNDAY. Notwithstanding that we are just as quiet here as it is possible for us to be, the newspapers will have accounts of skirmishes every day, and have even told of a reconnoissance to Culpeper. Our cavalry pickets are about two or three miles out, just this side of Brandy Station, with the rebel pickets in sight. A perfect amnesty exists between them, both parties watering their horses in the same brook. "Jeb" Stuart has his headquarters at Culpeper, with his cavalry; so far as we can learn there are very few rebel infantry north of the Rapidan, the main body of Lee's army being beyond around Orange Court House. . . .

AUGUST 26, WEDNESDAY. The weather has become hot again. . . . Monday morning General Newton sent for me to ride around with him on a tour of inspection of the different camps. We went through every part of the corps, taking all by surprise, as there was no notice whatever of his coming given by the general. I was proud to find that all the batteries were in a creditable condition, their camps decidedly in better order than the infantry. At Stewart's battery the guard was turned out to salute in as good a form as it is possible to do it here; and this was the only camp guard in the whole corps so turned out. I was so much pleased when I came back that I issued an order informing the batteries of their general creditable appearance, and under cover of that spurred them up to more care, and greater efforts to appear as well as to be soldiers; also giving directions as to improving their camps. I had only just sent my order off when I got one from corps headquarters, covering the same ground as to directions about their camps, drainage, and protection of tents by the erection of bowers. The general was terribly disgusted with a large part of his command: the absolute filth of many of the regiments, and the total want of an exhibition of respect to their commanding general in most of both officers and men. . . .

The other day General Meade issued an order on the duties of the chief of artillery of this army.* It is a kind of halfway thing as regards his powers, while it clearly makes him responsible for the "condition of all the artillery, wherever serving." It makes us responsible to General Hunt as to the equipment and supplies, as well as regards the instruction and discipline of our batteries; yet gives him no control over those supplies, or any power to regulate leaves of absence, or do anything else much. In fact, all the good it might do is annulled by it saying: "He will

---

* Brigadier General Henry Jackson Hunt, it will be remembered, had been chief of artillery of the Army of the Potomac at Fredericksburg; had suffered some curtailment of authority under Hooker; but after Chancellorsville was restored to full command again, and had handled the Union artillery with great ability at Gettysburg.

give no orders that would interfere with the military control exercised by corps and division commanders over batteries attached to their troops." Hunt has been working very hard to get his duties defined, and this is the result of it. I wish they would let me draw up an order for them. I believe it could be done so as to put us on a true artillery footing, and at the same time not interfere in the least with corps commanders having a proper control over the batteries serving with them. . . . AUGUST 29, SATURDAY. The quiet of our life here was disturbed yesterday afternoon and evening by a grand sword presentation to General Meade by his old division, the Pennsylvania Reserves. The sword, belt and sash were very handsome, as they should be for $1,000—what they cost. The arrangements, too, were very well got up, and the supper wonderfully good for the field. From what little I have seen of General Crawford,* I should think he was just the man to enjoy getting up such a thing. . . . The division headquarters were dressed with evergreens and flags; a large ornamented stage erected for the presentation, and a number of tents put up for the supper. Crawford presented the sword in a rather high-faluting speech, and Meade replied lamely. He need not have asserted that the reserves did not run away at Groveton, for every one knows that most of them did; many of their own officers acknowledge it, and General Meade has cursed them for himself often enough. But at the time he probably saw all their behaviour through the jewelled hilt of the sword. Afterward Governor Curtin and other politicians took the stand and went in on the spread-eagle order; the Governor made a strong bid for the soldiers' vote at the approaching election in October.

After the speeches, the supper tents were opened. An attempt was made to get all the invited guests seated first, but without entire success. I looked at the crowd pushing and hauling to get near the tables; saw that it was a regular scramble, and gave up all the idea of getting anything to eat myself. As the next best thing I amused myself wandering around to watch the others, and take this opportunity to judge of the social status of our volunteer officers. There must have been 500 officers present. Of these, perhaps thirty were actual gentlemen; one hundred more may have had some pretensions that way; while the rest appeared little better than street blackguards. It must be remembered, however, that by far the greater part of them were from Pennsylvania regiments, and Governor Curtin has disgraced his state by commissioning a worse class of men

---

* Samuel W. Crawford, a Pennsylvania physician by birth and training, had commanded a battery at Fort Sumter during its bombardment. He was later promoted to be a brigadier general and commanded the Pennsylvania Reserve (thirteen infantry regiments constituting a division of three brigades) at Gettysburg. Despite Wainwright's animadversions, these regiments fought well; one with 394 men at Fredericksburg lost 211 killed and wounded.

than any other governor. Champagne as well as whiskey was in abundance, and soon began to tell: such a drunken scene as ensued I never saw before. A number of privates who had been brought in as guards were hobnobbing with their captains, holding each other up or hugging most affectionately. The Governor's staff of friends were no better: an old grey-haired, baldheaded man royally drunk was standing on one of the tables singing ribald songs. I was so disgusted and so ashamed of my uniform that I soon cleared out and wandered over to some of the staff's tents a little removed from the centre of gaiety. Here I found one or two officers who recognized me, though I have no idea what their names were, but finding I had had no supper, one of them belonging to Crawford's staff, and the only sober one among them, kindly went off and brought me some boned turkey and a bottle of champagne. I left early with the orgy still going on. Heard and Bache got home soon after; they had fared even worse than I had, not having tasted a thing.

I presume the drunkenness could not be helped, so long as the liquor was there, and men's nature will come out when they are drunk. That being the case, and the discipline of our army being what it is, the best thing to do is to have no more of such presentations until the war is over. Livingston tells me today that there was any amount of pilfering of knives, and forks, plates, and so on (officers supplying themselves with mess furniture!), and one man with shoulder straps on was seen carrying off half a dozen bottles of champagne.

We have had a good deal of fun about a Mrs. Fogg, who is down as an agent of the Maine Sanitary Commission. We have but one Maine regiment in the corps and two batteries; still the woman seems to have taken them under special protection. Lieutenant Twitchell she has made a pet of, and brought him over here to Smith's house, where she herself was stopping. Our doctors curse the old woman up and down as a meddling pest, doing ten times the harm that she does good. Her bringing Twitchell over here at last excited the General's ire, so that yesterday he ordered her out of the corps. The sanitaries no doubt do some good—perhaps a great deal in the general hospitals and just after a big battle—but when they send women down to poke around the camps with an unlimited supply of jam and sweet cakes, they are mistaken in their zeal. When their agents go still farther than this and attempt to run against regulations, they become a nuisance not to be borne.

Soon after Gettysburg, Sanderson proposed that the First Corps should erect a monument to General Reynolds. At that time we were on the march and could do nothing in the matter. Within the last week or two we have been talking the matter over among the old staff and with some of the colonels. Bache and Heard and I have at last agreed among ourselves on a general plan, and I today rode over to the division headquarters and to the Pennsylvania Reserves to propose it. All seem anxious to carry the matter out. . . .

AUGUST 31, MONDAY. One whole month today we have been lying here doing nothing. Not that I find fault with nothing more being attempted at this time, for I do not believe that we should have succeeded had we tried; but I do think that General Meade might have been a little more liberal in granting leaves without injury to the service. I should have liked much to have been at home myself for a fortnight, and might have been as well as not for all the good I have done here. . . .

Recruits continue to come in slowly; some real conscripts at last, not substitutes, and a very different sort of men, strong, healthy and orderly, while most of the substitutes are simply rascals who never intended to serve, but merely wanted the bounty or purchase money offered. It is well enough to talk about volunteers, but I am decidedly in favour of conscripts. Certainly they are more desirable than volunteers who are bought with money. There have been a great many attempts at desertion by these substitutes, even to going over to the enemy. I do hope they will keep on shooting them just as fast as ever they are caught, for society will be benefited at any rate by so doing. We get no accessions to the batteries as yet, nor have I heard of any steps being taken to fill us up; meanwhile each trimonthly shows some diminution in my aggregate. . . .

RAPPAHANNOCK STATION, SEPTEMBER 3, THURSDAY. All quiet, perfectly quiet on the line of the Rappahannock. People talk of the excitement (!) of army life. They know nothing of the ennui of weeks and even months with nothing to do. . . .

The position of our corps remains just the same as it has been since the second week of our arrival here. The same troops are on the south side of the river, and all my own batteries are in position. The camps are now all in pretty fair condition; drills of some sort are had almost every day; most of the regiments have sunk wells; and considering the season and location, the men may be said to be remarkably healthy, the average of sick for the last month being only seven in one hundred present. Our corps headquarters remain at the Smith house, and some of the officers have become quite intimate with the family. I have not myself done any visiting there, though I believe they are really very nice people. The eldest daughter, some two and twenty perhaps, is quite pretty, and what is not by any means common in this part of the country, exceedingly neat. Kingsbury, our adjutant-general, is decidedly smitten, and quite particular enough in his attentions to warrant Papa's demanding an explanation as to what his intentions may be. They ride out on horseback every afternoon, he having a very nice saddle horse, and she looking well when mounted. General Newton, too, likes to lounge in the house, and be entertained by the family. He is very fond of music, and has Jackson and Carrington of his staff sing for him by the hour; they are both fresh from college, and so have a host of songs, which they render very fairly. On Sunday evenings they all get into the house, where Miss Laura accompanies with voice and piano. The commencement is always good, but the number of psalms and hymns in their repertoire being rather limited, they quickly fall back upon the college standbyes. . . .

I was at headquarters today; found it as dull there as it is here. In speaking of the newspaper rumours that the Secretary of War has referred McClellan's report to a committee, of which Major-General [David] Hunter is president, under the plea that it is too extended for the Secretary to digest himself, all think that the object is to kill the report. Those who know old Hunter say that he is not capable of comprehending it, be the report never so simple. . . .

SEPTEMBER 10, THURSDAY. At last and almost unexpectedly a leave of absence has come for me. My application was a sort of forlorn hope, and the reply is a most forlorn leave; only ten days, four of which are required to go and return. . . .

"THE MEADOWS," SEPTEMBER 20, SUNDAY. Safely at home for a week past. Tomorrow I must start on my way back. A week and a day is a very short time to see one's friends, and look after one's business; but it is better than nothing. Fortunately Lewis has proved himself faithful and quite capable to run the farm part of the place. I pretended to look over his accounts; a mere pretense to be sure, still enough to make him think that they were closely scrutinized. I intended to write up my books, but found that it would keep me really busy through nearly all my stay; which I did not choose, being on a pleasure trip. The road and grounds about the house are not looking quite as well as I like to have them; nor have any improvements been carried on in my absence. But Lewis has worked his crops just as well, and more economically than I was able to do when running the machine myself, so that, almost for the first time in my farming experience, I have had funds on hand all the year. The gardener has been drafted and is in great trouble about it. Mr. Kelley says there is no doubt about his getting clear, and that he will help him to get the matter through. In Kelly's good hands I feel quite safe about it.*

The draft I find the universal topic of conversation here. Everyone is personally interested in the matter, or was a week ago: now they know their fate in this county, so far as the drawing goes. Of all in this neighbourhood who I hear were drawn, I also hear that they will get off or pay; one or the other. Indeed, there seems very little prospect of the draft bringing us any material reinforcements. So soon as a man is drawn

* This was of course Wainwright's close friend William Kelley, who had been the unsuccessful Democratic candidate for governor in 1860. Of the farm manager Lewis we know nothing.

everyone begins to pity him, and set to work to help him get off. This is not limited to the "copperheads"; the most rabid "Republicans" head subscriptions to raise the $300 commutation for great hearty young men, who should under no circumstances be allowed to remain at home at such a time as this. The amount of false swearing which is being done is perfectly frightful. The truth is that the whole affair has been mismanaged from the start. Its originators allowed the terms "conscription" and "forced draft" to get in, words which can be used by their political opponents to great advantage; such party cries as are always of more weight with the mass of the people than the wisest logic. . . .

It is singular to see the inconsistencies into which the members of the dominant party are forced in order to support the measures of their leaders. But the cry of "copperhead," "rebel sympathiser" has such a power now, and the name is so freely applied to everyone who dares to have an opinion in the slightest degree at variance with those in power, that few have strength of mind enough to utter them. There is John DePeyster, who openly advocates the most radical measures, and privately in his letters to me denounces the draft, the Administration, and all its satellites. To be sure, with him it is not the result of fear, but of obstinacy. He hates the South from simple hatred, not because he opposes "State Rights" and loves the negro: with him the war is a war between the States of New York and others on one side, and South Carolina and others on the other side, and a war between the "Republican" and "Democratic" parties. He, being a "Republican," goes in for his party, right or wrong. This is the case with the vast majority of the people, too. Having adopted their party, they only see their country *in it;* cannot see beyond it on any side, and blindly obey their leaders, whose only desire is to keep themselves in power. Taking special pains to sound them since I have been at home, I find almost everyone of my neighbours to be a "mild State Rights man," as DePeyster calls it. That, under certain circumstances (that is, when it supports their own pet notions), their allegiance is due to their State against the United States. . . .

I dined one day at Bard's and met Cruger, Delano, Aspinwall and one or two others. Was much surprised to find how rabid they had become within a year. Delano always was inclined that way, but Cruger was an old Whig, and Bard an "anti-war Democrat" last year. Now Aspinwall is the only one who does not see everything through "negro" spectacles. All the rest were very violent in their attacks on McClellan. I did not dream of educated gentlemen having become so radical, and talked freely at first; but finding they were in the condition of the man who "would not see," turned the whole matter over for time to settle. I have met some men on this trip wild enough to assert that McClellan was a traitor. I had not supposed before that anyone really believed it, or that a man (save a member of Congress or a newspaper writer) could utter so base a lie. . . .

NEAR CULPEPER COURT HOUSE, SEPTEMBER 22, TUESDAY. Reached camp a little before dark, and found everything quiet.

SEPTEMBER 23, WEDNESDAY. Have had time to look around me today, get some idea of where we are and the lay of the land, as well as to report to General Hunt. Culpeper is quite a sizable place for Virginia, so near as I could judge without going through more than the outskirts of the town. The country immediately around is about half cleared, and being quite broken affords some good positions. Southeast of the village about two miles off, is a high knoll, or hill, wooded to its summit, called Poney Mountain, on which we have a signal station. They say that the view from there is very extensive, commanding the Rapidan for a long distance in our front. . . . My own batteries are lying nearby headquarters here. . . .

While I was at home I was struck with and noted at the time the enthusiasm manifested by the returned two-years' regiments for their old commander, and the excellent speech McClellan made on the occasion. This speech, it seems, was also discussed in the army here one evening at headquarters by Meade, Hunt, Sedgwick and others, and the General's expressions of strong affection for the old Army of the Potomac fully reciprocated. From this conversation has grown what is called the McClellan testimonial, which I find fully inaugurated in most of the corps. The circular setting forth the matter says: "It having been proposed by many officers of this Army to present to Major-General Mc-Clellan some mark of their respect which would serve as a memorial of the relations which have existed between them; it has been suggested that the privilege of joining be extended to the whole army, as an evidence that the warm feelings, which he has ever borne towards it, is fully reciprocated by both officers and men; and in order that all may unite in this object that it take the form of a testimonial from the Army of the Potomac to its old Commander." The circular also proposes a rate of subscriptions for each rank: ten cents for privates, up to twenty dollars for major-generals: and suggests a plan for carrying out the idea. Nothing has been done in this corps as yet: the circulars were sent to Bankhead, but he has not even circulated them yet. . . .

CAMP THREE MILES FROM RACCOON FORD, SEPTEMBER 24, THURSDAY. This evening we get a circular, unsigned, in these words: "The object of the proposed testimonial from the Army of the Potomac to Major-General McClellan having been misconstrued and the proceeding being considered as contrary to Army Regulations, it is deemed proper for these reasons by many who have united in it to proceed no further in the matter." What it means I cannot tell, except that several of the radical papers have spoken of it as a political move. The Washington *Chronicle* indeed denounces it most bitterly, and as that is a semi-official paper, it may be that orders from Washington have stopped it....

SEPTEMBER 27, SUNDAY. That which I have suspected for some time past is at last acknowledged by many of the radicals, namely, that they did not want the rebellion to be put down earlier. General Patrick tells me that when closely questioned most all those he met in Washington lately admitted it; and Major Hall, who was down here for a day, repeated to me a conversation he had with a Massachusetts Member of Congress in which the M.C. plainly said that he did not want to see the Union restored without the abolition of slavery. That there are and have been from the start many who sincerely believed that slavery was the first and only cause of the war, and that any restoration of the Union as it was could be but temporary, I do not doubt. Some men were honest in this idea. Whether they were right or wrong can never now be positively proved; I think them very far from the mark, and that having got negro on the brain they could see nothing else. The number who held this ground two years or eighteen months ago, however, was very small; President Lincoln certainly did not. But there was another lot of men, and a numerous body too, who were in power, and who knew that the return of the South to the Union in its old state would deprive them of power. The very instincts of self-preservation told these men that it would not do, and seeing that the doctrine of the extreme abolitionists if carried out would save the loaves and fishes to them they secretly adopted it. Secretly, because the mass of the people at the North did not then agree with them. These masses had to be converted to their doctrine: and in this conversion I confess they shewed a vast amount of cleverness. Having a perfectly honest but also a perfectly weak man as President it was easy to make him do as they chose. Then by a skilful manipulation of generals, half adopting their plans, and then placing every obstacle in their way, it has been easy to prolong the war until now. These generals being all conservative men, it was also easy and lay the cause of the failure to their conservatism....

Whether it would have been possible to restore the Union on its old basis, with a simple settlement of the State Rights question and an introduction into the Constitution of the doctrine of Federal sovereignty clearly defined, and the unity of the people as one nation, can now never be decided; for there is no doubt that the immediate extinction of slavery will be insisted on as well. The radicals having entire power in the nation have fixed the test of loyalty, and we *must* support to it, practically if not theoretically. But if this war could have been ended on the grounds above mentioned (and I believe that it could have been, finally), what a fearful loss of life, destruction of property, and breeding of hatred they are responsible for.

SEPTEMBER 30, WEDNESDAY. We changed our headquarters camp again yesterday, the spot where we were being found very wet. The soil here is like that on all the level land I have come across in Virginia, a light top and heavy clay bottom, so that the slightest rain makes it horribly muddy.

I was at Army Headquarters the other day and learned from General Hunt all about the McClellan testimonial. The evening that they received the New York papers with an account of McClellan's speech on Staten Island, he, Meade and several others were talking it over, and expressing the high opinion they had of McClellan as a man, and the attachment they still felt for him as their old commander. Among themselves they proposed to send him some little remembrance, and to ask some of his old personal friends to join with him. It was originated entirely as a private affair, and meant solely to show the General that the affection he had expressed himself as still entertaining for his old army, was fully reciprocated by themselves. With this idea, Sedgwick, Sykes, French, and others were invited to join. The two first in addition to accepting the proposition (which all did) protested against limiting the affair to McClellan's personal friends, and claimed that as the General's interest had been expressed for all his old army, so all should be allowed to join in returning the good will. "Uncle John," too, pledged himself for $20,000 in his corps.

So after talking the matter over, the circular issued was agreed upon. General Newton agreed to it, but was too cautious to take an active part in pushing the matters. Subscriptions were fully started in the other corps; when General Meade being in Washington, the President called his attention to it as a reflection on the government, and a breach of discipline, requesting him to issue an order stopping it. Meade replied that the presenting of testimonials to their ex-commanders had always been common in the army; that he had himself received one only a month ago, to which Mr. Lincoln had not objected, but had even approved, and that consequently he could not himself issue such an order, that it must come from the War Department. The next day the *Chronicle* comes out with its assertion that the testimonial is a political move, and tries to raise an issue on that question. Sooner than allow such a thing even to be supposed it was dropped at once. The amount of indignation felt in the army generally among those who served under McClellan is very great, but we are gradually getting accustomed to the tyranny of the ruling party, and learning to obey the curb and whip without kicking over the traces.

THREE MILES FROM RACCOON FORD, OCTOBER 4, SUNDAY. On Friday we got the rain which had been threatening for some days; it fell pretty steadily all day, and has made the country decidedly muddy. . . .

My battery commanders have been busy taking down the names of infantry men who want to be transferred to their companies. They have more than double the applications there is room for, and so will have a grand chance for selection if the thing is carried out. As yet we have received no further instructions in the matter; and there is a very strong opposition to it springing up, especially in some of the other corps, where the corps commander has himself issued orders on the subject. I heard of one regiment where over 300 of the men applied for transfer out of less than 400 present. I rode over to the Fifth Corps the other day to look at "C" Company. In Captain Martin's tent I met General Griffin,* who swore that not a man should be taken out of his division to fill up the batteries under the present artillery organization. He will, I have no doubt, do his best to prevent it, as he was very bitter against the brigading of the batteries, and will not scruple about the means if he sees any chance of bringing them back to his division. As usual he ranted like a crazy man, without rhyme or reason, but he is indefatigable in having his own way, especially when influenced by spite, and is consequently feared.

I found "C" Company looking abominably. The camp was pitched around anywhere, the horses tied to trees, the carriages dirty, and the men looking like slovens. Captain Barnes has been absent since the middle of August, reported sick in hospital; perhaps he is. I only wish that I had the battery under my command, so as to either reform it or get rid of Barnes.

OCTOBER 8, THURSDAY. There has been a great canvassing going on throughout the army this week, under a circular calling for a report as to what regiments, whose terms expire next summer, would re-enlist as a regiment; provided they were allowed to go home as an organization to recruit, in addition to the other inducements held out by existing orders. Almost all the officers are anxious to go, and some worked very hard to persuade their men into voting for going. Several regiments in this corps I believe have voted to go home; but their hopes have been suddenly dashed by another circular explaining that the object of the first was only to obtain information as whether such a proposition would be likely to meet with success in the army. It is just like everything else done by the War Department, a halfway measure; and the consequence

---

* Augustus Martin, of the Third Massachusetts Battery, was commander of the artillery brigade of the Fifth Corps; a total stranger to Wainwright. Charles Griffin, West Point, 1847, commanded the First Division of the Fifth Corps; an Ohio man, "bluff and bellicose."

is that the men are already backing down from their agreement to re-enlist.

Today we have an order from General Hunt, which prohibits battery officers recruiting from the infantry regiments, stating that the men required will be furnished under orders from general headquarters on the receipt of reports showing just how many men will be needed, after dropping from the rolls of the company all such men now absent as are not likely soon to return to duty, or are on detached service. This looks as if General Meade meant to do something, but it throws over all the nice lists of men wishing to join the batteries which I have sent up, and make me fear that the selection of the men will be left with the infantry officers, in which case we shall only get the refuse of their commands, or worse than none.

General Meade seems determined that as the McClellan testimonial is quashed all other officers shall be placed in the same category and has issued an order drawing attention to and explaining paragraph 220 Army Regulations forbidding all expressions of opinion with regard to their superiors by meetings or combinations of men or officers. . . . At headquarters I learn that the ire of Mr. Stanton was even more deeply stirred up than was at first supposed; an order was actually drawn up summarily dismissing from the service Generals Sedgwick, Sykes, and Hunt, together with a number of other officers, for the part they had taken. So petty was the big man in his spite that he even included little Bissell, of Hunt's staff, a second lieutenant, whose great sin was that he made himself useful in copying the circular stopping the subscription. A leading Republican member of Congress, who had a little more sense than most of the radicals, happened to see the order before it was issued, and at once took measures to stop it. Had the order come out it would have been a glorious roll of honour, on which not a few would have been proud to see their names inscribed. General Sedgwick claims that 12,000 men in his corps had subscribed $10,000 before the matter was stopped.* . . .

I also learned at headquarters that Meade was about ready to try a flank movement on Lee when the Eleventh and Twelfth Corps were taken away. This weakened him so that he was obliged to give it up. I hear that the troops sent to New York are returning now, but should doubt if they would strengthen us enough to make it safe to attempt anything. . . .

OCTOBER 9, FRIDAY. Reports came in from our cavalry on the left this morning that the rebels had entirely withdrawn from the river bank opposite to them: while the infantry reported that they had withdrawn

* Wainwright later crossed out the figure $10,000.

most of their pickets along our whole front. Of course this gave us to understand that we might expect active work again. Orders have just come for this corps to be at Moreton's Ford at daylight tomorrow morning, beyond which I have not yet been informed; but presume it means crossing. . . . My cold has about all gone, so I shall be ready to start in good order in a few hours.*

OCTOBER 10, SATURDAY. I got off at two-thirty o'clock with my brigade, having a guide to show me the way. The moon was still up when we started, but very little of its light got through the dense growth of scrub oak and pine on this slope of the hill. Our road was a very narrow and winding one, and my guide none of the best. We had not more than fully got into the wood before he lost his way, and after two or three mistakes became totally confused at last. I knew nothing of it myself, and it was too dark to see anything whatever. Carriages got stuck in trying to turn around, horses got baulky, and my staff who I had sent to find the right road did not get back. I kept moving most of the time, but where we went to I have no notion at this time. As the day began to break we found our way out, and pushed on as fast as possible. I was in a great worry at having got so much behind time when everything might depend on exactness; I was therefore much relieved when I found that but one division of infantry had got to the neighbourhood of the Smith house before me. This made it full two hours after sunrise by the time we were in a position to act. Fortunately no harm was done this time, as it was not in contemplation to force an immediate passage. . . . We remained in this state of waiting all day. . . . About sunset and just as I had got my command settled for the night we received orders to fall back to a point near our old camp between Culpeper and Stevensburg.† Men and animals were very tired, having been under such close restraint all day. The infantry straggled terribly and made awful slow work. Robinson would not let me pass his division without a written order from General Newton, which at last I rode ahead and got, and was able to get into camp about ten P.M. totally fagged out. Corps headquarters are at Colonel Slaughter's house; the night is raw, chilly, and disagreeable. Just as I was turning in orders came to move from here at three

---

* In his incidental remarks in the diary at this point Wainwright records that the nights have become very chilly, so that the rail fences of the countryside are fast disappearing; that two more deserters in the corps are to be shot; and that Charles Hamburg of the Swedish army is joining General Newton's staff as topographical engineer. "He can not be worse than 'Rats' the Russian or Wilcox the American," cynically comments Wainwright.

† Meade's intention had been to throw Newton's corps across the Rappahannock at Moreton's Ford as soon as Buford's cavalry, which had been sent to cross higher up, came down on the opposite bank. But as no word came of their approach, a retrograde movement was ordered.

o'clock for the north side of the Rappahannock. It is said that Kilpatrick who held our left in the vicinity of James City was driven in this morning, and that Lee is trying to re-enact the Pope campaign of last year.

KELLY'S FORD, OCTOBER 11, SUNDAY. We got but two hours' sleep last night, and were ready to start, according to orders, at three this morning. With the hour however came orders for us to hold on, and we were kept hanging around until nearly eleven o'clock. I know nothing worse than this being ready to start a couple of hours before daylight, and then detained until near noon. I cannot lie down and go to sleep as many can, so that smoking is the only resource left to me. Some of Buford's officers came up before we started, and informed us that they reached Moreton's Ford at sundown and camped on that side for the night. The officer sent to inform Newton of their crossing got lost on his way up, and did not reach us until midnight. Buford met with no opposition yesterday, there being no force opposed to him. He picked up quite a number of prisoners (rebel stragglers), waggons, and so on. It is queer that we should not have seen anything of his advance before we left the ford.

This morning he crossed to the far side; but meantime, the Sixth Corps having been withdrawn like ourselves, the rebels pushed a brigade of infantry across at Raccoon Ford and took post between him and Culpeper—obliging Buford to fall back on Stevensburg. As my batteries at the rear of our column went through that place, one of Buford's came into position on a knoll right alongside of the road, while his other guns were blazing away quite lively not over half a mile off; this battery opened before we were all out of the village, and a number of wounded cavalry joined our column. I fully expected to come in for a share of the scrimmage, but General Newton only hurried us off. I know nothing about how pressing and exact the General's orders may have been, but it seemed to me a shame that such an opportunity to bag a thousand rebels or so should be lost. From the way they pushed on the cavalry they evidently did not dream of a corps of infantry being so near; while the country afforded lots of places to have hid the corps until Buford could have decoyed them into the trap.

Our road was good and straight; the men marched along steadily, very few straggling to the rear, for though the rebels did not follow us up at all the firing about Stevensburg had a salutary effect. At Paoli Mills, where we crossed Mountain Run, I got a couple of batteries into position until all had passed over; but we were not disturbed at any time, and were all safely to the north of the Rappahannock an hour before sunset. The day has been very fine, and after we got started I rather enjoyed the whole thing; there was just enough excitement to make it pleasant,

while the selection of positions for my guns in case of necessity at different points gave me plenty to do. . . .

Now for a good long night's sleep, after two of watching.

OCTOBER 12, MONDAY. This has been a day of rest for our corps, whatever it may have been for the rest of the army. We are the farthest down
the river, and as Lee's movement evidently was up, there was little
chance of our being disturbed. I have heard nothing as to what the
other corps are doing today. . . .

This has been a lovely, soft autumn day, just such an one as rests
body and mind when there is nothing to do. The rest has been most
welcome to man and beast too, thoroughly tired with two nights' work.
My five batteries are all in beautiful positions: Breck up at a mill where
there is a small ford, say a mile above Kelly's, Cooper on a high knoll
below the ford, and the other three on the open ground. It is a lovely
place for a fight. After getting them all right, and giving instructions to
repair and be ready for an instant move when called on, I turned in
regularly and had a long sleep. This evening I have written a letter
home and received one from there under date of Friday last. It tells me
that my gardener had got frightened lest he should be held by the draft,
and had therefore taken leg bail and cleared out for Canada. The man
was a fool, as most men are. . . .

Ten-thirty P.M. Have just returned from posting my letter at corps
headquarters. Lee is trying to shove around our right after all, and we
are to push for Warrenton Junction before him. We shall get off in a
couple of hours.·

THIRTEEN

MEADE AND LEE AT HIDE-AND-SEEK

The two armies, as Wainwright's record shows, had been maneuvering without actually coming to grips. Both had meanwhile sent reinforcements to the forces battling in Tennessee. When Meade had learned that Lee had dispatched Longstreet with two divisions to Chickamauga, he felt emboldened to move forward to the Culpeper line. That was all. His army actually outnumbered Lee's two to one, but he still refused to fight. Then in October Lee learned that two of Meade's corps, with Hooker in command, had gone West to take part in the Chattanooga campaign. With characteristic energy, the Confederate leader undertook an offensive movement.

In this the Southern army displayed all the nerve that was lacking on Meade's part. They were poorly uniformed, poorly shod, and poorly fed; since Gettysburg their ranks were sadly depleted; and Lee himself was half ill with what he called rheumatism in the back. But Lee had good reasons for trying to seize the initiative. Even a moderate advance would intimidate Meade sufficiently to prevent him from letting any more of his troops be sent to the West. Moreover, if Lee could push Meade well back toward the Potomac and keep him there, he would spare the people of northern Virginia the hardships of occupation, protect the central Virginia railroads from raids, and give himself more room for strategic action when the spring of 1864 came.

As it would be unwise to deliver a frontal assault on Meade's position on the ridges about Culpeper, Lee undertook a flanking movement to compel a Union retreat. This was at first successful. Meade did evacuate the Culpeper line, and moved back across the Rappahannock. The morning of October 12 found Lee trying to cut off his retreat up the Orange & Alexandria Railway and strike him a heavy blow before he could place the Union army in a strong new position behind the stream and hills of Bull Run.

In this effort Lee was destined to fail, but not before some spirited fighting took place. At Bristoe Hill on October 14, Lee's advance corps under A. P. Hill attacked Meade's Third Corps. This was Sickles' old corps, now commanded by that stout, red-faced West Pointer (class of 1837), William H. French, who was later to be accused of drunken mismanagement of a critical operation. The zealous Hill failed to perceive that Meade's Second Corps (the corps of Gouverneur K. Warren, temporarily under John C. Caldwell, a Vermonter out of civil life) was behind a railway embankment nearby. The result was that, thanks in large part to the artillery of the Second Corps, the Confederates were thrown back with heavy losses. Wainwright took no part in this.

But Lee's offensive taken as a whole was a success; as we have said, he pushed Meade back forty miles, and destroyed a stretch of railroad that the Union forces had laboriously to restore.

* * *

BRISTOE STATION, OCTOBER 13 [1863], TUESDAY.   This day has been a good twenty-four hours long; I might almost say I was in the saddle from midnight to midnight. We got off at one o'clock this morning, all feeling fresh and well, under a superb, clear sky. With good roads we pushed on lively, and were within a couple of miles of Bristoe Junction when day broke. Here we halted for half an hour to form the troops and learn the state of matters at the junction, when finding all clear we pushed right on, and took position facing to west. The Third Corps began to arrive soon afterward; say about nine o'clock. Both corps were drawn up in line of battle, and fully expected an attack, for Lee's advance struck Gregg's division of cavalry at Sulphur Springs yesterday afternoon. So near as I can learn the state of affairs, General Meade felt so doubtful as to Lee's really meaning a turning movement, that yesterday morning he sent the Second, Fifth and Sixth Corps forward again to Culpeper, leaving the Third at Freeman's Ford. They met with no opposition to speak of, but had no sooner got there than, General Meade receiving Gregg's report that Lee was actually at Sulphur Springs, they were ordered back. Now we all know what Lee is trying to do. But we have lost a whole day, so that he is about as near Centreville as we are; while his men are doubtless fresh, as, except at the start, he has had no occasion to make night marches.

General Meade arrived at the junction about noon, and soon after our corps was again started out to take the lead in the race for Centreville. We have had about thirty miles march of it from Kelly's Ford to this place, pretty near all of it in the dark. Here we arrived about eleven o'clock. . . . The day has passed off without any fighting that I have heard of; there has too been a certain amount of pleasure in the excitement of passing trains and seeing the way things are managed. The whole army lies tonight well together between here and the junction, so there is no danger of our having a repetition of the Pope blunders. If Lee wants to fight he must fight the whole army. General Meade's dispositions so far as I know them have been admirable, and never have I seen orders so well carried out.

CENTREVILLE, OCTOBER 14, WEDNESDAY.   When the day broke this morning we were already astir; but though I went around to all the divisions, and did move some of my batteries a short distance, I could learn nothing of our surroundings in consequence of the heavy wet fog which lay close to the ground over the whole of this part of the country. . . .

Our men did not march so well today; there was a good deal of straggling to the side of the roads. About two hours after starting we fell in with the head of the Sixth Corps on the other side of the railroad. They were marching beautifully, company front, well closed up, and gaining on us, though we still had two divisions ahead. I felt ashamed of the way our men were marching, and so did General Newton, but he had no right to expect discipline and vigilance in the corps when its head is so lazy and self-indulgent. I had five batteries in a body opposite the head of the Sixth Corps, which I closed up to section front so soon as we struck open ground, and marched them so, with the cannoneers at their posts, the rest of the way whenever I could. Were the country more open I would always march section front. As it is, the constant lengthening and closing of the column, caused by narrow bridges and other obstacles, is a great objection. This does not hold with a column of infantry, however, for they do not stretch to any greater length when marching by the flank, and when in company front at full distance. . . .

At intervals during the day there has been a great deal of cannonading: either the rebel cavalry hanging on our rear, or our own trying to detain the head of their column I suppose, for I have heard nothing concerning. About an hour before sundown, however, we were all roused by a genuine fight, which made noise enough while it lasted. It seems that quite a gap had formed between the rear of the Fifth Corps, and the head of the Second. So that Hill got in between them at Bristoe Station, and was forming some of his command on the very ground we occupied last night as near as I can make it out, when Warren came out of the woods on the east of the railroad with his leading division. Both were surprised, but Warren shewed the most gumption, for though both saw at once that possession of the railroad cut was the turning point, the rebs tried to gain it by a double quick, while Warren just hallowed to his Irish brigade, "run for the cutting." Paddy knew what that meant; it was speaking in his own language. The possession of the cut enabled Warren to get his line formed and three batteries (Ames being one), into position. The serving of these batteries is said to have been something very fine and to have shaken the rebel line terribly; a lively charge, immediately on getting his men formed, completed an actual victory; and Warren marched on with 400 or 500 prisoners, and five captured guns. Crawford was sent back to help him, but did not arrive in time to do anything. Soon after dark the whole army was safely on the north side of Bull Run. . . .

OCTOBER 17, SATURDAY. We have now lain here quietly for three whole days, without any symptom of attack on Lee's part. There is no doubt that he thought to get around us and cut our communications with Washington, or at least pick up some advantage over us on the way. But he has failed totally. Not a waggon has been lost or destroyed so far as I can learn, and in the only engagement he was badly whipped. Meanwhile we are very comfortable here; we are near Washington, have a very strong position, well covered with earthworks, and everything in good order. On Thursday, the day after our arrival, Taft's battery, six Parrott twenty-pounders, and Sheldon's "B," New York, were sent to me. General Newton remodelled the works around the hill, and with forty-four guns I felt as if this, the key of the position, was quite safe. It was pleasant work, and such as Newton is at home with. I enjoyed it most thoroughly for I was all the time gaining information. . . .

CENTREVILLE, OCTOBER 18, SUNDAY. In commencing the third volume of this journal I also commence the third year of my service as a soldier. Two years ago yesterday, I, with most of the other officers of my regiment, were mustered into the service for three years. As I look back to that time, it seems but as yesterday, yet what changes have taken place among those who then took the oath of office in the First New York Artillery! How much more have I myself gone through than I ever supposed really likely in my boy day-dreams! Of the field and staff of the regiment mustered in as such then, I am the only one so borne on the muster rolls; of the eight captains then commanding companies, Bates of "A" and Wilson of "F" alone retain the position, and old Wiedrich of "I" is the only one of the four captains who afterwards joined us who continues in the same post. For myself, and what I have gone through during these two years, the first feeling cannot but be one of wondering gratitude to Almighty God that he has kept me from all harm. I cannot boast of any great display of ability, I did not expect to find myself a military genius; but I have been able to perform all the duties which have fallen to me quite as well as I expected to, and in no case have been subject to reprimand by my superior.

These and hosts of other half-formed thoughts concerning the future as well as the past ran through my head on this lovely, bright, quiet Sunday, as I wandered about the little village and strolled over to my batteries on the hill. The dozen houses which composed the village lie on the same ridge as the old works erected here and about half a mile west of the summit. The right of our corps rests on the village and extends along the ridge as far as the summit. Its whole front is covered with a line of rifle pits behind which the men's tents still are ranged though all chances of an attack are passed by. Today everyone seems lazy, as if they were determined to take their fill of do-nothing against hard work ahead. The new Swedish topographical officer is the only one at work. I have come across him a number of times during the day, making most elaborate drawings of the position, which can be of no use now, except for him to display when he returns home and talks of his battles in the American war. His companions on the staff have taken a great dislike to the poor fellow, so I felt sorry for him, and stopped to talk and look at his work, which is certainly a marvel of neatness and system. . . .

Mr. Kelley has got me another gardener in the place of my deserter. I am very sorry to see a letter of McClellan's in the papers endorsing the Democratic candidate for governor of Pennsylvania.* In the purity of his own mind he has met some of the greatest scoundrels in that party without knowing them to be such, and has doubtless been led on to this. He makes a great mistake in allowing his name to be connected with politics at all. It is just what his enemies want him to do, and will afford them the means of decrying him to the people, who are now just in the state to believe any man a devil who opposes the Administration.

HAYMARKET, OCTOBER 19, MONDAY. I was correct in both of my expectations as to today; for we started in the rain this morning soon after sunrise. Our corps led off again over the stone bridge on the main road to Warrenton. This took me for the first time over the Bull Run battleground. My greatest surprise is that, once defeated, our army was not annihilated; for there was only the one narrow, high bridge, and no ford near. Neither can I see why we should have fought at all at this point last year, instead of falling back to Centreville. Captain Cooper tells me that even the waggons were not sent over the run until it was known that the fight was going against us. He describes the whole flat south of the bridge as jammed full of artillery, waggons, and ambulances at the time the retreat commenced; while the enemy had possession of the bluff down the stream, and batteries on it which commanded every part of it.

*The Democrats in Pennsylvania had nominated George W. Woodward for governor; the Republicans had renominated Andrew Curtin. Although the Democratic candidate was accused of disloyal utterances, McClellan on October 12 wrote a letter to the Philadelphia *Press* declaring his emphatic agreement with Woodward that "the sole great objects of this war are the restoration of the unity of the nation, the preservation of the Constitution, and the supremacy of the laws of the country"; that is, slavery was not involved. Later that fall Curtin defeated Woodward by a vote of approximately 270,000 to 254,000.

The more I learn of Pope's campaign, the more thankful I feel that I escaped taking any part in it.

We kept on the Warrenton road until we reached the Manassas Branch Railroad, and then turned off to this place. . . .

THOROUGHFARE GAP, OCTOBER 20, TUESDAY. The Iron Brigade came in this morning; they had got lost in the woods and wandered around a good part of the night.* They fired but few shot, small squads of rebs striking them once in a while. . . .

Thoroughfare Gap in the Bull Run Mountains is a short, narrow passage not wide enough for all its three occupants, a railroad, stream and common road, so that in places the last runs along the bed of the stream; and at all points is narrow, rough and rocky. The hills on either side are not high but wooded from base to summit. Here we have a very good position on an open ridge which forms a sort of amphitheatre around the opening to the Gap on this side. The day has been wet again; consequently our camp ground is wet and soppy. The waggons remained on the other side of the gap. . . .

BRISTOE STATION, 27, TUESDAY. We moved from the Gap to this place on Saturday last in a cold, disagreeable rain, which made everybody cross; so that I had several quarrels with my friend Robinson as to the right of way along the narrow roads. That general is not over amiable at any time, and when on the march such a day as Saturday was, he appears to be determined to see how disobliging and ugly he can make himself. . . .

Corps headquarters and my own tents are on the same knoll on which we spent the night of the 13th when on our way up. . . . It is a bleak position, but dry; so we have had full benefit of the high and bitterly cold wind which has prevailed ever since our arrival, and have been just about as uncomfortable as we well could. A tent without a stove is far from a desirable residence such weather as this. We keep big fires burning out of doors but the wind blows the smoke into one's eyes whichever side of the fire you get. A shovel full of hot coals in your tent helps along nicely if constantly and carefully replaced, but I look with envy on the niggers belonging to the construction corps who have good stoves in their Sibley tents. My own discomfort is increased by the want of a decent

---

* By the Iron Brigade, a name used by several units, Wainwright apparently refers to the body of Indiana, Wisconsin, and later Michigan men that had won fame under General John Gibbon; at Second Manassas it had lost one-third of its men, and it had fought bravely at Fredericksburg, Chancellorsville, and Gettysburg. Another Iron Brigade under General J. P. Hatch had gone out of existence in May 1863.

Wainwright paused long enough in Thoroughfare Gap to make out his reports, and notes that in his own brigade he had 425 artillerymen and 256 attached infantrymen; his proper strength being 912 men. He was informed here that the Common Council of the City of New York had forwarded him a stand of colors voted for his regiment.

servant. I could not get one when I was at home last month and have
been working along the best way I could with an orderly to take care of
my horses, and John Brown (Sanderson's boy) to look after my tent. He
is remarkably stupid even for a nigger, and almost useless. Ben (another
contraband), our cook, too gets worse instead of better, so I have written
to ask Mary to make another effort, so soon as they get settled in town,
to send me both cook and groom. . . .

The President has issued a proclamation calling for 300,000 more men
to fill up the companies and regiments now in the field. I hope this may
bring us some men, though I have very great doubts as to whether the
last previous call has been filled. Nothing has yet been done decidedly as
to re-enlistment of the old men who have served two years. If the new call
should through any means be fully answered it will fill up every organization now in service to its maximum, I should think. A few recruits of
one kind and another continue to arrive every day, but none for the
batteries. . . .

OCTOBER 31, SATURDAY.   We are still at Bristoe though we have been expecting orders to move as far forward as Catlett's Station, to which point
the railroad was completed two days ago. We hear that it is only intended
to restore the road as far as Warrenton, and that it will be open by
tomorrow. This looks as if we were to take up the line through there,
perhaps for the winter. Should we be condemned to spending six months
in this wretched country, I trust that our corps may have the good luck
to get Warrenton as its post. But I sincerely hope that nothing of that
kind is in store for us. So long as Lee destroyed the railroad at all, I
wish that he had done it so effectually, as to make it impossible to
restore it. In that case the country from Rappahannock Station to Washington could easily be made such a desert as would completely cover
Washington from any approach in that direction, and leave the upper
Potomac as the only avenue to be guarded. Another report says that
all idea of this army getting to Richmond is given up; that it is henceforth to be a mere army of observation, while the active operations are
to take place at the west. If so, there can be no need of so many men
here, and I for one should like to be shipped off south. . . .

NOVEMBER 4, WEDNESDAY.   Nothing of moment since my last entry; the
weather has been more moderate than it was a week ago, but very changeable: no rain, however, most fortunately. I have been amusing myself by
making the monthly inspections. The batteries of my own brigade have
not varied from the previous inspections, save perhaps by a small improvement. Of the two batteries temporarily with me, the Sixth Maine is
about as bad as any I have come across lately. Captain Dow addresses
also his men as mister; asks in place of ordering; has no idea what public

property he has on hand; his horses are wretched, carriages shoddy, and harness in wretched condition.* . . .

I was at Army Headquarters today, the first time in a long while. They are about halfway between Warrenton and the junction, on the north side of the branch railroad; a pleasant spot when you get to it, but not an easy one to find. While there, General Meade called me into his tent to ask about the lay of the land immediately around the railroad bridge at Rappahannock. The rebels, it seems, have fortified the knoll there on the south side of the railroad cut, making a strong tête-du-pont, which they hold in force. I was glad to be able to give him the information he desired. From the plans he had there, and the questions he put me, it was evident that we are again to push forward along this route. . . .

Today the express brought me the set of colours presented by the New York Common Council; they were beautifully boxed up, and consequently not at all damaged by the long delay on the road. They consist of a national flag and two guidons of very excellent silk and beautifully made, the stars being worked in floss silk. I do not know that I have ever seen handsomer ones; only the guidons are blue instead of yellow. As the afternoon was fine I displayed them in front of my tent, but not wanting them here, shall get Lieutenant Thomas to take them up with him to Washington, and ship them to Fourteenth Street for safe keeping.† My batteries here have got their camp in pretty good order and have had some drills. I intended to have tried a brigade drill today, but the Second Maine being ordered off prevented.

Mary writes me that I cannot get a cook under $45 or $50 or a groom under $25 or $30. I have answered that I must have them. These wages are enormous, but I cannot stand our present way of living, much longer. There is quite a fleet of Russian vessels in New York harbour, to the officers of which a semi-political ball has been given at the Academy of Music; it is said that Delmonico is to receive $12,000 for the supper. I cannot myself go this strong friendship for Russia and great hatred of England.

CATLETT'S STATION, NOVEMBER 6, FRIDAY. The orders to move came very suddenly at last; about two o'clock yesterday afternoon we were ordered to start at once for this place. It was four by the time we got fairly on the way, which threw the greater part of the march into the night. The road was execrable. I cannot imagine anything worse, and I believe I

---

* This officer was a brother of Neal Dow, the eminent temperance advocate, who though a Quaker became colonel of a Maine regiment, was twice wounded at Port Hudson, and finally was captured by the Confederates. Wainwright liked neither man.
† Wainwright's family had their winter home on Fourteenth Street in New York, then a thoroughfare of rather fashionable pretensions. His sister Mary looked after many of his general interests at home.

have traversed as bad roads the last two years as ever were seen. In many places we could not get through at all where the road once was, but were obliged to take all sorts of bypaths through the thick pines, where the carriages were continually stalling, or getting fast to the trees. I worked like a Trojan myself riding back and forth, hunting out new paths in the dark, and saw every piece up before I left off. It was then eleven o'clock. The infantry, taking the railroad track, got on much better; still it was two hours after dark when they got into camp. It does seem to me as if our marches might be better managed at headquarters. This move has been pretty much decided on for several days, and I cannot see any sufficient reason why we could not have been allowed daylight to move up here, especially as we have lain here all today. With daylight I now know we could have found another and better road around the worst part. As it was, what with horses played out and dying on the road, stocks, wheels, and harness broken, implements lost, and everything strained to the utmost, I think that $3,000 would not cover the loss to government in my command alone. . . .

It has been a busy day to me, shipping off a great lot of condemned horses and ordnance stores as well as the Second Maine Battery. I would not let this last take any good horses up to Washington with them, but had them exchange all such for poor ones in the other batteries. They had a horrible-looking lot when they went off, but can get enough good ones at Washington. . . .

KELLY'S FORD, NOVEMBER 7, SATURDAY. We started in due time this morning and reached our present position, about a mile in rear of the ford, by four P.M. The Second and Third Corps were ahead of us, which was the cause of our being so late. French led this column with the Third Corps; he did not wait to put a bridge down but so soon as he got his batteries planted and his men forward, Birney's whole division waded the stream, and attacked the heights on the other side, carrying them with the loss of only thirty-five men killed and wounded. The rebels were not in strong force at this point, nor much entrenched; so the resistance was not great. French reports having captured 254 prisoners. Bridges are now being laid, and the rest of this wing of the army are to cross early tomorrow morning.

General Meade has his headquarters near us tonight; I have just returned from there where I learned from Hunt and Patrick all about the doings of the other wing at Rappahannock Station, which resulted in a most brilliant little success. Sedgwick had command of that column, his own corps coming within sight of the rebel works about noon. Their tête-du-pont was found to be quite extended, and strongly manned. On the knoll to our right of the railroad bridge, they had made a good work and mounted four guns in it; from there a rifle pit ran around on the little rise to the wood, west of where our better pontoon bridge was, their bridge being laid at the same point. Early in the afternoon Sedgwick put a goodly number of batteries into position along the edge of the woods, which I should say was from 12,000 to 15,000 yards from the rebel works. At the same time half of Russell's brigade was pushed forward as skirmishers as near as it was possible to get them: the artillery keeping up a steady fire. The skirmish line thus thrown out was of nearly double the ordinary force. Having got up as near as they well could, the skirmishers lay down, and kept quiet until about sundown, when another line, composed of the other half brigade, was sent out as if to relieve them. So quietly and naturally was the whole thing done that the rebels were completely taken in. On the joining of the two lines, they formed a tolerable line of battle. The charge was immediately ordered, and they went in right over the rebel works. The rebs fought hard but they were surprised, and their fate was sealed by Colonel Upton, who had crept around meantime to their flank, and charging over the end of the work at the same time that Russell attacked in front, he got possession of the bridge. Sedgwick's whole loss as now reported is not much over 300, while Patrick tells me he received 1,344 prisoners from him. Four guns were captured in the works.

They were all feeling very jolly at headquarters over this success, and well they may, considering how cheaply it was bought. It seems to have been admirably planned and perfectly executed. I do not know with whom the idea originated; but "Uncle John," Russell, and Upton all deserve great credit. Tomorrow we shall doubtless push ahead again, and may calculate on a fight. . . .

❊ ❊ ❊

Lee, moving his army back across the Rappahannock, had what Wainwright calls a tête-du-pont at Rappahannock Bridge, and a body of troops at Kelly's Ford four miles downstream. Jubal A. Early held the bridgehead, and Robert E. Rodes the area of the ford. Lee expected them to protect his passage of the river. But about noon of November 7, as Wainwright indicates, Sedgwick at the head of the Fifth and Sixth Corps moved up opposite Early's position and began a brisk artillery bombardment. The Confederate works were strong, and Early held on tenaciously. Lee himself inspected the position, and felt as confident as his subordinates that the bridgehead could be maintained until next morning. Nobody expected the Union troops to make a night attack.

But that was just what "Uncle John" Sedgwick did. In David A. Russell of New York, a West Pointer in the class of 1845 who had been brevetted in the Mexican War, he had an especially dashing officer. As dusk closed in, Russell led a smart advance by two brigades, while Emory Upton (West Point, 1861), still in his early twenties, took in another brigade as skirmishers. Two regiments, the Fifth Wisconsin and Sixth Maine, made an irresistible bayonet charge. The attackers swarmed over the Confederate works and took the pontoon bridge over the river, killing or capturing the Louisiana defenders.

Meanwhile, the two North Carolina regiments at Kelly's Ford downstream under Rodes were defeated and in large part taken prisoner. The total Confederate losses in the two areas exceeded 2,000, a figure that stunned the Confederates and elated the Union camps.

❊ ❊ ❊

BRANDY STATION, NOVEMBER 8, SUNDAY. For the first time I feel inclined to find fault with General Meade today. I have always taken the ground that no one but the General himself and his immediate advisers know what information he has at the time of coming to a decision, and consequently we should be very careful in finding fault. Perhaps I am wrong in doing so now, but I do feel most decidedly that he has been overcautious today. Our men were not used up, as at Falling Waters, but on the contrary were very fresh, and full of ardour in consequence of yesterday's success. The country too is, or at least ought to be, perfectly known to Meade and his corps commanders. Lee was undoubtedly unprepared for the extent of our move last night, and had made preparations to go into winter quarters hereabouts.

When we commenced moving this morning I supposed that the General himself, with these three corps, would push direct for Culpeper, while Sedgwick advanced by the railroad with the Fifth and Sixth. It would, to be sure, have separated the army into two columns until we got near the Court House, but there was not much danger of Lee's trying to cut between them, if we pushed on rapidly and boldly. As it was, this corps pushed up immediately on the river, with Second and Third swinging around on our left; and so much time was lost in keeping the different parts of the line straight that it was near sundown when we got here. There was no opposition to this wing of the army: a few stragglers picked up and an occasional shot at some venturesome scout was all we saw of the enemy. They skirmished with the Sixth Corps in its advance, all the way, but did not show a line of battle anywhere; yet that corps reached here some time before we did. Lee was doubtless with his main force at Culpeper if he was not making for the south of the Rapidan. I fear that our chance, whatever it may have been, is now gone; a whole day and two nights are quite enough to enable Lee's army to entrench themselves thoroughly if they mean to fight, or to get safely across the Rapidan if they do not.

On the road up today we had abundant proof that the rebels expected to winter here, in the extensive and elaborate huts they were erecting. Whole villages of quite sizable houses were half finished, and thousands of shingles split out for roofing. . . .

RAPPAHANNOCK STATION, NOVEMBER 10, TUESDAY. We are once more in our old quarters at the "Smith house," where we spent so long a time last summer. The family moved up to Baltimore soon after we left here in September, and the house being without regular occupants since then has suffered much. All the fences around have been destroyed, and the walls of the rooms disfigured. The weather too has changed as much as the place. In August it was hot enough to roast one; today we have it cold and disagreeable enough for the ugliest kind of a November day at home. The wind blows a gale straight from the mountains which are white with the snow which fell last night. Odd squalls of it came whistling around the house when we got here after dark last night, making us glad to huddle around a blazing fire in the house, though most of the glass being broken out of the windows, the storm drove in there badly.

Yesterday morning Buford and Kilpatrick came into our front from either flank, and reported that the enemy were all on the south side of the Rapidan. All further move forward was therefore given up, and the army disposed to as to cover Brandy Station; this corps being sent back to complete the railroad from Warrenton Junction to this place. . . .

My new man turned up this evening; he is a powerful great Irishman, named James McClusky, and looks as if he might do well. I am so rejoiced to get anything that I am not likely to be exacting. They have some prospect of getting me a Frenchman as cook who has served on like duty in Algeria.

NOVEMBER 14, SATURDAY. Lieutenant-Colonel Patten, Colonel Bailey's father-in-law, writes me that the widow has not been able to draw the balance of pay due him at the time of his death "by reason of non-settlement of his property account." How in creation a man killed in action is to settle his property account I cannot see; nor can I tell how the survivors are to do it for him when all his papers were captured. If this is not running red tape-ism into the ground I don't know what is. And suppose he does die indebted to the government; is a man's life worth so little that it does not balance a few hundred dollars? It makes me more than mad to think that the widow of such a man as Bailey should be kept out of a few months' pay, merely because a form has not been filled out; while millions of money are being squandered on all sorts of most worthless trash. The matter in question was a waggon, four horses, and so on, drawn for regimental headquarters, which Bailey receipted for, instead of the regimental quartermaster. Suppose the whole thing had been captured by the rebs; who was to account for it, or even report such capture? . . .

NOVEMBER 18, WEDNESDAY. I was surprised this afternoon by a telegram saying that father is dangerously ill, and begging me to come home; I immediately took it to General Newton, and then sent my application up to headquarters with a note to General Williams, asking him to do what he could for me. I am now awaiting his return. I trust that this attack may not prove so bad as they anticipate, but as the old gentleman is now almost ninety, he cannot be expected to fight against it as well as a younger man. . . .

NEW YORK, NOVEMBER 26, THURSDAY. Left camp a week ago today, and reached here on Friday morning, without trouble. Found father much better: the doctor says it is wonderful that a man of his years should have shown so much vitality. He is certainly blessed with a strong constitution, which together with his enviable temper has preserved him from sickness almost all through life. This is the first he has ever been confined to his bed for a day within my recollection. Now he is up again and about the house. His age begins to tell on him now very decidedly; he has failed very much the last two years, since I left home. . . .

NOVEMBER 27, FRIDAY. This morning's paper states positively, and in such a way that I believe it, that the army cut loose from its base yesterday at daylight, and has gone no one knows whither. They talk of its turning up at Richmond and all such nonsense; but I hope to catch them yet before they get very far. . . .

RAPPAHANNOCK STATION, NOVEMBER 28, SATURDAY. Reached Washington on time this morning. At the provost-marshal's office in Washington they told me that the trains were running to Rappahannock Station, the Third Division of our corps holding the road, but that there was no use in my going out there, as the army had cut entirely loose from this road; that I would have a better chance of getting to them by waiting until the Aquia Creek route was open. I, however, determined to try this route first. There was one passenger car on the train which was crowded with officers and men, many of the former standing up while the latter were seated. A private of the Pennsylvania Reserves, who had served in Cooper's battery, recognized me and gave me his seat. This way of crowding officers and men in together on a purely democratic footing is very disgusting, and certainly might be avoided on a road like this, which is entirely under the control of the army. When we arrived here I found some twenty or thirty officers, who came out yesterday, waiting to take the train back to Washington; they too told us that our chances were hopeless this way, and persuaded most of those who came down to go back. But I determined to hold on, especially as the troops here being a

part of our own corps I knew I should have as good a chance as anyone. So I footed it up to General Kenly's headquarters, about half a mile
from the station.*

The General and Captain Baird, his adjutant-general, received me
most kindly, and offered to make me as comfortable as they could; but,
like everyone else they said there was no chance of my getting out from
here. They too think that the army will open a new base at Aquia Creek,
though I cannot find out exactly on what ground this supposition is
based. They say that there was a great deal of heavy cannonading yesterday afternoon, some claiming to have heard musketry. This only confirmed me in the idea that there will be an opportunity to get out from
here. For if there was a fight, the wounded must be sent in, and this is
the nearest point; also the prisoners if any were captured. A real victory
would certainly be announced; and without one Meade cannot advance
far. So I dined with Kenly, smoked and gossiped away the afternoon: he
having sent orders down to the station that he should be immediately
notified were there any arrival from the army. About eight o'clock word
came up than an escort had arrived from the army, with dispatches, and
would start at daylight tomorrow on their return. . . .

* * *

While Wainwright was absent at his father's bedside, Meade had begun
his abortive Mine Run campaign. He crossed the Rapidan at Germanna
Ford, which is some seven miles due south of Kelly's Ford on the Rappahannock, and marched west with five corps toward Rapidan Station. His
object was to force Lee out of his lines on the upper Rapidan. The Confederate cavalry, however, immediately discovered the movement. Lee
placed his army on the western bank of the tributary of the Rapidan called
Mine Run, squarely in front of Meade, and entrenched it there. There
seemed some chance that Meade would really give battle. On November
29 the Union forces began a brisk artillery fire across the Run, while Lee
further strengthened his earthworks. On the 30th, in bitter cold weather, the
Confederate cavalry reported that Meade's men seemed to be forming a
line of assault. But as no attack came then, or on December 1, Lee made
preparations for taking the offensive himself.

At dawn on December 2 the Confederates were ready to leap at the foe.
The gunners manned their pieces, and the infantry were alert. But Meade
was gone!—he had stolen away during the night. "I am too old to command

---

* John Reese Kenly, a Maryland attorney and veteran of the Mexican War, was now a
division commander in Newton's First Corps.

this army," commented Lee. "We should never have permitted those people to get away."

* * *

MINE RUN, NOVEMBER 29, SUNDAY. From the captain of my escort, and conversation since my arrival, I learn that the army broke camp on Thursday morning, the object being to surprise Lee and get between the two halves of his army which had been ascertained to be rather widely separated. Things did not go as Meade expected, however; none of the corps reaching the positions expected the first night, and the Third not even crossing the river. On Friday morning they all pushed forward again, but the Third Corps lost their road, and ran into Ewell's corps and had to fight. This was the firing heard by Kenly. Our men claim to have had the best of the fight, but it so delayed matters that the point was not reached until yesterday afternoon, when Lee was found to have got all his force together on the other side of the Run, where he was busy entrenching. The blame for the failure is pretty generally laid upon General French. . . .

NOVEMBER 30, MONDAY. The day opened and continued clear and cold. All hands were stirring early, full of anticipation of a great, perhaps decisive battle. General Warren, with his corps, the Second, had passed around to the Orange Plank road, where, he reported, he had found the right of Lee's line. There he had been strengthened by two divisions of the Third Corps, giving him about 30,000 men. Warren was to make the main attack, and when he was fully engaged Sedgwick was to push in on the other flank with the Fifth and Sixth. . . .

Everything was quiet until the signal gun was fired, when all the batteries on our right and centre opened. The Fifth Corps batteries were now covered by our corps, so General Newton desired me to take charge of them also. To this Captain Martin demurred, and as he had not received regular orders to that effect, I said nothing until General Hunt came along when I asked him to give the necessary directions. . . . During all this time we were waiting intently for signs that Warren was going in. Hearing no symptom of it General Hunt ordered us to slacken our fire, but keep ready for a renewal at any moment. Warren, however, did not make any attack; I hear that he found this morning that Lee had extended his right during the night and strengthened it so that there was no chance of an attack being successful. In this General Meade agreed with him on going over to our left. Consequently the whole thing fell through, and we hold the same position tonight we did in the morning, with small loss beyond the expenditure of a good deal of ammunition. . . .

STEVENSBURG, DECEMBER 2, WEDNESDAY. Yesterday we lay quiet all day; several plans were talked of I believe, but found to be impracticable when examined into. The day and following night were bitter cold, with a gale of wind blowing; everybody suffered terribly. There were rumours among the men of several of our pickets being frozen to death the previous night, but Dr. Heard tells me they are not true, a few severe cases of frozen feet and hands being the worst. Before dark it was determined to clear out, giving the whole thing up as a bad job. The Fifth Corps was to bring up the rear, and I was ordered to report to General Sykes with those of my batteries in position. The other corps having got well started, the Fifth hauled out about ten last night, Crawford's division leading with a battery placed between each of his first regiments for protection. . . .

On reaching the north side of the river General Newton informed me that he was ordered to cover the taking up of the pontoon bridges, so I had another hour's work putting batteries into position on the north bank. It was broad daylight when I got through. After ascertaining that I had made no mistakes in the dark, I turned in to one of the headquarters tents, which were all up, for a few hours' sleep. I was routed out by the guard taking the tents down this morning. The army was all across; the bridges up, except one boat which was ferrying over the stragglers. This one was soon taken out of the water, and then the cavalry, too, began to withdraw from the other side.

It was amusing to see the stragglers who came down after the boat was out; how they tried one way and another to avoid getting more wet than necessary. Many of them got a thorough sousing, probably the first bath they had had in a long time. Never have I seen so many stragglers from the army. Whether the awful cold weather, the changes of position in a dense wilderness, and the fear of a hard fight made more than usual, or whether the move to the rear was unexpected by them, I do not know. But when about halfway to the ford, in a place where the wood was somewhat more open, I saw thousands, literally acres, of them, cooking their coffee or sleeping around their fires. These rascals get very sharp about finding their way home. But I should think that there was rich pickings for the rebel cavalry all through the wood this morning of prisoners as well as blankets and overcoats. Many a poor reb will sleep more comfortably all this winter for what he picks up today, and will have cause to bless the Mine Run campaign.*

* The principal incident of this night march was the oversetting of Wainwright's headquarters wagon on a particularly vile stretch of road near Germanna Ford. Wainwright was elsewhere on the line at the time, and so escaped seeing Meade come up and fly into a fearful rage over the way the prostrate wagon was "stopping the whole army." Later Meade became calmer and told Wainwright politely that his baggage

About ten o'clock we marched for this place. The day has been much milder and fine; the road comparatively fair; but the troops marched like a mob; everybody was tired out, and feeling miserable. On the way we passed the Sixth Corps, lying in the woods, where they bivouacked last night. . . . When we arrived here, a couple of hours before dark, there was no one to give us orders where to camp, General Newton having stayed behind to gossip with his old Sixth Corps cronies. This way he has of indulging himself and not considering the comfort of his men is outrageous. I waited for him until near dark and then put my batteries in camp for the night, not knowing whether there were other troops to the right and left of us or not. The Sixth Corps came up soon after, General Newton with them; he has not made me change my dispositions tonight. . . .

PAOLI MILLS, DECEMBER 3, THURSDAY.   . . . Orders came to move to this place, which is on Mountain Run, about two miles from Kelly's Ford. . . . Orders have just been received to be ready to move again at four o'clock tomorrow morning. . . .

KELLY'S FORD, DECEMBER 6, SUNDAY.   I suppose that this is the best designation for me to give to our present location, as it is a point supposed to be held by our corps; though in truth the house around which General Newton's and my own headquarters are pitched is just about halfway between the ford and Paoli Mills. I have not yet learned what was intended by the orders to move at four o'clock on Friday morning; whatever it was, it came to naught; we only changed the position of headquarters. . . .

The idea here is that the successful defense of Knoxville last month was much more due to Benjamin than to Burnside. His own part of the affair, the artillery, certainly was perfectly managed. The rolling of lighted shells by hand into the ditch was entirely his arrangement, and much of it done by his own hands. His classmates (1861) here have a story that during the heaviest part of the attack Benjamin walked the top of the parapet, lighting the big shells placed there with the cigar he was smoking, and rolling them with his feet down upon the rebels below. Rather a strong story, but Benjamin is brave and cool enough to have given some foundation for it.

Another of my Camp Barry acquaintances distinguished himself quite as much at Knoxville, though he was not so fortunate in getting off. The General Sanders who with his little brigade of cavalry delayed the whole of Longstreet's corps for nearly three days was Bailey's classmate and chum, who used to brew cocktails and spin jolly yarns. Sanders was the last of four chums at West Point, all of whom have fallen in battle;

was being sent by another wagon. "Meade does not mean to be ugly," comments the diarist, "but he cannot control his infernal temper."

Gaston, killed in Sheptoe's fight with the Indians, Bailey at Fair Oaks, Bayard at Fredericksburg, and now Sanders at Knoxville. The three last were an illustrious trio. Bayard was the best known out of the army, but perhaps the others were quite his equal. They say that Sanders was actually engaged to my friend Susan Gaston, his old chum's sister. Poor girl! She has had a hard experience of war, with both brothers and lover killed in battle.*

DECEMBER 10, THURSDAY. Everything now so strongly indicates our remaining where we are that I have told my commanders to go to work and hut their commands. Most of them have already nearly got their men covered. Stewart has looked to his horses first, being lucky or rather energetic enough to secure slabs for his roofing. He and Mink went over to look at the sawmill one day: the lumber, of which there was a large pile when we passed a week ago, was all gone, save a lot of slabs. I told them they had better secure these; Mink put it off for a day, but Stewart borrowed waggons all around, armed a lot of his men, and had his party off by daybreak the next morning; thus securing them all. Mink reports some of the castings of the engine gone and all the belts. Ingalls, Chief Quartermaster, tells me he will get them for me if I will fix the mill so that it can be run for the army. I spoke to General Newton about a guard at the mill, but he says it should be attended to at Army Headquarters. If Newton had any snap he would be glad to make the necessary arrangements and so secure boards for his own corps first.

I have rather allowed than directed the huts to be put up; few of them are built as I would have them. When visiting Captain Reynolds's battery this morning, he showed me his men's work with pride, which was considerably lessened when I pointed out to him that his lines of huts were not straight, nor were they all of a size. He thought I was very particular and that the men should be allowed to suit themselves; but gave in when I pointed out how much easier it would be to keep in order a regularly laid out camp, to keep an eye on the men if there was one main street on which all the huts opened, and above all, that the men.

---

* Longstreet, advancing from Chattanooga early in November, laid siege to Knoxville in the last fortnight of the month. On November 29 he attacked Burnside's principal defensive position, Fort Sanders. The cannon here, a battery of twenty-pounder Parrotts, was commanded by Lieutenant Samuel N. Benjamin, of the Second United States Artillery. The strength of the works astonished the assailants, many of whom were caught in a deep ditch. "The guns flanking the ditch," writes General Jacob D. Cox, "raked it with double charges of canister. Shells were lighted and thrown as hand-grenades into the practically helpless crowd below." Longstreet was repulsed with about 1,000 casualties.

Fort Sanders was named for William Price Sanders, head of cavalry in the Department of the Ohio, who was mortally wounded November 16, 1863. General George D. Bayard of Pennsylvania, a cavalryman, died of wounds December 14, 1862.

themselves would take more pride, after it was built, in a really military-looking camp which would attract the commendations of passersby. It is the same old story with all our volunteer officers, no real pride in being a soldier. . . .

There are rumours about camp of Meade's removal, Pleasonton, Hancock, and Sedgwick being talked of as his successor. I trust that there is no foundation for them, and that Meade's report of the "Mine Run" campaign, as it is called, will induce the President to maintain him in his command. Since I have become fully acquainted with the history of this movement, I think more of General Meade than ever; especially of his *not* fighting. His plan, which I have already mentioned, was excellent, as were all his dispositions. Its failure was no doubt mainly owing to General French, who I find it generally believed was drunk. I cannot vouch for the truth of this, however, and hope it was not so. He certainly lost his way twice, and appears to have acted very queerly. Had Meade been supported by a good staff (which it is impossible to get) of officers regularly educated to, and thoroughly understanding staff duties, I believe that everything would have gone well. It would then have been their duty to conduct each corps to its proper position, and on them would have fallen the blame of failing to be there in time; certainly that of missing the road. As it is, we plunged blindly into an unknown densely wooded country with no guides except perhaps an old county map, or a stupid contraband. After the failure to divide Lee's army or to turn the right entrenchments, the only thing left was an attack in front of his lines. Meade believes that he could have carried the works at Mine Run, but after a heavy loss which would have totally unfitted the army to follow up their first advantage, as he ascertained that they had another and much stronger line of works already erected in the rear of Mountain Run about two miles back, thus making it a mere victory without actual advantage gained.

Patrick tells me that on Wednesday night, when Meade got back to his old camp, he was very much dispirited. Patrick's tents being up, the General came to his quarters, and talked very freely to him. He told Patrick that on laying his plan before the President, Mr. Lincoln approved it, telling him: "Only be sure to fight; the people demand it of the Army of the Potomac." Stanton told him he "had better fight and leave 18,000 men on the field, without result, than to come back without a battle." After repeating this conversation, Meade said: "I expect to be deprived of my command; but my men's lives are too valuable to be sacrificed for popularity. I could not do it." The radical papers are of course finding much fault with Meade. But I can already see that the men of the army are beginning to understand the matter, and that their confidence in their general is increasing. When it gets out that he was ordered to lose

18,000 men anyway, as such things always do get out, his not fighting will do as much for him in gaining the confidence of the army as if he had won a victory. . . .

DECEMBER 16, WEDNESDAY. The papers have pretty near ceased discussing the Mine Run affair, but are by no means satisfied to have us settle down for the winter. The public have got a taste for blood, and want more excitement. A week passed without reports of a battle with thousands killed and wounded—is very dull, rendering the papers hardly worth reading. There is very little chance of this morbid desire being gratified here, although we are not entrenched. . . . What we should have done on withdrawing from Mine Run was to move at once down to the heights south of Fredericksburg, and wintered there. So self-evident was this that everyone in the army, even the privates, expected it. General Meade wanted to do it, and urged the President to give him permission; but Mr. Lincoln was obstinate, fearing it might uncover Washington. Perhaps too, Mc-Clellan having failed to reach Richmond by his route, the Peninsula, and Burnside having in like manner failed by his, Fredericksburg, our military President is now determined that his own plan shall be carried out, so as to prove he was right.

Another reason why none of this army will be sent off is in the desire to get the men to re-enlist; which in fact will be almost a reorganization of the army, and will require all winter, in order to give the men their promised furloughs. The inducements held out are very great. Men originally enlisting for three years and who have served two, may now re-enlist the same as if they had served out their whole term, getting the $100 promised them at the close of it. In addition, they are to receive $300 U.S. bounty on their new enlistment, and being credited to their state and town on the new call for 300,000 men, are entitled to the state and local bounties. These have grown to be something enormous; in some places in Massachusetts $1,000 down is said to be paid. New York State pays $75, and almost every town or county something. The city gives $300, which with the state and U.S. bounties mounts up to about $1,000. . . .

DECEMBER 20, SUNDAY. This army and the country have met with a great loss by the death of General John Buford. He was decidedly the best cavalry general we had, and was acknowledged as such in the army, though being no friend to newspaper reporters, he was made no more of in their reports than Reynolds was. In many respects he resembled Reynolds, being rough in his exterior, never looking after his own comfort, untiring on the march and in the supervision of all the militia of his command, quiet and unassuming in his manners. As General Hunt said: "Reynolds and Buford are the greatest losses this army has suffered."

DECEMBER 23, WEDNESDAY. The cold spell still holds on; it is really severe, equal I think to anything we had during the whole of last winter. Today has been the coldest of all, not thawing at all even in the sun. I expected to move into my new quarters this afternoon, but a new order has put all notions of that kind to flight. This corps is ordered to move to Culpeper tomorrow, and go into winter quarters there. Consequently the whole corps is engaged today in one big swear. It is very hard on the men, who have just got themselves comfortably hutted, to be obliged once more to put up with the poor comfort of a shelter tent for a fortnight or so until they have once more built shanties for themselves. My own men will have another three weeks work to get up huts and stables, for which I pity them. So far as my own comfort is concerned, it does not matter much. All last winter I lived in a tent, and in two hours can make myself as well off as I have been here. Then there are certain advantages in the move, first and foremost of which is that all the country around here is low and very wet, while around the Court House we shall have high and dry ground. This alone I think will fully compensate for the move before the winter is over. I hope, too, to get all my batteries together where I can look after them more closely. I fully mean that this time they shall lay out their camps and build their quarters in a way that will do credit to the command.

CULPEPER COURT HOUSE, DECEMBER 27, SUNDAY.   We had a fine day for our short march to this place on Thursday. It was very cold, still and bright: the road was frozen hard, so there was no sticking in the mud. I walked a good part of the way to keep my feet warm. We reached the Court House soon after noon, but, as usual, there was no General Newton along to tell us where we were to camp; we therefore had to hang around all the afternoon waiting for him. Headquarters were to be in the village; that was all that anyone knew. About a couple of hours before sundown the General arrived, expressing surprise that somebody had not put the men in camp. He hates the labour of looking up positions for his corps; both the bodily labour of riding around to view the country, and the mental work of how best to locate his troops. As, however, he had to do it, he took Bankhead and myself and went out onto the hills south of the place. Should such a thing happen as Lee's crossing to attack us here, the high ground behind Mountain Run is the line to be taken up by the army; the duty of this corps would be to hold the enemy in check until the line was formed there. With this view I had to camp my batteries in such a position as would enable me easily and rapidly to move them onto the knolls south of the town.

Very fortunately, that position proved the most desirable for a camp in other respects of any around. I saw it from the heights lying snug and dry, well sheltered to the north by pines, a few hundred yards from the water, and about three-quarters of a mile from the station. I did not like to point it out, for there was a house in the centre of it, and I feared that the general might think it was that I was after. I find that the commanders who like most to get into houses themselves often make the most fuss about their subordinates doing the same thing. The spot was, however, so clearly the best for my camp that Newton could not help seeing it himself; when he pointed it out and told me I might camp there, I moved off at once and took my batteries over to the neighbourhood. On arriving I found the wood where I meant to put my batteries occupied by a cavalry brigade, the colonel commanding it having his headquarters in the house. As it was near dark, I had my men bivouac for the night, under the lee of a hill; while my own tents were pitched within the dooryard of the house.

After seeing them all located, I returned to the tavern in the village, where headquarters were, in search of some supper. The night was very cold, and the idea of one of Ben's beefsteaks eaten in a cold tent was by no means agreeable, when I knew that I could beg something better in a warm room. I stopped at headquarters for some time so as to give full opportunity for them to get the tents and stoves up. When I returned, about ten o'clock, I found a body of infantry bivouacked close to the railroad. Oh, how cold and miserable the poor devils looked, crouching around fires no larger than a tin pan, for there was no wood near. The ground was frozen too hard for them to pitch their little bits of canvas; and when they looked back upon the warm huts they had left at Kelly's Ford, how they must have cursed someone. As I rode along thinking how it was Newton's love of his own ease that had prevented these poor fellows from providing for their fires tonight, I was cheered up by the sight of my own men. Close behind where I had located them lay a large amount of pine and cedar brush, fresh cut: this they had hauled together; each detachment building for themselves a semi-circular wall of it four or five feet high. In the centre of each semi-circle was a roaring big fire, around which the men lay, well wrapped up in their blankets and paulins. I could not help stopping to congratulate them on being battery men; the whole picture was one of such absolute comfort.

On reaching my headquarters, I found that my staff had cozened with the cavalry officers in the house, and had fared well. I went in to see the colonel myself, and to express the hope that I was not intruding by pitching my tent in his dooryard for the night. He was quite polite about it, but evidently felt very grumpy at the prospect of having to move farther to the front, now that the infantry had come up. Orders to which effect he got the next day.

FOURTEEN

THE ADVENT OF GRANT

"All is quiet and mudbound in camp." So wrote the New York *Tribune* correspondent on December 29, 1863, from the Army of the Potomac; and mudbound the forces remained. Lee's army was intrenched along the Rapidan, a screen of regiments guarding that little river while the main force lay just behind, ready to reinforce center or flanks at need. Meade's command went into winter quarters between the Rapidan and the Rappahannock, with most of the infantry and artillery in or about Culpeper Court House, a pleasant, well-built little county seat. The Union troops would make no forward movement until the beginning of May 1864. But while the army waited for warm weather and drying roads, two significant changes were to take place. It was to receive a new general, Ulysses S. Grant, in place of the dilatory Meade; and it was to be reinforced and reorganized on a grand scale.

The Confederacy as 1863 ended and 1864 began had still two formidable hosts. One was Lee's, now so reduced that in spring he would be able to muster only 60,000 to 65,000 troops and some 200 guns; but valorous, determined, and better toughened and disciplined than ever. The Confederacy had nearly all its old fighting spirit, and early in the year lowered the age limit for conscripts to seventeen at the bottom, and raised it to fifty at the top. The other Southern army was Joseph E. Johnston's. Grant, taking command at Chattanooga in October, had flung the enemy out of his strong position on Missionary Ridge, and pursued him in full rout to Dalton just across the border of Georgia, inflicting a loss of 18,000 men. He would have smashed ahead through Georgia when weather and roads permitted, but he was wanted elsewhere, and had to leave that task to William T. Sherman.

Wainwright and his artillerymen made themselves comfortable for the winter at Culpeper. He oversaw the building of huts for his force, carefully aligned and uniform in style and size. For himself he had the comfort of a private house—"a square building of red brick, finished just before the war began, about the most absurdly planned house I ever was in." A family of poor folk shared it, but they occupied the basement and one room of the second floor while he took for his special quarters a high-ceiled southeast room, twenty feet square, with a fireplace. Five other officers had rooms. On Christmas Day they dined with a neutral Virginian of the neighborhood, who gave them roast turkey and a "glorious" bowl of milk punch. Wainwright was cheered also by the arrival of four large boxes and a barrel from New York, full of Christmas luxuries: canned soups, vegetables, peaches, mushrooms, and the like; mustard, chow-chow, Worcestershire sauce, and other condiments; dried prunes, dates, figs, nuts and candy; and a dozen bottles of sherry.

A serious re-enlistment problem was troubling the army. Great numbers of men who had volunteered for three years were approaching the end of their terms. They had to be offered strong inducements to re-enlist, both in bounties and in other favors. Meade had reported to the War Department on December 12, 1863, that the time of seventy-seven regiments would expire before the end of August 1864; but that his officers believed more than half of them would remain if given a thirty-day furlough as well as the Congressional bounty of $402. The grant of furloughs on a wholesale scale gravely reduced the field strength of the army.

* * *

JANUARY 7, 1864, THURSDAY. The weather continues cold for this latitude. Snow which fell on Monday has melted but very little since; the ground is frozen hard, and there is some prospect of another fall. If this weather holds, Lee may possibly be tempted to try something, for in spite of all care taken to prevent news going out of the number of men away from this army, he must be pretty well aware of our comparative weakness at this time. The papers too state that there is a great deal of disaffection growing in the rebel armies; the men are beginning to get tired of it. There may be some foundation for these reports, as deserters are beginning to come into our lines. On Monday four men from an Alabama regiment came over, and on Tuesday seventeen more from the same regiment. This is a large number, but they may be from the north of that state, where the people have never gone heartily with the disunionists. . . .

At last the movement in the corps to erect a monument to General Reynolds has been fairly started. It was a very great mistake putting it off so long, as a large number of those who were members of the corps under Reynolds have left. When I found at Rappahannock Station that my views on the subject did not meet with general approval, I left off taking an active part in the initiation of the matter. . . . My objections lay in the fact that the plan contemplates a glorification of the First Corps, rather than a simple tribute to the memory of General Reynolds by his former companions in arms. "The Association is to be composed of the First Corps as now constituted" is the expression of their resolution. Now there are a number of regiments with the corps, to say nothing of the whole Maryland brigade, who never served a day under Reynolds, while all the Pennsylvania Reserves, not now with the corps, have. . . .

I do not approve of the way in which they have limited their subscriptions, either. Fifty cents for an enlisted man is not enough; it should have been $1, and as much more as the individual was willing to give. Many of our privates are much better able to give than their officers, and would be glad to subscribe their $5 or $10. With the subscription from officers, it is even worse—$5 for all ranks; this is too much to ask from lieutenants and too little from colonels. It should have varied from $2 or $3 for lieutenants up to $20 or $25 for generals, or more if they chose. Stewart with his pay of $125 a month and family to support can illy afford to give $5, while I, with my pay of $300 and no family can much more readily give $50. . . .

JANUARY 10, SUNDAY. Having got my brigade work pretty well done up, I am now busy on regimental affairs. All the returns for November are in, and the sergeant-major at work consolidating them. Those for December too are so far received that I am able to come pretty near the state of the regiment at the close of the year. The aggregate for November was 1,139. For December it will be some few more, a turning point from which I hope to have it go on constantly increasing. . . . The regiment is widely separated, and will never act together as a regiment, but so long as it maintains its organization, I want to do all I can to keep up a regimental pride. I have also sent a circular to all the batteries urging the officers to do all that they can to induce their men to re-enlist, as well as to endeavour to secure recruits while they are at home on leave. . . .

There has been no news stirring for some time now. In want of it the army is full of camp rumours. One of these is of importance, and coming down from Washington may very likely have some foundation. It is to the effect that the First and Third Corps are to be broken up, and consolidated with the Second, Fifth, and Sixth. It would be a good move in my opinion, as a corps d'armée of 15,000 men is simply absurd, causing a vast increase in the amount of writing to be done, and the time necessary to get orders to their destination. Were all the companies reasonably full, and the army not stronger numerically than at present, two-thirds of the writing could be dispensed with, two-thirds of the clerks returned to the ranks, and one-half the officers dispensed with. If any consolidation does take place, this corps and the Third are the ones most likely to be broken up, for the commander of neither of them is popular at the War Department; and if there is any difference in the excellence of the different corps in this army, I think these two are the poorest.* . . .

There are other rumours to the effect that General Sickles has sworn to oust Halleck, and Governor Curtin has done the same as regards Secretary Stanton. Much ill feeling and some high words have doubtless passed between the parties; but such a thing is most too good to be true, for "when rogues fall out, honest men have their due," and these are not the days for anything so good as that. If these men have done any such swearing, the Secretary and Commander-in-Chief have two strong opponents who are not likely to stick at trifles in order to carry out their designs.

We are now required to make a daily report of men re-enlisting, by states; also of officers going and returning on leave; and a field return on the 4th, 14th, and 24th of the month, in addition to the regular trimonthly. General Meade is evidently anxious on account of so many men having left on furlough. Letters from home say that the streets are full of uniforms. . . .

JANUARY 14, THURSDAY. I have just got a curious report from Captain Cruttenden, my quartermaster, showing the number of horses drawn by each battery in the command since we left White Oak Church. The Fifth Maine, which started as a six-gun battery and was reduced to four guns, has drawn forty-nine horses; Cooper with four guns has drawn forty-five; while Reynolds with six guns has drawn but thirty-eight and Stewart only sixteen—a wonderful difference, showing how much depends on the care of its horses as to the efficiency of a battery.

Letters from New York speak of cold weather and good sleighing there as well as all over the country. I have opened a new correspondence with Mrs. Delano by which I hope to hear more of the city gossip. Her first letter tells me that they are taking hold of the proposed Sanitary Fair most energetically, the prospects being that it will prove a great success. Thorne writes me the particulars of the death of our old friend Rotch, who was carried off very suddenly by a return of the fever he got eighteen months ago when on the Peninsula as state agent. He is a terrible loss to his parents, and a very great one to his friends, all who knew him valuing him very highly. Our agricultural society, too, will miss him very much, for in many respects we have not his equal in the state.

General Hunt has gone off on a leave of absence. During the time he is

* Wainwright has already explained the grounds for his harsh judgment of the limp John Newton and blundering if not drunken W. H. French, heads of the First and Third Corps.

away, I am ordered to take his place at headquarters, in addition to my other duties. I cannot say that I rejoice in the privilege of thus signing myself Chief of Artillery of the Army of the Potomac; "le feu ne vaut pas le chandelle." I have enough to do here without riding four miles to Brandy Station every day through these bad roads; to say nothing of leaving my own bed and the contents of all those boxes behind me if I stay over night. . . .

JANUARY 17, SUNDAY. Being Sunday when no business is done at Army Headquarters, I am staying at home today, and trying to make it appear different from other days. In the first place, I went to church in the village, where I heard one of the chaplains preach a very poor sermon fifty minutes long; not a good way to induce men to attend. My other effort was more successful, being a Sunday dinner. On Friday still another box arrived from New York or I might properly say from The Meadows, for its contents consisted of long strings of sausages, pots of head-cheese, and a three-gallon can of okra soup. By looking after them myself and a constant blowing up I have managed to get "Ben" and "John" into something better than they were. "Ben" too is helped in his cooking by a great tin oven which Beraign sent me in place of a Dutch *bake* oven I ordered; this the darky pronounces to be "the goodest thing to bake in he ever se'ed"—roast is a word unknown in his vocabulary. Dr. Heard dined with us in honour of the extra spread, which consisted of soup, turkey, potatoes, and beets; then broiled quail; finishing off with nuts, dried fruit, cake, and candy. Backed by the sherry, which we drank out of tumblers in the absence of wine glasses, it made a very respectable feed for camp.

I manage to get through my triple duties as colonel of my regiment, commander of a brigade and chief of artillery of this army tolerably well, as fortunately there is not very much to do in either sphere just now. . . . I know but few of the officers at Army Headquarters well. Dr. Letterman, who has proved himself such a capable surgeon-in-chief, has been relieved, a Dr. McParlin taking his place. Letterman was married not long ago, and I suppose wants to get home post where he may enjoy more of the company of his bride.* . . .

JANUARY 19, TUESDAY. We have no more news as to corps consolidation; that is, nothing more decisive than the first report. Burnside has permission to raise his corps to 40,000 men. He is working for it in the different states himself very hard, and with good success, as I learn through the Talbots. They are to rendezvous at Annapolis and are probably meant for some expedition south so soon as spring opens. It is astonishing how a man who has shown himself so utterly unfit manages

---

* Dr. Jonathan Letterman, organizer of the medical field service in the Northern army, had married Mary Lee of Maryland in October 1863.

to continue getting independent commands. Hancock, who is just re-covering from the wound he received at Gettysburg, is also trying to raise his corps to a like number. He has entire sway in Pennsylvania, that being his own state and he hand and glove with the Governor. . . .

After four weeks of hard work my batteries have now about got their camps finished. The palm lays between Stewart and Reynolds, both of whom have tried their best: they are different in every respect. Stewart's huts are beautiful, all the same size, and near five feet high to the eaves; they are in two rows facing inward, the first sergeant's and office tent being at the foot of the street so that he can see the door of every tent from it; the street is about twenty-five feet wide, with a three-foot corduroy sidewalk all around it. His stable has the advantage over all the others of a board roof; the horses face inward and the sides are closed by split logs pinned into the uprights. Reynolds's huts are quite uniform in size, but they are too low; the chimneys are not all on the same side, nor do they all open into the street, which he has made more than double the width necessary. This he did so as to form his company in the street for parade. I tell him it will greatly increase the labour of keeping his camp in order. Reynold's stable is something unique, being the half of a hollow square, with his carriages parked in the centre. The ground was particularly well fitted for him to carry out this idea, which of a fine, dry sunny day will be very showy. The inner side of the stables is open: the other is closed with split logs set upright. Roof and floor are made in the same way, with not a nail in the whole thing. Mink has arranged his huts like Stewart's, only they are altogether too low, and he finds his ground rather wet. His stable, too, is planned the same, only instead of logging up close he has set up an eight-foot-high brush fence all around, and some five feet off, which I think is better as it will give more air while it is quite as much protection against the wind. Stevens has built very elaborate huts, quite equal to Stewart's, in one row, facing south, just under the lee of his clump of pines. . . .

JANUARY 28, THURSDAY. Last Friday I got out my order for drills and other duties. . . . I do not prescribe the exact time, nor the hours they are to give; only warn them that if any fail to work hard I shall do so. I require recitations in tactics and regulations three evenings in the week, and drill at least two or three hours each day: when the ground will allow of it, all else is to give place to the battery drill. Attention is also particularly called to the care of their horses. I hope to turn out a pretty good command by spring, if we lay quiet as long as I think we are likely to. . . .

JANUARY 31, SUNDAY. The convalescent camp at Alexandria has been broken up, and the ground and buildings taken for a camp of distribu-tion. My first instalment of recruits is there now. . . . New York, I hear, is all alive with returning regiments, and squads of recruits marching off.* I hope to be there before this day week. My return of re-enlisted men today shows 117; it is about done in my command. Have I mentioned that my surgeon, little Dr. Mosser, left me a month ago? He was really a loss as he filled his place admirably, giving perfect satisfaction to everybody. He was only a contract surgeon, and has gone home to Pennsylvania on invitation of his old master, who offers him a partnership with half the profits. As the practise is said to be worth three or four thousand a year, this is quite an inducement to a young man just beginning life. . . .

I am really without anything to enter today; have not been so hard pushed for material since last winter. The officers of the Third Corps gave a grand ball last week; an immense ball room was put up; supper brought down from Washington, and so on. It is said to have been a great success. I did not receive an invitation so was not there. There are lots of women in the army now.†

CULPEPER COURT HOUSE, FEBRUARY 4, THURSDAY. On Tuesday I sent up an application to be ordered on recruiting service for twenty days in order that I might look after my party, and took the application up to General Williams himself, who kindly spoke to Sedgwick about it while I was still there. General Sedgwick said that it would have to go up to Washington, but that he would approve it; so Williams recommended me to get a ten-days' leave meantime, as I wanted to get off at once. This General Newton has given me, and I start tomorrow. . . .

On the first of the month the President ordered a draft for 500,000 men to be made on the first of March if the quotas are not filled before that time. This is an increase on his original call, and will give my party a better chance, as some of the districts had nearly filled their quotas on the first call.**

* Up to January 2, 1864, more than 16,000 veterans of the Army of the Potomac had re-enlisted, a figure much larger than had been anticipated. Meanwhile, the reappearance of veteran regiments on furlough in their home communities had a great effect in the stimulation of recruiting. Ranks sometimes filled up as if by magic. The Tenth New York Cavalry enlisted 250 men during its furlough period.

† The army was so full of women, in fact, that according to *Harper's Weekly* of February 20, 1864, General Sedgwick's order a fortnight earlier for a reconnaissance had found nearly a thousand wives of officers and men in camp. The General Williams mentioned below is of course Seth Williams of the regular army.

** President Lincoln had issued a call on October 17, 1863, for 300,000 volunteers "for the various companies and regiments in the field from their respective states." New calls were now issued. By various means the strength of the Army of the Potomac was raised by the end of April 1864, according to its official reports, to 99,438 officers and men "present for duty equipped." But the character of the new recruits often left much to be desired.

I have been a good deal troubled about court-martialing some of my men. Formerly I could hold a garrison court, and General Reynolds used to order my grievous cases before some of the division courts. Now all regimental and garrison courts are done away with; the field officers of each regiment present are to constitute a court for the trial of such cases in their own rights as formerly came before these courts. But I have no field officers of any of the regiments to which my batteries belong, except "L" and "H," and so I cannot hold such courts. . . .

NEW YORK, FEBRUARY 16, TUESDAY. Left camp on the fifth and reached here the next day, to find all well. Last week I went up to Albany for a couple of days to attend the annual meeting of our State Agricultural Society, where I met many old friends and had a good time. . . . From there I went home to The Meadows, where I stopped until yesterday, driving down to thank Mr. Kelley for all his kindness.

At Albany I saw Governor Seymour, hoping to get part of some 800 unassigned recruits which are at his disposal. But he would only give them to me on condition of my taking a certain number of civilians with them as officers, which I would not do. These men had been raised for new companies, but those raising them not having procured enough to be accepted, the men were surplus. Some of those who raised them, the Governor felt, ought to have commissions with the men. There are several new regiments of heavy artillery raising, as also two extra companies for those infantry regiments which have been turned into heavy artillery. There is a great rush of the recruits to get into these regiments, as they are promised to have nothing but garrison duty to do. Some of the new ones I learn are 2,000 strong. . . . The Governor was very polite to me. . . .

Under the present system of getting recruits none of the men can appear on the returns as enlisted by my party. In each Congressional district there is a provost-marshal appointed from Washington, as also the examining surgeon. With them rests entirely the receiving and mustering of the men. The recruits are picked up by agents or brokers, who receive $10 to $20 for each man they bring up. These agents are of course men of that kind who are best at such work; great gab and small conscience. Should an officer try to enlist men they would all be down upon him as interfering with their business. All my party can do is to try and secure for the regiment the men who are enlisted by these agents. Mr. Pudney at Poughkeepsie is one of these brokers; and, so far as I could learn, an honest one; he is no doubt indebted in some way to Mr. Kelley for past favours and so only too glad to do as he requests now. Davis spends his time in Mr. Pudney's office, and tells me he has found him perfectly fair, and quite gentlemanly.

Provost-marshals are most of them politicians. Platt of the Pough-

keepsie *Eagle* holds the position in our district, and according to Mr.
Pudney's account is proving himself a great rascal. He has accepted
scores of men as volunteers whom he rejected on the draft three months
ago as over-age or physically exempt; many of whom, Pudney says, will
not be able to stand a week's service. Then he retains his recruits at
Poughkeepsie as long as he can before sending them to the depots, as he
gets so much for their rations and quarters, which of course he makes as
poor as possible. He has a large empty warehouse where they are crowded
together in a condition little better than the "Libby." Pudney told me
that he went there the other day to see one of his recruits who was sick:
he found him lying on a little straw on the floor, in a crowded room, for
there was no provision to separate the sick from the others. When he returned home he found his arms covered with lice from the sick man's
body!—and this man was a very respectable, well-to-do man before he
enlisted. Such treatment will cause the loss of a great many men by sickness and death; still more by desertion. Nor can one blame a decent man
who is driven to deserting from being shut up in such close companionship with the lowest dregs of society. . . .

FEBRUARY 26, FRIDAY.   I shall leave for camp tomorrow, though my time
is not quite up yet; but I begin to feel anxious to get back and look after
the condition of my command, as well as to attend to the assignment of
the recruits in my regiment, as they ought to begin arriving by this
time. . . . I now feel pretty confident that we shall start the spring
campaign with all the batteries full to the maximum.

I went to Albany again last week to report to Colonel Townsend, but
did not see him, and thanks to the loose way of doing business there,
was allowed to do what I chose with myself; so I have since then been
taking my ease here in the city, enjoying the hospitality of my friends.
When in Albany I saw Captain Stocking with his company on their way
back to camp. A number of his recruits have deserted. The rest were a
fine-looking lot of men. . . . Davis has exhausted Dutchess County and
moved over to Kingston to see what he can do in Ulster. Winslow writes
me that now they have got the bounties settled he expects to do well;
but that the great press is for the heavy artillery regiments, which have
more offering than they can take, as by going into these regiments the
men expect to avoid all marches and battles. . . .*

This city is all alive with recruiting. The agents have booths in the
park, and offices everywhere; from all that one sees in the newspapers
and hears everywhere the greater part of them must be the biggest sort
of rascals. Not content with the fee they are entitled to, they try to cheat
the recruit out of a large part of his bounty, and often succeed in

* Captain George B. Winslow, of the First New York Light Artillery, was soon to be
wounded in the battle of The Wilderness.

pocketing from a half to three-quarters of it. The provost-marshals are but little better as a general thing, conniving at if not taking part in the rascality. My little friend Theodore Bronson has shown a real devotion to his country in taking the place of provost-marshal, and attending closely to his duties. He can do quite as much good in this way as by going into the field, and I think deserves infinitely more credit. General Hays told me Theodore was the only honest man he had in that position. I have spent a part of several mornings in his office, seeing how the thing was managed, but he does comparatively little business; eight or ten men a day, for the brokers hate him, as he will not allow any but first-class men to pass and insists upon explaining to each recruit just how much bounty he is entitled to and paying it into the recruit's own hand. He has also caused the arrest of two or three of the most notorious rascals among the brokers.

He told me a number of capital stories of his dealings with these fellows; one of a great six-foot fellow who swore he would have the bounty money of one of his recruits, and threatened to take it by force, but was quieted by the sight of a big revolver in the hands of the little marshal. It must have been an amusing sight, the great hulking "rough" cowed by five feet of gentleman, but the little rascal always had lots of pluck. Another fellow who had given him an infinitude of trouble and had twice been released by one of our judges after being arrested, he at last found was himself a deserter, and has got him safe on Governor's Island this time; where he declares the man shall be shot, if there is any military law in the land. . . .

From the army they write me that everything is quiet and going on smoothly. The very day I left they were stirred up by orders to move the next morning. It only amounted to turning them out of their huts for a few days, and making a demonstration to keep Lee quiet while Butler captured Richmond. Butler's expedition marched up to Bottom's Bridge and back without firing a shot. Their army lost about 250 men in occupying Lee; "taking off his intentions," as my old Scotch herdsman used to say. "Why don't the Army of the Potomac do something?"! . . .

Society here is all agog about the great fair for the Sanitary Commission which is to open right after Easter. The fair itself is to be the greatest thing of the kind got up anywhere in the world; donations of articles to be sold are coming in not only from the city, but from all parts of the country and even from Europe. Nor are the articles to be sold confined to the fancy things usually offered at fairs, but are to include all sorts of useful things; so that one can almost furnish a house there, while our country cousins who make their spring visit to the city will be expected to do all their shopping within its limits. Not content with all this, the gentlemen's committee are soliciting subscriptions in cash to the funds of the fair. A. T. Stewart led off with $10,000, and every day the papers publish long lists of the donors of hundreds and thousands. In this way they have already raised several hundred thousand dollars, while the most sanguine begin to talk of a total of one million (!) being the result of the effort. I cannot fully sympathize with all this enthusiasm for the commission, nor do I believe that they can use properly so large an amount. But the moral effect of such liberality is excellent, not only by opening the hearts of the donors, but as exhibiting to the world at large that the people at home are heart and soul with the army (provided you will let them shew it in their own way). I would give a good deal to be here during one week of the fair, to see the thing: doubtless everyone who does see it will have to give a good deal.

❊ ❊ ❊

Wainwright's visit home had enabled him to see old friends in the metropolis; he mentions the Tallmadges, the Bronsons, and the Delanos. The city, full of soldiers on furlough and recruiting officers, was still more than 3,000 men short of its quota under the recent calls, and anxious to reduce that figure before a new draft began on March 10. Small-scale army movements were being reported from various fronts, and were not always successful. A Union column under General David S. Stanley, which penetrated within three miles of Dalton, Georgia, late in February, found the Confederates so strong that it had to retreat. And at Olustee in Florida on February 20 a force commanded by General Truman Seymour was defeated with heavy loss, nearly 1,900 men out of 5,100.

Everybody in New York, as Wainwright says, was talking about the Metropolitan Fair that was to open on April 4 for the benefit of the Sanitary Commission, and its great buildings on Union Square and Fourteenth Street were being filled with exhibits. General John A. Dix was president of the fair, and the Rev. Henry W. Bellows was president of the Sanitary Commission; but the planning and administration were chiefly in the hands of a Ladies' Committee that exhibited remarkable acumen and energy. They had arranged many features of interest for the crowds that attended, sometimes 12,000 or 14,000 people in a single day. An International Department represented all the principal nations of the earth; an Arms and Trophies Department and an Indian Department housed exhibits that interested everybody; a picture gallery presented many of the best paintings thus far collected by Americans; and a Knickerbocker Kitchen lent a quaint touch.

The United States Sanitary Commission, despite what Wainwright says in disparagement, had done an indispensable work for the care of the wounded and sick of the Northern armies. It was able to assert this spring that it had collected some $2,000,000 in cash subscriptions, and $9,000,000 or $10,000,000 in goods, and that by its own efforts, and the improved standards it helped to impose on the surgeon general's department, it had greatly reduced the mortality in the armies East and West. It cared for the wounded, recruited nurses and expert physicians and surgeons, saw to it that the camps observed proper sanitary rules, bettered the diet of the soldiers, kept a directory of the inmates of army hospitals, and maintained a home in Washington and transient lodges elsewhere for invalided members of the armed services. In short, it performed a multiplicity of tasks that the government was too busy, clumsy, or negligent to execute. But conservative men like Wainwright long looked upon it as a "fifth wheel to the coach."

* * *

CULPEPER COURT HOUSE, FEBRUARY 29, MONDAY. Got back all right this afternoon. Never before have my camp quarters appeared so comfortless on my return from a leave. It must be owing to my having been away so long this time, so that I fell into the bad habits of cleanliness and comfort. I remember the first night I spent in a bed after several months of camp life, I could not sleep, the sheets felt so queer: but this has not been the case since. I have gone back to the comforts of home on each leave as if I had not been deprived of them for half a year; only it has required a few days for me to get used to the close houses. Here I find my room dirty from the court martial having sat in it, and the mess absolutely cookless. The first trouble I shall have rectified tomorrow by a thorough scrubbing; the other I do not know how to mend. . . .

MARCH 3, THURSDAY. When I reached here I found the whole army under orders to be ready to move at short notice; from which state we were relieved today. The cause of this was an attempt to release the prisoners on Belle Isle near Richmond. I know not with whom the plan originated, but learn that General Meade has great confidence in its success, his scouts having reported that there are almost no troops around Richmond, and the prisoners are but slightly guarded. On Saturday, the Sixth Corps was moved to Madison Court House and Custer's brigade of cavalry sent on a secondary raid around Lee's left. Meantime Kilpatrick with some 3,000 cavalry crossed at Ely's Ford, and was to push with all speed direct for Richmond. The last heard of him was at the railroad near the South Anna Sunday afternoon: our next news will probably be by way of Fortress Monroe, unless we get it through the

Richmond papers. Having so good a start, they run but little risk with this fine weather and good road unless Kilpatrick attempts something rash. He has just lost his wife and only child, and they say he is gloomy and desperate; just in the state to try something wild. . . .

There is nothing more known on the subject of consolidation, though it is still believed to be probable. General Newton, I learn, has not been confirmed as a major-general. If this is so, the First Corps will doubtless have a new commander even if no consolidation takes place. I trust that we shall get a man with more snap, and that will attend to his business. General Barry is to go out as chief of artilley of Grant's command, he having no officer with him in that capacity at present; General A. P. Howe succeeds him in Washington as inspector general of artillery. I am sorry to lose Barry from Washington as he could often be of service to me, and was always willing to do what he could for me (if it did not cost him anything).* However, I ought not to say anything against him, for he has always been a good friend of mine; but then knowing his weak points, I have been careful not to run against them. He will have to do a great deal more before I can forgive him his treatment of Bailey. . . .

I have McClellan's official report, but have not found time as yet to more than glance at it. It evidently is not written for the popular eye, being a dry statement of facts, presented in the most military manner without any dressing up whatever. . . .

MARCH 6, SUNDAY. Kilpatrick has reached Yorktown, but Jefferson Davis still sits enthroned in Richmond, and our prisoners still suffer on Belle Isle. The whole thing has been a failure; resulting, so far as we yet know, in nothing but the burning of one or two railroad bridges, and the pretty thorough using up of most of the 3,000 horses. That is, if Dahlgren gets in safely: he was detached with 500 men and sent to cross the James above Richmond, but has not since been heard of.† These raids have never amounted to anything on either side beyond a scare, and proving

---

* William F. Barry, so prominent in the history of the artillery—he had advised Mc-Clellan to organize an overwhelming force of guns—had held an important staff position in the War Department since September 1862.

† Ulric Dahlgren, son of the admiral and ordnance inventor John A. Dahlgren, had lost a leg while on Meade's staff at Gettysburg, but had returned to service. He commanded part of Kilpatrick's brigade on its raid to Richmond, was led astray by a treasonable guide, and betrayed into an ambuscade, where many of his men were killed, wounded, or captured. "The guide," writes Regis de Trobriand in his memoirs, "was hanged to a tree with a stout rope; but the death of that wretch did not restore to life the young colonel, whose body lay among the dead." Among the papers allegedly taken from his pockets were documents instructing his troops to kill Jefferson Davis and his cabinet members. Whether the papers as printed were forged or authentic has long been a matter of dispute.

that once in within the enemy's line a good body of cavalry can travel either country with perfect freedom for a long time. When Jeb Stuart first went around McClellan's army at the Peninsula it was something new, and as it was not known how easily such feats could be performed, he deserved some considerable credit for it: the moral effect, too, amounted to something then. Now it is known that any sharp fellow acquainted with the roads could make the circuit of either army with 100 men, but he would cause very little scare and do very little harm. General Sherman has been trying a raid too out West, but on a very much larger scale; still, he does not seem to have accomplished any more than Kilpatrick. These raids make a big noise in the papers, and so glorify their commander; who is generally a man of that kind who court newspaper renown.

I understand that the army has been quite gay during my absence. The Third Corps ball was followed by one in the Second, to which many ladies from Washington came down; Barry brought his two daughters, who stopped with Mrs. Webb. I must go over, and call on Madame some day soon. General Rice, commanding our First Division, has had a bevy of girls at his headquarters, a private theatre and what not.* Heard says he was over there once or twice, and tells a good story of his mother when giving her name to a shop girl in Baltimore being asked if she was any relation to Dr. Heard of the First Corps, who the shop girl said she knew very well, having met him during her visit to General Rice, in the army. Imagine Mamma's disgust, she having just social standing enough to feel such a thing. . . .

We are existing without cook or waiter; that is all. Now my groom says he wants to leave. I am getting desperate, and shall turn pig, like the rest of mankind. General Newton still has his wife with him. Stewart and Reynolds have brought theirs down, too; the latter is exceedingly pretty and ladylike in appearance. The New York *Times* says that General Meade has been summoned to Washington to answer charges brought against him before the Committee on the Conduct of the War about Gettysburg, by Sickles and Doubleday. A pretty team!—Rascality and Stupidity. I wonder which hatches the most monstrous chicken. The weather continues fine; so that my batteries are having a good spell of drilling. Reynolds's park and stables look beautifully now that he has them all finished and his carriages painted up. His men are great on base-

---

* James Clay Rice, a Massachusetts man and graduate of Yale who was practicing law in New York when the war began, struggled up from first lieutenant in the Thirty-ninth New York to become division commander. Later this year he was to fight in the Wilderness, and to be killed near Spotsylvania Court House. The army had no more daring officer.

ball and have a lovely ground for it in front of the stables. Here too he
exercises his horses every day that he cannot have a battery drill. . . .

* * *

Wainwright is gentler in dealing with the raid by Kilpatrick's cavalry
division than Colonel Theodore Lyman was in the letters later collected
under the title *Meade's Headquarters*. Lyman, a Massachusetts man who
had gone on Meade's staff the previous September, wrote on March 5:
"Behold my prophecy on Kill-cavalry's raid fulfilled. I have heard many
persons very indignant with him. They said he went to the President and
pressed his plan; told Pleasonton he would not come back alive if he didn't
succeed; that he is a frothy braggart, without brains and not overstocked
with desire to die on the field; and that he gets all his reputation by newspapers and political influence. These charges are not new and I fancy
Kilpatrick has rather dished himself. It is painful to think of those poor
prisoners hearing the sound of his guns and hoping a rescue was at hand.
Now all that cavalry must be carried back in steamers, like a parcel of old
women going to market!" It was true that Kilpatrick had made lavish
promises to persuade Stanton to authorize his wild dash, in which he lost
340 men, killed or ruined well over a thousand horses, and left behind him
a large quantity of small arms. But Kilpatrick, though a stormy contro-
versial figure to the last, rose to be major general.

The gravamen of the charges by Sickles and Doubleday against Meade
before the Committee on the Conduct of the War was that he made and
promulgated an order to the army at the close of the first day's fighting at
Gettysburg to retreat from the positions then held; and that on the forenoon
of the second day's battle he gave another order to withdraw. The two
generals also asserted that Meade made no battle dispositions and formed
no battle plan; and that at the close of the third day's battle he was either
ignorant of the fact that the Union army had defeated Lee, or so uncertain
of the fact, that although abundantly able to make immediate pursuit and
crush Lee's columns, he refused to use his fresh and effective reserves and
allowed the enemy to escape. These charges precipitated a bitter controversy. Meade gave his own testimony before the committee on March 5,
utterly denying the statements of his opponents. Historians have rejected
the statements of Sickles and Doubleday that Meade wished to break off
the battle on the evening of the first day or the morning of the second. "I
utterly deny," said Meade, "ever having intended or thought, for one instant, to withdraw that army. . . ." Sedgwick, Hancock, Howard, Gibbon,

Warren, and Hunt all supported their commander. The failure of Meade to pursue Lee with instant vigor, however, remains a moot issue.

❊ ❊ ❊

MARCH 10, THURSDAY. Today we have a real pouring rain, such an one as we have not had before for a long while. I trust that now the time for active operations approaches we are not going to make up for the long spell of fine weather we have enjoyed by an equally long one of bad. Starting before daylight and marching halfway through the night, to say nothing of fighting, is bad enough under every advantage: but when you add cold rains and mud thereto, it becomes almost intolerable. I do not, however, expect an early opening of the campaign on our part, for so far as I can learn, we have not now over 60,000 men present in this army. A large number of re-enlisted men, including many of my own, have only just received their veteran furlough, and consequently will not be back before the middle of April. Of those who went off in January a number have been very late in getting back, and some have not returned at all. The regiments that went home as organizations are returning; I do not hear of any of them having been able to fill up to the maximum. Colonel Bragg of the Sixth Wisconsin told me he was about 600 strong.*

The newspapers say that we have from 200,000 to 250,000 more men in service now than at the same time last year. Where are they? I am sure that I cannot imagine, unless they are in the heavy artillery regiments around Washington and in the depots. Why don't they send the men to the army? Surely there can be no good reason for keeping them more than ten days or a fortnight at the depots. If they would only remember how necessary drill is to these new men, and how much their health depends on their learning how to take care of themselves in camp, before they start on active service; as well as their efficiency there, on their acquiring now some knowledge of what they have to do. Squads of a hundred recruits, or so, arrive every few days for this corps; but they ought to average a thousand a week to give the regiments here their proportion of the men said to have been raised. Some of them are terribly hard-looking chaps; regular "bounty jumpers"; who never intended to come into the field. Others are of a superior class and mean to do their best.

I met a most amusing incident with one of these last, belonging to the Fourteenth Brooklyn, the other day, as I was walking through the streets

* Edward S. Bragg, who had entered the war as captain of the Sixth Wisconsin, was now a colonel and would shortly be promoted a brigadier general; he fought effectively in all the campaigns of the Army of the Potomac after Malvern Hill. After the war he was to play a prominent role in the Democratic party.

of Culpeper. He had been placed as a sentinel there only three days after arriving, and of course without having received any instruction. I had just passed him when he called out "Halt! Halt! I say, you there, halt!" Turning around, I said to him pretty sharply: "Is that the way you speak to an officer?" His reply, "That's just it; you be an officer, be'nt you?" shewed me at once how green the fellow was, so I quickly informed him that I was. "Well," says he, "they told me I was to salute all officers when they went by, and I want you to show me how." The man was so honest and simple in his desire to do what was right that I really pitied him. But as I could hardly be expected to give him his first lesson in the manual of arms then and there, I advised him to apply to the first sergeant of his company so soon as he was relieved.

I have Major Fitzhugh's report up to the end of February complete, by which it appears that the recruiting party had secured 274 men up to that date; 31 were reported to him as mustered between then and the 6th inst. He had been down to Elmira, but does not seem to have got any accurate information there; the men, they told him, had been forwarded to Fort Schuyler. He says that he has official information of 404 men mustered into the regiment, and estimates that by the 20th of March 650 men will be enlisted for it altogether, but he fears large losses from desertion. The question has been up in New York as to allowing soldiers from the state to vote, and has been decided in the affirmative. Mr. Lincoln telegraphed the news down himself! I suppose he thought to make himself popular by so doing, and perhaps he will; but for myself I think it would be more becoming the dignity of the President to telegraph his thanks after a victory than such small news. I am sorry the thing has been so decided, as it will open a door for political discussion and influence which may be very damaging to discipline. A soldier's business is to obey; he forms a part of the executive, not of the legislative force in the country.

Most amusing stories are told of the number of re-enlisted men who have been married while on their thirty-five-day furlough. In some companies a third and even a half have been spliced while away. Some four or five hundred dollars cash in hand set the girls wild after the men, so that it was hard work to get clear of them. The most steady got married; the others let the women have it without marrying. My copy of the *Herald* the last week has been like a daily edition of *Punch* to me. Each number has had some very clever articles on the negro regiment which the Union League in New York have been getting up; and each night as I read them I have roared with laughter. The hits on ex-Governor King,* "the pink of propriety" and "flower of aristocracy," were capital.

* John A. King, who had been elected governor of New York on the Republican ticket in 1856, was a lifelong opponent of the expansion of slavery, and while in Congress

As it has been decided to employ niggers as soldiers, do it by all means; but why make more fuss over them than if they were white? No regiment leaving New York since the spring of 1861 has had half such an ovation. Really respectable ladies presented the colours, and threw bouquets to great buck niggers. William saw the regiment marching down Broadway, and says that had they been white men under the same length of drill, they would have been thought to march badly; being black, the *Times* and *Tribune* say they surpassed the Seventh. For my part, I wish all the negroes in the country were safely back in Africa.*

It is now certain that Grant is to have the new post of lieutenant-general, just created by act of Congress. This marks him officially as our major-general "most distinguished for courage, skill, and ability." I trust that he may prove himself so, and not only that, but equal in all respects to the greatest generals of history. But it is hard for those who knew him when formerly in the army to believe that he is a great man; then he was only distinguished for the mediocrity of his mind, his great good nature, and his insatiable love of whiskey. He will doubtless now be placed in supreme control of all the armies; and as the radicals must see that they have nothing more to gain by prolonging the war, we shall probably have matters pushed with great energy the coming campaign.

We are all agog now with regard to consolidation; the order carrying it out was expected today for certain. The division generals and all staff officers are shaking in their shoes for fear that they will be dropped from their present high estate. It is certain that this and the Third Corps will be sunk, but whether they will be absorbed bodily or broken into fragments is not known. My good friend Dr. Heard will certainly lose his position as he is junior corps medical director in the army. I shall be sorry to be separated from him, but there is not another member of the corps staff who could not easily be improved upon. For myself, it is a mere choice of commanders. At present I lean towards Hancock and the Second Corps, though when the time comes I shall probably leave it to chance to decide for me. I intended riding up to see Hunt about it today, but the rain has prevented. . . .

Congress has again extended the time for paying the extra bounties to the first of April. All ladies are ordered home out of camp: the first step towards activity.

MARCH 13, SUNDAY. We are now having real March weather, at least as

had assailed the Fugitive Slave Act in bitter terms. He was a son of Rufus King, a member of the Constitutional Convention of 1787, and minister to Great Britain.
* The Twentieth United States, a regiment organized against the opposition of Governor Horatio Seymour, but with the strong support of the Union League Club and such citizens as William Cullen Bryant and Peter Cooper, acquitted itself well, and was followed by two more regiments of colored New Yorkers.

to changeableness; no two successive days being alike. Still, the spring is opening. What little grass there is about here begins to look green; the birds have commenced singing of a morning, while the frogs and tree toads keep it up all the night long.

I went up to Army Headquarters on Friday. There they told me that the consolidation question was at a standstill, and that now the chances seemed to be that it will not be carried out at all; so much opposition being brought to bear by the generals who would be deprived of commands—reduced from a corps to a division, or from division to a brigade. Could the present corps be filled up to 25,000 or 30,000 effective men, it would be wrong to sink their past history: but as they are now only some 10,000 or 15,000 strong, it is absurd to have such large staffs and such a multiplication of papers.

I also heard that there were strong rumours again that General Meade was to be relieved. There is no doubt of his unpopularity at Washington, but their great trouble is to find some one to take his place. "Baldy" Smith is most talked of. I know nothing of him except his laziness at the first Fredericksburg, and his insubordination on the "mud march."

General Grant spent Thursday night at Army Headquarters. He was called out West suddenly, but expects to be back in ten days. He said while here that the people of Alabama and Mississippi were in a much more subdued condition than the secessionists of Kentucky and Tennessee. Also that there really had been over 10,000 deserters from the rebel armies out there since the battle of Chickamauga. Supposing this to be all so, the rebellion must be pretty well put down out there. Indeed, they have never shown the pride and obstinacy at the West that has been displayed in the older Atlantic States. It is here that they will fight the longest, as they have by far the hardest. Everything has aimed on their part to retain Virginia—and what a noble history hers would have been had her cause only been a just one! I cannot help admiring the constancy of the "Old Dominion" in the midst of such suffering and desolation as has been totally unknown to any other part of the country. Her people have not only poured out their money and their blood without stint, but from this state have come all the greatest and best men; Lee, Sidney Johnston, and Stonewall Jackson will always figure as the greatest and purest generals on the rebel side in this war.* . . .

I have finished reading McClellan's report, and it has given me a higher opinion of him than I ever had before; I now think him about as near being a *great* general as it is possible to come without arriving at it.

* Wainwright's belief that Albert Sidney Johnston had been a Virginian was as gross a misconception as his notion that the fighting at Shiloh, Stones River, and Chickamauga was somehow less fierce than that at Antietam and Gettysburg. Johnston had been born in Kentucky and became a Texan.

Certainly none of our other generals have come nearly so near to it, so far as I am able to judge them. Nine-tenths of the report is made up of copies of orders received or issued, correspondence, and extracts of returns. He does not attempt to explain away any of the charges made against him or excuse any of his failures, but makes a plain statement of the facts as known to him at the time, and then tells what he did. The whole report shows a man confident in the purity of his intentions, and the perfect honesty of all his actions. On all the points in which he is so much blamed, his besieging Yorktown, taking the line of the Chickahominy, and others, the report tells me little that I had not heard before; but in getting the particulars on these points, I am more than ever convinced that where he was not right he had good reason for being wrong.

The kindly way in which he passes over entirely, or just mentions without calling attention to, the great failures of his subordinates to do their duty, as in the case of Sumner at Williamsburg, and Burnside at Antietam, speaks volumes for the man. In no single instance is there the least attempt to shift responsibility on the shoulders of his subordinates. Through the whole report runs a care and consideration for his men, an actual love for his army, which is most beautiful. No wonder we all loved him if there is any truth in the old proverb that "love begets love." Where in the midst of all that the army was enduring, he fairly pleads for a few words of praise from the President, "not for myself, but such as I can give to my officers and men," I could hardly help crying. And Lincoln would not give it.

It would be hard to say which is the most intolerably disgusting in the light they appear here by their dispatches: the obstinate conceit of the President in his own ideas of military matters, the petty spite of Halleck, or the rancorous hate of Stanton. When calm history comes to be written, Mr. Lincoln must appear as one of the smallest of men, ever harping on trifles. But enough of this; 'twould be treason were it known at Washington that I did not think them demigods.

The report, too, shows wherein lay McClellan's strength, and where his weakness. The former was undoubtedly in planning: in the vast scope of his mind, taking in the whole field of operations, and his foresight as to what the enemy would do. In all these he is really great. I cannot see how any man acquainted with military art and science can think otherwise. Had his dispositions for the protecting of the approaches to Washington been carried out (but they were not even begun), there would have been no Banks scurry down the Shenandoah Valley, neither would there have been any waste of men and matériel by Frémont's wild goose chase among the mountains. More confidently now than ever before I say that had McClellan been allowed to land 120,000 men at

Altoona, we should have been in Richmond before the 4th of July, and the close of 1862 would have seen the close of the war. But then, where would now be the great question of emancipation; where the firm status of the Republican Union (!) party; where all the glory that other generals have earned?* . . .

MARCH 17, THURSDAY. The rain still keeps off; every attempt it has made has come to nothing, and here we are close to the equinox. This has been the first spring when it was possible to begin operations early. Never were the roads finer or the weather better for marching, but never before' has the army been so unready; not through any fault of its own or its general commanding, but entirely through the fault of those at Washington. There are so many interests to consult, and the political bearing of every step has to be so carefully weighed, that we are now not so far on as we should have been two months ago. It was just as easy for Mr. Lincoln to know last October how many recruits would be needed this spring as it is now, yet here he is just out with another call for 200,000 men. Had these men been raised so that they could have been sent to the army by Christmas, and had we been ordered into winter quarters by the 1st of December, all our re-enlisted men would have had their furlough by this time and the recruits would have been drilled into some shape.

This new call will make 700,000 men this winter, a vast army of themselves; enough, it seems to me, to fill up every regiment in the service to its maximum. Where the new men are I cannot conceive, and have given up trying to imagine.† . . .

* McClellan had written Edward Everett on February 20, 1863, while compiling his *Report on the Organization of the Army of the Potomac, and Its Campaigns in Virginia and Maryland:* "It is much easier to conduct campaigns and fight battles than to write their history—at least I find it so." He finished the report in time to date it New York, August 4, 1863. A well-organized and lucidly written statement, incorporating a full array of letters and telegrams, it was issued early in 1864 as a government document. Later in 1864 Sheldon & Company of New York published it in a neat volume of 465 pages, for McClellan had added to the official report what he called "a simple narrative of the campaign in Western Virginia." Though some of it had an ex parte tone, as a whole it did the author credit. It was of course used for campaign purposes after the Democratic party nominated McClellan for President.

† Throughout the war it was impossible on both sides, but especially the Northern, to reconcile the great totals of enlistments with the slender totals of men present, armed, and ready for battle. But as Thomas A. Livermore states in *Numbers and Losses in the Civil War,* "to invade and hold a constantly increasing territory required many more troops than would have been needed in the Union army for actual fighting, and many Northern soldiers were employed in non-combatants' work." The Army of the Potomac, as we have seen, opened the spring campaign in 1864 with just about 100,000 effective troops. Ben Butler commanded the co-operating Army of the James, with more than 35,000 troops, a force that moved up the James early in May to disembark at Bermuda Hundred Neck below Richmond. More than 40,000 men were kept in and

The order is out assigning Lieutenant-General Grant to the command of the armies of the United States headquarters to be in Washington and in the field. With him Halleck is to be a sort of chief of staff at the Washington headquarters. Sherman takes Grant's late command of all the Western armies. Report says that Grant means to accompany his army in person. General Hunt sounds the first note of preparation, calling upon us to at once see that the batteries are fully supplied with all matériel; to increase the number of our horses to 116 and 88 for six and four-gun batteries respectively; and advising some target practise where suitable ground can be obtained. . . .

At last we have got a cook, a white man American; he only got here yesterday, so I cannot say certainly how he will do, but he seems clean, and must be better than no cook at all. I do not expect anything wonderful from him, and suspect he is merely a common eating-house cook. I have told him to look around and hire a contraband to help him and to wait on table; I want him to hire the boy so that he shall have control over him. We are to pay him $35 a month. . . .

I rode to General Rice's the other day; his nuns, as he called them, had all left him but two. I have also been over to Andy Webb's, but Mrs. Webb was absent in Washington. Webb is in command of a division in the Second Corps, which he has in beautiful order; their camps far exceed any others I have seen in this army—especially that of the Twentieth Massachusetts. Webb told me that he had only been outside the limits of his division twice this winter. He is down on Governor Curtin for his appointments in Pennsylvania regiments, and read me a very sharp letter he had just written the Governor. I look upon Webb as one of the most conscientious, hard-working and fearless young officers that we have.*

MARCH 20, SUNDAY. Nothing of note has happened the last three days: on Friday there was a great stir under reports that Lee was going to take the initiative this spring, and was actually moving to attack us. . . . We have a signal station on Poney Mountain now, the same as last autumn, from whence they command a sight of several of the rebel stations. Our

---

about Washington. Sherman's army for the Atlanta campaign on April 30, 1864, numbered 110,000 effectives. Large forces had to be disposed in Tennessee (the Union used about 50,000 men in fighting at Nashville late this year), in the Shenandoah Valley, in Florida, before Mobile, west of the Mississippi, and at other points. Still, the Northern use of manpower was highly inefficient, and experts like Provost Marshal James B. Fry agreed with Wainwright that an efficient draft, without use of bounties or substitute brokers, would be the best means of keeping the armies full.

* Alexander Stewart Webb, mentioned earlier in the diary, was barely twenty-five when the war began, and might still be called a young man when it ended. Young as he was, he became Meade's chief of staff. Colonel Theodore Lyman wrote of him in much like Wainwright's terms: "He is very jolly and pleasant, while, at the same time, he is a thorough soldier, wide-awake, quick, and attentive to detail."

officers claim that they can read all the rebel messages, and they are regularly transmitted to General Meade. The news of Jeb Stuart having started on some expedition may have come through them. I have been intending all winter to go up onto Poney Mountain but have not yet accomplished it.

Kilpatrick's men have most of them returned to camp; they crossed the Rappahannock down near its mouth, and came through without loss. Poor Dahlgren is killed. He had to let his men disperse into small bodies; nearly all of them got in safely, but he is said to have been betrayed by his negro guide, and murdered in cold blood. All who knew him regret his loss exceedingly. It is said that General Hancock is getting recruits rapidly in Pennsylvania, and that large numbers are arriving daily for his corps. Morgan, who is with him in Pennsylvania, writes that there is little doubt but what he will fill his corps up to 40,000. If so, it will affect the consolidation project materially; most likely cause it to be abandoned entirely. . . .

Rumour says that a house has been taken in Culpeper for General Grant, which is very probable, as in his first order assuming command of the armies of the United States he says: "Headquarters will be in the field, and until further orders will be with the Army of the Potomac." The last call for recruits says that they are for the "Army, Navy and Marine Corps." In regulating the quotas of districts, all men enlisted in the navy are to be allowed. At the present time, too, there are a large number of men being transferred from the army to the navy: I have lost two or three men in that way.

* * *

The efficiency of the Army of the Potomac was now promoted by the consolidation of its five corps into three, under the leadership of the ablest and best-experienced generals: Sedgwick, Hancock, and Warren. The ablest division commanders were kept. Burnside's corps was also recalled from the West, at first to co-operate with the Army of the Potomac and shortly to be incorporated in it. In addition, an efficient cavalry corps was brought under the command of General Philip H. Sheridan, who came from Tennessee at Grant's bidding. The main Eastern army was thus welded into a formidable body under tried leadership. It had the assistance of Ben Butler's auxiliary army, which had been collected in the area of Fort Monroe to ascend the James, and of Sigel's auxiliary command, some 18,000 men holding the Shenandoah Valley and threatening Lee's communications with the West.

Hitherto the Union armies in various parts of the country had moved with little or no co-ordination. "I determined to stop this," writes Grant. His general plan was to concentrate all the force possible against the two main Confederate armies, Lee's and Joseph E. Johnston's. "Accordingly I arranged for a simultaneous movement all along the line." When the spring season gave opportunity, George Crook was to advance in West Virginia, Sigel in the Shenandoah Valley, and Butler up the James, while Grant himself struck across the Rapidan. In the West, Sherman was simultaneously to move against Johnston, and Banks was to throw his forces against Mobile. The Confederacy would be ringed with a contracting circle of fire.

Naturally, in the general shift and progress Wainwright felt more acutely than ever the importance of a reorganization of the artillery arm and an improvement in its standing.

❋ ❋ ❋

MARCH 24, THURSDAY. The long agony is over: consolidation is—not accomplished, but a fixed fact. The order was issued from Washington yesterday, and from Army Headquarters today. Bye the by I see that it is "by order of the Secretary of War," not of General Grant, so he does not mean to fight on that ground, and quarrel with Mr. Stanton at the start. *The* order consolidates the First, Second, Fifth, and Sixth Corps into two divisions each; it then transfers the First Corps to the Fifth, the First and Second Divisions of the Third Corps to the Second, and the Third Division of the Third to the Sixth. This will give four divisions to the Second and Fifth Corps, and only three to the Sixth, but I presume will make them about equal in numbers; which does not look as if there was much truth in the reports of Hancock getting so many recruits. Hancock retains command of the Second Corps, and Sedgwick of the Sixth. The Fifth is to be under Major-General G. K. Warren. The orders call it a temporary consolidation, and allow the divisions formed of the old First and Second Corps to retain the badges. But temporary will no doubt be permanent; the consolidating into divisions and retaining old badges is merely a way to let them down easy, for the thing will no doubt cause a great deal of ill feeling in the First and Third Corps.

I am looked on as a sort of traitor here, for having always favoured consolidation, but I tell them that I belong to the Artillery Corps, and not to the First. A number of general officers are relieved from duty with this army: Corps Commanders Sykes, French, and Newton, and Brigade Commanders Kenly, Spinola, and Meredith. The first is the only one I should think any loss. The order says nothing about artillery save that Hunt will assign eight batteries to each of the three new corps; tomorrow I shall go up to see the General, get my own position fixed, and see what

I can do as to securing the batteries that I want. I still lean towards Hancock, knowing little of Warren; perhaps, too, I have a penchant for the Second Corps. But I may not have a choice, and under any circumstances shall be most influenced by what batteries I can get. . . .

General Grant arrived at Culpeper today, and Halleck is with him. We were ordered to be in readiness to turn out in rear of our camps for inspection by him, if so ordered; but no order came. From what I heard at corps headquarters this evening, there was no enthusiasm shown by the men on the arrival of their new commander. I have not seen the Lieutenant-General yet, but probably shall in the course of a few days. I expected and rather hoped that we should have a good specimen of Virginia mud to show him when he arrived, for there was four inches of snow fell on Tuesday, more than in all the rest of the winter put together; but it is going off rapidly without rain, and as there is no frost in the ground, the water will soon sink off. . . .

Many officers of the regular artillery have long been trying to get a reorganization of their arm of the service, doing away with the regiments and making a corps of it, the same as the engineers and ordnance. Mc-Clellan and Hunt drew up a plan soon after Antietam, which was then approved by Stanton and Halleck, but nothing more has been heard of it since. Their plan contemplated uniting the artillery and ordnance in one corps, also the pontoniers. I believe I gave an idea of it some time ago. This last winter Barry, Tidball, and others in Washington drew up a proposition, which has now been reported in the Senate by Wilson. It merely does away with the regiments; but does not increase the number of batteries or of field officers; still it is a step in the right direction. Anxious to help on so good a cause, as also to secure more field officers of artillery for this army, I have written a letter to Senator Morgan asking a like organization for the Volunteer Artillery. This I mean to take up to Hunt tomorrow and get him to give me a good letter backing my application. As it was neither brigade nor regimental business I have not entered a copy of my letter anywhere; and as the rough draft in pencil will not keep, shall transcribe it here.

"Hon. E. D. Morgan, U.S. Senate. Sir: Seeing by the newspapers that a bill has been introduced in the Senate reorganizing the artillery of the regular army, I take liberty of addressing you on the subject of the organization of the same arm in the volunteer service. I am induced to take this liberty from the fact that our State has furnished a very much larger number of light batteries to the army than any other; and from the great interest you always professed while Governor of New York, in the welfare of the regiment which I now have the honour to command, that raised by the lamented Colonel G. D. Bailey.

"The bill I refer to provides for the abolishing of the regimental organization of the artillery, and forming it into one corps, with a certain number of field officers, the battery being taken as the unit of organization. I believe that all our best light artillery officers agree that such a change is expedient. My own experience constantly reminds me of the absurdity of a regimental organization of light batteries, which must necessarily be so widely scattered that the commanding officer of the regiment can have no control over them whatever; while the very fact of their belonging to his regiment makes him to a certain extent responsible for their condition. . . . My object is to recommend that the proposed organization be adopted for the volunteer light batteries as well as for the regular artillery.

"The act of Congress prescribing the organization of volunteer light artillery simply states that it shall in all respects agree with the organization of the Fifth United States Artillery, the only regiment of light artillery, organized as such in the regular army. At this time there are from the states east of Ohio *three* regimental organizations of light artillery: one from Rhode Island of eight batteries; one from New York of twelve batteries, and one from Pennsylvania of eight batteries; while from the same states there must be in all about a hundred light batteries in service; thus, only providing thirteen field officers for this large command.

"Both General Barry and General Hunt while commanding the artillery of this army have frequently complained in their reports of the great want of field officers. Were the light batteries of each state organized into a corps, and provided with field officers in the proportion proposed in the bill referred to above, this want would be provided for. The officers of light batteries also have a claim demanding some such change. No class of officers in our volunteer service stand as high as those of our light batteries. I say without hesitation that they are very far superior as a class in all respects to the officers of the same rank in either the infantry or cavalry. Yet for them there is not at this time any chance for promotion above a simple captaincy, except in the few regiments spoken of. I can point to several cases of captains of light batteries who, from this want of field officers, have for a year past exercised all the authority and borne all the responsibilities of a brigadier-general.

"Individually I have nothing to gain by the proposed change, for I already hold the highest rank known in our artillery organization. . . .

"I have taken the liberty of submitting the above to Brigadier-General Hunt, Chief of Artillery of this Army; whose opinion on the subject is of more practical value probably than that of any other officer in the service. I beg to submit herewith a copy of his reply fully endorsing the proposed change." . . .

Morgan ought to take hold of this matter, but I do not know that he will, for he may not see anything to be made out of it. Hunt's letter, when I get it, I mean to keep; I am sure of his approval, for we have talked the matter over thoroughly. . . .

MARCH 27, SUNDAY. My position is now pretty well settled, and I shall hereafter sign myself as commanding the Artillery Brigade, Fifth Corps, though I have yet received no order assigning me there. General Hunt told me on Friday that Hancock had asked for Tidball as his chief of artillery, and that he was coming down with his regiment: this left me no choice. . . .

General Newton issued his farewell order on Friday, and Warren assumed command the same day; he has moved his headquarters to Culpeper, but I have not yet reported to him, being at present in a sort of independent state; my order I am expecting every hour. Warren has issued his order consolidating the old divisions. . . . Warren has commenced by ordering all the stray officers out of the village: quite a number had quartered themselves in houses there even among those whose commands lay at a distance. Dr. Heard goes to the Artillery Reserve.

When in Culpeper yesterday I got a sight of the new Lieutenant-General as he was poking around the house he has since moved into. He is not so hard-looking a man as his photographs make him out to be, but stumpy, unmilitary, slouchy, and Western-looking; very ordinary in fact. It rained on Friday heavily a good part of the day; since then it has been clear and drying. A new order as to inspecting gains us a small step in artillery: hereafter we are to get our horses through General Hunt, and not through the corps quartermaster. . . .

MARCH 31, THURSDAY. The order finally organizing the artillery brigades did not come out until yesterday: it assigns me to the Fifth Corps, and gives me the batteries I expected; so now I have to go to work and organize my trains and staff. From the waggons and teams in the two corps I ought to be able to get a very nice outfit. The changes in my staff are likely to be my losing my commissary, Cranford, whom I shall be sorry to have leave me; and my surgeon, Richmond, whom I shall not regret much. . . .

On Tuesday the corps, that is the old First, no other part of the present corps being about here, was turned out for review by General Grant. The ground about a mile south of the village along the railroad was quite good. Warren knew enough to put the artillery on the right of the line where it belonged; I had the six batteries here out, all looking quite well. When we arrived Warren was already on the ground to assign each command its position: he promises to be a very different man from Newton in this respect. General Warren is a small man, about thirty-five years old, dark complexioned, with black eyes, and long, straight black hair; he has a little of the look of an Indian, and evidently is of a nervous temperament. Just as General Grant came on the ground it commenced to rain; he rode along the line in a slouchy unobservant way, with his coat unbuttoned and setting anything but an example of military bearing to the troops. There was no enthusiasm, and as the rain increased, we were quickly dismissed without passing in review.

I have a most capital letter from Hunt, "heartily approving" mine to Morgan. In it he very truly says: "The *battery* is the unit of organization for artillery, corresponding to the *battalion* of infantry, and *squadron* of cavalry; two, three or more of which constitute a regiment for administration, but for purposes of combat, a brigade. So, six or eight batteries constitute a brigade of artillery; a command fully as important and extended and much more complicated than a brigade of infantry, and requiring from the ground it covers and its distribution a large staff." He also gives the organization of the British artillery, as he received it from Colonel Turner commanding our arm of the service in Canada at this time; and who was down here last week. "A brigade of eight six-gun batteries" (just the command I now have) "is commanded by a colonel with the army rank of *major-general*"; then there are "two colonels and four lieutenant-colonels, one of these last for every two batteries." How different is this from our organization! . . . In this army there will be when we start about 280 guns; with one brigadier-general, four colonels, and perhaps two or three lieutenant-colonels and majors: on the British footing we should have at least five major-generals, one for each corps and the reserve; a lieutenant-general probably as chief of artillery of the army; seven colonels and fourteen lieutenant-colonels.* . . .

CULPEPER COURT HOUSE, APRIL 3, SUNDAY. The rain which commenced during our review on Thursday continued until Friday night; so that we are now in the full enjoyment of all the mud which properly belongs to this season of the year here in Virginia as well as on the Hudson. Today we have a high wind and some little sunshine, for which I am particularly thankful as I want to go up the railroad tomorrow to look a little after my batteries there. . . .

General Grant, I believe, has gone off for a time. He kept himself quiet while here; was very little seen or even talked of so far as I can learn. All the newspaper reports about the immense enthusiasm for him are bosh; as well as the stories of his having forbidden sutlers in the army, his living himself on pork and beans, and such stuff. I should fear that they would ruin him as they did McClellan, by leading the people to expect too much of him, were it not that their ideas at home have come down

---

* After Burnside's arrival the Army of the Potomac, according to Naisawald's *Grape and Canister*, had about 100,000 men with 346 guns. Wainwright did not count Burnside's batteries.

very much within two years as to what a general can do; and there seems
to be a determination now to find no fault with Grant whether or no. . . .
APRIL 7, THURSDAY. After ten days of most disagreeable, wet, snowy,
cold weather, we at last have one of warm sunshine; more like what one
expects in this latitude for the month of April. But I have not found,
and I have been here now at the opening of three springs in succession,
that there is so vast a difference between Virginia and New York during
the first half of April. On Monday I went up to Bealton Station to look at
the batteries there; it was so very muddy, however, that I did not go
about much. . . .

There are now quite a large number of men in this army applying for
transfer to the navy under orders allowing all such to do so whose
former calling in life fits them for that service; seven men in Phillips's
battery "E," Massachusetts, have applied for such transfer. . . .

Judging from the newspapers, New York must have run wild on
Monday at the opening of their great Sanitary Fair. It was made a
general holiday; all the troops and what-not turned out, and flags
flaunted in every direction. Mary displayed all my regimental colours
in the window in Fourteenth Street.

APRIL 10, SUNDAY. The equinox which did not come when the sun
crossed the line, or something quite worthy of it, has been upon us for
two days. All day yesterday the rain fell much in the way it did in old
Noah's time, and had it continued as long as it did with him, we should
have all had to take refuge on the top of Poney Mountain. This morning
opened clear and bright, but the rain began again at three in the afternoon and promises to keep it up all night. Mountain Run is a river,
and the rivulet which rises close by me here, a broiling stream; while
every low spot has become a lake. We have news of the railroad bridge
at Cedar Run being carried away; and others have probably shared the
same fate. There was no mail in this afternoon and may not be for
several days to come.

This rain insures our remaining at peace for at least one week more,
even if present orders did not point to tomorrow week as the earliest
period Grant can have in view for a start. All sutlers and citizens are
ordered to quit the army by Saturday next; this is usually the first
premonitory symptom, just as the clearing out of all the sick who are
unable to march is the last one before actual orders. I have had a great
deal of comfort in my sutler this winter: not a complaint has reached me,
either of him from the men, or of any of the men from him. At General
Patrick's headquarters they speak of him as really an honest and trusty
man, most rare qualities in a sutler. He has kept us well supplied with
poultry and mutton through the winter; occasionally with game and fish,
several times of late bringing us shad. . . .

A War Department order assigns General Phil Sheridan to the command of the Cavalry Corps with this army; he has previously been at the West, in command of infantry. I know nothing more of him, but a change I think was needed; neither Pleasonton or Stoneman proved themselves equal to the position. The same order unites the Eleventh and Twelfth Corps in one, to be called the Twentieth, under General Hooker. I wonder how old "Joe" will like the come-down; they have dropped him very gradually, one step at a time, till he is now somewhere near his proper level. Howard is to have the Sixth Corps, another new consolidation; Slocum whatever Sherman chooses to give him.

General Warren interprets "extreme cases" in the question of leaves very strictly: "the dangerous illness or death of any relative will not hereafter be so considered." He thinks that if soldiers can die without their wives coming to them, the rule should work the other way also. The Ambulance Corps has this winter been regulated by act of Congress; the system adopted is pretty much that which we have had in this army for a year past. . . . My trimonthly yesterday shewed an aggregate of 1,785 officers and men, including the four temporarily attached batteries. . . .

I have a letter from Major Hall about the new organization of the volunteer artillery proposed in my letter to Senator Morgan, copies of which and General Hunt's I sent to him; he had shown it to Vice-President Hamlin, who had entered strongly into the subject and had promised to see Senator Wilson on the subject. Hall intended also to send copies to the Maine Senators, and is not only working in the matter, but is quite sanguine of success. He tells me that he has twenty-one batteries now under him with over 3,000 men. . . .

We are almost as much interested in the Sanitary Fair down here as they are in New York. The papers are almost spelled; I cannot say that I read the full account, but enough to give me some idea of it. I should judge that it never was equalled in its kind. The jam seems to be something fearful even now that they have put the price of admission up to a dollar. Tallmadge sends me a little paper published for it, called the "Spirit of the Fair," but it is rather a series of short literary articles than any account of their doings. The subscriptions for the army sword is the most exciting part of it for the army; the contest lies entirely between Grant and McClellan. . . .

As yet we get no intimations as to when or which way we start, but things do not look as if it would be any earlier than in previous years. The taking up of two hundred locomotives by government looks like a great sudden concentration of troops on some distant point; a tremendous re-enforcement of this army from the West or vice versa. For myself, I want until the end of next week before I shall be quite ready. This leaving everything until the last moment is detestable. There is no reason whatever why all the changes made in the last three weeks should not have been carried out three months ago, when things would have got into working order; officers would have known their commands and their commands them.

The fair in New York grows as a wonder every day; the crowd is so great that it is only by the hardest pushing one can get about. The sword votes are recorded daily in the papers like election returns; so many hundred for Grant, so many for McClellan—outside of these there is now no real competition. Each vote represents a dollar; some people put down a hundred at once for their favourite general. . . . A book of autographs presented by Mrs. McClellan brought $500. . . .

APRIL 17, SUNDAY. We have had another wet spell since Friday; yesterday it rained steadily. The spring is more backward and colder than it was at this time last year; much as in 1862. I trust we are not going to have a whole summer of rain as we had then. . . .

On Friday I got the order assigning the battery of heavy artillery to my command. They have had terribly bad weather to get their camp in order, which has come very hard on them as over half the men are recruits, and the rest have always been accustomed to garrison duty. The Fourth New York Heavy was originally commanded by a brother of General Doubleday, who I believe proved to be worthless; then de Russy was colonel and now Tidball; the two last ought to have made a good regiment of it. They look very much like rats drowned out of their holes as I pass the camp. . . .

APRIL 21, THURSDAY. Since Monday morning we have had fine, bright sunshine. The peach trees are in blossom, and the leaves of the earlier forest trees bursting out from the buds. Still the snow lies white along the ridge of the Blue Mountains, and the nights continue to be cold. . . .

My monthly return of yesterday shew an aggregate present of 1,611 . . . for the troops around here. We have two more warning notes of a start, viz: the shipment of the most sick today, and the regulation of supplies to be taken at the start and the means of carrying them. Three days full rations in havresacks, three small in knapsacks, and ten in waggons, or sixteen days supply in all. Ten days forage is to be taken. How absurd such orders are! What are the animals to do the last six days? Or are they to live on nothing? From the start they are cut off from their hay fourteen pounds, and the allowance of grain reduced two pounds, so that they may be said to be placed on half allowance. When will our commanders give up this penny-wise-and-pound-foolish plan? If their proposed operations require sixteen days' food for the men, they should require the same amount for the animals. . . .

APRIL 24, SUNDAY. Spring is upon us now, almost at a jump. The last three days have been fit for June; fires are abandoned and replaced by open doors and windows. Today the air is heavy with the moisture of a strong south wind, betokening rain. With the warm days have come clouds of rumours as to the spring campaign and all that is to be done. The newspapers are full of dark hints, principally meant to make the public believe that the editors and correspondents know more than other people; which is all bosh. Every officer returning from Washington brings down his pockets full; quartermasters, having more transportation than anyone else, bring the most and the biggest. But among them all I have yet to see the man bold enough to attempt predicting what the first move of this army will be. One report says that Burnside's corps has left Annapolis, in steamers for somewhere; another that Baldy Smith, of whom Grant is said to have the very highest opinion, is getting up a strong army on the Peninsula.* Common sense would say that these two were to make one command, to advance on Richmond from the James while we looked after Lee here; but then common sense has always been the rarest of the military qualities at Washington, and one cannot well imagine Burnside and Smith acting together after all the trouble they had at the time of and after the "mud march." . . .

I have figured out our transportation allowance, which is about as absurd as it well can be. I often wonder whether General Meade himself apportions the waggons or whether it is done by Ingalls; also, whether whoever draws up these orders has a special spite against artillery horses, or is utterly ignorant. The order allows one waggon to each battery for baggage, mess furniture, desks and the like, and three waggons for subsistence, and forage. Ten days' small stores and one day's meat for 140 men, about the average of my batteries, will with its forage take up one waggon (Captain Cruttenden says more), which leaves us two waggons to carry ten days' forage for 120 horses, or 6,000 pounds per waggon, beside the forage for its own teams! Five days' forage is all we can possibly manage, and then the loads will be very heavy at the start. As for loading five days' more on my artillery carriages, I can't and won't do it. Such absurdities as this take away all my pleasure and pride in my command. I wrote it all out for Hunt and sent it up to him. He replies in a most characteristic note, beginning: "The Jews of old were required to make brick without straw; anybody could do that if not responsible

---

* Grant had recommended General W. F. Smith for promotion to the rank of major general after Chattanooga, and was annoyed when confirmation was delayed. "I found a decided prejudice against his confirmation by a majority of the Senate," he writes in his memoirs, "but I insisted that his services had been such that he should be rewarded. My wishes were now reluctantly complied with, and I assigned him to the command of one of the corps under General Butler. I was not long in finding out that the objections to Smith's promotion were well founded."

for the quality of the bricks delivered. You lose one waggon and are required to increase the forage carried from seven days to ten. Now that
beats the Jews." Hunt is evidently discouraged, and beginning to give
up all hope of our ever getting what is right. . . .

APRIL 28, THURSDAY. We have got back one more waggon for each
battery, which gives us three for forage instead of two; still we ought to
have one more, for though I have taken eight from the ammunition train
to carry forage for the batteries in, we shall be loaded too heavily should
the roads be bad at the start, and will have to set out with some on the
carriages. One forage waggon is to march with each battery. I have
had all my train out for inspection. It looked very well: the mules are
good and in capital order, the waggons all newly painted, and new
covers marked with cross cannon and the corps badge.

My train now comprises 103 army waggons and eleven ambulances,
and 781 horses and mules; the grand total of carriages of all sorts is 225,
which when on the march, allowing fifteen yards to each, will cover just
about two miles of road. Hunt writes me that the howl with regard to
their losing one waggon per battery was universal, and thinks that with a
little practise, so that we should "howl in unison," we might really be
able to accomplish something. There is just where the trouble has lain;
several, I think most, of the artillery officers have heretofore leaned
towards their corps commander, and for their own advancement have
sought to please him; they have identified themselves with the corps to
which they were attached rather than with the arm in which they belong. . . .

We are entering on this campaign with the term of quite a number of
the regiments almost out. The question arises, how will these men behave when they have only a few weeks to serve before going home?
Meade has considered it of sufficient importance to issue an order on the
subject, exhorting them "not to suffer the honourable fame they have
won to be tarnished by acts of insubordination"; at the same time warning them that "extreme measures" will be resorted to to stop any such
trouble if necessary. Yesterday I notified both General Hunt and Warren
that all my preparations were complete, and I was ready to move at any
time. . . . Lieutenant-Colonel Comstock, Grant's senior aide-de-camp,
was expected back from Chattanooga last night with information as to
the state of readiness in Sherman's army.* Burnside's corps did embark

* Cyrus Ballou Comstock, of Massachusetts, West Point, 1855, had been chief engineer
of the Army of the Potomac until March 30, 1863, and then for a time held the same
post in the Army of the Tennessee. He was Grant's aide from the spring of 1864 until
after the end of the war. "He had somewhat the air of a Yankee schoolmaster buttoned
in a military coat," writes Colonel Theodore Lyman. But he was an officer of great capacity and energy.

according to the rumours in my last entry, and disembarked on Monday at Alexandria. He is to relieve the half of this corps now guarding the railroad; but after all the fuss made about him, and his big corps it is not to be supposed that he will remain there all summer. . . .

The great fair is over in New York. The sword goes to Grant; McClellan was ahead at the close of the public subscribing, but afterward they claim to have received $1,000 from somewhere outside the city in votes for Grant; it was given by the Union League in New York, who pretend that in this way they are supporting the Union. All the ladies engaged in it are completely used up: many of them sick; and at least one, Mrs. D. D. Field, has died from sickness brought on while there. Lydia, my black cook, who did not want me to come and fight for the freedom of the slaves, now says that she "wishes a pestilence would carry them all off if they are to be set free without any means of being taken care of; for then they would fall by the hand of the Lord; now they are falling by the hand of man." . . .

CULPEPER COURT HOUSE, MAY 1, MONDAY. We are still here but expecting orders hourly almost. . . . Things here look so very near a move that the chances are decidedly against our being in our present quarters for a regular Thursday entry in here this week. Our sick were all sent off yesterday. Burnside's division of negroes has relieved the half of this corps on the railroad so that it will be here tomorrow. The rest of Burnside's command is near Rappahannock Station. One division they say has not joined him yet. So near as I can make out, Grant will start from here with about 125,000 men, including all Burnside's corps and the cavalry. One-third of the number are green troops, but there are only a few new regiments, and the army was never in better condition, take it altogether. The number stated, I am confident, is not over 5,000 out either way, as I have excellent means of knowing. It is enough anyway; quite as many as Grant and Meade together can take care of, and properly used ought to be sure to use up Lee. The weather continues very fine. The roads and all the country are just in the very best condition. Everyone here is in good spirits and those at home full of expectation.

---◦◦◦◦---

FIFTEEN

THE BATTLES OF THE WILDERNESS
AND SPOTSYLVANIA

"The Army will move on Wednesday, the 4th May, 1864"; this sentence began the orders issued from headquarters on May 2. Promptly at midnight on the 3rd, General Sheridan led the way with two cavalry divisions, the infantry following. Five bridges were rapidly laid across the two-hundred-foot expanse of the Rapidan at three fords—Germanna, Ely's, and Culpeper Mine; and the long trains of artillery, ambulances, wagons, and other vehicles spent all the first day and most of the second getting to designated points beyond the stream. The transfer of the force was efficiently managed. "This I regarded as a great success," Grant wrote later, "and it removed from my mind the most serious apprehensions I had entertained, that of crossing the river in the face of an active, large, well-appointed, and ably-commanded army, and how so large a train was to be carried through a hostile country and protected."

The movement was prelude to a fierce, bloody, indecisive battle, which raged on singularly difficult ground: the "wilderness" south of the three river fords named, an area of woodland with thick tangled undergrowth drained in part by Wilderness Run. The thickets of bushes and low trees covering the rocky, hilly terrain impeded both sight and action. As Grant's and Lee's armies came into full collision on May 5, the troops fought while groping their way. Precision of movement was impossible. Colonels could seldom see all the companies of their regiments, and brigade commanders could rarely comprehend what their left wing was doing while they watched the right, or vice versa. At many points the opposing lines came upon each other by surprise, sixty or eighty feet apart, and fired through the undergrowth at point-blank range.

Each corps, as it moved into this desperate battle, had its own artillery brigade. In Hancock's Second Corps the brigade was commanded by Colonel John C. Tidball; Sedgwick's Sixth Corps had Colonel Charles H. Tompkins as head of its brigade. Wainwright of course commanded the brigade in Warren's Fifth Corps. Management of the artillery was particularly difficult in dense scrubby pines and brushwood, and hard enough when the batteries next to the highways—the Germanna Plank Road, Orange County Turnpike, Orange Plank Road, and intersecting roads. By the night of May 6 the battle was substantially over. Grant had not dislodged Lee from his front and had to try a new flanking march.

❋ ❋ ❋

MAY 3 [1864], TUESDAY. Everything is packed, and we only wait the hour of midnight in order to start. Orders have been coming in thick and fast all day; an army is as bad as a woman starting on a journey, so much to be done at the last moment. . . .

It seems that notwithstanding General Meade's appeal to their honour, there are a number of men inclined to be fractious under the idea that their term of service is already out; he now sends notice that all such be shot without trial if they do not step out to the music. . . .

I found yesterday that General Warren, I suppose by order, was building several redoubts on the heights south of the town, and rode around to see them, thinking that I might be called upon to have something to do with them, especially as the General asked me to examine whether the parapets were too high for light guns. I thought to meet him there but did not. I, however, came across General Wadsworth. The old gentleman was talkative as usual, and said that he did not know very much about engineering, though he did claim to be otherwise pretty well up in military matters. I agreed with him perfectly as to his ignorance of engineering, and thought he would be wiser not to attempt to use terms belonging thereto. . . .

This afternoon General Warren had his division commanders and myself at his quarters, shewed us his orders, and explained tomorrow's move. This Fifth Corps leads off, followed by the Sixth; we are to cross at Germanna Ford again and go as far as the Old Wilderness Tavern tomorrow. The Second Corps, all the heavy trains, and also the Reserve crosses at Ely's Ford and goes to Chancellorsville; the Ninth Corps* does not move until the next day. We are to try to get around Lee, between him and Richmond, and so force him to fight on our own ground. My batteries, with two forage waggons each, start at midnight, pass through Stevensburg, and then follow in rear of the First and Third Divisions. The ammunition and all the rest of the waggons, together with half of the ambulances, move off to Chancellorsville and we are warned that we shall not see them again for five days. The night is soft but cloudy, with some signs of rain; now the roads are capital. Our general officers, that

---

* This was Burnside's corps. It had not brigaded its artillery, two batteries being attached to each of the four divisions.

I have talked with, are very sanguine; Grant is said to be perfectly confident. God grant that their expectations be more realized.

When I reached Warren's quarters Wadsworth only was there. He insisted on having my opinion as to which way we were to move, whether around Lee's right or left; and when I told him I had no opinion, having nothing to found one on, declared I must be a regular, I was so non-committal. Would that it were characteristic of all regulars never to give an opinion on subjects they knew nothing about; and if the people at home, newspaper editors and correspondents, and also the politicians at Washington, would take a leaf out of the same book, it would save the country millions of money, and many a poor fellow in our army his life. During the interview I could see that Warren paid especial deference to Griffin, whom he evidently fears. I do not wonder much at it except that Griffin has no influence; but then, he is such an inveterate hater, and so ugly in his persecutions. I was gratified at being summoned with the division commanders. . . .

OLD WILDERNESS TAVERN, MAY 4, WEDNESDAY. It was nearly two o'clock this morning when we got our orders to haul out. I had managed a few short snatches of sleep before that time, but do not improve in my ability to go off at any moment and in any place. There is a kind of weird excitement in this starting at midnight. The senses seemed doubly awake to every impression—the batteries gathering around my quarters in the darkness; the moving of lanterns, and the hailing of the men; then the distant sound of the hoofs of the aide's horse who brings the final order to start. Sleepy as I always am at such times, I have a certain amount of enjoyment in it all. We got off without much trouble.* . . .

Great care was taken not to make any more fires than usual, so as not to attract the attention of the enemy; otherwise the darkness and distance were a quite sufficient cover to our movement. Through Stevensburg, on towards Shepherd's Grove for another mile or so, and then across country through a byroad, we had it all to ourselves. When we arrived at the head of the Germanna Plank Road we had to wait an hour for the two divisions which were to precede us to file by. It was nine o'clock by the time I reached the ford. After crossing, General Warren directed me to divide the batteries among the infantry divisions for the march through the Wilderness. . . . I hated to break them up so on the first day's march, before I had time to look after them all, but an unbroken

---

* Wainwright had forty-eight light guns; that is, eight batteries of six guns each. Eighteen of these were three-inch ordnance guns; twenty-four were light twelve-pounders; and six were twelve-pounder Parrotts. He had in addition a battalion of heavy artillery, which he does not define, but which probably means 24- and 32-pounder howitzers, and a group of ambulances.

string of artillery over a mile long was certainly somewhat risky through these dense woods.

We moved on very slowly, although there was a division of cavalry ahead of us, and did not all get up here until near dark. The First and Third Divisions went into position immediately on the west side of the road. . . . Meade's headquarters are with the Sixth. Grant is still on the north of the river, I believe. Sheridan is up among the barns belonging to the old tavern. I went up there towards dark to see Kingsbury, and took a look at our new cavalry leader; he is very short, close built, with rather a jolly face, but not a great one. He dresses and wears his hair much in the Bowery soap-lock style, and could easily pass himself off for one of the "b'hoys."* . . .

We had no rain during the day; but some this evening, with a prospect of more during the night. I understand that all the other armies started today also: the campaign opens with a combined move. Orders have just come for us to move tomorrow morning at five o'clock to Parker's Store, on the Orange Court House Plank Road, the Sixth Corps moving up to this point.

LACY HOUSE, MAY 5, THURSDAY. This is the second anniversary of my first battle and has been celebrated in due form. Two years ago, I went into the battle of Williamsburg on the 5th of May; one year after I was in the battle of Chancellorsville; today we have been at it for the third time, and though I have not been under very much fire myself, I have had quite a smell of gunpowder, and am two guns short tonight. We have made no progress today, and virtually hold the same position we did yesterday.

The corps started punctually, Crawford leading with the Third Division; followed by Wadsworth with the Fourth, then Robinson, and Griffin to bring up the rear. The batteries moving in the same way they did yesterday. So soon as the Fourth Division was stretched out along the road, I passed on to the front, with Warren's permission and at his request, to join Crawford. The road to Parker's Store is a narrow country road, most of the way through a dense wood. I reached Crawford just as the head of his column came into an opening of some twenty or thirty acres around a house belonging to one Savarra, about two miles from the Lacy house in a straight line, and one from Parker's Store. It stands on

---

* Compare Theodore Lyman's description: "a small, broad-shouldered, squat man, with black hair and a square head . . . looks very like a Piedmontese . . . makes everywhere a favorable impression." A New Yorker, Sheridan had graduated at West Point in 1853 and was only a lieutenant when the war began. But his star rose rapidly after he took command of the Second Cavalry Brigade in the West in July 1862, and he had won the gratitude of the nation during the Chattanooga campaign by storming Missionary Ridge.

high ground, so that we could plainly see the store and the Orange
Plank Road which runs by it. There was a small body of our cavalry
at the store, perhaps a regiment. The head of Crawford's column had
not crossed the little open ground around Savarra's house, when we saw
our cavalry driven away from the store along the plank road. Crawford
halted, and sent back a report of it, with request for orders. . . .

So soon as I learned that Griffin was to attack on the turnpike, I
hurried back to that point. On reaching an opening about half a mile
back of Crawford, I found Wadsworth going into position there. It was
a pretty good spot, though small. At the same time we heard firing on
the turnpike and orders arrived for Wadsworth to join Griffin. There
was evidently a woods road which led from this opening to the turnpike
near where the firing was going on, and by taking which Wadsworth
could probably have struck on the flank of the force engaged with
Griffin. I believe, though I am not sure, that he said to me he should
like to try it. From there I went back the road we came to the Lacy
house, and then along the ridge on which it stands to the turnpike. Here
I found Phillips's battery and two sections of Winslow's: the first news
that greeted me was that Winslow's other section was captured and he
himself badly wounded. From the stragglers and wounded men coming
back down the road, there was no doubt as to Griffin having had the
worst of it. Riding forward I met them carrying Winslow back; he was
shot through the fleshy part just below both shoulder-blades, the ball
coming out over the spine. Soon after I met Captain Martin whom I
had given charge of the three batteries with Griffin, and who told me all
about it.*

* It was here that the battle of the Wilderness really got under way. When Warren's
Fifth Corps reached Old Wilderness Tavern, advanced Confederate forces under Ewell
were but three miles away. Griffin of the Fifth Corps, marching west along the Orange
Court House Turnpike early on May 5, reported the enemy just in front of him, and
supporting troops were ordered up. Meanwhile, Griffin's division was directed to press
the enemy. A sharp encounter between Griffin's troops and Ewell's force followed. For
an hour and a half the battle raged, and the turnpike was soon crowded with walking
wounded and lines of ambulances with serious casualties. Griffin, a man of hot impul-
sive temper and blustering language, later declared that he had driven Ewell back
three-quarters of a mile, but the failure of other commanders to come to his aid so
exposed his flanks that he had to fall back. Thus he had to abandon two guns—a loss
which sorely mortified Wainright. When Griffin made an oral report to Meade that
afternoon, he was so abusive in denouncing his fellow officers that Grant, who was
standing by, exclaimed: "You ought to arrest him!" But Meade knew the man's ways,
and replied: "It's only his way of talking."

General Romeyn B. Ayres, who is mentioned here, a graduate of West Point in 1847,
had commanded a division at Gettysburg, and was now leading a division in Warren's
corps. A hard fighter, he rose to be major general. It will be seen that Wainright
thinks highly of Ayres's sportsmanlike temper, and badly of Griffin. It will also be
noted that the regulars of Griffin's command had fought poorly.

It seems that our cavalry, who were at Robinson's Tavern yesterday afternoon, were withdrawn during the night. This morning Griffin pushed along the road to cover the passage of the rest of the army. Advancing with Ayres's brigade of regulars on the right of the road, and Bartlett's on the left, he drove the enemy half a mile or more, Winslow's section being pushed up the road on a line with the skirmishers, and firing. On reaching a small piece of open ground, beyond which the road rises quite an ascent, and bends off to our right at the same time, the rebs made a sharp charge on Ayres's right, lapping him a little, and drove his whole brigade in confusion around behind Bartlett and across the road; Bartlett's men too were very shaky. Winslow's section was just at the foot of this rise at the time, and everyone says had been handled beautifully. . . .

General Ayres told me that the loss of the guns was due entirely to the bad behaviour of his brigade and no blame could in any way be attached to the battery. General Bartlett, whom I found with his mouth fairly glued shut, from excessive thirst and hallooing, spoke of them in the same way as did Martin. Griffin alone, on whom the whole responsibility really rests, seemed inclined to shift it off of his shoulders.

I have no idea at what time of the day all this occurred: they say it was about noon, though it does not seem to me that it could have been nearly so late; still it may have been as General Warren stopped me at the Lacy house to put some of the batteries in position there, which took me some time. The Lacy house stands high facing about south and looking down on to a little valley, through which runs a small stream, little more than a ditch. The ridge on which it stands runs away to the north, bearing a little west: along this I placed Phillips, Rittenhouse, Mink, and Cooper: they looked directly towards Parker's Store and the Savarra house, where Crawford was. Griffin fell back to within a few hundred yards of where this ridge crosses the turnpike and formed his line there. There was a sort of opening at this point on the right of the turnpike, the ridge turning sharp off to the northeast. On this open I placed the two remaining sections of Winslow's battery under Lieutenant Richardson, and also brought a section of Phillips's guns onto the road itself to reply to a section of the enemy's which opened fire along the road from the top of the hill beyond where Winslow's were lost. I only had them reply slowly when the reb guns opened as there was nothing else to fire at. The rifled guns opened several times on the rebels as we noticed columns passing the Savarra house, but we could not judge much of the effect, as the distance was from 2,700 to 3,000 yards. It, however, afforded me a chance to judge of the relative merits of the Parrott and three-inch gun at that distance. I found that the elevation required was the same for both; nor was there any perceptible difference in the accuracy. The preference of the three-inch lies in the ammunition and in their greater lightness and shortness. . . .

So ends our first day's fight in this campaign. I have not heard anything as to Hancock's loss, but it must have been at least equal to ours, for he was much longer engaged; 6,000 men will do pretty well for a beginning. The Ninth Corps they tell me is at the ford and will join us tomorrow morning.

MAY 6, FRIDAY. I cannot pretend to give an account of today's fighting except so far as I hear reports of it, for almost none has come under my immediate observation. Certain orders and movements I saw, and certainly heard enough noise. Grant ordered us to attack along our whole front this morning at five o'clock, but Lee got ahead of us, and pitched into Sedgwick's right. The fight there, all musketry, was hot but not very long: report said that we had the advantage. At five o'clock Hancock went in very hot. He had all his own corps, Getty's division of the Sixth, and the two remaining brigades of Robinson's from this corps. Wadsworth, too, was over there, so that the actual force at that point was equal to two corps. We could hear the firing and the shouts—they were I think ahead of anything I have ever heard before—and see the dense mass of smoke which hung over the woods. We knew from these that Hancock was gaining ground, and at one time even looked to see him in possession of Parker's Store, but he did not get so far as that.

Soon after sunrise the head of Burnside's column arrived, and passing the Lacy house, moved to fill up the gap between Hancock and ourselves. They went into the wood by a road from the south corner of the opening here, and pushed on I don't know how far. . . . Burnside himself remained at the very opening of the road, where he fixed his headquarters. The number of staff officers who kept continually riding back to him was something wonderful; nor did his division commanders seem satisfied with sending, but came themselves a number of times: so that I got a very poor impression of the corps.

About noon Hancock was attacked in his advanced position and driven back to the Brock road. This was another very hard fight, and we all waited most impatiently to hear Burnside's men begin, but not a shot was fired by them; at least none to speak of until it was quiet again in front of the Second Corps; then there was an hour or two of musketry but amounting to nothing. There is a great deal of feeling here about this, and I could see that Warren and Meade were very sore about it too, though the latter said nothing. Burnside somehow is never up to the mark when the tug comes. In the evening, about their usual time, Lee pitched into Hancock again, and they had a third heavy fight, but without any gain on either side I hear.

In our own immediate front and that of the Sixth, which lay on our right, all was quiet, from the repulse of the enemy in the morning until dusk. I think that there were but three divisions all told along this front, and one brigade; everything else having been sent to Hancock. Burnside's negro division were guarding the road to the ford. During the morning I posted batteries along the ridge in continuation of Winslow's to the left of the turnpike: the wood was comparatively thin here, and much was cut by the men to make breastworks. Richardson still remained on the right of the road; then moving to the left. . . . Thirty-four guns in all gave us a mighty strong line had the rebs pushed up that far. But our infantry line was very thin; it lay in advance of the batteries. . . .

This day's fight has been a terrible one. Our losses are variously estimated at from 10,000 to 15,000 at headquarters, and we hold no more ground than we did last night. Among our lost is General Wadsworth reported killed within the rebel lines; Getty, Webb, and Baxter are said to be wounded; and a General Hays in the Second Corps killed. There is some hope that Wadsworth is not dead, but the reports are very positive; he and his men are said to have fought superbly. I know nothing of the plan of battle, if indeed there was any, or could be in such a dense wilderness; but I cannot help thinking that had Burnside pushed in as he was expected to, things might have been very different. Lee's losses, too, must have been very heavy, as he was the attacking party quite as much as we were. Patrick tells me he has received about 1,700 prisoners: these report that General Longstreet was wounded on Hancock's front today. My own command has not fired a shot. Burnside and his staff occupy the Lacy house. We have our tents pitched in the courtyard at night and taken down in the morning.

❉ ❉ ❉

On the morning of the second day of heavy fighting, May 6, Hancock's corps on the Union left vigorously attacked along the Orange Plank Road. He had A. P. Hill in his front, with Longstreet arriving to support him. Using an unfinished railroad cut that provided a concealed approach to the Union flank, Longstreet threw four brigades against Hancock's line. Part of the troops of Francis C. Barlow's and Gershom Mott's divisions at once gave way. Hancock exerted every effort to restore his battle front, but had to withdraw. It was in the course of Longstreet's successful attack that the brave General James Wadsworth fell with a bullet through his head, the Confederates trampling over his lifeless body. But later, partly in consequence of a blunder by General William Mahone, who in the confusion fired into his own Confederate forces and wounded Longstreet severely, Hancock was able to regroup his troops and hold fast.

Meanwhile, Sedgwick and Warren on the center and right of the Union line repeatedly attacked Richard S. Ewell, but failed to shake him. Here John B. Gordon managed to find an exposed flank where Sedgwick's command was ensconced in the woods. Late in the afternoon Lee ordered Gordon to lead his Georgians to assault it. By a brilliant advance the Georgians drove back two of Sedgwick's brigades, and captured their generals, Alexander Shaler and Truman Seymour, along with several hundred men. Then as darkness set in, both sides dug intrenchments. General Burnside with his Ninth Corps had been expected by Grant and Hancock to arrive on the field in time to fight throughout the day. But it was not until two o'clock in the afternoon that he joined in the battle, and he accomplished little.

Union losses in the Wilderness have been estimated at some 17,600 men; Confederate losses at about 7,750. The North felt the loss of Alexander Hays, with his splendid record in nearly all the battles since Yorktown, as much as that of the fine-spirited Wadsworth. Longstreet, who was at first thought mortally wounded, recovered. The Northern public read with chagrin of the "disgraceful stampede," as Theodore Lyman termed it, of some units in Sedgwick's corps; but many of these were troops with a bad record, called "Milroy's weary boys."

※ ※ ※

MAY 7, SATURDAY. Things have been quiet all today: no movement of importance has been made on either side so far as I can learn. Our skirmish line was pushed forward in the morning, but Lee was everywhere found strongly entrenched and consequently no attack was made. The losses in this corps have been very heavy; some 6,000 or 7,000 as near as I can ascertain. My batteries remain as they were and have entrenched themselves. . . . The two regiments of heavy artillery serving with the Reserve were brought up, and temporarily attached to the corps; and my battalion of the Fourth New York was united to them; even my ordnance battery was put into line, and all headquarter and waggon guards were ordered to the front. Grant evidently means to fight all his troops. The Heavies who must number over 3,000 strong formed a brigade under Colonel Kitching, Sixth New York Artillery, and were placed on the left of the Third Division, across the valley road to Parker's Store.

About dark, General Warren informed me that the whole army was to move during the night for Lee's right, and shewed me Meade's order. I wish that I could have got a copy of it. So near as I can remember all trains were ordered to Chancellorsville; we were to lead off the troops so soon as it was quite dark. . . .

MAY 8, SUNDAY. The night was cloudy, and exceeding dark: we struck the road just where the turnpike to Chancellorsville, and the Germanna Plank Road cross, in such a way as to make it more of a fork than a crossing. The Ninth Corps was moving out on the turnpike, and caused some confusion as it was difficult to distinguish the two roads in the dark. . . . So soon as I had all started I tried to push up to the head of the column to join General Warren, but could not get a step beyond Richardson's battery. The road, which was not wide and made a thorough cut all along here, was literally jammed with troops moving one step at a time. Never before did I see such slow progress made: certainly not over half a mile an hour, if that. Nor could I get around them, for it was so dark that you could not see at all where your horse was stepping.

As we pushed along in this way, every lighted pipe being distinctly seen in the darkness, a lot of pack mules from one of Griffin's head brigades, who had got frightened at something, came down the line on a run. Their great wide packs cleared a broad road through the middle of the line, and their numbers were constantly increased by other mules and horses which they frightened in their passage as much as themselves. I thought the little grey quartermaster's horse that I was riding was going with them, for he reared up the bank, which I could not see, and fell over backward; he did not, however, get off, nor was either of us hurt at all.

When we reached the Brock road, we also struck the right of the Second Corps. They had thrown up a breastwork along the west side of the road, and made a wide slashing in front of it, while the men lay asleep along either side of the roadway. So tired were they that even the passing of the batteries did not awaken them. Along here I managed to get a little ahead but not much until the day began to dawn, so that we could see where there was an opening. I then pushed on at a quick walk until I got clear of the Second Corps. Soon after it was light enough to see I came across Andy Webb, who I was delighted to find was not wounded on Friday as reported. Beyond the lines of the Second Corps Ayres's brigade were lying down, as there appeared a complete block ahead. Having a clear road, I started my little grey into a slashing trot, at which I found him a marvel, and did not draw rein until I reached Meade's headquarters at Todd's Tavern; when I found I had one staff officer and one orderly with me.

The whole cause of this delay, this dragging along at a snail's pace, I found caused by a couple of hundred yards of wet road, over which the water ran an inch deep, and where the men were picking their way one at a time. Beyond this I rode nearly two miles without coming across anything that could be called a column. At Meade's headquarters I found them all asleep, but thought this straggling of the column of sufficient importance to wake Williams up and tell him of it, as I did not know what might be depending on time. Every officer and man was doubtless very tired and the night was very dark, but it is to me impossible to understand the perfect indifference with which officers allow their men to lag and break ranks for such little things. The fact of our march at night was enough to tell every man that we wanted to reach some place without Lee's knowing it; and one would think that a desire for their own safety would spur them all up to do it, so as to avoid a fight.

When I reached General Warren, who had halted Robinson's division about a mile and a half beyond the tavern, I found them all quietly eating their breakfast, waiting for Merritt* to open the way with his cavalry. Perhaps it was on account of my having made such a fuss along the road about the time lost by our corps, so that I felt chagrined; but I certainly thought then that both Warren and Meade were not pushing matters as much as they ought, considering how important it was to reach Spotsylvania Court House before Lee; and now that we have not got there at all today, I am quite sure of it. Warren had no control, I presume, over the division of cavalry under Merritt which was ahead of us; but he should have, as ranking officer at the head of the column, been charged with the securing of a good position at the Court House and have had control of all troops engaged in doing this, or else Meade should have been on the ground himself. I feel sure that had our column been properly pushed we might have got up to Merritt at least an hour before daylight; which would have given the men that much time for rest and breakfast. If then Merritt had pushed ahead at five o'clock, with Warren's corps close behind him, there is no doubt we should have been ahead of Lee, and got hold of the Court House.

About six-thirty o'clock Merritt reported that the enemy were too strong for him, and Warren was ordered to clear the way for himself. The General appeared decidedly crusty this morning; why I do not know. He went on with Robinson's division, taking Martin's and Breck's batteries, but directing me to remain where I was and send up other batteries as he needed them. This I did not consider my business; it was for me to make arrangements to have the batteries brought up as needed, but my own place at the opening of a fight is undoubtedly alongside of the corps commander. It was some time before I got orders to move up all the batteries, and a sharp engagement had taken place, our leading divisions being driven back. . . .

* Wesley Merritt, West Point, 1860, who has been casually mentioned before, commanded a cavalry division under Sheridan.

When I got up to the Alsop house I found Richardson and Mink in position to the left and front of it, pointing down the eastern or northern road, and Breck to the right front of the house commanding the other road. The line of infantry was being formed about a quarter of a mile beyond the house facing southeast, its right where Walcott's battery was. I put Cooper in on the right of Breck, and Phillips in front of the house, both facing at right angles to the other batteries so as to fire southwest down the open valley spoken of. Rittenhouse was left in reserve and Stewart to move forward with the troops. So soon as our line was formed and a part of the Sixth Corps had come up, which went in on our left; the line was again advanced. . . . I went with Stewart down the right-hand road, picking up Walcott on the way. . . .

As we came down to this point, the rebel sharpshooters opened a very ugly fire on us from the other side of the valley, say four hundred yards off, especially from the wood to the left of the road where they lay thick behind large fallen trees. A couple of batteries of twelve-pounders also opened, from over the open part of the opposite knoll to our right of the road, a very ugly fire of shrapnel, their guns being entirely hid by the knoll. I immediately put Stewart's leading section in on either side of the road, and the rest of his guns on the right; ordering Walcott in on the right of him. Walcott's men did not behave over well, nor did he push them forward as well as he might. . . . Stewart was as usual himself, also what old men he had left, but his young recruits were inclined to dodge, and once when a couple of fresh limbers came up with ammunition they got quite a scare and attempted to limber up. All this obliged me to keep in the open ground among the guns myself, until I could get them quieted down and firing to please me.

The rebel guns, just equal in number and description to my own, were, as I have said, quite hid by the knoll behind which they stood; we could only see the puffs of smoke from their explosions. It followed as a matter of course that they fired too high. My own gunners did the same, and it was with great difficulty that I got them down. At last, however, I did so as to make almost every shot strike the top of the knoll just on what was to us the skyline. When I had also got them to burst their shot as they struck, we shut the rebs up in five minutes; probably their guns were withdrawn.

The whole affair lasted half an hour, and was one of the prettiest little duels I have seen. The enemy had decidedly the advantage in ground, but they lost it by keeping too much under cover; otherwise it was a very even match, both sides firing shrapnel entirely. Had they run their guns up to the top of the knoll so as to get a good sight of us, the chances are that we should have got the worst of it, for their skirmishers hurt us badly. From behind the logs where they lay, a dozen or twenty would

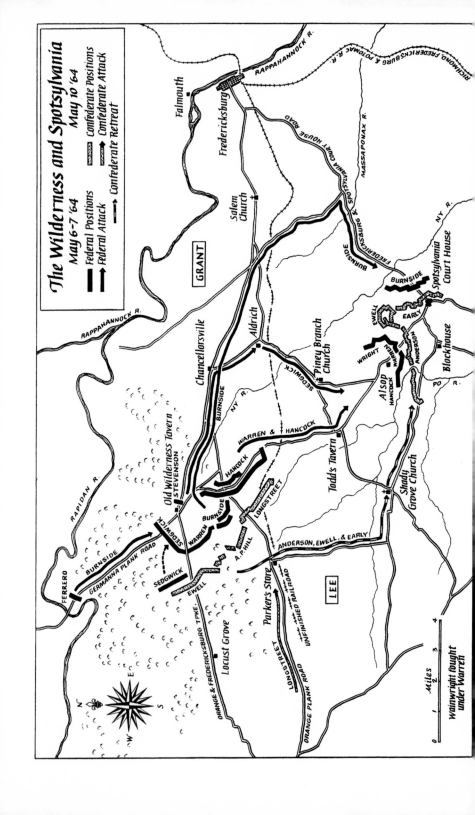

The Wilderness and Spotsylvania
May 6-7 '64
May 10 '64

Federal Positions
Federal Attack
Confederate Positions
Confederate Attack
Confederate Retreat

GRANT

LEE

RAPPAHANNOCK R.

RICHMOND FREDERICKSBURG & POTOMAC R.R.

Falmouth

Fredericksburg

RAPPAHANNOCK R.

Salem Church

RAPIDAN R.

BURNSIDE

FERRERO

Old Wilderness Tavern

STEVENSON

GERMANNA PLANK ROAD

SEDGWICK

WARREN

SEDGWICK

EWELL

Locust Grove

A.P. HILL

Burnside

Burnside

HANCOCK

LONGSTREET

LONGSTREET

ORANGE & FREDERICKSBURG TPKE.

ORANGE PLANK ROAD

Parker's Store

UNFINISHED RAILROAD

ANDERSON, EWELL, & EARLY

Chancellorsville

BURNSIDE

NY R.

Aldrich

SEDGWICK

WARREN & HANCOCK

Todd's Tavern

Piney Branch Church

HANCOCK

ALSOP

Shady Grove Church

SPOTSYLVANIA & FREDERICKSBURG R.R.

FREDERICKSBURG & SPOTSYLVANIA COURT HOUSE ROAD

MASSAPONAX R.

BURNSIDE

BURNSIDE

WRIGHT

EWELL

WARREN

EARLY

ANDERSON

Spotsylvania Court House

Blockhouse

PO R.

NY R.

Miles
0 1 2 3 4

wainwright fought under Warren

N S E W

fire by command at the same object. They let fly at us when I first arrived with most of my staff and orderlies; being all on horseback in the open ground, it is a great wonder that none of us were hit. Supposing that the fire was drawn by the evidence of a general officer, I sent all off into the wood. . . . After I was alone the rascals fired several times at me in the same way so that I got off my horse, and placed the little grey as a bulwark between us; until turning so as to speak to Stewart, I exposed myself without thinking, when instantly a score of minies whistled around my head, and kicked up the dust at my feet. None of them hit me, but one went through the grey's left breast right under my arm. . . .

Our men and the batteries, meanwhile, as well as the enemy, entrenched themselves; but after dark Stewart and Walcott were withdrawn to the Alsop house, where they were all parked on the plain around. Corps headquarters were on the edge of the wood in rear of the house. The day's fight has been anything but encouraging. Lee by this time has all his force in our front, and tonight will doubtless make his position secure. Grant will not be able to force his way through by this route without a hard fight if he succeeds then. Our men did not go in today with any spirit; indeed, it is hard work to get any up after marching all night. . . .

I feel awfully tired tonight, now the excitement is over, having had not a wink of sleep for forty hours; and pretty miserable, too, for my waggon has broken down again, and we are consequently minus everything, forcing me to sponge upon corps headquarters for my supper and night's lodging. They received me very kindly, and served a very good meal considering: their purveyor goes along himself and furnishes the whole concern: very different from what it was in Reynolds's time. There are also two other civilians at corps headquarters: Hendricks, a reporter for the *Herald,* and Reverend Doctor Winslow, Sanitary Commission Agent. The former seems a nice sort of a man and as he sends off a messenger every evening with his report, I may be able to get letters through.* At any rate, I shall be able to give him an exact account of any officers who fall, and they will know at home that I am safe if I do not figure in the *Herald*'s list. Dr. Winslow is a famous old trump. I met him first on the field of Chancellorsville and introduced myself, he being an own cousin of father's; I was astonished tonight to see how well he bore all the fatigues and inconveniences of this hard life; he was as jolly as anyone and made himself agreeable to all. Warren was colonel of Duryea's Zouaves, with which the doctor and his family first entered the service, and is very much attached to him. I say the "doctor and his family first entered the service," for they all came, he as chaplain, his wife as nurse, and three boys in the line.

* This was L. A. Hendricks, well known for his vivid report of Chancellorsville.

ALSOP FARM, MAY 9, MONDAY. About midnight we were awakened with orders that no move would be made today; we were to rest, fill up supplies of all sorts; make returns so far as possible, and straighten out generally. Notwithstanding all my trouble, I find I am already beginning to fall short of forage, General Warren having ordered Captain Cruttenden to abandon a lot at Chancellorsville in order that the waggons might be used to carry wounded.

I have been feeling very ugly all day. This morning General Warren said to me, "I want you to remain here so that when I want any batteries I can send for them." I asked if I should then bring them up, but he said no, he "wished me to remain with the Reserve and he would send an officer to show the battery where to go." I cannot understand this. Had I failed in doing what he ordered at any time, or been off gossiping when wanted, there might be some reason for it. I told him that I would leave my adjutant-general with the reserve batteries to order up such as were sent for, but he insisted on my remaining myself. I do not know how to act in the matter. Of course I have obeyed the order and have not left the hill all day, but I do not know whether it would be best to demand an explanation now or to wait patiently. I certainly cannot and will not occupy any such position longer than is necessary, but if things are to go on in this way will ask to be assigned somewhere else, so soon as this campaign is over. Above all things, though, I would avoid doing anything which could possibly be construed into making trouble at this time, or preferring my own interests to those of the service.

Being as it were, then, kept at home all day, I have seen nothing, and only know from hearsay what has been going on. Mink and Richardson went down before daylight to the ground where Stewart and Walcott were yesterday. Quite strong works had been thrown up during the night, but the rebel sharpshooters still made it hot there. . . . Quite early in the day these skirmishers inflicted a terrible loss on us by killing General Sedgwick. He was shot dead a few feet from Mink's left piece, near the rejunction of the roads. No greater loss could have befallen us; certainly none which would have been so much mourned. "Uncle John" was loved by his men as no other corps commander ever was in this army. His name will henceforth be linked with Reynolds and Buford; nor do I know of another worthy to be associated with them. General Wright, on whom Sedgwick has always placed the greatest reliance, succeeds him in the command. . . .

I hear nothing tonight of our moving straight to Dabney's Mills, and fear that Grant has been foiled on this route as he was along that passing Parker's Store. Prisoners say that Longstreet was shot through the left lung. My waggon is up tonight so that I have my tent pitched and mean to get a bath and clean clothes on before going to bed. Communications are opened through Fredericksburg to Aquia Creek, so we can hardly be said now to be fighting on General Lincoln's line.

* * *

"More desperate fighting has not been witnessed on this continent than that of the 5th and 6th of May." So Grant writes in his *Personal Memoirs*, and survivors of the Wilderness would have agreed. But an equally desperate and still more lethal combat was now beginning—the battle of Spotsylvania Court House. Grant's determination was to give the Confederates no respite.

Immediately after being brought to a stop in the Wilderness, Grant issued orders to advance against Lee by the left flank. He heard from Washington that Sherman had probably attacked Joseph E. Johnston in the West that day, and that Ben Butler's Army of the James had reached City Point safely. He feared that Lee might swing back to the Richmond area, with his customary energy and alacrity, to crush Butler. By marching out of the Wilderness and moving southeast, he could at the same time outflank Lee and place his army in a position to protect Butler.

The result was the movement that Wainwright has recorded. Warren set his Fifth Corps afoot on the morning of the 7th along the Brock Road toward Spotsylvania Court House and was followed by Sedgwick. But Lee's troops were also moving, by parallel roads—and got to Spotsylvania first. Just how this unhappy event took place has always been a matter of controversy. Grant thought it was largely an accident; a Confederate commander, Richard H. Anderson, who had succeeded to the command of Longstreet's corps, would have bivouacked in the woods on the night of the 7th, but, finding them on fire, could not stop and so marched straight on to the key point. Meade thought that Sheridan had let Merritt's cavalry block the way of the infantry. Sheridan retorted that Meade had given blundering orders. Wainwright has plainly expressed his view of the matter. The important point is that Lee was able to entrench himself at Spotsylvania squarely across Grant's lines of advance. This was on May 8 and the ensuing night.

Thus on May 9, when Grant ordered heavy attacks, a bloody battle developed around Spotsylvania and on the headwaters of the little Po stream south and west of the hamlet. (The Mattaponi River, which joins the Pamunkey to form the York River, is formed by the junction of four streams, the Mat, the Ta, the Po, and the Ni; the Po and the Ni being particularly troublesome because they have abrupt banks, and at some places wide marshy bottoms.) In the confused fighting on the 9th, Lee held his positions, which made a rough semicircle enclosing Spotsylvania on the northwest, north, and northeast. One of the principal events of the day was the killing of General Sedgwick by Confederate sharpshooters. General H. G. Wright, whom we have already encountered, took his place. Both sides prepared for a life-and-death grapple on the 10th.

* * *

ALSOP FARM, MAY 10, TUESDAY.   This has been a day of hard fighting and heavy loss, without a commensurate gain, if indeed we have gained anything. Of the fighting I saw nothing for until late in the afternoon, when it was about over, I was kept on the hill. No one can tell the humiliation and chagrin I suffered all the time while waiting in my tent or pacing the narrow limits in front. I can imagine now what would be the feelings of an officer unjustly placed in arrest at such a time, without even knowing of what he stood charged. To hear the firing of my own guns all day; to see the long columns of troops moving from place to place, followed by the hoorah, the fusillades, then the yell of the enemy in their counter charge, while tied hand and foot so that I could take no part in it, was a misery beyond my powers of description. General Meade was on the hill several times; he asked me what I did there, when I was only too glad to tell him the whole state of the case, lest he might think me in disgrace or shirking. His reply was, "I never treated you in that way when you were with me." I also saw Hunt and told him the trouble, but he could do nothing. He said that Tidball was just as badly off, for that on the day we started Hancock issued a printed order, assigning nearly all the batteries to divisions, and placing them entirely under the control of the division commanders, while at the same time it held Tidball "responsible for them whenever he is present on the line." This is being worse off than I am in some respects.

When late in the afternoon, say five o'clock, all our attacks had failed, and General Warren was afraid that we were likely to be ourselves driven from our works, he sent me word to "bring" a battery to the front. I did not wait for the word to be repeated, but started out with Stewart at once; nor did I return to my quarters until I had visited all my batteries in position. Warren himself sent me to look to the right of his lines, but the compliment of calling upon me when he was in trouble does not cover the insult of consigning me to inactivity for two days. From Warren's manner and all, I do not believe that he meant it as an insult in any way, and I am much inclined to the idea that it was some crude plan of his to secure a prompt obtaining of batteries; a plan made concerning that of which he knew nothing. Still the effect, as to the appearance of disgrace and distrust, were the same, and cannot but injure me in the eyes of all who saw me doing nothing at such a time. I thought again to remonstrate with him this morning, but feared it would tend to make him obstinate, and my position worse than ever.

Mink and Richardson returned this morning before daylight to the position they held yesterday, where Griffin had caused a strong line of works to be thrown up a little in advance, and well protected with traverses. About ten o'clock they began firing by Griffin's order, and kept it up all through the day with but little intermission. I should say they must have expended one hundred rounds per gun; a terrible waste, at least two-thirds of it, but Griffin kept insisting that they did not fire enough, and I was helpless to prevent it. They were lucky in escaping with only two or three men wounded between them. Mink was struck on the ankle by a spent ball about noon, which obliged him to leave; it did not break the skin, but bruised him so as to cause his foot to swell terribly, and be very painful. Ritchie took command of the battery then.

Breck and Rittenhouse moved over to the right of the corps at ten A.M. to aid in the movement of the Second Corps across the Po. They took position on the edge of the wood some four hundred yards in rear of the W. W. Jones house, and engaged the rebel batteries on the opposite side of the Po, firing a good deal; Breck reports a total of 231 rounds during the day. When I went over there in the afternoon at the time our men were driven back and there was fear of an attack on our right flank, the Second Corps having been withdrawn from there, I moved these two batteries farther forward, so as to give a chance to Cooper and Walcott to change front with them if necessary. These two last batteries I had loaned to Tidball, at General Hunt's request, in the afternoon when the enemy were pressing the rear of the Second Corps at the time it was withdrawn. They went as far as the Pritchett house, but were not engaged.

Phillips remained on the hill. Stewart I moved to the front by General Warren's order at one time, but there was no position for him there to do what Warren wanted equal to the one he had left; so I sent him back to the Alsop house, where he went into battery on the right of Phillips.

I saw none of the hard fighting, and only know that a number of attacks have been made all along the line by portions of the Second, Fifth, and Sixth Corps. So far as I can find out they seem to have been weak affairs in almost every case, and unsupported; and mere shoving forward of a brigade or two now here now there, like a chess-player shoving out his pieces and then drawing them right back. There may have been some plan in it, but in my ignorance I cannot help thinking that one big, well-sustained attack at one point would have been much more likely to succeed. None of those made accomplished anything except Upton's, which was very brilliant, as he carried the works at the point of the bayonet without firing a shot, and brought out nine hundred prisoners. But he was not supported at all, and had to fall back at once. Probably his loss was smaller than that of any of the unsuccessful brigades: men will never learn that the greatest safety is in pushing ahead. Upton will certainly get his star now: 'tis a thousand pities that Grant has not the power to confer it on the spot.*

The Third and Fourth Divisions were the attacking party from this corps. They tried the rebel lines by the John Perry house, behaved badly, suffered heavily, and did nothing. The Third Division in particular is said to have 'acted abominably, breaking all to pieces, so that Warren was obliged to rally them himself, colours in hand. I believe these reports, for when I went out with Stewart's battery I found the Pennsylvania Reserves forming away to the rear of Griffin, and not two hundred yards from the knoll where Cooper and Walcott belonged, while Warren still grasped the staff of his corps flag. He held it short, for it had been shot in two in his hand just before. The little general looked gallant enough at any rate. Mounted on a great tall white horse, in full uniform, sash and all, and with the flag in his hand, he must have made a prominent mark at any rate. Cutler's men did but little better than Crawford's. General Rice was killed.† Meade has his headquarters close by us tonight. Having had a look at matters, I feel somewhat better tonight, and hope that Warren will not repeat his stay at home order tomorrow. Success seems to have attended Sherman so far; we have a telegram from Washington tonight saying that he was victorious in his first fight at Dalton; not a very big affair. Butler too reports himself as landed south of the James and in possession of the railroad between Richmond and Petersburg.

MAY 11, WEDNESDAY. One day fighting and then a day of rest seems to be the new order. Yesterday was fighting day; this has been a day of rest,

---

* Colonel Emory B. Upton, commanding a brigade in the Sixth Corps, made a spirited attack at six in the afternoon of May 10 upon the well-entrenched position of General George Pierce Doles, which lay about six hundred feet from a pine forest, in clear and open ground. Upton formed a column of four lines inside the woods, which charged, burst through the Confederate abatis, reached the parapet, and swarmed inside the works. Here he took the second line of entrenchments, seized some guns, and extended his hold laterally. He had punched a gap in the Confederate front that offered the Union forces a great opportunity. But his reinforcements failed to arrive, while fresh Southern troops poured forward and by nightfall restored their line. Immediately after the attack Upton, who was badly wounded, was made a brigadier general. Grant had received authority to promote officers on the field for special acts of gallantry, and he now exercised it.

† Samuel W. Crawford commanded the Third Division in Warren's Fifth Corps, all his regiments belonging to the Pennsylvania Reserves. Lysander Cutler of New York led a brigade in the came corps. General James C. Rice.

so called. That is, we have not made any attacks nor been attacked; but all hands have been on the alert, not knowing what might turn up. To officers of sufficient rank to have any responsibility such a day is almost as tiring as one of actual fighting, for they are kept on strain the whole time by reports of the enemy moving here and gathering there. I have lain quiet myself most of the time, only riding around to visit the different batteries; "D" and "H" of the First New York were not withdrawn last night; Griffin kept them firing constantly since nine A.M. when the enemy opened a battery on them, but was soon silenced. "At that time," Richardson reports, "I received orders from General Griffin to shell the woods in front and keep up a steady fire during the day. Fire solid shot at no visible object, and, so far as I could see, with no effect." Mink says that they have expended a whole campaign allowance of ammunition (250 rounds per gun), in the three days at this point. I can only account for such a waste on the ground that Griffin was scared, and made a noise to keep his men's courage up. The battery officers all say that he was constantly complaining that they did not fire enough. Two-thirds of this ammunition was absolutely wasted. . . .

It is now eight days since we left Culpeper, during seven of which there has been more or less fighting. It is said now that the men stood up to their work much better yesterday than they did in the Wilderness, and that the losses on both sides are very heavy. Our total loss up to this time is variously estimated at from 20,000 to 30,000; including four generals killed, Sedgwick, Wadsworth, Hays, and Rice; five wounded, viz: Getty, Robinson, Baxter, Morris, and Shaler; and Seymour a prisoner.* The old First Corps has been most unfortunate in this respect; of its five general officers retained on consolidation, Cutler only remains.

An unusually large proportion of the wounds are slight, owing to the fighting being mostly in the wood. Richmond papers of Saturday last say that they have had six generals killed. The weather has been very hot and dusty, so that the men have suffered much, while the wounded must have undergone intolerable agonies during the long ride from here to Belle Plaine, where our base now is. This afternoon we had a nice refreshing thunder shower, which will help us much. Water is good in this district, and ice is found in sufficient quantities for all hospital uses. I have just signed my return of casualties from the start up to five P.M. today. It sums up four men killed; four officers and thirty-four men wounded; one officer and six men missing; total forty-nine. . . .

---

* Brigadier General George W. Getty commanded the Second Division of the Sixth Corps; Henry Baxter a brigade of the Fifth Corps; Gilbert P. Robinson a brigade of the Ninth Corps; and Alexander Shaler, William H. Morris, and Truman Seymour each a brigade in the Sixth Corps. These were six very capable officers.

It was on May 11, as most of the troops rested, that Grant telegraphed Halleck: "I propose to fight it out on this line if it takes all summer."

The next morning, at the first glimmer of daybreak, Hancock delivered a mass attack of 20,000 troops against a salient of "mule shoe" shape in the Confederate lines. The night, as the men moved into position, had been dark, chilly, and rainy. A fog hampered their movements as dawn broke. They had to advance over ascending and heavily wooded ground, part of it marshy. Burnside with his Ninth Corps simultaneously attacked the other side of the salient, but the heaviest work fell to Hancock.

Despite all the difficulties of the terrain, Hancock's troops pushed forward at quick step until within a quarter mile of the enemy entrenchments. Then, with a tremendous cheer, they rushed up to and over the breastworks. Once inside the salient, they had to wage a violent hand-to-hand battle; much of the struggle was at such close quarters that men dared not fire, but used their guns as clubs. The Union forces quickly captured 2,000 troops (some early reports, as Wainwright notes, said 4,000), and twenty guns. They also took two generals, Edward Johnson of Kentucky and George H. Steuart of Maryland. This was so important a success that it did not much matter that Burnside was meanwhile beaten off.

It was so important, in fact, that Lee felt it necessary to restore his lines. "He made the most strenuous efforts," writes Grant, "to regain the position he had lost. Troops were brought up from his left and attacked Hancock furiously. Hancock was forced to fall back; but he did so slowly, with his face to the enemy, inflicting on him heavy loss, until behind the breastworks he had captured. These he turned, facing them the other way, and continued to hold." This was the battle of the "bloody angle" or "the salient." The narrow limits of the angle intensified the desperation of the fighting on both sides. At one time the ranks on each side were crowded four deep by reinforcements.

"Our losses were frightful," writes a Union participant. "What remained of many different regiments that had come to our support had concentrated at this point, and had planted their tattered colors upon a slight rise of ground close to the Angle, where they stayed during the latter part of the day." Pack mules brought up three thousand rounds of ammunition apiece at a time; and the men, firing three to four hundred rounds each, fought on with their mouths encrusted with powder from biting cartridges. The continuous fire cut and tore the heavy logs of the breastworks until their ends resembled hickory brooms. Early next day, the 13th, this participant helped bury the mounds of dead on the Union side of the works. Then he peered over the other side. "Hundreds of Confederates, dead or dying, lay piled over one another in those pits. The fallen lay three or four deep in some places, and with few exceptions, they were shot in or about the head." The trenches had run with blood.

Hancock held most of his ground, and the Union forces could regard Spotsylvania as a partial victory. But still Grant was checkmated, and had to try another flanking movement.

❊ ❊ ❊

LAUREL HILL, MAY 12, THURSDAY. This place, where my own and corps headquarters are pitched tonight, is about a mile and a half to the left and rear of the Alsop house; and is the spot where the Fifth Corps hospitals have been established. . . .

This has been a day of fighting fully equal to any that we have had as to severity and loss, but for once with the advantage decidedly on our side. The Second Corps had all moved around to the left of the Sixth during the night, and at daylight made an attack in force, the whole corps being thrown in at once. I do not know any of the particulars of it, and saw nothing but the long line of prisoners as they came to the rear. General Meade in his congratulatory order says Hancock captured forty guns and seven thousand prisoners, "driving the enemy entirely from his works." The number of guns and prisoners is very likely overestimated; nor has Lee yet entirely left his works. Still, we have made a big haul of prisoners, and certainly got more guns than have ever before been taken or lost at once by this army; being the whole of Johnson's division of Ewell's corps together with Generals Johnson and George Steuart. We also still hold the line so far as first taken but no more; while Lee has spent the whole day in efforts to recapture it, making such fierce attacks that although our men were now behind works, it has been all they could do to hold their own with the whole of the Second and Sixth Corps, and the First and Fourth Divisions of this. Our loss during the day is estimated from 5,000 all the way up to 10,000.

Of course nothing has been talked of all day by those at the rear save this morning's success; every incident reported, whether true or not, is rapidly passed from mouth to mouth through the whole army. The following is fact. When the two rebel generals were brought to Hancock, he, having known them both before the war, offered his hand. Johnson took it and behaved like a man, but Steuart, who is from Baltimore, drew himself up and said that "under present circumstances he could not take General Hancock's hand." Hancock at once replied "under no other circumstances would it be offered to a rebel." It was very good.

Officers just in from the captured salient, where the fighting is still going on, say that there has been no one spot like it in the whole war.

A perfect rampart of dead lie on either side of the captured works. A number of the guns have not been got over the works yet, and neither side is willing to let the other take them off. I do not know exactly why we have withdrawn all the guns from our right, the Second or Third Divisions remaining there; whether we are to move away from here altogether tonight, or whether there is to be another grand attack in the morning. I hear that 20,000 reinforcements are expected up tonight.

MAY 13, FRIDAY. It commenced raining last night and has kept at it pretty steadily all today. The day has been a veritable day of rest to the men and all, for both sides were too much exhausted to do anything, even if the weather had been more propitious. Lee has given up all hopes of recovering the ground lost to Hancock, and has fallen back about a mile at this point to his second line. . . .

Patrick tells me a good story about starting off the prisoners. He was alone at the time, all his officers being away. He therefore desired the adjutant-general of Steuart's brigade to assist him in forming that command; but General Steuart would not allow him to do it. Patrick then called off the different regiments of the brigade, with the names of the commanding officers, and the companies in the same way. Seeing this, the adjutant went up to General Steuart and told him that he might as well help, for their whole organization was as well known by Patrick as by himself.

Our reinforcements have not yet made their appearance. We need them, for this army is very rapidly dwindling. General Grant, I hear, says that he never knew what fighting was before. A new move is to be tried tonight, the order for which has just come. This corps is to move around to the left of Burnside and attack at daylight tomorrow. It is a terrible night for a march, though it be but seven miles. The infantry are to move along in rear of our line of works, while I take the road around with the batteries. I am to get a guide when I reach Army Headquarters about two miles from Laurel Hill.

The last three days I should have had very little to do under any circumstances; but General Warren has shown no disposition to treat me differently, though he has not reiterated his order about remaining with the Reserve. I have found no previous commander who did not shew me more consideration, though he made so good a commencement. I have talked the matter over with Patrick, in whom I have great confidence. He confirms me in my determination to grin and bear it until this campaign is over, and then ask to be relieved, unless matters change for the better.

Today I received the first letters from home since leaving Culpeper. Though only ten days, it seems months since I last heard, making the answers to questions written before that read very queer; the subjects having been entirely forgotten. The latest was dated on the 6th. They had just heard of our starting, not of the commencement of fighting. I have got a line off almost every day, Mr. Hendricks, the *Herald* reporter, kindly sending them with his dispatches.

In our domestic affairs we manage to rub along, not expecting much luxury in eating or comfort in sleeping such times as these. I wonder how I manage to get on with only four or six hours' sleep, who need eight or nine ordinarily; but excitement does wonders. Dr. Thompson's boy acts as cook. He does quite tolerably, considering; better a good deal than Ben. Fried potatoes in his "pièce de résistance." My old black gets no better, they tell me; I have not seen him since we left, and I fear it is a hopeless case. The little grey which was shot on the 9th is going to recover from his wound. We have our spring waggon back, and part of the headquarters guard, but I fear that there is no chance of my getting my battalion of heavies, or even all of Dexter's company. My artillery horses are suffering badly from want of sufficient forage; but the number hit in action has been quite small, exclusive of those lost with Winslow's section on the 5th. . . .

BEVERLY HOUSE, MAY 14, SATURDAY. My march last night was a hard one and a most extraordinary. I started at ten o'clock with all the batteries, making, together with their waggons, some one hundred and twenty carriages. The night was dark as Erebus to begin with, but a dense fog and drizzling rain increased the darkness soon after midnight. Our road at first lay directly to the rear, and was encumbered with endless trains on their way to Belle Plaine. I had to exert the full force of my authority and constantly appeal to the spread eagle on my shoulders in order to get past these endless trains. Sometimes even these did not avail, when main force had to be resorted to, and their waggons forcibly turned out of the road.

My orders were to be at the Beverly house by the first break of day, and if the thing was among the possibilities I meant to do it. When, after moving some four miles, I came to the bridge over the Ni River on this road, I found a waggon upset right in the middle of it; the bridge timbers had given away, and the waggon gone through. It took us a long time to repair this damage in the dark, but meantime I got my column nicely closed up and ready to cross without a break so soon as the bridge was repaired. Notwithstanding this long delay, the rear of the waggons which had got over was but a few hundred yards beyond. I made these fellows haul off to the side of the road until I got nearly up to Army Headquarters. . . .

At Meade's headquarters I found my guide and sent him on with one of my staff to see what the matter was, and clear the road if it was possible; at the same time riding myself a mile or more up the road. The case proved hopeless. The string of waggons was unbroken, and no possibility of their freeing the road until the trouble, miles ahead, was removed. For hours I paced the ground in front of the quiet tents where almost everyone was asleep, or sat cowering over the wet embers of the camp fires. Duane, who seemed the only officer stirring, invited me in and proffered the universal drink; by no means unacceptable on such a night. But I was too nervous to sit still and liked it better out-of-doors, where I could watch every foot gained by that horrid train. If it was General Meade's intention that I should move by this road, and I presume it was, as my guide is furnished here, he should have informed Ingalls of it and held him as chief quartermaster responsible that the road was not blocked. The behaviour of General Warren to me the last week made me doubly anxious to get to the appointed spot at the appointed hour. When, then, my guide about half past one o'clock informed me that he had found a man who said he could take us a short-cut through the wood, I at once jumped at the offer, and started.

We left the road in front of Meade's headquarters and crossing the field in which they were, plunged immediately into a dense wood. Through this we went for nearly two miles, by a mere wood road only just wide enough to drive the carriages between the trees; up and down the steepest hills and over the roughest gullies. How we did I do not know. The more I think of it the more I wonder at our success, for it was so dark that the lead drivers could not see the carriages ahead of them, and only kept the road by driving their horses' noses against them all the time. Our guide made but one mistake, and that he discovered before more than one carriage had gone wrong. I could not discover how he managed to discern the road; to me I was surrounded by the same blank darkness on every side. My guide properly rode a white horse which I could distinguish at twenty paces, no more; from him I stretched my staff out Indian file so as to keep up connection with the leading battery and at the same time leave interval enough between the guide and the first carriage to enable him to discover mistakes before the batteries went wrong, as to turn around there in the dark was impossible. We reached the open ground so that the rear of the column came out just as day was breaking. I felt a great relief as I saw the last of the one hundred twenty carriages climb the hill into the open ground, and at once galloped again to the head.

Just where we struck the road I found Burnside's headquarters, and his "butterfly cavalry" picketing the road from there on. . . . By the time my whole command was parked at the bridge, there not over 3,000 infantry up, yet I had marched twice as far, and been detained half the night near Meade's headquarters. They say that the men got lost in the wood on every side, and that the mud was ankle deep the whole way. Of course any attempt at the intended attack was hopeless for

today, as it was noon before the greater part of the corps was got together, and the Sixth commenced to arrive. This is the second night
march of the Fifth Corps rendered useless by the men not keeping up.
I doubt if it was possible last night, but there was no excuse the night we
left the Lacy house.

There has been more or less skirmishing during the day, and my
batteries have done some firing, but we have had no heavy fighting. The
Ninth Corps has held the north bank of the Ni River for some days
with detached posts up to this point. Today they straightened out their
left flank so that it reached up to within one division front of the
Fredericksburg road. . . . The road itself is very nearly straight from the
bridge to the Court House, its direction about south-southwest. Spotsylvania Court House, which we can plainly see, is a village of not over
a dozen houses, including the Court House itself, the tavern, and two
churches. The two first buildings stand directly facing our road, and we
can plainly distinguish the road running along their front, which is the
one we wanted to get. This is being a good deal nearer our object than
we were yesterday, but does not insure its accomplishment.

The Beverly house stands on a slight knoll, two little branches of the
Ni running past it on either side. East of it on the other side of the
Ni is a large high open plain on which the Sixth Corps deployed today:
this is the estate of Mr. Anderson, who has a fine large house in the
centre of it.* Southeast from us, a mile off, a small open knoll rises
out of the wood to a height which completely commands us here. It
had a small house on it this morning, from which the spot is known as
the "Jet House," though the building itself was burned this afternoon.

So soon as he had men enough to make a strong skirmish line, General
Warren sent some three hundred men over to hold this Jet house; while
I placed Cooper and Breck in position close to the Beverly house, and
bearing on the same point. I also pushed Rittenhouse up the Fredericksburg road to where there had been some Ninth Corps guns, I presume,
as there were works thrown up. The rest of the batteries remained in
park near the bridge. Rittenhouse threw a few shots at the Court House,
while Cooper and Breck had quite a little squabble with a few guns the
rebs got at the Jet house while they held it. This same Jet house, lying
in the wood away out on our left, and commanding so good a view in
all directions, came very near proving a trap for a number of our
generals, including Meade himself. Our little outpost of two or three

* The Anderson house, back of which Meade made his headquarters on May 17, is described by Colonel Theodore Lyman as one of the best he had seen in Virginia. "It is a
quite large place, built with a nest of out-houses in the southern style. . . . Anderson
was reputedly a rich man, but he had carpets on very few rooms; most were floored
with hard pine."

hundred had been relieved by Upton's brigade of the Sixth Corps; and
Upton had just commenced to entrench himself, when a strong force
of rebs pounced upon him so suddenly that they were within an ace
of making all prisoners. . . .

It has rained pretty much all day. The whole country is a sea of mud,
especially around the house here, where the ground has been trod up
by men and horses. Indoors the floor is covered with an inch of mud;
but notwithstanding that, Warren, his staff, myself, and my staff are
spreading our blankets on the muddy floor for our night's lodging. The
roof leaks, too, so that small streams of water drop through onto us;
while a few signs of blood around show that the house was used as a
hospital early in the day. Such a pig sty one would hesitate to enter at
home—certainly without thick-soled boots and turning up one's pants.
But here it seems a blessing, and I expect to sleep soundly, for it is
near forty-eight hours since I closed my eyes. We lay tonight in our spurs,
fearing the enemy may try us, as our men have been too tired today to do
much in the way of entrenching themselves. All my batteries have been
moved to the north side of the bridge for the night.

MAY 15, SUNDAY.   A quiet day, although it is Sunday, which is somewhat
extraordinary for, without its being intended, Sunday has seemed to be
heretofore the day of hardest work. Perhaps it is only because the day
being properly a day of rest, we notice it all the more when it ceases to
be so. By "a quiet day" I only mean comparatively so, for skirmishing
is going on incessantly, and more or less wounded constantly coming
in from the front, but there has been no attack on either side, nor any
artillery firing on our side. The Second Corps has passed around to the
left of the Sixth, leaving the Ninth as the extreme right of our line.*
Cooper and Rittenhouse returned to the positions they held yesterday
and have covered themselves with good earthworks. The rest of the
batteries remained in park, but were kept harnessed from daylight except for an hour or so in the afternoon, when they took it off to clean the
horses down.

My poor horses are suffering terribly under this hard work. It is the

---

* Lee's and Grant's armies were maneuvering slightly for position. Grant wrote Halleck
on May 16: "We have had five days almost constant rain without any prospect yet of it
clearing up. The roads have now become so impassable that ambulances with wounded
men can no longer run between here and Fredericksburg. All offensive operations necessarily cease until we can have twenty-four hours of dry weather." Both armies had been
burying their dead. On May 13 Grant had recommended the promotion of Sherman and
Meade to the grade of major general in the regular army; Hancock's promotion to be
brigadier general of regulars; and the promotion of Wright, Gibbon, and Humphreys to
be major generals of volunteers. "General Meade has more than met my most sanguine
expectations," wrote Grant to Stanton. "He and Sherman are the fittest officers for large
commands I have come in contact with."

same old story of corps commanders insisting that their artillery shall be hitched up all the time, even at night frequently. They have no consideration for the horses, nor will they learn that a battery can be harnessed in less time than a regiment of infantry take to put on their equipments. We have had our teams on half rations, five pounds of grain a day and nothing else; notwithstanding which, there is hardly a sack of grain in my whole command, and Cooper, who is the most improvident of my commanders, has had no feed whatever since Friday. I hope for something of a supply during the night, but am not certain as my waggons have been repeatedly taken away from Cruttenden to carry wounded, and then seized by other quartermasters, as he has no assistant that he can send with them. I know almost nothing as to my ammunition train, save that so far Dexter has kept us well supplied and reports having sent to fill it up again. He is better off than Cruttenden in that he has an officer under him to go with his waggons. The supplies for the men keep abundant; I have heard of no failings in this respect. The wounded, too, have all been sent off which could be moved. A few hundred bad cases, I learn, were left in the hospitals at Locust Hill. But tents, supplies, and surgeons were left with them, and also a small guard to keep off marauders until the ground should be occupied by responsible bodies of the enemy.

Hendricks gets a paper now and then, but no mail reaches us; at least no letters for me. The reports in the *Herald* I think are more accurate this campaign than any newspaper reports I have seen before. We hear good news from Sheridan with his cavalry: he passed right through here the day after he started, and had we come on at the same time we could doubtless have got possession of the Court House at least. Grant's flanking move was not extended enough to deceive the enemy. From here he struck the Orange Railroad at Beaver Dam, and destroyed a lot of it; also three or four trains and any amount of rations, beside recapturing several hundred of our men, prisoners on their way to Richmond. There is a rumour that in a subsequent fight with the rebel cavalry "Jeb" Stuart was killed, their best cavalry general.* . . .

MAY 16, MONDAY. Another day of quiet: Grant seems to be nonplused

---

* Jeb Stuart was dead at thirty-two, leaving an imperishable legend behind him. His opponent, Sheridan, with 12,000 cavalry had begun a raid toward Richmond on May 9, with the object of pushing as far as Butler's army on the James, getting provisions there, and returning; he could play havoc with Lee's communications, and perhaps bring Stuart to battle. Learning of the expedition, Stuart moved to halt it. He wrote another officer at daybreak on May 11: "I intersect the road the enemy is marching on at Yellow Tavern, the head of the turnpike, six miles from Richmond. My men and horses are tired, hungry, and jaded, but *all right*." In the sharp battle of Yellow Tavern later that day he was shot in the abdomen by a Union trooper. Carried into Richmond, he died on the evening of May 12.

and to have got to the end of his tether. Things remain just as they were yesterday. We got a little feed for our horses last night, but we have orders not to feed more than four pounds a day, barely enough to keep life in a horse provided he had nothing to do. Under this I have got permission, however, to have the horses of the batteries not in position unharnessed, save for a couple of hours at daylight, and in case of any firing on the line; which is a great relief. I got two or three tents up today for my headquarters under cover of the hill by the Beverly house, where I am much more comfortable than with the crowd in the house. It has cleared off at last, and the ground is drying up rapidly. I managed to get a bath and clean clothes in my tent, which was a luxury no one can imagine who has not been living as we have since we left Culpeper. I cannot imagine how the line officers of infantry manage, for they have no means of carrying aught with them beyond what they have on their backs. They must simply go dirty: a fortnight without a change is something awful to contemplate.

I got a couple of hours to run up to Army Headquarters this afternoon. They being only some three-quarters of a mile back from the bridge, near the Harris house, I could hear any alarm on our front and return in five minutes. I learned there that by the last returns our losses are over 35,000 up to last night; which is more than I supposed More than 20,000 fell in the Wilderness, beside some 6,000 reported prisoners. These are about all the prisoners we have lost, while we have nearly double that number of the enemy. Their loss in killed and wounded must be near two-thirds as great as ours, which with the 10,000 captured will make a hole in their strength.*

General Meade has got a new kink as to his artillery; the Reserve not having been needed so far in this campaign is to be broken up, or sent off to Washington as useless. The last is Meade's plan but Hunt tells me he means to hold on to all the organizations he can, and wants Meade to reduce the number of guns to a battery rather than send off the batteries themselves, so that they can easily be filled up again if needed. General Horatio Wright has been appointed Sedgwick's successor in command of the Sixth Corps by the President; he has held the position by seniority since Sedgwick's death.

MAY 17, TUESDAY. Have been busy all day reorganizing my command, for it almost amounts to that. Late last night the order came to reduce

---

* No treatment of losses is fully satisfactory. General Andrew A. Humphreys in his volume on *The Virginia Campaign of 1864–65* computes the total of Union killed and wounded in the two battles of the Wilderness and Spotsylvania at 28,407; adding the report of missing, the grand total was 33,110. Confederate losses are not accurately known, but were smaller, for the Southerners fought largely from entrenchments, and as Wainwright says, showed greater skill in protecting themselves.

all batteries to six guns, shipping off the surplus guns and ordnance stores at Belle Plaine. We are to retain six caissons to each battery, all the ammunition, and every serviceable horse. The change has at least the advantage of enabling us to put the remaining guns in complete order, and has given all my batteries, save "D" New York, a full supply of horses. The column which started for Belle Plaine this noon looked sorry enough, and will have hard work getting there with the teams sent. To make good the guns lost in this way four batteries from the reserve have been assigned to each corps, so that we have the same number of guns with which we started. . . .

A number of stragglers, runaways from the battlefield, have been brought back to the army; who are ordered to be tried at once, and executed where found guilty. The reinforcements are said to be fairly on their way up at last. General Warren asked for some heavier guns last night, and Taft's battery of twenty-pounders was sent up this afternoon, but not posted, as our line is to be advanced tonight to where our pickets now are, about three-quarters of a mile from the Court House. A big move is on foot for the night. The Second and Sixth Corps are to return to the old ground on the right and pitch in there; great things are hoped from it by Grant. I fear he will not find Lee asleep.

❊ ❊ ❊

Bad news reached the Union army on May 18. General Franz Sigel had been defeated three days earlier in the Shenandoah Valley, at New Market; this being the famous engagement in which a battalion of Virginia Military Institute cadets, mere lads, fought bravely under one of their professors. Sigel had to retreat, and was shortly relieved from a command. At substantially the same time Ben Butler's Army of the James was defeated by P. G. T. Beauregard at Drewry's Bluff below Richmond. His force of 15,800 men was almost enveloped by some 18,000 Confederates, and he was compelled to withdraw into the historic bottle of Bermuda Hundred—a triangle of land where the Appomattox River joins the James. The Confederates promptly corked the bottle by a line of entrenchments. Butler planned a stroke against Petersburg, but when Grant ordered him to send nearly two-thirds of his effective troops to assist the struggle against Lee, he was left powerless to take the offensive.

Grant now, on the 18th, undertook a new blow against Lee's left, in the hope that the enemy had weakened it to meet the previous Union concentration on his right. He ordered Hancock with the Second Corps and H. G. Wright with the Sixth to attack at dawn. The troops moved forward at four A.M., only to find that Lee had erected new earthworks of the most formidable nature, protected in front by heavy slashings and lines of abatis. A storm of musketry and artillery swept the attackers. After several attempts they fell back, and Meade ordered the movement discontinued. A simultaneous attack by Burnside with his Ninth Corps on a different segment of the line also broke down. Meanwhile, the artillery of the Fifth Corps, as Wainwright indicates, kept up a heavy fire for several hours.

It will be noted that entrenchments were playing a much larger part in the fighting than in earlier years; the Confederates in particular prepared heavy defensive works. It will also be noted that the Union troops moved by night marches and delivered their assaults at first daylight. The combats were unprecedented in intensity. Savage fighting had continued for fourteen hours without cessation in the Bloody Angle of Spotsylvania, and was almost as hotly sustained at other points. The war was becoming brutal in other respects. "The wagoners and train rabble and stragglers have committed great outrages in the rear of this army," writes Theodore Lyman.

Both Lee and Grant were being reinforced. The defeat of Butler enabled Beauregard to send part of his troops to the Army of Northern Virginia; the retreat of Sigel released other Confederate veterans in the Shenandoah Valley. Grant's losses were being repaired, as Wainwright states, by reinforcements—the War Department reported that it sent him nearly 28,000 officers and men between May 4 and June 12, 1864—and by new recruits. Fighting was to go on steadily until November, and no corps was to see more of it than Warren's, in which Wainwright led the artillery; for that corps saw its total casualties in the six months of May–October 1864 rise above 11,000.

❊ ❊ ❊

MAY 18, WEDNESDAY. The movement last night was carried out on time, so that two divisions of the Second Corps attacked at daylight. But they found that Lee had covered his front here with acres of slashing, which was almost impenetrable of itself; rebel batteries too swept the whole front, and infantry enough were there to make success impossible. Our men, especially the Irish Brigade, are said to have behaved admirably. They made a number of attempts to get through the fallen timber, but were unable to reach the rebel works. Our losses are said to have been considerable; that for the enemy could hardly have been anything. All attempt on that flank is given up, and now the whole army, including the Ninth Corps, is to be swung around again on to our left.

The troops having been all withdrawn from our left, Warren had to stretch his command out so as to cover more front and also protect his own left flank. At daylight I sent Major Fitzhugh with Hart's, Bigelow's,

Richardson's, and Walcott's batteries, sixteen light twelve-pounders, to the Anderson house, where they had a beautiful position completely protecting our left rear, where the country was all open. . . .

Meantime Crawford was pushing forward on Griffin's left, seeking a good position with a shortened line. Major Roebling was with him, and brought word that he had opened a capital position for batteries. I at once returned with him to look at it, and finding it all that he described, moved Cooper's, Phillips's, and Breck's batteries around there, placing the former as senior captain in command of them all when once in position. The place was an ugly one to get into, or out of, but perfect when reached. A straight ridge of some 300 yards in length fell off gradually in front to a small rivulet and marsh; at the rear it descended abruptly for twenty-five or thirty feet, so sharp that we had to level places for the limbers to stand, but they were beautifully protected. The crest was so narrow that most of the guns were sunk in the rear of the bank. This line formed an angle of about 60 degrees with that held by Griffin and was separated from it by a swamp some 150 yards wide; so that Fitzhugh's and Cooper's batteries covered each other's front to perfection. Cooper, too, had an excellent oblique fire on the Court House; but a projecting wood on his left prevented his seeing the rebel lines much to their right of it, while at the same time it hid him from their batteries in that quarter. . . .

I had not got these last three batteries fairly in position when the sound of Hancock's attack reached us. This was the signal for us to open, which we did, and were at once answered by the rebels. The engagement lasted a good three-quarters of an hour, and was very sharp, the practise being excellent on both sides, and the range short. The enemy fired from twenty guns that we could see, and some shots came from a battery on our left which was hidden by the woods. I had twenty-six guns firing, and succeeded at last in silencing all of theirs.

At different times during the day one side or the other opened fire, so that there was a great deal of noise to no effect. I did all I could to avoid a waste of ammunition, but Warren repeatedly ordered me to fire, and Griffin insisted upon the batteries with him keeping at it pretty steady. At one time I feared that they would use up all the ammunition I had and sent word to General Hunt that such would be the case if Warren insisted on a continuance of it all day. This brought Hunt over, and he managed to make Warren less exacting on this point. Cooper's batteries expended about ninety rounds per gun; Fitzhugh's near one hundred and fifty. My loss was three killed, and seven or eight wounded. Griffin's infantry suffered a good deal, which showed the folly of his provoking the enemy's fire when they were inclined to keep quiet. I could not see what damage we did to them, but it was certainly equal to what we suffered, though their works were very strong, and they understand protecting themselves better than our men do. . . .

During the day I visited the Anderson house, which is really a fine as well as comfortable residence; the view from the top is extensive and beautiful. The females of the family are there, and shoals of young niggers in every quarter. The Sixth Corps returning in the afternoon, my batteries there were withdrawn about three o'clock.

Since leaving the Alsop house, Warren seems to have got over the freak he had of fighting the artillery through his aides, and today has allowed me to attend to my own business. I know nothing as to what put such a notion into his head; and am willing to forget it all, if he chooses to treat me decently hereafter. I fear, though, that he is apt to take freaks, and when excited does not consider much what he does. With my forty-eight guns I have now an effective strength of 1,550 officers and men, and 1,180 horses. The heavy artillery battalion I do not pretend to report or know anything about.

MAY 19, THURSDAY. The rifled batteries remained where they were yesterday except that Taft was sent off to Washington, and was replaced by Bigelow, the Fifth Corps being now the extreme right of the line. Cutler's right was drawn in so as to rest on the Ni about four hundred yards above the bridge, his line passing close to a small deserted house on the right of the road. Here I posted Stewart and Mink on either side of the house so that they could command the valley so far up as it was open, which was only a few hundred yards. . . .

Everything remained quiet during the morning, even Griffin being willing to pass a day without the noise of cannon. The rest of the army passed quietly in rear of us to our left, the Second Corps being the last. All my spare caissons, forges, and so on were sent to the Anderson house to be out of the way. About five o'clock in the afternoon Ewell made a bold push to get possession of the Fredericksburg road in our rear, and did succeed in pushing his left across it, picking up a few waggons and men. His right struck Kitching's brigade, and drove them at first, his men not being accustomed to skirmishing. But General Tyler with a division of new troops, reinforcements, and mostly heavy artillery, happened to be coming up just at that time, and was at once put in to strengthen Kitching and extend his right.* Birney also brought up his

* John Howard Kitching of New York, who had entered the service in 1861 as captain of the Second New York Artillery, was now colonel and shortly to be brevetted a brigadier general. He died early in 1865 of wounds sustained at Cedar Creek. Robert Ogden Tyler, whom we have met before, was a division commander in the Second Corps, and a very good one. He was soon to be made a major general of volunteers and brigadier general in the regular army.

division and Ewell was repulsed with loss so that he left his dead on the field. . . .

Most laughable accounts are given of this fight. To nearly all of Tyler's command it was the first for both officers and men; they consequently went in very much jumbled up, and doubtless did fire at our own men in some few cases, but not nearly to the extent talked of. Our loss was probably double what it would have been had the officers seen more service. The best account of it is given by one of the quartermasters, who claims to have seen it, as follows: "First there was Kitching's brigade firing at the enemy; then Tyler's men fired into his; up came Birney's division and fired into Tyler's; while the artillery fired at the whole d——d lot."

This evening I got a batch of letters from home down to the 13th. They had not then received any of my pencil notes, which I have sent off nearly every day; but the papers had given full accounts, and they were congratulating themselves on my name not being in the long lists of killed and wounded, which certainly look fearful in print. Mary is greatly exercised over the loss of the two guns in the Wilderness, under the idea that I am blamed for it; which I am not, the whole responsibility resting on General Griffin. Of course, the whole city was in a state of terrible anxiety, while they appear to have received a better idea of our success than we have here. I also got a letter from Major Reynolds.* . . . He gives the following as the idea prevalent through the Western army: "We expect Lieutenant-General Grant will march right into Richmond: if he fails it will be because he has not his old troops with him. The Army of the Potomac never did anything." Reynolds and the Twentieth Corps of course know better than this, but their easy victories at the West have given them this notion. Had they been here the last fortnight, they might have been induced to say with Grant: "I never knew what fighting was before."

The trial of deserters has been pushed forward rapidly. Several are to be shot tomorrow morning. Now is the time to do it; the punishment should be so sure and speedy that cowards will be more afraid of running away than of standing. The Sixth Corps reports that they found our hospitals at Laurel Hill unharmed, and a rebel guard over them. Arrangements were made to send for all such as could be moved. . . .

MAY 20, FRIDAY. The days have been clear of late, not very warm; but there is a heavy fog every night, which keeps things in a state of chronic dampness and nastiness; bad and uncomfortable enough for us who lodge under a roof, and must be much worse for *outsiders.* I have met

* Gilbert H. Reynolds, formerly of the First New York Light Artillery, was in the Twentieth Corps under Hooker, now beginning the Atlanta campaign, and later to take part in Sherman's March to the Sea.

with two losses while here, which prove that I have not my man John (or Charles) with me, viz: my leggings and poncho stolen while hanging out to dry. I shall feel the want of them badly when it comes on to rain again; especially the leggings as I have no high boots. During this wet weather and night alarms I have found the advantage of lace bootees over boots, for those who wore the latter, getting them wet during the day, did not dare to take them off at night lest they should not be able to get them on again in their wet state. We are all getting used to this wretched life now. I am astonished to find how little sleep I can get along with, when kept up by constant excitement.

Things have been very quiet today; no attempt on either side. Indeed Lee seems to have determined to act altogether on the defensive of late; and Grant to be quite nonplused as to what to do: he evidently has not found any weak spot opposite our left, or there would have been fighting today. Now he has concluded to give Spotsylvania up altogether as a bad job, and we have orders this evening to march in the morning. I am to withdraw all my batteries before daylight, and previous to that to erect brush screens in front of them on the works so that the enemy will not know that they are withdrawn. I suspect that they will make a shrewd guess at it, however. The wounded are all to be sent to Fredericksburg, and everything indicates a longer detour this time than heretofore. . . .

MAY 21, BIVOUAC, SATURDAY.   Our corps started at ten A.M. this morning, getting off without any serious trouble, though the enemy did open from some of their batteries and knock over a few men. We passed the Ninth and Sixth Corps just beyond the Anderson house, the latter of which covered the rear, and followed a road about parallel to the Ni River until we reached Guinea Station on the Fredericksburg road. Here we turned to the south, and crossing the Mattaponi River near the railroad bridge that was, are spending the night on its right bank. This river, which together with the Pamunkey goes to form the York, is itself formed by four branches of nearly equal size, the Mat, Ta, Po, and Ni; whether the river gets its name from uniting those of its branches or vice versa I do not know; but the arrangement is both clever and pretty. At the spot where we crossed this afternoon it should properly be called the Taponi River, as the Mat branch does not come in until you get farther down.

Our march today has not been a severe one, the roads being good and unobstructed. . . . We are bound for Hanover Junction: at least that is the point Grant hopes to get possession of before Lee. If we succeed it will be a great thing. The Second Corps has made a longer detour to the east than we have, going from here to Bowling Green. Our new base is to be at Port Royal on the Rappahannock.

So has ended the battle of Spotsylvania Court House, for I suppose that properly speaking all our fighting around that point was one battle.

Yet it bore more of the likeness of an irregular siege than of a pitched battle, for all the engagements were actual assaults on works. Grant was foiled there as he was in the Wilderness, so that the victory, so far as there was any, rests again with Lee. Yet we did somewhat better than in the Wilderness; for, as near as I can learn, our losses have not been nearly so great, while the enemy's have been heavier. I may be mistaken in this, but believe I am correct.

This evening we have orders "to be prepared to move tomorrow at four A.M. The object being to take up at that time a defensive position in this vicinity. . . . This is rendered necessary by difficulties having been met by General Burnside in getting to the position assigned him." . . .

SIXTEEN

COLD HARBOR:
GRANT MOVES TO THE JAMES

The Union advance being frustrated at Spotsylvania, even Grant realized that Lee's position was impregnable to direct assault. He therefore began a new movement to turn the Confederate position by a flank march; sending Hancock's corps south and east along the Mattaponi to Milford Station on the Fredericksburg & Richmond Railroad. At that point he was about forty-five miles north of Richmond. The flanking movement, immediately observed by the Confederates, tempted them to an attack, which was repulsed. But it delayed the general advance of Grant's troops so that once more they found the enemy ahead of them. Two rivers, the North and South Anna, unite to make the Pamunkey. On the morning of May 23 the Union forces came to the banks of the North Anna—and found Lee firmly planted on the other side! But planted is hardly the right word, for Lee was as usual in active movement. Hancock reported: "The enemy was seen in large force marching in column on the opposite bank, evidently en route from Spotsylvania."

Though Lee had priority, he was temporarily unable to hold the line of the North Anna. Warren's corps found a neglected point on the stream and, after an advanced brigade plunged over and the engineers built a pontoon bridge, crossed to the south side. Hancock's men, with some hard fighting, soon made good a passage farther downstream. Lee was thus left in an unpleasant predicament. But he brilliantly extricated himself. He thrust his center between the two wings of the Union army, Warren's downstream and Hancock's upstream. If battle began, Grant would be unable to reinforce either wing except by ordering the other to make a double crossing of the stream.

"To make a direct attack from either wing," Grant wrote Halleck on May 26, "would cause a slaughter of our men that even success would not justify. To turn the enemy by his right, between the two Annas, is impossible because of the swamp on which his right rests. To turn him on his left leaves Little River, New Found River, and South Anna River, all of them streams presenting considerable obstacles to the movement of our army, to be crossed." The Union commander therefore decided to withdraw across the North Anna, and begin a new advance—a march east and south to cross the Pamunkey. And once more Lee fell back by a shorter line, so that the Union troops no sooner got over the Pamunkey than they again encountered the whole Confederate army ready for battle.

"I am afraid," General Meade had told a fellow officer at breakfast on Sunday, May 22, "the rebellion cannot be crushed this summer!" The prospects grew darker day by day. Grant's army was now getting close to the area in which McClellan had fought with such ill success in his Peninsular campaign of 1862.

❈ ❈ ❈

NORTON HOUSE, MAY 22 [1864], SUNDAY. We formed line of battle early this morning, but Lee did not make his appearance so we started at noon, and had only some ten miles' march to this place. I fear that Grant has made a botch of this move also, for Lee is certainly ahead of us now. If the demonstrations on his part which kept the whole army idle through most of today were intended to hold us until he had got sufficient force at Hanover to keep the place, they have probably succeeded.

This corps led today. Had we pushed on at daylight we should have had a fight with Longstreet this afternoon, for he was only a few hours ahead of us and we have been picking up stragglers from his command ever since we started. We must have over three hundred of them; a brigade of cavalry ahead of us would have secured five times as many and had Sheridan been here, instead of no one knows where, we should have been sure of the junction. I say this because our information is very accurate tonight, coming from so many prisoners and hosts of contraband. . . . The batteries marched today divided among the divisions, as Warren was afraid of an attack. Several are in position tonight commanding different roads, and the rest in camp near here. We were fortunate enough today to pick up a little corn in the country, so that my horses have an extra feed tonight. . . .

JERICHO MILLS, MAY 23, MONDAY. We had a fight today, and though I feel sad at the heavy loss in my own command, especially for poor Davis, I cannot help also feeling very exultant, for I do believe that the artillery saved the day. General Meade sends the following to Warren tonight, dated ten-thirty P.M.: "I congratulate you and your gallant corps for the handsome manner in which you repulsed the enemy's attack." I presume he includes the batteries in the corps, but I think that they ought to have had especial mention, particularly Mink's. But to the history of the day.

We started at five o'clock this morning, Cutler leading, then Crawford; the batteries moving as they did yesterday. A squadron or two under Colonel Pope had joined us during the night, and led the advance today. We kept the telegraph road pretty much all the way until we struck the North Anna at the railroad bridge at eleven o'clock. The bridge had been destroyed; the banks were high and ugly, while the enemy had several batteries in position on the other side. Hancock soon after came up, and it was found that we had got into the position assigned to the Second Corps. . . . The detour of course took time, so that it was after three when we again struck the river.

Jericho Mills are about four miles up the river from the railroad bridge. The ford here just above the mills is excellent; the descent on the north side is good, that on the south very sharp. Both banks are high, precipitous, and clear of trees. Griffin's division was now leading, Rittenhouse being the foremost battery. So soon as he came up I wheeled him into an orchard on the left of the road, and put him in position in front of Mason's house there. Ayres's brigade soon pushed over the ford, climbed the opposite bank and formed on the plain; followed by the rest of the First Division and then by the Fourth. . . . Breck's battery I moved down the river about six hundred yards where they could get a good oblique fire on the opposite plain. The rest were parked on the roadside until the pontoon bridge was completed, and the road on the other side rendered more practicable. So soon as this was done I crossed myself with the twelve-pounder batteries, leaving Fitzhugh on the north bank with the six-rifled batteries. Crawford's division crossed also at the same time. The deployment of the troops on the opposite bank was a beautiful sight as we watched it from the north side.

The plain on which the troops formed south of the river embraced about two hundred acres of open ground. Directly in front was a wood some one hundred and fifty yards through to a country road, along which Griffin formed his line of battle. Crawford's division connected with his left, bearing back toward the river to a deep ravine which served as a cover to his flank. The ground here was much broken, with several orchards and clumps of trees. I placed Hart and Stewart here close to a barn, in rear of Crawford's right, where they had a good position, and were already protected by some half-built rebel works. I left Captain Cooper here in charge, as he had been acting as division chief of artillery to Crawford the last two days, and I had no confidence in Captain Hart, save as a good fighter. Mink I then moved over to the right, where Cutler's division was to form. Matthewson, Walcott, and

Bigelow remained near a small barn at the head of the ramp. . . .
I started with all my staff to ride around the right of the division on to
the top of the ridge. But just as I got in rear of the right regiment, the
enemy came over the ridge and fired. As they were in line of battle along
the ridge, their fire of course struck each regiment obliquely on its
right flank. Had our men been accustomed to manoeuvre under fire, they
could easily have formed line by a quarter wheel of regiments to the
right, but as it was, the whole first brigade and a part of the second
broke most disgracefully. A few officers and men remained, about
enough for a good skirmish line; the rest ran to the river and many
of them quite crossed it. This was a very ticklish moment; our whole
right was open, and unless the enemy could be stopped they would seize
our bridge, and make sure work of Griffin and Crawford, for we had no
troops in reserve on the plain except my batteries. I felt that now was
the time to show what artillery could do.

The instant the enemy opened fire I sent Captain Davis to bring Mink
up, and so soon as it was plain that our infantry would not stand, I
started Lieutenant Morris off for Matthewson and Walcott. Mink had
not waited for orders, but forming his battery in line, was moving forward
when Davis reached him; then with his cannoneers holding by the traces,
he came up at a steady swinging trot. Anxious as I was (for whether with
good cause or not, I felt that the safety of the whole corps rested on me
and my command), I could not help a glow of pleasure and pride as I
watched the four little guns moving straight through the fugitive
infantry and forming on the very ground a whole brigade had abandoned. Matthewson with "D" Company came up almost equally well,
and Walcott was not very far behind him. These two batteries I placed
on the right of Mink at intervals of about fifty yards. Although Mink
had checked the enemy's advance, all three batteries opened within
canister range, and did not spare ammunition.

So soon as I had given them their instructions to hold on at all hazards,
I rode back to Bigelow's battery, which had unlimbered just where they
were and was firing over the wood in front. Here I found General
Warren. He had evidently been a good deal scared, as he had ordered
all three of the batteries to fire from that point when Morris came up
for the other two. I stopped Bigelow at once, and represented to the
General that his shot must fall just about where Griffin's men were, and
would do more harm than good. Meantime the fight had extended along
nearly our whole front; the enemy opening from several batteries opposite Crawford. It was heaviest in front of Griffin, where our artillery
could not get at them. Had they pushed their main force in on our right
instead of the front, it is very doubtful if the batteries could have held
them. As it was, the fight lasted until dark, very weak at last to be sure;

but our infantry were so shaken, that the batteries had to keep up a steady fire. The roar of the twenty brass guns in position was continuous; Hunt tells me that at Meade's headquarters it sounded as if the whole army was engaged. The rifled batteries had also contributed somewhat to the noise; Breck farthest down the river, and Sheldon farthest up did excellent service, as their range of fire covered both flanks. Major Fitzhugh acted very promptly and well, making excellent dispositions of his command. . . .

The bad behaviour of Cutler's first brigade is a strong instance of how panic at times seizes a whole command. No brigade in the whole army had a higher reputation than the "Iron Brigade." Its pre-eminence in the old First Corps was very generally acknowledged, yet one-half of it ran clear across the river without firing a shot, and two-thirds of the other half were brought back with difficulty by their officers to support the batteries, a service in which they have always taken especial delight.* The greater part of the Second Brigade had stood firm; and falling back, with a part of Griffin's division, extended to the left of Mink's battery. General Griffin also sent Bartlett's brigade to the right which drove the enemy, stopped by the artillery fire, back near half a mile into the wood across the railroad. We got a large number of prisoners, seven or eight hundred I believe; and the enemy's loss in killed and wounded must have been heavier than ours. General Meade came up just about the time that the fight was over. . . .

Among the prisoners taken was a young officer, who was brought up to headquarters about an hour after dark. Our headquarters were just below the head of the road leading down to the bridge, and consisted of a big fire of rails. At the time Warren had gone to Meade's headquarters; his staff, my own and most of Griffin's were sitting around the fire talking. Griffin asked the man who he was and how he came to be taken so long after the repulse, and not wounded. He said he was an adjutant-general, but would not tell of what command; that his brother had fallen in the fight, and he was looking for him when captured. He was very uppish and would answer no questions, not even as to what regiment his brother belonged to, though Griffin told him that he only asked so as to know where he most likely fell, and even offered to send

---

* Wainwright adds that Cutler appeared stunned. "The old man has not been at any time during this campaign what he was last year; he is evidently very much broken, and lost his head entirely when his men behaved so badly." Lysander Cutler of Wisconsin was in fact fifty-eight this year; wounded twice during the war, he did not long survive it. Wainwright also records with sorrow that his batteries lost eight killed and nearly fifty wounded during the day's fighting.

Of the artillery officers named, who are mainly familiar to us, the trusty Charles E. Mink, George Breck, and Albert S. Sheldon belonged to the New York volunteer forces; Aaron F. Walcott and John Bigelow to Massachusetts volunteer units.

him under guard, to look for him. The fool was so taken with his own consequence that he would hardly say anything, even when told that we knew from other prisoners exactly what troops they had engaged. We, however, had him sit down among us, gave him whiskey and tobacco, and amused ourselves with his absurd airs and obstinacy until General Warren's return. Warren put a few short, sharp questions to him, but got no answers. He then again offered to send him, under guard, to look for his brother, and on his refusing this offer, ordered him to the rear, saying that he was a fool or something of that sort. The fellow at once replied that "he had heard on their side that Warren was a good general, but no gentleman." I heard Warren murmur, "If they only think me a good general I don't care to be considered a gentleman"; which I believe to be true. . . .

General Warren has not given me one word of commendation for myself or my batteries. Perhaps I am altogether mistaken in supposing I did anything, and show my ignorance by thinking so. But the batteries certainly behaved well, and lost five to one in proportion to the infantry engaged; so he might have said something to me that I could transmit to the men.

MAY 24, TUESDAY.   This morning we found that the enemy had fallen back somewhat from our front. . . . The Second Corps also found their front free this morning so that they crossed without opposition. But the two corps are over three miles apart, and Lee comes down to the river between us. Our generals seem to have been all day in making up their minds how to unite them, and not have found out until too late to more than get ready today. This afternoon the Sixth Corps crossed here and formed on our right, coming up into the wood where Griffin's right was. My three batteries on that flank remained where they were. . . .

MAY 25, WEDNESDAY.   The position of the two armies here is certainly a very queer one. Lee still holds on to the river with his centre, while we have crossed both above and below him, but all our efforts today have failed in forming a junction of the two flanks. There has been a good deal of fighting on the part of the Ninth Corps and a part of this, in which Crawford got pretty roughly handled. This is the first time that Burnside has put in any force since the Wilderness, and from the talk of some of our officers, the work was not very well done. Lee was found entrenched in a strong position, his line running almost due south at right angles to the river. Burnside pushed through the wood so as to get sight of his line but reported it too strong to storm. . . .

QUARL'S MILL, MAY 26, THURSDAY.   There has been no fighting today; Grant finds the enemy too strongly posted to allow us any chance of carrying his works, and Lee appears inclined to act entirely on the defensive. The batteries on Griffin's front have, of course, done some firing;

so have those of the Sixth Corps to his right. I withdrew Mink and
Richardson during the morning and parked them with the Reserve,
back of the Matthews house. The infantry have been busy all day
destroying the railroad in our rear for two or three miles to beyond
Noel's Station. I went out to Griffin's line this morning; the pickets
on both sides are comparatively quiet today. From his front where the
railroad enters it we have a good view of the rebel line, which is strong—
much better laid out and heavier than ours, as they always are. I was
glad to get a copy of an order from General Meade forbidding the use
of ammunition waggons to bring up either commissary or quartermaster stores. I have had a great deal of trouble with my waggons being
seized by some quartermaster for this purpose when they have gone down
with wounded and so been separated from their train.

A council of war met last night or this morning, I don't know which,
when it was determined to make a bold stroke, viz: to cut clear of our
communications altogether, and push to get around Lee's left, shoving
right on for Richmond. I do not know enough of the country, or the
state of the two armies, to have an opinion of my own as to its prospects
of success. Warren and Hunt, I know, were both strongly in favour of it,
and are much disappointed that the plan has been abandoned. But
General Grant changed his mind this afternoon, and decided to try again
to turn Lee's right. Can it be that this is the sum of our lieutenant-
general's abilities? Has he no other other resource in tactics? Or is it
sheer obstinacy? Three times he has tried this move, around Lee's right,
and three times been foiled. His dispatch sounds very well, "I mean to
fight it out on this line, if it takes me all summer"; but officers and men
are getting tired of it and would like a little variety on night marches
and indiscriminate attacks on earthworks in the daytime. There must
be a pretty continuous line of entrenchments now, all the way from here
to the Rapidan, or half a dozen lines rather; and if we keep on they will
by and bye join on to the works around Richmond. . . .

MONGOHICK CHURCH, MAY 27, FRIDAY. We started this morning at daylight; all my batteries moving together in rear of the leading division.
At Carmel Church we met the waggons which should have been up
yesterday with rations and had to halt for a couple of hours to issue.
Meantime the Sixth Corps closed up alongside us, and the Second came
up the other road; so that what with the hundreds of waggons, and the
three corps, it seemed to me inextricable confusion. There was a large
open plain here which was completely covered with carriages of one kind
and another. When we came to start, only two of my batteries were able
to get up close to the infantry, the others having to wait for a clear place
in the road. Consequently I got separated from the rest of the corps,
and then took the wrong road, being misled by empty ammunition wag-

gons; so that after going a mile or two I found myself on the Bowling Green road. At is was hopeless to attempt to work myself back through all the waggons and as the country was safe, I took the first good road to the right and determined to trust to my Yankeeism to find a new way around. In this I succeeded perfectly, though after a good deal of anxiety. . . .

We struck very near the head of the infantry column when we rejoined it. I would be quite willing thus to increase my march one-third in length if I could have the road to myself, as being much less fatiguing to my horses than the shorter march with constant haltings when in rear of infantry. From the time I rejoined the column until our arrival here we had a hard and tedious march; the road was cut up and muddy, while the sun this afternoon has been hot. This country is better than any we have come across yet, with some really fine plantations and comfortable houses. A portion of the corps lies tonight at Brandywine with headquarters and the artillery.

DR. BROCKENBROUGH'S, MAY 28, SATURDAY. We started this morning soon after four o'clock, the artillery in rear of the three divisions of infantry; reaching the Pamunkey River by nine, nearly opposite Hanovertown.* There was a bridge here which quite unexpectedly was found to be guarded by a small body of the enemy. General Meade had camped beyond us last night, and not looking for any opposition, started on ahead, when the rebel pickets fired on him. In order to save the bridge, if possible, he at once brought up his headquarters guard and ordered them to charge it. They had quite a brisk little fight, but succeeded in securing the bridge from entire destruction until Griffin came up, when he put a brigade over. Wright, who had crossed a couple of miles farther up the river, also sent a division down, and among them all we picked up quite a little batch of prisoners. We were all across by noon, and the corps moved up onto the high ground about a mile, together with half of the batteries while the rest remained under the bank with the trains.

Fearing that Lee might attack us here . . . the corps was formed in line of battle, and well entrenched. Our right, under Griffin, crossed the road and connected with the Sixth Corps; from there we stretched along an open plain for a mile or more until our left under Crawford struck the Totopotomoy. The main force was placed on the flanks, the centre being held by batteries, with the Fourth Division and some detached brigades in a single line. Warren laid out the lines here himself,

* Hanovertown, twenty-two miles or so from Richmond by road, had originally been called Page's Warehouse, and in 1751 came close to being chosen capital of Virginia. It had been a place of detention for British prisoners during the Revolution. Edmund Ruffin, the agricultural reformer and political radical, had lived at Marlbourne not far away. It is not to be confused with Hanover, seat of Hanover County.

and for once they were made with some knowledge. The men and many of the officers too looked with wonder at the great openings he left in the re-entering angles. He liked the work and was consequently in good humour, so that I had a very pleasant time aiding him. Along this line I placed Cooper, Stewart, Bigelow, Barnes, Breck, and Phillips, or rather, all but the first and last were in the line proper, Cooper being on the road at the right; and Phillips I took out of the works to a spot in the wood where he could command the valley of the Totopotomoy. Our line faced nearly south. With the exception of a few shots exchanged by Crawford's men with rebel cavalry pickets, there was no disturbance on our front. Towards dark the Ninth Corps crossed at the same place we did and went on out to Hawes Shop to relieve the cavalry.

The name Pamunkey brings to one's memory the campaign of 1862, and makes those of us who then belonged to the Army of the Potomac feel as if we were approaching known ground. But how few of those now here took part in that campaign; how many lie at Bull Run, Antietam, Gettysburg, and all the way from here to the Rapidan! When last I saw the Pamunkey myself, it was from the windows of the steamer which was taking me home, miserably sick. That was nearly two years ago. Take the officers, too, the then corps and division commanders: Sumner, Heintzelman, Keyes, Porter, and Franklin had the corps; Sedgwick, Richardson, Kearny, Hooker, Casey, Couch, Sykes, Morell, Smith, Slocum, and McCall had divisions. Not one of them is in this army now, and could I recall the brigade commanders, I should find but few of them here either. Meade, Hancock, and Birney are all I think of at this moment. . . .

This house of Dr. Brockenbrough is a large establishment, which, if it ever was really in order, must have been fine. There are a number of fine trees in front of it, and an extensive garden, though full of weeds. We managed to purchase for our mess a fair amount of peas, asparagus, and lettuce, all which were a great treat, although we could get no butter to cook them with. They also gave us a taste of strawberries; they are not ripe yet in any quantity. The roses and honeysuckle about the house, all untrimmed and uncared for, I think finer than any I have ever seen before. We passed through several fine places today. One in particular was very extensive, quite equal to what we read of in books as to the number and order of the negro huts; it must be a kind of model plantation. There is considerable grass, too, in this country, so that my horses have had quite a bit this afternoon.

What with the fine day, the beautiful country, and the getting south of the Pamunkey, everyone is in great spirits this evening. The general notion is that Lee will not make another stand this side of the Chickahominy, if he does not fall back within the outer works of Richmond itself. His army must be growing smaller (we have over 12,000 prisoners), while we are rejoicing now in daily reinforcements. Even I am beginning to think that we may be in Richmond by the 4th of July.

This place seems like a paradise tonight, after my bath and good supper. All is as quiet as if there was no war; the frogs and crickets make the only noise; the fireflies are brilliant by their infinite numbers. One must go through such a three weeks as we have had to know all the luxury of such a spot, such a night, and a good pipe.

NORMAN HOUSE, MAY 29, SUNDAY. At two o'clock this morning we received orders to be ready to move forward at five A.M., but did not start until eleven, when General Griffin led off with his division and Rittenhouse's, Mink's, and Richardson's batteries; Crawford, Cutler, and the rest of my command following. Lockwood's (the new brigade) remained observing the lower part of the Totopotomoy. . . .

I do not see why we are so long getting at our new position. It was just so when we went to the North Anna; starting the first day with almost a forced march, and then dwindling down to what could be done in a few hours. They talk about McClellan's slowness in getting up the Peninsula. It was quite as rapid as our movements here, without the excuse which he had of green generals and an unorganized quartermaster department. I do not believe that we have met anything beside cavalry today, yet our corps has not averaged over three miles; the Ninth has not moved at all, and the others cannot have gone far.

My battalion of heavy artillery has now gone entirely; an order from Meade unites all the battalions of the regiment in the Second Corps. It directs that they "will be relieved in their present duties by details from the foot artillery regiments now with the Fifth and Sixth Corps." This may mean that another battalion is to be assigned to me, or simply that my details as teamsters, and so on, are to be replaced. Major Arthur, with all the command not on daily duty, left at once. . . . Our nearer approach to a base of supplies is shown by allowing the full ration of grain to the horses again. They needed it very badly, for they are beginning to be very poor. Our trains go down the north side of the Pamunkey to reach the White House.

❊ ❊ ❊

As Grant and Lee maneuvered their armies southward, Warren's Fifth Corps and Burnside's Ninth Corps crossed the Pamunkey River at Hanovertown, on the left or eastern flank of Grant's army. Lee by May 28 had taken up a defensive position on the Richmond side of Totopotomoy Creek. Two days later, on the 30th, Warren's troops were in position on that stream. They had crossed the Pamunkey, as Wainwright records, with little trouble. But now they were in for a hot battle. In the area of Bethesda Church, to which Warren had moved up on the Shady Grove Church Road, one of Jubal A. Early's brigades attacked the Fifth Corps with great vigor. At first he drove the Union forces back and, as Grant says in his memoirs, threatened to turn the left flank of the army. Later Warren concentrated his forces, repulsed Early, and drove him back more than a mile. Wainwright offers a spirited account of the fighting.

On the evening of the 30th, Grant received word that General W. F. Smith with his corps had arrived at the White House on the Pamunkey, a reinforcement of the first importance. His troops were ordered to march directly to the vital road junction at Cold Harbor, north of the Chickahominy. This was a point that Sheridan's cavalry seized on the 31st, and held until both Wright's and Smith's corps arrived—though Smith, through a confusion in orders, did not reach the place until mid-afternoon of June 1.

On that day another terrible battle between Grant's and Lee's armies began. The Confederates under Anderson, who had succeeded to Longstreet's corps, were seen moving along Warren's front. Both Warren and Wright were ordered to attack vigorously. Some rather confused fighting, in which the Union artillery was heavily engaged, followed. The struggle grew hotter late in the afternoon, and Wright and Smith by a stubborn assault gained the first line of the entrenchments the enemy had thrown up, taking nearly a thousand prisoners.

"While this was going on," writes Grant, "the enemy charged Warren three separate times with vigor, but were repulsed with loss. There was no officer more capable nor one more prompt in acting than Warren when the enemy forced him to it." He was under great strain, which no doubt accounts for the shortness of temper described by Wainwright. Darkness stopped the struggle, which was to be renewed with greater fierceness on June 2.

* * *

VIA HOUSE, MAY 30, MONDAY. The whole corps crossed to this house this morning, the rest of the army advancing, too, on our right. The Via house stands in an opening of some one hundred and fifty acres, with an extensive wood on the south and west of it. A small farm road runs from the house nearly due south, through this wood, to the Shady Grove Church road, distant about three-quarters of a mile. Along the north side of this latter road, and west of the former, is a long narrow opening of seventy or eighty acres, with a house in the centre known as the Bowles house; from this opening the Shady Grove road passes west for half a mile or more to an irregular opening of considerable extent where are a number of houses. Along to this point Griffin pushed his division, when the enemy opened on the head of his column with a battery up the road.

Major Fitzhugh then brought Mink up to reply, leaving Breck and Richardson in a little open halfway to the Bowles house, while Griffin got his men into line of battle. Meantime Crawford advanced down a farm road leading from the front of the Bowles house straight south . . . to the Mechanicsville pike. . . . Some two hundred yards before reaching the pike it crosses a little stream. . . . As Fitzhugh was with Griffin I rode out the road taken by Crawford, and had just mounted the bank beyond the little stream when firing commenced up the pike. At the time Colonel Hardin's brigade was ahead of me; about half of it deployed as skirmishers in the wood to our front and right, while the other half were carrying rails and throwing up breastworks around the Tinsley house, close to where I was. The other two divisions were north of the stream facing west.

Now the enemy came in from the south and along the pike, making their whole attack on Hardin's brigade, which had no line formed and was not in condition to receive it. I waited to see how much of an attack it was, which I soon found out, for in five minutes Hardin's brigade were running, and the other two divisions, finding the enemy quite on their flank, were rather indiscriminately hurrying back to the Shady Grove road. . . . I pushed at once for headquarters, where my batteries were, things looking very squally for a complete turning of our left. When I went up the road, the reserves had much the appearance of "the devil take the hindmost."

Before I reached headquarters I met General Warren, who desired me to bring three batteries to the junction of the Shady Grove road with that from the Via house. I hurried out Rittenhouse, Walcott, and Bigelow as fast as I could through the narrow road blocked by the Fourth Division, which was also moving up. Here I posted Bigelow to sweep the road and open ground by the Bowles house, while Walcott and Rittenhouse took position on the road (eastward) facing south, Rittenhouse's left piece close to the garden of Armstrong's house. Warren remained at this point himself until the fight was over, holding the Fourth Division in reserve. It was an anxious time for fifteen or twenty minutes; the fighting was very near us, yet we could see nothing of it owing to an intervening wood. But for some time I expected to see the rebs come shouting out around the Bowles house. . . .

Had the enemy, which proved to be Rodes's division, been in position to follow up their first advantage instanter, they would have been successful; but while they were forming for an advance, Crawford too had to reform his men, and Griffin to withdraw his division from its advanced position. All this occupied time, so that it may have been half an hour from the first firing until their charge on our position. During this time the enemy opened from one or two batteries near Bethesda Church, firing remarkably well. The loss must be about equal, I suspect, on both sides. Perhaps theirs is the heaviest, as doubtless many of Crawford's men now supposed to be missing will turn up; they always do after such a little stampede. . . .

MAY 31, TUESDAY. A beautiful warm, summer day, and one of peace and quietness. I fear that Lee has once more cried check to our lieutenant-general, so that Grant finds himself obliged to make a new combination. I only hear that the Second and Sixth Corps found earthworks all along in front of them. For myself, I am quite content to lie idly in the shade today, and get all the enjoyment I can. I rode all along our line in the morning so as to know its whereabouts and outlook. It all remains the same as it was last night. The Ninth Corps, or a part of it, were going into position, on Griffin's right, connecting it with the Totopotomoy. There has been no fighting on our front; hardly a shot between the opposing pickets.

We needed this as a day of quiet too, for nearly the whole of Crawford's division have gone home, it having been decided that the term of the Pennsylvania Reserves dates from their muster into the state service. This takes some three or four thousand men out of this corps, which was already small. A thousand or so of the reserves' re-enlisted men and recruits remain; these have been consolidated into a couple of regiments, and to them have been added the Maryland brigade, Kitching's heavy artillery, and perhaps some others to make a new command for Crawford temporarily. Cooper's battery, as part of the reserves, also goes out of service properly today; but he has so many recruits that the organization will still be efficient as a four-gun battery, there being over a hundred enlisted men present. Captain Cooper himself went off with forty-four men. He says that he will return so soon as the men are mustered out and paid to serve out his full three years as captain, which will take him until August. I am sorry to lose him even for a couple of weeks at this time, for he is perfect in a fight, while I do not think much of his lieutenants.

This being the last day of the month, the quiet comes very well, too, for enabling us to make up some of our returns in form; for we have had nothing but field returns since we left Culpeper, which are very inaccurate. . . . I have taken advantage of the day, too, to have my man do some washing; also to get my hair cut *en zouave*. Last night I got letters from home down to the 21st; ten days nearly on the road. Fortunately my little notes have not been so long in getting to them, though irregular; that of the 15th they got on the 18th. My letters contain nothing of moment. Newspapers we have several days later. They tell us that Butler is completely shut in at Bermuda Hundred, able to do nothing whatever; so that affair amounts to nothing. Sigel in the Valley, too, had come to a full stop and has now been replaced by old Hunter. Mr. Lincoln certainly does hold on to his fourth-rate men, however fond he may be of disgracing his best generals. . . .

BETHESDA CHURCH, JUNE 1, 1864, WEDNESDAY. This morning the left of our corps was swung around across the Mechanicsville pike: the Fourth Division to the south of the pike advanced into an open wood there, and extended from the pike across a small road which leads to Walnut Grove Church. At that time General Warren desired me to see if I could not plant batteries to fire down this road, and also where we crossed the pike. From a bend in the Walnut Grove Church road just after entering the wood we could see the rebel works distant some 1,200 yards; the road running straight from that point for three hundred yards through the wood and then across open ground. It was a very ugly place, as I could not put in more than two guns, while the enemy had several batteries behind their works which could fire on us. However, as Warren was in one of his ugly tempers, I ordered Rittenhouse to try a section, and fire only in reply to them. The enemy opened on him before he got his guns planked, but we did get them in and leaving them there, I went out the pike to see what show there was there.

The wood on the south side of the pike extends almost half a mile beyond the church. From there the ground is sowed with small scrub pines and bushes which prevented my seeing to the west along the road; but there was open ground due south where I could get a good oblique fire on the rebel works. This was on our skirmish line, and some distance beyond the line of battle. I walked out there with the officer in charge of our pickets, and found everything very quiet. He said that they did not fire at one or two men; but that the bushes in front and quiet near, too, were full of rebs, so that he did not believe it possible to put a battery there. Still, I determined to try it, cost what it would, and ordered Sheldon up with one section of his battery ("B," First New York). I took him out first to show him the ground, and directed him to have his men throw up some dirt first so as to cover themselves a little. They had not got fairly to work when the rebel skirmishers opened a perfect shower of balls upon them, wounding two of the men and Captain Sheldon. Finding the place altogether too hot to attempt anything, I ordered the section back. Sheldon's wound is a horribly ugly one, the ball striking him full in the chin and passing out at the back of the neck. No arteries can have been cut or he would have died at once, but I fear there is small chance of his getting over it.

I then returned to Rittenhouse, who I found could do nothing except provoke the enemy's fire, which was very accurate and ugly. During the time I was with him, they burst three spherical case-shells within a space of ten yards square, and almost between his guns. It was a great wonder we were not all hit, the balls flew about so thick; one entered the tree against which I was leaning, hardly an inch above my cap. The only man hit, however, was a sergeant who lay near me. I at last gave him permission to withdraw his guns as I found he could do no good, but to remain just outside the wood ready to take position with his whole battery in case of the enemy attempting an attack by that road.

The reason why I was so determined to try these two points was that General Warren sent me an order this morning "assigning" Phillips, Stewart, and Richardson to Griffin's division. The order was entirely unexpected, for we had got along very well together for the last ten days. I can only explain it by supposing that Griffin has asked for it, and Warren been afraid to refuse him. I know that Griffin is set on breaking up the brigade organization of the artillery because it did not originate with him and because he commands a division.

General Warren has been in one of his pets all yesterday and today, as ugly and cross-grained as he could be. One would suppose that a man in his position would be ashamed to show that kind of temper. When I reported to him the result of my efforts, he grumbled to himself something of which I could only catch a few words, to the effect that he could get nothing done. He has remained most of the day in the grove in front of the church, where are a number of benches. I have kept within call as much as possible so as to give him no chance to find fault with me if I can help it; only leaving when he sent me on some duty. He has pitched into his staff officers most fearfully, cursing them up and down as no man has a right to do, and as I wonder that they allow. I certainly would not stand it for one instant; and as he may let out on me, I have thought much as to just how it would be best to act and what I should say, did he try it.

The three batteries assigned to Griffin have been, at least one of them, in position near the Shady Grove road, but having been taken entirely out of my hands, I have no control over them and have not been near them. I also recalled Fitzhugh from in charge of them. Not content even with getting three batteries assigned to him, Griffin has been continually during the day telling General Warren that here was a good place for batteries and where artillery could be of service; not on his own front, but in front of other divisions. Indeed, he seems today to want to run the whole corps.

When early in the afternoon Cutler had pushed his skirmish line to the far edge of the wood south of the pike, Griffin rode up and said something to General Warren; whereon the general turned to me and said, "General reports that there is an excellent place for some of your guns out there. I wish you to see what can be done." I at once mounted my horse with Griffin, who started off at a gallop. At the same time he turned to me, saying, "You will think a d——d ugly place to put a battery, and I tell you before hand that you can't keep your horses there, and will lose lots of men, but then you will have a capital shot at the enemy." We dismounted at the mouth of the Walnut Grove Church road, and walked or rather crept from tree to tree along the left side of it out to the skirmish line; whence we certainly had a fine view of the rebel line for over half a mile of its length, distant from 800 to 1,200 yards. They had a very strong earthwork thrown up, and I could count with certainty a dozen guns perfectly protected.

Here Griffin—an artillery officer!—wanted me to put a battery, 150 yards outside our line of battle, without any cover, under the concentrated fire of the enemy's guns, and within two or three hundred yards of their skirmishers, who made it so hot all the time that a single man durst not shew himself. Of course, I told him that I should not put a battery there without positive orders from General Warren, and then did not see how I could get them up the road in daylight. He said that I could have the cannoneers cut new roads through the wood!—but "that he did not suppose I would put a battery there; he would not were he in my place." I felt like asking what he meant then by recommending it to General Warren, but don't want to quarrel with him.

Later in the afternoon Griffin again came up and said that two batteries could be put in on his left, where I tried to place Sheldon in the morning. I told him that I had already lost an officer and two men there, and that it would require darkness in order to throw up cover; but he talked much about his division being there now, and that he would have the works thrown up. General Warren was very cross at my reporting against the other place and finally told me to let Major Fitzhugh try if he could not get a couple of batteries in there. I gave him Rogers and Bigelow, and told him to try to get them around north of the pike through the woods. In less than half an hour Fitzhugh returned and said that the thing could not be done, that the pioneers had hardly commenced digging when several of them were shot down, and the rest would not work.

But now General Warren gave positive orders to put the batteries there; so I was obliged to tell Fitzhugh that it must be done, though we lost all our guns and men. Warren said the artillery was terribly afraid of losing its guns; he did not see that they were worth more than ambulances or waggons, and grumbled away at a great rate. But he was in the midst of it when we heard peal on peal of musketry down there, then the rebel yell, and a real hot fight just at the point the batteries were to go. I said nothing, but saw that Warren was getting fidgety. Presently he asked me if I thought Fitzhugh had got the guns there. I told him that there had been time enough, and the major was always prompt in obeying orders. Now I was very confident they were not there or I should have either heard them fire, or heard that they were lost; but I meant to let him believe they were gone just to see whether he really thought losing guns no more than losing ambulances. Two or three times afterward he said to me: "Colonel, do you think those guns are lost?" "Do you think Major Fitzhugh got them into position?"—but I let him think they were gone.

The fight lasted some fifteen or twenty minutes, when the enemy were repulsed. They had passed directly over the ground where the batteries were to go, and would have captured them had they been there. But fortunately Fitzhugh met General Ayres, who asked him where he was going, and on being told said that the enemy were just advancing to the attack at that point (it was outside our line of battle). The major told him that he had no option in the matter, his orders were positive from General Warren to put the batteries there. Upon which Ayres ordered him back, saying that he would be responsible for it. But enough of this. I have had almost as unpleasant a day as that at the Alsop house, save that I have not been kept idle.

Some of the other batteries were parked near the wood south of the church to be ready in case of need out there. After dark, our line was pushed forward to the far edge of the wood on either side of the Walnut Grove road; and I moved four batteries out there, thinking it of no use to put out any unless I sent enough to have some effect. . . .

The cavalry fight yesterday afternoon was at Cold Harbour, some six or seven miles to our left. Last night the Sixth Corps was taken from the extreme right and sent around there; where they, together with the Eighteenth Corps, had quite a big fight. Report says that we were successful. The Eighteenth Corps has just joined us, under Baldy Smith, from the Army of the James which is shut up at Bermuda Hundred. Have heard no firing to speak of on our right, where the Second and Ninth Corps still are. Tonight we sleep on the church benches, either inside or under the grove, as we please.

JUNE 2, THURSDAY. The artillery ball opened early this morning, and was kept up in a most lively manner all day. Lee must have received a big supply of ammunition, I should suppose, if one might judge from the amount his batteries expended today. So soon as it was light enough for them to see the advanced line our Fourth Division had taken up, and the Fourth batteries I had placed there, they commenced a furious cannonade from all their line, rendering it a very hot spot to be in or to get out of. I could not make out how many guns they had to bear on this point, but should think about twenty. Our men answered manfully, and were at no time silenced by the rebel fire though they had every advantage over us. Their fire was a converging one from three-fourths of a mile of line, besides two guns in a detached work on our left which almost enfiladed us; while their skirmish line was only two or three hundred yards out from our guns. Still it was wonderful how few men I lost. Hart had one killed, and five wounded; Rittenhouse and Walcott one wounded each; Barnes none. They all lost more or less horses, the getting out and in with the limbers being an ugly job.

About ten A.M. Crawford put his men in on the left of the Fourth Division, so stretching through the wood in that direction, across a small rivulet to the Jenkins house, a distance of half a mile from the Walnut Grove Church road. Here there is an opening of some two hundred yards, and then a wood for a like distance. . . . In this first opening I placed Cooper's battery under Lieutenant Miller, and Sheldon's under Lieutenant Rogers; while I took Breck on beyond the other house, and beyond our extreme left, where he had a capital position but no supports at first, there being an interval of some five hundred yards here between the left of the Fifth Corps and the right of Birney's division of the Second Corps, which had moved around from the extreme right during the night. There was, however, no danger, as the wood on either side was held by our men, while he had full room to move about; afterward the officer commanding Birney's right brigade sent a regiment down by him. After this I found a place for Bigelow about halfway between the Jenkins house and Barnes's battery, just in the side of a ravine: a position difficult to get in and out of, but perfectly covered, and with a beautiful outlook along all our front to the right.

By noon, when I had got these four batteries established, we were on a more equal footing. Miller and Bigelow soon drove out the two guns they had in the little detached work; then, by throwing solid shot along their skirmish line to the right, they freed the other batteries to a great extent from that annoyance. Afterward Bigelow turned his attention to the wood on Rogers's left, and drove their skirmishers almost entirely out of it, so that ours advanced nearly up to the end of it near which was the detached work spoken of.

General Warren seemed in better humour today, and all my batteries except Mink being now in position, we got along very well together. He visited the line to the left during the afternoon, and even went so far as to commend Bigelow's position, which with a perfect outlook is the most thoroughly "perdu" of any I have ever seen. He may not have been well yesterday, which would be some, though not sufficient, excuse for his behaviour.

About five o'clock I received orders from General Warren to withdraw two of the batteries out of the Walnut Grove road, and to take them with Mink, who had not been in position, as also all the forges and so on, around to near the house where Breck's battery was; and to remain there with them myself keeping a sharp lookout, as he was going to take one of the divisions over there to fill out to Smith's corps, while the Ninth swung back to the church; and that he would be over himself presently. Meantime I 'would leave Major Fitzhugh there with the other two batteries, who were also to be brought back to the church. I accordingly withdrew the four batteries: leaving Rittenhouse and Hart with Fitzhugh, I took Barnes, Walcott, and Mink through the road which our pioneers had opened during the day, and parked them as directed; the distance being about two miles.

We had just got there, and I was out with Breck's left section, when there was very heavy firing back by the church, commencing with musketry and quickly followed by a most rapid cannonade. I did not know what might happen where I was, especially as Birney's division was being withdrawn; so I remained where I was, but sent Lieutenant Wilbur over to learn how things stood. I had lost three of my staff, and now had none but Morris and Canfield to get as aides, and the latter was left with the major; I therefore impressed Lieutenant Wilbur into the service, and believe I shall keep him with me until he gets an order to join his own battery "K." He got back after dark. . . .

It seems that as the Ninth Corps fell back, the rebs followed them up with a line of battle, when they—well, I don't know certainly what they did, except that they brought up on the south side of the pike. Finding themselves successful there, and our right also swinging back, they charged through the wood north of the pike, advancing a battery up the road at the same time. They succeeded in catching a great part of Griffin's skirmish line, and were not stopped until almost through the wood to the Tinsley house. Fitzhugh at once put Hart across the road beyond the Tinsley house, and Rittenhouse on his right, where they drove off the rebel battery and with Bartlett's brigade stopped the attack from the west. To shew how near the rebels came to success, Bartlett formed outside the wood and yet within fifty yards of it in order to cover the road from Bowles's house. The two batteries were on this line, while Stewart took position on the other side of the house, facing and firing north; Phillips and Richardson were to the east of the Bowles house road, and nearly back to the pike. It must have been a very hot place in that corner around the Tinsley house, for our line made a perfect right angle there

with the enemy close up on both the sides. The Ninth Corps do not seem
to have covered themselves with glory. . . .

* * *

Grant's primary object in seizing upon Cold Harbor, where five roads
meet, three of them reaching down toward the Chickahominy, was to hold
it as a point of departure for crossing that stream, and throwing Lee back
into the defenses of Richmond. The place was not a harbor, not a town,
not even a hamlet, but simply a crossroads. It might originally have been
Cool Arbor, but more probably drew its name from the English usage of
calling roadside inns that offered shelter without fire "Cold Harbor." Lee
was, of course, determined to prevent any forward movement by Grant to
the crossing points over the Chickahominy.

Grant had disposed his army, facing Richmond, with Hancock's corps
on the left, Wright's and Smith's corps at the center, and Warren's corps (in
which Wainwright fought) with Burnside's corps on the right. The left,
which was nearest the Chickahominy, rested on a road, and the right on
Totopotomoy Creek. Lee's entrenched army was squarely in front of Grant,
behind Cold Harbor, much of it in thick woods. On June 2 Burnside had
been ordered to mass his forces on the immediate right and rear of Warren,
and his effort to carry out these orders, exposing his lines, had provoked
the Confederate attack of that day, in which many Union prisoners were
taken. The attacks were not pressed with much vigor; nor, for that matter,
did the Union forces, after checking them, follow up the repulse with any
energy—a fact that irritated Grant.

Meanwhile, Grant had determined to attack along the whole line at
dawn on June 3. "The corps commanders," he tells us, "were to select
the points in their respective fronts where they would make their assaults."
His plan was that Hancock, Wright, and Smith should do the heaviest
fighting, but that Warren and Burnside should lend support by threatening
Lee, and should attack fiercely if a favorable opportunity occurred. At
seven A.M. that morning, Grant rather belatedly gave Meade instructions:
"The moment it becomes certain that an assault cannot succeed, suspend
the offensive; but when one does succeed, push it vigorously and if necessary pile in troops at the successful point from wherever they can be taken."

Meanwhile, at early daybreak, four-thirty A.M., the Union lines had
sprung from behind their rather primitive parapets and moved forward. At
various points they were quickly entangled in thickets; at others they
splashed through marshes. Lee was ready, and the roar of his guns and
musketry was tremendous. Within a quarter hour or little more, the issue

was clear. As the war correspondent William Swinton writes: "There was along the whole line a rush—the spectacle of impregnable works—a bloody loss—then a sullen falling back, and the action was *decided*." Grant had met a stunning defeat. He was compelled to write later: "The assault cost us heavily, and probably without benefit to compensate. . . ." He should have omitted the word "probably." But the battle continued to rage at various points the whole day.

* * *

JUNE 3, FRIDAY. The day opened with a big battle to our left; where the Second and Sixth Corps attacked at daylight. The Fifth Corps being strung out on a line some five miles long could do nothing save demonstrate and fire artillery. Soon after daylight, I received orders to return to the Walnut Grove Church with the three batteries I had taken away last night. On arriving there I found matters as I described them to be last night; the Ninth Corps having thrown up works along the south side of the pike. Burnside was to have attacked with his whole corps at daylight, as a diversion to the attack on the left, but as usual was not ready until the matter there had been decided.

So soon as I had got to the church, I sent Barnes and Walcott out to the position they held yesterday, on the left and right of the road to Walnut Grove Church, and placed Mink on the left of Stewart. Some four hundred yards to the east of the church, on the north side of the pike, stands a house belonging to one Curry; just back of this house the little stream commences which crossed the Bowles house road, running west nearly parallel to and some two hundred fifty yards from the pike. The ravine in which it runs is quite deep, but the banks slope gradually on either side, and are almost free of trees. On the south bank of this ravine Phillips and Richardson were posted to the east; Stewart and Mink to the west of the road to Bowles's house. The enemy's skirmishers were some hundred yards back on the north bank, with batteries stationed just where Breck and Richardson were on the 31st of last month, so that our relative positions were exactly the reverse of what they were that day.

About ten o'clock, perhaps earlier, our line facing north commenced to advance together with the Ninth Corps on its right. The progress made was very slow at considerable loss, the artillery advancing by battery with the line of battle. After we got possession of a small nameless house directly north of the Tinsley house Stewart and Mink did not suffer so much; but the rebel battery in Breck's old place showed how good a position it was. The whole move was a gradual swinging round of our right; Bartlett's brigade finally coming around at right angles to the pike on a line with that of Ayres, and the Ninth Corps stretching from there north-

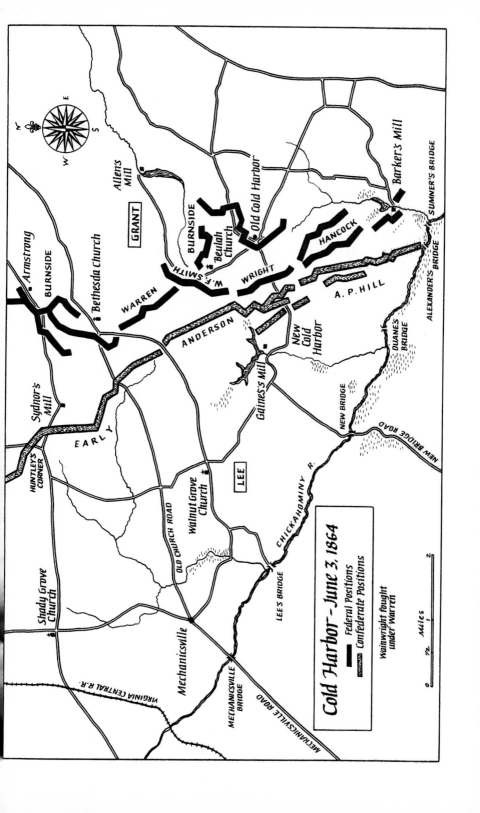

Cold Harbor – June 3, 1864

▬▬▬ Federal Positions
≈≈≈ Confederate Positions

Wainwright fought
under Warren

Miles
0   ½   1   2

east to the Armstrong house, with their skirmishers across the Shady Grove road. It was late in the afternoon when this was accomplished. Stewart and Richardson suffered severely. . . . The enemy, too, must have suffered severely by our fire if the twenty dead horses which we counted on the ground where their batteries had been is any criterion.

While this was going on, the rebels made a savage charge up the pike and through the wood north of it, getting to within canister range, but were repulsed by Ayres's brigade together with Hart's and Rittenhouse's batteries. Breck had gone back to his old position on the extreme left; while Miller, Rogers, and Bigelow, remaining close by the Jenkins house, had all twelve batteries in position, and engaged throughout a good part of the day, using an immense amount of ammunition. Their reports tonight show a total of 3,435 rounds expended, equal to seventy-one rounds per gun, and making about eighteen tons of iron thrown at the rebel lines; an amount which one would think ought to have some effect, but probably did not, if we may judge from the small amount of harm their fire did us, which was almost if not quite as heavy as our own. Their shot were rolling all over the plain around the church in every direction, their endeavour I presume being to enfilade Burnside's line in our rear. My total loss during the day has been one officer and four men killed, and sixteen men wounded; also thirteen horses. . . .

So far as news has reached us, the fight of Cold Harbour this morning must have been terrible, and though it was short, our losses were something fearful; while the enemy's were probably small, for they were behind very strong works, and had many small swamps in their front. Our men are said to have carried the line in one place notwithstanding, and captured three guns. Tyler's division of heavy artillery were all cut to pieces. He lost a leg himself, while Colonels Morris and Porter were killed. I hear, too, that Captain Ames of "G" Battery is wounded, making the *fifth* out of the six captains of the regiment with this army who has been hit; one of them, if not two, mortally wounded.

The day has been rather a pleasant one to me, as I have been free to move around from one battery to another without any unreasonable demands being put upon me. I mention this, as I feel that I am standing on the edge of a volcano which may burst out at any moment, and in the spot least looked for. This evening I saw it in its fury though its lava did not reach me. General Warren went over to Burnside's headquarters before dark, leaving no orders whatever for the night, and did not return until ten or eleven o'clock. His staff were yawning around a fire under some trees on the plain, where he had his tents up last night, but were afraid to put up a tent or even order their supper without his consent. I had established my headquarters about a hundred yards off, where we had had our supper, and were all ready to put up tents, but waited to learn whether we remained here all night or not. I was talking with some of the corps staff, when the general returned, and seeing no preparations for the night, he ripped out at his staff generally and poor little Marvin in particular. I used to think the Charleston hackmen the most profane in the world. Our army swears as badly as did Uncle Toby's in Flanders. I have heard Meade in one of his towering passions. But I never heard anything which could begin to equal the awful oaths poured out tonight; they fairly made my hair stand on end with their profaneness, while I was filled with wonder at the ingenuity of invention and desperate blackguardism they displayed. So soon as I gathered that we were to remain, I called my staff and went home; far enough off, fortunately, to be out of hearing.*

JUNE 4, SATURDAY. The batteries not with Griffin's division remained in the positions occupied yesterday; the four on the left, Barnes's and Walcott's firing more or less during the day, but not so much as yesterday. Griffin's three batteries were withdrawn and went into park near the wood southeast from the church; the Ninth Corps having taken up the right of our line as far as the stream beyond Tinsley's house. Save the artillery fire and a good deal of picket firing, all was quiet along the line. The enemy's batteries fired more than ours did today. Rifled balls whizzed over our heads and twelve-pounder shot was constantly rolling about the plain; I counted six and eight at a time thus expending themselves. As the men got accustomed to them, they began to think it great fun avoiding these spent balls, for hardly any of the shells burst. One round shot struck the horse of one of General Warren's orderlies on the saddle flap, knocking the man down, who was standing on the other side leaning against him. At the time it caused a general laugh, but the orderly found afterward that his horse had two ribs broken.

The more we hear of the fight yesterday, the more severe it proves to have been. The order issued for the attack to the corps commanders was the same which has been given at all such times on this campaign, viz: "to attack along the whole line." I would give a great deal to know if this mode of attacking works is Grant's or Meade's idea. The orders come to us as from Meade, but I cannot think it is his, having the opinion I have of his ability as a general. After the failure yesterday, there was a still more absurd order issued, for each command to attack without reference to its neighbours, as they saw fit; an order which looked as if the commander, whoever he is, had either lost his head entirely, or

---

* Warren may have acquired part of his mastery of profanity at his birthplace on the Hudson, and a good deal more of it at West Point; but his education in the art was doubtless completed when he was working as army engineer on the Mississippi River, helping survey the Delta and make plans for improving the Rock Island and Des Moines rapids.

wanted to shift responsibility off his own shoulders. The newspaper correspondents speak of Grant doing this and that, hardly ever mentioning Meade's name. Here we see nothing of General Grant; I hardly heard his name mentioned. Burnside, however, is not under General Meade's command. Whoever was responsible for this extended mode of attack is getting no military credit, nor the love of the men who are about used up by it. No optional attacks yesterday were made; everybody felt that they had had enough.*

Burnside swung back his extreme right today from the Armstrong house, and has commenced a small redoubt on the north of the road about three-quarters of a mile from the church; I suppose as part of the siege operations which I hear are ordered this morning. 'Tis said that the two lines of works at some points of the Second Corps front are not a hundred yards apart; from these it is now designed to push regular approaches siege fashion. Burnside's men are great at throwing dirt. All this army have got to be very expert diggers, being able to do a full day's work with no other tools than a tin plate and their bayonet; but the Ninth Corps far surpasses all others that I have seen both in the height and number of their breastworks. From what I have seen . . . here and in the Wilderness I have but a very poor opinion of their general officers, and consequently of the whole corps. There is an immense amount of galloping to and fro all the time, and two or three men with stars on their shoulders are always around Burnside, but from the start the corps has done nothing; it has been put in very little, and when sent forward always stuck at the first impediment. Burnside's best staff officer, Benjamin, was wounded at Spotsylvania; Lieutenant-Colonel Monroe now reigns in his stead, as chief of artillery of that corps.†

JUNE 5, SUNDAY.   A comparatively quiet day along our front; everything remaining pretty much as it was yesterday. General Warren issued an

* This criticism of Grant's generalship at Cold Harbor, widely voiced at the time, has been accepted by nearly all subsequent writers. Once more the futility of a frontal assault delivered against an unshaken foe had been demonstrated, as Burnside had demonstrated it at Fredericksburg, and Lee at Gettysburg. As Theodore Lyman wrote at the time, "Put a man in a hole and a good battery on a hill behind him, and he will beat off three times his number. . . ." The order given some hours after the failure of the first assaults that each corps commander should renew the attack without reference to his neighboring commands was especially stupid. It came from Meade, but its origin was of course with Grant. The corps commanders transmitted the order to the division heads, and they sent it down to the brigade and regimental officers. Yet not a man in the army stirred. Their immobility gave a silent but emphatic verdict against further useless butchery.

† William H. Benjamin had entered the service in 1861 as major of a New York cavalry regiment, and rose to be brigadier general. J. Albert Monroe, former commander of a Rhode Island battery, now headed the dozen field batteries of the Ninth Corps. Burnside's forces were to make a sorry showing again at the Battle of the Crater.

order today reorganizing the corps; the number of divisions is maintained, though in reality the corps itself is not larger than one big division, such as Porter's was while we lay in front of Yorktown—say some sixteen or eighteen thousand all told. But Crawford and Cutler being the ranking generals, it would hardly do to deprive them of their commands, yet they were the ones which I have no doubt Warren would have liked to get rid of. The new organization takes Ayres's brigade, the regulars and three New York Zouave regiments from the First Division, substituting what was the Third Brigade of the Fourth Division. . . . The Second Division, to be commanded by General Ayres, will consist of his own old brigade, the Maryland brigade, and Colonel Kitching's heavy artillery. . . .

The same order assigns three batteries each to the First and Second Divisions, and in its fifth section says, "the remaining six batteries will constitute the Reserve Artillery of the corps." This cuts my command down just one-half. But there is no use in my trying to do anything, for yesterday I got a note from General Hunt, whom I had informed of the first assignment of three batteries to Griffin, in which he says that he had laid Warren's order before General Meade, whose answer was: "The power of the corps commander to distribute the batteries for service is necessary, but you will retain their administration and supplies as heretofore." I have not a doubt as to this being General Griffin's work, but am helpless to prevent it. Tonight we are to move over towards the centre of the line about Cold Harbour, and there become a reserve until the new organization is complete. . . .

COLD HARBOUR, JUNE 6, MONDAY.   The corps have had a busy day of it, first in carrying out the new organization, and next in trying to clean up a little. In order to carry out my part of the new arrangement I ordered Rogers, Rittenhouse, and Walcott with their batteries to report to General Ayres. In notifying corps headquarters of this selection, I asked "for explicit information as to what authority, if any, I as chief of artillery of the corps retain over the batteries assigned to the First and Second Divisions, and whether they will continue to draw their supplies, make reports, and receive general orders through these headquarters." . . .

The cleaning operation is one that must have become fearfully needed by the line officers and men of the infantry. What with the mud and dust which they have alternately been called up to march through and sleep in, and the fact that for a week at a time they have stood or lain in line of battle, night and day, the amount of dirt accumulated must be great. The men have been really better off than their company officers, for there have been times when they could get an hour or two to strip, wash themselves and their clothes, and so prepare for another spell. The officer cannot strip by the roadside in the midst of his men; the operation is too familiar if he wishes to maintain his position. Nor is he even so well off as to change of clothing, for being required to move about more, his overcoat, canteen, and small havresack are about all he can carry; while his servant, who in theory is supposed to carry his master's change of clothing, five days' rations, and cooking utensils, besides what he needs himself, being a contraband soon loses everything intrusted to him except the eatables and frying pan. There should be a pack mule for the officers of each company, as in the French army; but then companies should not be allowed to dwindle down to ten and a dozen men.

Field officers, being allowed two horses, can make one of them a pack horse and so get along tolerably well. Some of the company officers, too, manage to keep a pack animal, generally some poor lame picked-up animal who is pulled and pushed along by a nigger, in everybody's way and with his pack forever falling off. Major Arthur told me today that his officers had got a change of clothing through the Sanitary Commission. I was glad to hear of the commission being of such service, even though it was a misappropriation of the clothing which had been sent down in large quantities for the hospitals—where it was not wanted, the medical department having a sufficient supply. The agent not being able to dispose of his goods as intended, begged the regimental surgeons to take it; and Arthur's surgeon distributed what he received among the line officers of the battalion. He tells me that it was almost impossible for the officers to keep clear of lice, do what they could. Today all the baggage waggons are up, which have been miles away from us since we crossed the Rapidan, and everyone is fitting himself out for another spell of hard work.

Almost every day on this campaign I have been obliged to remark, even more than ever before, how superior is the position of a light battery officer to even a colonel of infantry, so far as comfort goes, in times of general discomfort. They have a mechanic and tools always close at hand, and their little cart to carry the mess-chest, a bag each, and the company desk, while either a tent is stuck in on top of the forage waggon, or if their battery is in position, they have their paulins. All these enable them to go through such a month as this last with quite as much comfort as a general officer with his spring waggon, and at times they are better off, as their cart, being ordnance property and part of the battery, is never sent to the rear, but moves with the battery at all times.

JUNE 7, TUESDAY.   Finding that we may remain here yet for several days, and that the spot on which we had lighted for our headquarters was too filthy to be policed, we moved this afternoon over into the courtyard of R. Burnet's house, where we have all our tents up, and things really very nice. Judd, the sutler, made his appearance this morning from the White House, with quite a little batch of stores for the officers of the brigade. Butter was the thing most rejoiced over generally, but I cannot manage the sutler's butter and would rather go without. A few dozen of ale, however, were a real treat, and we have a couple of bottles of champagne laid by for the Sunday's dinner. An ice house close to our tents is by no means a thing to be despised.

The First Division moved off this morning, taking its three batteries along, to the left of the Second Corps so as to stretch our line to the dispatch station on the railroad. How all these names bring up recollections of two years ago! The rest of the corps remains quiet at present. General Warren still keeps his headquarters around the Leary house, though it is a wretched spot, being right at the corner of two roads where trains are all the time passing, and covering them with dust. The General will not move. He appears to have sunk into a sort of lethargic sulk, sleeps a great part of the time, and says nothing to anyone. I think at times that these fits of his must be the result of a sort of insanity; indeed, that is perhaps the most charitable way of accounting for them. He has not got along well at Meade's headquarters lately, though I know nothing as to wherein the trouble has lain. General Meade's headquarters are only about half-a-mile off, and Grant quite near them. I was at the former last evening, and saw Generals Hunt and Patrick. . . .

We have an order from Meade's headquarters today about one Edward Crapsey, a newspaper correspondent who had been writing some blackguard libel about him, Meade; in which Mr. Crapsey is sentenced to be "paraded through the lines of the army with a placard marked "Libeller of the Press," and then kicked out. I fear that the General will hurt himself by this, for these newspaper fellows stick very close by one another when an outsider attacks them. But I rejoice to see one of the rascals shown up, for they make more trouble than their heads are worth, with their lying accounts of affairs in the army; raising false hopes among the people, and almost always giving false ideas as to the merits of an officer, for they praise those who treat them, and ignore those who will have nothing to do with them. For my part, I should be glad if none were admitted to the army.*

---

* Meade had allowed his unbridled temper to lead him into a serious blunder. Edward Crapsey of the Philadelphia *Inquirer*, who had been captured by Mosby's troopers at The Wilderness but had escaped, was highly esteemed in his own city and in press circles. He had lately sent the *Inquirer* a dispatch outlining the respective roles played by Meade and Grant in leading the army. Meade, he wrote, controlled all details; "he is entitled to great credit for the magnificent movements of the army since we left Brandy." Grant exercised supervisory authority. Crapsey added: "History will record . . . that on one eventful night during the present campaign Grant's presence saved the army and the nation too," with further remarks intimating that after the check at The Wilderness, Meade had wished to retreat back across the Rapidan, but Grant insisted on moving ahead. While this was not true, Grant's tenacity had undoubtedly

JUNE 8, WEDNESDAY. My work is now about all done up here, as they have not yet called for my report of the campaign, or for back returns; so I have time to rest and think. The mere feeling of no prospect of a fight at any moment is a delightful one; I have, too, quite a number of letters from home, which though stale are still interesting. The newsboys whom the Prince de Joinville mentions as selling the papers on the line of battle in 1862 are not with us now, the wiseheads at Washington having seen fit to stop the sale of papers in this army since we left our winter quarters; a most absurd arrangement as all who choose get them down through the mail. Had I supposed that the regulation was to last so long, I should have had a copy of the *Herald* sent me in the same way. My latest home letter is dated on the 31st ultimo.

They have had quite a time in New York over the publication of a *bogus proclamation* of the President, stating that Grant was in great straits, everything looked dark for the country, and appointing a day of fasting and prayer on that account. The *Journal of Commerce* and *World*, in which papers it first appeared, were notified to stop their publication; which was a way of proceeding quite Napoleonic, and a little too strong for this country yet, though we are fast getting to it. The publication of the papers was only suspended for a few days, when on proper explanations, or because they found in Washington that they had gone too far, the interdict was withdrawn. Great blame is laid on Mr. Lincoln for this arbitrary proceeding, but he, poor fellow, I am sure is not to blame; I doubt if he was even consulted in the matter; every day he seems to have "less influence with the present Administration."*

The last letter of mine they had received was that of the 25th, after the North Anna fight. . . . Everyone at home is said to be intensely anxious, and to suffer more mentally than we do; which I have no doubt

---

done much to keep Meade (whose despair of victory in 1864 we have noted) up to his work. The article stung Meade the more because Doubleday and Sickles had accused him of showing the white feather at Gettysburg. While he might have been justified in expelling Crapsey, his brutal treatment of the man was indefensible. Angry newspaper correspondents, at a meeting in Washington, promptly agreed that Meade's name should not be mentioned in dispatches again except in connection with a defeat, and for six months ignored the general. If Meade had any political ambitions this ring of silence stifled them; it is even possible his maltreatment of Crapsey cost him the Presidency.

* The New York *World* and *Journal of Commerce* were innocent victims of a hoax. An adventurer named Joseph Howard, Jr., stealing some Associated Press flimsies and envelopes, delivered the false proclamation—declaring the Virginia campaign a failure, calling for a day of fasting and prayer, and demanding a draft of 400,000 men—late at night on May 17–18. His object was to make money on the gold market. As it was steamer day, danger existed that the fabrication would cause trouble in Europe; and Stanton lost his head. As many said at the time and Wainwright suggests, the United States was not a country to tolerate bayonets in editorial rooms.

is the case, for of all conditions that of uncertainty is the most trying. They are enrolling for another draft, which the men in charge say is to be put right through without delay; which I do not believe. The government have dallied and truckled to popularity too long to begin now to push a thing of this sort right through.

All articles appear to have gone up to enormous prices: cotton is one dollar per pound, a price never dreamed of before; beef twenty cents for the quarters, while gold reached 194½ on the 30th! To balance this, some ladies have formed an association to use American goods, dress plainly, and set an example of economy in all respects. I think with Mary that it will all end in smoke, the members finding themselves in the same quandary as Ned Thorne's wife, who was said to be very earnest about it, but could not find where to begin. . . .

The siege operations progress very slowly; so slowly, indeed, that their progress is invisible. Everything is consequently at a deadlock. Will Grant move once more to the left and take up the line by White Oak Swamp? Will he now try cutting loose and a dash around to the west of Lee? Or what will he do? Neither of the above appear to me desirable, and I don't believe he can break through here. I see nothing left but to cave in entirely, admit that *"my plan"* (that is, Mr. Lincoln's) is not the way to get to Richmond, and then take McClellan's with the James River as his base.

Our losses have mounted up to something fearful, and even now are daily added to by hundreds. It is only in the number of prisoners and guns captured that we can shew any advantage over Lee. General Patrick tells me that 10,400 of the former have passed through his hands, while perhaps 1,600 have been sent off direct by Sheridan.* Our loss is not over half this number. Grant may be waiting to see what Hunter's move will bring out. Our latest news from him is in yesterday's Richmond papers, which announce that he had won a decided victory at Staunton. If Crook and Averell join him he will have quite an army, and should he succeed in taking Lynchburg something may come of it. Sherman by newspaper accounts seems to get on, but very slowly. He has not made very many more miles than we have, though he has had next to no fighting. Butler remains "bottled up" in Bermuda Hundred, and matters

---

* The losses of Grant's army from the crossing of the Pamunkey to the end of the fighting about Cold Harbor (May 27 to June 12, 1864) are carefully estimated by General A. A. Humphreys at 12,970. Of these nearly 6,000 were killed and wounded in the general assault of June 3, when many Union soldiers felt so certain of death that they pinned slips of paper with their names to their uniforms. Confederate losses are unknown, but for the fifteen-day period probably did not exceed 5,000. Many wounded lying between the lines after the fighting on June 3 died of exposure, for though Grant proposed on the afternoon of the 5th a cease-fire for bringing them in and burying the dead, hostilities were not interrupted until the afternoon of the 7th.

along the coast are in a state of status quo; not ante bellum, however.
JUNE 9, THURSDAY. Cutler's division has moved over on the left of Griffin; not as extending the line of battle, but stretched in detachments and a picket line along the bank of the Chickahominy to beyond Bottom's Bridge. Sheridan with two divisions of cavalry watches the roads beyond this and I believe patrols the country as far as the James River.

I rode today as far as Griffin's division for the exercise and to see the country. When I started, it was my intention to visit the works on the front of the Second and Sixth Corps, but I found that the sharpshooters made it dangerous to do so at any time; which kept me from going there, as my only object was curiosity. The salient of the Second Corps where Gibbon effected a lodgement on the morning of June 3 in the enemy's line is said to be not fifty yards from the opposing works. Ames's battery and two others are in this place; they have to draw their guns to the side of the embrasure to load. General Hunt has got down a number of coehorn mortars, which are in use on the line; these little pieces he believes can frequently be used to advantage in such fighting as we have had, and wishes a battery of them to be attached to the artillery brigade serving with each corps.* . . .

In my ride I could at times see our line of earthworks, which are stronger than any I have before seen. As I looked at these immense diggings I was reminded of the great cry made two years ago against McClellan, because he had used the shovel at all. Were all the earth thrown out by his army on the Peninsula including that in front of Yorktown for road, approaches, and everything, made into one mound, and that thrown on this campaign into another, the former would be hardly visible in comparison. Yet Yorktown was a regular siege; the digging done after leaving there would barely make one night's work for this army. *Spades* were said to be *trumps* with McClellan; what are they then with Grant? . . .

I heard at Army Headquarters that General Grant had himself likened this campaign to the celebrated battle of the Kilkenny cats, adding "that we had the longest tail." When the commanding general himself admits that his only dependence is on being able to furnish the most men to be killed, not much can be said for the science of the campaign; especially as the estimates now are that we lose two to one. The original three-year regiments, too, are beginning to go home; the Second Wisconsin follows

---

* The coehorn mortar, named for its seventeenth-century Dutch inventor, was a smoothbore muzzleloading piece usually of 4.6-inch caliber. The standard brass coehorn weighed only 164 pounds detached, or 296 pounds when mounted on an oak carriage, and was hence easily portable. Their high-angle fire, throwing a seventeen-pound shell from fifty to twelve hundred yards according to the size of the charge, was devastating.

the Pennsylvania Reserves day after tomorrow, and I am sorry to say take eleven men from Stewart, which will reduce him to under a hundred present. My batteries are fast losing men so as to be able to run no more than four guns, if they had them, and to find their extra caissons rather a burden. . . .

JUNE 10, FRIDAY. We have now lain here for five days, quite a rest, and are cleaned and fixed up so that we again feel like civilized beings. Even the other two corps have had something of a rest, though not so much of an one as we have. Tomorrow morning we start again at four A.M. moving by Basley's Mill and Prospect Church to Moody's on the New Kent and Bottom's Bridge road, the order says. This takes us on to ground I have been over before. The order does not tell us what is designed by this move, and I ask no questions. . . .

The men of the two armies have settled down very quietly here, those on the respective skirmish lines having agreed not to shoot. There has also got to be a good deal of intercourse between them, exchanging papers, coffee, and tobacco; all of which is again strictly forbidden. I am glad to see that now we are near our base Meade has reduced the number of days' rations the men are required to carry themselves to four instead of eight as it was.

To get back to an old subject. I have received two letters from Mr. Kelley with regard to my proposition as to a change in our artillery organization. In the last he enclosed one from Governor Seymour stating that he had read my paper and approved it heartily, and that he is ready to do anything in the matter I may desire. . . . Just at present my artillery enthusiasm is about all taken out of me, so that I do not feel much like pushing this or any other matter with regard to it. Were General Meade not so seemingly prejudiced against our arm, we might get matters improved; but as it is every step gained by hard work all last winter has been demolished by a scratch of his pen. . . .

PROVIDENCE MEETING HOUSE, JUNE 11, SATURDAY. Our march to this place was made without any incident to vary it. I followed the two divisions of infantry with the half a command left me. The road, though sandy, and somewhat dusty, was good, not having been cut up by previous travel. . . . Though we have had frequent rains this spring, they have not been long or severe, and the sun has come out brightly afterward; whereas in 1862 it seemed as if it would never stop raining. Neither is the sun so intensely hot as it was then on the few clear days we had; but the weather keeps almost too cool for comfort, so that winter clothing is still very agreeable. Today we have it warmer, as perfect a June day as is possible to get up.

We are bound for the James River, south side. At least so says rumour, or indeed something more than mere rumour, for the information comes tolerably direct, though not through authorized channels. Cruttenden's clerk was up this evening and told Morris that they were shipping everything at White House, and that the quartermaster in charge had said his orders were to form a depot at once at City Point. I had him cross-questioned so as to find out what truth there was probably in it, and found that the information was got very direct. Here was a pretty instance of how movements are kept secret in our army. While every precaution is being taken at the front to prevent the enemy suspecting what is up, the exact point of our destination is freely spoken of by the quartermaster's department, and as a matter of course comes up by every teamster, who tells it to all the men he knows; and officers, even generals of divisions, first learn the plan of campaign through their enlisted men. Once out, you cannot blame everyone for circulating the information; but the quartermaster who received the order, and to whom alone it was at all necessary that our destination should be known, ought to be dismissed at once, and sent to prison for the rest of the war, if he divulged it to a single person. By tomorrow Lee will no doubt know it, if he has not received the information already.

The change to the south of the James will be something quite new. What the country down there may be I do not know, but hope it is more open than some we have had. Another week will now probably give us a chance to learn something about it. We shall at any rate have a base of supply quite close to us, and ought to be more comfortable than we have been on our way here. What became of Mr. Lincoln's desideratum, "not to uncover Washington"?

LONG BRIDGE, CHICKAHOMINY, JUNE 12, SUNDAY. We did not move until late this afternoon, six o'clock, so that we had a whole day in camp; which I had my batteries commanders take advantage of to make out inspection papers for their serviceable horses, which have got to be quite numerous. I received back from Army Headquarters the application for the Fourth New York men and Captain Dexter, with the endorsement that they must all be at once returned to their regiment. It can't be done on the march, however, and General Hunt tells me to hang on to Dexter as long as I can. It has been a beautiful day; very enjoyable here off from the rest of the army.

We started at six o'clock, by which time I learn that all the army was to be in motion. The infantry moved on the side of the road all the first part of the way, so that though I started last, my six batteries were soon up with the head of the column. There I rode most of the way with General Warren, who was in a good humour today, and quite conversable. We took a byroad which carried us pretty straight to this place, where Long Bridge used to be but is not now. The engineers are busy making it good with pontoons, so that we expect to cross by midnight.

We have not seen a sign of the enemy on the march here, nor has the cavalry which was directly ahead of us. There was a great charm in moving on such a beautiful clear night through the quiet country, and over good roads. The air had something exhilarating in it so that everyone moved along cheerfully. For my own part, I enjoyed it most thoroughly. . . .

JUNE 13, MONDAY. About midnight we commenced crossing on the bridge to the south side of the Chickahominy. The troops were bivouacked a little beyond the bridge, leaving room for the train to be parked between them and the river. I turned my command in on the left of the road so soon as we got up the hill, where it was joined to the Ayres's three batteries. As we were to remain here until morning we next chose a big tree for our cover, had a fire made, stationed a guard, and stretched ourselves out for a nap. It always takes me some time to get to sleep when I do not go regularly to bed, especially if there is anything going on around: this night I got but very little sleep, being absolutely kept awake laughing.

The spot we had pitched on for our nap was a delightful one, under a great spreading tree and with a good sod beneath. But it was only some twenty feet from the road leading up from the bridge, and though the bank was six or eight feet high on this side, the fire was plainly visible to the waggon guard and stragglers who were crossing until near daylight; which fire was a strong attraction to that class of men generally known in the army as "coffee boilers"—men who seldom keep in the ranks, but hang on the rear of the army so long as their rations last, if there is any work going on, and always have a little tin pail with water in their hand ready to boil coffee half a dozen times a day.

Now our new guard, from "B" Company, are many of them recruits, nor is the discipline of that battery strict enough to give even the old men much idea of the proper order to be maintained around headquarters. Finding the "coffee boilers" disposed to make use of our fire, I told the guard not to allow it. He reasoned with them, and asked them to leave, telling them that it was headquarters. I called to him to make them go but he did not understand the word fully; that is, was unconscious of his power as sentinel. At last one fellow not only persisted in stopping, but was impudent into the bargain. Jumping to my feet, I seized him by the collar and seat of his breeches, and with a shove and a pitch tossed him into the road. It was the work of an instant. As the man fell, a great waggon came galloping up the road. I was frightened for a moment lest it should run over him, but as he rolled safely out of the way, I kicked his cap and coffee pot to him, and then instructed my sentinel that he must give but one warning should others come, then drive them off with his sabre; those were orders and he would pass them to his relief. At the time I was angry, for I have no sort of patience with this class of men. But my anger was soon turned into laughing by the next man who came on guard and to whom the instructions were literally given.

This was a little fellow, one of your liberal, earnest men, who do everything with their whole heart. He had not walked his post long before one fellow, not minding his warning that it was "a headquarters fire and he could not boil his coffee here," persisted in putting down his pot. Not another word did the little man say but went right at him, striking right and left with his sabre; not being ground, of course it did not cut. A number of these disappointed fellows had now gathered at the foot of a tree close to the road, and were urging each newcomer to try his luck at our fire. A cavalry man whom they persuaded into it received the same treatment, only worse than his predecessor; as he was a little inclined to show fight, this raised a cry of "Cavalry against Artillery," and some quite good jokes on the subject. Others were ugly and blackguarded our little sentinel, who walked speedily up and down his post, not uttering a word.

I was getting very much interested in the matter, and began to wonder what we should do if they made a fight, for our guard had but two sabres among them. At last someone in the party below threw a stone at the sentry. This was too much for the little fellow; making a jump directly over me as I lay there, he lit right among them, and without waiting for an answer to his reiterated question, "Who threw that stone?," struck on every side, driving the whole party before him. Wrapped in my blankets I pretended to be asleep, but laughed until my sides ached, as the farce was kept up for half an hour or more. This morning I find that General Warren, who was just across the road, had had the same trouble but none of the fun.

So soon as the men had got their coffee this morning, we pushed forward about a mile from the bridge; while Wilson's cavalry and Crawford's division advanced along what is known as the Long Bridge road as far as it intersects with that over White Oak Swamp, close to where Hooker's division was camped before Fair Oaks. General Warren was with them, and sent Barnes's and Hart's batteries down. The object of this move was to mislead Lee as to our intentions, giving him to suppose we meant to advance on Richmond along the north bank of the James. . . . While this was going on, the Second Corps crossed at our bridge and passed on, having left Cold Harbour at dark last night. The Sixth and Ninth Corps (the latter of which was placed last week under Meade's command, and so became once more a part of the Army of the Potomac) crossed at Jones's Bridge lower down. After the Second Corps came the First and Fourth Divisions of this, under Griffin. . . .

* * *

Grant had decided as early as June 5 to make his next flank movement carry his army south of the James River. It was not feasible to continue holding a position northeast of Richmond supplied by the Fredericksburg Railroad, for that supply line was too vulnerable. Nor was it possible to attack Lee's entrenchments frontally without another staggering loss of life —and the North was already rebellious over casualty lists. Grant believed that once south of the James River, he could besiege Lee in Richmond, cutting off his main sources of supply. He had been disappointed by the auxiliary armies under Ben Butler and Sigel, though Hunter as Sigel's successor showed a little more promise; now he would depend on his own heavy striking power. As he put it, he meant to "hammer continuously."

Warren's corps, only ten miles from the Long Bridge over the Chickahominy, led the way in this change of base. After crossing the bridge, he made a feint that, threatening a direct advance on Richmond through White Oak Swamp, covered the movement of the other corps. The army effected its fifty-five-mile march across the Peninsula to the City Point area without difficulty. Lee, of course, discovered the retirement within a few hours after it began, but he made no effort to harass it, moving instead toward Richmond. He was momentarily in the dark as to the Union movements. But once Grant reached the north bank of the James, he had the problem of getting his troops across that wide stream.

Here a delay occurred: the pontoons for a bridge were late in arriving. During the wait Hancock's corps was ferried across the river to Windmill Point. But it was not until midnight of June 14 that General Benham finished the bridge, which was a difficult piece of engineering; it was more than 2,000 feet long, and the channel boats had to be anchored in nearly eighty feet of water. Over this bridge, Theodore Lyman tells us, at once passed "a train of wagons and artillery thirty-five miles long; more than half the infantry in the army and 3,500 beef cattle; besides 4,000 cavalry; all of which was chiefly accomplished within the space of forty-eight hours!" By the afternoon of June 16 Grant's whole army, in fighting trim, was on the south bank.

The previous day Lee had received a frantic message from Beauregard: "If not reinforced immediately, enemy could force my lines at Bermuda Hundred Neck, capture Battery Dantzler, now nearly ready, or take Petersburg, before any troops from Lee's army or Drewry's Bluff could arrive in time." And at two A.M. on the 16th Lee was awakened by another urgent message from Beauregard, who had moved to Petersburg: "I have abandoned my lines of Bermuda Neck to concentrate all my force here." Plainly, Grant was heavily threatening Petersburg.

The whole front of war had changed: it would now lie along the Petersburg-Richmond line.

* * *

DR. WILCOX'S HOUSE, JUNE 14, TUESDAY.   We passed the Second Corps in camp, and hauled into an open field near here about one o'clock this morning where, too sleepy to do or think of anything, I turned in so soon as I could get a tent up and my bedding unrolled. This morning I found that we are in a large, dusty field close to the main road, and about three miles west from Charles City Court House. The Fifth Corps infantry, together with Griffin's batteries, had gone on about half a mile beyond the Court House. I rode out there, so soon as I had got my breakfast, to report for orders, and was glad to get permission to remain where I was until we cross, which we expect to do tomorrow.

While I was gone Fitzhugh and Morris had moved my headquarters to this place, and having all our waggons with us just now, we are this afternoon quite luxuriously arranged. Our tents are pitched on the south side of the house under a number of fine old locust trees. We have a fine grass field in our front, and a view of the James River in the distance. Dr. Wilcox's house stands about half a mile back from the river, and a couple of hundred yards from the road. For Virginia it is a good house, and in quite decent order outside and around. I have not been in it myself, though they say that the doctor's daughter, a married woman, is very agreeable. The Fifth Corps having been at Westover in 1862, only a short distance up the river, this family are quite well known to many of its officers.

While our tents were going up we rode down to the river bank. There is a dock at this place from which the Second Corps commenced to be ferried across the river in steamboats this afternoon, to Windmill Point directly opposite. The river here is about three-quarters of a mile wide; the bank on both sides high and steep. Around Windmill Point it turns south almost at right angles, so that a house on the bank here would look straight down the river three or four miles to where it again turns, opposite Fort Powhatan. The shore here is gravelly, offering a most inviting place for a bath. To look at the situation no one would suppose that it could be subject to fevers, yet the whole river bank is said to be.

We received orders this morning to be ready to move at noon, but they were soon countermanded. This afternoon I hear that there are not enough pontoons in the train sent down to stretch across the river. Having little to do, I have been amusing myself this afternoon with looking over the large batch of War Department orders received. By them I see that they are already immortalizing the generals who have fallen in this campaign by naming forts after them out west. I find nothing else in them worth noting here. I hear of no signs of Lee following us up at all, other than a few cavalry hanging around; just enough to find out where we had gone to. I fear that this delay with the completion of the bridge will enable Lee to make Petersburg safe. Smith's corps went around by boats direct from the White House to land at City Point. This with Hancock's, which is crossing this afternoon, may suffice to get possession of the place. Grant has gone up the river, to look after matters himself.

JUNE 15, WEDNESDAY. The bridge was not finished until some time last night. We are under orders to cross at daylight tomorrow. The Second Corps artillery and trains, and the Ninth Corps going over today. So I have another day of rest and comfort. It is a beautiful and lively sight to watch the crossing from the bluff; the bridge is about two miles below this point: over it is passing a constant stream of carriages, while two impromptu steam ferries are plying with the infantry at points between here and there.

Lying here on the James within a few miles of Harrison's Landing it is impossible not to be constantly reminded of 1862, and to be comparing the incidents of that campaign with this. They both had the same objective—Richmond; and both ended in the same way, failure and the James River. McClellan commenced his the first week in April; Grant the first week in May. Grant started with 125,000 men, of whom 15,000 were cavalry of two years' service; McClellan landed in from Yorktown 108,000 men, including Franklin, and had about 1,000 regular cavalry, and a regiment of cavalry greenhorns. Grant's officers had all been tried in two or three years of war, and their capacities were generally known to their superiors; McClellan had hardly an officer with the least experience in his then position. Now our quartermaster, commissary, medical, and ordnance departments are comparatively perfect; then they were about as imperfect as they well could be. Grant has probably received more reinforcements than McClellan did, but I do not know the numbers in either case. Grant has been backed by all the power at Washington; McClellan was thwarted at every step. Grant has lost 60,000 men in battle; McClellan lost little over half that number. Grant has had an army opposed to him of not over two-thirds his own strength; McClellan all the time had more than his own numbers in his front. Grant has inflicted a loss equal to about one-half his own; McClellan twenty percent more than he suffered.

This is about a comparison of the two campaigns and of the abilities of the two generals; yet the people wildly laud Grant to the skies and call McClellan a traitor, for the one has been continually fighting—"being in earnest," they call it—while the other would only fight when he saw some prospect of success. The army sees through spectacles of another colour, and do not appreciate the beauty of 3,000 or 4,000 of their number being stretched on the ground, when there is merely a bare chance that something may come of it. From what I hear all around the men are getting tired of this constant jamming, and unless General Grant finds some other way of fighting them they will show but little spirit in the matter. . . .

SOUTH OF THE JAMES, JUNE 16, THURSDAY. I left our pleasant camp at sunrise this morning and marched around to the bridge; here the division batteries joined me, but we were obliged to wait for a couple of hours before the bridge was free to us. The Fifth Corps infantry meantime were crossing at the two ferries. This bridge is really a wonderful piece of pontooning, equal I suspect to anything of the sort ever before done. It is. over a mile in its total length,* and the channel boats are anchored in I don't know how many feet of water. Yet I found it very steady in crossing, nor has there been the slightest trouble so far as I can learn.

After crossing I moved about a mile to where the road from Flower Landing (the other terminus of the ferry from Wilcox's) joins the one we were on. Here we parked up and waited till all the infantry were over, which brought it to three or four o'clock in the afternoon. The day was very hot, far more so than any we have had before this season; but we made ourselves quite comfortable under the trees of another Mr. Wilcox's house. Many of the men suffered a good deal from the heat. The ladies in the house, of whom there seemed a number, were very kind to these poor fellows; they could not have been more so had they been "Yankees" themselves instead of Virginians. This place is very different from any I have before come across in Virginia, in that the grounds around the house had been laid out and planted in the modern style, and shew that before the war they had been kept up in good order. But the most remarkable thing was the immense number of birds, and so tame too. Every bush and tree was full of them, so that it resembled a confined aviary more than an open garden. Their numbers, too, and the dense shade of the bushes, caused them to keep up a continual singing even in the heat of the day. As I lay on the grass I counted near twenty mockingbirds in sight at one time, besides as many others.

At intervals all today as well as yesterday we have heard firing in the direction of Petersburg. Now we learn that Smith's corps attacked there yesterday.

* Wainwright meant with the carefully built approaches.

SEVENTEEN

SIEGE LINES BEFORE PETERSBURG: THE MINE

General William F. Smith almost seized the glittering prize of Petersburg on June 15—but not quite. The town, when he arrived before it, was thinly fortified and defended, and his attack carried a long line of entrenchments, with some guns. But then, late in the evening, he stopped. He did not know how few the garrison were; an old illness returned upon him; his men were very tired; and he thought it better to hold what he had than risk everything by trying for further gains. The night was calm and the moon shone brightly. Had he delivered a new attack with all his strength he could probably have captured Petersburg and fortified himself along both sides of the Appomattox. But during the night Robert F. Hoke's division of Lee's army streamed into the town; new works were thrown up and old ones strengthened; and at dawn on the 16th the Union troops saw themselves faced by formidable entrenchments glittering with the arms of some of Lee's best veterans. A great chance had been lost. Smith paid for it by forfeiting his command, and the Union army by a ghastly ten-month siege.

Petersburg was now a powerful fortress serving as bastion to Richmond and shielding the communications of the capital. It protected the Weldon, Lynchburg, and Norfolk railway lines, the James River Canal, and important highways. As long as the Confederates held it they kept Richmond, only twenty-two miles away, safe from Grant's forces. The Union troops made another effort to storm the place late on the afternoon of the 16th. Hancock and Burnside simultaneously flung their corps against it, and they renewed the assault early on the 17th. But they failed with heavy loss. When Grant ordered still another attack on the 18th, his troops found that the enemy had withdrawn into a new and stronger line of fortifications closer to the town, and the charging Northerners were repulsed at every point.

Raids, forays, and minor attacks followed, but they achieved nothing; the Southern lines held fast. Meanwhile, Wainwright reached the Petersburg front with troops of Warren's corps, quite worn out by their arduous marching since leaving Cold Harbor. He had his first sharp fighting in the general attack on the 18th.

* * *

IN FRONT OF PETERSBURG, JUNE 17 [1864], FRIDAY. We travelled very slowly, with constant stops and then a few yards gained. Everyone was very sleepy, the heat of the previous day seeming to have taken all the vigour out of man and beast. My own men kept up, for unless with their battery they have no chance for any breakfast; but after every little halt more or less of the infantry were left asleep on the roadside. The provost guard which was immediately in my front could do but very little towards getting the stragglers along. Take it altogether, I do not remember ever to have seen such an amount of sleepiness on the part of both officers and men. Poor Morris slept like a top on his horse, and when he got off and walked he went so much to sleep that he did not know what was going on around him, and even walked on half a mile ahead of the command one time without waking. This was about two o'clock in the morning; when finding the provost guard and those immediately in their front hauled off the road and lying down, I took it for a general halt. All my staff were soon asleep too on the roadside. I tried it myself, but, though my eyelids ached from sleepiness, I could not lose myself even for a moment. Getting up then, I walked up the road five or six hundred yards: both sides were lined with men sound asleep just as they had fallen down; but one other did I find awake among the hundreds. All this time the sharp whiz of bullets was heard through the still night air, seeming as if but a short distance off, just beyond the wood at the outskirts of which we had halted.

We had probably been here for an hour or more when an aide came up and told me the corps was in camp about a mile on. I had been deceived by the halting of the provost guard, and they probably by the hundreds of stragglers in front of them. We at once now pushed on; I saw the general, got my orders from him, as sleepy as myself, parked my batteries, gave my own orders, and was asleep *in bed* as quick as it could be done. The sun was just rising as I turned in. I should make a poor private, I fear, with this inability to sleep unless regularly turning in; but once in bed I make up for all lost time. About eight o'clock I was awakened with orders to have my command in readiness to move at very short notice. After getting my breakfast and looking around, I found all the batteries on a large open space around Bailey's house; the infantry were in front of us; and beyond them we could hear skirmishing, and at times see the smoke of a cannon rise on the air, but a ridge of higher ground about half a mile off hid what was going on.

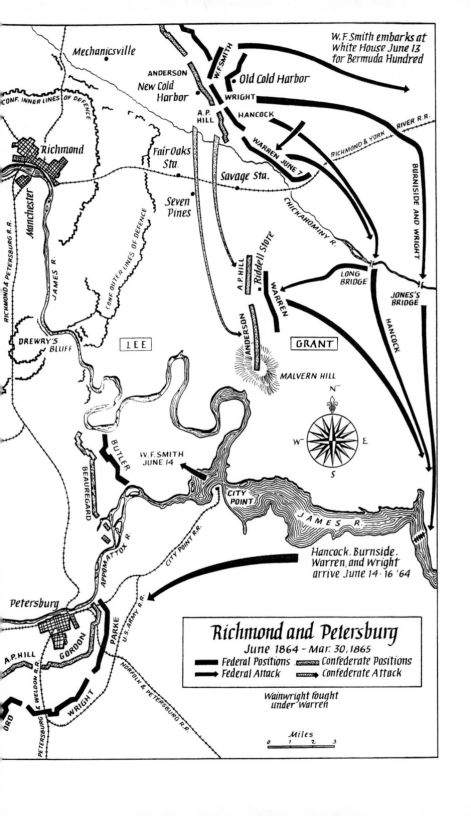

Richmond and Petersburg
June 1864 – Mar. 30, 1865

Finding no other orders came, I rode up to Warren's quarters, and afterward with him to the front. There had been a good deal of fighting going on all the morning by the Second and Ninth Corps; the former was off to the right, the latter reached to our front. Burnside's negroes, I hear, carried one work, capturing four guns and some prisoners; this I believe is the first time that they have been put in. . . .

AVERY HOUSE, JUNE 18, SATURDAY. We might say that we slept under fire last night, for odd shots were constantly coming over our way. . . . So soon as it was light, we found that the enemy had abandoned the rest of this line of works to our left around the Avery house with their main force, leaving only a strong skirmish line, which fell back fighting as we advanced. Cutler pushed forward at once, taking possession of the Avery house, and then through a piece of wood beyond. Our line fronted nearly due west all day. . . . All fighting this morning could hardly be called a battle, though there was an immense amount of iron and lead thrown from both sides and no inconsiderable loss. Lee was putting up an inner line of works, and not having them finished this morning, fought us pretty stiffly all the way back. His batteries were within the new line, but he had a double skirmish line out, and strong bodies of infantry in all the bit of wood we had to pass through. By nine o'clock all the batteries were engaged. Griffin's three batteries, "E" Massachusetts, "D" New York, and Stewart were on the left of the road to the Taylor house in the open ground: Ayres's three batteries as already mentioned, and the other six were strung along a farm road, and behind a hedge in front of the Avery house. . . .

We were under orders to be ready for a general attack along the whole line, but no hour was given. I intended to run these two batteries forward as the infantry advanced, and as soon as they crossed the ridge, some fifty yards wide only on top, they would descend again. I should be able to fire over them with safety until they were close to the rebel lines. Having arranged matters here, I rode along the edge of the wood to the left to see the ground there. While talking to General Cutler, word came that the attack would be made at three o'clock; it then wanted but a few minutes of it; only just enough time to get the men up and in rank. At the same time, too, I met Major Fitzhugh, who had come over to report, and see whether more batteries could not be used. He proposed to bring Barnes over to the left of Bigelow, to which I consented, as I was anxious to see that battery in a warm place, which it had never been before.

At three the attack was made, Hart and Bigelow shoving their guns up by hand directly behind the troops, and opening immediately. The fire along the whole line was tremendous on both sides, the batteries being in many instances within long canister range of each other. I cannot say that our men went in well, or at all as if they meant to carry the works. In five minutes they were coming back. Old Hart said the enemy were following them up, which at the time I also believed to be the case, and ordered them to keep on firing even through our own runaways. Finding several hundred men of the Fourth Division who had come back behind the ridge on which the batteries were, I rode down there, and tried to get them forward again, appealing to them for the honour of the old First Corps. I thought I had succeeded, as I got them into some sort of a line, but there was no officer with them higher than a first lieutenant, and they were from two or three brigades. One young adjutant who had been most busy in getting them formed now came to me and said the men would go if they had some officer of rank to lead them.

Very foolishly, as I now think, for I knew nothing of the real state of affairs in front, I cried out that I would lead them myself; and in the excitement of the moment I should have done it on horseback, I believe, had the men gone, but not over some two dozen would budge. Had they gone I should probably have made no more entries here. In some fifteen or twenty minutes the whole attack had proved a failure, though it was some time longer before all our men got back out of the valley; and a great deal of firing was kept up all the afternoon, though nothing more was attempted on either side. . . .

The attack this afternoon was a fiasco of the worst kind; I trust it will be the last attempt at this most absurd way of attacking entrenchments by a general advance in line. It has been tried so often now and with such fearful losses that even the stupidest private now knows that it cannot succeed, and the natural consequence follows: the men will not try it. The very sight of a bank of fresh earth now brings them to a dead halt. I hear that the loss in the Fifth Corps today will mount up to 3,000; the others, I suppose, in proportion. The loss in my own command is thirty, viz: one officer (Lieutenant Blake of "E" Massachusetts), and two men killed; one officer (Captain Hart) and twenty-six men wounded; of these last two in "D" New York, and one in "H" were injured by premature discharge of the pieces.

Whether the fighting of today may be called a battle or not, I cannot say. But there has been a good deal of shooting going on: all the batteries of my brigade have been engaged throughout the day, firing a total of near 4,000 rounds. It is seldom that I have had more satisfaction in a day's work, too: my officers and men have been prompt in the performance of every duty they were called on for, and performed them well, so that in looking back on the day's operations I feel perfectly satisfied with my command. I should also be more than ordinarily thankful for my own escape today without injury. During the attack I was on top of the knoll where Hart and Bigelow were, mounted, until our men began to fall back. . . . A piece of a laid-up shell passed through my pants and drawers directly under the right knee, cutting as square a hole at its entrance as if done by a pair of scissors. How it went where it did I cannot see, the holes looking as if the shot must have gone directly through the leg. A torn piece of the drawers, knit silk, striking sharp on the muscle under the knee, made one think that I was really hit. It is absurd now, but at the moment I sat down, after going a step or two, to see whether I was hit or not. During those fifteen or twenty seconds I believe that I imagined my whole future life on one leg. . . .

JUNE 19, SUNDAY. This has been a day of rest; that is, so far as remaining under a constant fire of musketry, and an occasional outpouring of artillery can be called rest. No new move has been attempted on either side but both have been busy strengthening their works. What our next move will be I am as yet in ignorance of. As to getting the men up to assaulting point, I do not believe it possible; never has the Army of the Potomac been so demoralized as at this time. Were McClellan in command siege operations would have begun this morning. But Grant I presume would think that a slow process; nor has he any siege train with him, every gun heavier than a light twelve-pounder having been sent off to Washington—unless Butler may have some. Will he keep on shoving off to the left? Perhaps for a little while, but he cannot now move his right from the James, and consequently the length of his tether is limited. . . .

General Hunt was here today and visited all our line. When he went out to Bigelow's battery we found it very hot; the bullets from the rebel line whizzed about our ears at the rate of at least thirty a minute. I do not remember ever being more scared, and we crept up to the guns almost on our hands and knees. Yet this is the same ground on which two days ago I rode about mounted, when there was a hundred times as much firing. Could there be a stronger proof that courage is merely a non-realization of the danger one is in owing to excitement, responsibility, or something of the sort?

I have met with a great loss today; one that it will be hard to make good—impossible down here. Night before last I broke the stem of my pipe, and today lost the whole out of my pocket when out on the lines with General Hunt. It was a present from Thorne just before I left home, and had been of infinite comfort to me through every battle I have been in, and on every march we have made. Besides being the sweetest pipe I ever smoked, it was a real beauty and had coloured most wonderfully; everyone who saw it admired it, and at least half a hundred have petitioned for it should I get knocked over. . . .

❋ ❋ ❋

Grant's general assaults on the Confederate lines at Petersburg having broken down with a loss of about 10,000 men, he resolved to try a less dangerous strategy. He began entrenching his own lines. At the same time he moved the corps of Hancock (now temporarily commanded by Birney, for Hancock's old wound prostrated him), and of Wright, as secretly as possible to the left in the direction of the Petersburg and Weldon Railroad. If he could seize this railway and cut the road to Lynchburg, he would seriously interrupt the supply lines to the west and south. A body of Union cavalry under James H. Wilson did reach the Weldon Railroad and begin tearing up track.

But Confederate troops under A. P. Hill, watching for an opportunity to strike, discovered a gap between the two Union corps. Thrusting his veterans into it, Hill attacked Birney's exposed flank with terrific effect. In rapid succession he hit the divisions of Barlow, Mott, and Gibbon, and rolled them back. The total Union losses in this action were fully 3,000, and 1,600 were taken prisoners by the Confederate troops under Mahone alone. Both Birney and Wright were forced back. The behavior of some Union officers and men was disgraceful. Theodore Lyman wrote: "I look upon June 22nd and 23rd as the two most discreditable days to this army I ever saw. There was everywhere, high and low, feebleness, confusion, poor judgment."

✳ ✳ ✳

JUNE 22, WEDNESDAY. These two days have only produced so far symptoms of a determination on Grant's part to stick to his old tactics. Having got the line strengthened, Burnside and Smith now hold from in front of the Taylor house to the Appomattox River. Cutler holds from there to the left, Griffin going around to the left of Ayres, and stretching to the Jerusalem Plank Road; across which and a short distance beyond Crawford has moved. Yesterday the Second and Sixth Corps were moved beyond this again, and were to have swung around on Crawford as a pivot today, so as to envelop more of the rebel lines and get possession of the Weldon Railroad. But in executing this move, the right of the Sixth got separated from the left of the Second in the wood; leaving a large gap, into which a considerable body of the enemy entered, and played the mischief with the flanks of both corps. So far as I can learn, our men broke at once, behaving miserably. The line of the Second Corps was just eaten up like flame travels up a slip of paper, until they reached the Twentieth Massachusetts, which regiment did know how to change front, and having done so, stopped the whole affair. We are said to have lost from 3,000 to 5,000 prisoners, and McKnight's battery. The guns are certainly gone, but I trust the number of prisoners is grossly exaggerated. Let us make the best we can of it, however; the whole affair has been very disgraceful to us.

I find myself rapidly being deprived of all command, and expect soon to be able to ask for a leave of absence, on the ground of having nothing whatever to do. Yesterday there came an order assigning Bigelow and Cooper to the Third Division, so that I am left now with but four batteries. Nor is Warren keeping to his own statement that the batteries are only assigned for service, not for administration, as two test questions have decided today. At Dr. Thompson's request, on the 19th I ordered a private of "E" Massachusetts to report to him as acting hospital steward. Captain Phillips, who I am sorry to say is shewing himself a tool of Griffin's, instead of obeying the order, refers it to division headquarters, whence it comes back to him with the endorsement "Captain Phillips will pay no attention to this detail." Phillips sends me no notice of this until he is asked why he has not obeyed the order; so that I am actually insulted by both Griffin and him. Yet what can I do? Such cases do not come against Regulations. As the only course left me, I referred the whole matter up to corps headquarters for Warren's decision; and now he says that I had no right to make the detail, but should have applied to have the man detailed, through corps headquarters. If this does not take the last remnant of control over the batteries assigned to divisions out of my hands, I don't know what remains for me.

The other case was an application I made to have Captain P. F. Nason, Eighteenth Massachusetts, detailed as acting ordnance officer; who I understood wanted to come, as he had served with the artillery brigade of the old Fifth Corps for two years. This application having been referred to Griffin, in whose division the Eighteenth Massachusetts is, he returns it to headquarters with the endorsement "that there is no such officer as Captain P. F. Nason in the Eighteenth Massachusetts." Yet he evidently knew that it was simply a mistake in the regiment, and put that on out of pure ugliness; for on the number of the regiment being corrected, he sends it to Phillips, who returns it with the statement that "Captain Nason is at present acting as adjutant of the division artillery." So I find a new command within my own starting up. All I can do is to wait and watch, in hopes that before long they will do something that will enable me to appeal to General Meade with a prospect of success. Should I do it, and get a decision against me, I should be worse off than ever. . . .

JUNE 24, FRIDAY. The weather has been waxing warmer the last two days, and today has been really a piper. We are not yet allowed to have our waggons up at the front permanently, so I have not got all my tents pitched, and still have Fitzhugh as a roommate. Fortunately I have next to nothing to do, but try to keep cool and kill time. The men in the trenches, though, must suffer very much from this great heat. Everything remains stationary in front of Petersburg. A large body of cavalry has gone off to try and cut the railroads south of Richmond; they are under Generals Wilson and Kautz.* I see no prospect of our being any more expeditious in reducing this place than McClellan was, in front of Yorktown. We have already lost three or four times as many men as he did there, and have done nearly if not quite as much digging. Yet operations have not begun here; it is neither a siege nor an investment as yet, nor do I hear of anything being determined on. As to these cavalry raids destroying the railroads so as to starve them out of this place and Richmond, it is all stuff.

I have been along our lines as far as the river; not, however, going up close where the picket firing was ugly, only near enough to get some idea of the lay of the land. The rebel position around the cemetery, and all the way from there to their left, is very strong. I do not think that we can do anything in that quarter. At the Appomattox we have a large battery of 4.5-inch guns; from it I got a good view of all the lower part of the town, and the railroad bridges. These last are very low; a mere skeleton of piles across the river, and consequently almost impossible to hit at a mile off. The captain of the battery, however, told me that he had stopped their crossing trains during the daytime. . . .

JUNE 26, SUNDAY. We have no thermometer around the Avery house, but Ayres has one at his headquarters which marked 101° in the shade yesterday. Today, if there is any difference, it must be still higher. As for the dust, it is beyond conception, lying like a cloud over the whole face of the country, there not being breeze enough to carry it off when raised

---

* James H. Wilson of Illinois, a brilliant young West Pointer of the class of 1860, was already famous. He had distinguished himself in the Vicksburg campaign and at Missionary Ridge; then earlier this year he had been named the first head of the new Cavalry Bureau in Washington, where he saw to the arming of cavalry with Spencer carbines; and now he commanded a division in the Cavalry Corps. He was to serve in the Spanish War and Boxer Rebellion and write one of the best of all books of military reminiscences. August V. Kautz, of German birth, had graduated at West Point in 1852, had been with the Army of the Potomac under McClellan, and now also headed a cavalry division.

But this particular expedition was destined to end in a sharp defeat. Encountering not only Fitzhugh Lee's cavalry but a large infantry force, Wilson and Kautz were routed and had to abandon many guns in a swamp. In a raid of some ten days' duration Wilson had covered more than three hundred miles and destroyed sixty miles of railroad; but he lost more than 1,500 men, and the Confederates soon repaired the track. The event added to the now widespread sense of disillusionment with Grant's leadership both in the army and throughout the North; the general feeling was that thus far he had been a sore disappointment.

by the thousands of waggons and horsemen which traverse the plain in every direction.

Nothwithstanding the heat, we put three of the coehorns in position yesterday, and fired a dozen rounds just to shew the men how it was done and get the range. It was astonishing that the men of Hazelton's company, not one of whom had probably ever seen a mortar fired before, should have made themselves in that number of rounds perfect masters, as it were, of their pieces. . . .

This afternoon I rode out to Army Headquarters, dined with Patrick, and spent the evening with General Hunt. We had quite a variety of vegetables for dinner, which, though not over-fresh, were a great treat to me, who have only once tasted aught in that line but old potatoes in months. Gibbon and several others were at Hunt's quarters. In discussing the campaign, I found that the loss of this army since we left Culpeper Court House is very generally set down at 90,000; a perfectly fearful amount. Gibbon says that the Second Corps has lost thirteen brigade commanders. . . .

JUNE 30, THURSDAY. At the present time we are doing nothing here, either to finish the war or to fill my journal. We have been flooded with orders about the monthly returns, and such like matters of detail and have been somewhat busy today in complying with the same. Apart from this, I have had nothing to do this week. Books we have none, so that time hangs heavy; as one might judge when I took to playing chess, a game about which I know nothing and which I never liked. Solitaire with cards has also come much into fashion here at Colonel Avery's, a poor but passable substitute for whist, which I cannot get enough to join in. Another amusement is playing with a litter of kittens which have been dropped since we came here. The house itself has been a great comfort through all this hot spell; standing high and free of trees, we have had all the air there was to be obtained, and the mere feeling of room was a great improvement over the confined limits of a tent. Since Tuesday the weather has moderated a good deal. Still, we are buried in dust, not having seen a drop of rain since the 28th of the month.

The cavalry expedition finished off most disastrously, and ingloriously. Everything had gone well with them up to yesterday morning. They had penetrated to the crossing of the Danville Railroad over the Roanoke, and destroyed some five and twenty miles of that road, as well as a good bit on the Lynchburg road. Wilson and Kautz had united, and night before last they had reached Reams's Station on the Weldon Railroad, on their way home. This point is not over ten miles from here, and they seem to have considered themselves safe within our lines, and to have been terribly careless, for yesterday morning they were caught by the enemy completely with their breeches down, attacked in front and flank, utterly stampeded and driven to the four winds. All their guns are gone, fifteen in number, including four mountain howitzers. The loss in men is entirely unknown, as they ran away so fast; but it is supposed that most of them will get in. . . . Lieutenant Fitzhugh came here himself without a hat, and with his clothes almost torn off of his back. Our affairs seem to go worse on this side of the James River than they did on the other; we are not only beaten, but disgracefully. I fear that the truth is that all the fight is gone out of our men. Grant has used the army up, and will now have to wait until its morale is restored before he can do anything. In all this bad behaviour, though, I have yet to hear of a single battery disgracing itself.

I have said nothing about War Department orders this month, having enough else to fill up; nor as to Banks's incompetency on the Red River. In looking over the orders I find nothing of moment, save one in which the President commutes the death punishment of all deserters to imprisonment during the war. Poor, weak, well-meaning Lincoln!

AVERY HOUSE, BEFORE PETERSBURG, JULY 3, 1864, SUNDAY. The midsummer month opened with intense heat; Friday and Saturday were fully equal to anything in that line we have had. Today it has moderated a good deal, while the sun is partly veiled by clouds, which, however, fly too high to afford much promise of rain. This heat may be one reason for our doing nothing, though I cannot learn that Grant has yet made up his mind what to try. Siege operations are said to be talked of. The men have lain very quiet in the trenches during these hot days, Burnside's negroes being the only ones that have done any firing. . . . I was at headquarters again today, but learned nothing new save the report that siege operations were to be begun. On my way there I called on General Crawford, who I found entertaining Governor Curtin and a couple of other Pennsylvania politicians with punch and champagne. Crawford was (confidentially) tight and his friends decidedly boozy. . . .

The *Army and Navy Journal* of a week ago contains the speech of General McClellan at the laying of the cornerstone of the Soldiers' Monument at West Point. It was an exceedingly good on, eloquent in places far above what I supposed him capable of; nor will his bitterest enemies be able to lay their finger on one single sentence in it which they can twist into anything to use against him.

JULY 7, THURSDAY. Grant appears to have got so far in making up his mind what he had best do as to have determined to hang on here at any rate. Since Monday we have been busy pushing out and strengthening our line. Last night Griffin and Crawford shoved up to the outer edge of the wood northeast of the plank road, which brings our line here about seven hundred yards from the great angle behind which this road enters the enemy's lines, and not over one hundred and fifty yards from their pickets at the chimneys of the burned Gregory house. . . .

Early is said to have crossed the Potomac, without opposition. I have only heard it as a report, but think it probable, as I have no confidence in Sigel who is (or was) in command in the valley. Report also says tonight that part or all of the Sixth Corps has gone to City Point for shipment up to Washington. It is to be hoped that the President (alias the politicians) will not get so frightened as to order us all up there. As a partial offset to Early's advance in the valley we have news of the capture, or rather sinking, of the *Alabama* by the *Kearsarge* (one of old Welles's new jaw-break names) commanded by Lieutenant Winslow. It was the only fair naval fight of the war so far; and most fortunately occurred within sight of the French coast, and near enough to some parts of England for them to hear the guns. I am not one of those who find fault with the whole Church of England and all Englishmen for their attitude toward us. Still, that they have acted scurvily about those privateers there is no doubt, and one cannot help rejoicing that the crew of one of them was taken as prisoners into an English port. As to Semmes's escape, the right or wrong of the matter depends entirely on what intercourse Winslow had with the English yacht; though it is a thousand pities that he was not caught and hung, simply "pour encourager les autres."

Another evidence of being settled here is the getting up of our heavy baggage, books, and writing material. By books, I do not mean to read, but books to write in. We are making history, not studying it. This arrival, of course, is followed by a stream of orders, circulars, and demands for reports. We have two months' back writing to bring up, which will keep the clerks busy and give me a little occupation, which will be a change from playing at solitaire all the day. . . .

Two more newspaper correspondents, Swinton of the *Times,* and Kent of the *Tribune,* are ordered out of the lines "for publishing incorrect statements respecting the operations of the troops." I wonder what the particular "incorrectness" was, for full half of all the statements of all correspondents are incorrect. Another circular desires corps commanders to furnish the names of such officers as deserve promotion to generals. If Warren's conduct has been any indication of his opinion, he will not send mine up. Indeed, he damns so generally right and left, that he will have hard work to recommend anyone consistently unless he does it for a salve. Well, I would rather go without the star then be damned into it; one of his pleasures he has not yet indulged in at my expense, but then I see as little of him as possible. . . .

The Fourth of July passed without any very great observance by the army. An attempt was made by the Sanitary to furnish the men with fresh vegetables, but although the amount in the aggregate was doubtless large, so that it will figure well in the papers, the distribution was very much of the "penny ice cream and two spoons" order—three onions or two tomatoes to a man. Having some of my Christmas box still on hand, we made quite a spread for us, Bankhead helping us to eat it. The "pièce de résistance" was salmon and green peas, both of which were canned somewhere in France at least a year ago. Still, they were as fine and delicate as when first put up; quite equal to any I have ever eaten. The salmon we had cold, as it had been soused. Although we all nearly dined of it, and I did quite, there was as much more left for the next day. 'Tis singular that our people cannot learn to can these things as well as the French; or rather it would be were not the French the best cooks in the world, while the Americans are the worst. Our sutler brought us some champagne, but it was of the poorest Jersey brand. I could not drink a glass of it myself, and stuck to a bottle of common madeira I found in my box.

Speaking of drinks, General Burnside would appear to like them as well as his staff. I was over there one day to call on some of them, when happening to enter his camp near the General's tent, I found him sitting in front of it in his shirt sleeves, alongside of a great pile of boxes labelled ale, cider, and whiskey. The General insisted on my taking some, so I drank a pint of cider with ice, which was most excellent. Indeed, I found Burnside himself so hearty and agreeable that I made but a very short call on his staff. Our cook brings us the bad news that there is no more ice in the house here. It is almost a necessary this hot weather and must be got somehow if possible. Captain Steele tells me that it can be bought at City Point for two dollars a hundred.

JULY 10, SUNDAY. Siege operations here have been at last determined on; the order, which I have not yet seen, was issued yesterday. I only know that the approaches are to be made from the front of this corps and the Ninth. Our line has been straightened along its whole length; that is, the worst of the crooks have been taken out, for the line itself is a curve. Our right is not over five hundred yards from the rebel works, but the ravine, which begins by the plank road, is quite deep here, and about equidistant between the lines. There is a spring at the bottom of this ravine which is used by both sides, though the opposing pickets have a code of signals by which they avoid meeting there. At the plank road the pickets are not more than twenty or sixty yards apart, within easy talking distance. Our lines being now permanently settled—that is, made so strong that we could not be driven from them save by a regular assault—all picket firing has again ceased. I spent nearly the whole of this morning is passing along our lines, on foot, made some sketches of the bearings of the rebel batteries, and took a good look, without being disturbed by a single shot, until I reached the extreme right within range of the lines opposite the negroes, when a few shot were fired. . . .

The parapet along Griffin's and Ayres's front was very good and well built; Cutler's was by no means equal. The whole shewed an improvement on anything I have seen made by our men before, which work was not laid out by the engineers. As yet no guns have been moved up to the new line on our front. Ayres is preparing a place on his front for the three batteries with him. This may be said to be the opening of the first parallel. I shall look with great interest on the ensuing steps of the siege, as a comparatively new study for me; as at Yorktown my position did not allow me to see all I wanted, nor did I know enough to profit by all I did see. McClellan was in front of Yorktown only a month when he had completed his works; we have now been here over three weeks, and have just determined what to do. Slow McClellan!

The Sixth Corps has gone up to Maryland, and lucky it was that they were able to hurry them off, for there appears to have been no troops, or only worthless ones, there before. A part of the Nineteenth Corps, which was coming here from New Orleans, arrived at the same time and was sent right on. So there can now be but little fear as to the safety of Washington although our last reports from there state that Early was within sight of the Capitol. Never have the greycoats got so near before, or given our blessed Congress so great reason to be scared. This will afford an excuse for another call for half a million of men, and indeed we want some of them; for of the 700,000 actually raised, on paper, within the last year, not more than 400,000 have ever joined the army. . . .

We are still without rain, and as there has been so much turning up of the dirt, the slightest wind renders the dust intolerable. It fills our tents even here at headquarters, where there is but little passing close by, making everything very dirty. At home they have had a fine shower. Mr. Chase has resigned his place as Secretary of the Treasury. It is one radical at least out of the Cabinet, and would Stanton only go too, the army at least would be thankful. Senator Fessenden, who succeeds him, has a good character and has not shown himself so rampant as many. . . .

❊ ❊ ❊

Lee, who knew that the area north of Richmond had been left open, at the beginning of July sent Jubal A. Early with about 12,000 men into the Shenandoah. This was a tempting field, for General David Hunter had recently been repulsed at Lynchburg, and compelled to retreat from the Valley. Advancing rapidly, Early drove the Union forces under Sigel out of

Martinsburg, crossed the Potomac, took Frederick, and made ready to march on Washington. The Confederate object was to compel Grant to give up his hold on Petersburg and move to the relief of the capital. Thus he would fling away all the gains in two months of bloody fighting and marching.

But the war had passed the stage at which either the Administration or the generals could be so easily scared. On July 6, a day after the Confederates entered Hagerstown in Maryland, Grant detached part of the Sixth Corps to meet the threat. These troops reached Washington and Baltimore at once. At this time the Nineteenth Corps was arriving in the James under General William H. Emory, known chiefly for his Far Western services before the war. Grant at once ordered it to proceed to Washington. When Early reached the suburbs of Washington on July 11, he saw that its defenses were being heavily manned by fresh troops; and after some skirmishing around Fort Stevens, and the destruction of Montgomery Blair's house at Silver Spring, he withdrew. He was soon back across the Potomac.

But if he had not succeeded in weakening Grant south of the James, Early had caused great irritation and chagrin in the capital. Congressmen, Cabinet members, and public were outraged by the fact that the Union armies, now so heavily outnumbering the Confederates, had actually been unable to prevent the enemy from reaching the outskirts of the capital and threatening its capture. At one moment Lincoln had even proposed that Grant leave his Petersburg headquarters and take personal command of the forces defending Washington. The episode fortified the gloom of the hour. Many Northerners agreed with Gideon Welles that Grant "displays little strategy or invention."

Lincoln, as many besides Wainwright expected, did call for more men. Acting on the basis of an act passed by Congress on July 4, he issued a proclamation on July 18 for the enlistment of 500,000 additional volunteers.

❊ ❊ ❊

JULY 12, TUESDAY. The whole corps has become one vast bee hive; immense details are at work everywhere. Cutler and Ayres are strengthening their works, while Griffin's and Crawford's men are throwing up two redoubts to cover our left flank. . . .

General Orders No. 29, headquarters Army of the Potomac, dishonourably dismisses Second Lieutenant Donald Gillies of the One Hundred Twenty-Fifth New York Volunteers, "he having tendered his resignation on the ground that a wound received in the battle of Gettysburg has so intimidated him that he has become constitutionally a coward." I know nothing more of his case, but it seems to me a pretty hard one; for I am a firm believer in a morally brave man being so physically, that is nervously, timid as to have no control over himself. Lieutenant Gillies may have acted honestly and conscientiously in thus resigning, and should at least have had the matter explained to him and been allowed to withdraw his resignation. Perhaps all this was done, or perhaps there were circumstances of which I know nothing. A month ago Lieutenant Fuller of "L" Battery sent up his resignation on much the same grounds, but did not state them in the paper. His wife and mother, who are entirely dependent on him for support, harped so continually on what they would suffer should anything happen to him, that he had become completely unstrung, and was so nervous under fire that it was apparent to the men, who had lost all respect for him. I forwarded his paper approved, merely stating that it would be for the interest of the service to have his resignation accepted, but it was returned. . . .

JULY 14, THURSDAY. Last night Ayres's three batteries were moved forward up to the new line where the whole twelve guns are in position together, due east from the "great salient" of the rebel lines, distant about eight hundred yards. Our works progress rapidly; as yet they are confined to securing our own position with redoubts and batteries; being of a defensive rather than an offensive character. The Second Corps have been wheeled to the rear, and are now at work on a line of defence facing that way, and extending from the Jerusalem Plank Road near the small redoubt I don't know how far.

General Warren is now in his element: so far as I can learn he is his own officer of the trenches, and commander of the working parties. There is nothing that he likes so much as overseeing work, and consequently is in a most agreeable humour. I spent some hours with him yesterday in the large redoubt, which one might easily believe he had undertaken to build by contract, and certainly has pushed forward with most wonderful rapidity. It is an immense work, five hundred feet front I believe, and perfectly square. Bigelow and Breck are to move their guns into this work, so soon as it is ready for them, and I was much surprised to have the General expressly leave the selection of position for the different pieces entirely to me, as also the building of the platforms and magazines. He is a queer mixture: one might have thought that he had the greatest confidence in his chief of artillery, who heard him today explaining all his plans about this work, and consulting most confidentially with him. I am becoming more than ever convinced that he has a screw loose, and is not quite accountable for all his freaks. . . .

JULY 17, SUNDAY. Dry, dry, dry; the leaves are like brass so far as their giving any moisture goes. The dust is intolerable; such as can only be equalled in the Sahara during a simoon. It has got so driven into the dark blue of our men's coats that even the neatest of them look shabby. The great heat, however, has passed, but left its mark in a large increase of fever patients in our hospitals. The division hospitals are nearby, but a vast one for the whole army has been established at City Point, so as to avoid so far as possible the sending of any men out of the control of the army, and so be able to get them back to duty so soon as possible. General Meade has just ordered the issue of daily rations of fresh vegetables, potatoes, onions, and cabbage, which if it can be done will contribute greatly to the health of the army. In another order I think that he has made a mistake; viz: in ordering all the musicians down to the hospital as nurses, cooks, and the like. We have little enough music in the army as it is, while a good tooter may be worthless as a nurse or cook.

A third order reads very queer to me, thus: "Until further orders the employment of *females* as officers' servants is prohibited." I did not know there was such an animal within the limits of this army, and have not seen a petticoat the last month. True, perhaps they don't wear them down here, but, like the contrabands, mount the cast-off garments of their masters.

The work on the two redoubts, or rather on the large one, for the other is finished, progresses well; but it was an immense undertaking, having room enough in it to hold one of our present brigades. I can hardly suppose that there was any call for quite so large a work, and am inclined to think that it was a hobby of Warren's. They say that Burnside is tunnelling for a mine somewhere, but I have heard nothing particular about it as yet. The enemy are quite as industrious as we are, erecting new batteries, and strengthening their parapet all along. . . .

General Hunt shewed me today a copy of a letter he had sent up to Humphreys, Chief of Staff, as to artillery control; really as to my own position. It was brought about in this way: one day, Wednesday last, I believe, we were going along our line together with Duane,* and when at the point held by Ayres's batteries the engineer in charge there complained to Duane that the firing of our batteries induced the enemy to continue firing in return, which had caused the loss of several of his working party and obliged him at times to stop work; and that a coehorn mortar battery on the right was particularly troublesome in this respect. Duane at once turned the complaint over to Hunt, who pitched into me for it. But I told him that the coehorns as well as all the batteries but two were taken entirely out of my hands by General Warren's order,

---

* James Chatham Duane, West Point, 1848, well experienced in all activities connected with the building of bridges, siege works, and defensive fortifications, was Chief Engineer of the Army of the Potomac.

so that I could not control them at all in this respect. When we got around to where Hazelton was, the general blamed him for firing so much; when he brought out his excuse, a note from Warren directing him "to serve his mortars and receive orders according as General Ayres directs," with another from Ayres in effect putting him under Colonel Kitching. Kitching, who is a nice fellow and first-rate officer too, is rather a busybody, and complained that Hazelton did not fire enough. General Hunt desired me to send him copies of these orders, which, with others, he has enclosed in a communication covering the whole ground of his and his subordinates' control over the artillery, especially at this time. Like all Hunt's dealings, it is straightforward and plain spoken, and being backed by tangible proofs of his statements, I trust may produce some effect. Meade, having a strong bias against the artillery or towards the corps commanders, which is the same thing, it is very hard work to get up a case at all likely to gain his decision on our side.

JULY 19, TUESDAY. The news of the day, most welcome too, is the arrival of rain. Even in the midst of a siege, those things which add most to one's comfort hold the first place in interest. After many attempts during the night, it made an actual commencement about eight o'clock this morning, and has continued falling softly but steadily all day; every drop sinking into the ground. . . .

Our works do not seem to me to progress as rapidly as they did. General Warren has tired of being overseer, and does not spend his whole day among the workmen; finishing off, too, is slow work in this as in pretty much all constructions. The engineers have just traced out an irregular work, to be enclosed in the corner of the wood close to the plank road; it is within one hundred yards of the rebel pickets at the Gregory chimneys, and having rather an ugly lookout for them is not likely to be put up with so little disturbance as the others have. . . . Large parties, too, are at work on a series of covered ways connecting the approaches to the different works; in widening the sunken way immediately behind the parapet along the whole line, draining it, and building proper banquettes. I am getting impatient for this sort of preliminary work to be finished, and the approaches to begin.

During the past week there has been considerable increase in the number of deserters who have come into our lines; and these say that many more would come if they could get a good chance. A large number have been from Florida regiments, who say that their whole brigade is planning to come over. Whether this report had any foundation or not is doubtful; but it is certain that that brigade was relieved from duty on the front the very morning after the report was brought to us. I am sorry to have to say, too, that the number of desertions to the enemy from our army is a good deal larger than ever before. . . .

JULY 21, THURSDAY. We are having cool weather after our rain; the nights really cold with their heavy dew. The dust, too, is already beginning to get up again. Work still goes on steadily. . . . The new work at the plank road gets on slowly. I was right in my surmise that the rebels would not like it; they make it so hot for the workmen there that it has already been christened Fort Hell by the men.

The mine which General Burnside is making causes a good deal of talk and is generally much laughed at. It is an affair of his own entirely, and has nothing to do with the regular siege operations, or the engineers with it. The rebels somehow, probably from deserters, have got information of it, and the men there seem to laugh at it too, as their pickets are constantly asking after its welfare. I know nothing about it myself save that it is somewhere opposite the Taylor house, where Burnside's lines come up very close to those of the enemy. Our engineers say that it is badly located. Neither they, Meade, nor the other corps commanders have any belief in its success. There are rumours, too, that the enemy are mining somewhere on Smith's front.

I have a letter from E. E. Heard dated July 9th. He is with Sherman as medical director of the new Fourth Corps commanded by General Howard. He is delighted with Howard as commander, as everyone who serves with him is. Their corps, he says, is a first-rate one, but the whole Western army is very much behind this in organization, though much has been done since Sherman took command and they got a number of Army of the Potomac generals there. . . . Bliss had been mustered out, and Jackson had just gone home with a flesh wound in his right arm. In a postscript he says: "Captured a factory the other day and four hundred women"; further deponent saith not. When the doctor wrote, they were lying quietly at the Chattahoochee River, within ten miles of Atlanta. Had had no general engagement; only marching, bushwhacking and small affairs. This morning General Grant sends us a copy of a telegram from Sherman dated "near Crosskeys seven P.M." of yesterday in which he says they are again moving; had crossed the river and seized the Atlanta and Dalton Railroad.

Yesterday's Washington papers contain a proclamation from the President, calling for 500,000 more men, who will be accepted as volunteers for one, two or three years; the number to be made up by a draft in all localities which have not filled their quota in fifty days. Also another proclamation suspending the Act of Habeas Corpus in the State of Kentucky.

JULY 24, SUNDAY. Certain changes in the plan of operations here were decided on on Friday night which will tend to hurry up the first scene in the tragedy. It was determined to adopt Burnside's mine, which has been successfully made, and try that way of getting into the rebel lines.

The point on the enemy front under which the mine is placed is a re-entering angle, which is greatly against it; but on the other hand, Burnside has pushed up to within one hundred fifty yards of their works, and from that spot it is not much if any over five hundred yards to the top of Cemetery Hill, from which the town is completely commanded, and which may be carried by the rush if the enemy have no other works there. I am myself inclined to think that they have a second line at least partially made along the top of the crest. Yesterday I spent the whole day with Hunt and Duane on our line, deciding where artillery to cover the assault was to be placed.

Two batteries of four guns each are to be added between Ayres and Fort Hell; the works on the right, which are miserably planned, are to be rebuilt, and two large mortar batteries are to be erected for ten- and eight-inch pieces. This has started us all into activity again, and I can now take hold with a will, too, for General Hunt's protest has produced good fruit. Yesterday Warren issued an order placing the coehorn battery (the immediate bone of contention) entirely under my control, and sort of backing out of his previous position as to the other batteries. The order itself would not give me much satisfaction, had not Hunt shown me the whole of the papers today. His communication, which as I said was very strong, was referred to General Warren. Warren's endorsement on it was very queer, merely complaining that Hunt had not come to him instead of making a formal complaint; it made me think of the wail of a whipped school boy more than anything else. Humphreys then, by Meade's order, wrote him a long and pretty sharp letter which gives me assurance that I may act as if his order had distinctly placed all the artillery in position under my control. . . .

JULY 27, WEDNESDAY. There have been some changes in the position of troops since Sunday, but all has continued quiet on our front. Yesterday the Second Corps was withdrawn from our rear; two divisions of it, rather, and moved down to City Point. . . .

JULY 28, THURSDAY. The works preparatory to the explosion of the mine are progressing rapidly. I have been all along our line with General Hunt today, making the final arrangements as to the placing of the guns. Saturday is now fixed on as the day of assault. I did not expect it so soon, and consequently gave Major Fitzhugh permission this morning, before I knew it, to go down and see his brother, who is on the river somewhere near City Point, and to remain overnight, which I am very sorry for now, as I need him here. The present plan is for twelve guns on the extreme right, twelve more where Ayres's batteries are, ten in two works between there and Fort Hell, and eight in that work; six of these siege guns. I have not yet quite decided on what batteries to place in each position; but have six batteries of the Sixth Corps placed at my disposal.

Fort Hell is not finished but has progressed so far that it will be in good condition by tomorrow night. They are at work on the magazine today, and laying platforms; the parapet is very high, and equally strong. The works on the right are a botch, and must be altered somewhat before they are used at all, as they do not all look the right way; the entrance to them, too, is very bad. The great mortar battery, for ten-inch mortars, is on the spot where Ayres's batteries were at first. . . .

Mortar practise has got to be quite the fashion on both sides. I have not allowed any of the pieces on our front to be fired since I regained control of them, except when the enemy persevered in firing. But Burnside has blazed away pretty freely, all his artillery being subject to the division commanders. The enemy, too, have a number of coehorns with which they frequently drop shells on our side, so that half our men have become underground tenants, and the whole ground in rear of the lines is one great rabbit warren. Van Reed has built most spacious and sumptuous bomb-proof quarters for himself and men, where I sit in perfect safety. Rogers and Walcott are not much behind him. Notwithstanding all their firing, I have not heard of a casualty from them. Bombs, unlike cannonballs, move so slowly that one can see them coming and has time to get out of the way. One came over today and fell into the covered way through which I was riding in rear of Cutler's line, but I had time to get around a corner before it exploded. As when we first saw it, it was almost directly over my orderly's head, he was a good deal scared. They tell some very laughable stories about them. . . .

* * *

The plan for the mine had originated with Lieutenant-Colonel Henry Pleasants of the Forty-eighth Pennsylvania, a regiment largely composed of miners from Schuylkill County—Pleasants himself being an experienced mining engineer. When he submitted the idea to Burnside through his division commander, the general accepted it with alacrity, and Pleasants set to work next morning. The army engineers were scornful. So long an underground passage had never been dug under such circumstances, they said; the miners were likely to be crushed or suffocated; the scheme was senseless. Meade was so influenced by their views that he was grudgingly and coldly tolerant. But Pleasants persevered. When the authorities refused him timber, he sent to an outside sawmill; when they denied him mining picks, he had ordinary picks remade; when he could get no wheelbarrows, he had the earth carried out in cracker boxes.

The site for the mine seemed favorable. The Union lines had been carried at one point part way up a hillside crowned by fortifications, with the cemetery hill beyond commanding all Petersburg. Inside the Union lines was a ravine deepened by the cut for the Norfolk Railroad, with its bottom shielded from enemy view by Union works. Pleasants opened a horizontal gallery into the slope, 510 feet long, with lateral galleries of 38 feet on each side at the end. Here were placed eight magazines, each containing a half ton of powder. Begun June 25, the work was finished July 23, without accidents—and at last the army engineers accepted it.

The massive assault arranged to follow the explosion was entrusted to Burnside's Ninth Corps. It was not the best choice, for it had suffered so much in recent campaigns that a conglomerate of new troops had been placed in it. "For myself," Regis De Trobiand writes in *Four Years with the Army of the Potomac,* "I am convinced that if Hancock or Warren had had charge of the affair, we would have carried everything in a few hours." But Burnside naturally felt he must complete the enterprise. He chose as head of the attacking column a division of colored troops on whom he placed special dependence.

The artillery engaged in the attack was at last, except for a few pieces, squarely under Wainwright's supervision. He placed it in position, gave his officers careful instructions, and rejoiced in the grand total of ninety-one guns. Warren on the eve of the assault issued an order explicitly placing the whole force under his command.

※ ※ ※

JULY 29, FRIDAY.   Had a hard day's work today, not getting to bed until half-past one at night. Major Fitzhugh did not return until after ten this evening, so I had to do everything myself. All my guns are in position and the officers have full and particular instructions, so that knowing my men I have every confidence that the artillery part of the affair tomorrow on this front will be well done. All day I have been passing from one position to the other, hurrying up the works, for the batteries on the right were not fixed last night, and all had more or less to do to them. This part of the business has given me a good deal of worry, as I had no men or officers to set to work myself. How I wished for my battalion of heavies today. But by night all were rendered serviceable, or in the way to be so before morning. General Hunt did everything for me in his power; he is a host at such a time. I had to send teams to City Point for the siege guns to occupy Fort Hell.

So soon as it became quite dark, we began moving guns into position. It was a most favorable night, just light enough to see our own way about, without enough for the enemy to discern our movements: with a gentle breeze blowing directly from them. While in Batteries One, Two, and Three, on our extreme right, I noticed that I could not hear a sound of the axes which were employed in cutting away a bit of timber some three hundred yards to the rear of that position, and so felt sure that the enemy could not hear our carriages moving. By midnight I had seen every gun in its place, and instructed, questioned, and cross-questioned all my commanders; each one of whom I had taken to his position during the day and pointed out to him exactly what he was to do. . . .

General Hunt's order of instructions is so very clear, full, and admirable that I am induced to copy most of it. He says: 1. "The batteries are not to open tomorrow morning until the signal is given, which will be the explosion of the mine under the battery in front of the advanced position of the Ninth Corps. 2. Immediately on the mine being sprung, the batteries will all open. The greatest possible care will be taken to avoid interfering with the storming party, which will advance so soon as the mine is sprung and over the ruins of the explosion. So soon as an entrance is effected here strong bodies of troops will move to the right and left behind the enemy's line to clear out his troops, and to the front to gain the crest and, if possible, to enter the town. A careful watch must be kept on these movements so as to avoid the possibility of interfering with the advance. 3. The fire will in preference be turned on those batteries which command the point of assault and the ground over which the troops will move." The rest of the order is in the same strain, pointing out what the assaulting column is expected to do, how we shall aid them, and how avoid interfering with them.

Before getting Hunt's directions, I had myself issued an order covering most of the ground of his, but have also sent his to each commander. Mine will be most welcome to the men, as it closed by ordering a ration of whiskey at midnight. . . . The mine is to be sprung at half-past three, which gives me just ninety minutes in bed tonight.

JULY 30, SATURDAY. The mine has exploded but we are not in Petersburg. The affair proved a fiasco, a most miserable fizzle. Never before have I felt that the Army of the Potomac was disgraced; failed it has frequently, and botches its commanding generals have made of more than one piece of work, but the army itself has always come out with honour. The only comfort I have tonight is that the artillery part of the business was *perfect:* even Meade and Warren admit that we did our whole share, accomplishing not only all that was expected of us, but everything that was wanted. . . .

But to particulars, and first as to the ground. The rebel lines in this part are tolerably near straight, running north and south from the foot of Cemetery Hill to the great salient. Behind them the ground rises in a gentle slope to a considerable height; along the top of which, and parallel to their works, is the Jerusalem Plank Road. I should say it might be an average of three or four hundred yards between the lines and the road. All this ground is open, without wood save detached trees, until you get near the cemetery, where there is a small copse in a little ravine. The battery under which the mine was placed was about a hundred and fifty yards in front and to their right of this copse. How the ground lay beyond that to their left I cannot say, as the view from our front is bounded in that direction by Cemetery Hill, which rises directly from this little ravine. Perhaps a hundred yards to their right of the mined battery, a small branch of Poo Creek comes out of their lines, running in something of a ravine; at this point their works are thrown out at right angles for a few yards, then run off south again to the great salient. Here at the creek crossing they have a strong battery with several guns in the re-entrant angle bearing down the little ravine, directly across the most advanced front of Burnside. Halfway between there and the salient is another battery thrown somewhat forward, redan fashion.

The great salient, beyond which their works trend back to the southwest, is an immense work, the exact shape of which I could never make out; but the parapet looks as if it were twenty feet high, and the whole place seems to be strengthened in every way. A few yards to the rear of this and overlooking it, they have lately been putting up a square redoubt, not yet entirely finished. Their works to their right of the salient did not bear upon the point in dispute. On the crest they had two batteries. . . .

At three o'clock we were all up. Day was hardly dawning; breakfast did not take long. When Fitzhugh and Dresser went to their posts, after sending a couple of aides to see that all was right with Hexamer and the rest, I planted my flag where I had indicated that headquarters would be during the affair, immediately in rear of the great mortar battery. From a mound of dirt here I could see the whole rebel line from Cemetery Hill south, and all my own batteries from Fitzhugh to Phillips. The covered way from here also led to all the batteries, and was wide and high enough to ride through on horseback. When I reached my post our lines were all alive. No fires had been allowed, but the men had made a cold breakfast and were ready for work; every piece was loaded and pointed, while the officers of each battery could be seen looking earnestly for the signal. Many of the infantry, too, had mounted the parapet and were gazing in the direction of the expected explosion. In the rebel lines, on the contrary, perfect stillness prevailed. On my first looking at them with my glass I could not see a soul stirring—to be sure it was then only just light enough to discern them clearly. Soon, however, they began to wake up, and as the first lookers-out noticed the unusual stir on our side, they quickly gathered knots of men around them on the parapets. The morning was very fine, clear and mild, with a gentle breeze.

Half-past three, the hour fixed, passed with no explosion. The match had gone out, but Lieutenant-Colonel Pleasants went up the gallery and lit it again. . . . This caused so much of a delay that it was a quarter past four when it went off. I will not be positive about the exact minute, for though I timed it, I did not note it down and am not sure of my memory. By this time the enemy had become thoroughly awake and aware that something was up. Whether any of them knew what it was or where the mine was located is doubtful.

Not sixty seconds elapsed from the moment the doomed work rose in the air before every one of our batteries opened. I do not know which got off the first gun, but think it was Mink. The rebs were about as prompt as we were, and replied along their whole line. The infantry, too, poured out rolls of musketry. It was a grand and most impressive sight and sound; in some respects the finest I have seen. The roar was not greater if equal to that at Gettysburg, but there was more variety of notes in it from the number of siege guns and mortars here. Very quickly the whole of our front was covered with a dense cloud of white smoke, so that all objects were obscured from my view save a dim view of the men handling their immense ten-inch shells immediately at my feet, and the rise of a great black ball, with a fiery tail, rolling over and over high up into the air until it was lost in the smoke.

To my view the explosion itself presented nothing but a column of black and white smoke rising perhaps a hundred yards into the air. I presume the guns of the battery and most of the men in it were carried up too, but they were so enveloped in the smoke and dust that I at least could not see them. Our fire was splendid. It was not ten minutes, I think, before the enemy were completely silenced; then I was delighted with the promptness with which nearly all my batteries slackened off their fire to one in which they could take deliberate aim, and watch the course of each shot. The infantry, too, ceased after a time, and I was again able to see something of what was going on. All I could make out was that our men were in possession of the mined battery, as I could discern a number of flags there.

I looked in vain, however, for the prompt movement along the inside of their lines, to right and left; nor was any such move made at any time during the day, or so far as I can learn, even attempted. I expected to see a cloud of musketry smoke pushing perhaps slowly but surely along the inside of their works toward the great salient, while the men of this corps moved over as fast as the line in their front was captured.

Indeed, I was even debating in my own mind how I could get the guns off that immense pile of dirt, should we not be able to hold the line; and what chances the redoubt in rear of the salient had of holding out after they had lost that work. Another thing I noticed, which struck me at the time: I could not see any large bodies of troops passing from our lines across into the rebel works, but a continuous stream of single men or little squads.

So completely did we subdue the enemy fire from their line of works that after the first spurt, they did not throw over a score of shells into our lines. Even their infantry were silenced, save now and then when some one man would venture a shot through an embrasure. Their whole line of works was much damaged, especially the great salient; a number of embrasures completely destroyed, and at least three explosions of ammunition made which I take to have been chests as they did not any of them appear great enough for magazines. So completely were they silenced that the greater part of the time our infantry stood in a line along the top of the parapet, completely exposed, out of curiosity to see what was going on. They, however, at times opened briskly from the two batteries on the crest, and from one in the redoubt, on the mass of our men in the crater of the mine; especially after ten o'clock. At such times all my guns that would bear were opened on these batteries, and would soon silence them for the time. . . .

Between one and two o'clock, when Burnside was drawing back from the clump of wood, the rebs followed our men up and a brigade attempted to charge down the slope on to their flank from near the batteries on the crest. I had gone home myself at this time completely worn out, and somewhat feverish from the exposure to the sun, which had become very hot. But Lieutenant Dresser tells me that every battery all the way to Fort Hell opened on them at once. He says that he never saw such a sight; the whole slope seemed covered with a rain of shrapnel, the dust rising where it struck exactly as it does on the road at the first large drops of a shower. There did not seem to be a square foot of ground on the whole slope that was not peppered.

My loss today has been almost nothing. Major Fitzhugh got a flesh wound in the side from a musket ball, just a twenty-day affair, and Phillips had one non-com wounded severely. . . . Nor can the loss of the infantry in this corps amount to anything much. In Burnside's and Smith's I fear, though, it has been heavy. It always is in badly managed affairs, and his men were evidently so crowded in the crater that a single shell exploding among them—and I saw three go off at once in their very midst—must have hurt a great many.

Since returning to camp I learn that the brigade which was to have charged first would not go, and another had to be substituted, by which much time was lost after the explosion. Where was the "forlorn hope" of volunteers, supported by the picked regiments of the corps? I also learn that when the niggers went in they did well at first but would not hold. It was they who first carried the second line in the clump of wood, but afterward they ran from it almost without firing a shot; a whole brigade ran from about five hundred men. A Colonel Russell who was over here this afternoon commanded one of the black regiments. He says that his men behaved admirably in the excitement of the first onset, but soon lost heart; also that every man who was hit yelled and groaned most hideously, which tended to demoralize the others. As both the traits are natural to the negro character, I have no doubt of his correctness.

A third trouble was that after the first charge the men were not moved over in order, but were directed "to make a run for it" and re-form their companies after they got over. Consequently all was confusion in the crowded crater; the good men trying to find their own command and the cowards to hide from it. This alone was sufficient to cause a failure, and is about the most disgracefully unmilitary thing I have heard of. The general officer who gave such an order, or allowed it to be given, ought to be shot. I hear too that, though there was a good part of the whole corps over, not a single division commander crossed from our lines, and that Burnside was not where he could himself see how things were managed. This last I trust is not true; of the other troubles there is no doubt.

After being up all last night, I hoped to get a good sleep tonight. But either something is up, or Meade has got a scare on, for he insists on all the siege guns and mortars being hauled out at once, and I have been run down with telegrams from Hunt on the subject up to midnight. The first directions were simply that I might withdraw such batteries as, on consultation with General Warren, I did not need for defensive purposes; this at seven P.M. I also had to repair my own batteries, giving instructions how to do it. This was all settled, and I in bed and asleep when, at eleven o'clock, came another telegram saying: "All the siege artillery is ordered to be moved at once; the matter is urgent." So I had to detail teams to help them out and what not. I fear that Captain Boker, who had charge of the matter, did not think me very amiable, and perhaps not very energetic; but I was clean used up from want of sleep and the hot sun. I have not been perfectly free from fever for the month past. That is the truth of the matter, though I do not like to acknowledge it even to myself.

JULY 31, SUNDAY. All was quiet last night and has been today, though Meade fully expected a counter-attack on our left and rear from Lee. Last night Hancock returned to his former position; and today there has been a truce about the mine for the burial of our dead, and the removal of the remaining wounded. The crater was evacuated soon after dark last night. . . .

I have learned nothing additional today about yesterday's failure, being busy with the month's returns, and getting everything straight once more. Tomorrow I shall try to get up to headquarters and hear what I can there. The President is at City Point today, whither Grant has gone to consult with him. Did he come down to enter Petersburg in triumph, or, hearing of the fizzle, has he come to insist that "the Army of the Potomac shall do something"? I really could not blame his requiring almost anything to wipe out the disgrace of yesterday; but I much doubt his ability to comprehend the greatness of it. Our loss is now estimated at 2,300. . . .

AVERY HOUSE, AUGUST 2, TUESDAY.   Everything has continued quiet since the failure of Saturday last. Lee has made no attempt to return the compliment. As is always the case after a failure, the camps are full of rumours of a change in the command of this army. . . . Many are inclined to throw the blame of the failure upon Meade. I do not myself think that he is free, but cannot see what fault can be laid at this door, which is not equally close to Grant's. The whole planning of the mine was Burnside's: he actually ranks Meade, and indeed was his commander at one time in this very army. Both these circumstances made it delicate to interfere in minutiae, or to any extent, until Burnside had failed. So soon as this became certain, however, Meade ought to have stepped in and directed everything. So, too, Grant being Meade's commander, and equally present, should have acted when Meade failed to do so. Everyone I have talked with believes that it could have been made a successs in spite of Burnside's miscarriage.

From General Hunt I have learned certain facts which account for the whole thing; but make Burnside's capabilities—for I suppose he has more than the average—perfectly inexplicable to me. Hunt considered the silencing of the guns in the enemy's re-entrant a matter of the first importance, and to make sure of it had erected a very strong battery of fourteen siege guns behind a small wood near the Taylor house; all of which guns would bear on the battery of the enemy's when the wood was cleared away. To be sure that this was done, he sent a note to Burnside, by Warner, late in the afternoon reminding him of it. Twice again during the night he sent Warner down to see if it was done, and, if not, to remind Burnside of it.

The last time Burnside replied that as the matter of the first importance now was to keep the enemy ignorant of any special movement on our side, he would not cut the trees down until the mine was exploded, when a strong party of axemen should be there, who could get them all down in a few minutes. The consequence was, as might have been expected, that the trees were not cut at all, and this great battery was unable to fire at all in that direction. How easy it would have been for Burnside to send an officer out to listen if the chopping could be heard even so far off as his own lines!—when I know he would not have heard a sound. How different he is from Reynolds, who went himself out to our skirmish line at Fredericksburg while I withdrew Stewart's battery, so as to be sure to know if any sound of the move could reach the enemy.

But another thing Hunt told me is still more wonderful. Burnside made no arrangement for his column to get out of his own works! Nor did any of his subordinates think of it. The obstructions in front of them at this point had been made as strong as possible on account of their nearness to the enemy; and no arrangements having been made to remove them, the men could not get through without breaking ranks, or marching by the flank. Imagine an assaulting column with a frontage of four men! General Hunt tells me that he did actually remind Burnside that the enemy's works had an abattis in front, and that it would be necessary to send pioneers with the first of the column to remove it; but that he supposed Burnside had sense enough to let his men out of the works he had built himself. I only wonder that Burnside did not think Hunt insulting to remind him of any of these things. Where was the common sense of the division and brigade officers who commanded the assaulting column, that they did not themselves see that such a matter was provided for? Surely such a lot of fools did not deserve to succeed. . . .

* * *

Wainwright's statement of reasons for the failure of the mine assault is essentially accurate. A court of inquiry composed of Hancock, Ayres, and Nelson A. Miles declared that the main causes of the disaster were, first, the want of judgment in the formation of the troops to advance; second, the halting of the troops at the crater when they should have kept on to the crest of the hill; third, the poor use made of pioneers, working parties, and tools; fourth, want of proper directions for certain parts of the attacking column; and "fifth, the lack of a competent leader of high rank on the scene of operations to order matters according as circumstances demanded." Primary blame was placed on Burnside, and secondary blame upon four division commanders.

Grant writes in his *Personal Memoirs:* "The effort was a stupendous failure. It cost us about four thousand men, mostly, however, captured; and all due to inefficiency on the part of the corps commander and the incompetency of the division commander who was sent to lead the assault." Meade was anxious to try Burnside before a court-martial and prepared charges that Grant disapproved; but the general was relieved of his command of the Ninth Corps on August 13, returned home, resigned, and afflicted the Army of the Potomac no more. The division commander, James Hewitt Ledlie of New York, has been stigmatized by Grant as both inefficient and cowardly, but did not resign until early in 1865. Colored troops under General Edward Ferrero were denied permission at the last minute to lead the attack, as Burnside had planned, Meade having a prejudice against them. When they came in later, they fought as bravely as the whites, but Ferrero failed as grossly as Ledlie to furnish proper control. Meade stayed at heaquarters well to the rear, where he heard the din of battle but could see nothing.

The siege of Petersburg continued under the hot August sun. A complicated system of trenches had been dug on both sides, each army having at least two main lines of embankment, with many traverses. Many troops stretched blankets or shelter tents as awnings over their rifle pits; some used branches of trees. Officers' quarters were often dug deep and wide, making snug caverns that not even a Whitworth bolt could penetrate. Sharpshooters kept a keen outlook for unwary targets, and fired savagely at night to drive in the working parties who emerged to erect new works. The Union army, at first hard beset for water, had sunk wells in all the area behind its lines, and now had a full supply. Photographs and drawings show that batteries were heavily protected by thick walls of sandbags or baskets of earth. But mortar shells could drop anywhere. Some soldiers made "gopher holes" into which they swiftly dived when they saw a shell approaching.

* * *

AUGUST 4, THURSDAY. Yesterday I wrote my report of the mine affair; it was very short and very simple. After designating the position and field of fire of each battery, I had nothing more to say than that they all did what was required of them. The whole number of rounds fired by the guns and mortars under my command was 4,274, plus what the extra coehorns fired, of which I have got no report. . . .

By orders just received I see that Howard has in the Army of the Tennessee the command left vacant by McPherson's death. Also that Hooker is relieved of the command of the Twentieth Corps at his own request, and is succeeded by Slocum. I think it likely that Hooker was disgusted at not getting McPherson's place. At last accounts Sherman was still outside of Atlanta. Is it going to be another Petersburg for him?

AUGUST 7, SUNDAY. It is three days since my last entry here, and yet I have about nothing to record. The weather all last week was very hot; not up, thermometrically, to what we had some four or five weeks ago, but more sultry and oppressive; from five to eight o'clock P.M. is the worst part of the day, when it seems almost impossible to breathe. The nights, however, are cool enough to sleep very comfortably; and the flies are quiet at that time also, though during the day they almost drive one crazy. Perhaps they are not quite so bad yet as they were at Harrison's Landing, but they soon will be unless we get out of this place.

AUGUST 10, WEDNESDAY. In the absence of anything to get up excitement here, we make a big rejoicing over Farragut's victories in Mobile Bay. Our first information was from a Richmond paper brought over by a lieutenant who deserted to us on Monday morning; which report was official to Davis's Secretary of War, and was published to our army. It is dated August 5th and says that Farragut passed the forts into the bay that morning with seventeen vessels; also admits that what fleet they had there was destroyed. This morning papers (Richmond) have another dispatch saying that Fort Powell was abandoned and blown up, and that Fort Gaines was disgracefully surrendered on Monday morning, without resistance. . . .

A dispatch from Sherman dated August 7th and published by Grant on the 9th says that he is progressing nicely. The language is such as I should suppose would please Grant, but sounds to me unmilitary, and undignified from a man in Sherman's position: "There is no peace inside or outside of Atlanta" and "a used-up community" are a little loud for a dispatch from Sherman, however well they might sound in that of a newspaper reporter. . . .

AUGUST 14, SUNDAY. A long letter from Major Reynolds dated August 1st is very gloomy as to the state of matters in the Western army. He is a strong Hooker man, and of course feels badly at that general's leaving the corps. He pitches strongly into Sherman, whom he styles "a man of very small calibre, envious and jealous of Hooker." The Twentieth Corps, he claims, has done all the hardest fighting, but Sherman will not allow them or their commander any credit. There may be some truth in this, but I fear that Hooker's own jealousy and bad habit of detracting from everyone else had most to do with his being overslaughed. Reynolds says that "there were several opportunities, when the whole of Johnston's army might have been destroyed." That he heard Freeman himself say, "that when McPherson marched through Snake Creek Gap to Resaca, there was but one small brigade of rebels there and had he taken the place as he might and could have done, we would have taken the whole rebel army—at least all their trains and artillery." "At Resaca," he says, "we had 110,000 men, Johnston about 40,000." If this is so, I cannot

myself see how Sherman is deserving of quite all the credit he gets.* . . .
WELDON RAILROAD SIX-MILE HOUSE, AUGUST 18, THURSDAY. We started pretty well on time this morning, Griffin's division leading off, followed by Phillips and Richardson, then Ayres, Crawford, and Cutler, with their batteries. The morning was very close and hot, so the men very soon began to fall out badly, and our progress was not so rapid as it might have been; although after we started Warren received a message from General Grant which he repeated to me, saying that if he pushed on lively he thought we might get into Petersburg. . . . We struck the Weldon Railroad at this house, which is marked on the engineer map with the name of Blick, but seems better known in the country as "the Yellow Tavern," or "the Six-Mile House." It is a large yellow brick building standing directly on the public road, and was used as a tavern, no doubt, before railroads came in and destroyed all these wayside inns. This road is known as the "Halifax road," and is one of the main roads leading out of Petersburg. The Weldon Railroad runs close alongside of it at this point. . . .

On reaching the railroad, which we did between nine and ten A.M., Griffin's division was formed along the road in front of the tavern, facing west, with a strong skirmish line in front, and a post down the road (south) at the next opening, say six hundred yards. Ayres's division formed facing north, and pushed up toward Petersburg. He had not advanced beyond the Blick house when the enemy opened a battery from the other side of the wood north of that. Martin, "C" Massachusetts, at once replied to them and the division pushed on to a narrow belt of wood to a small opening beyond where the railroad bends off to the eastward, and where there is a small house called the Davis house; Martin moving forward with it. Here Ayres struck the enemy in some force, or rather they struck him before he was fully formed, and after a sharp little fight drove him back on the double-quick to the Blick house. In this fight Martin lost one man killed and four wounded, and got his guns off with considerable difficulty. I at once ran two other batteries at a trot up to the Blick house, but the enemy did not follow Ayres.

❊ ❊ ❊

* It was true that Hooker was greatly piqued by the fact that when the command of the Army of the Tennessee fell vacant through the death of James B. McPherson—killed at thirty-five—he was not given the place. He was senior to the other generals in line for the place; he had held higher posts. But Sherman feared that both his habits and his temperament unfitted him for the leadership of the entire army, and so had O. O. Howard given the prize. Hooker departed on July 28, 1864, and was shortly sent to the Northern Department. As for McPherson, the animadversions here quoted upon him are unfair. It is true that his withdrawal from the Resaca area on May 9 to entrench himself at Snake Creek Gap was sharply criticized at the time. But he had good reasons, and he was unquestionably one of the most brilliant of all the younger Union generals.

The Weldon Railroad (so called) ran from Petersburg almost directly south through Weldon, North Carolina, to Wilmington, where it connected with the east-west line to Atlanta, Chattanooga, and Memphis—or rather, the remnants of that line. Weldon was an important junction, for it also had a line running in a southwesterly direction to Raleigh, Charlottesville, and Columbia, South Carolina. To cut and hold the Weldon line was therefore an important Union objective. Richmond and Petersburg had another lifeline with southwestern Virginia, Knoxville, and Chattanooga: a set of connecting railroads running through Lynchburg, of which the Richmond & Danville, the Southside Railroad, and the Virginia & Tennessee were the most important components. To sever this line became another of Grant's important aims.

The Weldon line was now quickly put out of commission. But in the last phases of the war the Southside Railroad continued to bring supplies from Lynchburg to the Confederate troops holding Petersburg, though wagon haulage became necessary over the final miles. Meanwhile, from Danville the Richmond & Danville brought food and materials directly into Richmond. The worn rails, the shaky bridges, the rickety locomotives and slab-wheeled cars might be said to constitute arteries, but they were badly clotted.

More fighting occurred along the Weldon Railroad on the afternoon of August 18 and on the 19th. The Confederates brought up eight guns on the second day, which Wainwright very smartly silenced. When a Maryland brigade and other Northern troops retreated in disorder, Union losses reached 3,000, mostly prisoners. "This is a horrible loss," wrote Wainwright; "disgraceful too, as there was not so very much fighting; still, Lee did not succeed in his object, or come anywhere near it, viz: the driving back from the railroad." Then on the 21st Wainwright had a brilliant chance with his artillery.

❋ ❋ ❋

AUGUST 21, SUNDAY. We have had a love of a fight today. For once it was all on our side, everything was well managed, and Lee got a lesson which I guess will keep him from attempting this place again. When I add that there was not the slightest interference with my command, that the artillery really did nine-tenths of the work, and that even Warren is said to praise it, one will not wonder at my calling it a love of a fight.

Day was just breaking, and I had not quite got on my shoes, the taking off of which and one's sabre constitute undressing in our present situation, when word came in from the signal station that the enemy were massing for another attempt down the railroad. It was some time, however, before they opened the ball, giving our men leisure to get breakfast, and me time to renew my instructions to the batteries. During the night General Warren had thought better of his dispositions, and had withdrawn both Ayres and Crawford to the line of batteries, where I found their men busy entrenching when I first went out. My instructions were almost entirely to "Fire low, low! low!!" The ground was good, and every shot must strike the ground before entering the wood; also "Fire solid shot almost exclusively!" Never before had I had so good an opportunity to test this low flight of shot through woods, so I was determined to give it a full trial, in which it more than fulfilled my expectations. These orders, of course, applied to the fire on the rebel infantry, not to the reply to their batteries.

Long after eight A.M. the enemy opened from the old place beyond the Davis house, and also from the west somewhere near the Flowers house. As near as I could make out they had twelve guns in each of these positions; some, however, counted eighteen in the former. All our batteries at once replied slowly. It was a very ugly fire for us, coming from two directions, and all converging, while ours necessarily was a divergent fire. The whole plain within our lines was crossed in both directions by this fire, while at times long-range shot would come in from the northeast. It was amusing to see the skulkers trying to get away, but this time they were fairly caught, for the provost guard kept them on the plain, while the shot coming in three directions prevented every cover from being perfectly safe. I saw lots of them actually lying half buried in the mud. . . . The rebel infantry first shewed advancing from the Vaughn road, by the little road leading from the Blick to the Flowers house, but each time they attempted to come out that way their lines were broken and driven back by a well directed fire from Hart and Mink. . . . On our north front, too, all their attempts to get a line of battle out of the wood were frustrated by the beautiful firing of the batteries on that front, though some of their skirmishers did creep half the distance across. . . .

I was out looking at the position taken by Jones's section, when word was brought me that the enemy was advancing from the northeast and that a battery was wanted. . . . Though the most serious attempt so far, the enemy had no better fortune, and the whole thing was over by the time I could get to that part of the field. Prisoners, of whom Potter in making a counter-charge captured some one hundred and fifty, state that they were formed in three lines, but that the first line was destroyed by the artillery fire before it got out of the wood. Their second line managed to advance to within three hundred yards of our line, but could not stand against a direct fire of canister and a cross-fire of case-shot from six and twenty guns. Major Roebling, who went out through this part of the wood in the afternoon, says that he never saw anything equal to it; the whole ground being ploughed up by our shot, while hardly a tree is struck higher up than he could reach while on foot.

The enemy's last attempt was made on our west front. Seeing Cutler's line ending in the air, they evidently did not understand the position of the First Division "en echelon" to the rear of it. This attack was made by a South Carolina brigade under General Hagood. Marching down through the deep wooded ravine directly opposite the tavern, they had completely turned Cutler's flank and were coming up on to the plain, sure of success, before we discovered them. Their yell, however, was stopped in their throats before it was well out. Never were they in so perfect a trap! As they reached the crest, their line facing nearly north, Matthewson had a fire directly on their right flank, and at short canister range. Phillips and Anderson, too, almost enfiladed them, while Barnes got a beautiful oblique fire on their rear. The right of Griffin's division, too, took them in the flank and rear, while Cutler's left brigade quickly changed front to face them. So completely were they surprised that the whole brigade stood still and threw down their arms. Our fire was at once stopped. The men mounted the parapet and cheered, while Captain Daly, Cutler's provost-marshal, went out to receive their surrender, with a guard from that division.

On getting up to General Hagood, in advance of his guard, that officer drew a pistol and shot Daly; when the greater part of the brigade escaped. Not looking for any such treachery, our men were not prepared to renew their fire on the instant, nor could they do it without striking the regiment which had gone out to bring in the prisoners. I have not heard in all this war of such a dastardly act before, and cannot but hope that the shot was not fired by General Hagood himself. His name at first was reported as Hayward, which really grieved me, as the Haywards of South Carolina are gentlemen.* We got several hundred prisoners as it was, Matthewson's men bringing in several, a thing battery men seldom have a chance to do. This ended the fight for today, though Lee did not withdraw from about the Flowers house until dark.

All my batteries behaved to perfection, Hart and Mink repeatedly changing front as the enemy tried our north or west front. The infantry really had very little chance to take part in the fight. Most of the casualties, on both sides, were caused by artillery fire, the rebels opening from all their guns after each repulse of their columns. The surgeons

* General Johnson Hagood was a rich fire-eater. A graduate of the Citadel, the well-known lawyer and planter, now in his mid-thirties, had fought at First Manassas and helped in the defense of Charleston. But this "gentleman" made himself infamous by the action which Wainwright describes. He offers a lame defense in his *Memoirs*, 18, 294, 295.

say they have never had so great a proportion of severe wounds, while of the two hundred wounded rebels which fell into our hands, not half are likely to recover. . . .

AUGUST 24, WEDNESDAY. Everything has been perfectly quiet here since Sunday. The whole loss in our corps and the Ninth was under three hundred; while we buried fully that number of rebel dead, and have five hundred sound prisoners. From their data their loss must have been at least three thousand, which about squares the account between the two sides for the operations at this place; but leaves us in possession of the railroad, which there is now no danger of our losing. General Grant sent us word this morning that the Richmond papers of yesterday are very despondent over their failure; as their authorities must be, too, as they have given the public no report of it, and what the papers knew was picked up from citizens. They say that they had five generals killed, but only give the names of two; this would be a very heavy loss. General Cutler on our side was slightly cut on the lip; besides him we had but one officer of any rank hit. The morning after the fight, General Warren paid the artillery a compliment, though I do not know that he intended to do it. He was grumbling at an order to hold all his disposable infantry in readiness to support the Ninth Corps if needed, and closed by saying that he "could hold this place with the artillery alone supported by a skirmish line; Sunday's fight proved it." . . .

We have not by any means been idle here the last three days; on the contrary, all hands have been busy digging, and, what is much better, chopping. I was delighted to see that Warren left to himself did just what, early in this year's campaign, I made up my mind was the proper thing when a line was established through the wood, viz: first of all cut down all the trees for two hundred or more yards in front of you; then, if you have time, throw dirt. In this way he has made is so that Griffin's division can hold all the three fronts south of the tavern; as even without opposition no man could get through the slashing inside of fifteen minutes, while roads are cut in all directions for us to move artillery as well as infantry to any point. . . .

Since the first day here I have posted all the batteries without any reference to what division they were assigned to. Sunday's fight, I think, has done me much good, and I trust that I shall have no more trouble from General Warren in this line.

Nine P.M. General Meade has just sent us word that the signal officers report large bodies of rebel infantry passing south out of their works, around our left; probably to attack us or Hancock tomorrow. I do not think that they will try it here again, though they may likely hit Hancock a crack.

❊ ❊ ❊

In the action at Reams's Station Lee now struck Grant's army a painful blow. On the morning of August 21 Hancock's corps, which had been north of the James, arrived in the lines around Petersburg, greatly fatigued from its long march. It was ordered to positions adjacent to those held by Warren's corps on the Weldon Railroad. Hancock spent the next two days tearing up trackage southward as far as Reams's Station, and on the 24th pushed this destruction three miles farther. Before he could recommence work on the 25th, however, A. P. Hill's corps, assisted by Wade Hampton's cavalry, appeared in force, and Hancock had to withdraw Gibbon's small division, with that of Nelson A. Miles, inside the badly situated breastworks that an earlier corps had built at the station. When the Confederates unleashed a series of powerful assaults, with devastating artillery fire, Miles's troops showed stubborn bravery, but finally abandoned part of their line; and Gibbon's force, which included many raw replacements, was driven back in confusion. At nightfall Hancock withdrew from Reams's Station. He had lost more than 2,700 men, of whom well over 2,000 were prisoners.

Yet Warren maintained his hold on the Weldon Railroad, and the Union works were permanently extended to that position. The army at once constructed a series of strong redoubts connecting its new lines with the old ones on the Jerusalem Plank Road.

* * *

AUGUST 25, THURSDAY. The reports last night proved correct; Lee hit Hancock at Reams's Station today, and hit him terribly hard too, driving him away from there in great disorder, capturing 1,000 prisoners or more, and nine guns. It was about as thorough a thrashing I guess as the Second Corps has ever had. We were under arms pretty much all day, but made only one abortive start to go to their help; though I think that Warren was anxious to do it. I came very near being in thickest of myself however, and equally near to being captured without a fight.

As the morning was passing away without our hearing anything from Lee, and there being some cavalry down the railroad, I thought it a good chance for me to make myself acquainted with the country in that direction, and so rode a mile or more down the Halifax road. I had just started on my return when I met Colonel Bankhead, who told me he meant to ride down to Reams's Station. I rather doubted the wisdom of it, merely from curiosity; but thought I would ride part way there, which resulted in my going the whole distance. We were alone without orderlies, and only met a few cavalry patrols on the road. The inhabitants looked at us with considerable curiosity, though most of them must have seen Union officers before, as there have been several raids down through this region the last two months. One young woman, from her remarks to her mother, seemed wonderfully taken with my moustache, which to be sure has got to be quite long, and being waxed "en militaire," I presume was something new to her unsophisticated eyes.

We got off our horses and passed an hour at Hancock's headquarters, talking with him and his staff. As we entered his lines they struck me as very badly laid out and quite untenable in case of a strong attack. . . . We had been there but a few minutes when musketry firing began to the south, in which direction Gibbon's division had gone to destroy the railroad. It was not heavy, only skirmish firing and spurts of small volleys. After a bit Lieutenant-Colonel Morgan came in, and reported that things were going well, Gibbon gaining ground, and that he could use a section of artillery to advantage. Things continued about in this way while we remained, which was not long after Morgan returned to the front. Indeed, from the first, I was anxious lest I might be wanted at home, and lest the enemy might interpose between us and there, necessitating a long detour to get back. We galloped along briskly but had not gone a mile before the musketry fire became heavy at the station, mingled with artillery. . . .

We do not yet know the particulars of Hancock's fight with certainty, save as to the loss of the guns. He had only two divisions, Gibbon's and Miles's, with him, and they are both very small. Roebling, who hovered around there until dark, says that our men fought very badly, and that the guns might have been recovered if the men had behaved well. He is so much given to swaggering that I do not place implicit confidence in his statements, but should not be surprised if there is some truth in this. It is a bad affair anyway, and will do much to revive the rebels' spirits from the depression of Sunday's thrashing. . . .

AUGUST 28, SUNDAY.   The later reports of Hancock's fight do not alter the main features as we got them that night. He says he had but 6,000 men there, and claims to have punished the enemy severely, repelling I don't know how many attacks. His lines turned out, just as might have been seen before, untenable against artillery fire save from directly in front; so soon as the enemy got a battery or two to the north of him the shot which passed over his line facing that way struck his south line in the rear and sent them kiting. Miles's division (he was not there himself) did not behave well, especially some heavy artillery; but then they were the ones who got struck in the rear. Mott, with his division, some 5,000 strong, was on his way out, but his guides mistook the road and led him off into the woods somewhere. On Friday he retook the ground without any opposition, and held it until yesterday, burying the dead. The Second Corps has now been withdrawn within the old lines to the east of the Jerusalem road. The rebs either suffered so much or found the hour so late that they could not follow up their advantage, and appear to have cleared out in considerable haste the next morning. . . .

AUGUST 31, WEDNESDAY. My brigade return shows a few over 1,500 present, and a gain in the aggregate belonging to the command of nearly one hundred over last month, mostly by the recruits sent down to Stewart. The six batteries of my own regiment with me report thirty-three men gained, but then they likewise report thirty lost. I trust that this month we shall receive more recruits, and from letters received by my officers, I think there is little doubt but we shall. The bounties offered all over the country are enormous; $600 local, beside state and general, seems to be about the lowest figure. They are paying that in New York City, while in New England and some of the country districts $1,000 and even $1,500 are said to be offered. This is all wrong. Not one cent should be offered, but the draft put straight through. When the war is over, the excitement dead, and this fearful debt to be paid, people will begin to see their folly. Heavy artillery service, which swallowed so many of the recruits last winter, is now at a discount; Cold Harbour and Petersburg have brought it down to the level of common infantry in the eyes of those who look for comfort and safety on enlisting. Light battery service, on the contrary, is better understood now, and they say there is quite a rush for it. . . .

The corps, though not engaged in any fight since the 21st, has been by no means idle. The engineers have laid out two four-bastion redoubts, one directly where the Blick house stood; the other just east of the railroad, and south of the woods. They are both large (not equal in area to the square redoubt on the plank road, however), and have called for an immense amount of work. General Warren has taken them in hand himself and pushed them on with great rapidity. . . . We have, too, another very certain evidence that General Grant intends to hold on here until he gets possession of Petersburg, and that he does not expect that to happen very soon, in the building of a railroad to this point. It branches off from the old City Point and Petersburg road about seven miles up from the former place, runs between Army Headquarters and the Avery house, and is building up to here with great rapidity, as there is but very little grading done, and where the valleys are too deep to run down into it is carried over on trestle work. The only cut is to the right and rear of the Avery house, where the rebs could get the range of passing trains and have been firing at it a good deal; here they mean to sink it into a covered way. It will be a vast convenience to us, and a great saving of mule flesh and oaths.

The New York papers we got yesterday morning gave us Stanton's dispatch concerning the affair at Reams's Station, in which he almost makes out a victory for us, dwelling much on the reoccupation of the ground the next morning, as if the enemy were driven away then. Twice as much is made in the papers of this fight as of ours on the 21st, for which there are two good reasons. First, Hancock keeps a reporter and seeks newspaper reputation, while Warren does neither; and second, Hancock's fight needs bolstering, ours does not. . . . Somehow that fight of ours seems to be very little talked of, though it was really one of the most brilliant and perfect affairs of the whole campaign. Hamlin, the *Herald* reporter who did so well all the way from Culpeper down here, has given himself up to the quartermaster's and commission's since we got to Petersburg and was not present during the fight! When he came out afterward, we ran him pretty hard about it; and though what I said was mere badinage (with a good deal of truth mixed in), it was quite sufficient to insure my not getting any mention in his report. Had the thing only been bungled at the commencement so that a couple of thousand lives were lost, it would doubtless have been a great battle. . . .

There has been some fever broken out among the troops here, so we get the quinine and whiskey ration again. Politics have caused a good deal of talk lately owing to the meeting of the Democratic convention at Chicago this week. If they will pass a strong war platform, up and down against secession, keep out all the Vallandigham set, and nominate good men, I think there is not a doubt of their success; so thoroughly disgusted are all thinking men with Mr. Lincoln's weakness and the rascality of every one around him. By tomorrow or next day we may learn the result. . . .

Sherman has got on faster with Atlanta than we have with Petersburg. On Friday night we got a telegram from the operator at Marietta, saying: "Our advance entered Atlanta two hours since." Yesterday came one from Slocum, saying that his corps, the Twentieth, occupied the city, and that a battle had been fought by the main army in East Point (wherever that is) in which we were successful. Today we have a long one from Sherman himself, from which he seems to have managed well, and Hood miserably; as he got between two wings of Hood's army, beat one, and cut all the railroad communications. The fight was at Jonesboro, south of Atlanta. Sherman claims 1,500 sound prisoners and ten guns, while his own loss he reports at only 1,200. The whipping of Hood's army is even better than the gaining of Atlanta. As Farragut has complete possession of the harbour of Mobile, Mr. Davis must feel as if his domain were being badly intruded upon at the west. Which way will Sherman go now? He has a large army, and cannot lie idle very long.

The Chicago convention have adopted a real political platform, one that can be read two ways. To be sure, this is what all parties do, but this is not the time for double-facedness, and with the bad behaviour, and almost, if not quite, disloyal avowals of so many of their leading men, there was especial reason why the Democratic party should have been square and explicit. Their platform will kill their candidate if he accepts it. They have nominated General McClellan, for which I am very sorry. First, because I do not want him to have anything to do with politics; and second, because I do not believe him enough acquainted with rascality to deal with the men at Washington. He would either be killed like Harrison and Taylor, or obliged to give way like Lincoln. An honest, fair man has no more chance there than he has of making a fortune as a horse dealer. I trust the General will not accept the nomination. Standing on that platform, I cannot vote for him; but if he will say plainly that he does not approve their platform, state one of his own in accordance with the views he has always expressed in his letters and speeches, and they will accept him so, there would not be much doubt of his election. Still, I should prefer that he would decline altogether.

We are beginning to live tolerably here; the sutler bringing us up a few luxuries. The camps are full of watermelons; poor enough things at home, but very acceptable here before breakfast. When Fitzhugh returned he brought a basket—half a bushel—of peaches with him, which lasted only a couple of hours; I believe I ate thirty of them. General Patrick tells me that flour sells in Richmond for $320 a barrel, and that there are but *three* butchers in the whole city who have meat for sale. This is getting down to pretty hard commons for the inhabitants and cannot be borne long; it must tell on the spirits of the people and react on their army. Indeed, we see it in the deserters, who come in in considerable numbers again. These report that Petersburg is almost deserted by its inhabitants and the houses in the lower part much damaged by our fire.

SEPTEMBER 11, SUNDAY. The event of the day is the opening of our railroad to this point. Two engines (or the same one twice) came up here this afternoon. It will take a few days more to make the turn out, and so forth, when our long hauling will be done with. Their platform here is to be rather near headquarters for my taste; not more than one hundred yards in rear of the tavern, which will bring the teamsters very close around it. The grade of the road is not exactly as true and level as that of the Hudson River, but as trains will not be required to make more than six miles the hour, it will answer all our purposes. Our sutler says that he will now be able to get us up a few more luxuries. . . .

We are now quite settled on our new line, so that the army certainly has no fears that Lee will ever regain possession of this road. Indeed, one report says that he is building a branch from a station some fifteen miles south of here to go around our left, and so draw his supplies this way in spite of us. The next question is, what will Grant's next move be: another shove to the left? Unless he strikes for the Danville Railroad and succeeds, I see no great use in extending our lines farther in this direction at such a distance from the rebel works.

-------~∞~-------

EIGHTEEN

BRINGING LEE TO BAY

Grant's Virginia campaign down to mid-August 1864 could be termed a failure. Most of the Northern public so regarded it. Dejection overspread the land, rendering even the bravest men apathetic, and converting the fainthearted to defeatism. Merchants and capitalists longed for peace; the hundreds of thousands of families that had seen sons or husbands killed, crippled, or sent to Southern prison camps wondered if the struggle would end except in general exhaustion. Horace Greeley spoke for countless others when he wrote Lincoln on August 9: "I beg you to inaugurate or invite proposals for peace forthwith. And in case peace cannot now be made, consent to an *armistice for one year.*" The chairman of the Republican National Executive Committee and owner of the New York *Times,* Henry J. Raymond, doubted whether Lincoln could be re-elected. "The tide is setting strongly against us," he wrote the President on August 22. Many party leaders believed a stronger candidate should be found. John Milton Hay, Lincoln's secretary, declared on the 25th: "Everything is darkness and doubt and discouragement."

It was not the Army of the Potomac that rescued the Administration and nation from this Slough of Despond. The great and brilliant victories that stilled the defeatism were won elsewhere. Farragut, winning the battle of Mobile Bay on August 5, followed it with the reduction of Forts Gaines and Morgan by the 23rd. The chief remaining port of the Confederacy was thus closed. At the beginning of September Sherman's army entered Atlanta, first defeating John B. Hood of Texas, who had succeeded Joe Johnston, in a series of spirited battles. Then in mid-September Grant visited Sheridan, who had taken command in the Shenandoah Valley, and ordered him: "Go in." The dashing cavalry leader within a few days won two important victories over Jubal A. Early—victories whose effect was the more important because Northerners remembered how close Early had come to capturing Washington, and how many times Stonewall Jackson had smashed the Union armies in the Shenandoah. Then on October 19 Sheridan won his crowning success at Cedar Creek.

Yet the Army of the Potomac was by no means idle. Never losing its grip on Lee's forces before Petersburg and Richmond, it battled them first on one front and then another, and drove continuously toward Lee's vital communications with the Carolinas and Georgia. One effort by Hancock to cut the Weldon Railroad had brought on the sorry battle of Reams's Station, in which Union troops were defeated with the losses just noted. Still, Hancock destroyed much track. Northern superiority in numbers was plainly winning in a war of attrition. This fact became clearer when late in September Grant's troops, in a surprise attack, captured Fort Harrison, one of the most important points in the outer defenses of Richmond. Efforts to recapture the fort failed, and Lee had to dig new entrenchments behind it. Anticipating fresh movements by Grant in October, Lee told General Samuel Cooper: "I fear it will be impossible to keep him out of Richmond."

Reinforcements were steadily reaching the Union troops.

* * *

SEPTEMBER 21 [1864], WEDNESDAY. Our receipts are now considerably more than our losses, so there is every prospect of the regiment soon being full to the maximum allowed by law, which it has never yet been. The men coming to me are a fine lot generally; farmers' sons and others from northern New York and some from Canada who are attracted by the high bounties. We have not had such men enlisting since the first furor of patriotism. They are intelligent, will easily learn, and most of them I think have too much self-respect to either desert or be troublesome. Still there are a number physically unfit for the service, so that we are obliged to have a board for the examination of those so reported, almost constantly in session. The worst feature is most of them only having enlisted for one year.

Grant's visit to the Valley seems to have worked wonders. Since yesterday noon we have been all jubilant over dispatches telling of a really complete victory gained by Sheridan over Early, in which, after a pretty hard fight, he appears to have sent him kiting through Winchester and up the Valley. The fight was on Monday, and at three P.M. yesterday Sheridan is reported at Cedar Creek. Sheridan claims to have captured 3,000 well prisoners in the fight, five guns, nine flags, and all their killed and wounded. With such a body of cavalry as he has with him he should have picked up many prisoners yesterday. Eight rebel general officers are reported killed and wounded. He gives no estimate of his own loss, but reports three general officers wounded including Upton, who I trust is not seriously hurt; the other two are cavalry generals. Also, General David Russell is killed. This last has thrown a gloom over the whole affair to all who knew Russell, for he was one of those we cannot afford to lose; one of the Reynolds and Buford school, straight-forward, honest, conscientious, full of good common sense, and always to be relied on in any emergency.* This is certainly great news and may produce greater. We all look forward now with eagerness for the next event.

On Monday I had a talk with one of our chief scouts, just come in, who told me that Davis's Cabinet were to leave Richmond that night for Gordonsville; that all the rolling stock of the Danville Railroad was being transferred to the Central, and that Lee had removed all his siege guns from Petersburg. This, *if true,* and I think most of it was, would indicate a determination to abandon Petersburg, and make their line from Richmond to Gordonsville, which would be wise at that time. Now, however, that there is good prospect of their losing the Valley, and so endangering their hold on the Central Railroad, they may hang the tighter on here for their Southern communications.

SEPTEMBER 25, SUNDAY. Sheridan is still doing good work in the Valley. On Thursday, he reports after manoeuvring all day he attack Early at four P.M. in his lines, which were strongly posted at Fisher's Hill, carrying everything before him, and capturing sixteen guns. . . . At times I cannot help thinking that these victories are the beginning of the end, the death-blows to the rebellion. Certain it is that either Sheridan has an overwhelming majority of numbers, or the life has gone out of the rebels, for his best troops are from the Army of the Potomac, which has never before been able to gain such complete victories as these. We received Sheridan's dispatch on Friday evening, and yesterday morning Hancock fired a salute of one hundred guns in honour of it. The newspapers give us long accounts of last Monday's battle of Winchester or Opequon, as it is indiscriminately called, but relate nothing particular as to its main features beyond what we got in the first dispatches. Our loss in killed and wounded very nearly equalled that of the enemy. Upton's wound is said not to be serious. General [Robert Emmett] Rodes, who tried to make us one visit on the hill the second night of Gettysburg, I see was killed.

Here everything continues quiet, though we are looking for orders to move at anytime should Sheridan's victories open up an opportunity

* David Allen Russell, West Point, 1845, commanded an especially efficient division. Sheridan had known him since the days in 1857 when they labored in Oregon to pacify the Rogue River Indians. He pays tribute in his *Personal Memoirs* to Russell's "judgment and sound practical ideas"; his "true manliness, honest and just methods"; and "the lovable traits of his character." At Winchester, Russell concealed his first wound until a second killed him.

to gain anything here. I have never seen the time when the army thought the war so near its close. The men are in good spirits, and I think will behave well should anything be attempted. The weather all through the last of the week was very windy and disagreeable. . . .

SEPTEMBER 30, FRIDAY. On Wednesday night Ord's and Birney's corps were crossed to the north of the James, and attacked the rebel works at daylight at a place called Chapin's Bluff, carrying them and capturing sixteen guns.* This is said to be quite an important point for us to hold as threatening the rest of their works. Still it is miles away from Richmond, and if we are to get but one important point per month I fear we shall be well on into another year before we reach the key point. . . .

This morning, however, we did get off, General Griffin leading, followed by Rogers's battery; Ayres with Hoffman's brigade next; then the remaining five batteries. The two divisions of the Ninth Corps followed close behind. We did not take a single waggon of any sort with us, not even an ambulance, leaving all parked in rear of the tavern here to be sent for when needed. The whole force of the two corps comprised about 12,000 muskets. This shows the size of our army when that number, equal to Hooker's old division at the time we left Budd's Ferry, has two corps commanders and four generals of division along, to say nothing of the eventual appearance on the ground of General Meade; or of the forty pieces of artillery. . . .

General Warren had got all the pioneers of the Fifth Corps in a body under his own command directly in rear of his advance; and as soon as we entered the wood he set them to work widening the road, and cutting a second one alongside of it, so that there should be no blocking in case of wheeled vehicles of any kind having to go back and forth. This was done without stopping the advance of the column at all, and even

---

* Birney and Edward O. C. Ord moved on the 28th against Fort Harrison, which was connected by strong entrenchments with the Confederate works on Chapin's Bluff. Two days later their surprise attack took the thinly defended fort, but Ord's efforts to seize Chapin's Bluff, which protected an important Confederate pontoon bridge across the James, broke down.

Grant's stroke in capturing Fort Harrison north of the James impelled Lee to weaken his forces at Petersburg. This gave the Union troops an opportunity to hack at his communications to the south, and Grant ordered Warren to move with his Fifth Corps toward Poplar Springs Church and its roads. The movement, which involved the Ninth Corps also, was successful. Though the attacking forces on October 1–2 lost about 2,900 men killed, wounded, and missing, or more than three times the Confederate losses, they established themselves on the Weldon Railroad and Vaughan Road south of Petersburg, and not far from the Boydton Road running southwest from that city. They thus made the Confederate position, already insecure, still more precarious. Wainwright gives a spirited brief account of the fighting.

the men seemed to realize that their work was better laid out for them than usual, which incited them to greater activity.

About two hundred yards beyond Poplar Spring Church the road crossed by descending into a deep ravine; here Griffin's advance first struck the rebel pickets. A few shots drove in these outlying posts, and another hundred yards or so brought them to a large open space on the north of the road, known as the Peeble farm. Skirmishing up the hill across this field they drew, as soon as reaching the top of a little crest, an artillery fire from a redoubt about six hundred yards north of where they left the road. There was no place into which I could get a battery to reply at that time, and even Griffin did not ask for one; or, if he did, General Warren did not order any out. There was skirmishing here for the better part of an hour, our men working up the ravine which brought them near to the redoubt without exposing them to its fire. . . . The rebs made a fair fight; it was Archer's brigade with one battery, but at last our men worked around to the right so as not to have more than fifty steps to go after leaving cover, when they carried the redoubt with a rush. I had never seen a work with a ditch carried before, and it certainly was different from the ideas we got from books and pictures. There was no line of men marching up to the work, nor any contest on the crest of the parapet; half a dozen men straggling to the top seemed to carry the work, so far as I could see—not but what there were plenty more close behind them.

The work proved to be a square redoubt of some one hundred feet to the side, with a high parapet nearly finished, and bearing the name "Fort McRae." . . . Here properly ended the work of the Fifth Corps for the time. It was now the business of the Ninth to take up the fighting and push the enemy. Our loss had been a mere nothing, one hundred or so killed and wounded. We had got forty or fifty prisoners, one three-inch gun, one limber, three horses and three sets of harness. This was the first gun this corps has captured since leaving Culpeper, and I did not see that General Warren looked upon it quite in the same light that he would have looked on the capture of so much value in ambulances or army waggons, though he did express the opinion the other night that the loss of guns was no more than the loss of an equal amount of any other property. . . .

The Ninth Corps were a long time getting into line and then moved very slowly over the Pegram farm in a northwest direction as far as his house to the west and the wood to the north. Here they halted, and Parke seemed unable to determine what to do.* Warren got impatient and rode out there; wanting to see all I could I rode along. Looking west

* John Grubb Parke, West Point, 1849, now commanded the Ninth Corps in succession to Burnside; a good officer, universally liked, but here very hesitant.

from Pegram's house, we could see quite a line of red dirt thrown up, and men still working, about one mile off. To the east of a line drawn due north from the house is quite an extensive wood getting thin and ending at this line. Riding out here a short distance, we could see the continuance of their line sweeping around to the north of us. It evidently was not half finished, and I doubt if it was even half manned or armed; but the country was all open in front; so broken, however, that troops could have been pushed across it through the hollows so as to be but little exposed to the fire from the works. Parke, however, hesitated and though I could see that Warren was urging him all in his power, it was of no avail. . . . After several hours' delay Parke at last got his dispositions made. . . . Between four and five in the afternoon, after all the day had been wasted, General [Joseph H.] Potter's division was ordered forward through the woods in front of him. His skirmishers were at once pretty heavily engaged, but he certainly had time to get nearly if not quite through the wood, which is open for Virginia. How far he went I do not know, but shortly before sundown the enemy attacked him on the flank, captured several hundred, and sent the whole division back on the run. At the same time they opened from several guns in their works at the west and their skirmish line on that front advanced.

It was just getting dusk when Potter's men came back out of the crowd. I was about halfway out from Fort McRae to the Pegram house; the skulkers were playing wounded and hurrying off to the rear; heavy firing was going on to the north and west, and I thought things began to look very blue. So when Parke's battery came back on the trot, I concluded his whole corps were on the retreat and rode back myself. . . . I met General Warren just after passing Mink, who desired me to place the other batteries so as to hold the knoll on which Pegram's house stands in case of our being driven back. This I did at once, bringing the four batteries there into position and sending their caissons over in rear of the crest. . . . This done, I returned to the spot where the road passes through the captured line of works, as the spot where I could most easily be found.

Here I found General Meade and his staff, who had just come out. . . . Shortly before the fight was over, Warren sent for another battery, when I took pleasure in showing Meade how quickly Rogers could answer the call. I went out with him and put him in on the left of Mink, where he fired half a dozen rounds of shell into the wood. It was now quite dark and the fight about over, though occasional bullets whizzed over our heads. One of them took off a twig from an apple tree under which I was passing, which striking in my eye, gave considerable pain for a few minutes. After this there were no more alarms to speak of. It had commenced to rain, and General Warren made his headquarters in Peeble's house. I was just looking about for supper and a place to sleep when the General desired me to take half the batteries back to the tavern and to remain there myself as he was very apprehensive of an attempt to break through in the morning. . . .

About ten o'clock General Meade came in. He had directed a train to come up to this point for him, but it had not arrived and through some mistake did not get up until after midnight. General Crawford had returned to his own quarters, so I did my best to make Meade, Humphreys, and Lyman* comfortable; the rest of his staff had ridden on. The General was quite affable, as I have always found him in my own personal intercourse with him. He told me that the thousand prisoners lost by the Ninth Corps today just about balances the account between the two armies under this head since we left Culpeper. I was surprised to hear this, not supposing we were enough ahead on arriving in front of Petersburg to meet our heavy losses since then.

Our object today was to get possession of the Boydton Plank Road. We got within sight of it, but a mile of open country lies between our left at Pegram's and their works along that road. Had Parke pushed on vigorously immediately after passing us he might perhaps have carried it north of Pegram's, though it is hard to say, as we did not get any view of their works in that direction. I doubt, however, whether we could have held them unless an immediate advance of the whole army were made. The two corps out on the left were not strong enough to do much in so isolated a position; 12,000 men are not many when one-quarter of them have handled a musket for less than six weeks. There must have been a host of stragglers too, for the whole country I passed over on my way in was covered with fires, and men boiling coffee.

YELLOW TAVERN, WELDON RAILROAD, OCTOBER 1, SATURDAY. The rain of last night has continued all through the day, steady and heavy at times; making it hard on our men in their new lines, where they have been obliged to entrench themselves. . . .

OCTOBER 5, WEDNESDAY. All has been quiet since my last, and our new line is now pretty well established. A small attempt was made on Sunday by Mott's division to do something towards the Boydton road, but without results. As near as I can learn the total loss in this last extension of our lines is near 3,000; one-third of which loss was in prisoners from Potter's division. . . . The engineers are laying out works along the new line: a square redoubt just west of the Flowers house, another on the Squirrel Level road, a large one close to Pegram's, and one or two more. These are all being connected by strong breastworks. . . .

* This is Wainwright's first mention of Theodore Lyman, whose letters give so interesting a picture of Meade's headquarters; Lyman for his part makes but one equally casual mention of Wainwright.

An order has just come making a new disposition of troops along the lines here. The Second Corps is to stretch to the left beyond Fort Alex Hayes while we extend to the right to meet it, so as to give Parke all his corps. The change will be made tomorrow, and will probably entail some change in the position of my batteries. . . .

OCTOBER 9, SUNDAY.   The change in the position of troops along our lines was made on Thursday. . . . General Warren went off Friday morning on an eight-day leave, Crawford succeeding to the command as next in rank. . . .

General Warren issued an order against racing through the camps by officers, which was much needed; but it read like Warren himself, and said quite unnecessarily: "The General commanding does not object to horse racing properly conducted." The weather has changed since Thursday, becoming cold and windy; outdoor fires are of but very little use when the wind blows so hard, and as we have no stoves for our tents, they are far from comfortable. General Warren's being absent is rather fortunate for me just at this time, as I had taken complete possession of his sitting room in the tavern, which is tolerably tight, and quite comfortable with a good fire. Here I spend a good part of the day and all my evenings reading or writing. The railroad station has not proved so great a nuisance, from being so close to us, as I expected it would. They have already commenced to extend it further on, so as to supply the Ninth Corps.

Since we have again settled down politics have once more begun to occupy much of the talk; I know no other way to express it, for it is mere talk. I have received circulars from Governor Seymour containing the law of New York State with regard to soldiers in the field voting. I do not approve of their voting at all; but, if they must, I think the New York plan by which each man's vote will be deposited in his own town the best. I do not at present intend to vote at all myself, but am trying to get Fitzhugh to pair off with me, which he is half inclined to do. Should I vote it will be for McClellan, or rather against Lincoln. Seymour certainly will not get my support. I do not hear much of the talk, nor know anything as to the state of parties in my own command. . . .

OCTOBER 13, THURSDAY.   We have been quite quiet here since Sunday; but rumours of an early move are prevalent, some of them even going so far as to prophecy the fall of Richmond before the election comes off. I have no hope of that long-desired event being so soon brought about, but fully expect another winter of it on the sacred soil. There are, however, certain indications of the commencement of the end of the rebellion in the character, numbers, and reports of the deserters who come in. Every morning more or less who have crossed the lines the preceding night are marched up to headquarters. Nor are they all of that wretched, ragged class of stragglers and shirks who have come in previously, but a number of real men, soldiers, are mixed in, who say that their cause is played out; that they have no more hopes of success, and give it up. This feeling they report as prevalent throughout Lee's army. They say that he has several times of late massed troops to attack us, but that the men shew so little inclination for the fray that the attempt was abandoned. At the same time, they say that if we attack them they will fight as hard as ever. . . . Meantime our men are gaining confidence, and if we can be successful in a few more small affairs, the morale of the army, which was so fearfully shattered by Grant's brutal attacks on the way down, will soon be restored.

The question of the "Valley of the Shenandoah" seems to be solved for the present by Sheridan's falling back below Strasburg. He could not remain where he was on account of the difficulty of obtaining supplies. . . . While falling back Sheridan's cavalry seems to have had a brilliant fight on Sunday last. I say brilliant, as they do not appear to have been obstinately opposed. Sheridan's dispatch is even more buncombe-ish than usual. His style is undignified, unsoldierly, and to me disgusting; "I directed Torbert to finish this 'saviour of the Valley' " (Rosser, the rebel cavalry commander), and such like expressions. He reports the capture of eleven guns beside waggons, ambulances, and the like, making thirty-six pieces of artillery captured in this Valley campaign.* Considering how many we have lost in this same Valley in years gone by, it is fitting that we should get some of them back there. . . .

My own three years were out yesterday! I came very near forgetting it, for so accustomed have we become to it, that three years of war do not seem so much to look back upon as one did at the time of my first anniversary. I have been trying tonight to recall some of the thoughts and feelings which came across me during the first months of my service, but find it almost impossible. Even the dreams and expectations I then indulged in have so completely passed from my mind that I cannot now say what they were. Fortunately I had not indulged in any very wild imaginations of personal glory; my highest ambition then was to earn a solid name in the army as a first-class officer in my own arm of the service. Indistinct visions of some occasion on which I might gallop half a dozen batteries into possition at the decisive moment, as General

---

* Sheridan had been laying the fertile Valley waste in the most ruthless manner, destroying the harvest, and killing or driving away all livestock; he was aggressively pugnacious, and of implacable temper. The action that Wainwright mentions was that which Sheridan called Tom's Brook, culminating in a twenty-six-mile chase of General T. L. Rosser's troopers by Merritt and Custer: "a general smashup of the entire Confederate line," writes Sheridan. Sheridan's style was that to be expected of a man of rough temper who had received only the most rudimentary education before he was admitted to West Point. It grated on others than Wainwright.

Sénarmont did at the battle of Friedland, and so save the day,* were soon dispersed by the densely wooded country in which all our fighting has been done. At the North Anna, to be sure, there was a very slight approach to something of the kind, but I never heard of any credit being given to me for it. The artillery is in fact an arm of defense rather than of offense; its glory is in coolness and obstinacy, qualities which do not excite general admiration like the dash of a charge.

How completely, too, have my ideas of great men changed in the last three years; not but what I still believe in geniuses like Gustavus, Napoleon, and a dozen others perhaps, but when you leave these out and come down to the ordinary man called great, the illusion is completely dispelled, and I see how a mere lucky hit or the fortunate combination of circumstances have given most of them their reputations. I say now without hesitation that there is not a great man living in this country; certainly not a great general in either army or anything approaching to it. The objects of the war, also, have completely changed: the real question of the salvation of the Union has been so completely overlaid by the insurance of a continuation in power of the Republican party that it is only by digging deep down that I can find the object for which I alone am fighting. The Almighty alone knows what will be the real issue to the country of this contest, though there is not now a doubt as to the military rebellion being put down. One thing is clear: that I never can be sufficiently thankful to a kind Providence for my preservation in life, health, and limb through all the bloody three years of war.

OCTOBER 16, SUNDAY. All continues quiet here. As the time for the Presidential election draws near, politics absorb more and more of the time and thoughts of officers and men. The camps are full of civilians sent down to secure the soldiers' votes for one side or the other. His party being in power at Washington, the friends of Mr. Lincoln of course outnumber their opponents two to one. There will no doubt be a great deal of influence exerted by some officers over the men under their command. It is easily done without laying themselves open to court martial, and if only exerted in the right way, there is no danger of Stanton listening to any complaints. I do not try to learn anything about the way things political go on in my own command, fearing that I might hear of something which I should feel obliged to condemn, and not have the power to punish.

General Crawford is quite a politician, strong on the side of those in

---

* Wainwright had read French military history. At Friedland, Napoleon ordered Alexandre Antoine Hureau, Baron de Sénarmont, to use thirty-six guns to take the Russian artillery in flank, which he did with crushing effect. Later he used his artillery to sweep the bridges across which the Russians were retreating.

power; from his talk one would be led to believe that nothing but certain ruin was in reserve for the country should Mr. Lincoln not be elected. From what I have seen of the man, I have not a doubt he would be as strong the other way, did he think his bread buttered on that side. Hunt, on the contrary, is an out-and-out Democrat, besides being a warm personal friend of McClellan. He holds that the re-election of Lincoln will prolong the war another four years, and then result in the breaking up of the Union. I do not believe in the extreme views of either side. The rebellion must cease in another year from mere inanition, in my opinion. The two parties are equally corrupt, and equally far from my views in their extreme doctrines; while I believe both of the Presidential candidates to be sound, and almost identical in their personal views. Both of them, too, are wanting in nerve. But Mr. Lincoln is much the worse, I believe, in this respect. We know that he is already completely in the hands of the radicals of his party, while there is at least a chance that McClellan, if elected, may not fall into the same snare on the other side. . . .

Last night we had an oyster roast at our headquarters. There have been several at corps headquarters, and this was a sort of return match. Our outdoor fire is on a raised hearth, with back; we had a barrel of James River oysters, which though small were a treat. The whole barrel disappeared, and having a couple of bottles of good Scotch whiskey, we closed with a good hot punch.

OCTOBER 20, TUESDAY. This evening we can think and talk of nothing but another victory gained by Sheridan in the Valley. His dispatch is hardly as bombastic as some of his others, though the little word "I" is to be found in almost every line of it. Sheridan was in Winchester at the commencement of the fight, and General Wright in command. The rebels were the attacking party, and completely successful at first, driving our whole force back four miles and capturing twenty pieces of artillery. Their second attack at one P.M. was repulsed, and at three P.M. a counter-attack made resulting in a complete victory on our part and the capture of forty-three guns (including the twenty lost in the morning, I suppose), whole trains of waggons, and many prisoners.

I am very sorry for Wright; the fact of defeat when he was in command and victory on Sheridan's return sounds very badly. Neither can I understand the audacity of Early attacking an entrenched force three times his own numbers. On Monday General Grant said that he had ordered the Sixth and Nineteenth Corps down here; it is possible that they may not have been in the first fight, which would explain much. At present, our knowledge is confined to the mere fact of the victory. General Crawford has sent out a circular authorizing the bands of the corps to play until one A.M. in honour of the victory. I should not suppose that the musicians would be over-thankful to him for the permission; but they are still at it (midnight), while the men, by their frequent cheers, seem determined to make a night of it. Wright, Ricketts, and Grover are all reported wounded, and a General Bidwell killed on our side.* Sheridan gives no estimate of his losses, but I fear that Early got a large number of prisoners in the morning.†

Last Monday the army was honoured by a visit from Secretary Stanton. He came to these headquarters in a waggon, drove to one or two works not in sight of the enemy, and returned, no doubt fully informed as to the state of matters down here. General Meade sent us word that he was coming, and ordered the troops to be held under arms, in their camps, for his reception. This was done, but our commander, Crawford, was not on hand. His laziness and self-indulgence proved too strong for his toadying, and when he reached corps headquarters at a gallop, the party had already gone on to Parke's. It was nuts to all here, and afforded great fun.

I have got half a dozen more three-inch guns, so that "B" Pennsylvania, "E" Massachusetts, and "L" New York are once more six-gun batteries. Ritchie, too, is mounted, and we have just drawn one hundred twenty-five horses. It will take a little time yet to get the command with its increased armament quite straight; four more batteries want extra sections. We have five hundred recruits, too, or one-third of the command, received in the last ten weeks to be broken in, as well as one-half the officers in new positions. . . .

OCTOBER 23, SUNDAY. From full reports received from Sheridan and the newspaper accounts, it is now evident that his victory is even more complete than it at first appeared to be. He now claims thirty guns captured and sixteen hundred prisoners. Early's army, they say, is entirely broken up. It was a very bold attempt on his part, well executed, and so far as I can understand it, really one of the most brilliant affairs of the war.

* This was Daniel Davidson Bidwell, who had been commissioned colonel of the Forty-ninth New York from civil life in the fall of 1861. He had since fought through the Peninsular campaign and in nearly all the Eastern battles since, including South Mountain, Antietam, Fredericksburg, Chancellorsville, and Gettysburg; and he had risen to be a brigadier general in the Sixth Corps.

† In this battle of Cedar Creek nearly 31,000 Union troops engaged about 18,500 Confederates. The Union loss was 5,665, of whom about 1,500 were missing; the Confederate loss was 2,910. Wright really had the Union troops under firm control by the time his superior got back; but, beyond question, Sheridan's electrifying return gave the troops the ardor and confidence that made their charge irresistible. The fragments of Early's command were now recalled to Richmond, while Sheridan's Sixth Corps resumed its position before Petersburg. Both men, however, later returned to the Shenandoah. Thomas Buchanan Read's poem, "Sheridan's Ride," soon helped to popularize Sheridan's exploit.

The enemy completely surprised Crook's corps under cover of a dense fog, and were inside of their lines before the men could unroll themselves from their blankets. The Sixth Corps, which was some distance to the rear, was not compromised at all in the defeat, but had to fall back in order to cover the retreat and reformation of the rest of the troops. General Wright had fully restored his lines, and was ready to receive the enemy when Sheridan came up. Sheridan made no change in Wright's dispositions until after the repulse; yet in neither of his dispatches to General Grant does he give Wright any credit whatever, but leads one to suppose that it was he alone who saved the day. The best informed here believe that Wright would have done quite as much had Sheridan not come up.

Our loss appears to have been heavy, especially in officers; the most severe is the death of Colonel Lowell, commanding a cavalry brigade. No officer from civil life stood so high in the estimation of the army. He was the brightest star among the many good officers, a gentleman from Massachusetts. Colonel Mackenzie, too, was wounded severely. He graduated at West Point in 1862 and was already commanding a brigade; I do not know him well but he is much thought of by the old officers.* Perhaps, should the war last a couple of years longer, some great general might come up out of the classes of 1861 and 1862; Upton, MacKenzie, and some other give great promise. . . .

Report says today that there are a number of ironclads coming up the river; this may indicate a combined movement on all parts of the rebel lines, or it may only mean an attempt to break through on the river line. Something may be tried yet before the election, but it is so near now that it cannot be expected to change the result in any way. Recruits are coming in every day in constantly increasing numbers. Still, they are only recruits, and one old three-year soldier is really worth three of them; which is just about the proportion of our gains to our losses. Desertions to the enemy, too, have become fearfully numerous in our army, a thing almost unknown before. They are all "bounty jumpers"; men who enlisted simply to get the money, and who not having been able to escape on their way down, now go over to the other side, not to fight with them, but to be sent by blockade runners to the West Indies, or by the underground railroad to Canada, from whence they

---

* Charles Russell Lowell, an honors graduate of Harvard, refused to leave his command when first wounded, and then received additional wounds of which he died. Ronald Slidell Mackenzie likewise refused to leave the action when wounded, a fact that Sheridan noted in dispatches. Young Lowell, a nephew of the poet, had just been listed for promotion to the rank of brigadier general. He had recently married a brilliant and beautiful young woman, Josephine Shaw, sister of Robert Gould Shaw, who was killed leading the Fifty-fourth Massachusetts at Fort Wagner.

again come into the country at some point where they are not known; again enlist, and receive a second or third $1,000 bounty. One New Hampshire regiment in the Ninth Corps is said to have lost three hundred men in this way, and it has been found necessary to withdraw them from the front line. A letter was found in the tent of one of the men which explained the whole process.

General Warren returned on Friday; ten days with his wife does not appear to have sweetened his temper at all, from what I hear. I see very little of him myself, except when obliged to officially. Our notions are not at all similar, so I deem it best to keep on the most punctilious terms with him. I have today got six more light twelve-pounders, so as to increase "D" and "H" First New York and the Ninth Massachusetts batteries to six guns each; this gives sixty guns in the corps, twenty-six rifled and thirty-four smooth-bore. . . .

Election matters are still in the ascendant. Most of the New York troops have sent off their votes. . . . All have to be sworn to before some commissioned officer of the State. Captain Breck tells me that he has been occupied several days swearing McClellan voters among the infantry in his neighbourhood, several of the regimental commanders refusing to allow it in their camps. I swore three officers at Baxter's headquarters this evening, but do not know how they voted. I was told yesterday that Lincoln has a majority of about fifteen votes in every hundred in my command. In the First Connecticut Artillery, out of one thousand voters, Lincoln is said to have a majority of twenty. This regiment probably has more old soldiers than any other in this army. The new men, thousand-dollar patriots, all vote for Lincoln, while a majority of the old soldiers go the other way. The army vote, however, will be decidedly Republican.

OCTOBER 26, WEDNESDAY. Another move is on foot; we start at daylight tomorrow. Our whole corps is to go, with four days' rations on the men and sixty pounds of ammunition; that is to say, the three divisions of infantry are to start, with every man they can scrape together in the ranks, leaving only a small brigade from each to hold all the lines, supported by the artillery. I am to take but ten rifled and twelve smooth-bore guns with us while the remainder hold the closed forts here. All waggons, save the few taken with the column, are to go tonight to City Point. As the Second and Ninth Corps are to move in equal strength, we shall make quite a force, and great results are confidently expected. . . .

Last night I sent off my proxy to Mr. Gillender to cast my vote for McClellan; I did not send any other vote, and if possible should have voted for McClellan as President, and Johnson for Vice. Indeed, Pendleton being on the same ticket with McClellan almost deterred me from voting at all, and I know has taken hundreds of votes from him in the army. Separated from Pendleton and the Chicago platform, McClellan would have received at least two-thirds of the votes of this army. I was at last induced to vote from sheer distrust of those in power now, and the belief that any change must be for the better. As to the radical newspaper charges that McClellan would acknowledge secession if elected, they are absurd nonsense. Major Duane has just returned from home, where he saw McClellan a number of times. General Hunt told me yesterday that Duane related to him a conversation he had had with McClellan, in which the General stated that should he be elected, he expected to be very unpopular the first year, as he should use every power possible to close the war at once, should enforce the draft strictly, and listen to no remonstrance until the rebellion was effectually quashed. If Fitzhugh had been willing to pair off, I would rather have done that than to have voted, but he would not.

I have just now (ten P.M.) got an order to be ready to start at four A.M. tomorrow instead of at daylight. This cuts short one's sleep a good deal, so must off to bed. We are to make another trial at turning Lee's right so as to get possession of the South Side Road. We shall have to go a good distance to accomplish this, as Lee has made that flank very strong for as far as we can see. I do wish Grant would try something else than this everlasting turning; he has not varied his plan of attack one iota since we left Culpeper. Lee must know exactly what is coming now, so soon as he learns that the army is in motion. . . .

OCTOBER 28, FRIDAY. Back at the old spot again, and nothing accomplished! Nothing save a few hundred more men laid under the sod, and a thousand or two carried off with a ball in their body or minus a leg or arm. Two years ago such a failure would have raised a hornets' nest about the ears of the commanding general, but now the country is accustomed to it, and the whole thing will be glossed over in some way. I am curious to see how it will be done, for there is no doubt that the expectation of great things, which was uncommonly strong throughout the army, came down from Grant's headquarters. . . .

The Second Corps did all the fighting in this expedition, and from all accounts deserve credit for their good behaviour. During the night Hancock withdrew from the Boydton road, and this morning crossed the Run at this point. About noon the whole army returned to their old positions, getting into their former camps before dark. I hear that Hancock places his loss at about 1,500 and that of the enemy opposed to him as more. The entire loss in this corps will not reach two hundred, while that of Parke's cannot be over three hundred. We have now a thousand prisoners. I suspect one side suffered about as much as the other, so that it may be called a drawn game, save the loss of morale in our army from not having succeeded in what we set about.

❊ ❊ ❊

Grant hoped in this last important movement of 1864 in Virginia to cut the Boydton Road and the Southside Railroad. For this purpose he used Parke's Ninth Corps, Warren's Fifth Corps, and a part of Hancock's Second Corps, with David M. Gregg's cavalry. He in fact reduced the forces manning the trenches around Petersburg so drastically that he took 43,000 men, leaving only 14,000 behind. To oppose him, Lee had only 28,000 men south of the Appomattox.

But the whole enterprise was mismanaged. Parke and Warren struck the Confederate line at about nine o'clock on October 27th. But Parke failed to break it, being in fact repulsed. When Warren sent Crawford's division across the small stream called Hatcher's Run, in an effort to turn the Confederate flank, the troops lost their way in an almost impassable swamp, their ranks becoming broken and confused. It was only after two hours of exhausting struggle that the command was brought up to the Confederate flank. Meanwhile, Gibbon's division in Hancock's column tried to establish some connection with Crawford; but it, too, became so bewildered in the densely tangled woods of the swamp that it failed in the effort. Crawford and Gibbon were less than a mile apart, but neither knew where the other stood.

Taking advantage of the situation, A. P. Hill launched an attack from the Confederate lines with all his characteristic vigor. Mott's division gave way, abandoned two guns, and fled in confusion to the rear. Hancock was sorely pressed by five brigades of cavalry under Wade Hampton, who attacked his advanced positions. Darkness ended the fighting in something like a stalemate; the Confederates had at first gained some ground, and then lost it. But the Union forces were withdrawn on the 28th to their old positions. They had accomplished nothing, though they outnumbered the Southerners by more than two to one; and they lost 1,600 or 1,700 men killed, wounded, or captured.

❊ ❊ ❊

OCTOBER 31, MONDAY. The newspapers try to make the best of our failure last week, taking their cue from Grant's dispatch to Washington, in which he calls the move a "reconnoissance." This affords a vast deal of amusement in the army, considering there were greater exertions and preparations made for this expedition than any previous one. There must have been near 40,000 men on the trip, but not more than a quarter of them were really in the fight. I was told at Army Headquarters that the official reports put our entire loss at 1,904.

As to where the blame of failure lies, the idea in this corps is universal that it belongs first to the Ninth Corps, which was so late in starting. Parke had but little over a mile to go from the southwest corner of his works; and the enemy not holding that country at all, he should have made himself perfectly acquainted with it, so as to have determined on his dispositions before starting. The second cause of failure was the really impenetrable and immense stretch of wood south of the Run. Had Crawford got through this he would have struck the force in front of Hancock in the flank, and the enemy having no strong works at the bridge of the plank road, we might have got over with them. I do not think that Crawford could be blamed for not getting through: by pushing harder it might possibly have been done, but the chances are that his command would have got scattered and picked up by the rebels, as they themselves were by Crawford.

The result has not lessened my own want of confidence in these flank movements. . . .

NOVEMBER 9, WEDNESDAY. I have had a small spree, a very small and quiet one so far as I was concerned. Being at Hunt's quarters on Sunday, he asked me to go on a trip to Norfolk with him; so I got a thirty-six-hour leave on Monday and went, returning yesterday afternoon. A new steamboat had come down to try for a lease by the quartermaster department as mail boat between here and Washington, and Ingalls was making a sort of trial trip in her. We started about ten A.M. from City Point, reaching Norfolk two or three hours before dark, and left there on our return about midnight; but, owing to the fog, had to anchor until daylight and then made but slow progress up, until the fog cleared, arriving again at City Point after noon. The party on board consisted of Generals Ingalls and Hunt, Berlin and Worth of Hunt's staff, Lieutenant Dunn of Grant's staff, two other officers and myself. . . . We were neither a brilliant nor a rowdy party so all went off quietly, the whole keeping sober. We took our meals on board the boat, and fared quite sumptuously.

At Norfolk, General Hunt went off in search of some old friends he had there, and to look after a couple of houses belonging to him in the town. I strolled around the town until dark, and then played a couple of games of billiards with Ingalls at one of the hotels. I was very much surprised to see the amount of business being done in Norfolk. The streets were full of loaded drays; every shop was occupied, open, and seemed to be doing a heavy business, especially in the retail drygoods line, some of which establishments were really equal to those of a first-

class city. I saw no ladies in the street, but throngs of very questionable
females, and any quantity of negresses dressed in the most extreme
fashion. The whores are said to be amassing real fortunes there, as it is
the nearest point to the army where they are allowed to come. All this,
however, does not begin to account for the amount of business in the
place; much of it I suspect is contraband. . . .

On our return to City Point we went up to General Grant's headquarters. He is still in tents, pitched on the bluff, without any pretensions
to display. Ingalls, who is now chief quartermaster on his staff, is the
only one having a house; but then, he always took care to be better off
than anyone else. While Hunt went in to have a talk with General
Grant, I made Patrick a visit, not having seen him for a good while. Hunt
came over then. The two old fellows croaked a good deal, but their heart
strings being opened, they let out much which interested me exceedingly,
but which I dare not commit to writing. Patrick, from his position,
has an opportunity to find out pretty much all that is going on behind
the scenes at Washington. He told me that there was positively a long
list of officers in the War Department whom Stanton had determined to
decapitate so soon as he was sure of his re-election (Lincoln's election
being really Stanton's); fifty of the number are in the Army of the
Potomac.

From newspapers we received today, and telegrams, we know enough
of the election yesterday to show that the democratic hopes of a great
change in public sentiment has not been realized; at least the change
has not become great enough to induce people to swallow the Chicago
pill. The result among those troops who cast their vote in the field in
this corps was as follows:

	Lincoln	*McClellan*	*Lincoln's Majority*
PENNSYLVANIA	2,962	1,642	1,320
MARYLAND	1,228	44	1,184
MAINE	290	74	216
MICHIGAN	363	252	111
WISCONSIN	333	67	266
	5,176	2,079	3,097

For my own part, I am delighted that the election is over, and trust
that having entire power secured to them now for another term of four
years, the Republican party will prove itself more conservative than
has been feared. McClellan resigned his commission in the army a
fortnight ago; what he will undertake for a livelihood I do not know.
The voting in the camps went off with perfect quietness. General Warren
issued an order for commanding officers to look to the matter, and have

it finished as early in the day as possible, lest the enemy might take advantage of its being election day to attack us. . . .

NOVEMBER 13, SUNDAY. We have had our change in the weather already. Today the wind has been high and raw, with a slight flurry of snow, the first of the season, so that I already find my addition and fireplace a comfort. If this corps is to spend the winter in its present position, I shall want to move my headquarters from this particular spot: it is completely exposed to all the wind and fearfully muddy. Beside which, we are now beginning to experience the disagreeableness of the railroad station being so near, in the accumulation of sutlers' tents and so on close by. One of the greatest nuisances I find a preaching tent a little way off. They have a ranter in it who hollers as loud as if he hoped to include the rebel picket line at least within his audience; the groans and cries of his hearers, too, are sometimes fearful. . . .

NOVEMBER 17, THURSDAY. General Grant and I had one of our long talks on artillery organization, appointment of officers, and other matters when on our Norfolk trip; and at his request I have put my views on the latter point in the shape of a communication to him. The main thing I want to accomplish is requiring all enlisted men to pass an examination before being commissioned, and all other recommendations for promotion to pass through his hands so that he may have a sort of veto power over the whole. I am getting all my regimental returns up; but not satisfied with what I have sent, the adjutant-generals department is calling for all the back ones. I have written to say that I will make these up from the time I took command, so soon as we go into winter quarters and I can get down the papers stored at Washington. The colonel of the Ninth Connecticut [Thomas W. Cahill] has just been dismissed the service for failing to prepare proper rolls and records of his regiment. . . .

Speaking of company, it appears to have been quite fashionable for English officers to run down here from Canada; I have met quite a number. The pleasantest that I have seen this autumn were Lord Mahon and his brother Mr. Stanhope; especially the latter—who, however, is not in the army. They spent the best part of a day with me, visiting the left of our lines. My French officers have left after a protracted visit, taking with them, I suspect, a report of a thousand pages. We have very few visitors at artillery headquarters from other officers; Griffin stops once in a while to see Major Fitzhugh, and Ayres has looked in a few times. Colonel Winthrop dined with us the other day; he now commands the First Brigade, Second Division. He is very pleasant, a thorough gentleman, a most capital officer, and universally liked.* He and Ayres have

* Frederick Winthrop, who had been in the New York militia, was commissioned a captain in the regular army in the autumn of 1861. He had been a participant in most of the great Eastern actions from Yorktown to Spotsylvania, and had not only been

the finest headquarters in the corps (Warren's I think is the worst and mine next), though Crawford is at work on something very elaborate in the way of a house. Winthrop was on leave a short time since, and brought back with him an exquisite headquarters flag, the gift of his lady love. This is quite coming back to the times of chivalry, only that the flag was made by Tiffany instead of being the work of her own fair hands. . . .

NOVEMBER 20, SUNDAY. The works around our present lines are now all finished. All of them save Conohey are simple redoubts, while Fort Conohey is complicated enough to make up for all the rest and to afford illustration for a whole course of lectures on engineering. It has no recognized geometric form that I ever saw. It is located on the side of a ravine. One half, being on the level at top, is an ordinary open work; the other in the ravine has bomb-proof casements and embrasures commanding the ravine both ways, with a musketry parapet above. A loopholed stockade divides the two parts of the work. This fort has cost more labour than any other, has afforded an admirable lesson in engineering, and is one of the sights to show to strangers. Further than this I doubt the value of its elaborateness. All the works, front and rear, are protected by strong abattis and slashing, and are well built save Fort Howard and the batteries on either side of it, where the ground is so low and wet that it is really impossible to make them trim and neat looking.

The building of these works and the men's huts has so cleared the timber off the country here that it is hard work now to recognize it, and fears are already entertained of running short of fuel, near by, before the winter is over. . . .

NOVEMBER 24, THURSDAY. This is "Thanksgiving Day" all over the country, the President having appointed it as well as the government of the different states.* Great preparations were made in New York City to supply all the soldiers with a turkey dinner, and the papers this week have been full of accounts of the cooking and packing. Unfortunately it did not get down in time for distribution this morning, though the *cargoes* arrived at City Point last night. Captain Steele tells me that the proportion to this corps will be 14,000 pounds of turkey, one hundred

---

promoted to be colonel, but had been brevetted a brigadier general in August 1864. We shall hear later of his sad ultimate fate.

* Mrs. Sarah Josepha Hale, editor of *Godey's Lady's Book*, had carried on an unremitting campaign that led President Lincoln to appoint the last Thursday in November in 1863 as a day of national Thanksgiving. The idea could be traced back to the thanksgiving festival that the Plymouth colony had held in December 1621 in gratitude for a bounteous harvest. Washington had proclaimed a day of thanksgiving in 1789. Now Thanksgiving was becoming an annual festival.

barrels of apples, with cranberry sauce and pies in like quantity. As the officers are to get some as well as the men, teamsters, hospitals, and all, the above amount will have to be divided among about 24,000, giving rather over half-a-pound of turkey, one apple, and a bite of pie to each. When these things are done, it would be much better to confine it to one article and plenty of that. . . .

I had quite a talk with some of the deserters who came in this morning. Six of them were from Florida, a sorry looking lot enough; only one of them had a blanket, and all were very ragged. Those from other states were better clothed. One of them told me, in reply to the question whether he had been into the town of Petersburg lately, that they received two months' pay lately, and then he went into town to get an extra dinner for himself and chum; that it took the whole of his two months' pay to buy one meal for the two men of mutton, turnips, and cabbage. What would our men say to this? Would we have any army at all if we were reduced so low? Things have got to be high enough here with our depreciated currency, but flour is not yet $350 a barrel. . . .

NOVEMBER 27, SUNDAY. We have no news from Sherman other than the rumours published in the New York papers. Jefferson Davis no doubt knows exactly where he is, and as we have no word through rebel sources, it is fair to conclude that he has not met with any serious check as yet. The deserters who came in this morning say that they have not been allowed to see the Richmond papers for several days. All here continues perfectly quiet. General Hancock has left the Second Corps and gone up to Washington to organize a new corps now forming, to be composed entirely of veterans; that is, men who have served honourably not less than two years. This corps is to be called the First; the men to be enlisted for one year, and to receive a special bounty of $300, a sort of premium offered to those who refused to re-enlist in the field. The corps is to consist of not less than 20,000 men. General Humphreys, late Meade's chief of staff, succeeds to the command of the Second Corps. This puts the whole Army of the Potomac under engineer officers, Meade, Humphreys, Warren, Parke, and Wright all being taken from that corps.

Another change I am more glad of: Parke has effected an exchange with Birney of his negro division for one of white troops. This clears the Army of the Potomac of them. The radical papers laud the negro troops greatly, but this division has done almost nothing here. Perhaps they have not had a fair chance, there not being overmuch confidence in them here; where they have been tried they have failed, save in their attack on first reaching Petersburg.

The Thanksgiving dinner reached us the next day, and furnished a better feast than I expected; at least I know that my own men got their bellies full of turkey. Our headquarters mess received four turkeys, a dozen pies (very leathery), a barrel of apples, and cranberry sauce without end. Theo Bronson was one of the committee who came down in charge; he spent the day with me yesterday. The cause of the delay in getting the dinner down was a severe storm in the bay; some of the dinner came very near being lost. . . .

NOVEMBER 30, WEDNESDAY. The month closes very quietly, completing the first month since we left Culpeper without some sort of a fight; but even the pickets now are on the best terms possible. . . . The greater part of the infantry have now better winter quarters than they ever had before: the First and Second Divisions have theirs built in regular streets running at right angles to and just within the works. Crawford's men, who hold east from Fort Wadsworth, are not so far advanced, having to drain all the ground in rear of Fort Howard. One of the Maine regiments, though, has laid out and commenced building a model camp near Wadsworth. Instead of all building their own huts, the work is being done by a detail of regular axemen and masons, and shows such a use of the axe as could only be looked for from Maine woodmen.

My batteries have in a great measure completed their huts. Mink has got decidedly ahead of them all this time, not only as to the first completed, but also as to the excellence of his buildings. His not being in position has been some help to him, though the others have had very little more to do. His huts are six and one-half feet to the plate, and large enough for six or eight men and a corporal, so as to have a noncom responsible in each hut for the condition of matters in it. But his stables are a work of art, and lying close to the great corduroy road, attract a great deal of attention; the horses stand on split logs facing each other in two rows, and the whole is roofed with nine to twelve-inch trees split and hollowed into gutters which are laid alternately and gutter up or down so as to lap like Dutch tile. . . .

There has been a good deal of talk in the army as to Butler levying a tax on all sutlers' stores coming to this army. He is said to have a gunboat constantly cruising at the mouth of the James, which sends all sutlers' boats into Norfolk, where they are obliged to pay a tax before being allowed to proceed up the river: which tax he says is for the benefit of the hospitals. Many of the reports go much further even to asserting that he helps himself to the best of all the things which come down. The first statement as to his levying a tax is doubtless correct; my sutler informs me officially that he has had to pay it. As to its going to hospitals, that is all bosh; and if it did, why should this army be taxed to support General Butler's hospitals? A row is being made about it now, and it will doubtless be put a stop to. . . .

Stewart has asked to be ordered to his own battery "A" Fourth Artillery, which is stationed at Washington. Every necessary of life has become so high that he says it is now impossible to support his wife and children through the winter on his pay, while he remains in the field; whereas, by being stationed at Washington where they are, he can send the fuel he draws to them, and can buy most of their groceries from the post commissary. I am very sorry to lose him, but could not help approving his application on these grounds.

Under an order from Hunt's headquarters I have sent up the names of Captains Sheldon and Bigelow and of Lieutenant Prescott, Ninth Massachusetts, as having been absent wounded or sick over three months. They will doubtless all be honourably discharged. I am sorry to lose Captain Bigelow, but it is very doubtful if he would ever be fit for field service again. The other two are no loss. I have some half-dozen new commissions for the regiment, not near enough though to give us all the officers we want, as the regiment is now more than full. It has only ten captains, eleven first and fourteen second lieutenants, or thirty-five company officers, instead of sixty as it ought. . . .

WELDON RAILROAD, DECEMBER 4, SUNDAY. Early being completely used up, and the Valley of the Shenandoah so devastated by Sheridan that it can no longer furnish supplies for a rebel army, the Sixth Corps has returned to this army. Wright's headquarters and one division came up today. The Sixth is to relieve this corps, and we are to go into reserve. It is very hard on our men, who have just got their huts completed, to have to turn them over to others and build afresh themselves. Being in reserve, too, probably means being held ready to go anywhere we may be wanted, and to do all the odd jobs that may turn up. It will probably be the most uncomfortable position we could be placed in. . . .

General Meade has at last been made a full major-general in the regular army to date from our fight here on the Weldon Railroad; though I cannot see why that date should have been chosen. There has been great opposition to his getting the promotion on the part of the radicals at Washington; and it is said that Hancock has tried very hard to get it himself instead. It was only when General Grant went up to Washington, and personally insisted upon it, that the Senate consented to confirm him. As it is, he will now rank Sherman by date of commission. Brevets have been received by almost all at Army Headquarters, except [Marsena] Patrick and [Seth] Williams, though they deserve them quite as much as any others; being, I fully believe, the two most conscientious and hardworking men in the whole army.

DECEMBER 6, TUESDAY. We, that is, the Fifth Corps, are to move tomorrow morning at daylight. It is a mere raiding expedition for the purpose of destroying the Weldon Railroad so far south from Stony Creek as will prevent Lee from drawing any supplies from that direction. General Warren will have command, and in addition to all the infantry of his own corps, he is to have Mott's division of the Second, and Gregg's division of cavalry. This will make him strong enough to hold his own against any force Lee is at all likely to send against us, should he attempt to interfere. As speed of movement will be our main reliance for success, I am to take but four batteries of four guns each along. . . .

DECEMBER 6, AT NIGHT. The batch of brevets for this corps arrived this evening. I get all those which I recommended for officers who are still present with me; also one for myself. That is an official notice of the appointment from Secretary Stanton, the actual commission depending on the confirmation of the appointment by the Senate. I shall therefore wait until I am confirmed before I assume the title, as I should not at all like to have to fall back to colonel after having once signed myself general. My notice reads: "The President of the United States has appointed you for brave, constant, and efficient services in the battles and marches of the campaign, a brigadier-general of volunteers, by brevet," to rank from the first day of August last; which, I believe, is as early as brevets are allowed to date under the present law.

The notice was accompanied by a very handsome letter from General Meade, speaking of "highly meritorious services," the value of which is, however, greatly lessened from the fact of its being printed. Altogether I think that I ought to be satisfied with my brevet, for it is handsomely given, among the very first conferred in this army, and there are only some six or eight other colonels in the corps who get them. I remember nearly three years ago now one afternoon at Camp Barry, when our then Lieutenant-Colonel Turner and others were indulging in dreams of promotion, and of how it would feel to have a star on one's shoulders, that I said I would not have it unless I could carry it on a red ground. To that resolution I have stuck, for once at least I had a good opening for the star as an infantry officer. And now that I have got as near to a brigadier-general of artillery as the rules of our service admit, if I am confirmed I shall wear the star on a red ground. . . .

* * *

The movement of Warren and the Fifth Corps was designed to cripple the Weldon Railroad completely. Union lines had been drawn across it near its point of entry into Petersburg, but the Confederates still made considerable use of it by sending wagons to the point of stoppage to haul in supplies. Warren, with the help of Gregg's cavalry and of Mott's division from the Second Corps, was to march south and break up at least twenty-five miles of track down near the North Carolina line. Setting out on December 7, the expedition that night reached Nottoway. Little interference was offered by the enemy, and the mission was successfully accomplished.

The railroad was completely destroyed over about twenty miles, and the Union forces lost very few men.

* * *

NOTTOWAY RIVER, DECEMBER 7, WEDNESDAY. We have had a lovely day for this the first stage of our march; clear and soft as June, and an excellent road all the way. Gregg led out with one brigade of cavalry and a horse battery; leaving his other brigade to cover the right flank and the rear of the train, which, though reduced as low as possible, was quite long, as we had to carry a large number of tools, a good many ambulances, forage for all the horses, and a pontoon train. . . .

The head of the infantry column reached this place, Freeman's Ford, about two hours before dark. The cavalry had crossed by the ford, and one brigade of infantry found its way over in the same manner. So soon as the pontoons were got up, they began laying a bridge of some fifty feet. It was a canvas boat train, the laying of which, being new to me, interested me much. The frame on which the canvas is stretched is very simple and easily put together; the whole packing, when taken apart, into a small compass. I was too surprised to see what a weight these boats would hold up, and how little water passed into them through the canvas. The bridge was very quickly laid. . . .

It was ten o'clock before our headquarters waggons crossed, so that supper could be got ready. I was fortunate enough to get a nice steak and cup of coffee from the engineers soon after dark along with General Warren. I wish that we could find such a cook as the major had, for I have never eaten a nicer steak in the field, though it was cooked in a frying pan. Soon after I got the batteries over and in camp, I spread my blankets under the trees about fifty yards above the bridge head and went to sleep. The last thing I heard was the teamsters yelling at their mules as the train crossed the bridge.

This was one of the romances of camp life: the soft night air; the tall, leafless trees under which we bivouacked, and which stretched all along the south side of the river; the wide, open plain on the opposite bank; the bridge, lighted up by great pitch-pine fires; the noise of the men, horses and mules—all contributed to make a picture such as one dreams of. [Henry] Baxter's brigade was pushed on some three or four miles to Suffolk Court House; the rest of the infantry only moving far enough to cover the bridge well, and to leave room for the trains to park inside of the line they occupied.

DECEMBER 8, THURSDAY. I do not know how exactly to designate the spot where we camp tonight; it being merely at a house by the roadside. . . . The master of the house is not at home, having gone, so at least his wife told us, some twelve or fifteen miles off to get salt for putting down his winter's supply of bacon. The poor fellow might as well have saved his time and money, for he will find no pigs to slaughter when he gets back, our men having killed and eaten the two large hogs before dark. I arrived here about four o'clock, and the afternoon having come off somewhat cold, I went into the house to warm myself. Everything shewed the poverty of the inhabitants, though the house was a large one, and the builder no doubt at that time thought himself pretty well-to-do in the world. Now the white part of the household were evidently all living in one room: the family consisting, beside the absent man, of a poor sickly-looking wife, with a young babe at the breast, two other children, and a sister of the man, who I suspect was the backbone of the whole establishment.

In this room were two large four-poster bedsteads, and it seemed to be the only place where they had a fire, at the time of our arrival, for they were baking some cakes there in a dutch oven. These cakes consisted of nothing but cornmeal and water, with the addition of a small propor-tion of wheat flour; very uninviting, but they were eaten with relish (by the children who came in, white and black) with the aid of a little sorghum molasses. Being anxious to see what they were like, I got a taste, on the plea of never having tried the sorghum before; and came to the conclusion there were some who lived worse than the soldiers. The sister told me that this was all they had to live on now for the coming winter: about three-quarters of a barrel of wheat flour, and some dozen bushels of old corn. They have suffered badly from the three (including this) raids through here the past season, by which all their growing crops were destroyed, and the whole of their livestock killed. The little grain above-mentioned and some eight or ten very young pigs running about, is all they have left, and no money to buy more. She told me of fabulous prices charged in Petersburg for everything in their paper money; $5 for a paper of pins gives one the idea that pins are very scarce, or money, so-called, very plenty. . . .

From the ford we passed through Suffolk Court House, a small village with a rather pretentious stucco Court House. From there we followed a byroad until we struck the railroad. . . . As yet we have met with no opposition. Only a small body of cavalry has been watching our move-ment, falling back in front of Gregg's advance without even attempting to skirmish. We had one very small alarm about halfway from the Court House to this place, caused by a score of rebel cavalry cutting across the road between Gregg and the infantry column. . . .

If money, real money, and eatables are scarce in this part of rebeldom, there is one drinkable called "Apple Jack" which seems to be more than abundant enough. Gregg says that he has had over fifty barrels of it stove today; yet, notwithstanding every precaution he could take, very many of his men have got beastly drunk on it. One man I saw who had got so drunk that he could not stand; his joints were entirely powerless, and after every attempt to get him along his comrades left him by the roadside. This was just by the spot where the squad of rebs crossed; they tried to take him along but could not, so one of them shot him through the brain with his pistol while the others pulled off his boots, and left the body. The whole thing was done in a minute and within sight of where Gregg was sitting at the time waiting for Warren to come up. . . .

All the infantry were at work today destroying the railroad, and the work was pretty effectually done for some twenty miles between the Nottoway and Meherrin Rivers; the ties being all taken up and the rails heated and bent. Beyond this, we could do nothing save destroy a few culverts. Gregg's cavalry pushed on to the Meherrin and tried to burn the bridge there, but did not succeed. There were two strong redoubts well manned, on the opposite bank, and after a small attempt to get down to the bridge, it was given up as likely to cost more loss of life than it was worth.

I rode with General Warren to our advanced position some five hundred yards from the river, and had a good look at the rebel works. All, I believe, disliked to go away and leave them unharmed, but it would cost us at least one day's delay, and probably two or three hundred men; half our rations were gone, and the most dangerous part of our work, the getting back, still to do. While we were at the front, the rebs fired very spitefully all the time from the guns in their works and their skirmish line on this side the river. This fire cost Gregg some twenty or thirty men. . . . The day has been cold and blustery with a few showers. The men have been hard at work, and are very tired, so the general means to give them a good long night of it, as there is no saying what they may be called upon for tomorrow. Bellefield is about thirty miles from Petersburg, and the same distance from Norfolk. This is the most southern point that I have reached so far during the war, being within ten or twelve miles of the North Carolina line.

DR. BRIGGS'S, DECEMBER 10, SATURDAY. We only made a few miles on our way back today; the weather being very bad, and some time being consumed in finishing off yesterday's work of destruction. We also had to move with caution, keeping our train well covered at all points, and to get the troops in such positions before nightfall that we could be ready for an attack in the morning. . . .

Last night was very hard on the men; it began to snow soon after dark, followed by a fine rain and cold. This morning everything was sheeted with ice; each spray of the trees and blade of grass was completely coated, making the country a most beautiful sight when the sun came

out, but the roads terrible for the footmen. There was more drunkenness among the infantry than on our march out, and one of Stewart's men
had got royally tight. This was the only case of either drunkenness or
straggling I heard of in my own command during the whole raid. He
was in charge of the first sergeant, who got him up to his battery and
tied him behind one of the guns, where he marched the rest of the day,
and was made sober by the aid of a bucket of water thrown over him
every once in a while. My men have given me great satisfaction, as well
as my officers; the detachments keeping close to their guns all the time,
as we did not know but what we might be called into action at any
moment. . . .

The men had behaved so well up to this afternoon that I am doubly
sorry to have a long black mark to set against them. Still, if the story
told is true, there was great provocation; not enough to justify their
acts at all, but somewhat excuse them. It is said that some two or three
dead men, stripped, were found by the roadside by our advance, who
were supposed to be some of our men who had got very drunk when we
went out, and had then been murdered by guerrillas. Just north of
Suffolk Court House a naked body was found which was recognized
as a sergeant in one of the regiments; and while the men were burying it,
a negro came up and said that the man who shot the sergeant was in a
house which he pointed out, hid away under some cornshucks in the
garret. The lieutenant commanding the ex-sergeant's company thereupon took his men, surrounded the house, searched the attic, and found
a man hid there as the negro had described. Leaving the man there, he
set the house on fire, and burned the man in it. This is the story as told to
me; if all true, including the negro's testimony as to the identity of the
murderer of the sergeant, one cannot blame his comrades for taking the
law into their own hands.

But now comes the worse. The story spread almost instantly through
the column, and the sight of the burning house seemed to raise the devil
in the men at once. Scores of men left the ranks, and seizing brands from
the burning house, fired every building in sight. None escaped, large
and small, pig sties and privies, all were burnt, with barely time allowed
for the people themselves to get out, saving nothing. The negroes fared
no better than the whites. Every soul was turned adrift to find shelter
for the night as best they could. For this barbarism there was no real
excuse, unless exasperation and the innate depravity of mankind is one.
I did not see the actual firing until the last of our march, but could not
hear that the officers in command of the advance did anything to stop
it. So pitiable a sight as the women and children turned adrift at nightfall, and a most severe winter night too, I never saw before and never
want to see again. If this is a raid, deliver me from going on another.

This house, which belongs to a major in the rebel army, and is really a very handsome dwelling, was only saved by the commander of the leading brigade wanting it for his own lodging overnight. He just got orders to halt for the night in time to stop the firing, for the men had piled and broken a lot of the drawing-room furniture ready to light when he stopped them. I was delighted when Locke came up and claimed the house for corps headquarters, for the colonel commanding the brigade had only stopped the burning for his own comfort, and now he was turned out to make the best of the night in a tent. To be sure, I slept in a tent myself, not choosing to sleep in the room with all the corps staff; Warren had another room to himself, so I took his tent which had a stove in it. The night was bitter cold, with a very high wind blowing, and my stove came very near burning up my house too. . . .

YELLOW TAVERN, DECEMBER 12, MONDAY. Safe back again in our old quarters, without a fight, or any mishap, though we were absent the full six days for which we took supplies. We made a tolerably early start, and had no delay in getting our bridge down over the Nottoway, as the approaches on either side were already made. At that point we found Potter's division of the Ninth Corps, which General Meade, getting fidgety about our safety, had sent out thus far yesterday to meet us. By dark we were safely back in our old quarters. The expedition has been a success, in that it accomplished all it was sent out for, and with very small loss, and that mainly caused by apple jack; forty or fifty will cover all our other loss. It has been a hard march, however, on man and beast, owing to the badness of the weather after the first two days. . . .

DECEMBER 16, FRIDAY. Yesterday and today we have had excitement enough over news from the west and south. As misfortunes are said never to come singly, so good news has in this instance come upon us in a flood: nor is it any the less reliable or enjoyable because a good part of it reaches us through the rebel papers. *First,* we hear that Sherman has reached the coast, just below Savannah, and taken position in front of the rebel lines there. *Next* comes from Nashville a telegram saying that Thomas has attacked Hood, who has been threatening him for some time at that place, carrying all the left of his lines, and driving him five miles; capturing seventeen guns and about 1,500 prisoners. The battle was fought yesterday and our loss is said to be small. As if this were not enough, we have, *third,* a long extract from the Richmond papers with an account of Stoneman's raid up the Kanawha Valley; where he seems to be sweeping everything before him, destroying the railroad and supplies, and playing the devil generally. The same paper gives Hood's official report of the battle of Franklin, November 30, in which he claims to have captured 6,000 prisoners, but acknowledges a heavy loss himself, especially in officers, seven generals killed, six wounded and one captured. A postscript announces the capture of Fort McAllister by Sherman, which they say puts him in communication with our fleet, but does not "by any means involve the loss of Savannah." As to this last, we shall learn more by and by: we ought to be content with so much good news in one day. . . .

JERUSALEM PLANK ROAD, DECEMBER 30, TUESDAY. I shall sleep in the new camp tonight, though not very comfortably, for I have nothing but a tent with a little "monitor" stove in it, and the weather is very cold. All the batteries moved over yesterday and today, so this cold snap comes pretty hard on the men who have been for a month in good huts, and are now again brought down to shelter tents. Last year we changed camp to Culpeper Court House a week later in just such another spell of cold. Of course, but little has yet been done in the new camps. Another week of good weather will, however, make all who work hard comfortable; but near a month will be required by some of them, I fear, to finish all up as it will be required. .... .

Thomas's victory at Nashville proves to be the most complete of anything known in this war. His dispatch of the evening of the 16th says that he is still following Hood, and though he is unable to give the number of either guns or prisoners captured, he furnishes enough data for us to know that the latter must be near if not over 5,000; while the former is likely to mount up to forty or fifty. The wording in my copy, which says "our loss does not exceed *three hundred,*" must be a mistake.* Hood seems to have been completely routed, so that we shall probably hear no more of his army than of Early's in the Valley. It is said that Thomas received an order relieving him of his command the day before the battle; he had not moved quick enough to please them at Washington, but would wait until all his arrangements were complete. He pocketed the order and fought his battle; now he is safe from any danger of that sort. One hundred guns were fired at sunrise of the 18th here in honour of his victory. . . .

DECEMBER 24, SATURDAY. I start off on a twenty-day leave tomorrow morning, and so shall finish up the year's entries here tonight, and close this, my fourth volume, at the same time; in this it has worked out very nicely. I trust that the war will not allow of my filling another book, even so small an one as this. It is now nearly a year since I was off from my command, and I begin to feel anxious to see a little of civilization, lest I forget all about it. This continued cold weather, too, is an inducement to get somewhere inside of a house. . . .

* Thomas actually reported a loss of slightly over 3,000 in the decisive Union victory at Nashville on December 15–16; nearly 50,000 Union troops against 23,200 Confederates.

Last evening General Grant sent us a copy of a telegram he has received from Ord, now in command of the Army of the James, Butler having gone off on an expedition down the coast somewhere. This dispatch gives us the information brought from Richmond by a telegraph operator; it reads to me somewhat confused and I think must be taken with some allowance. He says that the fleet (i.e., Butler's expedition?) appeared off Wilmington on the 16th to 18th, and that Fort Fisher was captured on the night of the 20th. If so, Wilmington, the last seaport of the rebellion, is closed. Beauregard telegraphed the unconditional surrender of Savannah on the morning of the 20th, but does not say whether the garrison surrendered with the town or evacuated it. He reports hard times in Richmond, and the rebellion pretty well played out generally.* It is certainly on its last legs, unless something unforeseen turns up. Everything goes to show that they are running short of men, money, and supplies; and what is almost worse for them, they have lost heart too.

NEW YORK, DECEMBER 31, 1864, SATURDAY. Got home safe on Monday to dinner. I had a comfortable trip, my new title of general giving me a stateroom to myself; a good breakfast at the Eubaw House, Baltimore, where everyone was jubilant over a dispatch from Sherman dated in Savannah, and presenting Mr. Lincoln with the place as a Christmas present, along with 150 heavy guns, and 25,000 bales of cotton. Later news adds to the cotton, and gives us 8,000 prisoners, steamers, locomotives, and what not. There was no fighting nor, indeed, did Sherman have any since leaving Atlanta. As we get full accounts, his march to the seashore seems to have been almost a pleasure trip. . . .

I find all well at home here, and glad to see me. On Monday I hope we shall have a fine day, so that I can make a complete round of New Year calls. The papers say that the Senate have confirmed my brevet.

* Fort Fisher, of course, did not fall. Ben Butler's expedition against it and the port of Wilmington instead broke down. Of the amphibious force, the troops were tardy in arriving, and the warships found their fire ineffective. A "powder ship" with 213 tons of explosive that was set off near the fort did little but "wake everybody up."

But the Confederates evacuated Savannah on December 21 before Sherman could bring his siege guns into play; its principal defensive work, Fort McAllister, having been taken on the 13th by a division under General William B. Hazen.

NINETEEN

THE FINAL CAMPAIGNS

Wainwright returned to camp on the Jerusalem Plank Road south of Petersburg on the evening of January 15, 1865, after twenty full days at home. He had thoroughly enjoyed himself, for after making sure that all was well at "The Meadows" at Rhinebeck, he had spent his time with friends there and in New York, meeting the warmest of welcomes. "Indeed," he writes, "I think I have never during the war known the soldier so popular as now. The victories of last month and the almost certainty that the war is drawing to a close makes everyone's heart go out to the men in uniform." He got a new uniform, his old one being worn out, but kept to a colonel's garb. "I could not go a full brigadier-general's uniform. I think that officers should wear the same uniform in all respects when only holding brevet rank as would be the proper thing if having actual rank." He was also careful not to overstay his leave as many others did. "I do not like that way of doing things," he remarks; "I cannot keep my officers close down to orders if I am loose in the observance of them myself."

During his absence his men had prepared exceedingly comfortable new quarters. He had a hut about sixteen by fourteen feet, built of large uniform pine logs, hewn on three sides so that they fitted closely. It contained a good fireplace and chimneys and two windows; the floor was also of hewn pine logs. He had brought some cheerful wallpaper and some carpeting from New York. At once he caught up on camp gossip. "I find Butler universally blamed here for his not attempting Fort Fisher," he reports. "But I must say that I think his engineer officer reporting against the attempt relieves him from much of the actual blame in the matter." The fact was that Lee, anticipating this assault on the last Southern gateway with the outer world, had sent such heavy reinforcements to the fort that any attempt to take it would have been very costly. A stronger amphibious expedition against it was now being outfitted under General A. H. Terry, who was given 8,000 troops and Admiral David D. Porter's North Atlantic squadron of nearly sixty ships for the purpose. It was to take the fort and thus shut the port of Wilmington before Wainwright was fairly settled in his new quarters.

Lee and his army at Richmond-Petersburg were being caught in a gigantic pincers. While Grant held them immobile, Sherman's triumphant forces were moving northward. He was to reach Goldsboro, North Carolina, on March 23—and then he would be only 150 miles from Petersburg. Sheridan was soon operating in the Shenandoah Valley again and threatening Lynchburg. It was plain to all that the great drama approached its end.

✳ ✳ ✳

CAMP NEAR JERUSALEM PLANK ROAD, SIX MILES FROM PETERSBURG, VA., JANUARY 15, 1865, SUNDAY. On the 21st of December the President issued his proclamation calling for 300,000 more volunteers; under which order and the high bounties recruits have come in quite briskly. The men know that the war is pretty much over, and think that they will not be kept long, and may get off without any hard fighting. No recruits, however, were allowed to be received for either artillery or cavalry, there having been such a rush for these arms of the service last autumn; but a subsequent order allowed application to be made to fill up any companies of these arms by special recruiting service. . . .

JANUARY 19, THURSDAY. On Tuesday we got news of the fall of Fort Fisher; at first the mere fact, and then a dispatch from Colonel Comstock, who had been sent by General Grant with the expedition, giving the particulars. From it and from what we have since learned, it is evident that our men did very well, and were well handled; also that the enemy did not fight as they did at Spotsylvania and previously; while it is still more certain that had Butler made the attack before, the capture would have been much easier, as the works had been greatly strengthened since then, and the garrison nearly doubled. This closes the last seaport of the rebels. Wilmington for the last two years has been their main entrance for all foreign goods, the coast thereabouts being such as to render a perfect blockade of the port impossible. One may well ask why it was not closed two years ago by seizing Fort Fisher then. I never could see why it should not have been tried. . . .

The departments in Washington are ordered to be draped in mourning for the death of Edward Everett. This, I think, is the first time such an honour has been paid to a private citizen. Colonel Fitzhugh, Sergeant Thompson, Major Phillips, and Captain Steele all went off on leave last Tuesday. General Warren is still absent and Crawford in command of the corps. He has, as I think absurdly, taken a notion that some of the battery men have removed part of a bridge between his own division and this camp for firewood. I say absurdly for all the batteries haul their firewood in waggons, and therefore it is not likely that any would go to the trouble of carrying a single log one hundred yards or more. In the infantry each man gets his own as best he can, so that every step he has to bring it counts. However, I have had to place a guard at the bridge, until Warren comes back. . . .

JANUARY 31, TUESDAY. As nothing of importance had occurred, I made no entry here on Sunday leaving it until today, so as to close up the month. . . . General Warren returned from his leave on Friday last. General Meade is still absent; and Grant has been down to Fort Fisher to take a look himself at the state of things there. Lieutenant Canfield has gone off on his leave, and the battery officers are all getting theirs as fast as they can be spared. . . . The applications for furloughs are very brisk: not content with the number allowed my orders, the men concoct all sorts of pressing demands to get one. The number of wives who are dying, and of children almost killed by some frightful accident, is astonishing. All applications of this sort are required to be accompanied with the original letter stating the case, and some of these letters are very amusing to read. . . .

McClellan has gone to Europe with his family. Letters from home are full of the fall in the price of gold, cotton, and other goods; all seems to show a general opinion that the war is drawing to a close. A week ago old Blair the father went into Richmond on a special mission to try to bring about peace. The accounts of it we got in the papers tell us nothing that can be relied on, but that he reported his reception as most polite, and thought matters looked favourable. Mrs. Davis kissed the old man when he was presented, and my visitor of today, Mr. Campbell, who is chief clerk in the War Department, attaches a good deal of importance to that kiss. Today Davis has made a first step in the direction of peace by sending three commissioners in to treat, viz: Messrs. Stevens, Hunter, and Campbell. They came into our lines near the point where Burnside's mine was exploded, and went at once down to General Grant's quarters at City Point, where they are to wait for permission from Washington to proceed.* . . .

CAMP NEAR JERUSALEM ROAD, FEBRUARY 5, SUNDAY. It seems that General Grant has what he considers reliable information that Lee transports large supplies in waggons from Hicksford, to which point we destroyed the railroad, by way of the Boydton Plank Road. The object

---

* Lincoln had allowed Francis P. Blair, Sr., who was a personal friend of many Southern leaders, to visit Richmond; and he brought back word that Jefferson Davis was willing to send commissioners to confer with President Lincoln on the restoration of peace. The result was an abortive meeting February 3 on a transport in Hampton Roads; Lincoln and Seward talking with the three men named.

of this move is to endeavour to capture or destroy some of these waggon trains and to do what they can to break up this source of his supplies. Two divisions of the Second Corps moved this morning to Armstrong's Mills, the point where we crossed Hatcher's Run in November last and carried the crossing after a short skirmish. They are to remain at that point which, if I remember right, is some three or four miles from the left of our present lines, so keep open the connection with the main body of the army. The Fifth Corps was to cross further this way to go to a point about four miles beyond Armstrong's towards Dinwiddie Court House where it would remain as a support and base from which Davis's cavalry division was to raid on the Boydton road as far as the Court House about three miles beyond Warren's position. The corps started at six-thirty this morning. . . .

❆ ❆ ❆

Wainwright was disgusted by the outcome of the expedition whose start he thus chronicles. The Second and Fifth Corps, with Gregg's cavalry, ran into great difficulties when they tried to move by way of Reams's Station to Dinwiddie Court House to stop the passage of Confederate wagon trains over the Boydton Road into Petersburg. They drove back John Pegram's division, and killed that veteran officer. But a smart Confederate attack resulted in a hasty retreat. "Our men were regularly stampeded," notes Wainwright. "All the officers I have talked with say it was disgraceful beyond anything they have ever seen on the part of the Fifth Corps before." Union losses were heavy, and Grant tried by an extension of his lines to conceal the grim fact that on the whole the Confederates had the advantage in the encounter.

"General Grant, however, does not mean that the public shall get such an idea, and so has ordered our lines to be extended to Armstrong's Mills, which will give the papers a chance to talk about an advance of our lines three miles. I see no other reason for doing it. Any gain there may be for future operations by holding the crossing of Hatcher's Run at this point (if any real gain it is) will be more than counter-balanced by the loss of men through sickness, as also of drill and discipline. . . . It does seem as if Grant never could see further than the length of his nose." So runs Wainwright's acid comment.

❆ ❆ ❆

FEBRUARY 9, THURSDAY. First as to the late expedition. So far as I can learn it did not amount to much; all went well the first day; the Fifth Corps reached its destination in the afternoon, and took up a good posi·

tion. Gregg with his cavalry got onto the Boydton road, and destroyed a few score of waggons. But the attack on the Second Corps at Armstrong's Mills during Sunday afternoon was so sharp that Warren was ordered back to the Vaughn road crossing of Hatcher's Run the same night. . . .

I do not learn that the rebel commissioners accomplished anything. There is no doubt that the soldiers on that side expected that something would be done, for desertions to our lines fell from an average of twenty-five a night to five immediately after they came in. I am glad to learn that desertion to the enemy was about stopped among our men by the hanging process some two months ago; since then, only one single case has been reported. . . .

FEBRUARY 23, THURSDAY. If last week closed with a dearth of news, it has been more than made up the last four days, and we have been almost swamped with dispatches from General Grant telling the army of what is going on elsewhere. . . . The first dispatch came Monday noon, merely saying that "deserters and the Richmond *Journal* report the occupation by our troops of Columbia and Winsboro, South Carolina, and the evacuation of Charleston on Tuesday of last week." Later in the day we got a long dispatch of three closely written pages of extracts from the Richmond papers giving us a full account of Sherman's capture of Columbia, where he made quite a haul of Confederate government property, medical stores, and so on. . . . This was about news enough for one; and was at once followed by orders for me to fire a salute of one hundred guns at noon the next day, Tuesday; which was done well. On Tuesday we got news from General Gilmore, by way of Washington; his dispatch was dated at Charleston, February 18th, Thursday. The rebel troops evacuated the place the night before, and the mayor of the city surrendered it that morning. Everything in the city belonging to the rebel government and all the cotton warehouses were burned; but two hundred heavy guns in good order were left in the forts. Only the poorer inhabitants, with a few exceptions, remained behind. Yesterday's Richmond papers say that they are not allowed to publish any news of "the pending military movements in the Carolinas." . . .

Richmond they say is full of rumours of all sorts. Today they say General J. E. Johnson has been ordered to report to Lee, and it is believed will be put in command of the forces opposed to Sherman. These same papers speak of disturbances all over the country. "A desperate affair occurred last week Tuesday in Lunenburg company between some deserters, and some of the Ninth Virginia cavalry aided by citizens. Several on both sides were wounded." In Henrico County they report a band of one hundred returned paroled soldiers committing wholesale robberies. Other robberies by returned prisoners occur daily in the streets of Richmond. They also report a bill in their Congress to raise 200,000 negro troops as likely to pass. Davis must hurry them up or they will be too late to save him. All this has put our army into great spirits. . . .

The number of deserters coming into our lines steadily increases, averaging fifty in each twenty-four hours. Near seventy had been received at Army Headquarters when I was up there at noon today. An officer from that part of our line reported that 141 came in the night previous on the front of Second Division, Second Corps. He told his story very straight; still I cannot believe that the number was so great as that. . . .

CAMP NEAR JERUSALEM ROAD, MARCH 5, 1865, SUNDAY. Last week continued stormy to the end; if it held up one day it was sure to rain the next; so that I fear my visitors did not have much of a visit. On Thursday we rode to the right of the line, and got a view of the town we have now lain in front of nearly nine months, from the banks of the Appomattox, and also from the top of the Avery house. The Avery house looks very different now from what it did when we had our headquarters there. All the fences are gone, as well as most of the outbuildings, while the interior is much damaged. . . .

MARCH 9, THURSDAY. There was more truth in the rumours of Early's rout which we got from deserters than we were inclined to credit them with. Yesterday Grant sent us Sheridan's dispatch from Waynesboro, which is on the railroad about one-third of the way from Staunton to Charlottesville. . . .

We have no reports as to which way Sheridan went from Waynesboro, but I presume he at least threatened Lynchburg, though it is not probable he could carry the place. The road on which Staunton and Waynesboro are is not of very great importance, but at Charlottesville, which he no doubt captured without much trouble, he would strike one of the main lines between Richmond and Lynchburg. This road he will doubtless destroy largely. If then he can get down and break the James River canal in half a dozen places, Richmond and Lee's army will only have two railroads over which to procure all their supplies. It is possible that he may be able to cross the James and damage both of these, but it will not do to expect too much; and the heavy rains we are having will probably make the river unfordable at any place. The week so far has been one of almost incessant rain; yesterday it poured in torrents. . . .

Sheridan's movement and the apparent falling through of the rebellion makes me look for an early opening to the campaign; so that it behooves me to have my command in a condition to move at any time. I believe that about all the batteries have repaired, and got everything in order. I have just ordered a minute inspection of all the ammunition; also of the horses, with a report on the same. The former is returned as right in all respects, but we are badly horsed. Last year's campaign was the hardest on horse flesh we have ever had; and though I have tried my best to bring them up since then, have been very particular as to care and due exercise, and although all the batteries have had excellent stabling for them this winter, I find that we are likely to commence the campaign in bad order. This is mainly caused by a lack of long forage, without which a horse cannot thrive, do what you may; his belly must be filled and he can no more improve in condition on oats and corn alone than a man can on beef extract, or any other concentrated food. Thirteen pounds of hay per day is the regulation allowance; and in England eight pounds is allowed even for hunters and horses whose bellies it is desired to reduce as much as possible. The past winter our allowance has been reduced to five pounds, and the actual receipts have been between three and four pounds including wood. . . .

MARCH 12, SUNDAY. Three days of perfect quiet, without event here, news from the other armies, or even any orders of moment leaves me but very little to enter here this evening. . . .

I went along our whole line, from Hatcher's Run to Fort Howard, along with General Hunt today. The General was in most excellent spirits, and amused me very much as well as filling me with wonder at his memory. I happened to refer to the *Rejected Addresses** soon after starting; when he took it up, quoting page after page; and then almost whole volumes of comic poetry, interspersed with stories. Still he saw everything as we rode along and was just as much alive to the object of his visit to the lines as if he had been thinking and talking of nothing else. He is certainly one of the most wonderful men I have ever met. With a very retentive memory, he is always forgetting; most original and practical in all his ideas, he is most impractical in carrying them out. . . .

MARCH 15, WEDNESDAY. We have news direct from both Sherman and Sheridan. The former was at Laurel and said he would be at Fayetteville on Saturday last; had met no opposition, and found an abundance of all supplies save sugar and coffee. The news comes through Schofield, who admits a slight reverse with a loss of two guns and some prisoners on the 8th, but claims to have repulsed a severe attack by two corps of Johnston's army on the 10th with a heavy loss to the enemy.

From Sheridan we have a long dispatch dated Columbia, March 10. (Columbia is at the junction of the Rivanna and James Rivers). He reports the very worst sort of weather for his operations, but no other opposition than that caused by the constant rains, and the destruction by the enemy of all the bridges he tried to get over the James River. He

---

* This is more evidence of Wainwright's reading; the *Rejected Addresses* were a clever collection of parodies by James and Horace Smith published in England in 1812.

seems to have made very thorough work in the destruction of the railroads north of the James, and of the canal up as far as to within fifteen miles of Lynchburg. The latter he says has been the main source of supply to Richmond, as I supposed. He now proposes to finish up the canal, as also all the railroads north of Richmond, and then come down here by way of the White House. . . .

As might be supposed, this news has its echo here in loud notes of preparation. Yesterday the orders came, and the word "confidential" underscored at the top at once gave one to understand what he was likely to find below. We are not required to break camp yet, or to have forage and rations loaded up, only to keep the full supply on hand, and everything ready to start on very short notice. All sutlers and camp followers of every sort are to clear out at once. . . .

General Hunt has some hopes now of getting an order from Grant which will tend to put the artillery on a proper footing, and define our duties and rights. Grant at first admitted that he knew nothing about it, had forgotten most of what he learned at West Point, and was totally ignorant as to the organization in other armies. He says that he commenced out West by assigning one battery to each brigade, but found out his mistake. He approves the brigade organization, and promises to issue much such an order as Hunt wants so soon as General Williams returns from his leave. . . .

MARCH 19, SUNDAY. The weather keeps wonderfully fine and warm; more like May than March, even in this latitude. We had a small shower on Thursday evening, but not enough to do any harm. I hope we shall not have to make up for it with a cold, wet spell when we come to move. As it is, this fine weather is very acceptable in making our preparations. . . . My command is now ready to move whenever the orders come; the surplus guns and matériel have been turned in; and all are strong in men. . . .

Two of Sheridan's scouts came in yesterday, having been eight days in getting through from Columbia. They report that they had much difficulty in getting through the country owing to the swarms of rebel deserters everywhere; and they were in constant danger of being arrested and shot as belonging to the number. . . .

✻ ✻ ✻

Lee knew that time was running out for the beleaguered cities of Petersburg and Richmond, and for his army. At the beginning of March 1865 he had only about 50,000 soldiers left in his own army; in North Carolina Joseph E. Johnston had at most 15,000 to oppose the advancing hosts under Sherman and General John M. Schofield. On March 2 General Jubal A. Early's pitiful remnant of between 1,000 and 2,000 troops was destroyed by Sheridan's forces. The Union leaders claimed the capture of 1,600 men, eleven guns, and all Early's supplies. This left Sheridan free to raid far into the rear of Richmond, cutting lines of communication with the South, and then to join Grant with his powerful forces. The Confederacy had reached a point where, against converging Union armies of more than a quarter of a million men, it could pit only 65,000 or 70,000 effective fighters.

If the Confederate forces at Petersburg waited all would be lost; their only course was to strike a blow. Lee had John B. Gordon study the Union lines to ascertain if there was any point at which they might be broken. Gordon reported that this might be feasible on Grant's right, at that part of his works called Fort Stedman; and since A. P. Hill was absent sick, Gordon was given the responsibility of planning and leading the attack. If Fort Stedman could be captured and held, and an attack were then delivered on Grant's communications with his City Point base on the James River, the Union commander would have to abandon some of his lines on his left, or otherwise shorten his front.

Fort Stedman lay only one hundred fifty yards from the Confederate line, and could be dealt with by a surprise attack; five minutes would take the attackers over this distance. It was not a powerful fort; it had no bastion, and the ground behind it was almost as high as its parapet. At four A.M. a Confederate soldier fired the signal shot. "My alert pickets," writes Gordon, "who had crept close to the Union sentinels, sprang like sinewy Ajaxes upon them and prevented the discharge of a single alarm shot." Simultaneously his packed columns of infantry rushed forward. Within a few minutes the Confederates had taken Fort Stedman with nearly 1,000 prisoners, and were turning the guns inside upon the Union lines on the flanks. "The success," Gordon later recalled, "exceeded my most sanguine expectations."

But then everything went wrong for the assault. Gordon's detachments, assigned the task of capturing some small Union forts in the rear of Stedman, failed to find them. General John F. Hartranft with a division of the Ninth Corps made a powerful counterattack that forced Gordon's men back into the main fort. What Gordon calls a "consuming fire" was leveled against his ranks from both flanks. Large numbers of his men chose to surrender rather than endure it. In the end, the Confederates had to retreat, and the Union forces triumphantly reinstalled themselves in their old positions. When the sun went down, Meade's casualties stood at a little over 2,000; those of Lee's army at between 4,000 and 5,000.

* * *

MARCH 26, SUNDAY. Yesterday morning the long quiet of the winter was broken at the first streak of dawn by a very decided attack on our lines. It was a well-conceived affair, a complete surprise, and successful in its first step. If the rebels had as much fight in them now as they had at Gettysburg, they might possibly have driven us out of this entirely, though I am by no means sure of it, for after their first dash all would have been open country and daylight. Our works are strong, and the artillery even of the Ninth Corps I do not believe would be easily stampeded. As it was, their attempt has resulted in real and well-merited glory to the Ninth Corps; in considerable loss to them, and but little to us. Just such an affair as it is good to begin a campaign with, and especially encouraging to the new troops.

I had no occasion to take part in the fight myself, and saw nothing of any part of it. It was very singular, too, that the firing did not awake me, for a single carbine shot on our rear line has repeatedly brought me out of bed; while yesterday morning a score of batteries were firing their best for near half an hour and I did not hear a sound—at least it did not rouse me. A very strong case in evidence that when one's mind is fixed the ear can detect the different directions from which the same sound comes, when one is asleep.*

I was first awakened by Berlin, who came in with an order from General Hunt to turn out all my batteries, and to send word to General Parke that they were at his service. I was partially dressed in one minute and out of my tent. The sun was not yet up; the roar of artillery was constant and very loud; squads of the battery men were standing in their parks and one or two officers were up. Most of the camp, though, were still asleep, for reveille had not sounded, and no one had had sense enough to rouse the camp. I called out to Mink's guard to turn out all the battery and pass the word on to the others. . . . Mink and Rogers were the first ready to haul out, so I started them off at a trot, and sent Captain Berlin to inform Tidball of it. It seemed to me as if no one had any life in them, as if no one moved; yet I believe it was not more than twenty minutes from the time of my getting Hunt's first order until the time the two batteries started. . . .

When, an hour or so later, the firing slacked off, I went up to Army Headquarters to hear exactly what was the matter, as I knew nothing beyond the fact that the enemy had broken through our lines at Fort Stedman. I left everything in camp ready for whatever might turn up and took Canfield and three or four orderlies with me.

* In this confused sentence Wainwright apparently means to say that a mind subconsciously alert can, even when sound asleep, detect minor sounds, while a fully relaxed sleeper may fail to hear even the loudest noises.

At Army Headquarters I found Hunt acting as commander of the army. General Meade and Webb had both passed the night with their wives on board the steamboat at City Point, and Parke has as much as he could do to look after his own command. The railroad from City Point was stopped, and it was some little time before Meade could return; indeed, the affair of the morning was quite over before he got back. . . .

Fort Stedman is, I believe, the farthest to the right of any of our enclosed work; at the point, near the Hare house, where we got nearest to the town. Our lines here make a slight salient angle, while those of the enemy form a much larger one, so that the two are less than a couple of hundred yards apart. The attack is said to have been made by two divisions, small ones I judge, and was under General Gordon. It was a complete surprise, hardly giving even the pickets time to fire, and many of the fort's garrison were taken in their blankets. They also carried two or three of the open batteries, on either side of the work, and captured most all the troops on the line there. But before they got to Fort Haskell, the next enclosed work to the left, its garrison were up, and the attack being a weak one, failed. . . .

Lee's intention doubtless was to seize the high ground around "Meade Station," clean out our line to the Appomattox, and so cut off our communications with City Point. But his troops were evidently not willing, and the reports of deserters, that their men would not attack, proved to be essentially correct. The time lost by Gordon's reserves not coming up enabled Parke to get a line formed on this ridge, and to garnish it with a number of guns from his left, so that the captured work became too hot for its holders; and when Hartranft's division was thrown forward, they recaptured all our line with comparatively little trouble. . . .

So soon as General Meade returned, he ordered an advance of the whole Second and Sixth Corps to take the rebel picket line, which was very strongly entrenched so as to make almost a regular line of works. This was done, with the gain of some six or eight hundred more prisoners, and the new position held by a strong infantry force; the enemy failing in an attempt to retake them late in the afternoon. . . .

The whole army is feeling very jubilant today over the affair, and as General Meade said to me this morning, "wish they would try it every day." What will be the next move?—a very few days will now show. Reports that Lee is getting ready to withdraw are very thick; also some rumours that Johnston is falling back to join him. . . .

MARCH 27, MONDAY. Signs of an early move thicken around us so fast that I want to keep well written up, though as yet no orders have come. This morning Sheridan's cavalry arrived. I met them in the woods between here and Ninth Corps headquarters. They looked as if they had had a hard march of it: the officers very seedy. I saw several of my acquaintances, formerly commanders of horse batteries, but now most of them colonels of volunteer cavalry regiments, and commanding brigades. Sheridan has shown great good judgment in getting these appointments. Such men as Pennington, Bardoe, and Fitzhugh, young, enterprising, and ambitious, who have served with the cavalry for several years, are just the ones to make dashing leaders. They were full of stories about their late raid, which appears to have been perfectly successful, and very thorough in its destructions. The dry weather has made the roads excessively dusty, and I do not know when I have seen such a dirty-looking lot of men. . . .

NEAR HATCHER'S RUN, MARCH 28, TUESDAY. Strong as the evidences were yesterday, I did not expect the orders to move which came this morning, quite so soon. They were issued from Meade's headquarters yesterday, but did not reach me until this morning. Since then, we have been all activity, breaking up our camp in which I have taken so much pride, and packing off all surplus traps; for I moved up here close to corps headquarters this afternoon, with my little command, now reduced to a smaller number than I have had since I took charge of the artillery of a corps.

The move is ordered to begin tomorrow morning at three o'clock: the Fifth Corps leading off across Hatcher's Run, striking the Vaughan road some distance down, at its junction with the old stage road, where we are to open communications with the Second Corps, and then occupy a position near Dinwiddie Court House. . . .

At Army Headquarters I learned that Sherman was at City Point last night, and urged very strongly that this army should not move until he got into Virginia; but Grant was unwilling to accede to his advice. The only reasons I can see for not taking it are that Lee may be withdrawing anyway, and the possibility that Sherman, in getting here, might be detained so long that Lee could repair his lines of supply north of the James. Unless, indeed, Grant is jealous of all the praise Sherman is getting, his name being decidedly the most popular among the people now. . . .

❋ ❋ ❋

The day before the failure of the Confederate attack on Fort Stedman—that is, on March 24—Grant had issued orders for the general forward movement that he hoped would break the Confederate lines southwest of Petersburg, cut off Richmond, and compel Lee's evacuation. As Wainwright says, Sherman wished for a wait until he could arrive from Goldsboro, North Carolina, but that would not be until mid-April; and Grant, as he writes in his memoirs, was "determined to move as soon as the roads and weather would admit of my doing so." General Edward O. C. Ord now commanded the Department of Virginia. Grant had him come down from the north bank of the James on the night of the 27th, to take his place with a large command of infantry and cavalry on the extreme Union left. General Godfrey Weitzel, who had succeeded Ben Butler as head of the Army of the James, held chief command north of the river, ready to move into Richmond as soon as opportunity offered.

"Ord was at his place promptly," writes Grant. "Humphreys and Warren were then on our extreme left with the Second and Fifth Corps. They were directed on the arrival of Ord, and on getting into position in their places, to cross Hatcher's Run and extend out west to Five Forks, the object being to get into a position from which we could strike the Southside Railroad and ultimately the Danville Railroad." He adds that the two corps had to do considerable fighting in taking up their new positions, and that in the battle of White Oak Road, March 30 and April 1, they met heavy losses. The Confederate line covering Petersburg on the southwest, after crossing Hatcher's Run, extended west along White Oak Road. Five Forks, a point where five roads met, lay only a little over a mile beyond the terminus of this line.

Sheridan meanwhile, on March 26, ended his long marches at City Point. Horses and men were jaded; the general himself was tired. But he, too, had to play a part in the movement commencing on the 29th, and he was shaken and irritated when he found just what he was expected to do. Grant made it plain that he hoped to capture Five Forks, make the two railroads just named unusable, and end the war without losing his grip on Lee's army. Yet he knew that he might fail, that Lee might get away to the southward. If this happened, he wished Sheridan to join Sherman in North Carolina and unite with him in destroying Joe Johnston's army.

But Grant believed it would not happen. "I told him that, as a matter of fact, I intended to close the war right here, with this movement, and that he should go no farther. His face at once brightened up, and slapping his hand on his leg, he said: 'I am glad to hear it and we can do it.' " March 29 came with good weather. The roads had dried fairly well, and Grant moved out to the southwest of Petersburg, leaving around that city only a sufficient force to hold his entrenchments. As rain soon set in again, he had to stop to corduroy his roads, but he kept stubbornly on. Lee was about to have his right turned, and be encircled, unless he made some countermove. He told President Davis that the Confederate government might have ten or twelve days to leave Richmond.

＊ ＊ ＊

QUAKER ROAD, MARCH 29, WEDNESDAY. The day opened fine for a march, mild and clear; clouding up in the afternoon, however, and beginning to rain at sundown. General Ayres had the advance moving punctually at three o'clock, followed by "B" and "H" First New York, and the pontoons. Next Griffin's division followed by the other three batteries, and then Crawford with the trains last. As we expected a fight, everything was brought into fighting trim. . . .

We crossed Hatcher's Run without trouble near the W. Perkins house, where the main trains of both this and the Second Corps are camped tonight; and went on to our appointed place at the junction of the Vaughn and Stage roads. . . .

Before the First and Third Divisions had reached their positions, orders came changing our destination, and directing Warren to move down the Quaker road to the Boydton Plank. Whether this change was Meade's or Grant's doings I do not know, nor on what it was founded, but am inclined to attribute it to Grant's fondness for his old plans, and love for getting possession of more ground to the left. We certainly were moving farther off from Sheridan, whose operations we were supposed to be supporting. . . .

We crossed Gravelly Run without opposition, or much trouble. Crawford's division and Rawles's were halted here while Griffin pushed on. The open ground to the north of the Run is some three or four hundred yards wide; then comes a belt of heavy timber, on entering which we found the road stopped by felled trees, some of them very large, which detained Mitchell until they could be cleared. About one hundred fifty yards through the wood was an opening of some hundred acres mostly on the right of the road, around a house marked "R. Spain" on the map. Chamberlain's brigade was formed in line, the other two following in column; we had seen no sign of the enemy up to this time, and Warren had gone back to the Run. As Chamberlain's skirmishers advanced into the wood beyond, they first struck the enemy, who fell back rapidly until, as usual, they had developed Chamberlain's line, when they struck him hard along his whole front and on his left flank. The brigade held well, better than I have seen our men do for some time under similar circumstances, and fell back fighting. But when they got into the opening, the rebs had the advantage of cover, and yelled fearfully.

It was just as they gave this yell that the road was cleared enough for Mitchell to get his guns through, and as Fitzhugh, who had been forward with Griffin and knew the lay of the land, came back for him; I sent Mitchell forward, and galloped back to hurry up Rawles, and to find General Warren to know if I had not better send for one or two of the

batteries with Ayres. I met Warren just coming into the wood, and
Rawles whom I had sent for. General Warren told me to set up two more
batteries and to hurry up Crawford. My staff I had left with the corps
staff on the bluff above the Run, where I rode to give the orders for the
two more batteries. While there, Mitchell rode up to me saying, "I have
got it this time, General," and sure enough he had; his right arm hung
helpless at his side, while five steady streams of blood ran from the
fingers of his gauntlet. He had been hit almost so soon as he got his guns
into position, just above the elbow, smashing the bone all to pieces.
He would not bring a man off with him, but rode back half a mile alone.
Fortunately, Dr. Winne was standing by, who took charge of him at
once. Winne says that he will undoubtedly lose his arm, and probably
his life; but I hope not. . . .

The two guns opened with canister at once, doing splendid service. I
did not see it myself, but I realized the scene fully, for as I heard the
first report, the rebel yell ceased, and the next moment our men hurrahed. How often have I seen the same thing with the first notes of the
battery! The rebel charge hesitates, stops, and our men begin to rally;
then if you can get a counter-charge, all is safe. The other two pieces
were put into position on the right, and as the enemy fell back, the whole
battery, under Lieutenant Vose, was moved up near Spain's house; and
Rawles coming up then, Fitzhugh put one of his sections on either side of
"B." Chamberlain told me that he should have been gone had not the
battery got in when it did. . . .

Altogether the afternoon's result was favourable to us. We had the best
of the fight and had secured a short line of connection with the left of
our old works at Armstrong's Mills, along the rear of which a road was
to be opened by morning. It began to rain soon after dark, not heavily
but steady, as if it intended to continue. My spring waggon came up,
and when I returned from examining the new line, two tents were just
going up, and supper being got ready. Corps headquarters waggon was
not up for some unknown reason, and when Warren came back from
Meade's headquarters there was a scene. I was just near enough to catch
a word now and then: they fell on Locke and everyone around, and were
fearful, worse if anything than that night at Bethesda Church. The devil
within him seemed to be stirring all day, and I presume something had
been said at Army Headquarters which he did not like.

Presently Locke came over to me, and asked me to invite the General
to supper with me. This I had already resolved to do, but thought that it
would sound most easy, and as if I had not heard any of the goings on,
did I wait until just as it was being served.

Accordingly when all was ready I walked up, and said, "General, I am
lucky enough to have a pair of broiled chickens for supper tonight, and

as I see your waggon has not yet arrived, should be glad if you will come over and help eat them." He, however, refused, and for him, politely; but could not help damning his staff. "If a corps commander could not get his own supper" he did "not see why they should sponge on their subordinates, and he'd be damned if he would." I did not attempt to reason, but tried to tempt him by praising my supper, and saying that Fitzhugh was absent and I should have to eat it almost alone; but could get nothing more out of him.

Later and just before I turned in, I again tried him with the offer of a bed, but it was the same answer: "If I can't sleep in my own tent, I'll be damned if I sleep in anyone else's"; and the last thing I heard as I went to bed were his mumbled oaths as he sat under a tree in the same spot he had been in for two hours. I have not put this down so particularly save as proof of what I have for some time past been convinced, viz: that these awful fits of passion are a disease with Warren, and a species of insanity, over which he has no control. . . .

MARCH 30, THURSDAY. We have had a steady rain all day, not heavy however. Shortly before daylight our First Division was advanced from the wood to the junction of the Boydton and Quaker roads, the Second Corps moving up at the same time. . . .

❋ ❋ ❋

Grant's advance southwest of Petersburg to encircle Lee and cut his two indispensable lines of communication, the railroad from Richmond to Danville, and the branch from Petersburg called the Southside Railroad, was impeded by rain until on March 31 he vigorously resumed it. That day Lee attacked Warren's Fifth Corps and Sheridan's cavalry, gaining so marked a temporary success that Sheridan asked Grant for reinforcements. Orders were accordingly sent to Warren to move his corps to Dinwiddie Court House and report to Sheridan; but he was very slow in moving. Directed to march the night of the 31st, he did not get off until five the next morning, and then he let Gravelly Run, swollen by the rains, delay him excessively. Sheridan meanwhile moved forward without waiting. He struck the Confederate army at Five Forks, and by nightfall had won what he termed an unqualified victory: "We had overthrown Pickett, taken six guns, thirteen battleflags, and nearly six thousand prisoners."

This was on April 1. Grant, informed that Sheridan had carried everything before him, ordered an assault on the Confederate lines early the next day; and the result was another decisive success. Confederate morale was disintegrating, and the Southern ranks were crumbling. On the morning of the 2nd, a Sunday, Jefferson Davis was at church when a messenger tiptoed in and touched his arm. He hastily left, for Lee had sent word that his position had become untenable, and he was evacuating Richmond and Petersburg that night. The news spread at once throughout the Confederate capital, causing tremendous excitement and confusion. At eleven that evening a special train on the Danville Railroad, still precariously open, carried most of the high officers of government, including Davis, away to Danville. The last soldiers marched out before the sun rose high on April 3, leaving a city in which a mob of irresponsible men and women, black and white, had fired many buildings, and attempted a general plunder of shops.

It was Lee's intention to march his now demoralized army to the Roanoke River, and try there to unite his forces with those of Johnston. His immediate objective was Amelia Court House, and he reached this point on the morning of April 4. But Grant's forces, with the cavalry in the van, were hot in pursuit.

❊ ❊ ❊

BUTLER HOUSE, BOYDTON ROAD, MARCH 31, FRIDAY. The day opened wet, and though the rain held up before noon, it did not clear off, but came on again in spells at different times. About daylight a division of the Second Corps relieved our First and Third in the works they had thrown up along the plank road for half a mile or more to the left of the Quaker road junction. . . .

WHITE OAK ROAD, APRIL 1, 1865, SATURDAY. This has been the most momentous day of the war so far, I think; a glorious day; a day of real victory. But to begin at the beginning and tell what I saw myself. During the night, that is, soon after five o'clock and before daylight, I was awakened, and on joining Warren, he informed me that he was going to move to Sheridan's support with all his infantry; that Ayres's division had already gone down the plank, and he was just starting across country with the other two to try for the flank of the force opposed to Sheridan. . . .

About one P.M. I received an order from General Warren to take two batteries out to him, and started at once with Mink and Hazelton. . . . General Warren had not fallen in with any force of the enemy, and in accordance with orders from Meade had reported with his whole corps to Sheridan. During the morning Sheridan had again advanced with his cavalry from the Court House, the enemy falling back skirmishing to the White Oak road, where the Ford road crosses it, at a place called the Five Forks. Here they had a line of low breastworks thrown up rudely along the north side of the White Oak road, and extending for a mile of more to either side of the Ford road. . . .

When I got up to Warren the whole of the Fifth Corps was just about

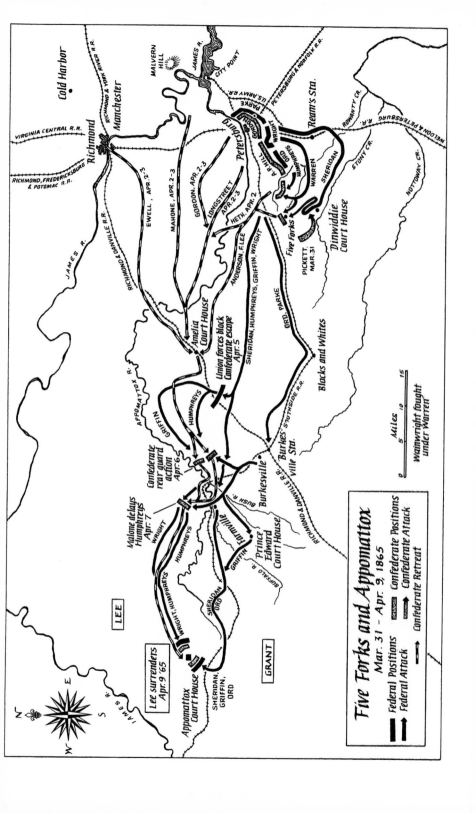

Five Forks and Appomattox
Mar. 31 – Apr. 9, 1865

to attack at this angle, and along the east flank, swinging around to the west with its pivot of the White Oak road. Ayres's division held the left, Winthrop's brigade crossing the road diagonally. Crawford was on Ayres's right, and Griffin in rear of Crawford. Much of this I have, of course, learned since, mostly from Ayres, who gave me a very clear account of the dispositions.

When I reached Warren, he was in conversation with General Sheridan, close behind Ayres's second line. Our skirmishers were just engaging, the men beginning to advance, and rebel bullets coming over our way somewhat thick. I waited several minutes for Sheridan to get through what he was saying before I spoke to Warren. As there was nothing for me to do, I then rode back out of the way of stray bullets, to an open ridge south of the road and not far from a small church, called Gravel Run Church, where our hospital was being established.

As our men passed through a narrow belt of woods, I could not see the actual charge on the works, only the smoke of the battle. The cheers of our men, however, told me that all was going well, and long files of prisoners coming in soon shewed that the works were carried. . . .

I do not think that it was over twenty minutes from the time I left Warren before I saw the first squad of prisoners turning down the road to the church. I then rode up to this road to learn what I could of the fight, and see the prisoners. Presently old Wiedrich came along, wounded in one arm, but in charge of a good thousand rebels, as near as I could calculate. These men all moved along cheerfully, without one particle of that sullenness which formerly characterized them under similar circumstances. They joked with our men along the line and I repeatedly head them say, "We are coming back into the Union, boys, we are coming back into the Union." It was a joyful and an exciting sight, seeming to say that the war was about over, the great rebellion nearly quelled.

But soon I saw that which was not joyful. In the very middle of these thousand prisoners, captured by his own brigade, came poor Winthrop; dead or at least very nearly dead, quite insensible and borne on the shoulders of four of his men.* He had fallen just inside the rebel works, himself one of the first to cross them; he never spoke or shewed any signs of consciousness. It was a glorious death to die, in the very moment of victory; a glorious funeral procession, the victor's body surrounded by the prisoners he had captured. But very sad to be shot down so young, so beloved, so promising, just as the fight appears to be closing, and after having gone through four years of it unscathed.

This procession of prisoners was soon followed by another quite as numerous or even larger.

* Frederick Winthrop, the New York brevet brigadier general previously mentioned by Wainwright with high praise.

I then passed out onto the White Oak road, and rode up it westward as the firing was rapidly becoming more distant. . . .

At the Forks I found two guns, three-inch, just in their works, and Pennington sitting on one of them. I stopped here and had a talk with him and several other cavalry officers, formerly light battery commanders. They told me that they had charged the works at this point and carried them with any number of prisoners. While there Crawford came down the Ford road, from the north, looking for Warren, and told me that there were more guns up the road which his men had taken. I went up the Ford road then. Some fifty yards up I found another gun, unlimbered and pointing east; perhaps a hundred yards further on two more standing in the road limbered, and one of them with three live horses to it. Also three caissons, much damaged, the spokes of the wheels being so badly cut as to be useless. This made a total of *five* three-inch guns. I rode some little distance farther but found no more guns. . . .

I turned back and pushed along the White Oak road to find Warren. I must have gone at least two miles, and about one mile west of the end of the rebel works before I found him. It was growing dark, the sun having already set; the bugles were sounding the recall; the pursuit was over, and the divisions getting together for the night. I told the General about the guns, and asked if I was to look after their removal. For this he referred me to Sheridan, as he said there might be some jealousy on the part of the cavalry.

We rode back together looking for Sheridan, and found him with his staff about a fire near the west end of the rebel works. Here I waited while General Warren had a short conversation with Sheridan. Then I dismounted, reported to Sheridan the number of guns I had found, and asked if he wished me to remove them; at the same time stating that Pennington claimed to have captured at least two of them. Sheridan was very pleasant, said that there was glory enough for all, and wished me to look after the guns.

Meanwhile Warren had ridden on with Bankhead. When I overtook them, they were both dismounted, and Warren talking earnestly. I also got off my horse, told Warren what directions Sheridan had given me, and inquired where corps headquarters would be for the night. Warren replied that General Sheridan had just informed him that he had relieved him from the command of the corps, and turned it over to Griffin; that he had given no reason for so doing, but referred him to General Grant, to whom he was to report for orders.

I was astonished at this news and could not imagine what the trouble was. The only thing that occurred to me was that Warren might have got into one of his ugly fits and said what he ought not to. But in that case he would have been relieved at once instead of its being put off until after the fight was all over. Beside which I had left them just at the commencement of the battle in apparently amicable talk.

Later in the evening I saw Major George Forsyth, Sheridan's senior aide, and asked him about it. He, too, expressed surprise at the removal and told me he knew of no cause; that soon after the rebel works were carried Sheridan had turned around and asked his own staff who knew where General Warren was. None of them had seen him since the advance on the line. Presently meeting Griffin, Sheridan put the same question to him. Then finding that neither Griffin nor his staff had seen Warren, he, Sheridan, ordered Griffin to take command of the corps. First, however, he inquired who was the ranking division commander. On learning that it was Crawford, he pooh-poohed; and then told Griffin that by authority from General Grant he placed him in command. . . .

I may as well put down here what Bankhead told me the next day; that in swinging around, Crawford's division separated from Ayres's, keeping off too much to the north; that Warren sent twice, the second officer sent being Bankhead, to recall him; and finally went himself and brought the division round. Griffin meantime seeing the gap left between the Second and Third Divisions, closed up on Ayres's left and took the place Crawford should have occupied. Crawford, I hear, says that there was a swamp in his way; of this I know nothing save that the First Division crossed the ground. It was Warren's having to go himself to bring Crawford back which was the immediate occasion of his removal, though it could not have been the actual cause.

This must, or certainly should have been, something very serious; otherwise Warren's removal in the moment of victory was a most cruel, not to say unjust thing. In talking of it since with General Bartlett who commanded a brigade in the First Division, I found he threw the whole blame on Crawford. He told me that a week or so before we moved, he went with Griffin and Ayres to Warren, and told him seriously that if he did not get rid of Crawford, Crawford would certainly be the cause of his losing his command; and referred to Spotsylvania and one or two other cases where, by his bungling or what not, Crawford had brought him into great trouble.

To me his removal at this time, and after the victory had been won, appears wrong and very cruel. It seems that even had he been removed just before, the victory should have covered up very big faults, and Sheridan should have restored him at once. . . .

I do not exactly like the idea of serving under Griffin; we have never got along well together, and I do not like him. It was one o'clock when I got to bed; up to that time and later there was a steady and very heavy cannonade kept up from dark along the old lines in front of

Petersburg. We can see the shells burst at times and watch the flight of
some of the big bombs. We start again at daylight.

The fight today was well planned. Ayres is loud in his praise of it. In
one respect, though, it was queer, viz: that cavalry attacked the works in
front, while infantry turned them. This I presume was owing to the
position of the two corps; our cavalry, too, are more mounted infantry
than anything else, all having carbines and fighting on foot. I did not
see any cavalry in pursuit of the enemy, but there may have been a few.

* * *

William A. Ganoe, one of the most careful historians of the United States
army, writes of General Warren: "At Five Forks, April 1, 1865, the last
decisive battle of the war, his corps, after conflicting orders, arrived with
dispatch on the flank of the Confederates and offered to the cavalry's hard-
pressed troops the signal aid that clinched the victory; but to the astonishment of his subordinates and others engaged in that critical action, he was
summarily relieved of command by Sheridan, who had been given authority by General Grant." Wainwright's narrative bears out this statement
as to the astonishment of Warren's subordinates. The experienced engineer
who had graduated second in his class at West Point; who had carried out
important surveys of Western rivers; who had been wounded at Gaines's
Mill and promoted major general after Second Manassas, Antietam, and
Fredericksburg; whose quick perception of the importance of Little Round
Top and skillful seizure of that eminence had been a decisive element in the
Union victory at Gettysburg, where he was again wounded; and who had
now commanded the Fifth Corps for a whole year of heavy fighting—this
rough but able officer was summarily deprived of his command by a general
known for his passionate temper, who had been suspended at West Point
for a year because he chased a superior there with fixed bayonet. Why did
Sheridan so humiliate his fellow New Yorker?

Colonel Theodore Lyman thought that Sheridan had nursed a grievance
against both Meade and Warren ever since the day when Meade accused
him of impeding the march of Warren's Fifth Corps to Spotsylvania, so
that the Confederates occupied that important point before the Union infantry arrived. Moreover, Grant felt a distrust for Warren because the corps
commander had a way, at times, of substituting his own judgment for that
of the lieutenant general. Grant admits in his memoirs that "there was no
officer more capable, nor one more prompt in acting, than Warren when
the enemy forced him to it." But he accuses Warren of disobeying orders by
failing to follow up the advantages he gained; and he asserts that Warren

was likely to show unexpected hesitancies, and make unwarranted objections, when his own superior demanded action. When, on April 1, Crawford's division of the Fifth Corps retreated to escape a severe crossfire from the Confederates, delaying the time table for the assault upon Lee at Five Forks, Sheridan thought Warren's dilatory ways intolerable.

"I had sent a staff officer to General Sheridan to call his attention to these defects," wrote Grant later, "and to say that as much as I liked General Warren, now was not a time when we could let our personal feelings for anyone stand in the way of success; and if his removal was necessary to success, not to hesitate." Thus Grant and Sheridan were jointly responsible for the removal of Warren for delays really attributable to Samuel W. Crawford, who had come into the army from medical school, and in lesser degree to S. G. Griffin, two division commanders (though Crawford had twice previously been a corps commander for brief intervals).

Warren was not a man to rest quietly under the stigma now placed upon him. Though he was unable to obtain a board of inquiry so long as Grant and Sheridan were in high authority, he finally appeared before one appointed in the Hayes Administration. It completely exonerated him, with praise, and with implied censure for the manner of his removal. Unhappily, the verdict came when he was three months dead.

❊ ❊ ❊

NEAR SOUTHERLAND'S STATION, APRIL 2, SUNDAY.   No fighting today for the Fifth Corps; only a hard and tiring march. There seemed to be considerable uncertainty as to how we had best move. I do not know all the ways the infantry divisions went, but my two batteries first started west along the White Oak road. I was still sitting by where our tents had been, trying to finish a short letter home, when cheer after cheer rang from the troops along the road. I supposed that Sheridan was riding by; for he excites the greatest enthusiasm among the men, and is greeted whenever seen with such cheers as I have not heard given to any officer since McClellan's day.

But this time I was mistaken—the hurrahs were for the fall of Petersburg this morning, news of which had just arrived. I know nothing more of it tonight than that the Sixth Corps carried the rebel works early in the morning at some point west of the Weldon Railroad, that the Ninth then carried those in their front, which were turned by the Sixth, and that all the other corps soon after advanced. Wild stories are told of the number of prisoners and great generals captured; none of which, however, have come to me very direct.

The fall of Petersburg caused our corps to counter-march, and push rapidly up the White Oak road eastward to cut off any of the enemy who might try to retreat by that way. . . .

Of course, yesterday's fight has been the great topic of conversation among the men today. Ryder, our corps provost-marshal, tells me that he sent off about 4,000 prisoners this morning; the cavalry claim to have captured as many more. Very likely some of the cavalry prisoners went to Ryder. If we got a total of five or six thousand it would be a large haul. We also have twenty colours. Most of the prisoners seemed glad to get in. One man I even heard exclaim, "It does me good to see the old flag again." . . .

ON RIVER ROAD NEAR DEEP CREEK, APRIL 3, MONDAY. There was an alarm on Crawford's front during the night, and considerable firing on the part of his men. Some stray body of rebels ran against while trying to join their main force. . . .

I pushed to the front myself and found Sheridan and Griffin at a small house near two miles from where we started from and at what appeared to be the end of this road. Sheridan's scouts had brought him word that Lee's army was passing near the Appomattox, and trying to cross at the mouth of Namozine Creek. Arrived here, he found that it could have been but a small force and they were all gone by. We waited here an hour or more, while the scouts were searching the country for the enemy, and for a road by which to get at them. These scouts were a motley set of men, near a dozen in number; not particularly hard or daring looking. All were dressed in partial rebel uniform, and certainly would never be taken as belonging to our men. From what I saw of them today, I was by no means favourably impressed with the accuracy of the reports which they brought.

While at this house, I saw a good deal of Sheridan; he appeared exceedingly affable and pleasant in his intercourse with his staff, but certainly would not impress one by his looks any more than Grant does. He is short, thickset, and common Irish-looking. Met in the Bowery, one would certainly set him down as a "b'hoy"; and his dress is in perfect keeping with that character. His Irish blood shone out today in the haphazard way he drove ahead, first on one road, then on another, seeming to think that infantry and artillery could go wherever his own horse did, and a whole corps turn in an equally small space. . . .

The scouts having finally reported that the enemy had passed by a path through the wood where the guns were found and that the road was practicable, the whole corps started off by that route. The five batteries had joined me by this time so they all moved together. We got about a mile pretty well but then began to stall. . . . All the rest of the day we moved rapidly; and by the aid of two or three more mistakes in the road have made a long march of it. As near as I can estimate it, all my batteries have marched full thirty miles. . . .

I had quite a talk with Crawford while waiting for the batteries to come up. He claims to have done more than either of the other divisions at Five Forks, to have captured all the guns, and so on. He complained somewhat of Griffin being put over him, but not so much as I expected. The cavalry I believe have been ahead, that is, to the west of us, all day. I have not heard of any fighting, but doubtless a good many prisoners have been picked up or come in voluntarily.

While at the Creek, we received a dispatch from Army Headquarters, saying that Richmond was evacuated last night. Weitzel found their works abandoned on advancing to attack them this morning. So, after three years of fighting, it is not after all the Army of the Potomac which enters Richmond as victors.* Petersburg itself, I learn, was not carried yesterday; Lee had an inner line of works quite close to the town, which he abandoned last night. They say that one of the hills was captured yesterday. To all intents the rebellion may be said now to be over; certainly it is on its last legs. If those legs are long enough to enable Lee to get around us and join Johnston in North Carolina, they may be strong enough to give us one more big fight. All the heart and spirit being gone, though, strength of leg is not likely to amount to much.

JETERSVILLE, APRIL 4, TUESDAY.   Another hard day's march; not equal to yesterday's however, for we have kept the roads; but these were badly cut up, many of Lee's teams apparently having gone over them before us. A pursuing army has hard work in this country, as we have found even from our first campaign on the Peninsula. This place is on the Danville Railroad, and about ten miles west of Amelia Court House, where Lee is said to be tonight, with his main force. So we have got ahead of him, and cut him off from his direct route to join Johnston. . . .

APRIL 5, WEDNESDAY.   In the same position, and Lee said to be still at Amelia, yet no fight. It seems to me queer for Lee must have known that there was only one corps of infantry here, until quite late in the afternoon. I cannot understand it; for it was a grand chance for him, if he has any large force with him. Now we are much too strong for him to break through and shall probably attack him tomorrow if he remains overnight. Our first work this morning was to rectify and entrench our line. Daylight shewed our position to be a capital one against an attack in front. What the cavalry left flank was I do not know; our own right he was not very likely to try, as a movement in that direction would throw him directly toward the other advancing corps. Our men built excellent works, and I got my guns in nicely advanced batteries, two at each of the roads running through our lines, and one between, so that

---

* It was of course the Army of the James.

I could cross a fire in front of our whole line. When the works were done, I almost wished Lee would attack, we had such a nice position, and our men were in such fine spirits. Meade and Hunt came up about three o'clock; the latter on seeing what a fine field of fire I had for my guns, asked if I was not sorry not to have had a chance to use them. A couple of hours later the Second and Sixth Corps arrived and went in on either side of us, our corps contracting its front somewhat. . . .

* * *

By this time, Lee's hope of gaining his objectives, Danville and a junction with Joseph E. Johnston's forces, had dwindled almost to despair. His hungry troops had marched into Amelia Court House on April 4 to find plenty of artillery ammunition but no food; and the wagons he at once sent out for supplies came back almost empty. The country was bare. As many of Lee's men were from southern Virginia and North Carolina, they were drifting away to their homes. On the 5th the main part of the army, wet, dispirited, and still hungry, set out southwestward on their circuitous way to Danville. But Lee and Longstreet, following on horseback early in the afternoon, proceeded only seven miles before they came upon the Union troops entrenching squarely in front. The path forward had been blocked. When Lee forced his worn veterans to undertake an evasive night march April 5–6, bad roads and a broken bridge slowed his columns to a crawl. On the morning of the 6th he heard that his wagon trains had been attacked, broken up, and captured; and that afternoon fresh Union forces, resisting the retreat at Sayler's (or Sailor's) Creek, practically destroyed the forces of Ewell and R. H. Anderson. The end was at hand.

Coming out above Sayler's Creek, Lee found the fact forced upon him. Writes Douglas Freeman: "It was such a sight as his eyes had never beheld: streaming out of the bottom and up the ridge were teamsters without their wagons, soldiers without their guns, and shattered regiments without their officers, a routed wreck!" Not far ahead lay Appomattox Court House.

* * *

WEBBER'S FORD, APRIL 6, THURSDAY. We moved out at daylight this morning, the Fifth Corps leading the infantry, for Lee's position at Amelia Court House, but soon learned from the cavalry which was ahead of us that he had cleared out during the night and passed around to the north of us. This corps then moved north to Flat Creek and from there to Paineville; where we struck a fine wide road which we followed until we struck the Appomattox at this point. . . .

The Second Corps struck the enemy's rear at Dentonsville or a little beyond, and kept up a running fight with it all the rest of the day. After three o'clock we could not only hear them, but distinctly see the smoke of their guns; still we were unable to get far enough ahead to close in on them at all, though we pushed as hard as it was possible for the men to go.

PRINCE EDWARD'S COURT HOUSE, APRIL 7, FRIDAY.   Another awful hard march; not so many miles passed over perhaps as yesterday, but many more hours on the road, and very much more fatiguing to man and beast. I did not get into camp until after eleven o'clock, and then was so completely tired out that I went to bed supperless sooner than lose half an hour's sleep. The Fifth Corps was again ordered to report to Sheridan; I presume because it was supposed to be the freshest, not having had any fighting yesterday. . . .

BIVOUAC, APRIL 8, SATURDAY.   Finding that Lee was not coming this way, but had struck for Lynchburg, we started early at a running pace. The Fifth Corps went out from Prince Edward's Court House by the road leading past the college, running north.* I should say. Some four miles out, near a small stream, we had to wait full two hours for the cavalry to pass us; Custer's division. . . .

The day has been a good one for marching, and the country level. Neither that we passed through yesterday nor today will compare in fertility or beauty with the counties north of the railroad; indeed, it is about as sterile as any I have seen. Most of it is wooded. We are now under Sheridan's orders, but divided from him by the whole Army of the James, which Ord by his superior rank thrust in between us and the cavalry, though the head of our column did reach Prospect Church a little before his did. Our march must have been full twenty miles, which would be a good distance had we been able to travel right along; but as we were twenty hours doing it, it was really as fatiguing as thirty miles would have been without the detentions. I forgot to mention yesterday that a dispatch from Webb reported the captures at Sailor's Creek at 12,000 men, 13 guns, 300 waggons, and 6 generals beside Ewell. . . .

APPOMATTOX COURT HOUSE, APRIL 9, SUNDAY.   I may head the account of this day in large letters, for its events close the rebellion. The Army of Northern Virginia under Lee has been its main strength, and today that army has surrendered. During three long and hard-fought campaigns it has withstood every effort of the Army of the Potomac; now at the commencement of the fourth, it is obliged to succumb without even one great pitched battle. Could the war have been closed with such a battle as Gettysburg, it would have been more glorious for us; more in accordance with what poetical justice would seem to owe to the Army of the

---

* Prince Edward, a county named for a son of George II, had at its seat, Farmville, an institution called the Farmville Female College; later a state teachers' college.

Potomac. As it is, the rebellion has been worn out rather than suppressed. The 9th of April will, however, be a day forever to be remembered with thanksgiving throughout our land.

Sheridan's cavalry struck the head of Lee's retreating army last night near Appomattox Station on the railroad, and was able to seize and hold the road to Lynchburg in advance of them; the main road at this point coming down quite near to the railroad. With the first break of day our corps was again in motion. On arriving at the station after a couple of hours' march, the corps was massed a short distance to the north of it. Ord's command was already in position and pushing slowly to the north toward the Court House, meeting with some resistence from Lee's advance. I could not see anything from where I was, but the musketry was at no time heavy; most of the firing seeming to be artillery. In half an hour or so I saw our divisions forming line and advancing, so I rode forward to see whether the batteries would not be needed. On my way, I met one of Griffin's aides with orders for me to move up two batteries as quick as possible. Taking "B" and "H," First New York, I pushed forward as fast as I could, but having no directions exactly where to go, nor anyone to show me the road, we lost some time by going astray, and in finding a road across an ugly ravine.

The country here is broken into abrupt hills, but is mostly cleared. On these hilltops I saw a number of abandoned guns standing, which had doubtless been used to oppose our advance. I could hear skirmishing all around to the front of me. On my left it was quite near, but we must have gone a mile and a half before I found the line of battle. Then, galloping myself to the top of a hill across which our line stretched, I found a superb position for my guns near a house, and just where the right of the Fifth Corps joined the Army of the James.

From here we could look down into a valley stretching to the north for some three miles. Immediately below lay the little village of Appomattox Court House, into which our skirmishing line was just driving the enemy. Beyond was one mass of men, waggons, and artillery; in the distance they appeared to be in utter confusion. Shells from the right and left were bursting in their midst, especially from the right away off to the north where the Second and Sixth Corps were. Little puffs of smoke, too, showed our skirmish line pushing in from the east, as far as the eye could reach.

I at once ordered Rogers up on the left of the house, leaving Mink below as the range was too great for his guns. Just as the guns were in the act of being unlimbered, a flag of truce came galloping up to the house in front of which Ord had his headquarters, when all firing was immediately stopped. Rogers and his men were greatly disappointed in not getting a last shot at the rebellion, for Lee's army presented a per-

fect target for long-range firing. . . . In about an hour we received
orders for a suspension of hostilities until three o'clock to arrange terms
of surrender. During this time both armies were to remain exactly as
they were.

We waited quietly until the time appointed; even the batteries away
to the rear were not allowed to move; so far as I could see the terms of
the truce were most scrupulously observed. . . .

Soon after three o'clock we received notice that the surrender of the
Army of Northern Virginia was agreed on. The notice did not reach
Humphreys 'until a little after the appointed time. The instant time was
out, he commenced to advance and his batteries opened a vigorous cannonade. For a few minutes we thought that the fight was opened in
earnest, but Meade quickly stopped it. The troops were ordered to remain just where they were. Our skirmish line, running through the
south end of the village, became a guard beyond which none but general
officers were allowed to pass; not even their staff could go with them.

I rode down to the entrance of the town, but did not go in as there was
nothing but curiosity to take me, of which I felt rather ashamed; nor can
I deny a certain amount of commiseration for the brave men who are
so humbled. An hour or so before dark, we received a circular announcing the surrender of Lee's army and directing that we go into camp,
make ourselves comfortable, and send for rations and supplies.

So ends the great rebel army: *the* army of the rebellion. For I doubt
if the force Johnston has in North Carolina amounts to very much, and
it is the only army worth calling such they have left east of the Mississippi. Setting aside the cause in which it was engaged, the history of the
Army of Northern Virginia has been a glorious one. There cannot, however, be much of it left in the valley below tonight, for since this campaign opened by the attack on Fort Stedman, we must have taken near
30,000 prisoners, while very larger numbers have no doubt deserted
since they left Richmond and Petersburg, seeking to reach their homes
across the country.

The day has been cloudy with rain at intervals. I have brought all my
batteries up to near where Rogers and Mink were and have pitched my
tents on the best bit of ground I could find. Bad enough it is with mud
raised by this sopping rain, but should we remain here long, I will
search for a battery. Tired and sleepy does not begin to express my state
tonight, and that of all the Fifth Corps at least. How thankful the infantry must be that there is no picket duty! I am going in for a twelve-
hours' sleep.

APRIL 10, MONDAY. Another wet, nasty day. This morning we got copies
of the correspondence between Grant and Lee, and the terms of the
latter's surrender. It seems that the Second and Sixth Corps came up with

the enemy at this place some time on Saturday. Lee skirmished with his rear guard until the rest of his force had entrenched in a good position. Grant, knowing that Sheridan and Ord would cut him off on the other side, did not attack, but that afternoon sent in a summons for him to surrender, offering very good terms. This Lee refused, and yesterday morning tried to break through Sheridan's cavalry on the road to Lynchburg. The arrival of Ord's infantry stopped this; when finding his case hopeless, Lee sent in to say he was ready to surrender. Grant offered the same terms as the day before; all officers and men to be allowed to go to their homes on parole not to serve against the United States until exchanged. . . .

The rebel officers, with very few exceptions, express themselves as perfectly satisfied with the terms of the surrender, and say that if the government will only show the same spirit of kindness, and goodwill that the army has, all will soon be right, and a real peace again extend over all the land. God grant it may be so. . . .

I rode in to look at the rebel camp today, but found that the lines were not yet open for general passing. I was, however, far more fortunate than I expected, for I chanced to get down to the lines while Grant and Lee were having their last interview, which gave me an excellent opportunity to see the latter. The interview lasted near half an hour. Lee had eight or ten officers with him, and Grant some of his staff; Griffin was also present and one or two other general officers of our army.

Lee is a fine, English-looking man, somewhat stout, with a florid complexion and white hair; his appearance is decidedly that of a gentleman. The meeting took place near a small stream, in the road, and all were mounted. What its object was, or what was said on either side, I do not know. In the tavern I saw Longstreet, Pickett, Gordon, Heth and a number of their other generals. The grey uniform is very handsome when good, and new; setting off a fine-looking man to great advantage. . . .

Tonight the men are celebrating the surrender with improvised fireworks. It was some time before I could make out how they managed to obtain what appeared to be hundreds of Roman candles, but at last discovered that they were shooting rebel fuses from their muskets with small charges of powder. These exactly resembled the balls thrown out by Roman candles. The effect together with the camp fires was really beautiful. . . .

------------◦∞◦------------

TWENTY

EPILOGUE: THE GRAND REVIEW

Three days after Lee's surrender, his troops marched to a point near Appomattox Court House where those who had muskets, about 8,000, stacked them; another 18,000 surrendered unarmed. As paroles were distributed, the Army of Northern Virginia ended its glorious career. The Northern forces, marching back to the James and Richmond, were shortly transported to Washington. With surprising ease and rapidity, in due course, the great armies of citizen soldiers melted back into the working population from which they had sprung. First, however, a mighty pageant did honor to the armed host, which the patriotism of the nation had created to perform an immortal task of unification and liberation. The adjutant general on May 18 issued orders for a review of the Armies of the Potomac, of the Tennessee, and of Georgia by the President, the Cabinet, and other distinguished persons.

The principal reviewing stand was erected in front of the White House; the starting point for the columns was the Capitol. At nine o'clock on May 23 the bugles sounded, and General Meade, surrounded by his staff, led the first platoons past banks of tumultuously cheering people. After him came the cavalry corps under Merritt; the provost marshal general's brigade; the engineer brigade under the builder of the memorable Rappahannock and James River bridges, Benham; the Ninth Corps under Parke; the Fifth Corps under Griffin; and the Second Corps under Humphreys. In the Fifth Corps nobody rode more proudly than its veteran artillery leader, Brevet Brigadier General Charles S. Wainwright. That night Sherman's troops bivouacked near the Capitol; and promptly at ten on the 24th he led forth his great orderly array, not so well dressed as Meade's, but bronzed and hardened by their epic marches.

"Soldiers!" ran Meade's farewell address, "having accomplished the work set before us, having vindicated the honor and integrity of our Government and flag, let us return thanks to Almighty God for his blessing in granting us victory and peace; and let us sincerely pray for strength and light to discharge our duties as citizens, as we have endeavored to discharge them as soldiers."

❋ ❋ ❋

MAY 20, 1865, SATURDAY. The grand review is settled on for next week. The Army of the Potomac, including what cavalry there is here that belonged to it, and also the Ninth Corps, on Tuesday; Sherman's army on Wednesday. We shall have near 80,000 men in rank, so it will be a big thing, though not to be compared with McClellan's grand review; for this is to be a street affair. Hunt astonished me yesterday with the information that General Meade had volunteered to let him have all the artillery in a body, and command it as a corps. It is no more than is due to General Hunt, who has been the soul of our artillery, and has made it what it is, by far the best arm in the service. The whole effect, too, will be very much finer; forty batteries in one mass moving up Pennsylvania Avenue battery-front will be a sight worth seeing. I had gone up to Hunt's quarters to see if something could not be done to get such an arrangement, but without much hope of success; so I was delighted to learn that there was a good prospect of its being done. I say a prospect, for as yet there is no definite arrangement, and I hear that Meade today is doubtful; says that he fears so much artillery will not be able to get free when it reaches the narrow streets of Georgetown. . . .

MAY 22, MONDAY. I carried out my plan of spending Sunday in the city and going to church. My waggon is now quite useful, and as stylish as any general's I see about. They gave me a good room at Willard's; two, I may say, for the first one they pronounced a mistake about two o'clock Sunday morning, when I was routed out of it to make room for *five* girls. It was a large room with two beds, but still tolerably close packing, three in a bed, I should think, such a hot night. My second room was quite as good as the first; they required that I should give that up by ten o'clock this morning, which I was quite ready to do. Washington is getting very full. I met a number of familiar faces, and some old friends from home, to say nothing of officers whom I have not seen for years. I did not pretend to call by name half of those in or out of uniform who spoke to me. Everyone was in a state of most joyous excitement, and the whole thing very pleasant. . . .

We have a long order for the review, very well arranged, too, it seems to me. Merritt is to command the cavalry corps, Sheridan, of course, being unwilling to appear under Meade. He left this morning for New York on his way to take command in Texas. Merritt and Custer start for the same destination right after the review. The artillery arrangement has all fallen through, the excuse being that there would be too much of it; but from what I hear, I have no doubt that Hazard instigated General Humphreys to object. I know that he told Humphreys that all his pride and that of his batteries was in the Second Corps and a lot of other stuff, evidently meant to curry favour. So each brigade is to march in rear of its own corps. As Tidball and Hazard both have six batteries, I have got an order for Ritchie to report to me for the day; and also permission to take what horses I need from my other batteries in reserve to make my teams look well. All hands have been hard at work polishing guns and brasses, cleaning carriages, and blacking harness. I have been most particular to have an extra amount of labour bestowed on the horses. All the ammunition has been taken out of the chests and temporarily placed in waggons, so that the carriages will run light, and there will be no danger of accident. As all the batteries have nearly double the complement of men present for four guns, only the most soldierly in appearance will be taken. The batteries in reserve feel very much disappointed that they cannot take part in the review. I chose Ritchie as a better-looking battery than Matthewson, and I wanted light twelve-pounders.

MAY 23, TUESDAY. The grand review of the Army of the Potomac is over, and it has received its share of praise. Everything went off to perfection. The weather, which had been so unpropitious, seemed to join in doing its share in our honour. Only a few hours before we started the clouds broke away with a gentle northerly wind which cooled the air and dried the mud, without rendering it dusty. I hauled out punctually at four o'clock, and the head of my column was just approaching the Long Bridge as the sun rose bright and clear. After crossing the bridge we passed up Maryland Avenue along the south end of the Capitol and so out into the open lots near the hospitals, on the ground where the cavalry camp was during the winter of 1861–62. We moved out left in front so as to avoid counter-marching.

It was not much after six o'clock when the Fifth Corps was occupying its prescribed position along Pennsylvania Avenue east, the head of the column at First Street east. As nine o'clock was the time set for the movement of the column, I had three hours to look around me, and get my breakfast. For this last I went out to Hall's camp; Hall, formerly captain of the Second Maine Battery under me, now lieutenant-colonel of Maine artillery and brevet-brigadier-general commanding the camp of artillery instruction. Camp Barry, as it is called, occupies the ground on the right of the Bladensburg Pike just out of the gate.

I have an impression that I described the camp after my visit to it some eighteen months ago; at any rate, my object this time was to obtain a breakfast, which I did, and a good one too. I even went further than that and borrowed a general officer's sash from Hall in honour of the occasion, not being the possessor of such a thing myself.

After my breakfast, I rode around to look at the collected troops. The cavalry were formed on Maryland Avenue east. Their camp had been on this side of the river. The Ninth Corps crossed last night and bivouacked east of the Capitol. They were now formed on East Capitol Street. The Second Corps crossed the river after us, and was massed in the side streets.

I did not see the head of the column start. Meade no doubt had a full staff, for no officer who could by any possibility claim a right to be there would be left out at such a time. At least, I found it so, and would have had no difficulty in doubling the size of mine had I been willing to let them in.

The cavalry under Merritt came next to headquarters, looking remarkably well and soldierly for our army. Its young brigade commanders, nearly all of whom I knew as battery officers, gave an air to it. But its artillery was beautiful, the show of the day, in fact; six horse batteries under old Robinson were got up with all the care for appearance which he, an old sergeant, could expend on them. As they had lain in camp either here or at Winchester all winter, they were in tip-top order. In some things, though, I think that I beat them: not each battery separately, but in the uniformity of the whole. Their horses, however, were in much better condition than mine, and the cannoneers being on horseback, of course, made more show.

I had taken my stand opposite the north end of the Capitol, which was hung with flags and decorated with mottoes. Among the last I noticed one: "The only debt we can never repay; what we owe to our gallant defenders." I could not help wondering whether, having made up their minds that they *can never* pay the debt, they will not think it useless to try.

On staging erected along the north side of the Capitol were the Sunday School children of Washington: the girls all dressed in white, armed with a great quantity of flowers to strew the victors' way. They were so liberal with these to the cavalry and head of the Ninth Corps that we who came afterward got hardly any. Merritt was almost buried in wreaths and bouquets. I remained there until I could see Tidball's artillery started; the Ninth Corps following the provost-marshal's and engineer brigades, which came directly behind the cavalry. His batteries looked well, better than I expected. The horse batteries had marched in column of sections, and I was particularly desirous to see if Tidball could get around the Capitol with battery front, so as to arrange accordingly. I found that he did it easily.

The Fifth marched with the First Division leading; then the Second, the Third, and the artillery. Company front was limited to twenty files, so many of the regiments were able to make a respectable appearance, and the whole appeared uniform. The column was closed in mass with diminished intervals between brigades and divisions. Each brigade was followed by six ambulances, three abreast. My batteries moved thus: Stewart, "B," Fourth U.S.; Hazelton, "D," First New York; Mink, "H," First New York; Ritchie, "C," First New York; Rogers, "B," First New York; and Rawles, "D" and "G," Fifth U.S. This put all the brass guns together and made it uniform. The cannoneers were mounted on the boxes, all had on good clothes, sacks, and sabre belts, with letters and numbers on their caps. I regretted more than ever not having a trained corps of buglers, but as I had none I directed them not to play at all.

My own get-up was rather shabby, I not having a decent full-dress coat; I was obliged to appear in a double-breasted sack. But I was over-shadowed by the handsomest flag in the army; backed by Berlin in his braided Swedish uniform, and Appleton in a very high-falutin' get-up. The nuisance of carrying a drawn sabre so long I did not relish; but was not guilty of the gaucherie of saluting with it in return for the cheers on the march, as some generals did. As it is not at all sharp, I could let it hang by the knot when I had to lift my cap.

The infantry marched very well, judging from the Second Corps. I did not see the Fifth; nor was there a single delay of more than two or three minutes at a time during the passage of the whole column. Two or three times on the route I heard three cheers called for me by name. At first I thought that it was from some persons who knew us opposite Willard's. I happened to look up at the proposer, who hesitated for an instant at the name, and saw he had a newspaper with the program of the review in it. As I expected, we got hardly any of the flowers; they were getting scarce when we passed by.

The President, as reviewing officer, was in a stand erected directly in front of the White House. With him were a host of notables. A stand for foreign ministers was on the same side of the street. Opposite was a number of stands for Meade's and Sherman's friends, and so on.* I was so intent on getting my salute just at the right time, not being much accustomed to this sort of work, that I saw nothing and missed a bunch of flowers thrown to me individually by a very pretty lady.

After passing Seventeenth Street, the column quickened its pace. By placing a pontoon bridge at the entrance of Georgetown for the Ninth and Second Corps to cross, while the Fifth passed on to the aqueduct bridge, all blocking was avoided. Just before getting to the circle, I wheeled my batteries down a wide street to the right into some open lots,

* Sherman, who like Sheridan had his private resentments, pointedly refused to shake the hand of Secretary of War Stanton when they met in the reviewing stand.

and then started them again in column of pieces for home under Fitzhugh, who got them all back to camp by five o'clock, much earlier than I expected.

Greatly relieved to have it all done, and well done, I rode back to join Hunt, who had asked me to come to him in General Meade's stand if I could. The guards at first refused to let me pass, but catching Webb's eye, he passed me in. I found a warm welcome at once from a host of ladies—Mrs. Webb, Mrs. Hunt, Mrs. Colonel Craig, her mother, her sisters, and a number of their friends, including the widow, Mrs. Douglass, and a very pretty Mrs. Smith Cliff from New York. It certainly is pleasant to be made much of by pretty women, especially after four years of absence from female society. Any man in uniform was, of course, the rage today; but I felt that I was especially honoured by General Hunt's party of ladies, and was flattered thereby as it could only be a reflection of his own regard.

I remained there until the end of the column had passed, which was about two o'clock; when we all walked around to Colonel Craig's in I Street, and had a lunch, spending a very pleasant hour or so. It might be said that I stuck to the artillery, even among the ladies; so, of course, that arm of the service was pronounced the finest part of the show. But Hunt tells me that the President several times repeated the same opinion, and that Meade is more than sorry he did not carry out his first idea of passing it all in a body.

Several were kind enough to say that my brigade was the best. I think so myself, but am hardly a fit judge. I know that it was the most uniform in appearance, and according to my ideas the most soldierly. Hazard had the band of Tidball's regiment, which of course added to his display; but as they were mounted on very poor horses, it looked like the militia cavalry bands in New York. . . .

MAY 24, WEDNESDAY. Sherman's army had as good a day as ourselves overhead, but it was a little dusty underfoot; not enough to speak of, but still enough for the dust to show. I saw the whole command pass, and was most of the time with the same party as yesterday. As they were to change their camp to this side of the river after the review, the men had more traps on than ours, and each brigade was followed by its pack mules and contrabands, who interested most of the spectators more than anything else.

The two armies were much alike in most respects. What struck me most in Sherman's men was their magnificent physique. I doubt if such another body of men of the same number can be found together in the world. The great predominance of the American type, too, was striking. It was generally thought that they marched somewhat better than the Army of the Potomac. All these differences are accounted for by the fact that the Western armies have lost far less men than we in Virginia, and consequently four-fifths of Sherman's men are old soldiers while full a half of the Army of the Potomac have not been in service over a year. Their officers, however, were very slouchy, from General Logan down, and all much less soldierly-looking than ours.

The artillery could not compare with ours; Reynolds's brigade with the Twentieth Corps, indeed, was the only one that shewed the hand of the brigade commander at all. I was amused and much struck by a reply I had from one of the Miss Woolseys in answer to my question why she liked Sherman's army better than ours; an opinion I have heard widely expressed by the outsiders, and pretty generally taken up by the newspaper reporters. She said the Army of the Potomac marched past just like its commander (Meade), looking neither to the right nor the left, and only intent on passing the reviewing officer properly; while Sherman's officers and men were bowing on all sides and not half so stiff. I told her she had paid the greatest compliment to the Army of the Potomac I had heard.

No doubt this was one of the main causes of the greater admiration for the Western army. We are not a military people.

So we have ended the two grand reviews without a single accident or drawback. I have never seen anything of the kind in Europe, but judge from pictures that they understand making much more of a show of it than we do. All the ornamenting of the streets and buildings was very crude. Nor could we show the variety, style, and showiness of uniforms to be seen in a European army. Still, it was a grand sight: 130,000 citizen soldiers, with everything for service and not a particle for appearance. Had it been more like a European review, it would have been less American. . . .

APPENDIX:

Officers of the First New York Light Artillery

Charles S. Wainwright was so closely identified with the First New York Regiment of Light Artillery, and kept so closely in touch with its officers, mentioning them often in his diary, that a full roster is useful for reference.

ADLE, JOSEPH W.
AMES, ALBERT N.
AMES, NELSON
ANDERSON, CHARLES L.
ANDERSON, WILLIAM J.
ATTIX, ABRAM S.
BABCOCK, DON CARLOS
BABCOCK, VOLNEY M.
BACKUS, CLARENCE W.
BAILEY, EDWARD L.
BAILEY, GUILFORD D.
BARNES, ALMONT
BARSE, GEORGE H.
BATES, THOMAS H.
BATES, THOMAS S.
BECKER, ANTON
BERLIN, CARL LUDWIG
BOWER, WILLIAM H.
BRECK, GEORGE
CAMPBELL, CHARLES H.
CANFIELD, MICHAEL
CANFIELD, WILLIAM J.
CHAPIN, DARIUS
CHAPIN, SYLVESTER
CLARK, ELA H.
COCHRANE, EDWARD B.
CONANT, FREDERICK W.
COOPER, DAVID B.
COOPER, WILLIAM S.
COTHRAN, GEORGE W.
CREGO, JR., HIRAM
CREGO, THOMAS H.
CROUNSE, LORENZO
CUNNINGHAM, JOHN

DAVIS, HENRY W.
DAVIS, MYRON J.
DECKER, JAMES E.
DEITZ, FREDERICK
DE MOTT, CHARLES
DE PEYSTER, JR., J. WATTS
DE PEYSTER, V. A.
DILLENBECK, JEROME
DUDLEY, EDGAR S.
EGGLESTON, GEORGE B.
ERDMANN, DIETRICH
EVERTS, FRANKLIN
FAIRBANKS, CLARK W.
FARRELL, THOMAS F.
FITZHUGH, ROBERT H.
FRANK, JOHN D.
FREEMAN, GEORGE W.
FREEMAN, HORACE W.
FULLER, BENJAMIN F.
GANSEVOORT, ROBERT H.
GIBSON, JOHN
GOFF, FREDERICK F.
GOODRICH, ADOLPHUS S.
GORMLEY, JOHN H.
GRAVES, DEMPSTER
HALL, ISAAC B.
HARDIE, JOHN H.
HARN, WILLIAM A.
HART, GEORGE P.
HAZELTON, JAMES B.
HENCHEN, FRANCIS
HODGKINS, THOMAS
HOOD, SAMUEL
HOWELL, JOHN H.

HUMPHRIES, CHARLES
IDE, ROYAL A.
JAMES, SAMUEL R.
JOHNSON, DELOS M.
KETCHUM, GEORGE E.
KIEFFER, LUTHER
KINGSBURY, JOHN T.
KINNIE, OLIVER E.
LAWTHER, ANDREW
LEONARD, NEWELL
LODER, EDWIN A.
LUDWIG, GOTTLIEB
MARSELLUS, JOHN W.
MATTHEWSON, ANGELL
MAY, JOHN
MCCLELLAN, SAMUEL A.
MCDONNELL, EDWARD
MCKNIGHT, GEORGE F.
MCQUEEN, NORMAN M.
MILLARD, JR., JOHN A.
MILLOTT, AUGUSTUS
MINK, CHARLES E.
NEWKIRK, EDWARD P.
O'DONNELL, FREDERICK
OSBORN, THOMAS WARD
O'SHEA, THOMAS
PARDEE, DANE
PARKER, ROBERT I.
PEABODY, JAMES H.
PERINE, DEWITT M.
PETTIT, RUFUS D.
PETTIT, WALTER D.
PHILLIPS, WILLIAM H.
REYNOLDS, GILBERT H.
REYNOLDS, JOHN A.
RICHARDSON, LESTER J.
RITCHIE, DAVID F.
ROBINSON, JAMES P.
ROGERS, ROBERT E.
ROONEY, CHARLES A.

RUMSEY, WILLIAM
RUNDELL, MARSHALL H.
SAHM, NICHOLAS
SCHELL, HIRAM H.
SCHENKELBERGER, JACOB
SCHMITT, CHRISTOPHER
SCHWARZ, GEORGE F.
SCOTT, ADDISON L.
SCOTT, WARREN L.
SEABURY, THOMAS F.
SEARLE, TYLER E.
SHELDON, ALBERT S.
SHELTON, WILLIAM HENRY
SKILTON, JULIUS A.
SKINNER, JAMES A.
SLAUSON, JOSEPH B.
SMITH, DAVID L.
SPRATT, JOSEPH
STOCK, CHRISTIAN
STOCKING, SOLON WALTER
STOCUM, JOHN
STOLPER, AUGUSTUS
STRINGER, WILLIAM H.
TALLETT, GEORGE H.
TAMBLIN, JOHN W.
THIERRY, LOUIS C.
TURNER, HENRY E.
UNDERHILL, EDWARD H.
VAN VALKENBURGH, DAVID H.
WAINWRIGHT, CHARLES S.
WARNER, EDWARD R.
WEBB, EDWARD P.
WELD, JOHN W.
WHEELER, CHARLES C.
WIEDRICH, MICHAEL
WILBUR, BENJAMIN W.
WILLIAMS, ALFRED A. C.
WILSON, WILLIAM R.
WINEGAR, CHARLES E.
WINSLOW, GEORGE B.
WOODBURY, JOHN D.

CPSIA information can be obtained at www.ICGtesting.com
Printed in the USA
LVOW131533080313

323402LV00001B/113/A